colourful characters . . . Wonderful, compelling . . . *The Sugar Barons* is an exemplary book; history as it should be written.   Andrea Stuart, *Independent*

Very impressive – a meticulously researched piece of work, and so engagingly written. It taught me so much that I didn't know about British Caribbean history. What a story!
        Andrea Levy, author of *Small Island* and *The Long Song*

A tumultuous rollercoaster of a book . . . Mr. Parker tells an extraordinary, neglected and shameful story with gusto.
                                                        Economist

In *The Sugar Barons*, Parker provides a glittery history of the British impresarios, heiresses and remittance men involved in Caribbean slavery . . . racy, well-researched history . . . *The Sugar Barons* provides eloquent testimony to the mercantile greed of a few and manifest misery endured by millions in the pursuit of sweetness.   Ian Thomson, *Guardian*

In *The Sugar Barons*, Matthew Parker weaves a fascinating and bloody tale about the period from the early 1600s when English sugar-growing dynasties such as the Beckfords, Codringtons and Draxes ran Barbados, Jamaica and other islands . . . *The Sugar Barons* is an antidote to the modern strain of neo-conservative history that says empire was rather a good thing.   Peter Chapman, *Financial Times*

Fabulously researched, the diary entries, letters and papers reveal a staggering level of corruption and cruelty. But despite the soap opera potential of the truly scandalous tales, Parker refuses to sweeten his matter-of-fact prose style for the casual page-turner. Instead he constructs, piece by piece, what amounts to a compelling prosecution of the slavery and Imperial greed that left a shocking legacy in the region.   *Wanderlust*

Able and well-researched . . . As Matthew Parker's engaging book demonstrates, by 1750 the sugar trade, like gas and oil today, had infiltrated so many aspects of national life that it had become a power in the land in its own right. Politicians courted it and men died in its service. It had become a national necessity.   Leslie Mitchell, *Literary Review*

Though *The Sugar Barons* retells a familiar tale, it does so with a vigour and panache which often eludes more academic studies . . . *The Sugar Barons* is an engaging reminder of the pivotal role of sugar and slavery in the shaping of an early British empire.   James Walvin, *BBC History Magazine*

A spellbinding account of how sugar transformed the West Indies into the most valuable, ostentatious and brutal colony in the British Empire . . . Today, as Parker notes at the end of this colourful and absorbing book, the great fortunes have vanished along with all but a carefully restored handful of plantation houses.   Miranda Seymour, *The Lady*

An enjoyable journey to a mercifully vanished world.
                    Wall Street Jounal

A rich, multifaceted account of the greed and slavery bolstering the rise of England's mercantile empire.   *Kirkus*

Gripping . . . extremely disturbing . . . This is a rousing, fluently written narrative history, full of color, dash, and forceful personalities . . . Parker's vivid evocation of the elite evokes the queasy moral rot beneath *la dolce vita*. *Publishers Weekly*

Successful both as a scholarly introduction to the topic and as an entertaining narrative, this is recommended for readers of any kind of history. *Library Journal*

Also by Matthew Parker

The Battle of Britain
Monte Cassino
Panama Fever
(Published in paperback as *Hell's Gorge*)

The Sugar Barons

Matthew Parker

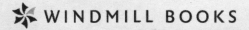

WINDMILL BOOKS

Published by Windmill Books 2012

2 4 6 8 10 9 7 5 3 1

Copyright © Matthew Parker 2011

Matthew Parker has asserted his right under the Copyright, Designs and
Patents Act, 1988, to be identified as the author of this work.

This book is a work of non-fiction.

First published in Great Britain in 2011 by Hutchinson

Windmill Books
The Random House Group Limited
20 Vauxhall Bridge Road, London SW1V 2SA

Addresses for companies within The Random House Group Limited can be
found at: www.randomhouse.co.uk/offices.htm

The Random House Group Limited Reg. No. 954009

www.randomhouse.co.uk

A CIP catalogue record for this book
is available from the British Library

ISBN 9780099558453

The Random House Group Limited supports The Forest Stewardship
Council (FSC®), the leading international forest certification organisation.
Our books carrying the FSC label are printed on FSC® certified paper.
FSC is the only forest certification scheme endorsed by the leading
environmental organisations, including Greenpeace.
Our paper procurement policy can be found at
www.randomhouse.co.uk/environment

Typeset in Ehrhardt by Palimpsest Book Production Limited,
Falkirk, Stirlingshire
Printed and bound by CPI Group (UK) Ltd, Croydon CR0 4YY

For my brilliant sister Caroline, with whom I shared many
West Indian adventures

CONTENTS

MAPS AND FAMILY TREES

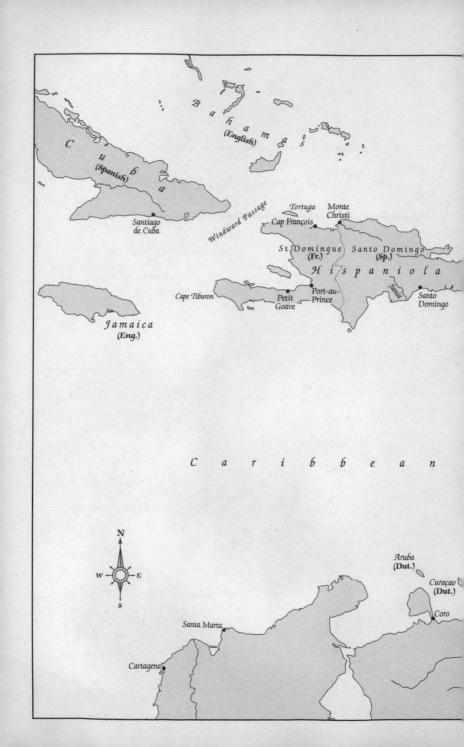

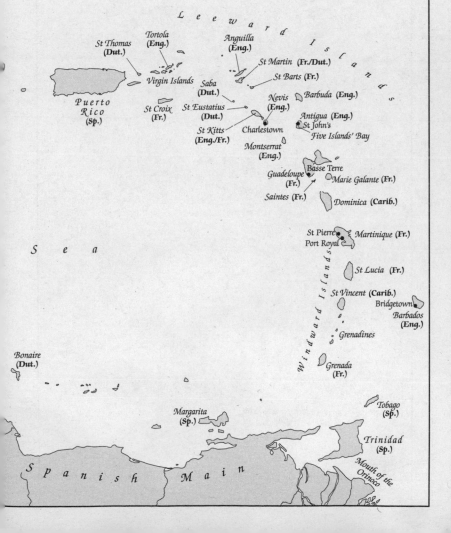

The West Indies and the
Spanish Main, c.1700

0   miles   200

A t l a n t i c   O c e a n

L e e w a r d   I s l a n d s

St Thomas
(Dut.)

Tortola
(Eng.)

Anguilla
(Eng.)

St Martin **(Fr./Dut.)**

St Barts **(Fr.)**

Virgin Islands

Saba
(Dut.)

Nevis
(Eng.)

Barbuda **(Eng.)**

*P u e r t o
R i c o*
(Sp.)

St Croix
(Fr.)

St Eustatius
(Dut.)

St Kitts
(Eng./Fr.)

Charlestown

Antigua **(Eng.)**
St John's
Five Islands' Bay

Montserrat
(Eng.)

Basse Terre

Guadeloupe
(Fr.)

Marie Galante **(Fr.)**

Saintes **(Fr.)**

Dominica **(Carib.)**

S e a

St Pierre
Port Royal

Martinique **(Fr.)**

St Lucia **(Fr.)**

St Vincent **(Carib.)**

Bridgetown

Barbados
(Eng.)

W i n d w a r d   I s l a n d s

Grenadines

Grenada
(Fr.)

Bonaire
(Dut.)

Tobago
(Sp.)

Margarita
(Sp.)

Trinidad
(Sp.)

S p a n i s h   M a i n

Mouth of the
Orinoco

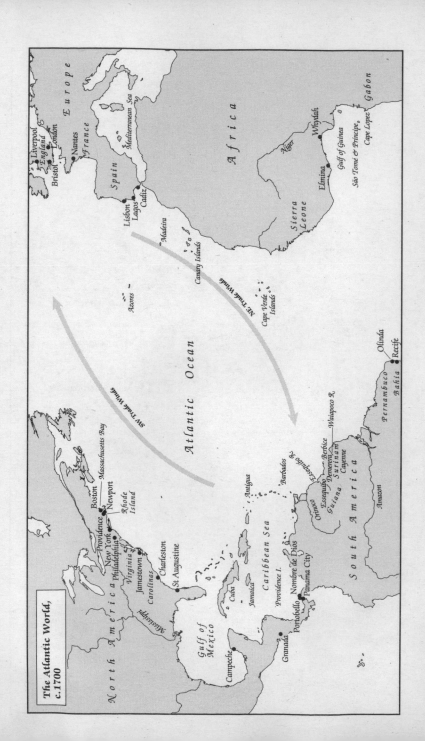

The Atlantic World, c.1700

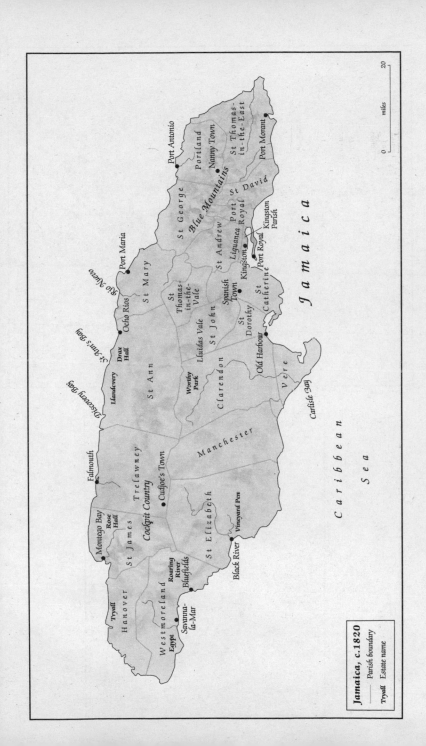

Jamaica, c.1820

—— Parish boundary

Tryall Estate name

Jamaica

Caribbean

Sea

Port Antonio

Portland

Nanny Town

St Thomas-in-the-East

Port Morant

St George

Blue Mountains

St David

Port Maria

Rio Nuevo

St Mary

St Andrew

Liguanea

Port Royal

Kingston Parish

Kingston

Port Royal

St Thomas-in-the-Vale

Spanish Town

St Catherine

Ocho Rios

St John

Llidas Vale

St Dorothy

Old Harbour

Drax Hall

St Ann

Worthy Park

Clarendon

Vere

Llandovery

St Ann's Bay

Carlisle Bay

Discovery Bay

Manchester

Falmouth

Trelawney

Cudjoe's Town

Cockpit Country

Montego Bay

Rose Hall

St James

St Elizabeth

Vineyard Pen

Black River

Hanover

Tryall

Roaring River

Bluefields

Westmoreland

Egypt

Savanna-la-Mar

0   miles   20

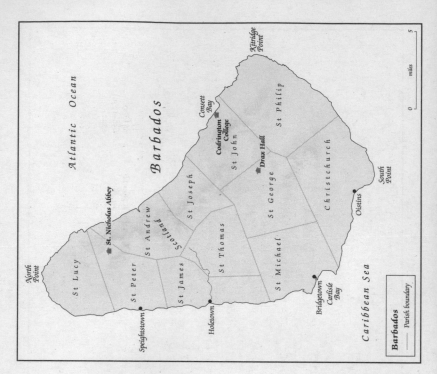

Barbados

— Parish boundary

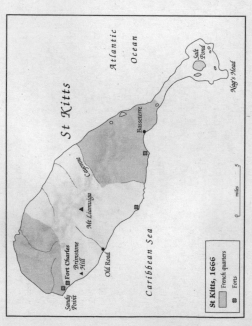

St Kitts, 1666

French quarters

Forts

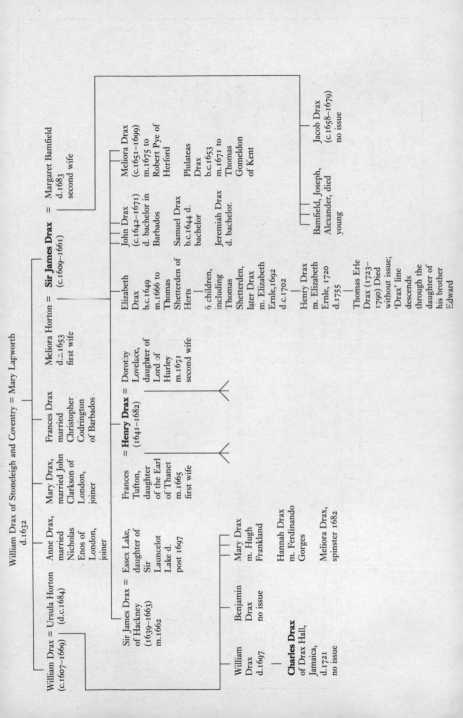

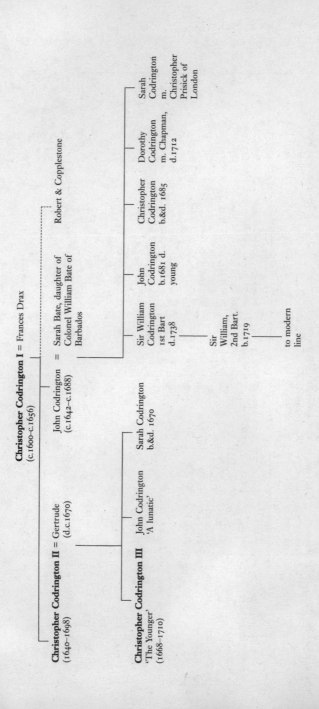

Christopher Codrington I = Frances Drax
(c.1600–c.1656)

Christopher Codrington II = Gertrude
(1640–1698)   (d.c.1670)

John Codrington = Sarah Bate, daughter of
(c.1642–c.1688)   Colonel William Bate of
             Barbados

Robert & Copplestone

John Codrington
'A lunatic'

Sarah Codrington
b.&d. 1670

Christopher Codrington III
'The Younger'
(1668–1710)

Sir William
Codrington
1st Bart
d.1738

John
Codrington
b.1681 d.
young

Christopher
Codrington
b.&d. 1685

Dorothy
Codrington
m. Chapman,
d.1712

Sarah
Codrington
m.
Christopher
Prisick of
London

Sir
William,
2nd Bart.
b.1719

to modern
line

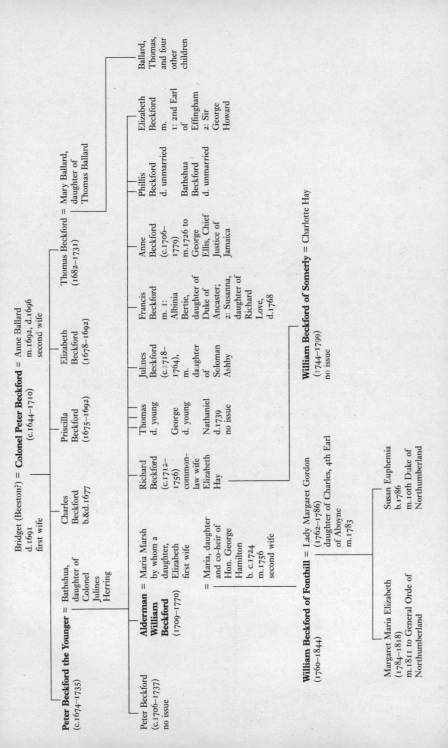

Bridget (Beeston?) = **Colonel Peter Beckford** = Anne Ballard
d.1691   (c.1644–1710)   m.1692, d.1696
first wife   second wife

Peter Beckford the Younger = Bathshua, daughter of Colonel Julines Herring
(c.1674–1735)

Charles Beckford b.&d.1677

Priscilla Beckford (1675–1692)

Elizabeth Beckford (1678–1692)

Thomas Beckford (1682–1731) = Mary Ballard, daughter of Thomas Ballard

Peter Beckford (1706–1737) no issue

Alderman William Beckford (1709–1770) = Maria Marsh by whom a daughter, Elizabeth first wife
= Maria, daughter and co-heir of Hon. George Hamilton b. c.1724 m.1756 second wife

Richard Beckford (c.1712–1756) common-law wife Elizabeth Hay

Thomas d. young

George d. young

Nathaniel d.1739 no issue

Julines Beckford (c.1718–1764), m. daughter of Soloman Ashby

Francis Beckford m. 1: Albinia Bertie, daughter of Duke of Ancaster; 2: Susanna, daughter of Richard Love, d.1768

Anne Beckford (c.1706–1779) m.1726 to George Ellis, Chief Justice of Jamaica

Phillis Beckford d. unmarried

Bathshua Beckford d. unmarried

Elizabeth Beckford m. 1: 2nd Earl of Effingham 2: Sir George Howard

Ballard, Thomas, and four other children

William Beckford of Somerly = Charlotte Hay
(1744–1799) no issue

William Beckford of Fonthill = Lady Margaret Gordon
(1760–1844)   (1762–1786) daughter of Charles, 4th Earl of Aboyne m.1783

Margaret Maria Elizabeth (1784–1818) m.1811 to General Orde of Northumberland

Susan Euphemia b.1786 m.1oth Duke of Northumberland

CHRONOLOGY

1509	Spanish settle Jamaica (Spanish Town established 1523)
1600	Dutch land on St Eustatius
1605	First English attempt to settle in Caribbean at St Lucia, fails because of hostility of Caribs
1607	Lasting English settlement at Jamestown, Virginia, established
1618–48	Thirty Years War: England, France and Holland v. Spain
1620	Establishment of Plymouth Colony
1623-4	English settle St Kitts; Dutch attack Bahia in Brazil
1627	English settlers, including James Drax, arrive on Barbados
1628	English and Irish settlers from St Kitts colonise Nevis
1629	English settlement founded on Providence Island
1630-40	Dutch seize Curaçao, Saba, St Martin
1632	English and Irish from St Kitts and Nevis colonise Antigua and Montserrat
1635-45	Dutch control northern Brazil
c. 1635	French settle Martinique and Guadeloupe
1639	Attempted English settlement in Trinidad destroyed by Caribs
1641	Spanish drive English settlers off Providence Island
1642-6	English Civil War
1647	Richard Ligon and Thomas Modyford arrive in Barbados
1650	Willoughby establishes English colony in Surinam
1651	Parliamentary force captures Barbados; First Navigation Act directed against the Dutch
1652	Hurricanes
1652-4	First Dutch War

1654	Dutch and Jews expelled from Brazil
1655	English take Jamaica from Spain
1657	James Drax knighted by Cromwell
1659	Major fire in Bridgetown, destroys more than 200 houses
1660	Restoration of Charles II
1663	Modyford to Jamaica; Barbados grants 4½ per cent duty to the King
1665-7	Second Dutch War
1665	April: Dutch admiral de Ruyter attacks Barbados
1666	French declare war on England, capture St Kitts, plunder Antigua
1667	Hurricane in Barbados; French capture Montserrat; Treaty of Breda grants Surinam to Dutch in return for New York; French conquests returned
1668	Another major fire in Bridgetown; 800+ houses destroyed
1670	Hurricane in Jamaica; Treaty of Madrid: Spain recognises English possession of Jamaica
1671	Quaker George Fox visits Barbados
1672-4	Third Dutch War
1673	Hurricane, fire and slave rebellion in Barbados
1675	Henry Morgan knighted
1685	Monmouth Rebellion in England against James II. Defeated rebels shipped to the West Indies
1688	'Glorious Revolution' in England
1688-97	Nine Years War (also known as King William's War, War of the Grand Alliance, First French and Indian War): England and Spain v. France, ends with Treaty of Ryswick: Spain cedes western region of Hispaniola to France
1689	August: English on St Kitts surrender to French
1690	July: English under Christoper Codrington recapture St Kitts
1691	April: Christoper Codrington leads unsuccessful English invasion of Guadeloupe
1692	June: Port Royal earthquake
1693	April: Christoper Codrington leads unsuccessful English invasion of Martinique
1694	French invasion of Jamaica
1702-13	War of Spanish Succession (Queen Anne's War). England and Holland v. France and Spain.
1702	July: French in St Kitts capitulate to forces of Christopher Codrington the Younger
1703	May: attempt on Guadeloupe led by Christopher Codrington the Younger abandoned
1706	February and March: French ravage St Kitts and Nevis

1710	December: murder of Governor Daniel Parke in Antigua
1712	July: French lay waste to Montserrat
1713	Treaty of Utrecht. Britain gains French sector of St Kitts, and wins *asiento*
1722	August: hurricane in Jamaica
1730s	Maroon wars in Jamaica
1733	Molasses Act
1736	Slave revolt plot in Antigua
1739	War of Jenkins's Ear, Britain v. Spain; becomes war of Austrian Succession until 1748; also known as King George's War
1751	George Washington visits Barbados
1756-63	Seven Years War or French and Indian War
1759	May: British occupy Guadeloupe
1760	Tacky's Revolt in Jamaica
1761	June: British North American colonials capture Dominica
1762	British capture Martinique, Grenada and Havana, Cuba
1763	Peace of Paris; British gain Grenada, Tobago and Dominica
1764	Sugar Act
1770s	Revolts in Tobago
1772-3	Carib Wars
1776-83	American Revolutionary War
1776	St Eustatius gives first official salute to American colours
1778	French control St Vincent and the Grenadines
1779	French regain control of Grenada
1781	Rodney sacks St Eustatius
1782	April: Battle of the Saintes off Dominica; Rodney defeats de Grasse; Jamaica saved
1791	Slave uprising in Haiti
1792-1803	French Revolutionary Wars
1794	British capture Port-au-Prince, Haiti
1794-1802	British occupy Martinique
1795	Second Maroon War in Jamaica
1796	Fedon slave revolt in Grenada
1797	Abercromby expedition captures Trinidad, ceded by Spain 1802
1808	Slave trade abolished in British Empire
1816	Bussa's slave revolt in Barbados
1831	Baptists' Revolt in Jamaica
1831	Huge hurricane on Barbados
1833	Slave Emancipation Act
1838	Apprenticeships end; true emancipation
1922	Sugar prices collapse

INTRODUCTION

'Hot as Hell, and as Wicked as the Devil'

On a voyage to Jamaica, but held at anchor for three freezing days off Deal because of unfavourable winds, Grub Street writer Ned Ward looked around him at his travelling companions. Seeking new opportunities in the West Indies was a decidedly mixed collection of his fellow British countrymen and women. It was January 1697, but it could have been any time between 1630 and 200 years later: the ship's company was a timeless array of the hopeful, disappointed and desperate. There was a salesman, recently fired; 'three Broken Tradesmen, who had lost their Credit'; 'two Parsons, who had lost their Livings; and several, like me', wrote Ward, 'who had lost their Wits'. The three women on board consisted of a widow, another woman in pursuit of an errant husband and a 'maid' who, 'I fear, had Lost her self'. The small party of passengers also included a decrepit ship's captain, an agricultural labourer deported for being caught up in a recent rebellion, and a young Irishman who had been got drunk and then been tricked into servitude on the plantations. All were going, wrote Ward, 'with one Design, to patch up their Decay'd Fortune'.

At last the vessel, the 400-ton *Andalucia*, weighed anchor and, enjoying a 'prosperous Gale', headed steadily westwards down the Channel. Past Land's End, she steered more southerly. After two weeks, the cold of January in England gave way to a 'pleasant warmth'. The route to the West Indies followed that taken by Columbus 200 years earlier: south past Portugal and modern-day Morocco, then across the open ocean to Madeira and the Canary Islands, where the vessel could pick up the trade winds blowing towards the Caribbean.

Like the others on board, and the tens of thousands of people who had already travelled to the West Indies colonies before the end of the seventeenth century, Ward, too, wished to patch up his 'decay'd Fortune'; in short, to make money and to reinvent himself as a success, rather than a failure. He was 30, and as a writer, his chosen profession, had made little mark on the world. He was wildly in debt and drinking far too much. What little money he originally possessed had been frittered away in a 'Wilderness of Pleasure and Enjoyment', chatting up women, consuming 'oceans of wine' and gambling with fellow Grub Street hacks. With his creditors closing in, he was now, he resolved, going to shun 'the Company of those who had nothing to do but Spend Money, for the Conversation of such whose practice was to Get it'.

He was heading for the right place, to a society whose guiding principle, perhaps its only principle, was to make money. It was well known in London that Barbados was currently England's richest colony, and Jamaica was on the way to taking over the title. Already, in a short space of time, families such as the Draxes, Codringtons and Beckfords had, from humble beginnings, become immensely, obscenely wealthy, selling the sugar from their plantations manned by enslaved Africans. In consequence, the West Indian islands had become for more than one state the foundation of their commercial and political greatness, and a test bed of national virility. The islands, in the most part minute specks in the sea, had therefore become bitterly contested between the rival great powers of the time, and were already dictating imperial policy.

Sugar itself would shortly become the most important commodity in the world – enjoying a position in the eighteenth century akin to steel in the nineteenth and oil in the twentieth. As a result, the tiny tropical islands became the strategic centre of the Western world, the hinge on which global history turned. Less than a hundred years later, the importance of Jamaica, the size of Yorkshire and smaller than modern-day Connecticut, would contribute directly to the loss by Britain of the North American colonies.

In Ward's time, emigrants from England to the Americas had a choice. But any with ambition for great wealth – or indeed hopelessly in debt – dreamed not of the prosaic settlements on the North American mainland, but of the West Indies. This was the place to get rich quick. As planters, eager for new recruits to the colonies, had been writing from the islands, even the most incorrigible jailbird from England could soon build up a great fortune.

Ned Ward, a professional cynic and wit, considered himself too savvy to believe all of this. He had heard, he wrote, 'extravagant Encomiums of that Blessed Paradise Jamaica, where Gold is more plentiful than Ice, Silver than Snow, Pearls than Hailstones'.

His disbelieving tone indicates that current in London were other stories of the West Indies: the appalling attrition from a host of unfamiliar diseases; the barbarously sticky heat; the natural disasters; the frightening Carib natives and vengeful slaves; the incessant warfare; the privateers and pirates infesting the sea lanes. In all, the risk, the strangeness, the extreme insecurity.

Ward does not seem to have minded the claustrophobic conditions on board the sailing vessel, his tiny, cramped cabin and the boredom of long weeks at sea. He passed the time playing his flute on deck, to the consternation of the ship's dog, and gambling at backgammon with one of the parsons. But before the coast of the Old World was out of sight, a fierce storm descended. It was late at night, and it struck a ship's company that was already unsteady, having been 'well Moisten'd' with 'an Exhilerating Dose of Right Honourable Punch'. A ferocious wind made standing on deck impossibly perilous, and thunder and lightning was followed by 'such an excessive Rain, that as we had one Sea under us, we feard another had been tumbling upon our heads'.

The storm raged almost all night, but the next day at first light an even greater danger presented itself. From high aloft, the lookout had spotted a sail bearing down on the *Andalucia*. They were off the coast of Morocco, near a port notorious for its Barbary pirates. The gravity of the situation was made clear to Ward by the speed with which the ship's crew cleared the decks, readied the 28 guns, distributed firearms and prepared to repel boarders.

As the other vessel neared, they could see that it flew English colours, but this was not trusted, and the *Andalucia*'s captain, by raising and lowering sails, did all he could to give the impression that his ship was better manned than it actually was. Only when the other vessel came into hailing distance was there relief: it was indeed an English ship, on the way to Africa to collect slaves. Ward and his fellow passengers celebrated with more punch.

Soon afterwards, they picked up the trade winds and started across the Atlantic. Around them the sea was empty and the sky enormous, its changing occasional clouds often the only diversion. They were now in the tropics and it was hotter than anything Ward had ever known. Had modesty not forbidden it, he wrote, he would have gone naked on deck. New to him too, were the sharks, turtles, dolphins and flying fish that could be seen from the ship.

The greatest fear now was of being caught in a calm, a situation that had seen many ships' crews starve to death. But luck was with the *Andalucia*, and after some six weeks at sea, they came in sight of the Leeward Islands gently curving in a chain to the north-west. Passing first Montserrat, then Antigua, Nevis and St Kitts, 'in a few days' they reached Hispaniola. From there, 'with a fresh Gail', it took only 24 hours before they were in sight of Jamaica.

Ward's pithy description of the island has become famous. He was not impressed. To be fair, he arrived in 1697 at a particularly bad time. Jamaica had recently suffered a catastrophic earthquake, and a hugely destructive invasion by a French army, which had laid waste to much of the western half of the island. In addition, it should be remembered that Ward's profession as a Grub Street hack demanded he write with impact, a clever turn of phrase and as much vulgarity as possible.

Jamaica, he wrote, was 'Sweating Chaos'. The climate was deadly: 'As Sickly as a Hospital, as Dangerous as the Plague.' Nature itself was also ill, producing wild disorders such as hurricanes and earthquakes. The food was bizarre and disgusting: the planters' favourite, the spicy Africa-originated pepperpot, was like consuming brandy mixed with gunpowder, 'an excellent Breakfast for a Salamander'; the local 'Cussue' apple was 'so great an Acid . . . that by Eating of one, it drew up my mouth like a *Hens Fundament*'. The pork was 'luscious', but, Ward warned, caused scurvy and leprosy.

Most disgusting of all, though, were the people. The men looked as if 'they had just knock'd off their Fetters'. The women, with nicknames such as 'Salt Beef Peg' and 'Buttock-de-Clink Jenny', were 'such who have been Scandalous in England to the utmost degree, either Transported by the State, or led by their Vicious Inclinations; where they may be Wicked without Shame, and Whore on without Punishment'. Neither sex went in for religion; instead 'they regard nothing but Money, and value not how they get it'. There was no 'felicity to be enjoy'd but purely Riches'. When not trying to get rich, 'They have this Pleasure in Drinking, That what they put into their Bellies, they may soon stroak out of their Finger Ends; for instead of Exonerating, they Fart; and Sweat instead of Pissing.'

This is perhaps a bit rich coming from Ned Ward, a man who had drunk away his twenties and was now himself in Jamaica purely to mend his fortune. Moreover, his lifelong Tory beliefs inform his disgust at the society he encountered on the island. Jamaica, he wrote, had been somehow 'neglected by the Omnipotence when he form'd the World into its admirable Order'. Proper rank and degree, the bedrock of English society, appeared to be absent. Instead, arrivals of whatever hue could be transformed by the island: 'A Broken Apothecary will make there a Topping Physician; a Barbers Prentice, a good Surgeon; a Balliffs Follower, a passable Lawyer; and an English Knave, a very Honest Fellow.'

The chance for such transformations, or new starts, was, of course, a primary motive for undergoing the dangerous adventure of emigration. The West Indies held out the promise of freedom, of opportunities for social mobility unknown in Europe. The apparent lack of 'order' was exactly what made it so appealing to those on the wrong side of the ancient hierarchy at home. Petty thieves or pirates could indeed become pillars of the colonial establishment. Second or third sons who might otherwise be destined for the priesthood or army could and did find themselves instead at the head of a newly dominant branch of the family. Women who were disgraced or 'lost', by their own fault or that of others, might indeed welcome Ward's snide assertion that 'A little Reputation among the Women goes a great way.'

Ward soon left Jamaica. Although, ironically, his career was transformed by the commercial success of his pamphlet, 'A Trip to the West Indies', published the following year, for him the island was a giant cesspit, inhabited by those beyond redemption: 'The Dunghill of the Universe, the Refuse of the whole Creation . . . The Nursery of Heavens Judgments . . . The Receptacle of Vagabonds, the Sanctuary of Bankrupts, the Close-stool for the Purges of our Prisons, as Hot as Hell, and as wicked as the Devil.'

PART ONE

The Pioneers

WHITE GOLD, 1642

'*The great industry and more thriving genius of Sir James Drax.*'
John Scott, 1667

On the Drax plantation on the small island of Barbados a secret experiment was taking place. It was some time in 1642 or soon after, by which point much of the land bordering the sea had been cleared and put to work in agriculture: tobacco, cotton, indigo, foodstuffs. But James Drax had established his own plantation away from the coast, in the uplands of St George's, and into that parish's rich red soil, far from prying eyes, he planted a new crop.

James Drax was later described by a contemporary as an 'ingenious spirit'. Certainly, he was fiercely ambitious and fearless, but also well-connected and willing to learn. In around 1640, as every embryonic planter suffered from a collapse of the markets for their Barbadian products, he had set sail to Recife, on the westernmost tip of Brazil, to learn a new technology from the Dutch and Portuguese – sugar. It was not just the techniques of planting that needed acquiring, but also knowledge of the complicated and difficult processes of manufacturing. While taking this all on, James Drax forged invaluable links with local sugar traders and, through them, with Sephardic Jewish merchants and bankers based in Amsterdam, the sugar-refining capital of the world.

Barbados is tiny – 21 miles by 14, with an area close to that of the Isle of Wight. It seems bizarre that the island would prove to be the location for an agricultural revolution almost unrivalled in modern times for its ultimate economic, political and human consequences. Yet Barbados's small size meant that everywhere was within fairly easy reach of the coast, crucial for transport, while its climate and distance from the equator are similar to those of the ancestral home of sugar cane – the islands of New Guinea. Both are hot, around 30°C, humid and wet.

It was in New Guinea that sugar cane, a giant member of the grass family, occurred naturally and was first domesticated. According to local folklore, two New Britain fishermen once found in their net a piece of cane. They threw it away, but recovered it the next day, and the day after that planted it in the earth. The cane burst into life and a woman came forth. She cooked food for the men and at night hid herself in the cane. At last she was captured, and became the wife of one of the men. From their union, the story concludes, sprang the entire human race.

Wild sugar cane had long been valued for the sweet pith that filled the inside of the otherwise bamboo-like reed. It is not hard to imagine a piece of cane, chopped for chewing, being discarded and then sprouting in the rich subtropical soil. From New Guinea, cane cultivation spread westwards, and in around 500 BC it was in India, where the cane also appears in numerous legends, that the juice obtained from crushing the plant was first processed into sugar through being boiled in a succession of ever smaller and hotter cauldrons.

By the sixth century AD, sugar cultivation and processing had reached Persia, from where it was carried into the Mediterranean by the Arab expansion (it was said that sugar followed the Koran). It was grown on Crete, Cyprus and Sicily, as well as the Mediterranean littoral, although the frosts of Europe and the aridity of North Africa made the yield low for the effort involved.

Spanish and Portuguese expansion in the fifteenth century carried the cane ever south-westwards, to warmer, wetter climes. In 1425, Henry the Navigator sent cane plants from Sicily to Madeira with the first Portuguese colonists. After a slow start, the island started producing huge yields. At the end of the century, Spanish colonists, after a long war against the indigenous inhabitants, took possession of the Canary Islands 200 miles further south, and also planted cane.

From the tiny island of Gomera in the Canaries, Christopher Columbus carried cane seedlings to the New World on his second voyage in 1493. Columbus knew sugar: he had traded it between Madeira and Genoa, and his first wife's family had thrived in the business. Thus it was an experienced eye that declared Hispaniola in the West Indies the finest place in the world to grow the crop. In the rich Caribbean soil, the canes Columbus had brought from the Canaries had rooted in seven days and then shot up with astonishingly fast new growth.

The western part of Hispaniola would, 150 years later and under different ownership, become the world's most productive sugar-producing hothouse. But strangely, the Spanish sugar industry on the island flourished only briefly and then rapidly declined. Along with the favourable reports, Columbus noted that the men brought over to tend the first sugar seedlings had fared less well than their charges. Most were dead by the time the first crop came to harvest. But the wider story of the Spanish failure in the Caribbean to tap the 'white gold' of sugar is more about the particularities of Spanish imperialism, the weaknesses that would soon allow other, less major European powers to muscle in.

For one thing, the mainland colonies, awash with precious metals, proved a stronger short-term draw for adventurers risking their lives gambling against the frightening new diseases of the tropics. In addition, there were monopolies and government interference everywhere in the nascent industry: all produce had to be shipped through Seville; heavy excise duty was charged on imports, which were then only available for purchase to a closed ring of those buyers who had been wise enough to lend money to the profligate emperor of the time. The powerful Church took its chunk of profits in the form of tithes; a monopoly on imported labour did the rest. For a brief time there were 100 sugar factories at work in Spanish Hispaniola; by 1600 there were only 11. This pattern was duplicated around the Spanish Antilles.

Thus developing the industry (and expanding the market) fell to the other nation of great Atlantic explorers, the Portuguese. In the 1490s, the islands of São Tomé and Príncipe in the Gulf of Guinea were colonised by Portugal and put to cane. When combined with the supply from Madeira, this made Portugal the world's leading sugar producer. The African islands, like Madeira, would for various reasons quickly fade from the picture, but not before they had acted as a nursery of cane technology for the next great expansion. In 1500, Portugal claimed Brazil, and within 20 years had created a huge industry in sugar, initially manned by the indigenous population, then, as it fled or died out, by imported African slaves. Numerous sugar factories were established by the 1520s, and from the 1530s the industry expanded rapidly, particularly around Pernambuco, Olinda and Bahia.

It was a golden period for Brazil. By the end of the sixteenth century, a narrow coastal strip boasted more than 120 sugar mills in what had now become the richest European colony anywhere in the world. James Drax, visiting in around 1640, would have seen all this: the fabulous opulence of the local planters, their tables laden with silver and fine china, their doors fitted with gold locks; the women wearing huge jewels from the East, precious fabrics everywhere and an army of prostitutes and slaves always hovering. A French visitor at the beginning of the seventeenth century has described his visit to a Portuguese sugar baron, who took his lavish meals to the sounds of an orchestra of 30 beautiful black slave girls, presided over by a bandmaster imported from Europe. All was afloat on a sea of easy profit – the Dutch estimated that in 1620, the Brazilian sugar industry made the equivalent of more than half a million pounds sterling a year, an astonishing figure.

Unsurprisingly, the Dutch, who had emerged after a long struggle against Spanish rule into their Golden Age as Europe's most extensive and successful international traders and bankers, wanted a piece of the action. When, for dynastic reasons, Portugal merged with Spain towards the end of the sixteenth century, her colonies became fair game.

The Dutch West India Company, licensed to make war in search of profits for its backers, was founded in 1621 to get its hands on some of this trade. Three years later, the Company, with a force of 3,300 men and 26 ships under the command of Admiral Piet Heyn, attacked a town on the coast of Bahia. The port's two forts were quickly captured and the defenders dispersed. Driven out the following year, the Dutch returned in 1630, landing 7,000 soldiers at Recife. This time, the hinterland was secured, and soon the Dutch controlled a large area of north-east Brazil.

The conflict had been hugely damaging to the sugar industry, with dozens of factories destroyed in the fighting or to prevent them falling into enemy hands. But new leadership of the Dutch colony from 1636 brought the industry to another high, with hundreds of Dutch merchant ships carrying Brazilian sugar to the refineries of Holland. With the control of Brazil, the Dutch owned the sugar business.

The Dutch leadership successfully encouraged the Portuguese sugar-growers to re-establish their plantations and increase production. But the planters always bridled under the yoke of the hard-working, money-obsessed Calvinist Hollanders. By the early 1640s, cooperation was breaking down and there was agitation in the countryside. This, together with a string of poor harvests during 1642–4 (possibly caused by soil exhaustion in the coastal lands), led the Dutch to look for new sugar acres elsewhere to supply the cargoes for their giant merchant marine and hungry refineries at home. Thus when Drax came knocking in the early 1640s, he found a welcome audience happy to help expand sugar production in the Caribbean basin.

The earliest accounts of Barbados at this time are partial and contradictory. All agree, however, that Dutch influence was crucial in the establishment of the sugar industry on the island in the early 1640s. The actual technology was Portuguese, as the language of the sugar factory – *ingenio, muscovado* – demonstrates. But it was the Dutch, as a 1690 account has it, 'being eternall Prolers about, and Searchers for moderate Gains by Trade', who were the engine of its transfer, as well as offering to provide labour, tools, easy credit, and the ships to carry away the finished sugar. Most early Barbados narratives also agree on the importance of James Drax, who was about 30 years old at the time. The same 1690 account suggests that 'a Hollander happened to arrive in Barbados, and . . . was by one Mr Drax, and some other inhabitants there drawn in to make Discovery of the Art he had to make it'.

Drax's was not the very first sugar to be planted in Barbados. That honour belongs to a Colonel James Holdip. But as an account from around 1667 has it, the colonel's efforts 'came to little till the great industry and more thriving genius of Sir James Drax engaged in that great work'.

According to a friend of Drax, bringing the business of sugar growing and processing 'to perfection' during the 1640s took 'divers yeeres paines, care, patience and industry, with the disbersing of vast summes of money'. Drax, an early account maintains, imported from Holland 'the Model of a Sugar Mill' for crushing the canes to extract the juice, and some copper cauldrons for boiling the liquid until it was ready to crystallise.

Whatever advice he had received in Recife, along with the infant cane plants, it did not all go to plan at first. Drax, who may have been in partnership with a kinsman, William Hilliard, made several mistakes over the first year or two of his new enterprise. Unlike cotton and tobacco, sugar is difficult and time-consuming to grow, and very tricky to process. It appears that Drax cut his first crop too soon – after 12 months rather than the required 15 or more – and made a mess of the manufacture.

Drax's first sugar was awful, 'so moist, and full of molasses, and so ill cur'd, as they were hardly worth the bringing home for England'. But he and his men stuck at it, learning from trial and error, 'and by new directions from Brazil'. Instead of planting the canes vertically into holes in the ground, they started laying them lengthways in trenches. This anchored the plant and prevented it being blown over on the exposed St George's hillsides, as well as producing new shoots from each buried knot. The vertical rollers that crushed the cane were strengthened with plates of iron and brass, and the correct boiling sequence was established in copper cauldrons of varying sizes.

As soon as Drax's first competent Barbados sugar arrived on the London market, it yielded a far higher profit than any other American commodity, fetching as much as £5 per hundredweight. Drax reckoned it increased his income per acre fourfold over any other crop.

The stunning success of his experiment would see James Drax and his heirs – as well as other families – accrue fortunes beyond their wildest dreams. More than that, it would decisively affect the course of history, the fate of empires and the lives of millions. Most immediately, however, it would radically alter the nature of the 15-year-old colony in Barbados.

2

THE FIRST SETTLEMENTS, 1605–41

'I think he will carry this island home in his pocket, and give it his son for an apple.'
Shakespeare, *The Tempest*, II: 1

The father of the British West Indian sugar empire was a second son of undistinguished, though not impoverished, Midlands stock. James Drax's father William was the Anglican vicar of the village of Stoneleigh in Warwickshire. James had five siblings who survived into adulthood; three of his sisters married middling artisans in London – two joiners and a goldsmith.

It has been suggested that Drax's unusual name indicates some foreign connection, most likely Dutch. Although this is possible, what seems more certain is that someone in his family had links with the Courteens. William and Philip Courteen were the sons of a Dutch emigrant to England, who had fled Holland during the tyrannous reign of the Spanish Duke of Alba. His trading company, with links to Holland (his son William married the daughter of a powerful Dutch trader), had been expanded by his sons to take in almost all of Europe, Greenland, the East Indies and the Caribbean. Recently, a director of the Dutch West India Company with experience in the Americas had been taken on board as a partner.

The Courteen Company was of the new model of trading businesses of the late sixteenth and early seventeenth centuries. In a very short time, the ancient overland trade routes, bestridden all the way with middlemen after their percentage, had been bypassed by the newly discovered ocean highways, a short cut to undreamt-of profit margins. Suddenly there was a new breed of businessman in London – the transnational merchant prince, with connections across the globe and the merchant fleet to link them all together under his control.

The Courteen brothers employed people of many nationalities and had fingers in many pies. One of their mariners was an Englishman, John Powell, a veteran Caribbean trader and pirate, who in 1625 found himself blown off course on a regular return trip from supplying one of the infant English colonies on the northern part of mainland South America. He steered his vessel, the *Olive*, to the leeward, west coast of Barbados, where he dropped anchor. His men briefly explored the heavily wooded interior, and then erected a cross, claiming the uninhabited island for their monarch by inscribing 'James, King of England' on a tree.

On his return, Powell told the Courteens of the 'goodness of the island', and through the efforts of the Earl of Pembroke, an enthusiastic promoter of colonial ventures, the brothers soon afterwards obtained a patent from the crown to establish a new settlement. The first vessel dispatched to Barbados was the *William and John*, commanded by John Powell's brother Henry, and carrying some 50 settlers, along with arms, ammunition and provisions. At some point on the voyage, they came across a Portuguese vessel, no doubt on the way from Africa to Brazil. The ship was over-powered, and 10 black enslaved Africans were taken on to the *William and John* – the English sugar empire's very first slaves. In mid-February 1627, they came in sight of Barbados, and could make out 'a great ridge of white sand' fringed by palms, above which could be seen a land 'full of woods'.

On board the *William and John*, a later report affirms, were all three of the later sugar pioneers – Holdip, Hilliard and James Drax. According to the available evidence, Drax was 18 years old.

Henry Powell took his men ashore on 17 February at a point, now known as Holetown, about halfway up the west coast, where a small stream flows into the sea. Huge trees, many 200 feet tall, clustered thickly right up to the edge of the beach, the outer screen of a jungle of such fantastic tangled thickness as to be virtually impenetrable. As before, there was no sign of human habitation, no footprints on the beach. In fact, Barbados had once supported an Amerindian population as high as 10,000, but a combination of raids by the Spanish and by the warlike Carib Indians, together with lack of water,* had meant that by soon after 1500 it was deserted. For the arrivals in 1627, then, it was an empty, virgin new world.

Mastering the strange new land would, however, require urgent hard work. The first priority was to build shelter – from the sun, the tropical rains and hurricane storms, and the insects and rats. Holdip later told the story of how he and Drax lived at first 'in a cave in the rocks'. Soon,

---

* Unlike the volcanic Leeward Islands, Barbados was formed primarily from coral, and the resulting porous limestone meant that water drained away rather than forming rivers.

primitive shelters had been built, each consisting of little more than a frame of forked sticks stuck into the ground, with palm leaves and reeds for walls and roof.

In the energy-sapping heat and humidity, clearing land for planting proved extremely difficult. The subtropical forest was immensely thick: 'growne over with trees and undershrubs, without passage'. Ponds and wells had to be dug. Tools were in short supply and rusted rapidly in the warm damp climate. Few of the settlers had performed this sort of work before, many of the trees had wood 'as hard to cut as stone', and most were lashed together by prodigious vines. There was a 'multitude' of black ants, which would drop on to the men's heads as they worked. Eventually, though, a small plot of land was cleared and sown with wheat, with the felled trees used to build log cabins near the beach.

The earliest accounts from the island give us a feel of what life was like for the first settlers. It was above all a battle against nature and the elements, the 'dayly showres of raine, windes', and the 'cloudy sultry heat' that made the air as thick as jelly. 'With this great heat', wrote another earlier settler, 'there is such a moisture, as must of necessity cause the air to be very unwholesome.' On the seashore, there was an 'aboundance of smale knatts . . . yt bite', which at sunset would descend on the men. The settlers slept in hammocks with their ropes plastered with sticky tar to protect them from cockroaches, ants and rats, and a fire lit underneath to drive away noxious flying insects. Night-time brought a cacophony of unfamiliar noises: the sawing, ticking and trilling of insects, the 'squeakinge of Lisards & other cryinge creatures'.

To supplement the by now elderly and unpleasant provisions from the ship, the settlers hunted for turtle and hogs. Almost a hundred years earlier, a Portuguese ship's captain had left some pigs on the island, and their numerous descendants, gorged on the tropical fruits and sweet-tasting roots of the island, were now set about with abandon by the English. In the meantime, however, Henry Powell, having left his nephew John Powell Junior behind as the island's governor, had taken a small group of men and set sail from Barbados to a Dutch settlement on the Essequibo river in Guiana. The governor there, Amos van Groenenwegen, was a friend of Henry Powell; they had been shipmates working for the Courteens. It is likely that Powell's visit was long planned, as the Courteens were amongst the backers of the Dutch settlement. In return for trade goods from England, Powell acquired seeds and plants – tobacco, Indian corn, cassava, sweet potatoes, plantains, bananas, citrus fruits and melons. He also brought back from Guiana to Barbados some 30 or so Arawak Indians to instruct the settlers in the growing of these new and unfamiliar crops. In return, the Arawaks were allowed a piece of land and promised that if they wished, they would be returned home after two years, with £50 sterling in axes, bills, hoes, knives, looking-glasses and beads.

It would be some time before many of the plants were properly established. A visitor seven years later reported a wide range of fruits, 'but not in any great plentie as yet'. Nonetheless, as more land was cleared, the English settlers, increased by another 80 after the arrival of John Powell Sr in the *Peter* in May 1627, concentrated on growing tobacco. This was why the Courteens had invested in the settlement, inspired by the success of the Virginia colony established 20 years previously.

The initial results were encouraging. The tobacco plants 'grew so well that they produced an abundance', which was carried back to London (in one account by Henry Powell, in another by James Drax), where it arrived on the market at a time of scarcity. The considerable profit was invested in another 50 men to help work the island.

But there was a problem. Barbados tobacco, it turned out, was of a very inferior quality. One of the first settlers, Henry Winthrop, sent his initial crop back to his father John in England in early 1628. John Winthrop (who two years later would found the Massachusetts Bay settlement) wrote to his son that the rolls of tobacco were so 'very ill conditioned, fowle, full of stalkes and evil coloured' that he couldn't sell them even for five shillings a pound.

But although the more enterprising settlers like Drax started to look around for another staple, most of the white settlers, swollen to 1,800 by 1629, persisted with tobacco, which remained quick and easy to cultivate. In the meantime, the growing population, even those at the top of the hierarchy, often went hungry – 'much misery they have endured', reads an account from 1629. Then, in late 1630/early1631, a combination of factors put the very survival of the colony in doubt. First, the price of tobacco fell sharply to a tenth of its previous value. Barbados's inferior product was now almost worthless. The island's hog population, hunted with reckless abandon, had dwindled almost to extinction. At the same time, a severe drought blasted the wheat crop. The result was what would soon be known as 'the Starving Time'.

Of course, colonies in the Americas had failed before, with disastrous, usually fatal consequences for the settlers. For a long time, the Caribbean had been a 'Spanish lake'; by the Treaty of Tordesailles in 1494, the Pope had granted to Spain the whole of the Americas bar Brazil, but with the fading of Spanish power after the long war of 1585–1604, a number of other European powers – France, England, Holland, Denmark, Prussia, Sweden – had scrambled for 'a place in the sun'. The first were the Dutch; before the end of the century, they had established settlements in Guiana, and in 1600 they landed on the tiny island of St Eustatius near St Kitts. Emboldened by their success, French and English merchants also sponsored a number of attempted colonies.

The West Indies had always been 'beyond the line'. As early as the mid-sixteenth century, the French and Spanish, unable to settle their disputes over the Americas, had agreed that there would be a line in the Atlantic beyond which accepted European treaties, and, in effect, accepted European codes of conduct, would not apply. The English, in treaties in 1604 and 1630, implicitly accepted the same agreement. Thus, from the earliest days of the Spanish empire, the Caribbean was a constant theatre of violence and war – declared or not – infested by privateers, pirates, corsairs, call them what you will. It was a lawless space, a paradise for thieves, smugglers and murderers.

French and Dutch privateers were in the vanguard. Indeed, on his third voyage, Columbus himself had had to take action to avoid French pirates. In 1523, a privateer squadron originating from Dieppe hit the jackpot, capturing the Spanish treasure fleet and a huge prize of gold bars, pearls, emeralds and sugar as well as the crown jewels and wardrobe of Montezuma. Generations of adventurers from a host of countries would be inspired to attempt to repeat the feat.

For the English, though, the Caribbean had a particular resonance (particularly for those, like Drax, of solid Anglican sensibility). After the lucky defeat of the Spanish Armada in 1588, and the foiling of the Gunpowder Plot in 1605, English identity and self-esteem had become ever more closely tied to a new anti-Catholic and anti-Spanish nationalism. The heroes of this new mood were the Protestant 'sea dogs', such as Hawkins, Drake and Raleigh, and their stage was the Caribbean. Hawkins was the first, trading illegally in the West Indies in the 1560s. The next decade saw Sir Francis Drake rampaging around the Caribbean basin, sacking Nombre de Dios in Panama (and bringing home £40,000 in loot), and then, in the 1580s, capturing and ransacking Santo Domingo in Hispaniola and Cartegena on the Spanish Main. All was justified as revenging the terrible cruelties of the Spaniards.

Because the West Indies was 'beyond the line', it made little difference whether countries were at war or not; no quarter was given or expected. But the raw pursuit of Protestantism and profit, not necessarily in that order, often had a wider strategic aim – to attack Spain at the source of its wealth. Thus during the struggles of the Counter-Reformation, the Caribbean basin became, not for the last time, the 'cockpit of Europe, the arena of Europe's wars, hot and cold'. The most effective way for the rival powers to sap Spain's strength was to commission privateers to attack its trade and bullion lines in the West Indies. This also promised the chance of great dividends for those who fitted out and provisioned the privateers; for the first time, merchants in London started investing in faraway imperial schemes.*

The exploits of the Elizabethan corsairs and adventurers were read about in England in the works of Hakluyt, Purchas and Raleigh as well as in translations from Spanish accounts. But it was soon apparent that the swashbuckling was only part of the story. Many ships' captains found that it was almost as profitable and far less dangerous trading clandestinely with the Spanish rather than looting their settlements with fire and sword. Furthermore, the curiosity of these men about the new, exotic lands proved highly infectious. From the first shipwreck of Englishmen in Bermuda in 1609, the idea of the 'paradise island', untouched by time, gripped the English imagination even as strongly as that of pirates. For Andrew Marvell in his poem 'Bermudas', it was a Garden of Eden. For Shakespeare, or, more exactly, his Prospero, the emptiness of the island gave free rein. There was no barrier to Prospero's self-assertion and his control over the lower orders of man and beast, and even nature itself. Raleigh described Guiana, where he disastrously ruined his life and reputation seeking a mythical 'El Dorado', as 'a country that hath yet her Maidenhead, never sacked, turned, nor wrought'. The inhabitants of Guiana, told by Raleigh that he was there to free them from the Spanish yoke, were for him just part of the scenery, a chorus to sing the praises of the great new conquistador. So if the deserted paradise turned out to be occupied after all, that did not matter. For Defoe's later Robinson Crusoe also, the 'natives' are part of the landscape, rather than the owners of it.

These intoxicating stories were complemented by a new English knowledge of the region. Drake watered and rested his crews at various of the Leeward Islands, burying his dead and sometimes trading with the native Caribs. Between 1584 and 1602 all Raleigh's Virginia fleets passed through the Antilles on the way. Hundreds more mariners had brought back information about where was dangerous and where looked promising. Thus,

---

* Between 1585 and 1604, more than 200 English privateers visited the Caribbean, carrying home between £100,000 and £200,000 each year in gold, silver, pearls and sugar.

although plundering and smuggling would continue unabated, a new impulse emerged alongside: settlement.

However much imperial strength had ebbed, the first settlements were concentrated nonetheless around the peripheries of Spanish power, probing at weak spots.

North of Florida, Spanish potency was negligible. Colonies still failed, but in May 1607, a lasting English settlement was established in Jamestown, Virginia. After early setbacks, it prospered, thanks to its cultivation of tobacco. In 1620 the Plymouth colony was started, and further north the Dutch were settling around New Amsterdam by 1624.

Partly inspired by Ralcigh's El Dorado fantasy, 1604 saw the first of many doomed English attempts to settle around the Waiapoco River, situated in a semi-no-man's-land between the Amazon, controlled by Portugal, and the Orinoco, held by Spain. The first British effort to settle in the Caribbean came the following year, when a relief ship for the Guiana colony lost its bearings and ended up depositing a group of 67 settlers at St Lucia. The small but mountainous island had not been occupied by the Spanish, partly because it was home to a tribe of Caribs, whose warlike and supposedly cannibalistic nature was fast becoming legendary. The Caribs were at first friendly with the English, but then fell out over a sword sold to them against the rules and then reclaimed without compensation. After a sharp exchange, the surviving 19 settlers fled the island. An attempt at nearby Grenada four years later met with a similar fate, though fewer escaped.

The experience of St Lucia and Grenada did not bode well for further colonising attempts in the Carib-dominated Antilles. Furthermore, the islands, although not occupied by Spain, were on the imperial shipping routes, and the policy of the Emperor was to expel any European found trespassing on his American domain.

Nonetheless, on 28 January 1623, Englishman Thomas Warner landed a small group of settlers on the island of St Christopher, better known as St Kitts, a mountainous island of 65 square miles, situated in the northern Antilles. Warner, described as 'a man of extraordinary agility of body and a good witt', was a younger son of gentleman-yeoman stock. He had been involved in one of the many failed English settlements in Guiana. There, he had been advised to look at St Kitts, seemingly fertile, well watered and neglected by the Spaniards. Warner had returned home and gained the support of London merchant and his Suffolk neighbour Charles Jeaffreson. His party was at first welcomed by the local Carib chief Tegreeman, and allowed to make a settlement at Old Road. The purpose of the colony, like Barbados four years later, was tobacco. By September, Warner had raised his first crop, only to see it destroyed by a hurricane. Undaunted and, frankly, with no other option, Warner's men set to planting again, but in the meantime, relations with the Caribs had deteriorated. The English were building a fort, something that seems to have displeased the Carib chief, and rumours started circulating that the Caribs were planning a surprise attack. Warner reacted quickly and ruthlessly. Having invited the Caribs to a lavish, drink-fuelled feast, he then had them massacred as they lay dozing in their hammocks. Only a few were able to escape across the water in their canoes.

This was not the end of the Carib threat, because there were other settlements on neighbouring islands within sight of St Kitts. Warner realised his appalling weakness in numbers, and so, when a French ship arrived carrying a crew of adventurers under Pierre Belain d'Esnambuc, he welcomed them and offered to join forces. D'Esnambuc, a protégé of Cardinal Richelieu, had sailed from France on a piracy mission, but after taking a beating in battle with a Spanish galleon, he had ended up beaching his wrecked vessel at St Kitts.

The Frenchmen were persuaded to accept the northern and southern extremities of the island, leaving the English a consolidated holding in the middle. They all agreed to maintain strict neutrality in the event of their parent countries going to war, and to render each other aid in the event of a Carib or Spanish attack. The former was not long in coming. In 1625, a large Carib raiding party arrived in enormous canoes, each holding up to 100 men, and attacked the French settlement of Basseterre. After fierce fighting they were driven back into the sea with help from the English.

This turned out to be the high point of Franco-English cooperation in the Caribbean. Before the end of the century, as Spanish power faded further and the French and English became the leading competitors in the West Indies, they would be constantly at each other's throats, both on St Kitts and in the wider Caribbean. But for a brief period mutual interest dictated friendly relations, at least for most of the time. Perhaps the similarities between Warner and d'Esnambuc helped. The Frenchman had been, in effect, a pirate before a settler. Warner, having carried his first tobacco crop back to London, took time off to go hunting for prizes in the Channel and the Baltic. On his way back to St Kitts, he tried an attack on Trinidad. Both men were essentially transitional figures between privateer-plunderer and settler.

Warner brought back more settlers with him, many from Ireland, and others from south-west England, and in 1628 a number crossed to nearby Nevis to start a new settlement on its mountainous 50 square miles. In St

Kitts, Warner now lived in a modest timber dwelling and had built a 'great tobaccoe house that stood to the windward'. Their product was far superior to that of recently established Barbados, and although it was a hard struggle, the colony prospered and its population continued to grow.

But on 7 September 1629, the annual voyage of the Spanish galleons, on their way to Panama, was diverted from its usual more southerly route and appeared off St Kitts in the late afternoon. Its 35 large galleons and 14 armed merchant vessels must have been an awe-inspiring sight, for the colonists put up little resistance. As night fell, entrenchments were thrown up along the shore, but when the Spanish landed the next morning, their troops made rapid progress. A counter-attack was led by d'Esnambuc's nephew, but when he was killed, the effort failed, and the defending force of English and French fled the battlefield. The majority of the Frenchmen managed to escape across the sea to St Martin, and 200–300 English took to the woods in the high centre of the island, but 700 English were forced to surrender. The Spanish admiral destroyed the tobacco plantations, but was merciful with his captives, sending the majority home to Europe with a warning not to return on pain of death; the rest were condemned to the mines of the mainland, a perennial hazard of crossing the Spanish.

As the conquering force sailed away, the refugees in the woods crept back to their ruined farms and started replanting. Soon after, a French contingent returned. The settlement recovered, and in the early 1630s established daughter colonies in nearby Montserrat and Antigua. But the Spanish and Carib threat remained.

So in comparison with Guiana and the new Leeward Island colonies, Barbados enjoyed key advantages. It was, for now, comparatively healthy, and its isolated position south of the galleon routes and upwind of the rest of the Caribbean islands had kept it free from hostile incursions. But the first few years of the colony were blighted by more than the 'Starving Time' food shortages of 1630–1.

No sooner had the Courteen-funded *William and John* left England with Barbados's first settlers, than James Hay, Earl of Carlisle, came forward to claim that the island had been promised to him by the recently deceased James I. Carlisle was a Scot who had come south with James Stuart, and as a court favourite had received an earldom and a number of lucrative government sinecures. But he was a man of spectacular extravagance and enormous appetites, and he was by now deeply in debt, in the large part to a syndicate of London merchants, who urged him to claim his rights in the West Indies and thereby repay at least some of what was owed.

Charles I had a habit of signing anything put before him, and in July 1627 he duly granted to Carlisle the whole of the 'Caribee Islands'.

The Earl of Pembroke protested vigorously on behalf of his grant and the Courteen interest, but in the meantime Carlisle leased 10,000 Barbados acres to the merchants' syndicate and dispatched a party of 64 men to take possession, led by a Captain Wolverston, who was to be the colony's new governor. As soon as they reached Barbados in June 1628, they arrested and imprisoned Governor John Powell and started clearing Courteen settlers off the allotted 10,000 acres around 'the Bridge' (later Bridgetown).

While the argument between Pembroke and Carlisle continued in London, in Barbados, might made right. In February 1629, Henry Powell returned to the island with nearly 100 men, enticed Wolverston to a conference, and then had him seized and manacled. John Powell was released and reinstated as governor, and all the Carlisle party's possessions were confiscated, including a large tobacco crop. Henry Powell then took this back to England to be sold by the Courteens, accompanied by Wolverston in chains.

But soon afterwards, the characteristic dithering of Charles I's court came to an end. Although most lawyers thought Courteen had the better claim, royal instructions were issued in May 1629 confirming Carlisle as the rightful proprietor. To the fury of the Courteens, who had by now sunk £10,000 into their venture, Carlisle had proved the more dextrous courtier.

A new Carlisle governor, Sir William Tufton, was appointed, and while he prepared to take up his new post, a deputy governor, Henry Hawley, was quickly dispatched to the island. Hawley arrived in August and initially made conciliatory noises to the Courteen settlers. But he then tricked the Powell group on to his boat anchored in Bridgetown's Carlisle Bay on the pretence of holding a conference. Once on the ship, they were arrested. Some of their number escaped by jumping overboard, but Governor John Powell and his brother William were stripped and chained to the mast for over a month. Eventually they were shipped to St Kitts, where they arrived just in time to be taken prisoner by the Spanish during their descent on that island.

A visitor to Barbados that year wrote of the islanders that 'there have beene so many factions amongst them, I cannot from so many variable relations give you an certainty for their orderly Government'. While tensions simmered between the Carlisle party, now established in the area near 'the Bridge', and the Courteens, based around Holetown, Henry Hawley was cultivating his own particular ambitions, aware that the island's isolation gave the man on the spot free rein to assert himself. The arrival of Governor Tufton in September precipitated a power struggle between the two men. When Tufton became embroiled in armed clashes between the Courteens and the Carlisles, Hawley seized the chance to have him arrested on trumped-up charges and promptly executed by firing squad. This *fait accompli* would allow Hawley to remain as governor for the next decade, running a spectacularly corrupt regime, during which he concentrated entirely on enriching himself and rewarding his friends and supporters. Drax and Hilliard were among those from the original Courteen party who now reconciled themselves to Hawley's victory and became close to the new governor.*

But the turbulence caused by Hawley's coup continued, magnifying the tensions and frictions that any small, isolated community would suffer, and contributing to the nature of the islanders as described to us in the earliest detailed account of life in Barbados, that of Sir Henry Colt. Colt was a settler – he was on his way to St Kitts to start a plantation – but he still carried the whiff of the corsairs, writing in his journal that his party were determined not to rest 'vntell we haue doone some thinges worthy of ourselues, or dye in ye attempt'. On his way to St Kitts, he spent two weeks in Barbados in July 1631. In 10 days' travel around the plantations, he wrote, 'I neuer saw any man at work.' To clear the forest, it appears, the settlers had now resorted to burning, leaving all the earth 'couered black wth cenders'. Nonetheless, the ground was littered with the stubs of half-burnt trees, and 'nothinge is cleer . . . all are bushes, & long grasse, all thinges carryinge ye face of a desolate & disorderly shew to ye beholder'.

In spite of this unfavourable impression of the new, still raw plantations, Colt – like so many later visitors – was entranced by Barbados, writing that of all the places he had seen, 'not any pleaseth me soe well'. He was amazed at the exotic fruit, the luxuriance of the tropical vegetation, how everything grew so fast, and wrote highly approvingly of the taste of the fish and turtle, 'between fish and fleshe of veale'. Best of all was the pineapple, tasting 'unto a great white ripe strawberry'. He would not be the last to praise this favourite fruit of Englishmen in the Caribbean. An account from a few years later described it in delighted tones as 'an

---

* The most tragic fall-out of the triumph of the Carlisle faction was that the Arawaks, stripped of the protection of their patron Henry Powell, found themselves enslaved. When news of this outrage reached the Dutch colony in Guiana, only the nimble-footed actions of the governor, Groenenwegen, in marrying a local girl prevented a furious Arawak uprising. Many years later, in 1652, Henry Powell succeeded in having three survivors of this original party freed. In 1676 an Act was passed prohibiting bringing Indian slaves to the island, as they were considered 'a people of too subtle, bloody and dangerous inclination to be and remain here'.

Aromaticall compound of wine and strawberries'. Nor would he be the last to look around and wonder how on earth shortages of food had come about in a land whose air and soil produced with such 'marvellous swiftness'.

For Colt, as for many others, the fault was with the inhabitants, who were squandering the advantages they had been given by the paradise island. 'Slowth & negligence must only cause this people to want', he wrote. Furthermore, as well as being idle, the settlers he met – almost all men, and mostly very young – were argumentative and usually drunk. Colt says that in their company he went from drinking two drams of spirits with a meal to 30, and reckoned that had he spent more time on the island, he would have increased his intake to 60. All this stoked what Colt called 'ye quarrelsome conditions of your fyery spirits'. During the two weeks of his stay he witnessed numerous quarrels, most arising out of very slight disagreements. 'Suerly ye Deuill ye spirit of discord haue great power in America', he wrote. No one could 'liue long in quiett' in Barbados.

Colt also reports that his ship, anchored in the bay opposite 'the Bridge', was constantly having to expel 'servants' who had sneaked on board hoping to escape the island. From the first days of the colony, and for its first 20 years, the majority of the labour force was indentured workers from the British islands. Henry Powell, when leaving for Guiana to collect seeds and plants, wrote that the 40 or so men he left behind were 'servants'; as early as August 1627, Henry Winthrop wrote home asking for two or three servants to be sent out, bound to him for three to five years.

The backers of new colonies, wherever they were situated, needed able and willing hands – to clear land, build forts, plant crops. Under the system of indenture, developed by the Virginia Company in the 1620s, young men and women contracted themselves to work for a master for a period ranging from three to nine years. In return, they were given passage to the colonies and subsistence during their tenure. Some were paid annual wages, but most were promised a one-off payment – usually around £10 – or some land (in Barbados it was 10 acres) at the end of their contract.

Some 30,000 indentured servants went to the Caribbean during the reign of Charles I (1625–49), with a similar number going to the North American colonies (making up more than half the total emigrants). Among them there were dissenters and the politically disaffected, but most were from the rural poor, suffering from the severe economic and social troubles in England during the 1620s and 1630s, which included persistent inflation, recurring depressions and bad harvests.

Some of the servants – the majority of whom were from the West Country,

East Anglia or Ireland – were tricked by merchants or middlemen into selling their labour, or even kidnapped. Others sold themselves out of desperation. But a large number, with energy and ambition, genuinely saw emigration as a route to a new freedom, be it religious, political, economic or social.

Few, however, can have known just what they were letting themselves in for. Indenture might have evolved from the traditional institution of apprenticeship, but it was much harsher. Indentured workers served for longer, could be sold on by their masters, were unable to renegotiate their contracts, and seldom emerged with a trade at the end of it all.

On crowded ships from England or Ireland many died from sickness, and the survivors would arrive weakened, shaken, and utterly unfit to start the hard physical labour expected of them. Few were equipped with suitable clothes or hats for the scorching tropical climate, and strict rules governed every aspect of their lives. A visitor to Barbados in 1632 commented that the indentured workers were kept more like slaves than servants, and two years later an attempted rebellion was only foiled at the last minute by an informer. Two brothers considered ringleaders, the Westons, were seized and one of them was executed as an example.

Unlike those stowing away on Sir Henry Colt's ship, some indentured servants did succeed in escaping their bondage, and many others left the island once their period of indenture was complete. Some settled in the English Leeward colonies – St Kitts, Nevis, Montserratt, Antigua – where land was more available. Others took up privateering or contraband trade with the Spanish Main – an English colony founded in 1629 by Puritan grandees on the island of Providence, close to modern-day Nicaragua, provided a useful base, as did Tortuga, just off the northern coast of Hispaniola.

Meanwhile, the French, from 1635, started the slow and painful process of driving the Caribs out of Guadeloupe and Martinique, and in 1638 English settlers made another failed attempt at colonising St Lucia. Other expeditions soon after also came to grief. A small party started a settlement in Hispaniola, but were never heard of again. Their bones were found in 1645 at Cape Tiburon. New colonies were also attempted in Trinidad, Tobago and Surinam, but all were wiped out by a combination of disease, starvation and Carib attacks.

In Barbados, the 1630s were hard times, particularly in comparison with what would come towards the end of the next decade. Even substantial landowners lived entirely without luxuries. The owner of hundreds of acres who died in 1635 left behind nothing much more than a battered chest, a broken kettle, three books and a handful of pewter plates. Nonetheless, immigration continued to rise, and with it the island's population, from under 2,000 in 1630 to 6,000 by 1636, and some 10,000 at least by the end of the decade, on a par with Virginia or Massachusetts. One study has shown that a fifth of all those who left London in the mid-1630s headed for Barbados, which soon had a population density unrivalled anywhere in the Americas. The island did little to advertise itself to settlers (unlike the northern mainland colonies), but clearly back in Bristol, London or Cork, Barbados still seemed exotic and full of outrageous possibilities, as indeed it would prove to be.

The immigrant population, inevitably homesick, went some way to trying to mimic the England they had left behind, re-creating customs and habits, organising parishes, building churches. It was a notable failure, particularly when it came to religion. As late as 1641, there were only 10 clergymen on the island for a population in excess of 10,000. Furthermore, many of the priests were themselves fortune hunters, or those who had for various reasons failed to make it up the ecclesiastical ladder at home. Most had no qualifications.

The general failure to create a 'home from home' stemmed from the heat and strangeness of the Caribbean, its position 'beyond the line', the raw tensions between servants and masters, and the profile of those who emigrated to Barbados. Studies of ships' rosters from the 1630s have shown that emigrants were overwhelmingly male – more than 90 per cent – and almost all very young. Seventy per cent were aged between 15 and 24. (It was similar for the tobacco plantation colony of Virginia; women, children and families tended to head for the markedly more God-fearing settlements of New England.)

With such a population, with 16 men to every woman, the establishment of family life, which underpinned moral stability at home (and in New England), was an impossibility. Even 10 years later, a visitor to Barbados would complain of the incest, sodomy and bestiality prevalent on the island.

The leadership of the island set the tone for the rest. The Earl of Carlisle had instructed that leases on land be granted (sometimes for life, sometimes for seven years) on the basis of 10 acres per white servant in each household. The purpose was to ensure for the colony a large white population, and therefore a strong local militia. But Governor Hawley formed an illegal syndicate with his brother, with William Hilliard and with one William Smart, in order to dispose of land claimed under the Earl's policy by themselves and their friends. Thus in 1635 Hawley claimed 40 acres for four servants, but then sold the land to William Smart, who sold it on to James Drax for £12. Over the following two years the Hawley brothers claimed 2,600 acres for 260 servants, even though they had never owned more than 60. Much of the land was then sold on to William Hilliard. At the same time, Governor Hawley was making a fortune through a poll tax and arbitrary fines and confiscations. Those who resisted were arrested and imprisoned or pilloried in the hot sun, with a favourite twist being to nail the victim's ears to the stocks.

Eventually though, Hawley overreached himself and heard that he would be replaced. To garner support, he invited influential Barbadians to form the island's first ever Assembly, with 22 delegates elected by wealthy freeholders in each parish (with Drax amongst those chosen). Nonetheless, in 1640 Hawley was arrested by the new governor, Henry Huncks, and returned to England as a prisoner.*

Huncks had served for six months as governor of Antigua, where he had gained a reputation as a drunken, vindictive tyrant and an unabashed seducer of his friends' wives. Arriving in Barbados, he declared that he did not care threepence for what people said about him, and set about installing his cronies in all the public positions in the island. Captain James Futter, a planter who had impressed Sir Henry Colt as a rare example of a skilful local farmer, asked in open court, 'If all the whore-masters were taken off the Bench, what would the Governor do for a Council?' He then pointed out that Carlisle himself was 'too much given to drink'. He received an hour in pillory in the burning midday sun for his outspokenness, but he was certainly right about the island's proprietor.

All the while, as the population grew, the island was being transformed. While the hard work of forest clearance proceeded slowly, many indigenous birds and other creatures were rapidly destroyed. By 1634, the hog population had been wastefully exterminated. There was fish still aplenty off the coasts, but in the heat it went bad so rapidly that the islanders started importing dried cod. A visitor in 1634 arrived under the impression that Barbados was the 'granarie of all the Charybbies Iles'. Instead he found that food was scarce and 'bore so high price, that nothing could be had, but it Cost us our eies'.

In other ways, little had changed between Colt's visit in 1631 and the end of the decade. Most striking was the continuation of the islanders' extraordinary and lethal alcohol intake.

A visitor to Barbados at the end of the decade wrote home that the

* Hawley would return to Barbados, and died in 1677 allegedly as a result of falling down the stairs of the Roebuck Tavern in Bridgetown while intoxicated.

islanders were 'such great drunkards' that they would find the money 'to buy drink all though they goe naked'. When they could not import wines, ales and spirits they made their own, initially 'mobby', made from sweet potatoes mashed then fermented, which reportedly tasted like 'Rhenish wine', and 'perino' from fermented cassava. Walking to church on a Sunday, the same visitor wrote in another letter that he came across people sprawled by the side of the road who had had their toes bitten off by landcrabs as they lay passed out. In 1641, a Reverend Mr John Wilson charged that the 'Inhabitants had pissed out 15000 [pounds sterling] . . . against the wall . . . by their excessive drinking'.

Henry Colt had declared in 1631 that the great hope for the island was in cotton. Although tobacco prices recovered after the slump of 1630–1, and many farmers continued to concentrate on producing it, a few of the more enterprising men moved into other crops. Fustic wood, a useful dye, was harvested, and indigo and ginger planted. Most important, though, was cotton.

Cotton was a more difficult crop to grow, and more capital-intensive than tobacco. Cotton gins and outbuildings were needed for its processing, and expensive canvas bags for its shipping. But with help from the Dutch in Brazil, those willing to work hard mastered the art impressively quickly, and what was more, the end product was highly regarded, unlike Barbados tobacco. By 1634 there were a number of cotton gins and warehouses in operation, and the value of the crop had surpassed tobacco by the late 1630s, finding a ready market in the mills of Lancashire, all too pleased to be released from their reliance on imports from Cyprus and the Levant.

The success of the switch to cotton kept the island afloat during the mid-1630s, and perhaps most significantly, demonstrated to investors among the merchants of London that there were planters in Barbados with competence and professionalism enough to be entrusted with the huge loans that sugar plantation establishment would require. As would be the case with sugar, the leading cotton producers were Hilliard, Holdip and James Drax.

By the mid-1630s, Drax, a Commissioner for Roads and a captain in the militia, had become a leading light in the infant colony, and the success story of his family. From the paltry evidence that survives, we know he was physically tough, solidly built and a stickler for debts being paid on time, which was something of a rarity in the free-wheeling colonies. Some time early in the decade, possibly after the death of his father in 1632, Drax's elder brother William and spinster sister Frances both emigrated to join their enterprising brother in Barbados. William and James went into partnership with a Thomas Middleton, started acquiring land in St George's parish, and commenced the arduous process of clearing away the thick forest.

In the mid to late 1630s, the young James Drax married Meliora Horton from a Somerset family who may have been his distant cousins. She was the sister, or possibly niece, of Ursula, who had married Drax's brother William. We can only speculate whether the marriages were love matches or planned by the families; whether James Drax met Meliora on a visit to England during this period, or instead William came out to Barbados with his new bride and Meliora in tow. It is known, however, that James and Meliora's first child, also named James, was born around 1639. He seems to have been a sickly child. A second son, Henry, was born two years later.

All the time, Drax was buying and selling land, steadily increasing his acreage, paying with cotton, which was fast supplanting tobacco as the currency of the island. By 1641 he had over 400 acres, making him almost, but not quite, the greatest landowner on the island. He was the first to have a significant number of enslaved black Africans working his plantations. He had 22 on one of his estates in 1641, at a time when no one else had more than a handful alongside their white servants.

But the end of the decade saw a disastrous fall in the prices of all of Barbados's staples. The value of its tobacco plummeted in 1638, and in 1640 the prices for cotton and indigo also fell, at the same time as the cotton growers recorded their most disappointing crop. A pamphleteer would write 10 years later that in the first years of the 1640s, the island was 'in a very low condition'. Merchants stopped calling there and supplies ran low. 'The inhabitants', we are told, 'being so wearied out with the small profits they reaped in their toylsome labours, daily run from the Island in Boats, being very much indebted both to the Merchants and also to one another.'

But one commodity seemed to be on the rise. During the 1630s, the price of sugar had remained low, as the Dutch shipped hundreds of thousands of tons from Brazil. But a combination of falling yields and political disturbance in Brazil had led to a sudden rise in its value. Drax saw his chance and took it.

At the same time, Barbados found itself freer than ever before to go its own way, to trade with whomever it wanted and make its own fortune. Governor Huncks was replaced in 1641 by the accommodating Philip Bell, an elderly and experienced Caribbean hand who was happy to leave the planters to their own devices; while in England, the beginning of the Civil War ushered in a decade of what turned out to be benign neglect from the metropolis.

Into the vacuum stepped the Dutch, who had by now established trading stations on small islands all over the West Indies. 'The Hollanders that are great encouragers of our Plantacions, did at the first attempt of making sugar, give great Credit to the most sober Inhabitants, and upon the unhappie Civill warr, that brake out in England, they managed the whole trade in our Westerne Collonies', reads an account from the 1660s. They also 'furnished the island with Negroes, Coppers, Stills, and all other things appertaining to the . . . making of Sugar'.

The stage was thus set for the triumph of sugar and everything that would go with it. With hindsight, for all its backwardness, tumult and impoverishment, the settler society of Barbados of the 1630s had been more economically diversified, relatively healthier and less brutal than what would follow. With the vital help of the Dutch, and with the leadership of James Drax and a few others, a new, radically different society was about to be created.

3

THE SUGAR REVOLUTION:
'SO NOBLE AN UNDERTAKING'

'If you go to Barbados you shal see a flourishing Iland many able men.'
George Downing, 1645

At the beginning of the 1640s, a crucial decade in Barbadian history, and, indeed, in the history of all of British America, a small number of planters such as Drax and Hilliard were in possession of fairly large estates, even though we know they were still far from cleared of forest. They had bene-fited not only from their apparent closeness to the corrupt Governor Hawley, but also from their early arrival in the colony. The first years of the Carlisle administration had seen large grants given out, averaging over 300 acres in 1630. But for the rest of the 1630s, with a handful of excep-tions, the grants had been smaller, in the region of 50 to 80 acres. So in the main, Barbados was an island of small farms, most owner-operated, usually by a single man with one or two indentured servants, or by a couple of farmers in partnership. A number were still struggling on with tobacco; others were now growing cotton, indigo or ginger for export. Most had some land in provisions and the odd pig or chicken scratching around the tiny board houses in which most of them lived. Much effort was still being expended in clearing land, and, short of tools, many had resorted to ring-barking and burning. Alongside the 10,000–12,000 whites were perhaps 1,000 black slaves and a handful of Arawak Indians. With the advent of sugar, all of this was about to change dramatically.

The Barbadians' mastery of cotton cultivation had been highly impres-sive. But sugar was on a different level, far more demanding in terms of the amount of labour, capital and expertise required for success. Planting, weeding and harvesting the cane and protecting it from rats and other pests was much more physically demanding work than producing cotton or tobacco crops, and that was only a part of the challenge. The canes had to be cut at exactly the right ripeness (during the dry months of January to June), and then, as they quickly spoil, the juice had to be extracted as fast as possible. This required the sugar planter to have a grinding mill of his own nearby, or at least access to one.

Once the canes had been fed through vertical rollers, powered at this time in the main by oxen, horses or men, the resulting juice (a green liquid, due to the innumerable tiny particles of cane in suspension within it) would, if left, quickly ferment. Thus the next stage of processing had to be immediate and on hand. The juice was then conveyed to a boiling house, where through a succession of operations, ever greater quantities of liquid were removed from the crystallising sugar. This was the most complicated process of all. Within the boiling house, usually situated adjacent to the mill, a series of four or five large copper kettles stood over a furnace. These were carefully scaled for size. The juice went in the largest first; the boiler, who needed to be highly skilled, skimmed impurities off the top of the liquid before ladling the contents into the next largest copper. As the receptacles got smaller, so they became hotter, until at last the sugar was thick, ropy, and dark brown in colour. Quicklime was added to aid granulation, and then the mixture was 'struck': at exactly the right moment, the boiler dampened the fire and ladled the sugar into a cooling cistern.

It was easy to get this wrong, as Drax had discovered with his first efforts. The head boiler, in order to determine how much lime temper the cane juice needed and the period of boiling, needed to know how the cane had been raised and treated, the type of soil it had grown in, how it had been harvested, and whether it had been attacked by insect pests or rats.

If everything went to plan, the planter now had a raw brown sugar called muscovado, combined with a liquid by-product, molasses. To cure the sugar, it needed to be packed into earthenware pots, the molasses drained for up to a month, and the remaining golden-brown sugar spread in the sun to dry before being sent in leather bags to Bridgetown, where it was packed into hogsheads, large barrels that held about 1,500 pounds of sugar. For an inland plantation like that of Drax, everything had to be carried to the coast by hand or on the backs of mules 'up and down the Gullies', 'for the ways are such, as no Carts can pass'. It seems that Drax, for one, had his own packing and warehouse premises in Bridgetown. The hogsheads were then carried away, usually in Dutch ships, which took them to Amsterdam, Hamburg or London, where the sugar commanded consistently high prices.

The whole process required very careful supervision, and a carefully laid-out and well-equipped works for which machinery had to be imported, assembled, maintained, and sometimes modified. To ensure exactly the right supply of cane to the mill during the harvest months, great care had to be taken with the timing of the original planting. The sugar plantation, then, was an integrated combination of agriculture and industry, with every part depending on the others, 'as wheels in a Clock'.

This was an immensely sophisticated production unit for the seventeenth century, at a time when agriculture at home in England remained hidebound and moribund. It says a great deal for the energy, hard work, and fierce, big-thinking ambition of the sugar pioneers that they mastered a process that has more in common with modern assembly lines than any sort of farming carried out in Europe at that time, and required a labour force much more complex than, for example, an English estate. And all far from home, in the enervating heat of the Caribbean. They must, indeed, have been as a contemporary described them, 'men of great abilities, and parts'.

In 1644, only Drax and his partner Hilliard, growing cane at the next-door estate, are on record as using sugar as currency, others still paying bills with tobacco or cotton. It appears that Drax was the first to build a 'factory in the field', and it is likely that, initially, Hilliard's sugar was processed there as well (although three years later, he would have his own *ingenio*, or factory). In addition, Drax persuaded a number of smallholders nearby to grow canes for his mill. But this was not a great success – they made a mess of it, and Drax began to come round to the idea of creating a self-contained unit, with all growing, processing and labour under his direct control. At the same time, he started rapidly increasing his slave holding: his first use of sugar as currency was to purchase 34 of the 254 slaves on the *Mary Bonaventure*. For payment he engaged with three London merchants to ship them 'so much Suger or other merchantable commodities as shall amount to £726 sterling'. In the same year, Drax erected the island's first windmill for grinding the cane. Built to a Dutch design, its heavy rollers could crush eight tons of cane a day.

Drax's secret experiment did not stay secret for long. Soon, more and more land was planted in sugar. By 1645, cane covered 40 per cent of the island's agricultural acreage. For those who made the switch, it was a shrewd move. The following year, the returns would be spectacular.

In 1645, a war of liberation broke out in Brazil as the Portuguese attempted to expel the Dutch. There was widespread destruction of cane-fields and mills, and a mass escape of the enslaved workforce. Effectively, sugar production was stopped for a year, sending the price of the commodity soaring. At the same time, the Barbados canefields, with much of the planting into virgin land and enjoying perfect weather conditions, produced a tremendous crop. Barbados sugar growers were suddenly rich.

Puritan minister James Parker, who had come to Barbados from Piscataqua, informed Massachusetts Bay Colony Governor John Winthrop in June 1646 that Barbados 'is now and like to be very wealthy . . . some have made this yeare off one acre off canes about 4000 weight of sugar, ordinarily 3000'. The immediate local result was a sharp rise in the price of land. According to one study, land that sold at 10s. an acre in 1640 sold at £5 in 1646, a tenfold increase. Certainly by 1647, land was selling for an average of well above £5 an acre, and more for the best situated. For this to make economic sense, as much of Barbados's small space as possible had to be planted in sugar. Indeed, all over the island the forests were now destroyed with renewed vigour and land previously given over to provisions was put to cane. 'Men are so intent upon planting sugar that they would rather buy foode at very deare rates than produce it by labour, soe infinite is the profitt of sugar', reads a letter of July 1647 to John Winthrop from Richard Vines, a doctor from New England practising in Barbados. Indeed, the rapid sugar 'rush' meant that suddenly Barbados could no longer feed itself, even if the harvest was good. Suppliers of provisions from Europe benefited, of course, but most important was the lifeline this now threw to the North American colonies.

Links between the Caribbean and North America had existed from the earliest times of English settlement. Pioneer traders had sailed south from New England during the 1630s to exchange pipe staves, needed for making barrels, planks, fish or candle oil for cotton and salt. From Virginia they brought oxen and horses. But they were few in number and most of their vessels were small, seldom over 50 tons. This contributed to the dangers of the journey at a time when many of the sailors were inexperienced and little was known of routes and currents. A great number were lost to shipwreck and other disasters.

But suddenly, in the 1640s, trade became much more important to the New Englanders. There was no market for North American products in England, so instead they had exchanged their agricultural surplus for the cash and metropolitan wares of the plentiful new immigrants. But at the end of the 1630s, the flow of newcomers came to a virtual halt, creating an economic crisis in New England. Credit dried up and the prices of land and cattle fell by more than a half. Leaders even considered relocating the colony.

According to John Winthrop, Governor of Massachusetts Bay Colony,

'These straits set our people on work to provide fish, clapboards, planks etc. . . . and to look to the West Indies for a trade.' In his journal, he wrote in February 1641 that 'The general fear of want of foreign commodities, now [that] our money was gone . . . set us on to work to provide shipping of our own.' Construction started at Salem on a vessel of 300 tons, and in Boston another of 150 tons was undertaken.

In around September 1641, the 11-year-old Bay Colony dispatched two ships to the West Indies. They were gone nearly a year, 'and were much feared to be lost'. Then one returned at last, carrying a good cargo of cotton as well as letters from Barbados.

It remained a dangerous journey, and not just because of storms or treacherous seas. Winthrop described a voyage starting in November 1644, carrying pipe staves across to the Canaries and Cape Verde Islands to be exchanged for wine and 'Africoes'. Both were sold in Barbados for sugar, salt and tobacco. It is likely the enslaved Africans from the Atlantic islands would be familiar with sugar cultivation and processing, and therefore extra valuable. Six months after setting out, the vessel returned safely to New England, but also brought news of another ship from Cambridge, Massachusetts, which had been set upon by Royalist privateers working out of Irish ports. A fierce battle had taken place off the Canary Islands as the attackers boarded the New England ship. They were eventually driven off, but only after several deaths and massive damage to the ship and its cargo.

By 1647, in spite of the risks, there was regular trade between the northern colonies and Barbados, much to the benefit of both sides. An ox that cost £5 in Virginia could be sold for £25 in Barbados, while Barbadians, increasingly dependent on imported food, could, with the right factor in New England or Virginia, obtain provisions much more cheaply than from Europe. New England now had a market for its surplus agricultural production, and to carry the trade, a shipbuilding industry was quickly established.

Rhode Island, to the south of the Massachusetts Bay Colony, peopled with those who had chafed at the restrictions of Puritan society, was by the end of the 1640s breeding horses specifically for sale in Barbados. This would soon become a staple export. At Newport, the first large wharf was constructed at this time. The earliest major departure that has survived in the record is of the 40-ton ship the *Beginningfirst*, fitted out in 1649 by carpenter-turned-merchant William Withington to carry 12 Rhode Island cattle, together with 'necessary Hay and corn for voyage to Barbados, and Guinney'. The return was via Antigua and Boston. In the same year a Dutch privateer, Captain Blaufeld, gave Newport the questionable honour of making it his base for disposing of prizes. In 1651, cultivated Royalist Francis Brinley moved to Newport from Barbados and established himself as the island's agent.

Inevitably some of the traders settled to establish themselves as local merchants, or even to start out as planters. Samuel Winthrop, as a four-year-old infant, had been with his father on the *Arbella* sailing to found the Massachusetts Bay Colony in 1630. In 1647, aged 19, he had carried wine from Madeira to Barbados, made a handsome profit, and then moved on to St Kitts to set himself up as a merchant. The following year, though, he wrote to his father that he had resolved on Barbados, 'where in all probability I can live better than in other places'. Part of the attraction, it appears, was the 'New England friends' already operating there who might be able to give him an opening.

William Vassall was a founder member of the Massachusetts Bay Company and had been on the Winthrop fleet in 1630. Wealthy and highly educated, by the 1640s he had tired of the strictures of the 'City on a Hill', and in 1648 relocated to Barbados, where he straightaway started buying land and influence, while trading between New England and his brother Samuel, who had remained in England. By the time of his death 10 years later, William was a substantial merchant in servants and slaves, Commissioner of the Highways and owner of a plantation in St Michael, as well as extensive New England property. Other ambitious and adventurous families were also in the process of spreading themselves into networks around New England, the West Indies and England.

Clearly for some New Englanders, the West Indies held the same attraction as for their cousins back in England. John Winthrop complained that in spite of the 'meagre, unhealthful countenances' of those West Indians who had appeared in New England, many of his community were selling up and heading south, so taken were they with the supposed 'great advantages' and 'ease and plenty of those countries'. But others saw the islands in a different light. In 1641, Governor Bell of Barbados had written to Winthrop asking that a number of God-fearing North Americans be sent down to inspire the island with some religious orthodoxy, but 'understanding that these people were much infected with familism, etc., the elders did nothing about it', wrote Winthrop. Bell tried again in a letter received by Winthrop in August 1643, 'earnestly desiring us to send them some godly ministers and other good people . . . but none of our ministers would go thither'. Eventually, though, some New England ministers did make the journey, and the letters back home of one have survived. The island abounded with heresies, complained the Reverend James Parker in a letter of April 1646. Everywhere was to be found profanity, 'divisions', argumentativeness, drinking. 'How oft have I thought in my hearte, oh howe happie are New England people!' he exclaimed.

But certain parts of Barbados society were changing. Christopher Codrington, the founder of a West Indian family of huge importance, had arrived in Barbados some time in the late 1630s. The middle son of three, he stood out from the other planters on the island: his family were long-established Gloucestershire magnates who traced their lineage back to a standard-bearer for Henry V at Agincourt; his elder brother was High Sheriff of Gloucester. This had made him the exception on the island, as no other planter had such aristocratic blood. Codrington also appears to have had Royalist sympathies, in contrast to the likes of Drax, Middleton and the other earliest planters, who instinctively took against Charles I's 'personal rule' and pro-Catholic leanings. Nevertheless, sometime in the late 1630s, Codrington married Frances Drax, sister of James and William, creating an important alliance between the two families. In 1640 their first son was born, also called Christopher. This son was destined to be at one time the most important Englishman in the Americas. Soon afterwards, Codrington the first, his father, started acquiring land and took up a place on the island's council. A second son, John Codrington, followed a few years later.

The bitter and bloody Civil War in England brought many more families of the ilk of the Codringtons to Barbados, particularly after the defeats of the Royalists at Naseby and Langport in the summer of 1645. Leadership of the 'Cavalier expatriates' was quickly assumed by Humphrey Walrond and his brother Edward from a wealthy landed West Country family. Humphrey, at this time in his mid-forties, had been given up as a hostage at the surrender of the Royalist enclave of Bridgwater in July 1645. He was imprisoned, but then released on agreement that he pay a huge fine. Instead, Walrond sold up his estates and, together with this brother Edward and son George, who had lost an arm fighting for Charles I, fled to Barbados.

Also captured at Bridgwater was 22-year-old Major William Byam. Like Codrington, he would become the founder of a great West Indian dynasty, and he too claimed distinguished blood. One of his ancestors, an Earl of Hereford, was supposedly one of the Knights of the Round Table. His uncle was Charles II's personal chaplain. Byam was imprisoned by the Parliamentarians in the Tower of London, but then given a pass 'to go beyond the seas'. He, too, headed for Barbados, together with his wife Dorothy, who not only boasted royal connections, but was also, according to a French priest who met her some seven years later, 'one of the most beautiful women ever seen'.

These new arrivals brought an aristocratic and metropolitan sophistication to the small island, as well as money and credit. Some bought up plantations, others acted as factors for the Dutch shippers who dominated Barbados's trade. They also brought a new attitude to the top echelons of island society – a sumptuous, showy style of living, where their extravagance and taste were there for everyone else to see and admire.

In April 1646, the besieged city of Exeter surrendered to Parliamentary forces under Sir Thomas Fairfax. Amongst the captured Royalists was 27-year-old Thomas Modyford, a barrister, the son of a prosperous Exeter merchant and mayor of the city. Appointed by the King as a Commissioner for Devon, he was part of the Royalist delegation negotiating the surrender of the city. Fairfax remembered that Modyford 'demeaned himself with much civility and mildness, expressed a more than ordinary care for easing the country, and for its preservation from oppression, and showed activity and forwardness to expedite the treaty for the surrender'. Such pragmatism and tact would serve Modyford extremely well during his subsequent spectacular career in the West Indies.

Modyford was fined £35 but escaped imprisonment. He decided that he was 'now willing to shift' and, like many of his fellow defeated Royalists, determined on a new start in the West Indies. But for Modyford, it was not the hopeful voyage of servants or the poor but a well-organised and determined act of colonisation. Modyford's brother-in-law was Thomas Kendall, a wealthy and influential London merchant with experience of the Caribbean trade. The two men now formed a partnership, and in the summer of 1647 two ships were dispatched, one from Plymouth, carrying 'men, victuals and all utensils fitted for a Plantation', the second, the Kendall-owned *Achilles*, from London, carrying Modyford and his immediate retinue and further manpower. The plan was to ship English trade goods to the Canaries and Cape Verde Islands, exchanging them there for horses and cattle. These would be sold in Barbados, then the party would proceed to Antigua to establish a sugar plantation on the plentiful empty acres there.

With Modyford at Exeter, and on his subsequent emigration to Barbados, was Richard Ligon, author of *A True and Exact History of the Island of Barbados*, by far the most vivid, sophisticated and considered contemporary account we have of these crucial, transformatory early years of the Sugar Revolution. Ligon was from a Worcestershire family of respectable name but diluted fortune; he was the fourth son of a third son. He seems to have been university-educated, probably at Balliol College, Oxford, and at some point forged links at court through the wife of James I. From his writing, we know he was well versed in architecture, horticulture, music and art. However, by mid-1647, when Ligon was coming up to 60 years old, he was in severe difficulties. Not only was he on the losing side in the Civil War, but he was also penniless and being pursued by his creditors. A large investment in a scheme to drain the Fens had backfired spectacularly, when a 'Barbrous Riot' had invaded and taken over his lands.

By the time of the fall of Exeter to the forces of Parliament, Ligon had attached himself to Modyford's retinue, and in defeat was just as keen to get away. He was now, he wrote, 'a stranger in my own Countrey', and, 'stript and rifled of all I had', was resolved to 'famish or fly'. With the approval of Thomas Kendall, for whom Ligon was useful as an understudy should Modyford 'miscarry in the Voyage', Ligon joined the party on the *Achilles* bound for Barbados.

Ligon wrote that he had travelled in his youth, and we know that his eldest brother Thomas migrated to Virginia, establishing the North American Ligon family, but it is very unlikely that Richard had been to the tropics before, as his account shares the sense of wonder and excitement shown by every first-time visitor to the West Indies.

Richard Ligon described himself as a man of 'age and gravity', but his boyish enthusiasm when, after a long voyage, the island of Barbados came into view, is plain to read: 'Being now come in sight of this happy Island, the nearer we came, the more beautiful it appeared to our eyes.' Soon they could make out 'the high large and lofty trees, with their spreading branches and flourishing tops'. Ligon pleaded unsuccessfully with the captain to lower some of the sails that were impeding this view, but soon he could see on the rising ground behind the beach 'the Plantations . . . one above another: like several stories in stately buildings, which afforded us a large proportion of delight'.

It was not only 'extreamly beautiful'; it also, for Ligon, held out the promise of a more orderly society than the one he had left behind. Just as the lofty trees they could see from the boat were nourished by the soil and in turn gave it shade, so for 'perfect Harmony', he mused, the 'Mighty men and Rulers of the earth by their prudent and careful protection, secure [the poor] from harms', receiving, in return, 'faithful obedience'. Thus, like for many other new arrivals, the island had already come to encapsulate Ligon's hopes for a better world and a reversal in his fortunes.

At Bridgetown he was impressed to see a large number of storehouses and in Carlisle Bay more than 20 'good ships' with 'boats plying too and fro . . . So quick stirring and as numerous, as I have seen it below the bridge at London.' But it was the strangeness and beauty of the island's

'infinite varieties' of unfamiliar tropical vegetation that made the greatest
first impression. Best of all was the royal palm, the most 'magnificent tree
growing on the earth, for beauty and largeness, not to be paralleled . . . if
you had ever seen her, you could not but have fallen in love with her'.

The new arrivals were brought back down to earth by the news that their
other vessel, which had set out before them, had 'miscarried'. This meant
that the Antigua plan had to be shelved: Modyford no longer had the labour
force needed to start a plantation on uncleared land. He thus decided to
remain in Barbados, 'til the times became better, and fitter for our remove'.
Consulting 'the most knowing men of the Island', Modyford was advised
that if you had money or credit, you were better off taking on a fully stocked
and operational plantation rather than starting from scratch, even if undeveloped land could be had far cheaper.

Governor Philip Bell introduced Modyford and Ligon to William
Hilliard, who told them he was 'desirous to suck in some of the sweet air
of England', and invited them to his 500-acre plantation in St Johns, which
bordered that of James Drax. Clearly Hilliard had undertaken what Ligon
called the 'hardships . . . tedious expectation' and 'many years patience'
required to establish a working sugar plantation. He now had 200 acres in
cane, which was considered the maximum that could be processed by a
single factory. His operation consisted of a 400-square-foot mill, a boiling
house and four other buildings for processing the sugar. There were also
stables, a smithy, storage for provisions and houses for his workforce of
'96 Negroes, and three Indian women, with their Children; 28 Christians'.
The list of 'stock' continues with: '45 Cattle for work, 8 Milch Cows, a
dozen Horses and Mares, 16 Assinigoes [asses]'. Apart from the sugar cane,
150 acres of the 500 was still wooded, the rest taken up with provisions
and pasture, with very small plots still in cotton, tobacco and ginger.

Hilliard's substantial investment turned out to be shrewd. After a month
of negotiations, Modyford agreed to buy a half-share in the plantation, with
the understanding that he would run the estate in Hilliard's absence. Before
cane had been planted and the sugar works built, the land had been worth
£400. Modyford was happy to pay £7,000 for his half-share, £1,000 down
and the remainder in three instalments over the next two years, paid for in
sugar from the crop. It was a fabulous return for Hilliard, but with the
sugar on stream, Modyford considered it a very good deal. He told Ligon
that he had resolved not to return to England until he had made £100,000
sterling – a staggeringly large fortune – out of sugar.

For three years Richard Ligon lived on the plantation, now called Kendal.
For some of the time he was employed in 'publick works' such as cutting

paths, but mostly he dabbled in his wide range of interests while working as a secretary and adviser to Modyford.

Like most newcomers to the tropics, he suffered in the heat. It was 'scorching', but above all suffocatingly humid, 'sweaty and clammy'. The result, Ligon found, was a numbing lethargy, 'a great failing in the vigour, and sprightliness we have in colder Climates'. He moaned about the biting cockroaches and mosquitoes, and, in particular, the chiggers that burrowed into his feet. But he was fascinated by the snakes, scorpions, ants and crabs and the melancholy-looking birds, as well as the vibrant night-time noise, which he described as resembling 'a pack of small beagles at a distance'.

After more than five years of penury in England, Ligon was now living the good life, pampered by Kendal's house slaves, including a beautiful Indian girl,* and moving among the great and the good of the island. He was clearly a regular visitor to the next-door Drax plantation. He described how Drax's men were busy felling trees, battling the ever-present vines, and how Drax himself lived 'like a Prince'. Almost uniquely on the island, Drax was rich enough to kill an ox for meat – for most they were too badly needed for work – and, Ligon noted, it was at Drax's house that he ate the 'best Virginia Botargo' (tuna roe) that he had ever tasted.

Indeed, Ligon wrote about food with the passion of a gourmand who has suffered years of hunger. He enjoyed the local pork, fish, fruit and spices, as well as imported beef, salt fish, spirits and beer. He chided the planters for overcooking or overseasoning some of their food, and instructed them in cooking and meat-dressing techniques, including the use of lemons, limes, mace, nutmeg and cloves. He had brought with him seeds of herbs such as rosemary, thyme, marjoram and parsley, and of vegetables including onion, cabbage, radish and turnip, all of which, he claims, he planted successfully. During the dry months he attempted to make bacon, but this did not fare so well. Like many others, he reserved his greatest praise for the 'incomparable wine of Pines', which he described as 'the Nector which the Gods drunk'.

Ligon's employer and friend Thomas Modyford was also doing very well. As he wrote in a later letter, his partner in London sent 'all the supplies to me at the best hand, and I returning him the sugars, and we both thrived on it'.

Towards the end of his book, Ligon described how an investment of

---

* Ligon, who had what he described as a painter's eye for young female beauty, was particularly taken with Yarico, an Indian house slave who had the responsibility of picking the chiggers out of his feet. She was 'of excellent shape and colour, for it was a pure bright bay; small breasts, with the nipples of a porphyrie colour . . . this woman would not be woo'd by any means to wear Cloathes'.

£1,000, by clever trading between England and Barbados, could within a couple of voyages be grown to more than triple – enough for a down payment on a plantation such as Kendal worth £14,000. He estimated that 200 acres in sugar, such as grown by Modyford, could produce a profit of as much as £7,000 per crop, an astonishingly high return on the investment.

Ligon was alive to the many serious potential pitfalls, the 'many rubs and obstacles on the way', such as fire in the canefields or factory, the death of cattle needed to drive the mill, or losses of cargo at sea from shipwreck or piracy. For him, this made the bravery and skill of those that succeeded at sugar all the more impressive. Such was the 'difficulty', 'industry and pains' required, that those of 'a sluggish humour . . . are altogether unfit for so noble an undertaking'. But those with energy, industry and determination, he wrote, 'may make it the Ladder to climb to a high degree of Wealth and opulencie, in this sweet Negotiation of Sugar'.

Ligon, then, hugely admired the new sugar barons, whom he described as 'Giants'. He thought Modyford as able as any man he had ever known. In addition, he praised their 'civility', and found their 'dispositions' 'compliable in a high degree to all vertues' – 'Civilly intreating of Strangers'; 'Loving, friendly and hospitable to one another'.

Some, he admitted, were too 'fixt upon' profits, but others had the proper aristocratic attitude to wealth: that a (small) proportion should be expended on doing good for the public and in charity to the poor. Fellow Royalist refugee Sir Humphrey Walrond came in for particular praise: 'He being a Gentleman, that had been bred with much freedom, liberty, and plenty, in England, could not set his mind so earnestly on his profit, as to forget his accustomed lawful pleasures', namely keeping his table well stocked and bidding 'his friends welcom to it'.

The sugar planters, rapidly becoming rich and creditworthy, certainly aimed to impress, to establish their place in the order of things in what was still a fluid, young and unstable society. They succeeded with Richard Ligon, who was complimentary about both the new arrivals such as Modyford, and those emerging as the leaders of the old guard like Drax. But although on the face of it a propagandist for the island, Ligon was too intelligent and sensitive an observer to miss the darker side of the society and of life and death on the island, or the rapidly growing fallout from the Sugar Revolution.

4

THE SUGAR REVOLUTION:
'MOST INHUMAN AND BARBAROUS PERSONS'

'The conditions . . . were that the convicts should be carried beyond the sea as slaves, that they should not be emancipated for ten years, and that the place of their banishment should be some West Indian island. This last article was studiously framed for the purpose of aggravating their misery.'

Lord Macaulay, *History of England*

For all the bustling trade and activity, Ligon realised very quickly that he had arrived at Bridgetown at 'a sad time'. The inhabitants of the island were so 'grievously visited with the plague, (or as killing a disease)' that within a month after Ligon's arrival, he wrote, 'the living were hardly able to bury the dead'.

Sugar did not bring sickness to Barbados. The New World had been a spectacular melting pot of diseases since the time of Columbus: the Europeans brought smallpox and influenza, with catastrophic results for the region's original inhabitants; and from the earliest days of contact, any European voyaging to the tropics took his life in his hands. Countless thousands of Spaniards and others were laid low by tropical fevers. The carriage of West Africans to the region as slaves brought a whole new array of diseases to add to the mix, as well as providing existing illnesses with new vulnerable victims.

Sugar did, however, cause a rapid increase in the traffic coming in and out of Bridgetown harbour. Ligon estimated that it was as many as 100 ships a year by the late 1640s. These mostly cramped, unhygienic vessels, with poorly fed crews, were ideal nurseries for illnesses, which were then transferred to the ports.

Bridgetown, described by Ligon as having the 'bigness of Hounslo', was by this time home to some 1,500 merchants, artisans, servants and slaves. Its situation had been chosen due to the fine, easily defended harbour of Carlisle Bay, and because it was on low ground and therefore relatively protected from hurricanes. But as a consequence, it was also the unhealthiest place on the island. Ligon wrote that behind the town was 'a kind of Bog or Morass, which vents out so loathsome a favour, as cannot but breed ill blood, and is (no doubt) the occasion of much sickness to those that live there'. Indeed, the diseases from the ships found a happy new home in the bustling town, where rubbish and excrement were everywhere, picked over by dogs, vultures and rats. According to Ligon, at the height of the 'sad time', bodies were thrown into the bog behind the town, 'which so infected the water, as divers that drunk of it were absolutely poysoned, and dyed in few hours after'.

Heat, humidity, insects and atrocious hygiene had from the time of first settlement taken a grievous toll on Barbadians. Ligon was shocked to discover that hardly any of the first pioneers had survived. But this new outbreak was on a different scale. Ligon did not identify the disease, and was unsure whether it had been carried to the island by shipping, or was caused by 'ill dyet', and 'drinking strong waters'. It is most likely, however, that this was Barbados's first encounter with the horrors of yellow fever, carried from Africa in the slave ships by infected mosquitoes.

At the time it was called the 'Bleeding Fever' or the 'Barbados Distemper', and nothing was known about the transmission of yellow fever. It would be 250 years before it was discovered that the disease was spread by a particular species of mosquito. The yellow fever virus causes headaches, loss of appetite and muscle pain, followed by high temperatures, a raging thirst and agonising back pain. To catch the disease in Ligon's time meant a less than even chance of survival. The end usually came with the sufferer spewing up mouthfuls of dark blood – *'vomito negro'* – as the virus caused liver and kidney failure and multi-organ haemorrhage.

The epidemic was long-lasting and violently destructive. Dr Vines wrote to John Winthrop that 'the sickness' was 'an absolute plague'. In his parish they were burying 20 a week, and the fever took no account of its victims' strength or habits. 'It first seased on the ablest men both for account and ability of body', wrote Vines. 'Men who had begun and almost finished greate sugar workes, who dandled themselves in their hopes, were suddenly laid in the dust.' As late as the end of the following year, 'the plague' was 'still hott at Barbados'.

The chaos caused by the epidemic, together with a severe drought in

late 1647, caused 'a general scarcity of Victuals through the whole Island'.
Only the timely arrival of provisions from New England saved the colony
from starvation, but by the end of 1648, as many as 6,000 may have died
out of a population of less than 25,000.

Such startlingly high mortality rates would remain one of the most
remarkable – and influential – features of the sugar societies. For the next
150 years, something like a third of all whites died within three years of
arriving in the Caribbean. Those born there fared little better; few families survived for more than a couple of generations. Those who did were
exceptionally tough, or lucky. Only just over a third of marriages left
surviving children; the risk of early death dominated everything,
contributing to the settlers' fatalism, fast living and callousness.

The destruction wrought by the yellow fever epidemic of 1647–8 also
provided an impetus for a process already under way once sugar had been
planted. As the deceased owners' lands came on to the market, they were
snapped up by the likes of Christopher Codrington, the Walronds, and
other richer planters, who were steadily increasing their acreage. At the
same time, surviving small-scale freeholders with 30 or 40 acres found
that they could not afford the switch to sugar. Establishing the complicated *ingenio*, or factory, was prohibitively expensive for any without
considerable cash or credit, and to be viable, the works needed substantial acreage of cane to keep it supplied. All this also required the assembling of a large workforce for the labour-intensive new crop. With no
improvement in the profitability of tobacco, cotton, ginger or any other
of the now minor staples, a great number of smallholders were forced to
sell out to the new sugar barons, 'wormed out of their small settlements
by their more subtle and greedy neighbours'. Over a thousand Barbadians (later described as coming from 'the Soberest' part of the population) migrated to New England during the 1640s. Thus through the late
years of the decade, the average size of an estate on the island steadily
grew, as land was increasingly concentrated in the hands of the few.

A man of small means could 'make it' in Barbados, however, provided
he survived the diseases and the lifestyle. Ligon commented on how some
who had arrived with virtually nothing 'are now risen to very great and
vast estates'. Henry Morgan, who would become one of the richest and
most powerful Englishmen in the Caribbean, was probably a servant in
Barbados by 1650, having sold himself into indenture to avoid the life of
a poor Welsh farmer. We know of a servant, Garrett Sisters, who served
his term of indenture and returned to England, then came back to Barbados
in 1639, aged 26. He acquired land, married well, and by the time of his

death in 1679 owned 19 slaves. Sometimes, prosperity waited for the second generation. The saying was that a man went out poor to the West Indies, and his son came back rich. John Harwood was a Royalist soldier, sentenced to servitude in Barbados following capture at the battle of Newbury in 1643. In 1679, his son Richard secured the job of overseer for Henry Drax, James's heir, and the following year is recorded as owning a few acres on his own behalf. Two years later, he became agent to a London merchant and absentee planter. In 1686 he was elevated to the lofty heights of the island's council. Another who started out working as an overseer for Henry Drax was Samuel Osborne. Both his parents were dead by the time he was 13 and he inherited just seven slaves, a few gold rings and £150. By the time of his death in 1736, he owned 10 plantations totalling 2,700 acres, possibly the greatest ever landholding in Barbados.

Nonetheless, for servants arriving in Barbados hoping to establish themselves on a small piece of land, the prospects were now grim. For one thing, the planters and merchants, who controlled the council, appointed by the Governor, and the assembly, elected by a handful of rich whites, did not want to see large numbers of subsistence farmers on the island. This would reduce trade and the labour force available to work the sugar fields. Furthermore, by the late 1640s, there was simply no land left on the tiny island to give to servants who had completed their indenture period. In 1647, the proprietor was forced to concede that 'the land is now so taken up as there is not any to be had but at great rates, too high for the purchase of poor servants'.

There were other changes to Barbados society and the type of immigrant at this time. In the 1630s, supplies of willing immigrants had been plentiful, but the next decade saw the birth rate in England fall, wages rise, and, of course, the wholesale slaughter of the Civil War, which killed a larger proportion of the population than any other conflict except World War One. At the same time, the switch to sugar increased the demand for labour, with the unhappy result that a growing share of those arriving in Barbados were now unwilling immigrants.

The earliest theorists of colonialism had seen overseas settlements as outlets for surplus population, which otherwise might provide 'fewell of daungerous insurrections', in particular those who were 'lewed and lasy felowes'. And from the outset, Barbados had received a number of forcibly deported prisoners of war, vagrants and criminals. On Ligon's ship were a group of servant women, 'the Major part of them, being taken from Bridewel [prison], . . . and such like places of education'. In addition, a number were tricked or physically coerced on to ships sailing for the West Indies. But these sources of supply suddenly became much more important in the late 1640s and 1650s. At this time, to be 'Barbadosed' took on the meaning of the more modern term 'Shanghaied'. Children were even stolen from their parents and sent to the colony.* One incident came to the attention of the authorities when a ship 'lately fallen down to Graves End', was found to contain 'children and Servants of severall Parents and Masters so deceived and enticed away, cryinge and mourninge for Redemption from their Slavery'. The greatest numbers, however, came as a result of the fighting of the Civil War, which saw at least 8,000 Englishmen joining the sugar estates of Barbados between 1645 and 1650. Cromwell found that he could sell his Royalist prisoners of war as servants in Barbados, and thus rid himself of potential enemies while clearing a profit at the same time. Some took their families with them, only to find themselves separated at their destination. 'They were sold', one account tells us, 'the husband in one place, the wife in another, and the children in another place so as not to receive any solace from each other.' And after Cromwell's victories at Drogheda, Worcester and Dunbar in 1649–51, there was a large influx of Irish and Scots to the colony (and also to the Leeward Island settlements). After Drogheda, Cromwell wrote that 'When they submitted, these officers were knocked on the head, and every tenth man of the soldiers killed, and the rest shipped for Barbados.' These Irish servants, in particular, were found to be 'fiery spirits', and came to be feared by the planters to the extent that the Governor of Barbados was soon pleading with Cromwell to send no more, even though the new sugar plantations remained hungry for labour.

Cromwell responded by instigating a new policy after 1655 of issuing pardons to criminals on the condition that they go overseas. This greatly increased the flow to Barbados of 'felons condemned to death, sturdy beggars, gipsies and other incorrigible rogues, poor and idle debauched persons'. In a fit of Puritan zeal, 400 women from the brothels of London were shipped to Barbados in 1656, 'in order that by their breeding they should replenish the white population'. A visitor to the island at this time, not without reason, described Barbados as 'the Dunghill wharone England doth cast forth its rubidg: Rodgs. Hors and such like peopel, which are generally brought heare'.

These newcomers, as well as the political prisoners – 'traitors' – were generally treated as was considered their due – with great cruelty. The

*Soon afterwards, the word 'kidnap' entered the English language, its original definition being 'to steal or carry off children and others for service on the American plantations'.

account of one party, shipped to Barbados after the Pennruddock Royalist uprising in 1655, furnishes us with details. The prisoners were kept below decks for nearly three weeks at Plymouth; during the six-week voyage they were 'all the way locked up under decks amongst horses, that their souls, through heat and steam under the tropic fainted in them'. On their arrival at the island they were sold, 'the generality of them to most inhuman and barbarous persons', and then set to work 'grinding at the mills, attending the furnaces and digging in the scorching land'. They were, it is clear, the absolute chattels of their masters, and 'bought and sold still from one planter to another, whipped at the whipping post for their master's pleasure, and many other ways made miserable beyond expression or Christian imagination'.

Richard Ligon's account supports this, although with an important caveat. 'As for the usage of the Servants', he wrote, 'it is much as the Master is, merciful or cruel.' The aristocratic Cavalier newcomers like the Walronds, says Ligon, took a paternalistic approach to getting the most work out of their servants, feeding and clothing them well and receiving in return 'love' and 'diligent and painful labour'. The implication, then, is that the old-timers, hardened by 20 years' struggle on the island, were the 'cruel masters'. This seems to have been the case with sugar pioneer James Holdip, who would later be described as 'extremely hated for his cruelties and oppression'. But James Drax does not seem to have fitted this rule. He was greatly admired by Ligon, and praised for 'feeding two hundred mouths'. Moreover, most of his workforce were now slaves rather than servants. Ligon said that Drax 'keeps them in such order, as there are no mutinies amongst them'.

Clearly Ligon was shocked by the treatment of the servants by the 'cruel masters', and he described in vivid detail their 'very wearisome and miserable lives'. On their arrival, they had to build their own shelters out of sticks, vines and leaves or otherwise sleep on the ground in the open air. The next morning, they were summoned at six and sent to the fields 'with a severe Overseer to command them'. They had a meagre meal at eleven, then worked on until six in the evening. Often they would be forced to sleep in clothes soaked by rain or sweat, with disastrous consequences for their health. Any complaints led to a doubling of their indenture period, or brutal punishment. 'I have seen an Overseer beat a Servant with a cane about the head till the blood has flowed for an offence that is not worth speaking of', Ligon reported. 'Truly, I have seen such cruelty done to servants, as I did not think one Christian could have done to another.'

Thus as the cultivation of sugar – with its attendant intense and back-breaking labour – remorselessly spread, so for most of its inhabitants Barbados became a place of terror, discipline and coercion. Indenture had started as a personal relationship based on a voluntary contract. Now most servants were treated as less-than-human objects, as property. The ground was laid for the horrors of chattel slavery.

Ligon wrote of the white servants that the hard labour and inadequate shelter and food 'had so much depress'd their spirits, as they were come to a declining and yielding condition'. The overworked servants responded, then, in the main, with what would later be considered 'black' attributes, but were in fact common to all slave classes regardless of race: stereotypes of sullen docility and childlike passivity. This led, in turn, to further coercion and brutality on the part of the overseers, who would, it was reported, beat them like 'galley slaves' to force them to work.

Very occasionally, the worst abuses came to the attention of the authorities. We know of one incident when two planters were imprisoned and forced to pay compensation after hanging a servant, John Thomas, 'by the handes' and putting 'fired matches betweene his fingers', a torture that cost Thomas 'the use of severall joynt's'. On other occasions the servants responded to ill treatment by setting fire to the canefields or factories of their masters. The cruel James Holdip was utterly ruined, losing £10,000, when his vengeful servants burnt his plantation to the ground.

In 1649, an extensive plot amongst the servants was uncovered in the nick of time. According to Ligon, a large group of servants, greatly 'provoked' by 'extream ill usage', decided to rise up, cut the throats of their masters and seize control of the island. But on the day before the uprising was scheduled to start, the plot was betrayed and the ringleaders seized. They were extensively tortured, and then no fewer than 18 were hanged. Soon afterwards a raft of laws was passed to further govern the lives of the servants: they now required a master's permission to marry; any servant convicted of striking their master faced a further two years' service; all servants had to have a pass from their master to leave the plantation. If they disobeyed this, they served an extra month for every two hours' absence.

However, by this time, the servant and wider poor white population was starting to decline. Some finished their indenture period and, finding no land to settle in Barbados, headed for other islands; a number escaped; very many died from a combination of overwork, hunger and disease. But the narrowly avoided 1649 rebellion confirmed the Barbados planters in their opinion that the white servants were an extremely dangerous threat and that they needed to look elsewhere for the enormous labour requirements of their sugar industry. Indeed, many were already doing so.

5

THE PLANTATION: MASTERS AND SLAVES

'*Slavery . . . is a weed which grows in every soil.*'
Edmund Burke

For some, the process whereby the sugar islands (all of which followed the model established in Barbados) became slave societies was simple, and had an air of inevitability. In 1645, a Barbados settler wrote to Governor John Winthrop Jr in Massachusetts explaining that the usual practice was to bring out servants from England – on as many years' indenture as you could get away with – to get a sugar operation up and running, 'and in short time [to] be able with good husbandry to procure Negroes (the life of this place) out of the encrease of your owne plantation'. Indeed, by the time that sugar took over the island's land and economy, a pattern was established of using the profits of servant labour to invest in enslaved men, women and children shipped from West Africa.

Why did the English planters choose this terrible option? Were not the English in the Americas supposed to be radically different from the notoriously cruel Spaniards? Slavery had disappeared from England hundreds of years before, 'liberty' was a national watchword – wasn't slavery 'un-English'? In 1618, an Englishman called Richard Jobson was in West Africa trading for gold and ivory when he was offered slaves to buy by an Arab middleman. Shocked, he replied, 'We were a people who did not trade in any such commodities, neither did wee buy or sell one another, or any that had our owne shapes.' The Arab merchant was surprised, saying there were white people on the coast 'who earnestly desire' to acquire slaves. Jobson answered that 'They were another kinde of people different from us.' So how did the English, within only a few generations, become the world's leading slave traders?

Before this time, English people were far more likely to be the victims of slavery rather than its perpetrators. Slavery had been abandoned in northern Europe by the twelfth century, but it was still common around the Mediterranean, and thousands of English and Irish travelling there found themselves enslaved by Muslims. This would continue well into the eighteenth century. Islamic law forbade the forcible enslavement of fellow Muslims, but 'inferior' people such as Christians were fair game.

Slavery had always been about 'inferior' peoples – for the Greeks it was the 'barbarians', for Jews, the Gentiles (and vice versa) – but Muslims believed that they had identified the most inferior of all: black Africans. The Arabs were the first to develop a specialised long-distance slave trade from sub-Saharan Africa, bringing workers to drain the Fertile Crescent to grow cotton and sugar. In almost all cultures, colour of skin was seen from the earliest times as an indicator of status. The darker you were, the more likely to be a humble field worker; the lighter, the more chance it was that you performed skilled indoor work away from the sun, or, indeed, no work at all. Thus, increasingly, black-skinned African slaves were given the most degrading forms of labour by their Muslim overlords.

The rediscovery of the writings of Aristotle gave this idea of racial inferiority weighty support. Aristotle had suggested that some peoples were 'natural slaves' – like tame animals, unable to look after themselves, they needed masters almost for their own protection. Soon the characteristics of these 'natural slaves', as decided by Aristotle – excitability, emotional immaturity, lack of reason, sometimes sullen stupidity – were being applied to black Africans.

In terms of numbers, though, most slaves in the Mediterranean were still white. From the early thirteenth to the mid-fifteenth century, Italian merchants transported tens of thousands of Slav people as slaves (hence the word 'slave') to the region, a good proportion of whom were used for the production of sugar. But the capture of Constantinople in 1453 stopped this flow, causing the Italian merchants to look westwards for a new source of supply.

Almost from their first voyages of discovery, Portuguese mariners had been bringing Africans back to Lagos to be sold as slaves. In 1444, 253 were landed in the Algarve, with 46 – the 'royal fifth' – being given to Prince Henry the Navigator, who rejoiced at the prospect of their conversion to Christianity, as well as at the income he got from selling them on. A contemporary witness wrote of the 'piteous company' of slaves: 'Some kept their heads low, and their faces bathed in tears, looking one upon the other. Others stood groaning very dolorously.'

A great number ended up in Lisbon, where, by the mid-sixteenth century, slaves would number 10,000, a tenth of the population. Here, they often functioned as decorations, denoting social standing. The Portuguese loved African music and enlisted slaves to perform at plays and other public entertainments, even royal functions. Marriage between white and black was not forbidden, and there were even some high-profile free blacks.

But a large number also ended up working in the sugar cane fields, where it was a different story. Sugar has a long association with slavery. It is certain that the cane carried by the Muslim expansion into the Mediterranean was to a large extent slave-grown and slave-processed, particularly in North Africa. When wages skyrocketed after the Black Death in the mid-fourteenth century, the labour-intensive industry relied even more on coerced workers. Then, when the Portuguese and Spanish started growing sugar on the Atlantic islands close to Africa, black slave labour became the norm for the crop.

To function, the institution of slavery requires the suppression of spirit, intelligence and initiative on the part of its victims. Sugar, with its mind-numbing, simple but repetitive and physically exhausting tasks, demanded exactly the same thing. Sugar and slavery were found to be a perfect fit.

So, the first stepping stones to the slave islands of the Caribbean were the Atlantic possessions of Spain and Portugal. Although there were a number of waged and indentured labourers, the mainspring of sugar production was handled by slaves imported from nearby West Africa. By the time of Columbus's first voyage in 1492, Madeira was already a thriving plantation colony worked by enslaved Africans, producing more sugar than the entire Mediterranean area. By the 1550s, there were nearly 3,000 slaves on the island, and many more in Portugal's African island colonies of São Tomé and Príncipe. São Tomé alone imported more African slaves in the first half of the sixteenth century than Europe, the Americas and the other Atlantic islands combined, and included wealthy Africans among its financial backers. The island, conveniently situated off the coast of West Africa, also acted as a gathering point for slaves to be re-exported back to mainland African buyers and on to the Americas.

Black slaves were shipped to the New World very soon after European contact. Of course, Columbus and his successors quickly enslaved the indigenous populations of the Americas, setting them to work in the fields and mines, with appalling consequences. But alongside them, from 1501 at the latest, were black enslaved Africans, with direct shipments from the continent recorded as early as 1518.

At the same time, the 'Indians' started receiving high-profile support.

As early as 1516, the Dominican priest Bartoleme de Las Casas was calling for the importation of African slaves in order to save the beleaguered native population of the New World. His campaign brought about the outlawing of 'Indian' slavery in 1542, although this was widely ignored. Most importantly, de Las Casas argued not against the idea that there were 'natural slaves' – simply that with the picturesque indigenous inhabitants of the Caribbean, Spain had chosen the wrong race. The distinction was also pragmatic. It was soon discovered that the Africans were hardier than the rapidly dwindling aboriginal population, who were poor workers, and were unable to sustain the physical and psychological degradation of slavery. An early Spanish account, while explaining that the growing of sugar made it 'requisite to send over blacks . . . from Guinea', marvelled that 'unless one happened to be hanged, none died'. Indeed, an African was considered to be worth four of the sickly Indians.

Not that African slavery did not present practical problems of its own to the Europeans. The same account that commended the black Africans' supposed resistance to disease commented that 'when they came to be put to the sugar-works, they destroyed themselves with the filthy liquors they made of those molasses'. Worst of all, this led to the black slaves fleeing 'into the mountains in whole gangs, revolt[ing] and commit[ing] murders and other outrages'. Rebellion ignited further tyranny and brutality in the masters, leading to more slave resistance. For Hispaniola, this must have had a good deal to do with the puzzling failure of the Spanish sugar industry on the island. In 1546, three sugar estates put up for sale could find no buyer because of the slave danger, and six years later, orders came that all new factories should be built of masonry and in the style of forts. This was understandable on an island with only 1,000 whites and some 7,000 'maroons', as runaway slaves were known. An Italian traveller of the time wrote that 'Most Spaniards think that it is only a matter of years before this island is taken over entirely by the blacks.' This would, of course, remain the perennial, ever-present nightmare of the white West Indian planters for the duration of slavery and beyond.

However, in Brazil, where the industry had succeeded spectacularly, there were more and more black slaves. In the 15 years after 1576, as many as 50,000 were imported, and possibly even more, mainly from Congo and Angola. And already, the plantations were showing all the signs of the familiar commercial enterprise of later days: excessive toil, especially during the harvest; severe punishments for minor offences; and fatalities because of dangerous machinery working badly. There also operated an assumption that the slaves would die within a short time and need to be replaced by continual imports.

The shocking cruelty of this system attracted opposition not just from the enslaved victims, but also from influential voices – including popes, kings and emperors – in Europe. A number of Dominican and Jesuit friars who had seen the slave trade in action denounced it as a deadly sin. The shipments continued, but by 1600 there were enough critics of the trade and of slavery for it to be foreseeable that abolition could come within only a few generations. But it was not to be, for at that point new players came into the business – the aggressive new Atlantic powers of northern Europe.

Whatever the protestations of Richard Jobson in 1618, the English had entered the trade as far back as 1562, with the slave-trading voyages of Captain John Hawkins. Hawkins was backed by a host of luminaries, including the Lord Mayor of London. Queen Elizabeth, who also enjoyed a proportion of the profits of these voyages, naively announced that 'if any African should be carried away without his free consent it would be detestable and call down the vengeance of Heaven upon the undertaking'. Both James I and Charles I licensed companies to trade in slaves, and by the 1620s, black slaves were to be seen in ports in England such as Bristol and London.

But English involvement was still minimal compared to the great maritime traders of the time, the Dutch. At first there were severe qualms: in the 1590s, several Dutch cities banned the selling of slaves within their precincts for moral reasons. Although Dutch factories and forts were established on the West African coast, the desired goods were gold and ivory, not slaves, and the leadership of the Dutch West India Company, having discussed the issue with theologians, decided that the slave trade was immoral and to be shunned. But independent traders grew steadily in number. It was a Dutch ship that in 1619 landed the first slaves in an English colony, at Virginia; cargoes captured on the high seas from the Portuguese often consisted of slaves, which the Dutch privateers were happy to sell on to any buyer. Then, in 1626, the Dutch West India Company abandoned its previous policy and started giving permission for the shipping of slaves from Africa to Dutch settlements in South America.

More than anything else, though, it was sugar that led the Dutch to take up the trade with gusto. In the late 1630s, with huge cane-growing areas of Brazil under their control, the Dutch started importing into the New World tens of thousands of enslaved Africans. At the same time, Portuguese slaving centres in Angola, the Gulf of Guinea and São Tomé were seized, bringing much of the trade under Dutch control. So when the 'Hollanders' helped transfer sugar to Barbados, they were looking for a market for their slaves, as well as new sugar producers for their refineries at home. It is unlikely to be a coincidence that James Drax, with all his Dutch connections, was the first on the island to make the switch from servant to slave labour.

Sugar did not cause slavery in the British Caribbean. Earlier settlements on Providence Island and Tortuga had been slave-owning, and there were a few thousand slaves, alongside the poor whites, working the Barbados cotton and tobacco plantations in the early 1640s, before the Sugar Revolution took hold on the island. But such was the early uncertainty about the institution of slavery that in 1638, the Governor was forced to confirm their status: that Indian and black slaves were to serve for life, unless contracted otherwise. Then, with the triumph of the labour-intensive sugar crop, the demand for slaves soared, and the composition of the island's population was altered for ever.

It was not just the example of Brazil and the encouragement of the Dutch, nor sugar's long association with slavery (and more recent links with specifically black African slavery), that led the Barbados sugar planters to switch their labour source. As well as debatable advantages in disease resistance, the bewildered and terrified new arrivals from Africa, speaking a huge variety of languages, were far easier to control than the turbulent Irish or English poor. In addition, racial, cultural and religious differences made it simpler to justify and rationalise the coercion considered to be required to get the gruelling work done in the extreme heat of the factories and fields. Most important of all, though, was the economic imperative. Slaves were cheaper.

With supply from the Dutch abundant, a Barbados planter could buy from a local trader an enslaved African for about £20 – less for women and children. This was in the region of twice the price of a five-year-indentured servant, but it was for life, and the slave-owner also owned any offspring the slave might have (as a contemporary put it: 'miserabell Negros borne to perpetuall slavery they and Thayer seed'). Furthermore, the planters decided that the black man was the better worker; some said he did the labour of three whites. A young George Downing wrote to Governor Winthrop in August 1645 that the Barbados planters had bought that year as many as 'a thousand Negroes; and the more they buie, the better able they are buye, for in a yeare and a halfe they will earne (with gods blessing) as much as they cost'.

The main suppliers were the Dutch, but English traders who had thrived in the servant trade, like William Vassall, Thomas Kendall and Martin Noell, simply switched their operations to dealing in slaves. Just as Bristol had been the centre of the servant trade, so now the city became a centre of the slave trade. Aggressive New England merchants muscled in, too. The first slave-trading vessel from there had arrived at Barbados as early as 1643. By the early 1650s, the leading planters, including Drax and his neighbour Middleton, had shares themselves in slave-trading vessels, if not outright ownership.

There has always existed a spectrum of freedom or dependency or powerlessness, from serfdom and peonage to indenture and actual lifelong chattel slavery. Even within slavery itself, there were degrees of freedom granted or won, depending on the enslaved person's usefulness or threat to his or her master.

Nonetheless, certain generalisations can be made about the institution of slavery, at least in the English Caribbean. A slave was defined as 'chattel' (a word derived from the Latin for livestock). This meant that he or she could be bought and sold, and lived under the permanent personal domination of his or her master or mistress. Alienated from family, culture, ancestors (even descendants, who would also belong to the master), the slave had no legitimate independent being except as an instrument of his master's will. It was a state of total degradation and dishonour.

The degradation of the slave gave the master a sense of prestige and superior identity. The slaves were property – the analogy frequently employed is with tame animals – and the greater the quality and quantity of that property, the greater its owner's status. The other safe generalisation is that the system, whenever or wherever it was to be found, relied on violent coercion to function, and on the continuing degradation of its victims.

Richard Ligon provided one of the very few accounts of how this system worked in Barbados in the late 1640s, and was one of the very small number of contemporaries to write in detail about the black slaves on the island (of course there are no black accounts at all from this time). He was not typical – he was far older, more educated and more sensitive than the sugar barons like Drax, Hilliard or Holdip, hard men who had survived through tough times and then prospered. But Ligon's narrative is uniquely detailed, and anticipated much of the confused attitude prevalent in later writings about slavery by sensitive English men and women in the Caribbean.

Ligon and Modyford's vessel the *Achilles* was originally supposed to pick up 'Negroes' as well as livestock during its stop at the Cape Verde Islands, but it is not clear that this actually happened (though we know that the ship, having dropped the Modyford entourage at Barbados, hastened to Africa to collect slaves). Ligon does not write about the 'Middle Passage', the journey the arrivals took to get to Barbados, but he clearly witnessed a slave sale in Bridgetown, which reminded him of a horse market in his native East Anglia, with the men, women and children spruced up and then assembled naked to be assessed by potential purchasers. Ligon described the original source of the slaves as 'petty Kingdomes' stretching from Gambia to Angola where 'they sell their Subjects, and such as they take in Battle, whom they make slaves; and some mean men sell their Servants, their Children, and sometimes their Wives'. Talking to enslaved Africans, he discovered that they measured time by the moon, but had only marked with this system the key moments in their lives, namely the 'notorious accidents' of being taken into slavery in Africa and then shipped from their homelands.

His description of the slaves, while condescending and obviously racist, also exhibits a sort of baffled pity for their hopelessness and alienation. 'Their spirits are subjugated to so low a condition', he wrote, that 'they set no great value upon their lives.' New arrivals in particular, Ligon reported, were 'timorous and fearful', extremely prone to suicide: starving themselves to death, or hanging themselves, in the belief that they would be resurrected in 'their own Countrey'. Humphrey Walrond 'lost three or four of his best Negroes this way'. Ligon described how the supposedly paternalistic Walrond responded by cutting off one of their heads and displaying it on a 12-foot-high pole, forcing his slaves to march around it. How was it possible to return to your country after death, he asked them, if the head is still here? This 'sad, yet lively spectacle', Ligon wrote, 'changed their opinions; and after that, no more hanged themselves'.

Ligon repeated the mantras of racial slavery. The blacks were 'as near beasts as may be'. They were 'natural slaves', inheritors of the curse Noah put on Ham's son Canaan, a passage in Genesis used by first the Arabs then Christians to justify slavery. They were idle, superstitious, dishonest, cruel, lacking intellect. Yet his actual descriptions for the most part tell a totally different story. At various times he called the slaves 'excellent workers'; they were fine swimmers and divers, and adept with tools such as axes. He wrote at length about their music, played on kettle drums of various sizes. 'So strangely they vary their time, as 'tis a pleasure to the most curious ears', he commented. 'If they had the variety of tune . . . as they have of time, they would do wonders in that Art.' Macow, one of the senior slaves on Modyford's plantation, amazed him by succeeding in building himself a theorbo, or large lute, having momentarily picked up Ligon's own.

Individuals like Macow do emerge, but on the whole Ligon saw the slaves as a group, particularly when it came to physical properties. He admired the torsos of the male slaves, 'well-timber'd ... broad between the shoulders, full breasted', and is one of the very few 'masters' to write about being sexually attracted to the young black women. During his brief stop in the Cape Verde Islands, Ligon encountered some 'pretty young Negro Virgins', and ended up, through an interpreter, elaborately praising their 'beauty and shape' and offering them English spirits. (Reading between the lines, he appears to have made a bit of an old fool of himself.) In Barbados he commented on the 'young [black] maids' who 'ordinarily [have] very large breasts, which stand strutting out so hard and firm, as no leaping, jumping, or stirring, will cause them to shake any more, than the brawns of their arms'. The latter phrase reminds us of the fact that these were manual workers – this was their primary purpose; the awkward gallantry Ligon showed in the Cape Verde Islands was now gone, even if his sexual interest remained.

The overall impression, then, is one of confusion and contradiction, at times reading like a battle between received – but still firmly held – views about blacks and slaves, and the evidence of his own experiences. The slaves were ignorant of 'Letters and Numbers', but the two slaves Ligon described in detail were both clearly resourceful and intelligent. They were compared several times to animals, but surprised Ligon by being 'Chast ... as any people under the Sun.' He said that in general they were not to be trusted, but then described how he saw a group putting out a cane fire by stamping on it with their bare feet and rolling on it with their naked bodies 'so little they regard their own smart or safety, in respect of their Masters benefit'.

Ligon several times tried to resolve this contradiction by saying that as a people the blacks were cruel and false, 'yet no rule so general but hath his acception'. Among them, he said, are some as honest and faithful 'as amongst those of Europe, or any other part of the world'. He could not decide which racist cliché fitted: the docile, pitiable slave or the resistant and troublesome.

One of these 'acceptions' was Sambo, who worked with Ligon on clearing the church paths. There seems to have developed between the two men something akin to friendship, however unequal. To find the right way through the thick jungle, Ligon employed a compass, which fascinated Sambo. Ligon explained the points of the compass, which Sambo 'presently learnt by heart, and promis'd me never to forget'. According to Ligon, the reason why the needle pointed north (described by Ligon as being because of 'huge Rocks of Loadstone' 'in the north part of the world') 'was a little too hard for him' and threw him into a 'strange muse'. To 'put him out of it', Ligon told him to hold his axe near the compass and move it about to see the needle turn. This so impressed Sambo that he decided he wanted to be made a Christian, so as 'to be endued with all those knowledges he wanted'.

Ligon promised to do his best, and brought up Sambo's plea with his master. It is not clear if this was Modyford; if not, then it is likely to have been Drax or Middleton, whose properties bordered Kendal. The 'master' explained the position: 'That the people of that Island were governed by the laws of England, and by those laws, we could not make a Christian a slave.' Ligon had a clever response ready: 'I told him, my request was far different from that, for I desired him to make a slave a Christian. His answer was, that it was true, there was a great difference in that: But, being once a Christian, he could no more account him a slave, and so lose the hold they had of them as slaves, by making them Christians; and by that means should open such a gap, as all the Planters in the Islands would curse him.' Ligon 'was struck mute, and poor Sambo kept out the Church; as ingenious, as honest, and as good a nature'd poor soul, as ever wore black, or eat green'.

Sambo may have been patronised and ridiculed for his reasons for wanting to become a Christian, but the issue of slave conversion would remain hugely important. When slavery was justified by the Church, as, most famously, in the Papal Bull of 1454, this support was clearly dependent on the conversion of those enslaved ('the Trade must be allowed', ran the argument, 'the Christian Scheme of enlarging the Flock cannot well be carried on without it'). In the same way, the defence of slavery, that their condition was 'bettered' by being removed from Africa to the West Indies, was also underwritten by the idea that the slaves would be Christianised. The fact that this did not happen would severely undermine the planters' defence of their practice.

Richard Ligon shied away from detailing cruelty to blacks. In his largely benign description of slavery, he refused to face the implications of his own evidence, for instance about slave suicide. In fact, he contributed to the formation of racial stereotypes. His is the first recorded use of the word 'Pickaninny' to describe a black infant, and his suggestions that the 'Negroes' were a 'happy people, whom so little contents' would become a stereotype of blacks in America. Ligon was more forthcoming about cruelty to the white servants, as if this somehow made up for the much grimmer position of the enslaved Africans. He even goes so far as to say that the bonded whites had 'worser lives', though his own account contradicts this. In his model of plantation expenses he recommends spending £58 16s on clothes for 14 white servants, but only £35 in total for 100 black slaves. When an ox died, he wrote, the white servants feasted on the meat; the blacks ended up with the head, entrails and skin.

Both the white indentured servants and the black slaves had very poor diets. Some planters imported salted fish of the lowest quality from Europe or North America, but the staples were cassava bread, and a porridge-like mush made from Indian corn, known as loblolly. This was particularly disliked by the slaves, who preferred to roast the corn on the cob, considered animal food by the Europeans. To drink was water for the slaves, and 'mobby' or 'perino' for the servants and poor whites. As the Reverend James Parker wrote to John Winthrop, the 'common people' 'are very meane in respect of provisions . . . though its true the rich live high'.

Indeed they did. The contrast with the diet of the poor was spectacular. Richard Ligon described in lip-smacking detail one feast he attended at the home of James Drax. There was beef, 'the greatest rarity in the Island' – great roasted breast, boiled rump and baked cheeks. The tongue and other delicacies had been made into pies 'season'd with sweet Herbs finely minc'd'. In all, there were 14 dishes just of beef. The next course brought pork prepared in three different ways, chickens, turkey, duck, veal and shoulder of young goat, all cooked in a variety of fruit, spices, herbs and wines. 'These being taken off the table', wrote Ligon, 'another course is set on.' This consisted of bacon, fish roe, pickled oysters, caviar and anchovies, together with olives, fruits and pies. The puddings and fruit kept on arriving, to be rounded off with Ligon's favourite, the magnificent pineapple, 'worth all that went before'. All of this was washed down with gallons of perino, English beer, French, Spanish and Madeira wines, together with sherry and brandy (Madeira, unlike other wines, which deteriorate in the tropics, improves in a high temperature and retains its quality almost indefinitely). Ligon evidently relished all this, or, more exactly, was impressed by it, but it is hard to envisage enjoying such a mass of food and alcohol at the hottest time of the day in the tropics.

Of course, the Jacobean court was well known for its Lucullan feasting. The Earl of Carlisle himself, Barbados's earlier proprietor, was famous for his culinary ostentation. Guests would arrive to ogle a vast table spread with food, at which point the whole thing was removed, thrown away and replaced with identical food just come from the kitchens. Such displays denoted status, and conspicuous hospitality was part of the code of the Stuart gentry. Nonetheless, the punishing heat aside, such extravagance in

Barbados, where so many provisions were expensively imported, and so much of the population was close to starvation, is shocking. The Drax meal, most of which must have been carried by hand up from the coast, stands as a vivid testament not only to the astonishing new wealth that the Sugar Revolution brought to Barbados, but also to the wild disparities in lifestyle and consumption.

Certainly, after a mere three or four years of growing and processing sugar, at a serendipitous time when later competitors – the French and Dutch – were yet to get off the mark, the soil was fresh and the price on a high spike, Drax was suddenly extremely wealthy. He boasted to Ligon that he had started his sugar business with only £300, but had now built up so much money that it was only a matter of time before he bought an estate in England worth £10,000 a year, 'and all by this plant of Sugar'.

At the next-door estate, shortly before Ligon's arrival in September 1647, a series of land deals had taken place that had seen Thomas Middleton become the sole owner of the Mount Estate in St George's parish, while the Drax brothers took control of Drax Hope and Drax Hall to the north-east of Mount. Soon afterwards, in May of that year, James bought out his brother William's part of the plantation for 'five thousand pounds ster-ling', and became the sole owner of an estate of 700 acres in what is still the most fertile part of the island – the high acreage that straddles the border of St John's and St George's parishes, where the soil is a rich, water-holding red clay, and the rainfall is abundant.

Drax's wife Meliora had by now produced four or five sons and two daughters, although neither she nor the children are mentioned in Ligon's account of his trips to the Drax estate, so we have to assume they were kept in the background. Instead, the field was given over to entertain-ments. Ligon reported several visits, in particular one on a Sunday. Drax, for all his Puritan background, was, apparently, 'not so strict an observer' of the Lord's Day 'as to deny himself lawful recreations'. This consisted, to Ligon's delight, in more showing off on the part of Drax. He was rich enough not only, uniquely in the island, to serve beef at his table, but also to recruit and use his slaves for entertainment, in the Portuguese fashion. One visit by Ligon was brightened by the spectacle of two of Drax's 'Portugal Negroes' giving an elaborate display of fencing, in which they were 'skilful' and 'nimble'. At the end of the show, they 'give their respects to their Master', followed by a song 'very loud and sweet'.

On another occasion, the slaves provided a different diversion for Drax and his entourage. A Muscovy duck was brought to one of his ponds and the Negroes were charged to catch it without diving under the water. This provided excellent 'sport' for the onlookers, until a newcomer, unaware of the ban on diving, caught the prey. It was a 'Negro maid'. Ligon pleaded on her behalf and she was allowed to take the duck away.

In these ways, successful planters like Drax demonstrated their wealth, their hospitality and their power. In fact, Drax himself came to personify the opportunities available on the island – the chance of riches from a small beginning; and the enormous power that a successful man could wield over his world and the people in it.

Drax may have been the stand-out success story of the 1640s, but other more middling sugar farmers and processors clearly shared in the new bounty. Inventories of estates made before 1647 rarely included beds. Farmers slept in cotton hammocks in low-slung shacks. But thereafter, even the smaller-scale planters moved to four-poster beds, and for the first time other furniture such as stools, chests and leather chairs start appearing in inventories, together with pictures, candlesticks, books, mirrors and lamps. Brass kettles and other kitchen implements replaced iron versions, and in 1648 silver objects made their first appearance, alongside other obvious tokens of wealth and success such as gold watches, silk stockings and lace handkerchiefs.

The torrent of cash that the Sugar Revolution poured down on the heads of those farmers fortunate enough to be well placed for the change and hardy or lucky enough to survive the ever-present threat of disease now made Barbados a serious market for English manufactured goods. By 1650, the tiny island of Barbados, less than 170 square miles, had a white population of more than 30,000. This was about equivalent to Virginia and Massachusetts combined, and on average far richer. A visitor to Barbados that year wrote that the island 'flourisheth so much, that it hath more people and Commerce then all the Ilands of the Indies'. Traders found that they could double their money bringing goods from Europe and then make a further 50 per cent on the sugar they carried on the return journey. By the end of the 1640s, 100 ships a year called at Bridgetown, the majority of them Dutch; four years later, that number had doubled.

Richard Ligon noticed a transformation of the island in just the three years he was there, from 1647 to 1650. When he arrived, the land was largely uncleared, provisions were short, and the houses of the planters low-roofed and unbearably hot and squalid. He himself designed a wooden frame house on a new style and scale for Thomas Middleton, and noted the vast improvements in lifestyle for the planters. It was all down to sugar. In just the few years Ligon was there, sugar-processing technology – and therefore output and profits – had improved enormously. By 1648, sugar had become the means of payment in 60 per cent of transactions on the island, and, as Ligon wrote, the 'soul of Trade in this Island'. If the process of the consolidation of the acreage into large estates, 'fit for plantations of sugar', continued, Ligon reckoned that Barbados would shortly become 'one of the richest spots of earth under the sun'. In fact, it had already become, quite suddenly, the wealthiest English colony in the world. In the 20 months before the end of the decade, the total value of Barbados exports had reached the amazing sum of £3,097,800.

It had helped enormously that during the short but transformatory period of the Sugar Revolution, Barbados had enjoyed minimal interference from home, and had basked in the advantages of free trade. Alongside this laissez-faire attitude to commerce had flourished a friendly, hospitable attitude between the rich white planters, and religious toleration found in few places in the world at this time. Jews and Roman Catholics were left unmolested, and Dutch, French and other foreign settlers made welcome. While the colonists in the mainland North American colonies fell out, often disastrously, over what seem now obscure differences of religious doctrine, in cosmopolitan Barbados most rubbed along fine and concentrated on the main deal: making money as fast as possible.

Not that the island was in any way complacent or laid-back. Every sugar planter faced severe risks: livestock, crucial for driving the mills, could be laid low by a mysterious illness; a crucial piece of machinery could break; fire could break out. Any of these could ruin an entire crop and see the descent of the planter into bankruptcy.

Perhaps even more worrying was the threat to the 'masters' inherent in the unequal and coercive new system from its victims – the servants and slaves. A letter from 1648 mentioned 'many hundreds Rebell Negro Slaves in the woods'. Ligon, whose book's accompanying map included an illustration of runaway slaves being rounded up, commented how the planters built their houses 'in the manner of fortifications, and have Lines, Bulwarks, and Bastions to defend themselves, in case there should be any uproar of commotion in the Island, either by the Christian servants, or Negro slaves'. The planters, he reported, collected supplies of water to see them through a siege or 'to throw down upon the naked bodies of the Negroes, scalding hot'. Nonetheless, Ligon considered it 'a strange thing . . . [the Negroes] accounted a bloody people', that they didn't 'commit some horrid massacre upon the Christians, thereby to enfranchise themselves, and become Masters of the Island'.

Richard Ligon's West Indian adventure ended in disappointment and disgrace. In his book he warned that in Barbados, 'sicknesses are there more grievous, and mortality greater by far than in England', and early in 1650 he himself became seriously ill. It started with a fever, and, as Ligon described with typical candour, led on to 'gripings and tortions in the bowels', with 'not the least evacuation' for a fortnight. This led to an 'excessive heat' within him, 'which stopt my passage so as in fourteen days no drop of water came from me'. Unable to sleep because of the 'torment', he fell to fitting, and was three times pronounced dead by his host Thomas Modyford. But he recovered, not, he wrote, thanks to the ignorant 'Quack-salves', but because of an effective cure: drinking in solution the ground-up dried 'pisle' of a 'green Turtle'.

With the help of Humphrey Walrond, Ligon got himself a place on a ship home. On 15 April 1650, after three months prostrate from sickness, he boarded a vessel for England, which left Bridgetown at midnight to avoid a pirate 'that had for many dayes layn hovering about the Island'. After more adventures at sea, Ligon reached home only to be promptly fined for his previous Royalist activities and then imprisoned for debt. 'We have seen and suffered great things', he wrote from his gaol cell.

Rehabilitated after the Restoration, he attempted to regain the lands lost to him during the early part of the Civil War, but with no success. He died in 1662 at Pill, a small village a few miles north-west of Bristol. In his will he left to his cousin his estate in the Fens, but it was never recovered.

Even in the bitterness of his cell, Ligon retained his huge admiration for the planter elite of Barbados, and for what he saw as the stupendous achievement of the Sugar Revolution. But very soon after his departure, the easy-going camaraderie of the colony's leaders would dramatically come to an end.

6

THE ENGLISH CIVIL WAR IN BARBADOS

'It may excite some surprise that I should have selected so small a portion of the globe as the island of Barbados as the field of my researches . . . but I believe . . . the history of Barbados is by no means barren of events which have materially effected the British Empire. If the navigation laws led to England's supremacy on the seas, that small island was the cause which led to the navigation laws.'

Sir Robert Schomburgk, *The History of Barbados*, 1848

While the fabric of the British Isles, from countries to cities, to towns, and even families, was torn apart by the Civil War, for a long time Barbados had remained isolated from the conflict. Individuals had sympathy or allegiance for one side or another and refugees from both parties washed up on Barbados's shores, but on the island a very English agreement was in place: don't mention the war. There was even a jokey forfeit for anyone who did: the compulsion to provide a roast turkey dinner for everyone in hearing. By the late 1640s, there were recognisable groups – the Roundheads led by James Drax, and the Royalists by the Walrond brothers, Humphrey and Edward – but friendships and marriages crossed the divide, and for now everyone pressed on with growing sugar and getting seriously rich.

In the same way, Governor Philip Bell pragmatically retained the neutrality of the colony, making it effectively independent. Both sides in England petitioned him, with threats and bribes, to declare for their cause, but Bell responded that 'against the kinge we are resolved never to be, and without the friendshipe of the perliment and free trade of London ships we are not able to subsist'. The needs of the sugar economy came before any principles; the island was doing well out of trading with all comers, and the longer they held out, the better the inducements from either side became.

But all the time, some kept the strength of their party feeling under wraps. As the King's cause faltered and failed, a number of young, impressionable Royalist officers arrived in Barbados, and were carefully taken under the wing of the Walrond brothers, who had begun to win a firm grip on the council and assembly and the sympathetic ear of the now elderly Governor, Philip Bell, through the cultivation of his influential wife.

News of the execution of the King at the end of January 1649 seems to have sharpened feelings on the island, with the Royalists experiencing what a contemporary called 'heart-burnings' 'towards those that wished the Parliament prosperity', none more so than the Walronds. While their loyalty to the royal cause was sincere, the brothers also looked to the events at home to give them a chance to take control of the island. Their first move in mid-1649 was to clear away a rival leader of the Royalist faction, the island's treasurer, Colonel Guy Molesworth. Playing on the fears of the Roundhead planters, they declared that Molesworth was planning to seize their estates to hand over to poor Royalist refugees. This was somewhat brazen, as it was exactly what the Walronds themselves were now plotting. But Drax was tricked into acquiescence, and combined with the Walronds to overawe the Governor and have Molesworth arrested. According to Molesworth's later testimony, he was 'by the malice and false suggestion of Sir James Drax and others' imprisoned for three months, and saw his friends tortured – mainly by partial strangulation – in the hope of extracting 'some pretence to take away his life'. Then, when that effort failed, he was expelled with his household of about 40 'in a vessel of no force and by that means fell into the hands of pirates to his utter undoing'. In his place, the Walronds got William Byam, a key Royalist ally and known 'malignant', appointed to the important post, along with responsibility for the island's arsenal and defence. In the meantime, pretending a Spanish threat, they had the island put on a war footing, with their supporters in charge of the militia.

Drax and his Roundhead party still had enough clout to block a proposed alliance with Bermuda, which had declared for the King in late August 1649 and now came to Barbados requesting official support and arms. The Walronds had backed the deal and were furious at the rebuff. Their response was to put it about that 'Independents' were poised to seize the magazines and put the King's supporters to the sword. A special 'Committee of Public Safety' was put together by Edward Walrond, which, sworn to secrecy, debated the 'quietest and most peaceable wayes of sending these malignants into Exile'. Diehard Royalist William Byam even argued that it would be better to kill than to exile the 'Independent' Roundheads, to prevent them stirring up trouble in England. An effort at compromise by Thomas Modyford, a moderate Royalist and above all a pragmatist, was hijacked by Edward Walrond, and what emerged from the secret meetings was a new Bill, backed by the assembly and Governor, which demanded from everyone an oath of allegiance to the King, and threatened severe punishment for any non-conformist religious practices.

This was too much for some of the more moderate Royalists, such as Christopher Codrington (whose two brothers had fought on opposite sides in the Civil War in England). While supposedly 'the worse for Liquour', Codrington revealed the contents of the plot to his brother-in-law James Drax (for which crime he was fined 20,000 pounds of sugar and ordered into exile). Drax quickly mobilised his remaining support and organised a blizzard of petitions against the Bill, while demanding of the Governor fresh assembly elections.

Governor Bell, desiring peace above all, now flip-flopped again, and at a council meeting sided with the petitioners, withdrawing the Bill on a technicality and agreeing to the demand for new elections. The Walronds and their party then stormed out of the meeting, leaving just two of the twelve councillors still with the Governor. In place of secretive political manoeuvrings, the Walronds now launched a pamphlet offensive. Bills started appearing all over the island, announcing the threat of a Roundhead plot and attacking in particular 'Colonel Drax, that devout Zealot of the deeds of the Devill'. One Royalist pamphleteer promised not to rest until he had 'sheathed my sword in [Drax's] Bowells'. Another declared: 'My ayme is Drax, Middleton and the rest. Vivat Rex!'

It was no idle threat. The Royalists were now openly arming themselves, and soon a well-mounted troop was at large in Humphrey Walrond's parish of St Philip. The brash young Cavaliers rode about swearing to slaughter all 'the Independent doggs' who refused to 'drink to the Figure II' (Charles II).

Governor Bell once more tried to put a lid on the growing uproar by publishing a declaration on 29 April 1650 'That no man should take up Armes, nor act in any hostile manner upon paine of death', but it was too late. The following day, the Walronds persuaded two impressionable militia leaders, Colonels Shelley and Reade, to mobilise their men to prevent a supposedly murderous plot by the Independents. Bell ordered them to send their soldiers home, but they refused, at which point the Governor turned to Drax, requesting that he raise his own force to preserve the peace.

Drax briefly had Edward Walrond and Major Byam under arrest, but he could only find about 100 men, far fewer than were now marching on Bridgetown under the King's colours with Humphrey Walrond at their head. There was no option left to Bell except to agree to the humiliating terms demanded by the Walrond party: complete Cavalier control of the arsenal and the body of the Governor himself; the disarmament and punishment of the Roundheads; and a declaration of loyalty to Charles II. The last was publicly made on 3 May.

So now the arrests started. Drax was one of the first, confined to his estate under armed guard. His neighbour Thomas Middleton was also seized, along with 90 more 'delinquents'. Drax was fined 80,000 pounds of sugar, twice as much as anyone else, and left the island soon afterwards for England, seemingly taking his wife and children with him. Others, perhaps with less local status, suffered more. Several prominent Roundheads were banished, and saw their estates confiscated. A Captain Tienman and a Lieutenant Brandon were disenfranchised, their plantations seized, their tongues cut and their cheeks branded with the letter 'T' before both were banished. Another, John Webbs, had his 'tongue . . . bored through with a hot iron'. In the meantime, the headstrong young Cavaliers celebrated by requisitioning all the island's best horses and toasted their victory in lavish style, even by the standards of the time. At one single feast, it is reported, 'vast quantities of Flesh and Fish' were consumed, along with 1,000 bottles of wine.

The Walronds' violent reign was to be brief, however. At the end of July 1650, Francis Lord Willoughby arrived, having been appointed by Charles II as the new Governor of the 'Caribbee Isles'. Willoughby had started the Civil War as a Roundhead but had switched allegiance to the King. Having fled England in 1647, he had served as vice-admiral on Prince Rupert's Royalist privateering fleet operating off the east coast and in the Channel.

Willoughby urged moderation, ending all sentences of banishment and dismissing the Walronds from official positions. In an attempt to secure an agreement with Parliament, he sent a Barbados planter whose brother had been one of the regicides to London to start negotiations. But by now news of the outrages against the Roundheads had reached England, along with a number of refugees including James Drax, his brother William and Reynold Alleyne, another influential Parliamentarian. Drax had corresponded from Barbados with the influential Robert Rich, the Earl of Warwick, so it is likely that he was given a chance to air his grievances at a very high level. Parliament responded by pronouncing the islanders 'notorious robbers and traitors', and, in October 1650, ordering a trade embargo, which also included other rebellious Royalist colonies: Bermuda, Antigua and Virginia. The embargo covered not only English vessels, but 'All Ships of Any Foreign Nation whatsoever'. Indeed, its primary purpose was to attempt, unsuccessfully, to stem the flow of arms and ammunition from Dutch vessels to the Royalist American colonies. In the same month it was resolved in London to send a fleet to subdue Barbados; by January 1651, the force was ready.

Willoughby heard about this the following month, and believing the Royalist cause to be far from lost, determined on resistance in spite of the contrary advice of his wife in England. 'If ever they get the Island', he wrote to her, 'it shall cost them more than it is worth before they have it.' In the meantime, he raised men, improved the island's coastal fortifications, and bought weapons and ammunition, mainly from the Dutch, but also from smugglers from New England. He also made an extraordinary pronouncement of colonial autonomy that now seems strikingly similar to the American Declaration of Independence of 140 years later. Why should Barbados obey 'a Parliament in which we have no Representatives, or persons chosen by us?' he asked, continuing: 'In truth this would be a slavery far exceeding all that the English nation hath yet suffered.'

Tied up with operations against Royalist privateers, the English navy took a long time before it sailed against Barbados. At last, in August 1651, under the command of Sir George Ayscue, it left Plymouth, having been joined by five merchant ships organised by the exiled Barbados planters. Loath to let armed conflict get in the way of easy profit, Drax, Alleyne, Hilliard (who had started as a Royalist, then switched sides) and others had successfully petitioned to be allowed to join the armada to take goods to Barbados and bring back sugar. Drax's cargo consisted of a valuable consignment of horses. As well as the merchantmen – almost certainly armed – the fleet had seven warships carrying 238 guns and somewhere near 1,000 men. Roundhead refugees had reported that conquest of the island would be easy.

In fact, Willoughby now had a considerably larger force at his disposal – some 6,000 foot and 400 horse – and the early part of October 1651 saw him in a confident mood. Prince Rupert's Royalist flotilla was on the way to the West Indies, it was believed. Wildly inaccurate news had just arrived via a Dutch ship that Charles II was at the head of a victorious army only 40 miles from London, that the population had risen to support him, and that Cromwell was dead. The Ayscue fleet, it was reported, now consisted of nothing more than desperate refugees from a defeated cause. On 15 October there were widespread celebrations across the island, with bonfires, dancing and feasting. Willoughby enjoyed himself at a huge evening banquet at a plantation some 12 miles from Bridgetown.

But while the Governor was feasting, the Commonwealth fleet had arrived in the darkness beyond the beaches of the west coast. Having heaved to for the night, early the next morning three ships from the fleet, under its second-in-command, Captain Michael Pack, sailed into Carlisle Bay, Bridgetown's harbour. There, they found at least 11 Dutch merchantmen illegally trading with the island. Although most were heavily armed, such was their surprise that almost all surrendered straight away. Hearing the news, Willoughby rushed to the town, and communicated to Ayscue that he would not surrender the island without a fight. The rest of the fleet then sailed into Carlisle Bay, right up to the main fort, where an exchange of fire took place.

Emboldened by his success, Ayscue ordered an amphibious attack on the main fort in the bay. A large number of longboats, packed with troops, was launched from the ships, but, as an eye-witness's account has it, 'so great was the repulse which they received, that they was inforced to make good their Retreat, with the loss of 15 men, and to betake themselves for sanctuary to their ships again'. This resistance was ascribed to the personal influence of Willoughby, who 'Rides the Rounds in person . . . from Fort to Fort'. So it was stalemate, with the Parliamentarians dominant at sea and the Royalists clearly superior in land forces.

Ayscue now opted for a policy of blockade and persuasion. The former was instantly successful, with no vessel able to approach the island and trade brought to a standstill; however, on 4 November, the council and assembly backed Willoughby's defiance, resolving to 'manfully fight' 'with our utmost power' for 'ye defence of this Island'. But Ayscue chipped away: swimmers were sent ashore by night to collect intelligence, get in touch with Roundhead sympathisers and, by raising the alarm, keep the defenders in a state of constant, wearying readiness; leaflets were distributed urging the island's inhabitants to come to their senses; Drax himself was sent ashore to contact Thomas Modyford in the hope of dividing the moderate Royalists from the diehards under Willoughby and the Walronds. On 8 November a letter arrived for Ayscue detailing the rout of the Scots at Worcester on 3 September, a defeat that signalled the final failure of the Royalist cause in England. This news was quickly conveyed to Willoughby, for whom, although he remained defiant, it must have been a hard blow.

But Ayscue now had his own problems. He reported that 'want of necessary refreshment brought our men into ye scurvye', so that 'we had not men Enough to rule our shipps much lesse to annoye ye Enemye on shore'. A more active policy was signalled by the launch of a surprise attack on 22 November against Royalist positions around Holetown. Two hundred men landed by night and got the better of a detachment of militia, spiking guns and taking 30 prisoners. Pressure on Willoughy further mounted when on 1 December Ayscue was joined off shore by a large force of 15 vessels on its way to Virginia to suppress Royalist rebellion there. The Commonwealth commander must have hoped that this would overawe the defenders, and again demanded Willoughby's surrender. Once more the Royalist was defiant, but each time he sounded less sure of himself.

In fact, the Virginia task force was in a sorry state, suffering severe sickness on board, but Ayscue was still determined to use its soldiers, many of whom were Scots captured at Worcester. On the night of 17 December, 450 men landed at Speightstown under the command of Colonel Reynold Alleyne. The Royalists responded quickly, engaging the raiders with 1,200 foot as well as a troop of horse. During fierce fighting, Alleyne himself was killed by a musket ball, but in the confusion of darkness, the defenders overestimated the size of the landing party, and, in the words of Ayscue, 'ye Seamen runninge in upon ye Enemye wth halloweinge and whoopinge in such a ffeirce disorder yt ye Enemye was soe amazed yt after a short dispute they all ran'. A hundred Royalists were killed, and 80 taken prisoner, along with guns, small arms and a quantity of gunpowder.

But the Virginia detachment could not linger due to their lack of water and provisions, and Ayscue could still not risk facing Willoughby in a pitched battle. However, his propaganda and the efforts of Drax were at last paying dividends. Moderates now demanded in the legislature that Willoughby come to terms. This effort was seen off, but Modyford seems to have made up his mind, helped, no doubt, by the generous terms Ayscue was offering in return for surrender. On 6 January, he drew up his regiment of 1,000 musketeers and 120 horse, and persuaded them to declare for Parliament rather than continue to submit to the tyranny of the Walronds. Contact was made with Ayscue, who then landed his army at Oistins Bay, whence Modyford marched to meet him. Together they had about 1,500 foot and 150 horse. Willoughby advanced towards them. The stage was set for a tropical Marston Moor among the palm trees and sugar cane.

On paper, Willoughby's forces were still far superior, but Ayscue's attritional blockade and propaganda had done their work. Nearly half of the Royalist army had melted away, leaving about 3,000 foot and a couple of hundred horse. Morale in the surviving ranks was low: they were tired out by constant night-time deployment; it was unbearably hot and humid. After brief contact, Willoughby fell back a couple of miles, then suddenly a torrential tropical downpour began. The long-awaited battle was a washout. According to Captain Pack, 'the soldiers could scarce keep a match lighted'. Ayscue was unable to advance to engage the Royalist forces, but at last Willoughby's resolve failed. After three days of almost constant heavy rain, Willoughby, 'seeing that the fire is now dispersed in the bowels of the island', asked for a ceasefire.

On 11 January, over drinks at the Mermaid Tavern in Oistins, a settlement was agreed whereby the island accepted the suzerainty of Parliament, and the imposition of a new Roundhead governor, Daniel Searle. The terms offered in return were generous: indemnity for all, and a return to 'as great freedom of trade as ever'. Willoughby, in particular, was favoured. His confiscated lands in England were restored, and he was allowed to keep the acreage he had recently acquired in Antigua, and in Surinam on the South American mainland, where, two years earlier, he had dispatched settlers to form a daughter colony for Barbados. Two months later, however, a new Roundhead-dominated legislature had their revenge on the Cavaliers, overturning the Mermaid Tavern agreement. Willoughby, the Walronds, Byam and a handful of other Royalist leaders were banished from the island. Willoughby returned to England, where he spent much of the next eight years a prisoner in the Tower of London, as a result of his dabbling in Royalist plots, but nonetheless survived to return to the Caribbean. Humphrey Walrond went to work for the Spanish emperor, while William Byam set off for the Surinam colony, which he thereafter ran for Willoughby as a personal fiefdom.

The agreement to allow free trade had on it the fingerprints of negotiators Drax and Modyford, planters who had benefited enormously from commerce with the Dutch. But soon after the agreement, it was made clear by Parliament in London that a new approach was now in place, based in part on the terms of the embargo of October 1650. In keeping with the dominant economic orthodoxy of the time, mercantilism, the First Navigation Act demanded that no colonial produce be shipped to England except in vessels owned and for the most part manned by Englishmen or colonials, and that European goods could not be imported by the colonies except in English ships or those of the country where the goods were produced. It was a measure to ensure that the English colonies benefited no one but the English at home, and was aimed directly at the great carriers the Dutch, showing the influence of the powerful London merchants who had underwritten the Ayscue expedition.

The Act was widely ignored; even Governor Searle profited from trading with all comers. When an English naval force arrived in Barbados five years later, they would find the harbour packed with Dutch vessels. But the

Navigation Act of 1651 remains immensely important as a marker for a new imperial direction. Before this time, the English colonies had been an informal association, bound together only by trade, families and shared cultural background. Business was in the hands of a rickety structure of royal monopolies, private individuals of many nationalities, and private charters. Now trade and empire were to be regulated – and vigorously expanded – 'in the national interest'. The Navigation Act pointed towards a new formal system, where the colonies provided for the metropolis an exclusive source of supply and a monopoly of shipment and marketing for the home country's vessels and ports. It also constituted the first instance of international commercial policy from London, as well as clear intent for English dominance in the Caribbean.

In this new climate of economic nationalism, Parliament was prepared to go to war to defend or expand the commercial interests of England. This is precisely what happened in July 1652, when conflict broke out with the Dutch. Soon, commercial advantage was replacing religious or dynastic differences as the main cause of wars between the great powers, with the Caribbean their constant theatre.

As intended, the Navigation Act marked the beginning of a process that saw England's merchant marine rise to international pre-eminence, and the resulting pool of skilled seamen man the world's most powerful navy. At last London began to rival Amsterdam as a centre of commerce. But the cost of this mercantile policy was borne by the English consumer, who paid higher prices for imported goods, and by the unity of the young empire. The restrictions of the Act and its successors not only caused a nightmare for those charged with enforcement; it also sowed the seeds for conflict between the colonies and the metropolis.

7

THE PLANTATION: LIFE AND DEATH

'[To work in a sugar boiling house] in short, 'tis to live in a perpetual Noise and Hurry, and the only way to render a person Angry, and Tyrannical, too; since the Climate is so hot, and the labour so constant.'

Thomas Tyron, 1684.

The Roundhead leader James Drax and the turncoat Thomas Modyford did well out of the new order. Their status enhanced by the chaotic events of the previous year, both were asked to join the new, slimmed-down six-man council. Drax, now a colonel in the militia, resumed his place as the host-in-chief of the island, and started work on a spectacular new residence to underpin his pre-eminent social position.

Drax Hall, built, it seems, some time in the early 1650s, still stands, the oldest surviving Jacobean mansion in the Americas. On the next-door estate, Ligon had designed a wooden house for Thomas Middleton, with airy spaces to catch the cooling breeze. But James Drax was having none of this. His house would be in the English manor-house style of the time, as befitting an English gentleman. The building was originally three storeys, with steep gables, stucco walls, and casement windows in the Jacobean style. It was primarily constructed of coral stone blocks, covered with plaster. There were five rooms on the ground floor, which was dominated by the main hall, with a handsomely carved arched opening leading to a stately, intricately carved staircase. Both were of local mastic wood. This staircase was the dominating feature of the house, and to a visitor in the hall gave the whole estate, the entire Drax undertaking, an almost tangible air of ancient prerogative and deserved riches, as it was designed to do (up the stairs and out of sight of the hall, and the banisters immediately reverted to normal and serviccable).

Drax Hall was small by later plantation house standards, particularly those of boom-time eighteenth-century Jamaica, and poorly suited to the climate. The ceilings were low, and although perched on a breezy hill with a vista all the way to the coast, the house was hot and stuffy. Nonetheless, it remains the first 'great house' of the Americas, a loud declaration that, less than 10 years after the advent of sugar, a new colonial aristocracy had arrived.

After a period buying and selling hundreds of acres, in 1654 Drax had some 200 slaves working a fertile, integrated plantation of something over 700 acres. This made him the richest planter in Barbados, if not all of the West Indies. With his sugar production, it seems, well managed for him, he branched out into commerce and shipping. We know that he had shares in a number of ships trading slaves and sugar between London, West Africa and the West Indies.* His enforced exile seems to have widened his scope from Barbados to the entire Atlantic.

With the construction of his 'Great House', Drax had affirmed his gentry status on Barbados; but at the same time, he seems to have outgrown the small island. In August 1653, the Governor, Daniel Searle, removed him from the council and stripped him of his rank as colonel in the militia. Thomas Modyford and a couple of others suffered the same fate at the same time. Perhaps Drax and Modyford had overreached themselves. Searle described them as 'unsatisfied spirits', and as among the 'more violent'. Maybe they had been too blatant in their illegal trading, even for the corrupt Searle, or had become too serious a threat to his authority. Neither took it lightly: from January 1654, both Drax and Modyford were organising petitions to Cromwell to be allowed to be reinstated to their former militia and political positions on the island.

Then, in the spring of 1654, quite abruptly, James Drax left Barbados, apparently never to return to the island that had been his home for nearly 20 years, and which he had taken such a hand in transforming. From the scanty and often contradictory information that survives – wills, court documents, inscriptions copied before they were lost – it is impossible to be sure of exactly why he left Barbados at this time, or whether he had intended to return to his new Drax Hall mansion. Some time in late 1653 his wife Meliora died, almost certainly in childbirth, with their third

* Drax's last deal in Barbados, which has survived in the records, was in late March 1654. He sold to fellow Barbadians Robert Hooper and Martin Bentley 'one-eighth part of the Ship *Samuel* and one-eight part of Pinnace *Hope*, llately set out from England for Africa for negroes, and one-fifth part of cargo and profits'. The cost was £454 sterling or '54,480lbs weight of good muscavado sugar', to be paid within the year, and part of the deal allowed Drax to select from the cargo 'two male negroes and two female negroes' from each vessel once they arrived in Barbados.

daughter, Plulateas. Her second son Henry, who many years later would commission an artist to make a likeness of his mother, was 12 years old. The resulting bust, whose accuracy cannot, of course, be guaranteed, shows a strong-featured, determined but kindly woman, an overlarge nose and slightly squinty eyes softened by a generous fleshiness around the neck. Certainly she must have been tough. In the space of 14 years, she had produced eight children who survived infancy, quite an achievement in Barbados at the time.

That said, she appears to have been in London when she died; it is likely that she and the children, or certainly the young ones, had stayed in England after Drax's expulsion, rather than return with him with the Ayscue fleet. His fourth son, Samuel, almost certainly went to school in England from about the mid-1650s, as he matriculated at St John's, Oxford, in 1661. We can be less sure of the location of the three eldest sons, James, aged about 15, Henry, about 12, and John, 11. Presumably they too were now in England being schooled there, and the Drax Hall estate run by attorneys or friends.

James Drax's first business in England was to find a new wife. With almost improper haste, an arrangement was made with another Somerset girl, many years Drax's junior, called Margaret Bamfield. From Drax's will, which has survived, it appears that the marriage involved several large financial transactions. James Drax and his brother William (in London since at least June 1653) borrowed the large sum of £5,000 from Colonel Alexander Popham, a Civil War officer and former Deputy Lieutenant of Somerset, who had become a senior politician of the Protectorate (now best remembered as an early patron of John Locke). In return, James Drax promised in a pre-nuptial agreement to will his new wife £300 a year after his death or a lump sum of £2,400. The deal shows the calibre of Drax's political contacts and also the immense scale of his business dealings. A loan of £1,000 to two of Margaret's brothers, one an ardent Royalist, might also have sweetened the romance. Margaret gave birth to a stillborn child, Bamfield, before the end of the year. In the meantime, James Drax started buying up land in various parts of England.

Drax, however, had not left Barbados for the last time without the razzmatazz due to a man of his pre-eminent status on the island. '[On] the day of his departure', an eye-witness account reads, 'he came to visit the Governor who entertained him and many others. Then, after dinner, he was accompanied to the place where the ship was to embark by more than two hundred of the island's most important people, all well mounted and marching two by two in a column headed by the Governor and Colonel

Drax.' As Drax arrived at the embarkation place, his ship fired a volley of all its cannons, and as he was conveyed to the vessel in a launch, his retinue left on the dock all fired their pistols in salute. Having watched Drax embark, the company marched back with the Governor in the same order in which they had come. The ceremony has an air of finality as well as demonstrating genuine gratitude and admiration for Drax's achievements from those who had benefited most.

Barbados was now generating enormous profits. This was its golden period. By the end of the 1650s it would be the most densely populated and intensively cultivated agricultural area in the English-speaking world. A visitor in 1655 called it one of the richest spots of ground in the world, and commented that the gentry on the island lived 'far better here . . . than ours do in England'. Indeed, there were few, like Drax, who were wise enough to move their profits to low-risk investment in England; most lived fast and spent recklessly.

In early February 1654, a vessel had arrived from the South American mainland carrying a party of refugees from a failed French colony in Cayenne. Among their number were 'gentlemen', servants and a young French priest called Father Antoine Biet. Biet stayed for three months on the island and left a detailed and articulate account of life in Barbados at this time. He was both impressed and at the same time shocked at what he found. 'They came here in order to become wealthy', he wrote of the English he met, and happiness seemed to be defined for them by conspicuous consumption. They lived 'like little princes'; gold watches were everywhere; and the most extravagant luxuries from England and elsewhere were all to be found in the island's well-stocked shops. The houses were sumptuously furnished, and men and women rode handsome horses, 'covered with very rich saddlecloths'. Neither was expense spared on clothing. Biet found the 'ladies and young women as well dressed as in Europe'. Unhappily for the ladies, it was a time when the fashion in England was for heavy, richly decorated fabrics worn over an intricate architecture of corsets, other wired supports and layers of petticoats. It was all vastly impractical, uncomfortable and even unhygienic, but strikingly, those who could afford it insisted on dressing for the climate at home, rather than for the heat of the tropics. If anything, the men were worse. To be wildly overdressed was a key indicator of status. One concerned doctor wrote that he had seen 'many men loaded, and almost half melting, under a thick rich Coat and Waistcoat, daubed and loaded with Gold, on a hot Day, scarce able to bear them'. Importers of fancy handkerchiefs, gold rings, gloves and ornate hats were now making a fortune.

Father Biet was quite clear about where the money was coming from: 'The wealth of the island consists of sugar', he wrote. Cane was planted in the countryside 'as far as the eye can see'. By the early 1650s, England was importing 5,000 tons of Barbadian sugar annually, a figure that rose to 8,000 tons by 1655. Nonetheless, the pioneer sugar barons now had a new challenge. From 1650, the return they secured for their crop started falling steadily as supply increased. The price of sugar in 1652 was less than half that of 1646, and it would continue to drop. The astronomical profit margins of the 1640s, as described by Richard Ligon, were now a thing of the past. But the planters responded quickly, upping output and efficiency, and thus the island continued to get richer throughout the decade.

Part of the vastly improved efficiency was down to labour. Although white indentured servants were still much sought after, the 1650s saw a steady increase in the proportion of the sugar workforce made up of enslaved Africans, up to about half, some 20,000, by 1655. After only a short period, it had been confirmed that these alien and alienated workers could be driven harder and fed and clothed much more cheaply than the fractious whites – especially after the practice was adopted of encouraging the slaves to grow a proportion of their own food. In addition, black women, unlike whites, were sent to the field gangs, and in general the price paid for new slaves fell as the trade became more efficient and extensive.

A large influx of Dutch and Sephardic Jews, after their expulsion from Brazil in 1654, brought to the island fresh expertise in sugar processing and trading, and from the early 1650s increasing numbers of planters used wind power for their mills, saving on lifestock costs. In all, the decade saw the widespread emergence of the integrated plantation, as pioneered by James Drax, and the full flowering of the new agri-industry. Indeed, a model was established that would survive almost unchanged for the next 150 years and would shortly be exported around the region.

The average size of a Barbados sugar estate rapidly increased from the late 1640s, and had more than doubled by 1657, with less efficient growers eliminated. With canefields and processing plants under single ownership, the supply of cane to the mill could be tightly controlled by carefully staggered planting in 10-acre 'pieces'. Father Biet, who visited the Drax estate and several others, described these integrated plantations as 'like villages', with a cluster of buildings around the plantation master's house, 'ordinarily handsome [with] many rooms'. Along with the sugar works, usually situated downwind of the main house, there would be dwellings for the servants and the slaves, with those of the latter made up of 'very inferior wood, look[ing] almost like dog-houses', according to another contemporary account.*

For the slaves and servants, work usually started at six. There was half an hour for breakfast between nine and ten, a noonday rest of between one and two hours, and work ceased at sunset. Most plantations had a 'Great Gang', consisting of the ablest men and women; on the largest plantations, such as Drax Hall, this could number as many as 100. The Great Gang did the heavy work of planting: digging trenches into which two-foot-long cane cuttings were placed, before being covered with a light layer of soil. Increasingly, as the earth wilted from the voraciously nutrient-hungry cane plant, manure would be collected and applied to the cane holes. A head driver, with a polished staff to lean on, and a short-handled whip, would be constantly on hand to increase the labourers' work rate.

The new plants sprouted within two weeks. A lesser gang of children or weaker adults, equipped with small hoes, would laboriously weed and further manure the young shoots until the plants were tall enough to suppress weeds themselves. The gruelling work of harvesting the canes would see the return of the Great Gang.

If this was the most back-breaking of the labours on a sugar estate, the processing was the most dangerous and stressful. Piling the cut canes into the three-roller mill was particularly perilous. 'If a Mill-feeder be catch't by the finger', wrote an observer of the first 'factories', 'his whole body is drawn in, and he is squeez'd to pieces.' An axe was always kept to hand to chop off, before it was too late, any limb caught in the crusher.

Sometimes the boiling houses got so hot that water had to be poured on to the roofs to prevent the shingles catching fire. As well as enduring the heat and stench, the workers were frequently burnt by the sugar. 'If a Boyler get any part into the scalding sugar,' said a contemporary, 'it sticks like Glew, or Birdlime, and 'tis hard to save either Limb or Life.'

Increasingly, plantations had other processing buildings as well. Many planters found it advantageous to further refine their muscovado sugar by 'claying'. The coarse, sticky brown sugar was set in a sugar mould smeared with moist clay. Water percolated through the mould, carrying away more of the impurities and molasses. This could be repeated up to six times, with the sugar on the top becoming progressively whiter. Clayed sugar brought a higher price in England, and was less bulky, reducing shipping

* This was German mercenary Heinrich Von Uchteritz, captured after the Battle of Worcester in 1651, who spent about four and a half months on the island in 1652 before escaping his bondage thanks to a visiting Hamburg merchant. He had joined a plantation with a workforce of 100 blacks and 100 whites.

costs. This further contributed to the efficiency of the sugar plantation, and concurrent falls in the costs of freight, commission charges and insurance rates also helped keep the money flowing in even as the price of sugar dropped.

At the same time, the slide in price had long-lasting and important consequences. Back home in England, consumption rocketed. For most of history, the English palate had made do for its sweetness with honey and fruit. The Crusaders brought cane sugar back from the Levant, and Italian merchants from Venice and Genoa brought cargoes of Egyptian sugar to London and Bristol from the fourteenth century onwards, but these were tiny quantities at very high prices. The lavish production of Madeira and then Brazil in the fifteenth and sixteenth centuries increased the supply to England, and thus lowered the price, but the market remained the super-rich, who used sugar as a medicine – it was prescribed for everything from fever to stomach ailments – or a preservative, and for the status its price and rarity conveyed. It was made into elaborate moulded displays, which signified wealth and distinction, and to have sugar-blackened teeth became a status symbol.

But the Sugar Revolution in Barbados changed all this. As production increased, and the price fell, consumption rose as much as fourfold in the 40 years after 1640. Much of the new demand was the result of other new tropical products coming onto the English market. London's first coffee house opened in 1652. Tea imported from China by the East India Company started gaining popularity at around the same time, and for the rich, chocolate from cacao became fashionable. All three needed, in most people's opinion, sugar to make them drinkable (tea, in particular, was drunk very sweet).

Alongside sugar in various states of refinement, a new product was also being marketed by Barbados – rum. From the Portuguese, the English planters had learnt to take some of sugar processing's by-products, skimmings and molasses, and having let them ferment, distil them into 'a hott hellish and terrible liquor', as a 1650 account describes it. Eventually called rumbullion, its first name, as reported by Richard Ligon, was 'Kill Devil'. Ligon records that it cost only half a crown for a gallon. He didn't like it, finding it 'infinitely strong, but not very pleasant to taste'. But others were less squeamish. Some was exported to Virginia, the Bermudas and New England, and as far as England, but an awful quantity was consumed on the island, particularly, we are told, by the 'meaner sort'.

The effect such cheap and strong liquor had on the health of an already heavy-drinking population can easily be imagined. Thomas Modyford commented that Spanish traders 'at their first coming wondered much at the sickness of our people until they knew of the strength of their drinks, but then wondered more that they were not all dead'. In the 1650s, Governor Daniel Searle tried to restrict the growth of unlicensed taverns, as he was concerned about 'the disableing and overthrow of divers manuall trade labourers or workemen and the impoverishing (if not ruine) of many families' due to drunkenness, but 10 years later a traveller reported that there were more than 100 taverns in Bridgetown alone.*

Visitors continued to marvel, as they had done from the first settlement, at the 'debaucht' inhabitants of the island. 'Drunknes is great, especially among the lower classes', commented Father Biet, going on to detail the frequent fist fights that this led to. But from his own account, it is clear that drunkenness was by no means limited to the poorer classes. The Frenchman described as typical a visit to a rich plantation, probably that of James Drax. As in Ligon's account from a few years earlier, the food was spectacular: 'nothing lacking in the way of meats . . . suckling pigs, turkey hens, capons, chickens . . . very good mutton . . . excellent stews'. He also carefully, and disapprovingly, noted the copious drinking – 'wines from Spain, Madeira, the Canaries; French wines . . .'

If, after Ligon's description of a feast at Drax Hall, we might have been wondering how they actually did anything for the rest of the day after such a huge consumption of food and alcohol, Biet provided the answer: those rich enough to have underlings managing their business didn't try. Instead, they subsided into a sybaritic torpor. 'After one has dined, and the table has been cleared', the French priest continued, 'a trencher full of pipes and another of tobacco is put on the table along with a bowl full of brandy, into which is put plenty of sugar.' Eggs were added, and 'the host takes a little silver cup, fills it with this liqueur and drinks to the health of whoever is in front of him. After he has drunk, he refills the cup and gives it to the person whose health he has just drunk; this person does the same thing to another, and this procedure is continued until there is nothing left in the bowl.' All the time, 'well built young slaves' refilled the pipes, which they then presented on their knees. 'The afternoon passes thus in drinking and smoking, but quite often one is so drunk that he cannot return home', the priest continued. 'Our gentlemen found this life extremely pleasant.'

Another visitor a few years earlier described the typical planter as 'A German for his drinking, and a Welshman for his welcome . . . if it raines he toapes [drinks] securely under his roofe . . . hee takes it ill, if you pass

---

* The saying went that the first thing the Spanish did when they started a settlement was to build a church, the Dutch a fort, the English a tavern.

by his doore, and do not tast of Liquor.' Others confirm that Barbadians took it as a severe insult if 'the trafeller dose denie to stay to drinke'. Soon, Father Biet found it too much: 'Sometimes I went along', he said of trips around the island, 'but, not taking pleasure in this visiting because one has to drink in a extraordinary way, I did not always go.'

Such heavy drinking was, of course, disastrous for the health of the islanders, as well as for their society and families. Furthermore, the rum was actually poisonous. From the time that rum was first distilled on the island, visitors had noticed the prevalence of what came to be known as 'Dry Belly-ache'. The symptoms were 'Tortions in the Bowells' – agonising stomach cramps. Sometimes the victim lost the use of his limbs, and for many the disease was fatal. Only in 1676 was the condition identified as lead poisoning, and it was not until 1745 that the pipes used in rum distilling were recognised as the cause.

Propagandists for the island, who could not deny the appalling attrition from disease, claimed that Barbados was healthy; it was the debauched habits of its people that explained the frightening death rate. But temperance was no guarantee of good health. A Swiss doctor who visited the island in 1661 commented that 'Most persons who come here from Europe will have to overcome an illness which the inhabitants call Contry Disease.' This, he wrote, made victims 'turn quite yellow, their stomachs and legs swell, and sometimes their legs burst and remain open'. The doctor blamed unfamiliar food, too much liquid and sleeping in hammocks in the open air, but the term was probably used to refer to a variety of diseases: gastrointestinal complaints such as dysentery or dropsy, caused by bad hygiene or the consumption of contaminated food or water – or the fevers that struck particularly hard during the wet season.

Life expectancy at birth during the seventeenth century in England was about 35. In the West Indies it was as low as 10. While in New England transplanted English folk could expect to live longer, and parent more surviving offspring than in England, in the West Indies the reverse was the case. In St Michael parish, which admittedly included Bridgetown, the unhealthiest place on the island, the register records four times as many deaths as marriages during the 1650s and three times as many deaths as baptisms. In London, the unhealthiest place in England by far, sickness was concentrated among the poor. Colonists, then, expected that rank would protect them, as it did to a large extent at home. But in Barbados, the great and the good were struck down as well.

For many, sugar was worth the risks presented by this extraordinary death rate. And sugar was now benefiting many more than just the Barbadians.

The ever-growing new trade began to swell the customs revenue back in England, while raising demand for insurance and finance services, as well as sugar refineries. Some two thirds of the Barbados sugar production was profitably re-exported to the Continent. New fleets of merchantmen were now needed to bring out equipment and supplies and return with the produce. Demand for processing equipment, packaging, building materials and vessels created new workshops, factories, saw mills and shipyards, both in England and in the North American colonies.

In the 1650s, the New England–Barbados trade really took off, helped by the partial removal from the scene of the Dutch, as well as other factors. The experience gained by North American mariners since the first trading voyages made the long journey, if not hazard-free, then certainly less dangerous. Barbados consumed more and more of New England's surplus foodstuffs and livestock. In return, the New Englanders not only brought back specie – vital for discharging their debts to England for manufactured goods – but also, increasingly, tropical products, particularly sugar, molasses and rum, were now finding a market in New England.

Much of the new trade was oiled by family and new religious connections. In 1655, Barbados was visited by the Quakers Mary Fisher and Anne Austin. Henry Fell followed the next year. Together, they found a small but influential constituency of spiritually starved Puritans ripe for conversion, including the important planter Thomas Rous. In 1656, Rous, with the unshakeable conviction of the rescued sinner, penned a diatribe entitled: 'A warning to the Inhabitants of Barbodoes who live in Pride, Drunkennesse, Covetousnesse, Oppression and deceitful dealings'. Castigating his fellow Barbadians, who 'Excel[led] in wickedness . . . cheating and cozening', he railed against the local propensity for violent greed, whoremongering, 'vanity, and folly, and madness', predicting that 'the wrath of God shall be revealed in flames of fire against you, ye Earth-worms'.

At the same time, Quakers were making a determined appearance in Rhode Island. In 1656 a party arrived from Boston, hoping that Rhode Island would provide them with the religious freedom they had been denied in Massachusetts. In the summer of the following year, more appeared, having been turned away from New Amsterdam. Two senior Dutch clerics living there wrote to Holland that in all probability the Friends had sailed to Rhode Island, 'for that is the receptacle for all sorts of riff-raff people, and is nothing else than the sewer of New England. All the cranks of New England retire thither.' An Anglican noticed that the Rhode Island settlement was 'a chaos of all Religions'. It was now uncharitably called 'Rogue Island' by the Bostoners. The island's 1663 charter from Charles II would end up giving unprecedented religious freedom to the colony.

The sanctuary given to the Quakers created strong links with Barbados that were crucial in driving the trading growth of Newport and of Rhode Island in general. More widely, by the late 1650s, the enterprising New Englanders were becoming known as the 'Dutch' of England's empire, trading whatever they could with whomsoever they wanted. Not even war would stop them – during the conflict between England and Holland in 1652–4, merchants from Newport, as well as commissioning the town's first three privateering vessels, brazenly traded with the enemy, setting a precedent that would later lead to major ructions in the empire. By the 1670s, English merchants were complaining that New Englanders were importing European goods and then selling them on in the West Indies at prices that severely undercut their own efforts, then selling the tropical products they got in return directly to Europe. 'New England is become the great mart and staple', the English merchants protested, 'by which means the navigation of the kingdom is greatly prejudiced, the king's revenue lessened, trade decreased, and the king's subjects most impover-ished.' It wasn't the fault of the New Englanders that their economy was simply not complementary to England's (then self-sufficient in foodstuffs and timber), but if the likes of Boston and Newport were to emerge as rival metropoles to the mother country, there could only be conflict ahead.

While offering the hope of trading wealth to New Englanders, Barbados was also providing investment for the English economy at home, as well as newer settlements in the West Indies and, indeed, the Northern American colonies. Perhaps even more important was the flow of settlers from the island, many of them experienced sugar planters or merchants, with bodies seasoned to the dangers of local diseases. Barbados remained a favourite destination for poor white emigrants from England, but losses to sickness, and, increasingly, onward migration, meant that the white population fell from a high of some 30,000 in 1650 to just over 25,000 a decade later.

So Barbados now became the 'mother' colony or 'hearth' of the English American empire. Some islanders moved on to the promising colony in Surinam. As in the 1640s, repeated efforts were made by Barbadians to settle other parts of northern South America, as well as Trinidad and Tobago. Between 1650 and 1662, nearly 2,000 spread themselves over Guadeloupe, Martinique, Marie Galante, Grenada and Curaçao. Others headed for the established, but comparatively undeveloped English settle-ments in Antigua, Nevis and Montserrat. Some 2,000 ended up in Virginia, bringing with them experience of the plantation system and of extensive black slavery.

The biggest single exodus was in 1655. On 29 January of that year, a powerful English fleet arrived at Barbados. Soon, Carlisle Bay was crowded with as many as 60 new vessels. On board were some 3,000 English troops. Their aim was grandiose: the ending of Spanish power in the Caribbean, and recruits were called for from Barbados to join the great design. More than 3,000 came forward, making this the most powerful expeditionary force the Caribbean had ever seen. They sailed at the end of March. Only a handful would ever see Barbados again.

8

CROMWELL'S 'WESTERN DESIGN': DISASTER IN HISPANIOLA

'Why did I go with such a rascally rabble of raw and unexperienced men?'
General Venables, 2 November 1655, Tower of London,
on the men under his command in the West Indies

The fleet had left England on 26 December 1654. A naval officer on the expedition, Henry Whistler, described the doleful scene on the wharf: 'This wose a sad day with our maryed men', he wrote. Husbands were 'hanging doune thaier heads, loath to depart'. Couples were embracing, 'sume of them profesing more love the one to the other in one halfe our then they had performed in all the time of thayer being together'. At two o'clock the fleet sailed, the wind blowing freshly at ENE. Whistler's ship briefly ran aground, but then got under way again. In the evening, light rain began to fall, and at midnight the wind veered SSE, 'a faier galle'.

This expedition represented an important new departure. It was no corsair raid, it was 'take-and-hold'. For the first time, England was to attempt to conquer colonial territory of one of its European rivals. For the first time, imperialism was to be directed by the centre; colonies were to be acquired by order of London, rather than by the actions of merchant syndicates, entre-preneurs or adventurers on the ground.

The fate of the men leaving Portsmouth set an unhappy precedent for further imperial wars in the West Indies. A year and a half later, both the expedition's commanders were prisoners in the Tower of London, and almost all of the men were dead.

Flushed with the success of conquering the Scots and Irish, and from the recent victory over the Dutch (who had agreed, however falsely, to observe the Navigation Act), Oliver Cromwell was looking for a new war to bolster his domestic position. The French seemed to fit the bill; indeed, an undeclared naval war had been continuing for some months. But in the end Cromwell decided that the Spanish provided the best target for his desire to fulfil what he saw as England's destiny of leading the opposition to the Church of Rome, of chastising the Antichrist. Since June 1654, a plan had been germinating for an attack on Spain's American empire, the source of its wealth, and therefore of the financial means to make mischief in Europe. At the same time, fighting Spain had a happy resonance with the exploits of the Elizabethan corsairs such as Raleigh and Drake, whose stories were being busily reprinted in the 1650s – safe patriotic fare after years of divisive civil war. Furthermore, while leading the Protestant cause, Cromwell also claimed to be revenging the cruelties of the Spanish in the Americas, and releasing the region's indigenous peoples from the 'Miserable Thraldome and bondage both Spirituall and Civill' of the King of Spain.

Oliver Cromwell undoubtedly saw the launching of this, his 'Western Design', in religious terms. But the mission also represents a moment when religious zeal as the basis of political action was beginning to fade away. In its place was emerging a steely pragmatism allied to a more modern commercial spirit. Cromwell saw England's destiny as the head of a navigation and mercantile system and looked to dominate trade in the West Indies. In the shorter term, he hoped for an instant profit from the overrunning of Spain's rich American cities. At the very least, the mission should be self-financing – the navy was by now over a million and a half pounds in debt.

There was no detailed plan of attack. Cromwell had consulted Thomas Gage, the country's leading expert on Spanish America and on all things anti-Papist. Gage had been born into a fiercely Roman Catholic family in Surrey in around 1600. First a Jesuit, then a Dominican, he lived and worked in Central America for some 15 years before returning to England in the early 1640s and renouncing his Catholicism in favour of a Puritan Anglicanism. (He confirmed his new loyalty by denouncing a number of former friends, including his brother's ex-chaplain, who was executed.) In 1648 he had published a book about the Americas full of tales of the corruption, decadence and strategic weakness of the Spanish American empire, as well as useful information for any invading army about fortifications, topography and infrastructure. The Dedicatory Epistle to Sir Thomas Fairfax, then the leading power in the land, urged him to 'employ the soldiery of this kingdom upon such just and honourable designs in those parts of America'. 'To your Excellency, therefore', he concluded, 'I offer a New World.'

'The Spaniards cannot oppose much', Gage told Cromwell, 'being a lazy, sinful people, feeding like beasts upon their lusts.' If Cuba and Hispaniola were taken, he said, Spanish Central America would fall to England within two years (Gage would join the expedition as chaplain to the General's regiment).

Also consulted was Thomas Modyford, in England at that time. He agreed with Gage that Spanish power was weak, and advised attacks on Guiana or Cuba. In the end, the official instructions were vague: 'to gain an interest in that part of the West Indies in the possession of the Spaniard'. Puerto Rico and Hispaniola were suggested as first steps, to act as staging posts for attacks on the mainland. Alternatively, or in addition, the capture of Havana, 'the back doore of the West Indies', 'wil obstruct the passing of the Spaniards Plate Fleete into Europe'. Cartagena should be taken as well, as this was where Cromwell wanted to situate the capital of his new empire.

With hindsight, these plans seem wildly hubristic, but on paper it looked easy. Cromwell planned a force of 3,600 regular troops from England together with the same number raised in Barbados and the English Leeward Islands. Drake had captured Santo Domingo on Hispaniola with only 1,000 men. The Spanish Antilles had seen a constant drain of settlers to the mainland, and few now had an entire population as big as the army about to descend on them. Spain had forced the English out of Providence Island in 1641, but this was something of a last gasp, and their power had become feebler since. Some fortifications had been recently repaired, but the confidence of the English naval gunners was high, having just proved their worth against the Dutch.

In the event, Spanish strength or weakness had much less to do with the dismal outcome of the 'Western Design' than did the quality of the English troops and of the expedition's planning, command and logistics. Neither the naval nor the land forces commander was first rate (nor, it would turn out, truly committed Cromwellians): the sailors were under the orders of an unscrupulous careerist, Admiral William Penn, father of the founder of the Quaker colony of Pennsylvania. In charge of the army was General Robert Venables, a Parliamentary army veteran, but indecisive and incompetent. In theory Penn was subordinate to Venables; in reality it was a split command, with the inevitable risks of rivalry and confusion. Furthermore, the two military commanders also had to factor in the guidance of three civilian 'commissioners' who secretly reported to Cromwell on their performance and loyalty. One was Daniel Searle, the Governor of Barbados; another Edward Winslow, who had sailed on the Mayflower in 1620 and been Governor of the Plymouth Colony, and was now a highly trusted expert on colonial affairs. The third was Gregory Butler, seemingly an old West India hand, described by one of Venables' officers as 'the unfittest man for a commissioner I ever knew employed'. He features little in contemporary accounts of the expedition, except for when he was so drunk during a parade that he fell off his horse.

The more junior officers were a mixed bag: some good, some awful. The private soldiers, however, were almost universally poor. The 'home' contingent had been recruited from the invincible New Model Army, but few officers let any but their most troublesome and feeble men go. There was also a general shortfall in the numbers required, so further recruiting was carried out by drum beat in the poorer parts of London and other cities. As was always the case, only those with little to lose came forward. Thus the English ranks were made up of 'slothful and thievish servants', criminals and debtors on the run.

The men recruited in the West Indies were, by all accounts, even worse. Some were small-scale farmers who, having found the Barbados acreage all snapped up, took their families with them in the hope of finding land to plant. Most, though, were the desperate and greedy; of all the migrants from Barbados to different parts of the Americas, those who went with Venables were characterised as the worst: 'the looser sort out of hopes of plunder', 'old beaten runaways'. Altogether, the men were described by Venables' wife, who accompanied her husband on the expedition, as 'the Devils instruments . . . A wicked army it was, and sent out without arms or provisions.'

The last complaint would prove perhaps most damning of all. The logistics of the expedition were a disaster. As the main fleet left Portsmouth, they were supposed to be joined by at least three further vessels from London. But the barque containing most of the army's pikes was still sitting in Deptford, as were the transports carrying horses and cavalry equipment, and, most importantly, provisions and heavy weapons in the form of siege mortars.

Thus the main force was compelled to wait in Barbados, scanning the horizon for the arrival of the missing arms and supplies. Weeks passed, during which the Spanish had plenty of time to be warned of the force's presence. Venables used the wait to drill his raw troops and attempt to replace the missing equipment: horses were requisitioned at huge cost; 2,500 half-pikes were constructed using cabbage palm shafts; and 1,500 mainly rusty matchlocks borrowed from the island's militia, though little ammunition or powder was to be found. (James Drax, never one to miss a trick, was soon applying for permission to export from England to Barbados replacement horses and weapons.)

But after eight weeks, with provisions on the island growing ever more scarce and expensive under the strain of so many extra mouths to feed, the commanders were forced to abandon the wait and set forth on 31 March 1655. Heading north-west, the armada stopped six days later at St Kitts, where a further 1,200 men were collected. Like the Barbadians, many brought their families with them. An officer from England commented that they looked 'rather as a people that went to inhabit some country already conquered than to conquer'.

Venables now had as many as 9,000 men at his command. Unfortunately, he only had provisions (of a very low quality) for about half that number. By the time the fleet left St Kitts, the men were already on half-rations at best and weakening all the time.

Only on 9 April was Henry Whistler, a naval officer on Penn's flagship, told that the target was Hispaniola. Two days later, with the island only 48 hours' sailing away, a huge row broke out among the soldiers. Commissioner Winslow had solemnly announced that all plunder from the island was to be reserved for the Protector and the 'Design'. Officers and men alike were put 'into a Great pachon'. Thus the army had already fallen out over the spoils of a victory yet to be won. As Henry Whistler commented, 'Wee . . . Ware asharing the skin before wee had Cached the foxx.'

On 12 April, the eastern end of Hispaniola was spotted by the vanguard. Alarmed reports soon came back that the shore was 'rocky, and a great surf of sea against it . . . in many places we saw the beatings of the water appear afar off like the smoke of ordnance'. Suddenly the amphibious attack did not look so easy. As warning beacons appeared in sight on the coast, and the population readied themselves for the attack, the armada's divided command squabbled about what to do next. Venables urged a direct assault on the city of Santo Domingo, the island's capital (and the oldest Spanish city in the New World). Penn, for the navy, insisted that this was impossible, with the winds in the wrong direction and the approach treacherous. At last a landing a short way down the coast was decided upon, with the aim being to attack the city from the weaker, landward side.

On the morning of the 14th, the English force headed west of Santo Domingo, steering for the mouth of the River Jaina, a short distance west of the city. But with the wind astern, and lacking an experienced pilot, the mariners took fright at running aground, and sailed past the landing point, not making shore until a spur of land nearly 40 miles from the city. Nevertheless, they found the small defences there unmanned, and some 7,000 troops landed unopposed.

As the men only had two to three days' short rations, there was no time

to be lost. The large column moved off, along a rough road running to the
east. Soon, enemy scouts were spotted, but no contact was made. Occasionally a small house would be encountered, but clearly all the inhabitants had fled, though not before taking everything they could carry,
blocking wells and burning the savannah to drive away the island's free-
roaming cattle. Very soon a critical problem emerged: the men had no water
bottles; the following day they found themselves crossing a wide treeless
drought-stricken savannah; it was punishingly hot. 'Our very feet scorched
through our Shoes', wrote Venables later. One of his soldiers reported:
'Our horses and men (the sun being in our zenith) fell down for thirst.'

At one time, they found themselves in thick woods. Although the shade
gave relief from the burning rays of the sun, the breeze was now gone,
and the heat was more intense and oppressive than ever. No water was to
be found. In desperation, men started drinking their own urine.

Then, suddenly, they found themselves in an orange grove in full fruit.
The thirsty soldiers gorged themselves, and loaded up as many as they
could carry. But for many, this was the final straw for their embattled
constitutions. By the evening, many of the men had come down with
diarrhoea.

The large force, it seems, lacked a guide with local knowledge. This
caused unnecessary lengthy detours and made finding water largely a matter
of chance. The column, unfamiliar with local topography, was also extremely
vulnerable to ambush. During the first morning, enemy horsemen appeared,
then disappeared in the distance. At last an officer of the scouts unwisely
gave chase to one and was not seen again. After that, occasional surprise
attacks – sometimes just a volley of fire followed by a swift disappearing
act – kept everyone on their guard.

Judging by eye-witness accounts, the progress of the army by the third
day resembled a desperate search for food and water as much as a military advance. Every building the soldiers encountered was ransacked in an
unsuccessful search for provisions. When a chapel was come across, the
'popish trumperie' was 'wasted'. On one occasion, the soldiers 'brought
forth a large statue of the Virgin Mary, well accoutered, and palted here
to death with oranges. Heere also they found a black Virgin Mary to enveigle
the blackes to worship.'

At last, the column's vanguard came within reach of Santo Domingo, and
a detachment from the Leewards regiment was sent forward to reconnoitre
the approaches to the city. Barring their way they found a small brick-built
fort, an outwork to the west of the city wall, screened by a small wood.

Officers, including Venables, who was, like his men, 'extreamly troubled with the Flux', made their way to the front to see for themselves. But at that point, a troop of horsemen came charging out of the wood. The English broke and ran; two officers next to Venables were killed, and the General himself, so one report goes, 'very nobelly rune behind a tree . . . being soe very much prosesed with teror that he could harlie spake'. Most of his men were similarly struck and fled in disarray.

A small number, however, stood their ground, repulsed the attack and wormed their way forwards to some earthworks between the outlying fort and the city. But they had no equipment for scaling the city wall. The men, one of them wrote, were 'fainting'. 'The great guns from the fort gawling us much. Thus wee lay without water, ready to perish and of hunger and want of sleep, till about midnight.' Venables, having recovered his composure, pulled them back and, against the advice of his commanders, ordered the English force to retreat to the River Jaina to regroup and re-equip.

On 19 April, after more losses on the march, a new camp was established there, and contact made with the naval force. While arguments raged among the commanders about what to do next, the spirit of the soldiers, already battered by defeat, fatigue, hunger and thirst, melted away. All the talk was of the strength of the enemy, in particular the 'cowboys' or 'cow killers' who had charged the vanguard outside the walls of Santo Domingo. For the most part, this opposition was not the decadent, pox-ridden Spaniards the Englishmen had been promised, but hardy blacks and mulattoes, tough, practised horsemen from years in the saddle rounding up – or, more exactly, slaughtering on the hoof – the island's wild cattle. Their principal armament had clearly made a great impression: 'Lances . . . a most desperate wepon, they are very sharp, and soe brod that if they strik in the bodie it makes such a larg hole that it lettes the breth out of the bodie emediatlie.'

As the troops waited for their commanders to make the next move, the initiative passed to the enemy. Men who ventured out of the camp to hunt for wild cattle to eat were almost always ambushed and stabbed to death with the dreaded lances. Outposts of the camp were raided and stragglers picked off. Soon the army was shooting at fireflies, thinking them 'the ennimie with light maches'. Even the noise of land crabs' legs knocking against their shells would create an alarm, and cause a large part of the army to run off into the woods.

And while the delay continued, the troops sickened further. Soon after the 19th, the rains started; the men had no tents or shelter. 'The abundant of frut that they did eate, and lieing in the raine dod case most of them to haue the Bluddie-flux', reported Henry Whistler. 'And now thayer harts wore got out of thayer Dublates into thayer Breches, and wos nothing but Shiting, for thay wose in a uery sad condichon, 50 or 60 stouls in a day.' Anyone so afflicted was soon far too weak to fight.

But Venables had not given up, despite the rapidly deteriorating state of his army. Over the next few days, their heavy weapons, consisting of a couple of artillery pieces and a single mortar, were belatedly landed, along with provisions from the fleet. Ladders were constructed for scaling the city walls, and on 24 April, the army marched once more eastwards against Santo Domingo.

Early the following day, having stopped two miles short of the city wall and camped without water, 'sufficiently faint and almost choaked of thirst', the English force approached the outlying fort. In the lead was a body of 400 men under the command of an Adjutant-General Jackson. The officer, who had acquired a reputation in Barbados for whoring and drunkenness, had taken the precaution of sending a more junior officer in the vanguard, while himself taking up a position in the safety of the rearmost ranks. This attitude seems to have informed the performance of his men. As before, the Spanish defenders counter-attacked with mounted lance-bearing 'cow killers'. The leading ranks found their Barbados-built 'half-pikes' too short to be of use against the longer lances of the Spanish cavalry. The junior officer was killed straight away, and within moments the English attack had turned into a rout.

As the vanguard fled back towards the main English force, their panic became contagious. The formation behind them let off a ragged volley from their matchlocks, and then they too wheeled round and fled. The line behind them actually lowered their pikes to prevent the flight, but then they also dropped their weapons and ran. Fleeing through a narrow gap between two hills, the melee was squashed into a narrow killing field. Some 600 died, most from a lance in the back as they ran away. Two hundred more fled into the woods 'whom the Negroes and Molattoes soon after dispatched'. Three hundred were wounded, most past recovery. A large number of officers also perished, and eight regimental colours were captured. The one-sided battle only stopped when the Spaniards, according to one English officer, 'were weary of killing'.

Once the Spanish horsemen had returned to their lines, Venables briefly considered pressing home the attack with the heavy mortar, but changed his mind and ordered it buried and the munitions destroyed. Once again, the English force retreated to the camp on the River Jaina. By now there were only 2,000 men fit in the whole army. Frightened of venturing out of the camp to hunt for food, the men started eating dogs and what remained of the horses so expensively procured from Barbados.

Winslow and the other commissioners urged a further attempt, but on the 27th, Venables made the decision to abandon the operation. By 4 May, all the surviving men were embarked, according to one soldier's account, 'in a most sad and lamentable condition, having never seen men soe altered in soe small a time'. The soldiers reckoned that their army of thousands had been routed by just 200 Spaniards.

Even while the shock of defeat was raw, the recriminations began. Adjutant-General Jackson, who had deserted his men in battle, was cashiered, his sword broken over his head, and was forced to serve as a swabber on board the hospital ship. One English officer commented that 'if all of like nature had been so dealt with, there would not have been many whole swords left in the army'. A number of prostitutes, dressed in men's clothes, were uncovered and 'severely chastised'. Most to blame for the cowardice shown by the English in Hispaniola, Venables reckoned, were the colonials, especially the men from St Kitts, who 'lead all the disorder and confusion'. The Barbadians, too, were 'only bold to do mischief; not to be commanded as soldiers, not to be kept in any civil order, being the most prophane debauched persons we ever saw, scorners of religion, and indeed so loose as not to be kept under discipline and so cowardly as not to be made to fight.' Venables' greatest anger, though, was directed at Penn and his naval force, which had conspicuously failed to support the efforts of the army.

In all, a heavy pall of disaster, division and defeat lay over the armada as it weighed anchor from Hispaniola and drifted westwards with the wind and currents. Commissioner Winslow, his heart apparently broken by 'the Disgrace of the army on Hispaniola', sickened and died on 7 May. As he was 'thrown overboard', the expedition lost the one man in the force with experience of setting up a new colony. Surprisingly, after what had just happened, such skills were soon to be sorely needed. A short time after the abandonment of the Hispaniola campaign, word trickled down through the ranks that there was a new objective, a 'smaller success': Jamaica.

9

THE INVASION OF JAMAICA

*'Many that are alive, appear as ghosts . . . out of a strange kind of spirit, desir[ing]
rather to die then live.'*

General Robert Sedgwick, on the English troops in Jamaica

'On Wednesday morning, being the 9th of May', wrote a soldier in Venables'
army, 'wee saw Jamaica Iland, very high land afar off.' Preparations were
made for invasion the following day.

In the island's capital, known at the time to the English as St Jago de
la Vega (and later as Spanish Town), alarming news arrived early the next
morning from lookouts on high ground over what is now Kingston harbour,
10 miles from the capital. A fleet had been spotted to the east, approaching
out of the rising sun. Soon afterwards, two fishermen, who had been out
catching turtles off the coast the previous day, reported in a terrified state
that they had blundered into a huge armada and had themselves only
narrowly escaped, paddling hard, to the safety of the port. They overestimated by a factor of two the strength of the fleet, at more than 70 vessels,
but had not failed to spot the red and white cross of St George flying from
the ships' masts: it was an English force of a scale previously unseen off
Jamaica's shores. In St Jago de la Vega church bells were rung and through
the streets drums were beaten, as the governor massed what paltry forces
he had and ordered them to the harbour to repel the hostile invasion.

Jamaica was, indeed, a 'smaller' target than Hispaniola, only a fraction of
its size and importance. Venables, having lost confidence in his troops,
urgently needed an easily won consolation prize for Cromwell after the
disaster outside the walls of Santo Domingo. Jamaica, thinly populated
and virtually undefended, hove into view at the right time.

Nonetheless, it was very different from any of the islands already settled by the English. The combined land area of Barbados, St Kitts, Antigua, Nevis and Montserrat is less than a tenth of Jamaica's 4,441 square miles. Furthermore, Barbados (by some distance the most important colony thus far) is small, relatively flat, and cooled to an extent by the trade winds. In spite of early struggles, it had shown itself to be a landscape that could be overcome and dominated by the English. Jamaica was radically different. It was a wild topography – mountains in the east rising to more than 7,000 feet, thickly clad in vegetation, with their summits cloaked in blue-tinged clouds. Below the 'cloud forests' lay thick woodland. Elsewhere there were barren savannahs in some places, lush rainforest in others. The interior also contained harsh, waterless uplands, and deep hidden valleys. Near the coast stretched rich alluvial plains, but they were isolated from each other by rivers and deep swamps. In stark contrast to Barbados, the English would find this a landscape impossible to master and subdue.

Columbus had 'discovered' the island on his second voyage in 1494, sailing into what is now called St Ann's Bay on the north coast. He called the bay 'Santa Gloria', 'on account of the extreme beauty of its country'. According to his reports, Columbus found Jamaica 'the fairest island that eyes have beheld; mountainous and the land seems to touch the sky'.

Jamaica was at that time the most heavily populated of the Greater Antilles, the coastline thickly dotted with villages. The Tainos, sometimes called Arawaks, had been in Jamaica for some 2,500 years. Arriving as colonisers from South America, they may have displaced earlier settlers who had migrated southwards from Florida. Although they had spread over the whole of the island, most Taino settlements were near the coast. There may have been as many as 50,000 at the time of European contact.

The Tainos, most evidence suggests, were a peaceful and gentle people. But Columbus met with a hostile reception, with 70 or so canoes launched into the bay towards his vessels, each full of shouting and gesticulating warriors. They soon dispersed when fired upon from the Spanish ships, but Columbus then weighed anchor and headed down the coast to what is now called Discovery Bay. Needing water, provisions and wood for repairs to his ships, he put a party on shore, guarded by crossbowmen and accompanied by a large dog. The former killed a number of Tainos, who also found the unfamiliar dog terrifying. Shortly afterwards, gifts of fruit and provisions arrived from local chiefs as symbols of submission.

Columbus returned to Jamaica in June 1503, and spent a year stranded there. Nonetheless, the island retained its charm for the explorer. Although he established that there was little or no gold in Jamaica, the island, for him, was 'otherwise a paradise and worth more than gold'.

Few of the Spanish colonists who followed in Columbus's wake felt the same way. The Tainos were forcibly set to work digging for gold, but when none was found, a majority of the more enterprising Spaniards left the island for the greater lure of the mainland. On the orders of Columbus's son Diego, a city was founded on the north coast, but this was soon abandoned as the small population gravitated to the south, establishing the colony's headquarters at St Jago de la Vega, six miles from the sea. By the time of the English invasion, the city consisted of a number of churches, a monastery and several hundred houses, some of brick and roofed with tiles, others only of rough mortar and reeds.

While the north and west remained undeveloped, on the southern plains farms were established growing sugar cane, cacao, pimento and cassava, mainly for domestic consumption, although a little was traded with passing Spanish galleons. The main activity, though, was hunting the cattle and pigs that were allowed to roam free. Pork fat and cow hides were exported to Spain, but on the whole the colony was a failure, more of a burden than a benefit to the imperial authorities in Madrid. The small number of ruling families quickly became inbred and suffered the bitter feuds attendant on most very small and isolated communities.

The island had been raided several times by English corsairs, but it was so poor and undeveloped that it was hardly worth the trouble, except for its richness in portable provisions. Part of the weakness of the colony was due to the elimination of the native population, and therefore workforce. Smallpox was perhaps the biggest killer, but many also died of other introduced diseases and of hunger as the imported livestock wrecked their unfenced provision grounds. Enslaved by the Spaniards, tens of thousands also died of overwork or wanton cruelty at the hands of their masters. Rather than live as slaves, many killed themselves, and women aborted their children. In 1598, an alarmed governor suggested an 'Indian reservation' to preserve the fast-shrinking population, but nothing was done, and by the time the English arrived just under 60 years later, they were almost all gone.

So in 1655, the population, including women, children and slaves, was only 2,500, outnumbered nearly three to one by the invading force under Admiral Penn and General Venables. There were perhaps only 500 Spaniards who could bear arms.

Nonetheless, after the humiliating disaster at Hispaniola, Venables was taking no chances. Before launching his troops, the general ordered that from then on, if anyone tried to run away, the person next to him should shoot him dead, or forfeit his own life. He seems also to have learnt another lesson from Hispaniola: the importance in amphibious warfare of close cooperation between the army and navy. This time, with helpful winds, the attack was vigorously led by the navy, which sailed a gunboat right up to Passage Fort, on the west side of Kingston harbour, and gave covering fire as a swarm of smaller vessels, packed with soldiers, was launched against the beach below. Before the keels of the boats had touched the sand, the men were leaping out into the waist-deep warm waters of the bay. Musket and cannon fire from the fort whistled around them, but no one was hit, and then the men were ashore, their 'determination', according to one account, causing the Spaniards to abandon their positions and flee. Venables had a different take, later thanking the wind for the fact that the men 'could not possibly row back, but must vanquish or die', but whether made bold by courage, threat or necessity, by three in the afternoon the English troops held the harbour as the Spanish soldiers retreated back to St Jago.

But Venables' trust in his men was not to be restored that easily. Having taken over a fortified but abandoned position on the road to the capital, the general called a halt to the advance. His men, 'wanting guides', were 'very weak . . . with bad diet', he later wrote. Indeed, the troops were sickly from their adventure in Hispaniola, and hungry, having been on half-rations since Barbados, but while they rested, the delay allowed the Spanish to evacuate the city, taking everything they could with them.

The next day, assured of overwhelming strength, the army marched towards the town. Shortly, a Spaniard appeared with a flag of truce. He was followed, an eye-witness wrote, by 'divers Spaniards, which seemed to be of quality, to treat'. With them they brought presents for the general of wine, poultry and fruit, and promises of cattle 'sufficient for the maintenance of the army, with other large overtures, and high compliments'. Clearly, the Spaniards hoped that this was another hit-and-run raid, for treasure or, more likely, provisions, and that the English would take what they needed and depart, as their countrymen had done before. Venables readily accepted the offer of food for his hungry army, but he also signalled that this time the English had arrived to stay. We have not come to plunder, he told them, but to plant.

Actually, this was the opposite aim of the majority of his men, particularly those from England, who had no desire for nor experience of tropical farming. They had travelled halfway across the world to loot the riches of Spanish America and were determined not to be disappointed. At two in the afternoon on 11 May, English troops entered St Jago. To their dismay, anything remotely resembling plunder had been carried off. All that was left was heavy furniture and a stack of hides, so common on the island that they were used to line the floors of slaves' dwellings. The hides were collected (and later sent on a Dutch ship to New England to exchange for provisions), but in their frustrated fury, the English soldiery laid waste to the town, ransacking churches and burning buildings, while frantically digging in the ground in the vain hope of buried treasure. Many of the buildings had to be rebuilt when the English remembered that they needed shelter.

After a further delay, the Spanish Governor, Juan Ramirez, at last arrived in the city to sign the articles of surrender. Ramirez, an onlooker wrote, was 'a uery sad creater' 'soe much eaten out with the pox' that he had to be carried in a hammock; 'the ennimie woas ashamed that wee should see him'. Apparently, Ramirez was afflicted with the 'French-disease'.

The articles deliberately echoed those imposed on the English inhabitants of Providence Island back in 1641: the Spaniards were to be shipped off the island within 10 days and forfeit all their property. In the meantime, they were ordered to supply the huge English army with cassava bread and 200 head of cattle a day. The Governor and two of his officers remained in English hands as hostages.

News of the terms came as a severe shock to the Spaniards sheltering in the hinterland behind St Jago. Most had been born in Jamaica and had never left the island; it was their home. While they debated what to do, they sent provisions as requested to the English in the town, but at the same time preparations were started for a guerrilla war in the interior. Indeed, the Spaniards had quickly decided that 'if they complied, they were utterly ruined, and desired rather to expose their lives to the hazzard of warr then to condescend to such termes'.

Four days passed before Venables realised he had been tricked. Suddenly the supplies of provisions ceased. Shortly afterwards, men started disappearing while out foraging for food or loot. It was soon apparent that rather than turning against their masters as the English had hoped, the island's slaves, together with the runaway maroons, had sided against the invaders, who, they were told, would treat them harshly. Small bands were formed under the leadership of Spanish officers. These lurked just outside the small sphere of English control, and preyed on those who ventured beyond the lines. Bodies of dead English soldiers started being discovered, stripped naked and horribly mutilated.

Efforts were made to pursue the Spanish into the hills, but the enemy melted away, only reappearing to pick off stragglers. It was, wrote one of Venables' officers, 'an impossible thing for an army, except well acquainted with the country, to follow or find them out . . . The excessive heat of the sun, the want of water in many places . . . did more weaken and disable them in ten miles march there, than forty in their own country.'

Even more serious for the fate of the English army was the lack of food. The island's planted acreage had supported a population of some 2,500; now there were an extra 7,000 mouths to feed. During the first days of occupation there had been no planning for managing food supply and the English soldiery had slaughtered cattle and hogs with abandon, but now, suddenly, there were none left who had not been killed or driven away by the Spaniards. Provision grounds were likewise sabotaged, and the army found itself on starvation rations of half a biscuit per man a day.

Thus the 'victory' in Jamaica became, for the men of the army, even worse than the calamitous defeat in Hispaniola. Henry Whistler reckoned that within 12 days of the landing, lack of food and water had halved the strengths of the companies.

Dysentery now swept though the malnourished ranks, so that soon 'they looked like dead men, just crept abroad from their graves'. By 14 June, there were 'not more than five field officers in health . . . two thousand privates were sick; and the rest grew very unruly and mutinous'. The day before, Venables had written home that 'our Men die daily . . . Fresh flesh and roots put them into Fluxes, which sweep them away by Ten and twenty per diem frequently.' Many of the dead remained unburied, 'others buried so shallow underground that they already scent through', wrote a senior officer the following month. Together with the garbage of the army, carelessly strewn about, 'the scents are here so noisome that in some parts of this town a man is not able to walk'.

As the strength of the English force steadily diminished, guerrilla attacks by the Spanish and their maroon allies grew ever more daring and destructive. 'The enemie lye still on the mountains, expecting our deserting this country', wrote an English soldier on 15 June in a letter home. At one point, maroon guerillas entered Spanish Town itself, burning several buildings. In all, it is estimated that as many as 1,000 men were killed by ambushes, usually when hunting for food. Within a short time, Venables was forced to ban his troops from venturing beyond the narrow confines of the city and the harbour. The men were forced to eat snakes, lizards and rats, and 'Neither', we are told by a Spanish source, 'did the English spare any of the dogs, cats, colts or donkeys which their bullets reached, so exceedingly hungry were they'.

The leaders of the ill-fated expeditionary force responded by scuttling back to England. Venables, to be fair, was seriously ill, with what he called a combination of 'flux' and 'fever', although the naval commander, William Penn, was the first to leave, setting sail from Jamaica on 25 June, with about three quarters of the fleet (leaving Vice-Admiral Goodson in charge of a force of 12 frigates). Penn, it appears, was keen to have his version of events in Hispaniola heard before that of Venables. At this time, it was rumoured in the army that the General had died, but instead, he was 'Convey'd on board in a distracted Condition', and arrived back in Portsmouth, still alive, on 31 August. Major-General Richard Fortescue was left in command of the army.

Cromwell was devastated by the Hispaniola disaster, which he saw as the Lord's punishment for his own iniquity. On hearing of the shock defeat there, he had shut himself in his room and become ill. When Penn and Venables showed up back in England, he was furious, and both were imprisoned in the Tower of London as punishment for deserting their men. A precariously held Jamaica was seen as totally inadequate return for the grandiose ambitions of the Western Design.

According to soldiers' accounts, the men of the army were, indeed, 'full sore' about the departure of their leaders. Furthermore, no one had been paid. Fortescue, Venables' replacement, wrote to Cromwell that the men of the army, who had come for plunder, now 'fret, fume, grow impatient'. The island had huge potential, he went on, but there was a desperate need for some more upstanding, 'Godlike' immigrants and servants who, unlike the vast majority of the army, might be willing to get down to the hard work of planting. Tools were also required, he wrote, along with well-equipped, experienced and disciplined reinforcements for the army to deal with the continued threat of reconquest by the Spanish and their maroon allies.

Fortescue was soon dead from sickness, leaving Lieutenant-General Edward D'Oyley in command, but Cromwell, wishing to make the most of the meagre prize of Jamaica, responded vigorously. Every male immigrant, he announced, would receive 20 acres, with 10 allocated per woman and child. A thousand each of Irish boys and girls under 14 were to be sent out and sold as indentured servants, and he ordered the sheriffs of the counties of Scotland to round up 'all known, idle, masterless robbers and vagabonds, male and female, and transport them to that island'. At the same time, appeals went out to other English colonies in America to provide the means to people the newly conquered territory. A number of Quakers from Barbados, who had made themselves unpopular by refusing to bear arms in the militia, were welcomed to Jamaica, along with Bermudans, as well as Jews expelled from Brazil by the Portuguese after the final defeat there of the Dutch.

Cromwell's great hope, however, was that the doughty Puritan North Americans, scratching a meagre living out of the stony New England fields – 'driven from the land of their nativity into that desert and barren wilderness, for conscience' sake' – would welcome a move to the warm and wildly fertile climes of the West Indies. In September 1655, an envoy was sent to New England to try to persuade them to move on to Jamaica. In his instructions Cromwell outlined his vision: 'Our desire is that this place [Jamaica], if the Lord so please, be inhabited by people who know the Lord and walk in his fear, and by their light they may enlighten the parts about them (a chief end of our undertaking and design).' In the meantime, 2,000 Bibles were sent to Jamaica for the edification of the troops there.

The New Englanders may have been supportive of Cromwell's aims, but with a few exceptions, they resolutely refused to migrate to this supposed 'land of plenty'. They were actually doing rather well, a large part through the ever-growing trade with Barbados and the other islands; and they had had enough contact with Jamaica to have heard of the 'prophaneness of the soldiery, the great mortality in the island; and the continual hazard to the lives of any peaceable settlers there, from the skulking Negroes and Spaniards'. In New England, in contrast, there might not have been such a hope of instant riches, but 'they lived more comfortably like Englishmen than any of the rest of the Plantations'.

Cromwell had more success with his appeal to the English settlers of the Leeward Islands. Governor Luke Stokes of Nevis responded enthusiastically, raising at least 1,000 men, together with women and slaves, to make the leap to the new colony. They were fetched by Goodson in three frigates and sent to the long-deserted eastern tip of the island near what is now known as Port Morant. This was an important part to occupy, for the good harbour there could easily have been taken over by the Spanish. It was also one of the most fertile parts of the country. However, it was long deserted for a reason: it was bordered by mangrove swamps that provided a home to countless malaria-bearing mosquitoes. Within two months, Stokes and his wife were dead, along with two thirds of the other immigrants. Soldiers sent to guard them from the ever-present threat of Spanish attack also died in droves.

But Cromwell's vision for his 'Western Design' had not been just about planting and settlement. Any foothold gained in the central Caribbean was to be exploited to harass, weaken and plunder the local interests of the Spanish (or of any other rival European powers). So at the same time as appealing for new settlers, the Protector sent orders to Jamaica for the creation of Courts of Admiralty (which dealt with the disbursement of 'prize' enemy cargoes and vessels, the proceeds being shared between the crew, the officers and the state) and for the commissioning of 'private Men of War to annoy and infest the Enemies of our Nation'. Admiral Blake's fleet was doing a good job of besting the Spanish navy in European waters, and this gave the energetic Goodson free rein to exploit Jamaica's strategic position, and to carry out his instructions to capture any foreign vessels he could at the same time as taking the fight to the Spanish Main. During the latter half of 1655, he brought in a number of prizes, as well as attacking Santa Marta near Cartagena, demolishing forts and burning the town. The big hope, though, remained the capture of the annual Spanish treasure fleet.

Cromwell also dispatched to Jamaica a new commissioner and military chief, Major General Robert Sedgwick, who arrived with some 700 rein-forcements in October 1655. Sedgwick was a pious Puritan soldier with an honourable military record in the Massachusetts colony. He had mixed feelings about the operations now being undertaken by Goodson: 'This kind of marooning cruising West India trade of plundering and burning of towns', he wrote home, 'is not honorable for a princely navy . . . though perhaps it may be tolerated at present.' He was concerned that unless towns like Santa Marta were taken and held, there would be little hope of carrying out their 'intentions in dispensing anything of the true knowledge of God to the inhabitants'. Such 'naked plundering missions' also ran the risk, he warned, of making the English appear 'to the Indians and blacks' 'a cruel, bloody, and ruinating people . . . worse than the Spanish'.

Such delicate sentiments, of course, had no place in the West Indies of the seventeenth century, and to do him justice, Sedgwick did have a more pragmatic side. Realising the importance of naval superiority, he started work on what would become the British navy's key West Indian base for the next 200 years and more.

Kingston harbour was protected by a sand spit, in places as narrow as 100 yards, just beyond the end of which lay a small island of just under 60 acres. This had been used by the Spaniards for careening ships but, a few shacks aside, it was empty. On the landward side was deep, well-sheltered water, a perfect harbour and anchorage. Sedgwick ordered the construc-tion of a fort on the island, which would command the harbour. Heavy guns were mounted, 21 by March 1656. A small stone tower was then built, mainly by men from the navy, the army being too debilitated. Traders came to sell to the garrison and labourers to work on the fort. The following year there was the 'fair beginnings of a town'. It was the start of what would very shortly become the dazzling and infamous city of Port Royal. As events would dramatically demonstrate, it was a wildly unsuitable place for a new city, only a few feet above sea level, consisting of unstable sands and in the midst of a zone battered by natural disasters. In addition, the island was small, lacking any fresh water, and only reachable by boat. Nevertheless, its advantages as a harbour seemed to outweigh everything, and soon the army's stores and headquarters were moved to the island.

Although the navy now enjoyed increasing success and relative good health, on land, the nightmare for the army continued unabated. Weakened by hunger, more than 100 men were dying each week from dysentery or fevers. Provisions grudgingly sent out from England – Cromwell complained about the expense of sending food to 'a place which abounds in all things' – were pilfered, purloined by corrupt officers or perished from careless storage.

When Sedgwick arrived in October 1655, he found the army 'idle . . . unworthy, slothful . . . in as sad, as deplorable, and distracted a condition, as can be thought of'. The bodies of dead soldiers lay in the streets and the bushes.

Those men still fit were expecting and hoping to be ordered against some richer Spanish target, and therefore get the plunder they came for, and, unpaid, they considered their due; the officers, it appeared, just wanted to go home. Thus neither was inclined to undertake the long-haul task of planting, nor, indeed, wrote Sedgwick, to 'do anything, however necessary, for their own benefit'.

A muster held the following month found that of the 7,000 who had landed in May, 3,720 were still alive, besides 173 women and children. 'Many that are alive', Sedgwick reported, 'appear as ghosts . . . out of a strange kind of spirit, desir[ing] rather to die than live.'

At the beginning of November another 800 men arrived as reinforcements. Those already there just felt sorry for them. 'Poore men I pitty them at the heart', wrote a soldier of the original party, 'all their imaginary mountains of gold are turned into dross.' In the same letter of 5 November, he described how half the surviving men were sick and helpless and how he himself was getting thinner all the time, having had no provisions from the army for 10 weeks. He had by now suffered 'with the bloody flux, rhume, ague, feavor'. In St Jago de la Vega, 'There were soe many funerals, and graves . . . it is a very Golgotha.' On the savannah outside the town, he reported, Spanish dogs were digging up the shallow graves of the perished English soldiers and eating the carcasses.

All the time, maroon and Spanish guerrillas in the hills and woods of the interior kept up their campaign, setting ambushes for the English soldiers seeking game, provisions or water. Sedgwick reported to Cromwell in January 1656: 'We now and then find one or two of our men killed, stripped, and naked.' In March he wrote, 'there scarce a week passeth without one or two slain'. The following month a mutiny had to be bloodily suppressed and its leaders hanged. Men started deserting to the Spanish, who rewarded most of them with instant execution.

By now, more than 5,000 men who had come from England and the other islands had died in Jamaica in 10 months. Amongst them was the renegade priest Thomas Gage, who had urged the 'Western Design' on Cromwell, and who had accompanied the expedition as a chaplain. In June, the hard-working Sedgwick was killed by a fever. His replacement from England lasted less than a year before dying of malaria and exhaustion.

This, then, was the less than glorious birth of what would become Britain's richest and most important colony. The island was a giant morgue for one of the most disastrous military expeditions of British history. And it had left as the founding stock of the new colony a mutinous, disease-ravaged and demoralised rabble.

Edward Long, the grand eighteenth-century historian of Jamaica, ascribed the 'disasters which befell the first race of settlers here' to the want of 'industry, unanimity, perseverance, and good order'. Although the death rate remained shocking, he wrote, 'they were the wretched victims to their own debauchery, indolence, and perverseness'. No doubt, this is to a large degree true. One English officer called the men of the army the 'very scum of scums, and mere dregs of corruption'. For its first adventure in aggressive, state-driven imperialism, England had put together a wretched army of the poorest-quality soldiers, moreover ill-equipped and ill-led. A large majority of the troops had paid with their lives.

But among them were men who, having had the courage to embark on a new and dangerous opportunity, had enjoyed the luck, and possessed the resourcefulness and the hardy constitution required to survive when so many others had not. Several of these tough, determined survivors would go on to found families of huge wealth and power. We know that Hersey Barrett, great-great-great-great-grandfather of Elizabeth Barrett Browning, was amongst the men from Barbados or the Leewards. He had brought his wife and five-year-old son with him on Venables' invasion fleet. The family would come to own vast and productive sugar estates and a number of grandiose 'great houses'. Another pioneer was Lieutenant Francis Price, probably recruited by Venables from among the less successful Barbadian smallholders, whose family would be within two generations the second-largest landowner on the island. The Beckfords, who became the grandest of all the sugar dynasties, may have had a family member or two on the expedition as well, and it has been suggested that Henry Morgan, who supposedly started out his spectacular West Indian career as an indentured servant on Barbados, was part of the force.*

On the death of each commissioner from England, military command in Jamaica was taken up by Edward D'Oyley. He was aloof and a harsh disciplinarian, but, as it turned out, an effective and astute leader of the colony in its hours of greatest danger.

In October 1656 he instigated a plan whereby land around Spanish Town and beyond was allocated to the soldiers regiment by regiment, in the hope that they could be ordered by their officers to start the cultivation of provisions and crops for export. At last, some cassava and tobacco was planted. It was hoped that this wider occupation would also squeeze the provision supplies of the enemy guerrilla force.

But D'Oyley's greatest concern now was the threat of reconquest by regular Spanish forces. Jamaica, however poor and backward, had been an integral part of the Spanish empire. Its apparent loss to a rival European power was a dangerous precedent Madrid was determined to reverse. Only internal rivalries within the Caribbean empire, and the spread of sickness from the English army to the Spaniards and thence with them to Cuba, had prevented an immediate counter-attack. But crack Spanish troops were known to be on their way from Europe, and the Governor of Cuba, at last receiving reinforcement and weapons from the Viceroy of Mexico, was massing soldiers and transport for a counter-invasion.

D'Oyley's answer to this threat was not to seek more soldiers, who could not yet be fed, but to look for a strong naval force to guard the coasts and prevent a Spanish army being conveyed from Cuba. It was hoped, furthermore, to put the enemy on the back foot with a continual campaign of harassment at sea and hit-and-run raids across the Spanish islands and Main. Goodson's handful of frigates and couple of hundred marines could only do so much. To achieve this aim, D'Oyley needed the buccaneers.

Even more directly than the planter pioneers, the buccaneers were the spiritual descendants of those English 'corsairs' who, during the Anglo-Spanish war of 1585–1604, had carried back a fortune from the Spanish Main in looted sugar, hides, logwood, indigo, silver, gold and pearls, and had thereby won themselves a place in the mythology of English adventures overseas. The nucleus of the buccaneers came from the Spanish

* Other prominent figures in the island's early history who came with the Cromwellian army are John Cope, Thomas Lynch, Samuel Long, Henry Archbold, Samuel Barry and Thomas Freeman.

THE INVASION OF JAMAICA

expulsion of the English and French settlers from St Kitts back in 1629. Those who escaped capture or declined to return to their ruined tobacco plantations relocated to deserted places in the Spanish Caribbean and vowed to take revenge on Spain, while at the same time guarding their independence and paying tribute to no one. An independent and international force, though almost always directed against Spain, they operated either out of Providence Island, near modern-day Nicaragua, or Tortuga, off Hispaniola's north coast, which was well placed for interception of Spanish ships in the Windward Passage. Over time, they attracted to their strength a large number of debtors, desperadoes and criminals, on the run from the various European settlements in the region.

Expelled from Providence Island, and periodically driven away from Tortuga, many buccaneers formed camps on the deserted northern shore of Hispaniola. There, they survived by hunting wild cattle and selling to passing ships the meat they had processed into dried strips on their 'boucans' or barbecues, hence their name. Sheltering under leaf-roofed sheds and sleeping in sacks to keep off the insects, they looked, said a French observer, like 'the butcher's vilest servants, who have been eight days in the slaughter house without washing themselves'. Soon, it was apparent that the best way to raise themselves above subsistence level was by taking over ships and selling the cargoes to the highest bidder. Even more profitable was raiding the peaceful Spanish coastal settlements. Thus developed the Caribbean's most formidable amphibious assault force, moreover one that expected no mercy from their Spanish enemies, nor granted any in return. Atrocities on both sides escalated in ferocity and horror.

Threatened by Spanish reconquest of Jamaica, Edward D'Oyley decided to make what later turned out to be a pact with the devil: he invited the buccaneers to come to the new Port Royal to dispose of their prize cargoes and loot, and to refit and spend the proceeds of their raids. In return they would act as 'freelance' auxiliaries to the official English naval force, who, of course, shared their goals: to snatch loot and generally cause chaos among the Spanish in the Caribbean. The chance to base themselves in a good, well-defended harbour at the strategic centre of the Caribbean Sea was welcomed. Within a short time, more than 1,000 buccaneers were operating out of Port Royal, with their loot and prize cargoes often reloaded on to New England or Bermudan ships as payment for provisions.

So the buccaneers now operated under commissions, or letters of marque or reprisal – official sanction from the English authorities. While still primarily motivated by the hope of Spanish pieces-of-eight and by the charisma and dash of their particular leaders, their efforts were led by the handful of English naval vessels left behind after the departure of Admiral Penn.

The deputy of this force was Captain Christopher Mygns, an aggressive and popular commander. Sent by D'Oyley on a wrecking mission against the Spanish Main, he was advised to attack settlements in secret and under cover of darkness. Instead, he arrived at midday with drums thundering and trumpets blasting, much to the terror of the Spaniards. After one raid with 300 men he returned to Port Royal with an estimated £200,000–300,000 sterling of booty, mainly in silver snatched during a descent on the Spanish town of Coro. Much of the treasure stuck to the fingers of Mygns and his men, causing the temporary disgrace and recall of the Captain, but his aggression and confidence were infectious.

In October 1658, the English came within a whisper of catching the elusive treasure fleet. Lying in wait at anchor between Cartagena and Porto Bello in Panama, they sighted the galleons on 20 October, but only two frigates were on hand to intercept them, the rest being away collecting water. The two vessels engaged the rear of the fleet, hoping to scatter the merchantmen, but the Spanish ships kept their formation and the silver proceeded unmolested to Europe.

Yet there were enough successes for the proceeds of prizes and raids to go a long way towards underwriting the young colony, in a way that planting could not yet achieve. They were Jamaica's only true income, and the demand from the buccaneers and privateers for naval supplies, provisions and entertainment drove the development of Port Royal and its hinterland.

In early 1657, the first crops planted by the regiments were ready for harvest. Helped by early rains, the yield was good, particularly for those Leeward islanders who had struggled on around Port Morant. In addition, fustic and other dye woods were now being gathered and sent back to England. In terms of simple survival, a corner had been turned. But in the same year warning came, through captured letters, that the plans of the Viceroy of Mexico to retake the island were now ready for launch.

D'Oyley took 500 men, and sailed in search of the enemy, whom he found on the north side of the island near Ocho Rios. About 500 Spaniards had landed and fortified themselves with trenches and a stockade of tree trunks. Undaunted, D'Oyley's men advanced, hacked their way into the stockade and drove the Spanish out. More than 100 Spaniards were killed and many more wounded. Some escaped back to Cuba, but most fled into the woods. English losses, though, were light.

The Spanish continued to land small parties of men from Cuba, and in May the following year, a larger party of nearly 1,000 established a new fort on the north coast at Rio Nuevo. This provided a sterner test for attackers: on high ground and protected by a deep river, it was equipped with six cannon, each firing four-pound shot.

D'Oyley didn't hear about the new Spanish base on the island until 12 days later; as before, rather than brave the hostile interior, he took a force of 750 by sea, landing a short distance from the Spanish position. Then, by circling round through thick woods behind the fort, he managed to find a weak spot. As his vanguard threw crude grenades into the palisade, scaling ladders were rushed up, and the fort breached. Three hundred Spanish soldiers were killed, against some 50 English.

The Spanish would not land again in such numbers, but the guerrilla war continued, with news of the death of Cromwell in September 1658 adding to the uncertainty of the English. Then, in 1660, a renewed effort against the guerrillas led to the discovery of a hidden, richly fertile valley where 200 acres had been planted in provisions to sustain the Spanish and their local allies. Soon afterwards came a decisive breakthrough when a key maroon leader, Juan Lubolo, was contacted and successfully persuaded to change sides. His men now hunted down the Spaniards and their allies, and by the end of the year, after one final unsuccessful landing of some 150 men, the Spanish at last abandoned their attempt at reconquest. Many hostile maroons, however, remained at large in the interior.

The performance of the English army in Jamaica over these three years was impressive, especially considering they were underfed, had still not been paid, and many did not even have shoes. D'Oyley continued to plead with London, describing a state of 'extreme want and necesitie' on the island. He wrote home that he feared 'sickness will reduce' the population 'to a small number; supposes it proceeds from excessive drunkenness.' He complained 'of merchants bringing strong liquors from all parts.' He was also vexed by the large numbers of men who, instead of planting, were joining the ever-growing privateering fleet operating out of Port Royal. Immigrants were not arriving in sufficient numbers to replace those dying of sickness. For one thing, settlement was discouraged by the widely held view that, after all their struggles, the restored King of England, Charles II, would hand the island back to his friends the Spanish without a shot being fired.

On 26 July 1660, D'Oyley wrote to London: 'All the frigates are gone, and neither money in the treasury, victuals in the storehouses, nor anything belonging to the State is left . . . the island has a sense of being deserted by their own country, which fills the minds of the people with sad and serious thoughts.'

PART TWO

The Grandees

10

THE RESTORATION

'Riches enlarge rather than satisfy appetites.'
Thomas Fuller, 1608–61

After his lavish send-off from Barbados in the spring of 1654, James Drax was given a warm welcome back in England from his friends in politics and business. He was soon involved in a partnership with his old friend and Barbados neighbour, Thomas Middleton, also in England, in a lucrative deal to deliver muskets to the island to replace those shipped out with Penn and Venables' ill-fated force. Other trading ventures – including slaves – almost certainly followed. For at least two years after his departure from Barbados, Drax remained in London, becoming a prominent member of the prototype committee of West India merchants and planters who met at the Jamaica Coffee House in St Michael's Walk near the Exchange in London. His bust shows a solid Puritan grandee in his later years, strikingly resembling well-known portraits of Cromwell, with shoulder-length hair below a short fringe, a prominent nose and fleshy lips. Evidence of his famous dinners can be seen in his large double chin; his expression is one of authority, but not without humour and kindness.

In gratitude for his partisanship during the Cavalier–Roundhead face-off in Barbados, and in recognition of his new but spectacular wealth and influence, James Drax was called in for an audience with the Protector in December 1657. Cromwell took the opportunity to bestow on him a knighthood. A contemporary account reporting the event described Drax as 'a Gentleman of much worth, and of great Interest in Plantations at the Barbadoes, where he formerly lived for some years'. Sir James, as he now was, took the chance to plead with Cromwell to prevent interference in Barbados from London, for free trade, the right to choose their own governor and to be allowed to spend their revenue as they saw fit – effective independence.

The death of Oliver Cromwell in late 1658 left a power vacuum and lack of direction to the colonies from the metropolitan centre, and Barbados and the other islands went about their business unmolested. In the meantime, Sir James seems to have worked hard on his new portfolio of English properties, all purchased thanks to the extraordinary profits from his Barbados plantations. A manor house and acreage were snapped up near Boston in Lincolnshire; property was purchased in Coventry and in Kent; while in Yorkshire, Ellerton Priory in Swaledale came under his control, along with adjoining lands.

It seems likely that this last purchase, and possibly some of the others, consisted of James Drax taking over the ownership from another part of the family – a Gabriel Drax is listed as the owner of Ellerton at the beginning of the seventeenth century, and Drax's family had originated from the Coventry area. Such a transaction was, of course, all about demonstrating that a new branch of the family was now dominant. Other *nouveau riche* sugar planters would follow this pattern.

Nevertheless, the centre of gravity for James Drax remained London, particularly the City and north-eastwards towards the smart merchant suburb of Hackney, where he must have had a residence, or at least some land. His local church, though, was St John of Zachary, which stood on the north side of Gresham Street, Aldersgate, and included the leading West India merchant Martin Noell in its congregation (it was destroyed in the Great Fire of 1666 and not rebuilt). At least one of Drax's sisters married there. He gave money for wine for the sacrament and for the 'ministers that precht for the Parson'. He also buried there three small boys – Bamfield, Joseph and Alexander – given him by his second wife, Margaret. At last, in 1658, a healthier child, Jacob, was born.

In 1656, Drax's eldest son was apprenticed to his cousin Abraham Jackson, a goldsmith. It was normal for the sons of gentry to be split between university, the Inns of Court and apprenticeships. In established families, the younger sons learnt a trade, while the eldest would go to university; in the newly rich Drax family, only the youngest two sons later matriculated, at Oxford. For reasons unknown, James the younger did not complete his apprenticeship. Instead, soon afterwards, his father sent him, aged about 18, to Barbados to run the plantations, for which he would receive an eighth share of the profits. He does not seem to have stuck at this either (or might have taken ill), as he was back in London by April 1659. This was when Sir James Drax, aged 50, made his will.

'It hath pleased the Lord of his mercy and goodnesse', he wrote, 'to bestow upon me . . . Lands, Tenements, Goods chattels . . . both in England and in the Island of the Barbadoes and else where.' His wife Margaret and her sole surviving son Jacob were to get his estate in Yorkshire, while the Barbados plantations were to be divided between the two eldest sons, James and Henry, the latter of whom had just turned 18. Clearly the sugar business was far and away the most important asset. All the annuities were to be paid from its profits: £100 a year each to seven younger children (a sizeable sum: the average annual wage at the time was about £8), and the same sum to his brother William and his wife Ursula. Other bequests bring the total up to more than £1,000 a year coming out of the sugar profits. (The poor of the parish of St John of Zachary were given £100, and there was £150 to buy cows for the poor of Coventry.)

The Restoration, though, presented Drax, and many others who had supported and prospered under the Protectorate, with a serious threat. Charles II returned to England in May 1660. As in Jamaica, in Barbados there were rumours of a deal done in exile in Spain – that the island would be allowed to fall into Spanish hands and the enslaved Africans taken as payment. In fact, Charles had no intention of handing over either valuable island. Instead, he wanted them under tighter central control and working harder for the benefit of the mother country.

Charles came to an agreement with the planters. Their sometimes makeshift land purchases of the turbulent previous 30 years were recognised, proprietory dues ended, and their sugar was given protected status. Foreign sugars were to be taxed to the point of unprofitability, thus delivering to the English sugar islands a monopoly of the home market. In return, Charles would receive customs revenue from the island at 4½ per cent of the value of all exports, and he insisted that the colonists buy manufactured goods only from England. Everything had to be transported in English or English colonial ships and tropical produce such as sugar could only be carried to England or another English colony, even if it was to be subsequently re-exported to the Continent. The Interregnum Navigation Act was therefore reapplied with stricter terms, subordinating the interests of the colonies to the idea of a self-sufficient empire engined by a mercantile marine, protected by a powerful well-manned navy. Just like Cromwell, Charles believed that the key to creating 'the greatest Dominion in the World' was to 'win and keepe the Soveraignty of the Seas'.

These Navigation Acts would determine policy for a century, and were, in fact, similar to the Spanish model, which sought to exclude foreigners from trade. The French, whose imperial policy was now led by Louis XIV's

Controller General of Finances, Jean-Baptiste Colbert, created a similar protectionist system shortly afterwards, setting the scene for confrontation to come.

Along with these new rules came a return to Barbados of a number of its former Royalist leaders, expelled after the descent on the island of Ayscue. Francis Lord Willoughby was appointed Governor of 'Barbados, St Christopher's, Nevis, Montserrat, Antigua, and the several islands of the province of Cariola' (which presumably included St Vincent and Dominica). While Willoughby delayed in London, he appointed Humphrey Walrond acting governor. The Royalists now went after Thomas Modyford, hated above all others for his treachery in 1651. Modyford, who had very briefly been governor at the end of the Protectorate, was tried for treason, but saved in the end by his kinship with the influential General Monk, Duke of Albermarle. When Willoughby at last reached the island in August 1663, he arrested Walrond for corruption. Walrond fled the island, but on reaching England was thrown into the notorious Fleet prison.

In England, Sir James Drax also had to face the events of 10 years earlier. Sir Guy Molesworth had barely survived his forced expulsion, and now blamed the 'malice and false suggestion' of Drax for his ordeal. The case came before the Lords, with Drax pleading the Act of Indemnity. But no one really wanted to open the can of worms of the plots and counterplots in Barbados at the end of the 1640s and beginning of the 1650s. The Lords decided they could not establish what had really happened, and Molesworth's petition was ordered to be 'laid aside'. Drax's friendship with Modyford and Popham, both related to General Monk, may have also assisted his cause.

It might also have been helpful that Drax himself seems to have borne no grudges from that bitterly divisive time, or held less firm political views than his Royalist detractors had alleged back in the days of the pamphlet war. In his will from 1659 he even left money to his wife's brother, Warwick Bamfield, an extreme Royalist. And now he was happy to work with the new authorities. In January 1661 he was appointed a member of a committee to meet at Grocers' Hall 'and inform themselves of the true state of the Plantations in Jamaica and New England'. Part of his role was to organise the shipment of £1,000 worth of brandy to Jamaica, and he was soon working in partnership with merchants Martin Noell and Thomas Kendall, sending tools and provisions also to Jamaica. On 18 February, along with a handful of other sugar and West India merchant grandees, he was given an audience with the King, and his knighthood was upgraded to a baronetcy.

He was still energetically going about West Indian business through the spring months, but then, sometime in the summer of 1661, he sickened and died of causes now unknown. He was about 52 years old, a good age for the time, especially for a man who had subjected himself to dangerous travel and disease-ridden climes. It was the end of a life characterised by energy, perseverance and wide-ranging talent, which, aided by good fortune and excellent contacts, had transformed not only Barbados, but the entire Atlantic world. The funeral was from the very grand Noell-owned Camden House in Chislehurst, and Drax's body was buried in St John of Zachary. Four shillings was paid, for the 'ringin ye Great Bell for Sr James Drax'.

Drax's eldest son, James, then aged 22, inherited the baronetcy as well as the half-share of the Barbados plantations, along with his 20-year-old brother, Henry. But the new Sir James styled himself not 'of Barbados', but 'of Hackney'. So while Henry held the reins in Barbados in the months after their father's death, his elder brother stayed in London.

Now a seriously eligible bachelor, the new Sir James didn't stay single for long. In March 1662 he married a rich heiress from a good family. But there was to be no heir. Twelve months later, James died.

The nomination of Henry Drax, the original Sir James's second son, as co-heir may have been insurance against poor health in the eldest son, James, or a reflection on James's performance at managing the estates or on his general conduct. Or it might have been testament to the high opinion that Sir James held of the ability and appetite for hard work of his second son. Either way, it was a sound move. Although he lacked some of the noisy flair of his father (no awestruck accounts have been passed down of any of his dinners), Henry would prove to be intelligent, industrious, and, on the whole, a good judge of character. Now 22, he found himself the sole inheritor of the Drax sugar business and was determined not to let down the family name.

Twenty years later, Henry would write down a series of instructions on how to run a sugar plantation. These have survived because they were copied by later generations, who saw them as the definitive model of good plantation management. Clearly, Henry was prepared to get his hands dirty: the 'Instructions' show that he involved himself in every aspect of sugar growing and processing and the challenge of managing a plantation work-force, down to the smallest details of spare parts for the machinery, and the supervision of key personnel such as the distiller, boiler and curer.

In the mid-eighteenth century, in a much-respected tract, an Antiguan called Samuel Martin laid out the qualities needed to be a successful planter: as well as an expert sugar boiler and distiller and an astute manager of both white servants and black slaves, you had to be 'adept at figures, and all the arts of economy, something of an architect, and well-skilled in mechanics', as well as 'a very skilled husbandman'. Henry Drax's 'Instructions' demonstrate that he had all of these qualities.

Later described as 'distinguished not only by gentle birth but by many virtues', and as 'intelligible . . . and of no faction, which is rare in Barbados', Henry had the priceless gift of quietly getting on with people. He resisted the dangerous temptation to 'empire build', expanding the Drax estates as established by his father by less than 100 acres to 800 by 1673; he was also noticeably astute in his choice of managers and overseers. The result was that his Barbados estates yielded income at a level only enjoyed by the most substantial landed aristocracy in England.

The success of Henry Drax's management of the family's Barbados estates can be seen in a comparison of his will, written in 1682, with that of his father from 20-odd years earlier. Where Sir James had lavishly handed out annuities of £100 to his extended family, for Henry the standard figure was £500, and in addition he gave sizeable one-off legacies.*

The terms of his will also demonstrate that Henry had made great efforts to create a more diversified portfolio of property, a process only just started by his father (in spite of his boasts to Ligon about aiming for an English estate worth £10,000 a year). Soon after coming into his inheritance, Henry invested his sugar money in land in Lincolnshire. Other purchases, including a town house in Bloomsbury Square, would follow over the next two decades. By the time his will was written, the scattered English estates were producing almost as much income as those in Barbados. Very few planters were wise enough to get their money out of Barbados in time in this way.

Henry was back in England from early 1664 to mid-1666 to sort out the estates of his recently deceased father and elder brother, and no doubt to see his sisters, who had all remained in England (in September 1666 his sister Elizabeth, aged 17, married Thomas Shetterden of Hertfordshire, 'by the consent of her brother Henry Drax and her uncle William Drax esq. guardians'). While in London, he also joined up with the society known as the 'Planters and Merchants trading to Barbados', and met and married, in February 1665, Frances Tufton, daughter of the Earl of Thanet. He was 24, she was 20. It was a highly prestigious match, even for someone of Henry's wealth.

---

* Among the beneficiaries were his sisters, nieces and nephews, his cousin, William Drax the Younger, son of his father's brother, and godchildren, who included among their number three Codrington children, his cousins through the marriage of old Sir James's sister Frances to the first Christopher Codrington.

Thus Henry succeeded not only in making money, but also in marrying it. All that was now lacking was what he evidently craved most – an heir to carry the Drax name forward.

Inevitably, given his wealth and his famous Barbados name, Henry was chosen for the island's council while still a young man, in June 1667. But he seems to have had little political ambition, or perhaps more exactly, he wanted to keep his head down and get on with the business of planting.

The contrast with his cousin, Christopher Codrington the second (whose father had married old Sir James's sister), could not have been starker. On the face of it, the cousins had much in common: both were first-generation 'Creoles' – that is, born in Barbados rather than elsewhere – who had both inherited substantial sugar acreage; Codrington was only one year older than Drax. But in other ways they were utterly different. While Henry made a solid success of his inheritance, Christopher Codrington would put together perhaps the most colourful, spectacular and controversial West Indian career of all.

The first Christopher Codrington died in 1656, leaving behind substantial scattered acreage, put together during his 20-odd years in Barbados. His eldest son, Christopher the second, was 16. His mother Frances brought up him and his younger brother, John and administered the estates until Christopher came to maturity, whereupon he married. Little is known of his wife, except her name, Gertrude, and the fact that she predeceased him. His brother John married the daughter of a rich planter and council member; it is likely that Christopher's match would have been of a similar if not even better status. It seems that Christopher inherited land in St Michael parish, and John an estate on the east coast in St John.

John Codrington, like Sir James's brother William, always played second fiddle to his more forceful and energetic brother. Although he would amass great wealth and would achieve high rank in the militia and gain a place on the council, he was always a distance behind Christopher.

There seem to have been two further brothers, Robert and Copplestone, but hardly anything is known about them. From the tenor of the scattered mentions of them in wills, it seems highly likely that they were 'natural', that is illegitimate (and possibly mixed-race) sons, something that would become a speciality of the Codrington men, and, indeed, of the sugar barons in general.

Christopher the second was a charismatic and easy-going young man, and undoubtedly highly intelligent. He was described as 'being of a debonaire liberal humour'. Unlike Henry Drax, his ambitions, even at this young age, took in leadership of the colony and, indeed, aggressive expansion in the wider region.

In this, he was in agreement with the returned governor Francis Lord Willoughby, whose earlier Surinam settlement was thriving. Willoughby envisaged English colonies spreading around the Caribbean following the Greek model of one colony giving birth to another. His first target was St Lucia, home to occasional Barbadian wood-cutters, a tribe of Caribs and a tiny, struggling French settlement. In 1663, he organised the 'purchase' of the island from the Indians. The price paid was 'divers goods, wares, and merchandizes . . . being of great value'. Organising all this as a trustee for the sale was the 23-year-old Christopher Codrington. (The following year Willoughby sent a party of 1,000 Barbadians to settle. Like previous attempts on St Lucia, the colony was a failure, with starvation, disease and Carib attacks ending the venture within three years.)

Codrington's evident support for Willoughby's vigorous expansionist policy greatly endeared him to the Governor. Three years later, at the age of just 26, Willoughby elevated him to the island's council. 'He is well beloved', wrote the Governor at the time, 'and free from faction, an ingenious young gentleman.' The same year Codrington was made a lieutenant-colonel of the militia. By 1668 he was a full colonel, the owner of at least one vessel trading amongst the islands and with England, and a father for the first time, to a son, another Christopher.

The young Christopher (the third) would grow up on an island being rapidly transformed by the riches from the 15,000 tons of sugar exported to England each year. In 1666 the Governor, Willoughby, described Barbados to Charles II as 'that fair jewell of your Majesty's Crown'. In 1668, two Bridgetown merchants declared that Barbados, then producing more than 85 per cent of the sugar imported to England, was 'worth all the rest' of the colonies 'which are made by the English'. A visitor eight years later called it the 'finest and worthiest Island in the World' and 'the most flourishing Colony the English have'. Per capita income was probably between a third and two thirds higher than in England and far ahead of the North American colonies. 'A mean planter', wrote a Barbadian in 1668, 'thinks himself better than a good gentleman fellow in England.'

This wealth was becoming ever more visible. John Scott, geographer to Charles II, who was on the island in 1667–8, noted that he had found 'by a rational estimate' that the 'plates, jewels, and extraordinary household stuffs' on the island were worth about £500,000. A visitor eight years later described the 'splendid Planters, who for Sumptuous Houses,

Cloaths and Liberal Entertainment cannot be exceeded by their Mother Kingdom itself'.

The establishment of the sugar industry had taken an enormous amount of hard work and energy on the part of the first sugar barons. According to an earlier visitor to Barbados, the enslaved blacks had a saying: 'The Devel was in the English-man, that he makes every thing work; he makes the Negro work, the Horse work, the Ass work, the Wood work, the Water work, and the Winde work.' Owners of smaller or undeveloped properties, or at least the successful ones, continued to graft, spending the day on long rides over their estates to check on the state of their crops, in constant battle against insects, weeds, drought or other setbacks, while closely supervising the welfare of their workforce, the processing, packaging and shipping of sugar, and the acquisition of provisions and other plantation supplies. But already a number of the richest planters had taken their feet off the pedal, delegating the hard work to employees, whilst themselves enjoying the luxury their new wealth now afforded. 'The Masters', wrote another traveller in the 1670s, 'for the most part, live at the height of Pleasure.' Indeed, an earlier account described how only 'the most inconsiderable of the Inhabitants' now actually did the work. The rest hired overseers and managers, and 'lead pleasant lives', making frequent visits to one another, 'endeavour[ing] to outvye one the other in their entertainments'.

In the countryside, a spate of building saw the old low-roofed wooden homes replaced by far more grandiose constructions in stone or brick, with tiled roofs, 'built after the English fashion for commodiousness and decency, as well as strength'. By 1681, they were 'now general all over the island'.

Few of these earliest 'sugar boom' mansions have survived the following centuries of hurricanes, humidity, termites and neglect. But St Nicholas Abbey* still stands in the northern part of Barbados, straddling the parishes of St Peter and St Andrew. Like Drax Hall, it was constructed in the 1650s out of coral blocks covered with plaster. Although also three-storeyed, it is smaller than the Drax residence, but its loving restoration makes it appear smarter. Like many contemporary Jacobean mansions in England, it looks very Dutch, with three curvilinear gables, each crowned with a tall finial.

* Unlike Drax Hall, which, amazingly, has remained in the same family since it was built 350 years ago, the ownership of St Nicholas Abbey perhaps more accurately reflects the impermanence and transitory nature of the island's inhabitants: the long list of former owners includes a string of different families, including such illustrious Barbados names as Dottin and Alleyne. It is now a tourist attraction and small-scale rum business. Sugar cane is still to be seen planted all around.

There are some concessions to the West Indian climate: the front of the house faces the vitally cooling north-eastern breezes, and there are no over-hanging gables, prone to be lifted up by tropical winds or hurricanes, but in each of the house's four corners rises a chimney, and the rooms are lavishly equipped with fireplaces, obviously totally redundant in the year-round heat of Barbados. A walled medieval-style herb garden is also part of the faithful copying of what must have been an off-the-peg design for a building back home in England.

On the east coast, right next to what is now the grandiose Codrington College, stands Consetts, probably built sometime in the early 1660s, and certainly before the end of the century. A big, square lump of coral stone, with Palladian details probably added later, it is quietly impressive, as it gazes out over the Atlantic. But it is also a great example of how the English built disease and discomfort into their early West Indian habitations – thick walls, no overhangs for shade, and small windows. Inside, the house is primitively divided in the medieval manner into three 'chambers', the parlour, dining hall and servants' hall.

Nonetheless, visitors to Barbados in the 1660s and 1670s were impressed. John Scott wrote that the new plantation houses were 'very fair and beau-tiful'. 'At a small distance', he added, they 'ordinarily present themselves like castles'. Together with all the sugar works and slave quarters, the plan-tations appeared from afar 'like so many small towns'. 'Delightfully situ-ated', reported another visitor, most of the 'pleasant Habitations' 'have pleasant Prospects to the Sea and Land'.

Bridgetown, situated on marshy ground below the reach of the cooling breezes, was noticeably less 'pleasant'. A visitor in the 1670s commented that the heat 'to Strangers at their first coming [was] there scarce toler-able'. But the town also attracted admiration for its 'abundance of well-built houses', 'Costly and Stately' and its 'many fair, long, and spacious Streets'.

Bridgetown was periodically visited by devastating fires. In 1659, a major conflagration destroyed more than 200 of the town's wood-built houses. Further 'Great Fires' were recorded in 1668 and 1673. Each time, though, the town was constructed anew, increasingly with 'well built' stone dwellings and other 'noble structures', warehouses and shops, 'well furnish'd with all sorts of Commodities'.

By the 1690s, if a contemporary illustration of the harbour is to be believed, Bridgetown was a prosperous and thriving mart, with numerous wharfs crowded with warehouses, residences and counting-houses, all looking distinctly gabled and Dutch, serving a bustling and numerous merchant fleet. Furthermore, it was now the hub of the Western Empire, the most crucial node in the emerging imperial system. A letter sent from London to Boston or Newport would almost inevitably travel via Bridgetown.

Outside the town, agricultural land now cost more than in England, and by the early 1660s, except for deep gullies, all the original forest had been cleared, and up to 80 per cent of the island was planted in cane. A governor in the 1670s noted that there was 'not a foot of land in Barbados that is not employed even to the very seaside'. His successor wrote that there was not even space 'to draw a regiment of foot on without great damage'.

Cotton was still produced by the island, mainly in St Philip, and tobacco grown by 'poor Catholics' in the inferior soils of the north of the island; elsewhere were small operations producing indigo, ginger and fustic woods. But sugar was king, accounting for up to 90 per cent in value of the island's exports.

It was not all plain sailing in the 'sweet negotiation of sugar'. The Navigation Acts, by removing international competition, raised shipping costs for the planters, and the 4½ per cent export duty bit into profits. Sugar growing itself remained, a planter lamented in 1687, 'a design full of accident'. In 1663, there was a plague of 'strange and unusual caterpillars and worms', which wreaked havoc. In 1667, there were numerous cane fires, as well as a hurricane. The following year saw a severe drought, followed by excessive rain, then another drought. An epidemic in 1669–70 carried off great swathes of the workforce.

Anything that hurt sugar production was potentially fatal for the planters' finances. Transforming Barbados into a giant sugar plantation had been extremely expensive. Planters had spent more than £1 million sterling just on slaves in the 20 years after 1640, as well as half again on servants, equipment, land and livestock. A visitor in 1671, while writing that 'The island appears very flourishing, and the people . . . live splendidly', added, rather ominously, 'what they owe in London does not appear here'. In fact, many a planter had 'spent' the proceeds of the sugar crop long before it came to harvest, and as it could take two and a half years – time for growing, processing, shipping and marketing – between planting and payment, the indebted planter was exposed to the risk of a change in the sugar price. With supply increasing, this was almost always adjusting itself downwards, by as much as half between 1652 and the end of the century.

But by improving efficiency and increasing the amount of land in sugar, the Barbados planters still made a very healthy return of about 20 per cent on their capital for the rest of the century, even after sugar from other

English islands had belatedly come on to the market. Part of this improved efficiency came, of course, from the ever-increasing use of slave labour. Two thousand enslaved Africans were imported into Barbados every year, and they continued to outperform the white indentured servants. Henry Drax, for one, had no time for white workers; 'the fewer the better', he wrote. By 1680 he had dispensed with their services on his plantations almost completely, with a labour force of 327 black slaves and only seven white servants.

With the Dutch officially excluded from the trade, most of these slaves were provided by a new company, the Royal Adventurers into Africa. Launched at the Restoration, its president was the King's brother James, and the King's sister had a share along with many prominent Cavalier politicians and grandees. When it was given a new charter in 1663, the King himself was an investor, along with, amongst others, the philosopher John Locke* and the diarist Samuel Pepys.

The Royal Adventurers company was emblematic of the new intrusive approach of the Restoration Stuart administration, and its official monopoly on supplying labour was disliked in the English West Indies almost as much as the Navigation Acts and the 4½ per cent. Care was taken to bring the most influential locals on board: the irrepressible Thomas Modyford was appointed the Company's agent in Barbados; in Surinam, William Byam was recruited. Nonetheless, the planters continued to lobby to be allowed to trade in slaves themselves, as well as to run interloping slave carriers. The Company shipped 3,075 slaves to Barbados in the seven months after August 1663, but struggled to get the planters to settle their bills. Soon the Royal Adventurers were in deep financial trouble, and in 1672 the business had to be relaunched as the Royal African Company.

The work of these new slaves went some way to making up for the falling sugar price. But of greatest importance was the effect this cheaper sugar had on consumption back in England. With the retail price slipping from 1.25 shillings a pound in the 1650s to 0.8 shillings by the 1680s, new consumers were created by the thousands. Annual per capita consumption in 1650 was barely a pound; by the end of the century it was five pounds. Thus what the planters lost in margin, they made up for in volume; by the 1690s, England was importing 23,000 tons of sugar a year, making it by far the most important commodity in the empire.

The unloading, storing and selling of all this sugar, which was worth

*Locke would later change his stance on the trade, writing: 'Slavery is so vile and miserable a state of man, and so directly opposite to the generous temper and courage of our nation, that it is hardly possible to be conceived that an Englishman, much less a gentleman, should plead for it.'

more than half of all imports from the colonies by the end of the century, was in the hands of a relatively small number of English factors. In 1686, 28 London merchants imported nearly half of all products from the West Indies by value. But the benefits from sugar's success were spread much more widely. The Crown, for one, made £300,000 a year from sugar duties by the mid-1670s.* A host of small-time merchants, some 700 by 1686, sent cargoes of foodstuffs, and, increasingly, luxury items, to the islands, where the whites, on average, consumed three times more by value than their cousins in the mainland North American colonies. All the sugar processing machinery – the coppers, the mills, the stills – were manufactured in England and shipped out. The tonnage of ships on the American trade doubled in the 20 years after 1660; all the vessels needed constructing, manning and victualling. In all, some 10,000 men were employed directly in the transoceanic trade.

In London, particularly, banks, insurance companies and brokers all participated in and benefited from the trade, while the number of refineries grew to more than 30 by 1695. Thus by the end of the seventeenth century, most English investors and merchants were in some way implicated in the economy fuelled by sugar and slaves.

The success of the sugar trade, then, helped shape a new direction for England. While in Europe the power of land still held sway, in England commerce and industry were becoming of central importance. There was growing urbanity: coffee shops and retail outlets proliferated; manufacturing boomed. And while trade with continental Europe stagnated, Atlantic commerce flourished above all. England was becoming, a pamphleteer of 1695 wrote, 'the centre of trade . . . standing like the sun in the midst of its plantations'. These, the country would 'refresh', 'but also draw profits from them'.

Yet it was not only the mother country that drew profits from the sugar islands. From the end of the 1660s, between 35 and 65 vessels entered Bridgetown annually carrying lumber and provisions from Boston, Salem or Newport. A street near the wharf in Bridgetown was renamed New England Street. Boston predominated, but shipping from Newport grew ever more substantial. Much of Newport's trade grew from an important link forged in the early 1660s, when Peleg Sanford, aged 22, arrived in Barbados from Rhode Island. Peleg was the son of the founder of the Portsmouth colony, John Sanford, who was also Governor of Newport and Portsmouth in the early 1650s. Peleg spent two

* Sugar paid import tax of 1s. 5d sterling per hundredweight of raw sugar or muscovado. Foreign sugars paid 3s. 10d. Colonial clayed, or semi-refined sugar paid 4s. 9d, the foreign version 7s.

years in Barbados, acting as an agent for a Rhode Island contact, as well as learning about the island – and the wider region – in terms of what it could provide, and what it needed to buy. In 1666 he returned to Newport, leaving behind two of his brothers, William and Elisha, to act as his agents.

His letter book from the subsequent five or so years gives a detailed picture of his business dealings, which were typical of the time for Rhode Island. From England, via Boston, Sanford received dry goods – nails, knives, kettles, pistols and hardware, as well as more luxury items – which he retailed in Newport. The money from this was invested in horses and provisions such as pork, beef, pease and butter, which he then shipped to Barbados. Often he would pay for the goods bought in London by trans-porting sugar direct to London from Barbados, but he also imported sugar, rum, molasses and cotton from Barbados to Rhode Island.

The letter book paints a picture of a thriving trade that was still oppor-tunistic, highly risky and slightly chaotic. At one point he wrote of the 'afat-ting of the swine' to take alive to Barbados; at another he ordered fine hatboxes and hats from his London agent, 'Mr William Pate at the Princes Arms in Market Lane'. ('Let them be Fashonable', he insisted, but 'not be very Beeg in the head'.) His business was also full of crises: debtors disap-pearing; friends or contacts being killed by tropical diseases; valuable cargoes lost though poor storage or fires on the ships, or arriving tampered with ('Ronged onboard') and worthless. There was a constant juggling act required to balance credit and exposure to risk. Sometimes the balls were dropped, and on at least one occasion Sanford found himself in gaol for debt.

Nonetheless, the profit margins were such that the operation prospered, and Sanford widened his scope to some of the other islands. In the early 1680s he became the Governor of Rhode Island, by which time the West India trade had become the cornerstone and most vibrant sector of New England's overseas commerce. In the same decade, the port facilities in Newport were much improved and extended, while in nearby Providence, the town's first wharf was built. By this time, more than half of the ships entering and clearing Boston were involved with the Caribbean trade, of which the New Englanders had a share coming up to 50 per cent, thereby playing an important role in nurturing and maintaining the plantation system in the islands. The fortunes generated by the West Indian trade were concen-trated in the hands of a relatively small number of individuals, and such earnings underpinned the creation of New England's first mercantile elite.

By 1690, a fifth of all Barbados exports went to New England, where rum distillation was starting to become big business. Unfortunately for the English islands, and for the unity of the Western Empire as a whole, enterprising

New Englanders had made an important discovery: trading with the French made for even better margins. The French did not make rum, due to protection measures in place for their home brandy industry. Thus their molasses were sold at only 30 or 40 per cent of the price charged in the British islands. In general, the French sold their tropical products cheaper and paid more for imports. Already there had been complaints back in London that New England, rather than Old, was reaping the benefit of the tropical colonies; trading with the French was an even more serious matter.

The New England traders were also increasingly serving the other English islands in the Leewards, which, a generation after Barbados, were now in the process of their own transformations.

The English Leeward islands of St Kitts, Nevis, Montserrat and Antigua would become sugar powerhouses, but for a variety of reasons their adoption of the cane monoculture lagged behind Barbados. Their environment was less easy to master: the volcanic Leewards have richer soils, but they are mountainous, or, in the case of Antigua, water-starved. In addition, the tobacco grown there was markedly superior to the Barbados weed, and so the incentive to abandon it was less urgent. It remained the dominant crop into the 1650s. Furthermore, the Leewards, though a more popular destination for poor whites, somehow failed to attract the richer expatriates like the exiled Cavaliers whose capital and credit had done so much to establish expensive sugar operations in Barbados.

Thus by the time of the Restoration, the Leewards were still like Barbados 15 years earlier, with substantial parts of the population involved in subsistence farming. There were also far fewer enslaved blacks, not that this made for harmonious societies. Like early Barbados, the social scene was crude, rough and lawless. In St Kitts, the cohabitation with the French, with the borders under constant guard, was a permanent source of negotiation and worry, and in Nevis and Montserrat, thanks to Cromwell's mass deportations in the 1650s, Irish Roman Catholics, whose loyalty to the English Crown was, to say the least, unreliable, made up the majority of the population. Throughout the West Indies, the relationship between the English and the Irish consisted of mutual loathing. All of this hampered development along the Barbados model.

The most unsettling factor of all, though, was the persistent danger from the Caribs.* Armed with clubs and fish-bone-tipped spears dipped in poison, the Caribs had been raiding European settlements since the time

* The threat is acknowledged in Willoughby's 1663 instructions 'to treat with the natives . . . or if injurious or contumacious, to persecute them with fire and swords'.

of Columbus, and were feared and mistrusted by all nationalities. A story in circulation held that 'The Caribbeans have tasted of all the nations that frequented them, and affirm that the French are the most delicate, and the Spaniards are hardest of digestion.' But having been driven out of the English Leeward Islands, and from Martinique and Guadeloupe by the French, the Caribs congregated at Dominica and raids intensified, particularly against thinly populated Antigua.

Sir Thomas Warner's son Edward was Antigua's first governor. In 1640, raiding Caribs abducted his young wife and two small children. In the process of making their getaway, the story goes, the Caribs killed one of the infants, who was crying, by dashing its head against a rock. Edward Warner set off in pursuit, later succeeding in rescuing his wife and surviving child.* Thereafter, Carib raids on Antigua became an almost annual affair, with melancholy records surviving of those carried away: 'Mrs Cardin and children, Mrs Taylor and children, Mrs Chrew and children, Mrs Lynch and children, Mrs Lee, wife of Captain Lee, and many other females.'

St Kitts, the mother colony of the English Leewards, was home by 1640 to some 15,000 inhabitants in its English sector (against fewer than 1,000 each in Antigua and Montserrat), and therefore had the manpower to defend itself against the Caribs. Nonetheless, raids continued. Then, in 1654, the St Kitts militia inflicted a sound defeat on a large Carib force, and for a while at least they were left alone.

The respite allowed the flowering of the sugar industry in the English parts of the island and in nearby Nevis, and a consequent rise in wealth. Unlike Barbados, though, the work stayed largely in the hands of the still plentiful white indentured servant population.

In Antigua, times remained desperately hard, with land uncleared and not enough men to do the work. In 1655 the Governor wrote to London that unless they were sent some servants, they would have to abandon the colony. But soon after, the first sugar estates were in operation on the island. By 1657 at the latest, Samuel Winthrop, who also had interests in St Kitts and Barbados, had established a small sugar works in Antigua at Groaton Hall, in the Wold North Sound region, manned by about 25 slaves. (Samuel would be described by a New England visitor as 'a reall Winthrop and truely noble to all'.)† In July 1660, a young Quaker, Jonas

---

* Warner, the story goes, then imprisoned his wife in a keep built for the purpose in a lonely nook, jealous of her violation by her former captors.

† In 1657, Samuel Winthrop, at great expense, sent his sons John and Samuel to Boston to be educated. He deemed 'that place more fit for it then this . . . I doe not find this country good for children'.

Langford, landed in Antigua from Bristol. Langford's sugar fortune, one of the first to be made on the island, would later end up in the hands of a resident of Rhode Island. By the mid-1660s the Leewards together were sending about 1,000 tons of sugar to London, a significant amount, even if dwarfed by the production of Barbados.

By the same time, sugar production was under way in the French islands of Martinique and Guadeloupe, helped by Dutch expertise and equipment.* The sugar pioneers of Barbados had stolen a march on the French, but the latter were now catching up quickly. A French settlement was also growing on the western end of Hispaniola, 'the most beautiful and fertile part of the West Indies and perhaps of the world', which became St Domingue, and is now known as Haiti. The French, driven by Jean-Baptiste Colbert's belief in the importance of colonies and commerce, were set on aggressive expansion. A number of very small islands abandoned by the Spanish came under their control, as well as territory taken from the Dutch. An effort was launched to drive the Caribs out of Grenada, the most southerly of the Windward Islands.

For the English Leeward islanders the Caribs were still considered the gravest threat, but the islands' overall governor, Francis Lord Willoughby, warned in 1664 that: 'The king of France pursues his interest in the Indies very high, and backs it with power of shipping and men.' Spanish power was fading, he wrote; 'the dispute will be whether the King of England or of France shall be monarch of the West Indies'. By the end of the following year, Willoughby was convinced that war with France was imminent. In fact, the young West Indian colonies of the English were about to face all of their potential enemies at the same time.

---

* In March 1663, a group of Dutch refugees arrived in Martinique, but were swiftly expelled under Jesuit influence as Jews and heretics. The party crossed to Guadeloupe and were welcomed by the Governor there, who was himself involved in the sugar industry. The Governor of Martinique realised his mistake and invited them to come to his island as well.

11

EXPANSION, WAR AND
THE RISE OF THE BECKFORDS

'Next day, when the march began, those lamentable cries and shrieks were renewed,
so as it would have caused compassion in the hardest heart: but captain Morgan, as
a man little given to mercy, was not moved in the least.'

Prisoners taken at Panama, described in *The Bucaniers of America*
by John Esquemeling, 1684

On 5 January 1661, Samuel Pepys wrote in his diary: 'The great Tom
Fuller come to me to desire a kindness for a friend of his, who hath a mind
to go to Jamaica with these two ships that are going, which I promised to
do.' The friend was 18-year-old Peter Beckford, son of an illiterate cloth-
worker from Maidenhead.

Although Peter's line would come to dominate, there were already other
Beckford family members involved with Jamaica, trading in cocoa, provisions and clothing. A Richard Beckford, who may have been a close kinsman
of Peter, had substantial land by the end of the 1660s (and took on another
1,000 acres in St Elizabeth in 1673), but remained as an absentee proprietor in London. Peter, later described as 'singularly fit', started out at the
bottom, working as a seaman, then a cattle-hunter and horse-catcher, then
as a buccaneer, then a wine trader.

Edward D'Oyley, who would remain as governor for a short time after
the Restoration, successfully urged the retention of Jamaica in the face of
the embarrassing fact that it was the principal conquest of the Cromwellian
era, which everyone was desperately trying to forget. But he was forth-
right about the difficulties the infant colony faced; after all, in the six years
since its conquest, 12,000 Englishmen had come to the island, but the
population in 1661 was less than 3,500. Furthermore, the transition to

planting remained severely hindered by a lack of shipping to take away the crops, and a lack of labour to harvest it. Planters were forced, he reported, to 'burn their Canes for want of hands'. The tiny number of sugar works – about 18 by 1663 – produced a lighter and finer-grained sugar than those of Barbados, but the principal export remained hides from cow-hunters like Peter Beckford, and the main crops cotton, indigo and, above all, cacao from the trees established by the Spaniards.

But few, D'Oyley complained, were interested in the 'dull tedious way of planting'. Most preferred to play the 'Lottery' of joining one of the privateer or pirate expeditions setting off from Port Royal. Many such adventures failed, leading those who had invested in them to flee the country to escape their debts; just sufficient, though, were successful enough to keep the hope of riches alive. Captain Myngs was back in Jamaica in late 1662, leading a force of more than 1,000 bucanneers (including Peter Beckford) against the important town of Santiago de Cuba. Four months later he brought back £100,000 from Campeche.*

D'Oyley, who had been responsible for recruiting the buccaneers in the first place, believed that official sanction for these raids, and the involvement of the Royal Navy, was not worth the 'plenty of money' they sometimes brought in. Each time a prize was captured, others were 'inflamed' to 'leave planting and try their fortunes. And no body is at all the better for that sume but the Alehouses where it is immediately spent' and the traders like Peter Beckford, who, D'Oyley complained, were importing for every £100 of 'necessary Comodities' '£500 of drink ... which deboches and impoverishes the people [and] causes frequent Mutinies & disorders'.

Jamaica staggered on in this fashion through a succession of short-lived governors until the arrival from Barbados in 1664 of the newly knighted Sir Thomas Modyford. Modyford, soon installed as governor, brought with him his enormous household, more than 1,000 slaves, and a new ambitious and positive attitude about the colony's future. His term of office lasted seven years, during which the population tripled to 17,000 (of whom just over 9,000 were black).

Before the end of the year, he was writing to London about the excellent harbours, wonderfully 'healthfull' climate, and, in contrast to Barbados, the abundance of building materials and the fertility of the virgin soil. Most of the old soldiers, he conceded, had 'turned Hunters', but with the profits from this, 'some of them buy Servants & Slaves and begin to settle brave Plantations'. Among them was Peter Beckford, cleverly investing

* Myngs subsequently returned to London, was knighted, and was then killed fighting de Ruyter in June 1666 in a battle off the North Foreland.

proceeds from hunting and buccaneering into planting. Some 'idle fellows' were still drinking everything they earned, but so many were now turning to farming that there was 'scarse any Place neere the Sea but is settled and many are gone into the Mountaines & find it the most healthful & fruit-full land which qualities doe sufficiently repay the difficulties'.

Modyford's experience as a planter in Barbados would be crucial to the development of Jamaica as England's most important sugar planta-tion colony, but this would not happen overnight. In the meantime, Mody-ford would throw himself with gusto into supporting the activities of the buccaneers, described by him in a letter to the King as 'no less than 1,500 lusty fellows'. England was not at war with Spain, but the West Indies remained 'beyond the line', and Spanish officials still aimed to exclude all foreign ships from the region. Modyford found himself, therefore, 'unwillingly constrained to reduce them to a better understanding by the open and just practise of force'. In 1664, a small party sailed up the San Juan river in Nicaragua in canoes and looted the rich city of Grenada, getting away with 50,000 pieces of eight. Soon after, St Augustine in Florida was attacked and ransacked, and the following year buccaneer admiral Edward Mansfield led 12 ships and 700 men on a daring raid on a town in the interior of Cuba. His second in command was a young Henry Morgan. The town's inhabitants were brutally tortured to reveal the hiding places of their treasures.

While in theory fighting against the monopolistic policies of Spain, the English were coming into increasing conflict with the Dutch, whose pre-eminent merchant marine was still threatening the Restoration govern-ment's vigorously held mercantilist ideas. Tension rose from 1662 onwards, and in 1664, the English Crown seized New Netherland (comprising the present-day American states of New York, Delaware and New Jersey). The greatest conflict, though, centred on rivalries in West Africa, where the English Royal Adventurers company was competing with the Dutch for the lucrative and ever-growing slave trade. An English force sent to the area at the end of 1663 to protect the Royal company's operations there took it upon itself to launch a series of devastating raids against Dutch outposts. In response, Admiral Michiel de Ruyter raced from the Mediter-ranean, and his fleet recaptured all that had been lost and more, as well as booty that included nearly 17,000 pounds of ivory. He then proceeded across the Atlantic, and in February 1665 a warning was received in Barbados that the island was de Ruyter's most likely target.

On 20 April, at six in the morning, news came to Bridgetown that the arrival of the Dutch fleet of 14 ships with 2,500 men was imminent. Just under three hours later, with the Admiral leading the way, the Dutch fleet sailed in battle order into Carlisle Bay.

De Ruyter's force held its fire. Only when it was within a short distance of the fort did it shoot 'a whole volley of small shott and his broade side', according to an eye-witness, the master of the ketch *Hopewell*, which was in the harbour. The fort returned fire, along with other ships in the harbour, and the rapid exchange of cannon balls and other shot caused considerable damage to both sides. Although casualties were surprisingly light, shops and residences in Bridgetown were smashed as the Dutch fleet fired '500 great shot into the town', some weighing as much as 30 pounds. De Ruyter, for his part, 'lost his mayne yard and two others lost theyre Topsayles . . . Wee damnified theyre sayles very much', reads the English eye-witness account.

At four o'clock, by which time the island's defenders had used up 33 barrels of gunpowder, almost their entire stock, de Ruyter raised red bunting to his masthead, calling a council of war. For an hour the fleet rode at anchor out of gunshot, the men busily repairing damaged sails while their officers debated what to do. Then the fleet withdrew from the bay, and stood away to Martinique 'in the confusedest manner that possibly could be'.

This was to be the only major attack on Barbados in its modern history. But de Ruyter's mission was not a total failure: having refitted at Martinique, he steered his force for Nevis, St Kitts and Montserrat, where he captured 16 English ships before being called back to Europe.

With the departure of de Ruyter's fleet from the theatre, the English launched a broad offensive in the Caribbean, in Charles II's words, 'to root the Dutch out of all places in the West Indies'.

Almost all the English islands participated, and from Jamaica, Modyford unleashed his Port Royal buccaneers. By the end of the year, virtually all the Dutch settlements in the West Indies were in English hands, along with valuable booty in slaves, cannon, horses and other merchandise.

Then the tide turned. In January 1666, France entered the war on the side of the Dutch. Although the move was motivated by European ambitions, Louis XIV sent out to the West Indies a substantial force of ships and men. The first blow fell on the English part of St Kitts. The English and French, living cheek by jowl on the tiny island, had come to an agreement that they would not make war on each other without explicit command to do so from home, and even then they would give three days' notice before attacking. Neither side, it appears, took the deal seriously. The English governor, Colonel William Watts, called in reinforcements from Nevis, as well as a force of buccaneers, but before he could launch his offensive, on 10 April the French attacked from the south-west, led by a body of slaves who set fire to the canefields. The French soldiers following 'fell upon the English on ye windward side of this Island . . . And Soe wasted, Slaughtered and burnt' all the way up the island until they reached their own territory in the north.

The English, outnumbering their enemy four to one, counter-attacked on the leeward side of the island around Sandy Point, and in fierce fighting the leaders of both parties were killed or mortally wounded. But then the English force, a mixture of hard-fighting buccaneers and much less effective planters, fell out among themselves, and the next day, unaware that the French were almost out of ammunition, capitulated on humiliating terms: all arms and fortifications were to be surrendered, and anyone unwilling to swear allegiance to the King of France was to be expelled. Eight thousand English, with their slaves, left the island, a large number to Virginia. Few returned to St Kitts, which would never again have a white settler population anything like the size before the war.

From Barbados, Willoughby urged the King to send forces at least equal to those now being poured into the theatre by the French and Dutch. At the end of June, two English men-of-war arrived in Barbados with orders to retake St Kitts. Willoughby, fearing this force was inadequate, commandeered a fleet of merchant ships, and raised 1,000 men from Barbados, as well as assembling 2,000 spare sets of arms for Leeward Islands recruits. On 18 July, they set sail.

The timing was highly risky, as Willoughby must have known – the hurricane season was almost upon them. Nevertheless, with the Governor on board, the armada headed north-west, capturing prizes at Martinique before coming to anchor off Guadeloupe on 26 July. That day, without warning, a massive hurricane struck. Almost the entire fleet, together with the men on board, was destroyed, driven ashore at Guadeloupe, with wreckage washed up on Martinique as well. Of Francis Lord Willoughby there would be no trace, except a couch, recognised as his own, 'and some peeses of a ship' washed ashore at Montserrat.

This devastating loss handed the French command of the seas, and doomed the English Leeward Islands to disaster. While the victors of the battle for St Kitts busily removed all the remaining sugar equipment and slaves from the English part of the island, a force of seven French men-of-war (the largest carrying 40 guns) assembled in Martinique, and at the beginning of November descended on Antigua.

Perhaps the best contemporary account, although somewhat confused on dates, comes from letters to his brother John Jr in New England written by Samuel Winthrop (who had already seen his holdings in St Kitts fall into the hands of the enemy). Having been prevented by contrary winds from attacking the main harbour and capital at St John's, the French landed at Five Islands' Bay, having dealt with its two forts, one being little more than an artificial mound. From there, they proceeded overland towards St John's, burning everything they came across and capturing the island's governor, Colonel Robert Carden. Near St John's harbour, some 200 English soldiers faced the 600-strong French force. 'Ye contention was verry smart for about ½ hour', Winthrop would report, '& our men withstood them verry resolutely, but, being overpowered with men, were put to flight, many slayne on both sides.' (By this time, Winthrop had put his wife and children on a passing sloop heading for Nevis.)

Most of the English were captured or killed, but the remnants retreated to Winthrop's house, 'having now other place left for defence, expecting ye enemy ye next morning'. But instead, a trumpet came with a summons to surrender. The English were happy to comply, especially as a Carib force, in loose alliance with the French, had landed on the windward coast and was causing havoc. Promising to return to collect arms and ammunition due by the terms of the surrender, and releasing Governor Carden, the French departed to St Kitts, although not before urging the English Antiguans to 'take up their armes to defend themselves against ye Indians'.

When the French returned, they found that reinforcements had been landed from Nevis and Barbados. Hearing that more English troops were on the way, they decided that they could not hold the island, but instead would 'land, attack the enemy, and, in case of success, place the island in such a state that the enemy can draw no sort of profit from it'. However, their plans were somewhat discomforted by their being met by another surrender party carrying a white flag. Having none of this, the French formed up into battle array and advanced on the English. Only two shots were fired against them, one of which hit an English sentinel. The English commander, a Colonel Fitch (or Fitz), rushed from the battlefield to organise the evacuation of his valuable slaves.

Having once again secured the island, the French commander took over Winthrop's house, removing all but 12 of his slaves (who had run away), but leaving his sugar works intact. Elsewhere the looting was much more thorough. After seven days, they left for Guadeloupe. 'In this sadd condic'on wee remained', wrote Winthrop, '& yt wch added to or afflictions were ye murthers & rapes wch ye Indians com'itted upon ye inhabitants after ye French departed, having, as they said, liberty to do so for five days.'

Governor Carden did his best to treat with the Caribs, but was lured away from his guard, attacked and decapitated. According to a lurid account that circulated for many years, Carden's head was then broiled, and carried back to his house and family, who were then taken into captivity.

Samuel Winthrop ended his account with news that an English counter-attack was rumoured. His livelihood depended on it: 'If wee prevaile', he wrote, 'I have yet wherewth to mainteyn my sonnes at schoole . . . Other-wise they will be put to trade or imploymt.'

Shortly after Antigua, Montserrat, with the aid of the majority Irish population,* fell to the enemy. Six hundred inhabitants of Montserrat arrived shortly afterwards in Jamaica, 'extremely plundered, even to their very shirts'. In all, according to the claims later put in, the English had lost from St Kitts, Montserrat and Antigua 15,000 slaves and materials for 150 sugar works, worth a total of £400,000. Early the following year, the valuable English colony in Surinam, weakened by disease and a shortage of arms, also fell to a comparatively modest Dutch force, who proceeded to retake other islands previously under their control. French and Dutch privateers ruled the seas, and Barbados, under effective blockade, faced starvation.

But at this point Louis XIV's priorities changed. While in the spring of 1667 Charles II sent out considerable forces to the Caribbean, Louis concentrated on his aims in Europe – namely the Spanish Netherlands (and thereby fell out with the Dutch). Led by a new Governor of the 'Caribbees', Francis Lord Willoughby's brother William, the English secured Nevis, and recovered and partially resettled Antigua and Montserrat. An attack on St Kitts in June by 3,000 men ended in defeat, but Surinam was retaken from the Dutch and Cayenne seized from the French. At the end of July, the Peace of Breda was signed. This returned all the colonies to the pre-war status quo, with the exception of Surinam, which was handed over to the Dutch in return for the New Netherland colony, renamed New York in honour of the King's brother.

The English took everything they could from Surinam and headed for the other islands. The colony's governor, William Byam, ended up in Antigua, where, he wrote, 'I am hewing a new fortune out of the wild woods.' He reclaimed the land given him by Willoughby back in 1650 –

* Montserrat is today the only country except for Ireland to have St Patrick's Day as a public holiday.

Cedar Hill and Willoughby Bay – and his descendants, marrying into the Warners, would become one of Antigua's leading families.

In 1670, the Leewards were separated from Barbados and given their own governor, and two years later William Stapleton took up the position, basing himself in Nevis, the only island to escape occupation by the French and therefore by far the most prosperous and populated. The fact that Stapleton was an Irish Roman Catholic must have helped draw together the antagonistic factions on the islands. The new governor took on large amounts of land himself and forcefully pushed the Leeward Islanders towards sugar production. As a consequence, the slave population more than doubled on the islands in the six years after 1672 to some 8,500. But it was a slow process; many of the white settlers expelled by the French never returned, and for some years half the land in Antigua and Montserrat remained unpatented and the other half scarcely developed.

In St Kitts, the French took until 1671 to hand back the English part of the island, and failed to return, as had been agreed, the slaves and sugar-making equipment they had seized. St Kitts never recovered its former population and importance. A settler wrote from the island in 1677: 'The wars here are more destructive then in any other partes of the world; for twenty yeares' peace will hardly resettle the devastation of one yeare's war.' Ten years after the invasion, 'the sad workes' of the destruction 'are not halfe worne out; nor is the island a quarter so well peopled as it then was'.

After the Peace of Breda, the local French and English governors tried to put together a deal whereby whatever was happening in Europe, they would remain at peace in the Caribbean. The failure of this agreement to be ratified in London meant that tensions would continue to rise between the two communities in the West Indies. William Byam, who had become Governor of Antigua, wrote to Willoughby in Barbados that 'the French are rampant among these islands'. Indeed, the French soon re-established naval supremacy, and continued to deploy Carib allies as their 'blood-hounds' in what amounted to a state of cold war with the English settlers. Continuing raids by Caribs, particularly on Montserrat and Antigua, meant a permanent state of readiness was required. In Antigua 'are kept every night 14 files of men on Guard against the Indians, and three nights before, and so many after the full moon, they are doubled, besides wch they make continual Rounds and Patrouls of Horse'. Occasional punitive raids on Dominica failed to end the Carib threat, which would only fade by the end of the century due to the ravages of yellow fever among the 'Indian' population.

*   *   *

On his monument in the churchyard of Spanish Town, Sir Thomas Modyford, Governor of Jamaica from 1664 to 1671, is described as 'the soule
and life of all Jamaica, who first made it what it now is'. (Another contemporary called him 'the openist atheist and most profest immoral liver in
the world'.) Certainly, as an experienced planter, Modyford could see the
agricultural potential of the island, whose soil, was 'rich and fat . . . every
where incomparable apt to produce . . . being always Springing'. He
persuaded the King to exempt the island from the 4½ per cent duty
imposed on Barbados, and now the Leewards, and to waive customs duties
in England until the island was properly established. In the meantime, he
handed out land with abandon: some 300,000 acres, triple the size of
Barbados, during his seven years in charge.

Modyford epitomises the sheer shamelessness of the planter of this early
period. He ruled as an 'independent potentate', and gave his family members
key positions on the council, the militia and the judiciary. Although in
theory land was allocated on the basis of how many family members, slaves
and servants immigrants brought with them, this rule, as in Barbados 30
years before, was widely ignored. The greatest beneficiaries were Modyford's own family; his brother and two sons found themselves owners of
over 20,000 acres in total.

In March 1669, Peter Beckford was granted 1,000 acres by royal patent.
Other founders of great sugar fortunes taking on land at this time were
Lieutenant Francis Price (frequently in partnership with Peter Beckford),
and Fulke Rose.* But very little of this acreage was sufficiently cleared for
sugar production, nor was there yet the large amount of labour that the
crop required. In 1667, an influx of Portuguese Jewish families from
Surinam, experienced sugar producers and traders, gave the nascent
industry a boost, but there were still fewer than 60 sugar works on the
island by 1670. Instead, most planters grew provisions, indigo, ginger,
cotton (much of which was exported to New England) and cacao. Only
when his cacao walks were wiped out by a blight in 1670 did Modyford
himself turn wholeheartedly to sugar.

The development of sugar production in Jamaica was slow because about
half of the male white population was involved not in planting but in buccaneering. Modyford himself encouraged this, and personally benefited to
the tune of several thousand pounds. After the end of the war in 1667,
during which the buccaneers had proved themselves a more than useful
auxiliary force, Modyford argued that these 'freebooters' of Port Royal

---

* Rose's widow would marry Sir Hans Sloane and his daughter into a Sussex family, the Fullers,
the next generation of whom would be key players in the sugar business in both Jamaica and London.

were essential for the defence of the island against French and Dutch privateers, and the continued threat of the Spanish, who, he wrote, 'look on us
as intruders and trespassers wheresoever they find us in the Indies and
use us accordingly'.

Led by Henry Morgan, the 1,400-strong Port Royal buccaneering force
attacked Porto Bello in 1668 (reportedly using monks and nuns as human
shields), and, most spectacularly of all, fought their way across the thickly
jungled isthmus to plunder and burn the city of Panama in 1671.

This last feat, accompanied by 'divers barbarous acts', proved to be a
step too far, and a severe embarrassment in Europe, where England the
year before had signed a treaty with Spain recognising English occupation
of Jamaica and the right of English vessels to be in the Caribbean (though
not to trade with Spanish colonies) in return for an ending of the destructive buccaneering raids. A new governor, Sir Thomas Lynch, was sent to
Jamaica with orders to arrest Modyford and suppress the buccaneers.
Lynch lured Modyford on to his ship, and then sent him home under
heavy guard. Morgan was also arrested and returned to England, as Lynch
then attempted to convert the buccaneers to planting. A few took him up
on his offer, but attacks on Spanish towns and shipping continued, and a
number of the buccaneers removed to Bermuda and became out-and-out
pirates, preying on ships of all nationalities. It was the beginning of what
has become known as 'the Golden Age of Piracy'.

Lynch continued the policy of handing out large grants of land, and
encouraged the nascent sugar industry. But there remained two Jamaicas:
one of planters, and one of buccaneers and (largely contraband) traders.
Five years later, Morgan's faction was back in favour, and he returned,
having been knighted for his services to his country's interest, to be deputy
governor. Although he sanctimoniously betrayed and sentenced to death a
number of his former shipmates, his drinking and carousing reached new
epic levels.

Meanwhile, however, a pattern emerged of planters building themselves
up to sugar production in stages. Land would be cleared, then planted
with pea crops while the tree stumps rotted, then potatoes and yams, and
perhaps indigo and ginger, with the land ready for canes by the third year,
and, all being well, profits from these minor crops sufficient to invest in
capital- and labour-intensive sugar production.

Among the first to start making serious money from sugar was Peter
Beckford, who in 1676 took over the 1,000 acres in St Elizabeth granted to
his kinsman Richard three years earlier. At the age of 33, Peter Beckford
had 2,238 acres in sugar and cattle, while at the same time continuing to

work as a merchant. He had also married well, to Bridget, the daughter of one of Jamaica's richest planters – she was probably the daughter of Sir William Beeston, or possibly a Lynch. Their first son, another Peter, was born around 1674, and was one of the first Jamaicans to be sent to school in England. Peter was followed a year later by a daughter, Priscilla. Another son, Charles, was born in 1677, but died in infancy. The following year a further daughter, Elizabeth, was born, then, in 1682, another son, Thomas. At the same time, although reportedly unpopular – described as 'a great incendiary' and as 'ruthless, unscrupulous and violent' – Peter Beckford became renowned for his 'great opulance', which 'gained him a superiority over most of the other Planters' and made him a leading light in the politics of the island. He was the first Custos of Kingston, a member of the assembly for St Catherine's, and from 1675, Secretary of the Island, the last a lucrative sinecure he purchased for £6,000. By then, it was reported, a personality trait had set in that would become an inherited characteristic of the Beckfords – violent megalomania. Apparently he thought 'himself the greatest man in the world', and took to 'carrying and using, too, a large stick on very trivial provocations'. Political opponents would find themselves physically assaulted and knocked to the ground.

During the 1670s, some 700 white immigrants arrived in Jamaica each year, with a large number coming from Barbados (by 1673, the population of Jamaica consisted of about 4,000 white males, 2,000 white females, 1,700 white children and about 9,500 Africans, almost all enslaved). They were not all the poor whites who had found the small island of Barbados unable to provide them with land of their own. Among them was William Drax, son of Sir James's brother, who had died in London in 1669. Through land patents and a number of small purchases, William Drax the younger put together a large plantation in St Ann's on Jamaica's northern coast. Thus, the second Drax Hall estate came into existence.

For the likes of William Drax, the reason for emigration was clear. As a 1675 report boasted, a sugar works with 60 slaves in Jamaica could make more profit than one with 100 'in any of the Caribbee Islands, by reason the soil is new'. As early as 1652, concerns had been expressed in Barbados that the soil was wearing out under pressure from the voraciously nutrient-hungry cane plant. In 1668, the Governor of Barbados complained that the island 'renders not by two-thirds its former production by the acre; the land is almost worn out'. While an exaggeration, the yield per acre was undeniably falling, from 1.35 tons an acre in 1649 to less than a ton per acre by 1690. One result was that the planters were no longer able to leave the cut canes to regrow (or 'ratoon'); instead they were forced to replant at least every second year. In addition, it became necessary endlessly to manure the fields. William Drax's cousin Henry, in his 'Instructions', written at the end of the 1670s, was obsessed by the need for manure, ordering that his overseer's 'Cheifest Care' should be to ensure the availability of a 'greatt Qwantaty of Dung Every year' and encouraging him to burn lime or collect human urine to create additional mineral fertiliser. 'Now is theire No Producing good Canes withoutt dunging Every holle', he stipulated. Naturally, this significantly increased the required labour – one estimate was that virgin soils such as in Jamaica needed one slave per acre, but Barbados needed two – because of the extra work that dunging and frequent replanting entailed.

The cost of the manure – some £10 sterling a year per acre – also ate into profits. Another planter decreed that 150 cows, 25 horses and 50 sheep were needed to produce the dung for 100 acres of cane. The Barbados planters had become more efficient by switching to wind power for grinding their canes – there were some 400 windmills in operation by the 1670s – but this also reduced the livestock on the island and therefore the available manure; by the end of the century there were many small operations producing nothing but dung.

The relentless march to sugar monoculture had also increased the prevalence of crop diseases, and the wholesale clearance of the island's forests had brought about a severe shortage of wood for construction and for fuel to heat the coppers in the boiling houses. Lumber had to come all the way from New England, and Barbados planters were even importing coal from England. Henry Drax ordered that cane trash be burnt and that trees be planted on his estates. The clearances had also led to serious soil erosion – an issue also addressed by Henry Drax in his 'Instructions' – to the extent that Bridgetown harbour was rapidly silting up as the wealth of the island – its soil – was washed from the hillsides. Slaves laboured, 'like Ants or Bees', collecting soil in baskets and carrying it back up the hill. It all led to more labour costs, and in spite of these efforts, by the end of the century something like a third of the island had abandoned sugar cultivation because of soil deterioration and sheet erosion.

In important other ways, too, the island looked back fondly to the earlier days of the colony. Royal geographer John Scott, who visited the island around 1667, and who wrote so admiringly of the planters' smart houses and expensive silver and jewels, ended his report with a curious note: although Barbados was 40 times richer than before the Sugar Revolution, he said, it was 'not halfe so strong as in the year 1645'.

What he meant by this was that the real strength of the island was its small white proprietors – 'interested men' with property to protect – who would 'defend the place', that is, man the militia, something at the front of everyone's mind after the terrible fate of the Leeward Islands during the war with France. But this 'middling' class of inhabitant was dwindling fast.

There was an anonymous report written on the island at this time, which took the same line: 'In 1643, [the] value [of Barbados], sugar plantations being but in their infancy, [was] not one seventeenth part so considerable as in the year 1666, but the real strength [was] treble what it is at this time.' The author of the report reckoned that before sugar there were 8,300 proprietors, and 18,600 effective men for the militia; but now there were not more than '760 considerable proprietors and 8000 effective men and the one half of these dissolute English, Scotch and Irish', who 'are fit to betray rather than defend so valuable a country'. Since 1643, the report estimated, at least 12,000 'good men . . . formerly proprietors are gone off' to New England, Virginia, Surinam and the other islands, and some 2,000 had perished in the recent war. At the same time, tropical fevers took a steady toll.

Some of these figures are dubious, but the trend they identify is undeniable. From a high of 30,000 in 1650, the white population had shrunk to 25,000 in 1660, 22,000 in 1670, then 20,000 in 1680 and 18,000 by 1690. And with each departure of a small freeholder, the island's white population became ever more polarised and unequal, divided between a small number at the top – 7 per cent owned more than half the land by 1680 – and an increasingly desperate and impoverished rump, many of whom stayed only because they lacked the 'courage to leave the island, or are in debt and cannot go'.

The same handful of planters who owned most of the land ran the government, judiciary and military, and continued to live in sumptuous style. A visitor at the end of the 1660s was shocked by the 'Intemperance' and 'Gluttony' of the planters. At one feast, he reported, more than 1,000 bottles of wine were consumed. In contrast, the poor whites never had enough to eat. After the Restoration, few indentured servants from England chose Barbados over the other islands, where there was still land to be had. But those who had worked out their time and remained on the island found life as a wage-labourer almost impossible. In the 1690s, the council fixed wages for whites at between 3d and 5d a day, but pork was 7d per pound, mutton 8d and beef 9d. 'There are hundreds of white servants in the Island who have been out of their time for many years, and who have never a bit of fresh meat bestowed on them', reported one of the Barbados governors in the 1690s. 'They are domineered over and used like dogs, and this in time will undoubtedly drive away all the commonalty of the white people and leave the island in a deplorable condition.' Few planters wanted to employ the poor whites, seen as idle, drunken and useless – black slaves were cheaper and better workers. 'Since people have found out the convenience and cheapness of slave-labour they no longer keep white men, who used to do all the work on the plantations', wrote Governor Atkins to London in the late 1670s. And increasingly blacks were being trained for skilled tasks that previously had been reserved for whites. As early as the late 1660s, Scott reported that he saw '30 sometimes, 40, Christians – English, Scotch and Irish – at work in the parching sun, without shirt, shoe, or stocking', while black slaves were at work 'in their respective trades in a good condition'.

Thus, while Barbados was in one way still fantastically rich – its 100,000 acres and 358 sugar works produced in the 1680s exports more valuable than those of all of North America combined – for the majority white poor it was 'a miserable place of torment', a 'land of Misery and Beggary', the worst place in the Americas to be a poor man. The only people who now came here to work, according to the Mayor of Bristol, were 'rogues, whores, vagabonds, cheats, and rabble of all descriptions, raked from the gutter'.

Some of the rich planters knew that their colony had taken a wrong turn. Christopher Codrington left the Council of Barbados on the death of Francis Lord Willoughby, but was reinstated by his brother William in June 1667. Then, when William returned on business to London at the beginning of 1669, Christopher, aged only 29, was appointed Deputy Governor, in charge of the island in Willoughby's absence.

As the King's representative, Codrington often found himself in the firing line. The assembly, dominated by the planters, was furious that they were being asked to pay for the upkeep of fortifications and the garrisoning of troops when they had been under the impression that this should be covered by the export duty of 4½ per cent (most of which disappeared into the hands of the collectors). He was also responsible for enforcing the deeply unpopular Navigation Acts, which meant seizing vessels trading illegally.* Nevertheless, he skilfully managed to carry out a delicate balancing act, keeping London happy while remaining popular with the assembly thanks to lavish dinners and by pushing for the money raised in Barbados to be spent there, as well as working for representation of the island in Parliament.

* In April 1669 he wrote to London that he was 'very glad to find himself so well backed by his Majesty's commands, since his former actions of this nature have with some gained him the imputation of severity'.

Above all, he demonstrated that he understood the serious challenges that the island faced if it was to be any sort of functioning society. Raising money by taxing the importation of liquor, he improved the island's fortifications against the threat of the French, built schools and hospitals, and all the time looked out for the interest of the 'poorer sort of this Island' – the men on whom Barbados depended for its security. Among 60 Bills he introduced were measures against cartels on provisions, 'An Act to Prevent Depopulations', 'An Act for the Encouragement of the Manufacture of this Island', and several Bills to 'prevent Abuse of Lawyers, and Multiplicity of Law-Suits'. (There were also purely practical measures, such as the building of a new public wharf, rules for 'the better hanging of coppers', and laws to prevent accidental cane fires.)

Henry Drax and others from the council were sent on trips to England to push the interests of the Barbadians. In London, the expatriate planters formed themselves into 'the Committee for the Public Concern of Barbadoes', meeting weekly at the Cardinal Cap tavern, in Cornhill, Friday afternoons at three. Drax was a junior member; he was far from pushy enough to be a politician – his greatest responsibility was the printing of literature – but his letters to Codrington show that he, too, understood the needs of Barbados, suggesting that people with land should be barred from buying any more, and that skilled trades should be reserved for whites, both measures designed to 'uphold the number of freeholders'. At the same time, his committee pushed to be allowed to import servants from Scotland (at that time barred under the Navigation Acts).

In all, Codrington showed himself for a time to be an immensely intelligent and capable governor, perhaps one of the best the colony ever had. But then he seems to have changed. In mid-1671, Barbados was visited by Sir Charles Wheeler, then Governor of the Leeward Islands. Wheeler wrote to London on 8 June 1671, and his letter contains the first hint of criticism of Codrington: 'The Deputy Governor is not an ordinary man,' he reported, 'believes he is a worthy one, yet he lies under great temptations, as all do who seek their profit from those whom they are to govern.' Clearly something happened around this time: from being described as 'liberal' and 'debonaire', in a short while Codrington would gain a reputation as a ruthless, money-obsessed tyrant, a bully and a philanderer. He was even, it would soon be rumoured, a murderer.

12

'ALL SLAVES ARE ENEMIES'

"'You know," observed Robert, "it appears to me that you are as much afraid of these people as they are of you."

"Of course we are," said Rider; "it has been a case of fear on both sides. Fear is in the very texture of the mind of all the white people here; fear and boredom and sometimes disgust. That is why so many of us drink."'

Henry de Lisser, *The White Witch of Rosehall*

The concern about the steady diminishing of the white population, and therefore the weakening of the militia, was not just about external threats to Barbados. As early as 1666, Governor Willoughby wrote to London that after the recent departures of whites to other islands and to Carolina, it was essential that they be replaced, or 'wee shall be soe thinned of Christian people . . . I feare our negroes will growe too hard for us'.

Because of the 'want of white people', a later report stated, Barbados faced dangers 'from without [but] much greater from within'. Whites were urgently needed not really for their labour (carried out more efficiently by the slaves), but for policing the enslaved Africans, whose number on the island was increasing at a furious rate.* This situation, of their own creation, was frankly terrifying for the white 'masters'; their island was becoming Africanised. The precariousness of the situation and the constant threat that this posed to their survival brought on amongst the planters a sense of continual crisis.

Perhaps the greatest fear of all was that the black slaves would unite with the poor, downtrodden whites and indentured servants to turn the

---

* Blacks were in the majority by 1660, and outnumbered the whites by two to one by the 1680s. By the end of the century, by which time a quarter of a million had been shipped to the English sugar islands, there were, according to most estimates, 50,000 enslaved Africans and fewer than 16,000 whites in Barbados: more than three slaves for every white person.

whole system upside down. Indeed, the planter elite was torn between their contempt for the 'other' whites, who, increasingly, were transported felons rather than the hapless poor, and their need for them to control the slaves. In 1661, just as the balance of numbers tipped towards the blacks, the government in Barbados passed laws to govern treatment of indentured servants and slaves (both profoundly different from labour systems familiar in England). These codified what had already been established, while shaping the future for both categories.

The aim was to persuade the poor whites to ally themselves with the planter class, in effect to choose race over class as their defining characteristic. In the 'Act for the Better Ordering and Governing of Negroes',* the Africans were described as a 'heathenish, brutish and an uncertaine, dangerous kinde of people'. The white servants, though still heavily policed in their behaviour, were carefully given better rights than the blacks – to food, clothing, general treatment and legal protection. Slaves who assaulted a white person of whatever status were to be whipped, then, on a second offence whipped some more and have their nose slit and forehead branded. While on paper the Act aimed to protect the slaves from 'the Arbitrary, cruell and outrageous will of every evill disposed person', masters could punish slaves in any way they liked, even to death, the only penalty being a fine, and this was easily evaded. Whites' rights to trial by jury (a fundamental right of English law) were confirmed, while blacks faced a kangaroo court of the master's local cronies. For whites, differences between men and women were legally recognised, but not for blacks. Black men were to be severely punished if they had sex with a white woman, even if it was consensual, although white men could rape black women with impunity.

This racism was a new departure, as planters, who had recently lumped together African slaves and 'dissolute English, Scotch and [particularly] Irish', came to realise the usefulness to their security of 'whiteness'. A pamphleteer writing at the time felt it necessary to explain to his readers in England that 'white' was 'the general name for Europeans'. And just as the 1661 Acts were copied throughout the English West Indies and in South Carolina,† so this new ideology of whiteness was spread from Barbados and carried around the empire.

* Only once in the Act was the word 'slave' used rather than 'Negro', which indicates both the squeamishness that the English had over the term 'slave' and also how increasingly status and race were being collapsed.
† Emigrants to South Carolina were not just poor whites, many of whom still held on in Barbados. A number were younger sons of the island's big planter families, such as the Sandifords and Halls. With no more room to expand there, lesser offspring were sent off with whatever members of the household could be spared. From the Caribbean they brought with them slaves, the plantation system

In the 1640s, Richard Ligon had been amazed that Barbados's enslaved Africans, whose number at that time, interestingly, he wildly overestimated, did not simply use their superior numbers to seize control of the island. He put this down to the Africans' fear of firearms, their successful 'de-manning' by the institution of slavery, the 'divide-and-rule' tactic that saw some given privileges (such as wives) in return for loyalty, and their inability – due to the many different languages they spoke – to combine with each other and therefore organise themselves as a united body.

As the balance of numbers shifted inexorably against them, even with the poor whites largely on their side, the planters tried, as much as was practical, to buy slaves for their plantations in small groups from different and previously competing tribes or nations. One commentator wrote that 'the safety of the plantations depends upon having Negroes from all parts'. But this was only going to succeed for a short time. A visitor from the late 1660s wrote that the slaves were 'passionate Lovers one of another; and though they are born in different Countries, and sometimes, when at home, Enemies one to another; yet when occasion requires they mutually support and assist one another, as if they were all Brethren'. Scott himself warned in the 1660s that 'the whole may be endangered, for now there are many thousands of slaves that speak English'.

Henry Drax, in his influential 'Instructions', was very careful to single out certain of the Drax Hall slaves for special treatment. Moncky Nocco, 'who had bene ane Exelentt Slawe and will I hope Continue Soe in the place he is of head owerseer', was to be given extra food – '10 pounds of fish or flesh a week to dispose of to his family' as well as 'a new Sarge Suit Every year and A Hatt'. A handful of others were also to be treated differently from the bulk of the workforce.

Most planters aimed, by insisting on continuous overwork and under-feeding, to keep their slaves in a state of exhaustion and physical weak-ness. This, in fact, took little extra effort. Enslaved Africans who had survived the brutal 'Middle Passage', the journey from West Africa to the Caribbean, during which as many as a quarter died from dehydration or

and 'mentality', a slave code, speech patterns and architectural styles. In all, Barbadians had a deci-sive role in shaping the new colony, creating a slave-based plantation society more similar to the islands than to the rest of North America. Lowland Carolina would soon have a population ratio of four blacks to every white, similar to the ratio in Barbados. Parts of Charleston's 'brittle, gay and showy society' of the eighteenth century would echo the Barbados atmosphere of a century before, and between 1669 and 1737, nearly half of the governors of South Carolina had lived in the West Indies or were sons of islanders. Seven of the early Carolina governors had Barbados backgrounds.

disease, arrived in Barbados so weakened that a further third died within three years. Henry Drax banked on having to replace some 5 to 8 per cent of his workforce per year.

Some, like Drax, came to understand that by starving and mistreating their slaves they were actually provoking rebellion and harming their own interests. After all, a sugar operation's slaves were by far its most expensive and valuable asset, often accounting for more than half the capital tied up in a plantation. As a governor of Barbados would write, 'our whole dependence is upon Negroes'. Henry Drax's approach, as outlined in his 'Instructions', was to ensure that 'there be not too much Severity . . . the weak hands must not be pressed'. 'Negroes Must Not by any means Ewer want.' So that they 'go through their Work with Cheerfulness', a wide range of provisions – cassava, plantain, corn and peas – should be grown, and each slave given two quarts of molasses and one pound of fish a week, with overseers and head boilers getting twice that amount. They should also have occasional rations of tobacco, palm oil and salt. Rum was to be doled out in the morning in wet weather and whatever else needed 'for the Incoragmentt of Ptickler Negros'. Although a doctor was to be employed full time on the plantations, Drax correctly identified adequate food as the most important factor in keeping the workforce healthy: 'The Kittchin being more usefull in the recovering and Raysing of Negroes then the Appothycaries Shopp.'

Henry Drax's 'Instructions', written as a guide for his overseer, Richard Harwood, are unusually detailed and generous, but his cousin Christopher Codrington, in his will written in 1698, also carefully stipulated the food and clothing that his slaves were to receive. In fact, both men wanted to see themselves as heads of families in the contemporary English paternalistic model. Drax referred to 'all the members of my family, black and white'. Codrington, who assembled his slave force from the Akan-speaking Coromantee people of the Gold Coast (considered by some to be dangerously warlike), told his son that 'They are not only the best and most faithful of our slaves but are really all born Heroes . . . Noe man deserved a Corramante that would not treat him like a Friend rather than a Slave.' According to his son, after the elder Codrington's death, his slaves paid regular visits to his tomb, lamenting and making libations, and promising that 'when they have done working for his son they will come to Him be his faithful slaves in ye other World'.

However far-fetched this story might sound, some enslaved men and women did show great loyalty to their 'masters'. Nevertheless, we know from the 'Instructions' that Drax's slaves were 'apt to Lurk and Meech from their Work' and constantly stole from him. If it was food taken, then the punishment should be light, he ordered, and his manager should 'Newer punish Either to Satttisfy your own anger or passin', the 'End' of punishment being the reclamation of the 'Mallyfactor'. (Drax hinted that he had hired Harwood precisely because he could control his 'passin'.) But no compassion was to be allowed to get in the way of profit. If they started stealing 'Sugar, Molasses or Rum, which is our money and the final product of all our endeavours . . . they must be severely handled being no punishment too terrible on such an occasion as doth not deprive the party of either life or limb'. Such punishments should be promptly applied, he warned, before the slaves 'when threatened do hang themselves'.

Thus the brutal reality of the plantation seeped through all the talk of 'cheerful work' and 'family'. Indeed, from the earliest days of extensive slavery in Barbados, more than anything else extreme violence underwrote and sustained the slave society. Admittedly, it was a time when in England the smallest felony would see a poor man put to death, and soldiers and sailors were regularly whipped to within an inch of their lives to enforce 'discipline'. Nonetheless, the brutality of the plantations was perhaps unprecedented in Western history; to be a slave in the Americas was worse even than to be a galley slave for the Turks or Moors. Every plantation had a whipping post, and many overseers excelled themselves with sadistic innovations. Some slaves, having been brutally lashed, would have salt rubbed into their wounds, or molasses poured on them to attract biting flies and ants. Father Biet, in Barbados in the 1650s, was shocked by the 'severity' with which the slaves were treated: 'If some go beyond the limits of the plantation on a Sunday they are given fifty blows with a cudgel; these often bruise them severely', he wrote. 'If they commit some other singly more serious offence they are beaten to excess, sometimes up to the point of applying a firebrand all over their bodies, which makes them shriek with despair.' On one occasion he visited an Irish planter on the eastern side of the island, a man whom he had befriended. As he arrived, he was confronted with the spectacle of a slave in irons in the middle of the courtyard. Apparently he had stolen a pig to eat. 'Every day, his hands in irons, the overseer had him whipped by the other Negroes until he was all covered with blood', Biet's account reads. 'The overseer, after having had him treated thus for seven or eight days, cut off one of his ears, had it roasted, and forced him to eat it. He wanted to do the same to the other ear and the nose as well.' Just under 50 years later, another French priest, Father Labat (a fascinating figure who was as much spy and military engineer as man of the cloth), reported from a visit to Barbados that 'The drunken, unreasonable and savage overseers . . . beat [the slaves] mercilessly for the least fault, and they seem to care less for the life of a negro than that of a horse.'

Such cruelty is testament to the growing fear that the whites felt for their slaves, and also to the slaves' continuing resistance. As the black population swelled and the number of whites dwindled, the 'masters' needed to be ever more vigilant; every two weeks, slave quarters would be searched for weapons; movement off the plantation was strictly regulated. A large part of the slave law of 1661 concerned dealing with the problem of runaway slaves. But even so, this level of sadism was extraordinary, a cruelty born perhaps out of the ennui and interminable isolation of the handful of whites on the plantation, fuelled doubtless by alcohol, leading to a loss of any sense that a human life was worth anything. Thus the institution of slavery, as has been written, 'led to a cycle of deformed human relationships which left all parties morally and aesthetically maimed'.

Few sensitive and intelligent visitors to Barbados in the seventeenth century, whether French or English, failed to be shocked by the severity of the workings of the slave system. But none really questioned the principle of slavery, only the practice. Father Biet conceded that 'It is true that one must keep these kinds of people obedient.' Father Labat, having condemned the cruelty of the overseers, explained that they were 'compelled to exceed the limits of moderation in the punishment of their slaves so as to intimidate the others and to impress fear and dutifulness upon them to prevent them becoming the victims of such men, who being usually ten to one white man, are always ready to rebel and attempt to commit the most terrible crimes to retain their freedom'. The French treated their slaves better, he wrote, but that was only because they were not so numerous, and thus not so great a threat.*

A visitor to the English islands in the 1660s called the slave trade 'barbarous', but conceded that the 'proud and insolent' blacks had 'to be kept in awe by threats and blows'. Punishment, he wrote, should be moderate, but this had more to do with practicality than compassion: if they were treated with 'extream ferocity', they tended to run away or commit suicide. He even went as far as to say that the Africans 'prefer

---

* An eighteenth-century historian of Jamaica would write: 'The French [are] less haughty, less disdainful, consider the Africans as a species of moral beings. The English consider them as productions which ought neither to be used nor destroyed without necessity. But they never treat them with familiarity, never smile upon them, nor speak to them.' Certainly, the *Code Noir* of Louis XIV was more benevolent than the slave laws in the English colonies. For slaves in the French colonies, rudimentary religious instruction and baptism were compulsory.

their present slavery before their former liberty, the loss whereof they never afterwards regret'. Another writer who was in Jamaica in the early 1670s complained that the slaves were starved and ill-treated, 'yet are they well contented with their Conditions; and if their Master is but any thing kind, they think nothing too much to be done for them'.

A threat to the status quo came with the visit to Barbados of the Quaker leader George Fox. During the next century, the Quakers would be at the forefront of the abolitionist movement, and they arrived on the island in 1671 with a potentially revolutionary idea: that the 'Negroes' were just as much men, possessing souls, as their masters.

After a difficult journey from England, involving storms, a leaky boat and a narrow escape from pirates, George Fox, together with a small entourage, landed at Bridgetown in October 1671. He spent three months on the island, during which time he addressed hundreds of whites and blacks, and had the opportunity to take a long, hard look at the slave society that had been created there. (He subsequently visited Nevis and Antigua, where Samuel Winthrop, 'being convinced, he and his Family received the Truth'. He then proceeded to Newport, thus further enhancing the Quaker-based links between that town and the West Indies.)

What emerged were a series of pamphlets published over the subsequent few years. In them, Fox appealed to the planters to 'deal mildly and gently with their Negroes, and not use cruelty toward them'. Deputy Governor Codrington was warned by Fox that God would require an accounting for the treatment of all Negroes and 'tawnies' in Barbados. Towards the end of their lives, the Quaker argued, the slaves should be freed and given the wherewithal to sustain themselves. His most trenchant criticism, however, was reserved for the Anglican clergy on the islands, who had spectacularly failed even to attempt to convert the Africans to Christianity. 'If you be Ministers of Christ', he wrote, 'are you not Teachers of Blacks and Tawnies (to wit, Indians) as well as of Whites? Is not the Gospel to be preached to all Creatures? And are not they Creatures? And did not Christ taste Death for every man? And are they not Men?'

This egalitarian message was deeply unsettling to the majority of the planters, for whom the 'heathenish, brutish' state of the Africans constituted a justification for their slavery. Furthermore, as Ligon had discovered, they were unsure about the legality of enslaving Christians. In addition, unlike for the Jesuits, busy converting slaves on the French islands, the Protestant tradition demanded thorough instruction before conversion, which would lead to the slaves mastering English and therefore becoming more able to unite against them, as well as fostering attributes of education and self-respect incompatible with slavery. They also greatly disapproved of the Quakers inviting blacks to their meetings: the occasions would surely be used by the slaves for plotting together.

Thus Fox and his followers were accused of teaching the slaves to rebel. In fact, the planters, at that time, had little to fear from the Quakers. Fox replied that this was a 'most false Lye', and that rebellion was 'a thing we do utterly abhor and detest in and from our hearts'. Instead, he said, they were teaching them 'to love their masters and mistresses, and to be faithful and diligent in their masters' service and business, and that then their masters and overseers will love them and deal kindly and gently with them'. Although a tiny number of Quakers did free their slaves between 1674 and 1720, a great number more were themselves major slave holders and remained so.

Nonetheless, the Quakers, who railed against the materialistic, gaudy and decadent culture of the island, were intensely disliked and ruthlessly fined and persecuted by the Barbados authorities, mainly on the grounds of disrupting Anglican services, and refusing to bear arms in the militia. By the end of the century, most had recanted or emigrated to Pennsylvania.

A tiny number of other Christians did take up the challenge laid down by Fox. In 1673, an eminent Puritan theologian, Robert Baxter, published *A Christian Directory*, in which he called it a 'cursed crime' that the planters considered the slaves 'equal to beasts'. But Baxter never visited the West Indies, and was not so concerned with the treatment of the slaves as with the fact that no one was trying to convert them – 'reasonable Creatures, as well as you' – to Christianity. He condemned as 'one of the worst kinds of Thievery in the world' the practice of those 'who go as Pirats and catch up poor Negro's or people of another Land, that never forfeited Life or Liberty, make them slaves, and sell them', but allowed slavery for those 'enemies' captured in a 'lawful' war, those guilty of a crime, and those who, out of extreme necessity, sold themselves. But the 'chief end' of anyone buying slaves, he concluded, should be 'to win them to Christ and save their souls . . . that they are Redeemed with them by Christ from the slavery of Satan, and may live with them in the liberty of the Saints in Glory' – a distinction that, perhaps, might have been lost on an enslaved African working in the canefields or boiling-houses of Barbados.

The Anglican priest Morgan Godwyn lived in Barbados for some years during the late 1670s, and his book, *The Negro's and Indians Advocate*, published in 1680, shows far more eye-witness experience of the chilling realities of African slavery in the West Indies. The wealth of the planters was wholly dependent on the labour of the 'Negroes', he wrote, but they were starved, 'tormented and whipt almost (and sometimes quite) to death', 'Their Bodies . . . are worn out in perpetual Toil for them . . . A Cruelty capable of no Palliation . . . other Inhumanities', he went on to describe, 'as their Emasculating and Beheading them, their choping off their Ears (which they usually cause the Wretches to broyl, and then compel to eat them themselves) their Amputations of Legs, and even Dissecting them alive'. All but the hardiest of their offspring died in infancy, he went on, as their mothers were ordered to leave them and return to work.

The 'brutality' of the 'Negro', he wrote, was a 'fiction'. In fact, the Africans showed more 'Discretion in management of Business' than most of the whites. If the Africans were 'beasts', what about 'those Debauches, that so frequently do make use of them for their unnatural Pleasures and Lusts?' Indeed, it was the planters who 'know no other God but Money, nor Religion but Profit'.

But, as with Fox and Baxter, the answer was not the abolition of slavery, but an improvement in the treatment of the slaves, and, most of all, their conversion to Christianity. Like Ligon before him, Godwyn failed to follow his arguments to their logical conclusion.

Thus, organised religion, so important to the abolition movement of the next century, failed to properly address, let alone end, the evil of slavery during the seventeenth century. It did not help that religion on the islands was moribund. Father Biet wrote of Barbados: 'To tell the truth, they have almost no religion.' At the end of the century, there were only 11 ministers for 20,000 Christians in Barbados, and even fewer in the other islands.

In London, the conversion of the slaves seemed to be self-evidently the right thing to do, and several governors were sent out with instructions to start this process. But although a few planters who returned to London with slaves had them baptised in England, on the islands the planters remained resolutely opposed. In 1680, the 'Planters' Committee' of Barbados told the Lords of Trade and Plantations that 'the conversion of their slaves to Christianity would not only destroy their property but endanger the island, inasmuch as converted negroes grow more perverse and intractable than others, and hence of less value for labour and sale'. They went on to argue that 'The disproportion of the blacks to whites being great, the whites have no greater security than the diversity of the negroes' languages, which would be destroyed by conversion in that it would be necessary to teach them all English.'

Morgan Godwyn's book remains a shocking description of the practice of slavery, and its impact is increased by the rarity of its viewpoint at this time. One other seventeenth-century tract, however, was even more vivid. Thomas Tyron was something of an eccentric; he would become rich writing self-help books, and was a great proponent of vegetarianism (and would number among his converts Benjamin Franklin). From a modest background, like Baxter he was a Dissenter, moving from Anabaptism to a more mystical faith based partly on the work of Jacob Boehme. For seven years in the 1660s he lived and worked in Bridgetown as a hat-maker. During this time, he had first-hand experience of slavery, and of its effect on both the slaves and their owners.

Most vividly, he put complaints into the mouth of an enslaved African. Slavery, says the 'Negro', is worse than death, starting with the horrors of the 'Middle Passage', where there were 'so many and so close together, that we can hardly breathe, there are we in the hottest of Summer, and under that scorching Climate . . . suffocated, stewed and parboyled altogether in a Crowd, till we almost rot each other and our selves'. Once on the island, the work was relentless and sometimes fatally dangerous: 'often-times we are forc'd to work so long at the Wind-Mills, until we become so Weary, Dull, Faint, Heavy and Sleepy, that we are as it were deprived of our natural Senses . . . we fall into danger, and oft times our Hands and Arms are crusht to pieces, and sometimes most part of our Bodies'. Appeals to the compassion or charity of the masters came to nothing, for 'Interest has blinded their Eyes and stopt their Ears, and rendered their Hearts harder than Rocks of Adament.' In turn, slavery had made the masters not only cruel, but corrupted by decadence: 'our luxurious Masters stretch themselves on their soft Beds and Couches, they drink Wine in overflowing Bowls, and set their Brains a-float without either Rudder or Compass, in an Ocean of other strong and various Drinks, and vomit up their Shame and Filthiness . . . to gratifie their raging Lusts, sometimes take our Women . . .'

Tyron's disgust and his sympathy for the enslaved leap off the page, but yet again, he fell short of calling for slavery itself to be abolished. Instead, like Henry Drax, he sought an improvement in the treatment and care of the slaves, not really for their sake, but for the efficiency of the industry, for the better production of sugar. For, he wrote, 'there is no one commodity whatever, that doth so much encourage navigation, [and] advance the Kings Customs'. Tyron's advice was in the end designed to help the planters, whose prosperity, he judged, was the prosperity of England.

Admittedly, a number of the Quakers did inch towards a condemnation of the institution of slavery, even if they never quite got there at this time. John Edmundson, who was with George Fox on his travels in the 1670s, came close, but he ended up more concerned with the morals of the slaves – in particular their polygamy, which was tolerated by the planters. But in 1675 he did issue a warning to Governor Atkins, who had accused him, along with the other Quakers, of encouraging the slaves to revolt: if they did choose to rebel 'and cut their Throats', Edmundson replied, the fault was with the masters for 'keeping them in Ignorance, and under Oppression . . . and starv[ing] them for want of Meat and Cloathes convenient'. In fact, Atkins was right to be worried: a large number of slaves had already been planning a rebellion for as long as three years. At the time of Atkins's conversation with Edmundson, it was almost ready to be launched.

The rebellion had been prepared with such secrecy that even the ringleaders' wives were unaware of it. Nonetheless, just eight days before the 'damnable design' was due to begin, the plot was discovered. A domestic slave by the name of Fortuna overhead an 18-year-old Coromantee slave discussing plans for the insurrection. It appears the young man baulked at the plan to kill the 'Buccararoes or White Folks'. Fortuna, who believed 'it was a great pity so good people as her Master and Mistress should be destroyed', persuaded him to go with her to tell Judge Hall. Hall rushed to inform Governor Atkins, who immediately mobilised the militia, declared martial law and arrested the known conspirators.

Precise details are hard to come by: it is possible that Atkins, subsequently reporting the plot to London, may have exaggerated in order to secure help with expanding the militia. But it appears that the plot was communicated through a network of African-born (rather than Creole) Coromantee slaves on a number of plantations, and may have originated in the Speightstown area. The aim had been for 'trumpets . . . of elephants teeth and gourdes to be sounded on several hills . . . in the dead of night . . . to give notice of their general rising'. Then canefields were to be torched, and the slaves were to 'run in and cut their masters . . . throats in their respective plantations'. Ultimately all whites were to be killed 'within a fortnight', although one report suggested that it was planned to 'spare the lives of the fairest and handsomest [white] women . . . to be converted to their own use'. An 'ancient Gold-Coast Negro' called Cuffee had been chosen as king, and was to be crowned on 12 June 1675. Already prepared was 'a chair of state exquisitely wrought and carved after their mode'.

More than 100 slaves were examined by a summary court, and 17 found guilty straight away. Six were burned alive and 11 beheaded, their bodies dragged through the streets of Speightstown and then burned. A report published in London the following year tells of how one of the leaders before he was burnt was called upon to give the names of others involved, which he appeared to be about to do. But another of the conspirators, 'a sturdy Rogue, a Jew's Negro' called Tony, shouted to him, 'Thou Fool, are there not enough of our Countrymen killed already? Are thou minded to kill them all?' The slave remained silent, and an onlooker shouted out, 'Tony, Sirrah, we shall see you fry bravely by and by', to which Tony replied, 'If you Roast me to day, you cannot Roast me to morrow.'

A further 25 were subsequently executed, and five hanged themselves in prison. The rest were either deported or sent back to their masters for a savage flogging. Fortuna was given her freedom, and the owners of the rebellious slaves killed were compensated for their 'loss of property'.

The extensive nature of the plot caused huge alarm amongst the slave-owners of Barbados. The following year, new laws were passed that reinforced the militia, further restricted the movement of slaves, and banned the musical instruments that were to have been used for communication. The Quakers were also blamed for enabling the plotting of slaves from separate plantations, and 'Negro' attendance at Quaker meetings was banned.

None of these measures, however, prevented further scares. In 1683, a plot was uncovered that, surprisingly, used notes written in English to spread the word, and three years later, 10 slaves were executed after it emerged that some blacks might have united with Irish indentured servants in an effort to overthrow the planters.

The most carefully planned and widespread plot in the seventeenth century occurred in 1692. It was highly organised and was put together, for the first time, by Creole slaves: those born in Barbados and in theory 'assimilated' in the island's system. Furthermore, the leaders were found to be from the elite, skilled enslaved workers – overseers, carpenters, black-smiths, boilers* – whose extra privileges, it had been hoped, would have divided them from the interest of the majority.

This leadership, which came from 21 different plantations, mainly in the St Michael, Christchurch and St George parishes, succeeded in identifying a moment of great weakness for the whites: the uprising was timed to take place shortly after the departure of much of the militia to Guadeloupe to fight the French. It was also able to achieve the difficult task of

---

* 'And such others that have more favour shown them by their masters, which adds abundantly to their crimes.'

persuading the downtrodden blacks of their own strength: plans were in place for the raising of four regiments of foot and two of horse, with officers named, from amongst the slaves. And the aim was more sophisticated than simply murdering all whites. The slaves, having secured their own plantations and, if necessary, helped out on neighbouring ones, were to proceed to Bridgetown to capture the arsenal, where an accomplice would be waiting to give them entry. A band of Irish co-conspirators was lined up to enter the town's main fort laden with alcohol to get the garrison drunk, whereupon the fort would be stormed, and its guns used to command the harbour and town. Once the island was under their control, the slaves would set up their own government, with their own new governor. 'The white women', a report later outlined, 'they were to make wives of the handsomest, Whores Cooks & Chambermaids of Others.'

It is not recorded who betrayed the plot, but apparently two slaves, Ben and Sambo, had been 'fully overheard . . . talking of . . . their wicked design' only ten days before the uprising was scheduled to take place. They were arrested and gaoled, and soon afterwards, a third slave, Hammon, broke into the prison to attempt to dissuade the two captives from divulging anything. But Hammon was caught and, in return for his life, implicated both Ben and Sambo, and another slave, Samson. What happened to the latter is unclear, although he was certainly killed. Ben and Sambo were sentenced to be 'hung in chains on a gibbet until you have starved to death, after which your head to be severed from your body and put on a pole on said gibbet, your body cut in quarters and burned to ashes under said gibbet'. The two slaves are reported to have heard this sentence 'patiently . . . without being in any ways moved'. They survived for four days before, their hopes for rescue fading and in an agony of thirst, they named names, in return for their lives, 'frankly confess[ing] (when it could not be help'd) what their design was'. Sambo, it seems, did not live long enough to enjoy the 'Governor's mercy'.

Ultimately, between 200 and 300 were arrested, although only about 30 were identified as ringleaders. 'Many were hang'd, and a great many burn'd', a contemporary noted. 'And (for a terror to the others) there are now seven hanging in chains, alive, and so starving to death.' One Alice Mills was ultimately paid ten guineas 'for castrating forty-two Negroes, according to the sentence of the commissioners for trial of rebellious negroes'.

Everyone among the white elite was deeply shaken. Governor James Kendall reported to London that: 'The conspiracy of our most dangerous enemies, our black slaves . . . put the inhabitants into so strong a consternation.' Appealing to London to send a permanent regiment to garrison the island, he wrote that 'these villains are but too sensible of . . . our extreme weakness'.

13

THE COUSINS HENRY DRAX AND CHRISTOPHER CODRINGTON

'All, or the greatest part of men that have aspired to riches or power, have attained thereunto either by force or fraud.'

Sir Walter Raleigh

Barbados, comparatively long-established and by far the most heavily settled of the English colonies in the West Indies, remained radically precarious and unstable. Yet another war with the Dutch from 1672 to 1674 saw the loss of many valuable cargoes, a hike in shipping costs, and a worrying increase in the public debt. Shortly after the uncovering of the first major slave plot, the island was hit by the worst hurricane in its history. On 31 August 1675, the sky darkened, and strong winds started swirling round, seemingly from all directions. Heavy rain, howling winds and lightning continued through the night. By morning, hardly a building or tree was left standing on the leeward side of the island. Two hundred people were killed, crops torn out of the ground or flattened, and two years' sugar production lost. The Governor reckoned the damage at more than £200,000 and with the destruction of food crops and shipping, famine was soon widespread. A year later, in 1676, a ferocious smallpox epidemic carried off thousands, particularly from amongst the enslaved Africans and children of all races.

Henry Drax's workforce seems to have been unaffected by the slave plot of 1675, in spite of the preponderance of Coromantees amongst his African slaves. Clearly, he also remained a very rich man, despite hurricane destruction and the sugar planters' shrinking margins. But his wealth proved to provide no protection for his own family, who had at least their fair share of Barbados's appalling mortality from disease. During an 18-month period up to the beginning of 1680, more than twice as many white people were buried than baptised in Barbados. A comparative analysis of households in Bridgetown and a town in Massachusetts from this time shows a mean number of children per family at just under one for Barbados, and more than three for Massachusetts. Furthermore, very few children who survived into adulthood in Barbados still had both parents alive. Sometime in the late 1660s, Henry Drax's first wife, Frances, died (his younger brother John, still in his twenties, also died in Bridgetown soon after). Desperate to produce an heir to carry the Drax name forward, Henry quickly remarried, while on council business in England in July 1671. It was another good match: his new, 21-year-old wife Dorothy was the daughter of John, second Lord Lovelace. Dorothy produced four children, but all were, as an inscription on her tomb reads, 'snatched away (alas!) too quickly'. None survived infancy; it is highly likely that at least one succumbed to the smallpox epidemic attacking Barbados at this time.

So, with a heavy heart, Henry Drax wrote his 'Instructions' for the running of his Barbados estates, and prepared to leave the island. His reluctance, and attachment to his Barbados home, is shown in his request for regular supplies to be sent to England of his favourite West Indian foods: 'Jamaca peper welle pickled in good wineger . . . green ginger and yams' (export was to be handled 'with the adwice and Asistnce of my Cozn Ltt. Colonel John Codrington'). On 22 April 1679, a ticket was granted for Henry Drax Esquire to sail for London on the ship '*Honor*, Thomas Warner commander'.

Ironically, the move to healthier climes backfired. No more children were forthcoming, and three years later Henry himself died, aged 41. His will was written only shortly before his death: in it, in an exceedingly rare example of planter philanthropy, he left £2,000 for the establishment of a 'free school and college' in St Michael. He had always deplored the practice, since the Restoration, of the rich planters sending their children back to England at the age of 12 to be educated there. Few ever returned, he complained, and those that did were 'utterly debauched both in Principalls and Morals'. Rich and far from home, it appears that the young Barbadians became loose-living and extravagant, and famous for 'the gaiety of their dress and equipage'.

Two thousand pounds was a very sizeable amount of money at the time, but nothing came of the school. The bequest was 'borrowed' by the hard-pressed assembly, and disappeared.

Henry's will requested that his funeral be 'not costly, only decent' and that he was to be buried with his father in St John of Zachary. Four hundred pounds was allocated to memorials to his mother and father, and a small sum for the poor of the parish. As well as his extended family, his godson Christopher Codrington the third was a beneficiary, as was his cousin William Drax. His wife found herself richer to the tune of a massive £8,000, as well as inheriting valuable property in London.

In the absence of an heir in his line of the family, the Barbados estates were to go to his sister Elizabeth's son, Thomas Shetterden, but with an important caveat: he had to change his name, 'and his posterity after him', to Drax. Should he be reluctant to do this, Henry stipulated, the plantations would go to his younger brother, with the same caveat that he change his name. (This young man already carried the first name 'Drax', so would have become Drax Drax.)

Henry's nephew Thomas duly changed his last name to Drax and lived for a time in Barbados until his death in 1702. His eldest son, Henry Drax, also spent some of his life inhabiting Drax Hall, but passed most of his time in England, where he became an MP for Lyme Regis and Wareham in 1719, in more than slightly dubious circumstances (both his sons would also represent the constituency). Nonetheless, the death of the first Henry, or, more exactly, his quitting Barbados in 1679, marked the end of the family's direct influence on the affairs of the island, once so crucial to its development.

Henry's cousin Christopher Codrington would also leave Barbados, but under very different circumstances. Sometime before 1671, when he was 31 years of age, Christopher abandoned his 'liberal, debonaire humour' and started gaining a very different reputation. The turning point seems to have been Codrington's takeover of a plantation called Consetts, situated in a beautiful spot on the east coast of the island in St John's parish.

This was one of the island's oldest plantations, established in 1635 by William Consett. It was also one of the most valuable: it had its own fresh-water spring and also contained rare clay deposits – essential for making the pots for 'claying' sugar. In addition, it boasted a fine sheltered harbour. This allowed the products of the plantation to be carried away by boat, avoiding the difficult 14-mile trek across the island to Bridgetown. By the late 1660s, the next-door plantation was owned by Christopher's brother John Codrington, and both William Consett and his wife Elizabeth were elderly and frail.

What happened next has been argued over ever since. It has been said that Christopher Codrington won the plantation in a game of cards. In a different, more convincing version of the story, the elderly Consetts made over part or all of their plantation to their friend and next-door neighbour John Codrington and his brother Christopher, to be theirs on their death, in return for a one-off payment to see them to their end of their lives. In another version, the deal was done with Henry Willoughby, son of the governor, or even with a third character known only as Turner. Alternatively, it may have been a combination of Willoughby and the Codringtons, with the estate lined up to pay Willoughby a large annuity while being inherited by Christopher Codrington. The facts are murky to say the least.

But we do know the outcome. The Consetts died in 1669, within weeks of each other, and Christopher Codrington took possession of the estate. Shortly afterwards, Henry Willoughby was invited to supper by Codrington. When he left that night he was fine, but when he got to his lodging he 'fell into a violent burning of the stomach' and died the next morning at seven o'clock. Many believed that Henry, as a rival claimant, had been deliberately poisoned.

Barbados was always a place of vicious rumour and counter-rumour, and it is impossible to be sure that Henry Willoughby was murdered by Christopher Codrington. But a judge who confirmed Codrington's ownership of Consetts was later accused of 'fraudulent proceedings', and an anonymous assessment of Barbados's councillors in 1670 describes Codrington as being 'accused of terrible crimes'.

Certainly Governor William Willoughby, Henry's father, previously a great friend and supporter of Codrington, turned sharply against him when he returned to Barbados in 1672. Having praised Codrington's stewardship of the island in his absence, Willoughby now criticised him for putting 'needless impositions' on the planters, and threw him off the council. Codrington was also stripped of his command of one of the island's militia regiments. According to a 1672 letter from Henry Drax, Willoughby now had 'a great prejudice against Codrington . . . and has the power . . . and the will to ruin him'. When Codrington (in an episode that shows his growing lack of judgement and general greed and megalomania) tried to develop a reputed silver mine in Dominica, Willoughby attempted to take the patent from under his nose.

Willoughby died shortly afterwards, but Codrington never sat on the Barbados council again, nor won the trust of the island's subsequent governors. An attempt in 1674 to regain his place was slapped down with the comment that Codrington 'was no fit man to be councilor'. Instead, he concentrated on the assembly, where he became everything he had fought against while deputy governor: a classic creature of faction and self-interest.

Soon after taking possession of Consetts, the Codrington brothers exchanged plantations so that John took over Christopher's land in St Michael in return for the estate next to Consetts on the St John's coast. Thus, in 1673, Christopher is recorded as owning 600 acres in the parish. By 1678 he had a very profitable plantation in operation, with 250 slaves, three stone-built windmills, a large boiling house with 17 coppers and a still-house containing four large rum stills. To celebrate his wealth, he commissioned from a silversmith in London the largest covered punch bowl ever recorded – 18 inches high, with a diameter of 17½ inches. Engraved on its side was the Codrington of Dodington arms, belonging to what was then the senior branch of the family (soon to be bought out and superseded by the West Indian Codringtons).

Having as deputy governor battled to enforce the Navigation Acts and the rule of law, Codrington now threw himself with abandon into illegal trading. A wharf and warehouse were constructed in Consett's Bay, where 'interlopers' could land slaves direct from Africa, in defiance of the Royal African Company's monopoly. It became a small entrepôt, engaging in some very profitable smuggling, and even in the taking of prizes. The RAC's factors complained several times about Codrington's operation, on one occasion in December 1678 writing to London that 'Christopher Codrington of this Island . . . is a great Favourer of Interlopers . . . [he], recd. The Gold, Teeth and Wax also the Negroes out of this last Interloper as wee are told and sccured them in his dwelling house, cureing house and boyling house, using this expression also as wee are told that he would warrant and secure them ag'st the Compa's Factors or any [one] else lett them come with what Authoritie or force they could.'

It may be that some events in his family life altered or soured the outlook of Christopher Codrington. He buried a daughter, Mary, almost certainly an infant, in St Michael's church in mid-1670. His second son, John, was, as his father later wrote, 'inflicted with an infirmity', elsewhere less charitably described as a 'lunatic'. It is very possible that his wife Gertrude also died around this time. Did these tragedies wear him down? Or was it what a visitor to Jamaica at this time described as one of the curses of slavery – the giving of 'unlimited power' to the slave-owner, and the corrupting influence of that 'absolute power over all the rest as slaves' that saw men such as Codrington 'guided only by his owne will', masters of everything but themselves?

Codrington's son, Christopher the third, remained all his life a defender of his father, whom he regarded with awe. He was probably educated as a young boy at Consetts by the Reverend Benjamin Cryer, the rector of St John's. But in 1680, aged 12, he was sent to England to be educated, and any companionship that he might have given his father was gone. In the same year, the elder Codrington made a concerted effort to be appointed to the vacant post of Barbados's governor, recruiting influential courtiers in London to push his case. But it seems that his reputation was beyond repair, and he lost out to Sir Richard Dutton, who immediately brought proceedings against Codrington, accusing him of embezzlement while deputy governor. Dutton was a crook of the first order, himself making a fortune out of his position, but he forced Codrington to pay back nearly £600 of allegedly stolen money. For a couple of years Codrington led the opposition to the new governor, but soon he had had enough. In 1683, he decided to move to new pastures.

In 1668, before the Consetts affair, Codrington had been granted through the influence of his then friend William Willoughby a 500-acre plantation in Antigua's Old North Sound division, known as Betty's Hope. This was just after the destruction of the French invasion and occupation, and its previous tenant, one Dame Joan Hall, had fled the island (she would later unsuccessfully try to retrieve her property). Codrington was then still concentrating on developing his Barbados interests, and although he ordered the planting of sugar on his new Antigua property, it was only ticking over 10 years later, with just two whites and 10 black slaves registered as living on the property in 1678. But as his reputation in Barbados soured, Christopher Codrington began quietly increasing his interests in Antigua, taking out a patent with his brother John for a further 400 acres in 1681. In 1684, the brothers obtained a lease for the nearby, largely deserted 60-square-mile island of Barbuda, previously granted to James Winthrop in 1668.*

Thus when Christopher decided to quit Barbados in the early 1680s, he had the nucleus in Antigua for what would soon become the most substantial estate on the island (eventually covering more than 1,000 acres and employing 800 slaves). In February 1683, he leased his Barbados plantations, now spanning some 750 acres on the St John's coast, to a Captain Higginbothan. The following year, to secure capital for development in Antigua, he raised a mortgage on the Barbados properties of just over £4,000, and another £7,000 the next year. While John concentrated on Barbuda, building a castle and developing the island mainly as a supplier

---

* John Codrington died in about 1688, his will giving a stark reminder of the precariousness of these new possessions, in comparison to relatively safe property in Barbados: the land in Antigua and Barbuda is covered by a caveat 'if estate lost or taken by enemies . . .'

The first farmers of Barbados grew tobacco, in an attempt to emulate the success of the Virginia colony

Busts of James Drax (*right*) and his first wife Meliora (*left*), commissioned by their son Henry. Drax was the first sugar baron, instrumental in making Barbados the richest place in the Americas.

A page from James Drax's will

St. Nicholas Abbey
(*left*) and (*below*)
Drax Hall, Barbados:
two of the oldest
surviving Jacobean
mansions in
the Americas

Ruins of the
sugar factory at
Drax Hall, Barbados

The earliest known map exclusively of Barbados, it appeared in Richard Ligon's *True and Exact History*, published in 1657. The map identifies 285 plantations by owner, and shows the early development of the leeward coastal region, while the interior remains overgrown and inaccessible. Vignettes depict planters hunting wild hogs and chasing runaway slaves. Curiously, a pair of camels is shown; Ligon wrote that 'several planters imported these beasts and found them useful in Barbados, but did not know how to diet them.'

Louise de Kéroualle, Duchess of Portsmouth, a mistress of Charles II, painted in about 1682. Black children became fashionable as 'toys'. When they grew up they would be returned to the West Indian plantations.

Charles II receives a Barbados pineapple, supposedly the first to reach England, from the royal gardener in a painting from 1675. The pineapple was adored by English West Indians and became a symbol of welcome, affixed to doors and door posts.

The Battle of Sandy Point, St Kitts, 1666.
The division of the island between French and English, originally to counter Carib and Spanish threats, caused continual conflict and devastating war on the island.

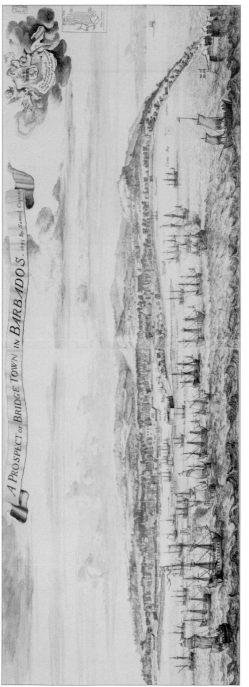

A Prospect of Bridgetown by Samuel Copen, 1695.
The port was a hub of the new Western Empire, a prosperous and thriving mart.

Cane holeing in Antigua, amongst the most back-breaking of the labours on a plantation, carried out by a 'Great Gang', which included women as well as men

A sugar 'factory' in Antigua, showing the different stages of boiling. This was highly skilled and dangerous work: 'If a Boyler get any part into the scalding sugar,' said a contemporary, 'it sticks like Glew, or Birdlime, and 'tis hard to save either Limb or Life.'

The violent and ruthless Colonel Peter Beckford, standing by an open window with a fort in the background, probably Fort Charles

Peter Beckford the Younger. By the 1730s, he had shrugged off murder charges and owned eleven Jamaican plantations as well as more than two thousand slaves.

Sir Henry Morgan, buccaneer and later Deputy Governor of Jamaica. A man of little scruple, great energy, and formidable self-destructive appetites.

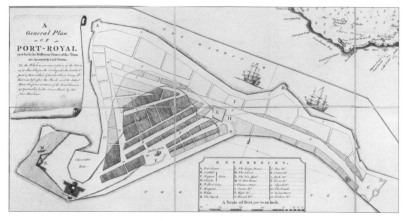

Port Royal in 1692, the 'Wickedest Town in the West'. The shaded area shows all that remained above water after the devastating earthquake.

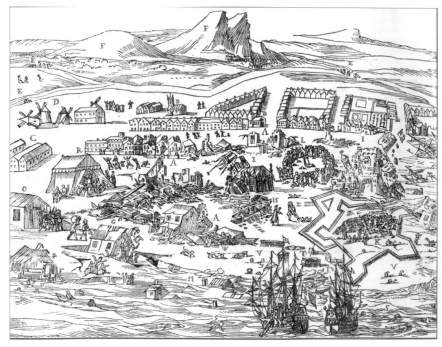

A graphic image of the earthquake of June 1692, whose original key included: 'K. The Earth opening and Swallowing Multitudes of People. O. Thieves robbing and Breaking open Dwelling Houses and Warehouses. P. Dr Trapham hanging by his Hands on the Rack of a Chimney and one of his children hanging around his neck, seeing his Wife and other Children Sinking. S. Dead Bodies of 400 floating about the Harbour. T. The Sea Washing the Dead Carcasses out of their Graves. V. People swallowed up by the Earth. W. The Dog's eating of Men's Heads. Z. Mr Beckford digging out of the Ground.'

of provisions and livestock, Christopher's priority was Antigua, where he joined the council in the mid-1680s, and was soon wielding great power and influence.

Codrington seems to have found the frontier society of Antigua liberating. Barbados was far from strait-laced, but there Codrington had old friends and relatives who had known him all his life. In Antigua, he seems to have dramatically loosened the shackles on his own behaviour, particularly when it came to sex. (Around this time, his brother John, a solid and reliable character, died.) According to an anonymous complaint sent to London, Christopher 'Keeps Continually about him a Seraglio of mulatoes and negro women and has by them no less than 4 or 5 bastards.' His will contains a list of his lovers and illegitimate children – 'Mary Codrington, daughter of Margaret who formerly waited on me, £300 at 21 . . . to my mulatta Cateen & her daughter Meliour their freedom, & £200 to the latter at 21' – all of whom seem to have been conceived after he left Barbados.

By this time, according to a detailed census compiled by Governor Stapleton, Antigua had a population of some 1,200 white men, 500 each of white women and children and just over 2,000 black slaves, of whom 800 were adult males. Montserrat had similar numbers, although comparatively more slaves; St Kitts had fewer whites and blacks, although a more equal gender mix; Nevis, which had escaped French depredation, slightly more of all categories, although still two males to each female. In total, the Leeward Islands had about half the white population of Barbados at that time, and about a quarter of the slave force. The islands were still some way behind Barbados on the road to the intensive sugar-and-slaves model. Nevis was the most developed, with the Governor's residence, nearly half the churches of the islands and the only well-built port, at Charlestown. But in 1680 Nevis councillors averaged fewer than 70 slaves per man, while in Barbados the island's councillors had nearly 200 each. In Antigua, the greatest planters, such as the Langfords, Byams and Winthrops, had even smaller households.

But like Barbados, there was increasingly concern about the lack of white settlers to police the growing black slave populations. In March 1687, a slave revolt saw some 40 or 50 slaves 'armed with guns' flee to the interior of Antigua, which, unlike Barbados, still provided the shelter of virgin forest. Mounted patrols were sent in pursuit; the first runaway captured had 'his leg cut off', and two weeks later a 'collision' between the blacks and the pursuing troops saw half the former killed and a ringleader, 'Negroe George', captured and sentenced to 'be burned to ashes'. In response to the rebellion, the Antigua legislature ordered that each plantation have a quota of white servants, and appeals were posted to London to send out 'the spawne of Newgate and Bridewell' to make up the numbers of the whites, but with little success. Thus the slave population rose steadily.

As the Leeward Islanders increased their sugar production – collectively up to about a third of the total of Barbados by 1680 – they found themselves heading inexorably towards the unhappy and unstable model of Barbados, with small farmers and freeholders dwindling to be replaced by a plantocracy of consolidated estates manned by black slaves. In addition, the insecurity of the Leewards was increased by the internal rivalries between the Irish and the rest, their lack of unity between the islands (refusing to cooperate on defence or even standardise their laws), and the ever-present and growing threat of their French neighbours, who throughout the late 1670s and 1680s were better supported from home with troops and ships, and looked ever more likely to descend once more on the vulnerable English colonies.

14

GOD'S VENGEANCE

'If thou didst see those great persons that are now dead upon the water thou couldst never forget it. Great men who were so swallowed up with pride, that a man could not be admitted to speak with them, and women whose top-knots seemed to reach the clouds, now lie stinking upon the water, and are made meat for fish and fowls of the air.'

Quaker John Pike, Jamaica, 19 June 1692

Jamaica's much greater proximity to the centres of Spanish power in the Caribbean meant that the old enemy was still a threat, notwithstanding the treaty made in Europe in 1670 and efforts by Jamaica's governors to improve relations with Spain by suppressing English privateering. Most dangerous was the Spaniards' inconsistency. A majority of the Spanish governors were corrupt and, when it suited or, more exactly, benefited them, would allow illegal trading by English vessels from Port Royal, whence they also came openly to buy much-needed slaves. But traders welcomed on one visit to a Spanish port would often find themselves seized on the next occasion, and 'made slaves ... and there used with the utmost of Rigor and severity'. 'We treat them on all occasions with all imaginable respect and kindness,' wrote Sir Henry Morgan to London during one of the three periods he was acting governor, 'and in return receive only ingratitude.' In December 1675, Peter Beckford, in his capacity as Secretary of the Island, wrote home that the Spaniards 'are daily taking all ships they can master, and are very high'. When the governor 'sent to demand satisfaction they answered they would look upon us as enemies'.

But in the same letter Beckford confidently asserted that if it came once more to war, then the Spanish, thinly stretched over vast areas, could be defeated. A far greater threat, he wrote, was presented by the French, who 'would prove very ill neighbours in war, and much more dangerous than the Spaniards'. The French had a powerful fleet in the theatre in 1677, causing invasion fears in Jamaica; and two years later martial law was declared on the island for the same reason. In the meantime, French privateers were a constant menace both on the high seas and for isolated coastal plantations. On one occasion privateers attacked the north-coast estate of a Widow Barrow, 'plundered all her Negroes, household goods and all she had, Tortured her to confess if she had money and then took away with him her maiden daughter, Rachel Barrow of about 14 years'.

Jamaica was still a wild and dangerous frontier. Its inhabitants were boisterous and unruly, even at the top, where the leadership was characterised by constant battles between the assembly and the Governor, and between factions made up of planters, merchants and buccaneers. A map drawn in 1677 shows a duel with pistols in motion. A few years before, an assembly meeting had ended with a drunken murder: a Captain Rutter was killed by a Major Joy, who 'had always been his friend, but the drink and other men's quarrels made them fall out'. The interior remained trackless, undeveloped, and infested with runaway slaves and servants. Jamaica in the mid-1670s had only four priests for the entire island, and the 2,000 white children had only one schoolmaster between them.

But even though much of the best land was still undeveloped (what would become, in the next generation, the island's finest plantation, the Prices' Worthy Park in Lluidas Vale, was still jungle and scrub), Jamaica was beginning to give up some of its extraordinary agricultural richness. Beckford wrote in 1675, 'As to the present state of the Island, no place the King has is more like to thrive, for they increase in planting to a miracle.' The increase in sugar production was, indeed, miraculous: by the 1680s, sugar had become the largest export by value, having increased tenfold since 1671. The number of sugar works had jumped from 57 in 1671 to 246 in 1684. Thirty years after Barbados, the Sugar Revolution had arrived in Jamaica.

Compared with Barbados, the cradle of the British West Indian sugar empire, Jamaica always possessed, and still does, more space, variety, fertility, potential and danger. For while Barbados still had a white population of which half could be deemed 'poor', Jamaican free society was almost straight away dominated by the biggest planters. As in Barbados, only those at the top could afford to switch to sugar. For the duration of the empire, crops such as indigo, ginger, dye woods, provisions and, later, coffee, remained important, but from the 1680s onwards, the wild profits – and political and social power – were in the hands of the sugar planters.

Many were from amongst the earliest arrivals: Fulke Rose, who earned a very good living as a doctor, also brought home some £4,000 a year from his sugar plantations; Francis Price, who had been part of the invasion force, now owned thousands of acres; Peter Beckford's sugar operation was in full swing, while he enjoyed substantial income as a merchant and money-lender, much of which was reinvested in further acreage. All three served as members of the assembly and were senior militia officers.

On the dangerously deserted north coast, those prepared to take the risk were also reaping the benefits of wonderful environmental conditions. For much of the coastline, steep hills border a two-mile-wide coastal strip. This flat and easily farmed land is watered by numerous streams that pour down from the higher ground and also bring down rich alluvial deposits. In addition, many of the streams were of sufficient strength to power mills to grind the sugar. One of the plantations enjoying these invaluable advantages was Drax Hall, established by Henry's cousin William in the late 1660s. Such was the space enjoyed by the Jamaican planters, unlike their cousins in Barbados, that plantations could be large enough to have 200 acres in cane (considered the maximum amount processable by one factory) and still have the majority of the land in provisions, livestock, woodland or fallow. Such was the Jamaican Drax Hall estate, one of the most profitable on the island for the next 70 years.

William Drax died in 1697, and the plantation went to his son, Charles Drax. Like Henry, both William and Charles served in the political establishment but largely kept their heads down and out of trouble. In addition, Charles seems to have been determined to create a new, physical Drax Hall in Jamaica, to rival the famous edifice in Barbados.

None of the earliest Jamaican great houses has survived the climate, neglect, natural disasters and the periodic vengeance of slaves. But recent archaeological investigations, together with a small illustration and various inventories, show the Jamaican Drax Hall to have been a large structure with limestone foundation walls a metre thick, rising to three storeys – highly unusual for Jamaica at the time – and some 10 rooms. In fact, it had much in common with the surviving Drax Hall in Barbados, which is unlikely to have been a coincidence: it had a steep, side-gabled roof, with sets of three triangular gabled dormer windows. Unlike Drax Hall in Barbados, it boasted an extensive porch extending the length of the house front, which faced out over the ocean.

The Drax Hall estate would soon have more than 300 slaves, a workforce that made the leap in sugar production possible. In 1676, Peter Beckford reported that 'the People of this Island are much dissatisfied about the Royal

Company', which was selling at 'Unreasonable Rates'. Jamaica was considerably further from the slave coast of West Africa than Barbados, and slaves that cost £17 in Barbados, Beckford complained, were priced at £24 in Jamaica. As elsewhere, interlopers filled the gap, finding Jamaica's long coast and numerous bays convenient for secretly landing their miserable cargoes. But by the 1680s, the Governor of Jamaica was able to write that 'The Royal Company now begin to supply us well, there being two Shipps with 700 Negroes in port.' In mid-decade, in one year alone – 1686–7 – more than 6,000 slaves were imported by the Company. Already, by 1680, the black population of Jamaica had surpassed that of the white – at 15,000 still about 5,000 fewer than that of Barbados. Soon the slaves would be in the majority, with their numbers concentrated on the large sugar estates, and growing at an extraordinary rate, particularly after the ending of the Royal African Company's monopoly at the end of the century and a consequent sharp fall in price.

The arriving slaves immediately found that Jamaica offered much more hope of freedom than the smaller islands. On Barbados, there was no interior into which to flee, but Jamaica had hundreds of square miles of trackless waste and jungled mountains, where the maroons, the runaway slaves of the Spanish era, still had well-established strongholds and independent settlements. There was also the hope of escaping by sea, something not wise to undertake from isolated Barbados. Between 1673 and 1694 there were six sizeable slave revolts in Jamaica, which affected almost every plantation on the island. In December 1675, one planter reported, 'many families were murdered' and 'now at this present there is at least one hundred Negroes up in arms at the north side, and have killed several white men, burnt and destroyed most the Plantations in St Mary's parish'. Parties of militia were sent to track down the runaways, but in many cases they were unsuccessful, and the maroon population steadily grew. A further supposed plot was uncovered in 1677, and the following year a plantation only five miles from Spanish Town was taken over by its slaves, who then put in place a well-conceived plan to join up with slaves from other plantations, some as many as 16 miles away. The uprising was crushed, but this network among slaves caused great concern to the planters; even worse, a slave was implicated who had previously been judged by his master 'so trusty a negro . . . I would have put my life in his hands'.

The white leadership of Jamaica responded, as had the other sugar islands, by attempting to increase their white population. In the early 1680s, an Act of the assembly stipulated that the master of five black slaves had to keep one white servant, overseer or hired man for at least three months of the year or pay a penalty of £5 for each white man lacking. But this measure failed, in effect becoming a revenue act. Up until the late 1670s, white immigration to Jamaica had been steady, but thereafter it fell off sharply, due to issues at home, and because of the reputation the island had acquired for high mortality and brutality. It did not help that, as in Barbados, the planters were 'verey severe' to their white servants, as John Taylor,* who visited the island in 1687, noted. While the 'master live at ease at full feed tables', Taylor reported, their poorly fed servants 'are att hard labour in the open feild, almost burnt up by the sun'. Repeated efforts to attract New Englanders largely failed. As a visitor to Jamaica wrote to John Winthrop Junior, 'All matters considered, I judge our husbandmen in Connecticut doe live better than a great part of the inhabitants here.' In 1684, 164 of the Monmouth rebels were sent to Jamaica by James II, where they were to serve for 10 years, but these sorts of numbers were never able to compete with the thousands of enslaved Africans now being imported.

According to John Taylor, it does not seem to have occurred to the typical Jamaican planter to deter rebellion by the enslaved population through better treatment. They paid no attention, he wrote, to the 'misery of the slaves', 'whom the sun and tormenting insects in the feild are like to devour'. Instead, the planters attempted to deter runaways and rebellious slaves through the harsh punishments inflicted on those recaptured or deemed to have been plotting to escape. Because of the untamed interior of Jamaica, white settlers had more to fear from their slaves than in the smaller colonies; this resulted in Jamaica becoming the most stark and brutal of all of Britain's West Indian slave colonies. For lesser offences, slaves were castrated or had a foot or hand chopped off. In 1677, a Joseph Bryan wrote to his brother about the 'cruel death' of a neighbour's slave who had apparently planned a rebellion: his legs and arms were broken, then 'he was fastened upon his back to the ground, a fire was made first to his feet and burned upwards by degrees. I heard him speak several words when the fire had consumed all his lower parts as far as his navel the fire was upon his breast he was burning near 3 hours before he died.' Bryan, fresh from England, was clearly shocked. But a year later, 'seasoned' to the fearful garrison society of Jamaica, he described a similar punishment meted out to a runaway as 'just rewards'.

---

* Taylor was born in 1664, on the Isle of Wight, the son of a minor gentleman. Having studied mathematics, he fought for James II during the Monmouth Rebellion. He had much in common with Richard Ligon, in his curiosity about the slaves and creole culture, and like Ligon came to the West Indies at a time of personal crisis (in his case a family argument), and left having been floored by illness.

Sir Hans Sloane, the famous naturalist, like Ligon before him, was intelligent and sensitive enough to see the enslaved Africans as individuals, rather than as a group, and showed unusual curiosity about their spiritual beliefs and family relationships. During the 15 months he spent in Jamaica in 1687–8, he also documented the island's slave punishments from this period, including mutilation and burning as described by Bryan: for the crime of negligence, Sloane wrote, 'After they are whipped till they are raw, some put on their skins Pepper and salt to make them smart; at other times their masters will drop melted wax on their skins, and use several very exquisite torments. These punishments are sometimes merited', he continued, the word 'sometimes' perhaps betraying his unease, but then concludes that the 'blacks' 'are a very perverse generation of people, and though [the punishments] appear harsh, yet are scarce equal to some of their crimes'. John Taylor also details slave punishments, its victims 'soe stuburn that with all this whiping, misserey, or torment, they shall seldom be seen to shead a tear, but rather at first laugh, and then afterwards stand scilent'. He also described the practices of forcing slaves to eat their own amputated limbs, and of rubbing molasses on to newly whipped slaves 'for the wasps, merrywings and other insects to torment'. But Taylor concluded that 'if you should be kinder to 'em they would soner cutt your throat than obay you'.

This deterrence seems to have worked for a short period, but in 1685 another serious rebellion saw 150 slaves up in arms. The Governor was forced to call up both regiments and more than 100 militia men, but more than 50 of the rebels escaped into the 'unaccessible mountains and rocks', from where they continued to launch attacks on outlying plantations. Of those captured, wrote John Taylor, 'some were burnt, others roasted alive, others torn to pieces with dogs, and others hanged and their heads and quarters set everywhere here and there on poles', but this now standard practice for unruly slaves failed to deter others. For the rest of the decade, the authorities were compelled to conduct an almost constant battle, with 'great troble and expence', against slave rebellions and the maroons of the interior.

While threatened from within, the island's leadership also feared the growing danger from France, and in the meantime struggled bitterly amongst themselves, with Peter Beckford, who would be elevated to the council in 1691, leading a planter faction that fought, with some success, to blunt the powers of governors sent out from London. One governor complained that 'so scandalous an Assembly was never chosen. At least two thirds of them sit up drinking all night, and before they are cool next morning vote whatver is put into their hands by Beckford.' Certainly the island, even by the standards of the West Indies, drank and caroused to an extraordinary extent, and no more so than in Port Royal, the 'Wickedest Town in the West'.

By 1680, Port Royal had grown into a town of considerable importance, in population second only in the English Americas to Boston. (Its value was underlined by its extensive defences – four forts, as well as a landward breastwork). Its fine harbour and central-Caribbean location had made it a hub of trade, with English, Portuguese, Spanish, Sephardic Jewish and Dutch merchants plying their goods, giving the town a distinctly cosmopolitan and tolerant as well as prosperous air. New England ships brought cheap provisions for the slaves, while ships from England brought goods for the master class (as well as a staggering amount of beer, ale, cider and English spirits). A visitor in 1682 called the town 'the Store House or Treasury of the West Indies . . . always like a continual Mart or Fair, where all sorts of choice Merchandizes are daily imported, not only to furnish the Island, but vast quantities are thence again transported to supply the Spaniards'. In one year in the late 1680s, 213 ships docked at Port Royal, almost as many as in all the harbours of New England combined.

The goods were loaded and unloaded at wharfs that ran along the landward side of the thin peninsula facing the harbour. On to this small area – less than 60 acres – were crowded some 800 buildings, many four storeys high to make the most of the limited space. Property in the town, according to an account from the 1670s, was 'as dear-rented as if they stood in well-traded streets in London; yet it's situation, is very unpleasant and uncommodious, having neither Earth, Wood, or Fresh-water, but only made up of a hot loose Sand'.

Notwithstanding these disadvantages, visitors such as John Taylor in 1687 found much to admire, including the Exchange, with Doric pillars and twisted balustrades, where merchants and planters met to transact their affairs. The planters, in particular, competed with each other in ostentation and showiness: 'the Gentrey', wrote Taylor, 'live here to the Hights of Splendor, in full ease and plenty . . . being sumptuously arrayed and served by their Negroa slaves, which always waite on 'em in liverys'.

According to Taylor, the rich planters with houses in Port Royal and nearby Spanish Town now did little work, but instead had 'English servants to manage their chiefe affaire and supervise their Negroa slaves'. In the comparative cool of the early morning and evening, they rode out in their carriages to plantations behind the towns, with the Liguanea region a favourite destination, 'as those of London doe to Isslington, Hackney and the Spring Gardens'. There, they enjoyed hunting, hawking and social-ising, all accompanied by 'a regalla of cream tarts, fruites, or what else they thinck fitt, but above all be sure they won't faill of a good glass of wine, and a jolly bowle of punche'. The less wealthy 'have noe other recre-ation, butt by enjoying their friends att the tavern . . . Also in the evening many young sparks and the common sort resort to musick houses [most, in essence, brothels] to devert themselves.'

In Port Royal, legitimate and illegal traders alike, along with the privat-eer fleet, created a demand for provisions – brought in from neighbouring farms – and for maritime services provided by rope-makers, carpenters, coopers, armourers and many other trades. In turn, the prize cargoes were sold on in the town, and luxury items purchased with the proceeds. Gold- and silversmiths did good business, as did shoemakers, tailors, hatters, and comb and jewellery-makers, who worked with the local tortoiseshell. All, apparently, 'live here very well, earning thrice the wages given in England, by which means they are enabled to maintain their families much better than in England', wrote Taylor. Even a cooper's wife could 'go forth in the best flowered silk and the richest silver and gold lace . . . with a couple of Negroes at her tail'.

However, it did not take long for visitors to Port Royal to realise that they were in the rowdiest city in the Americas. Taylor commented on the 'many taverns, and an abundance of punchy houses, or rather may be fitly called brothel houses'. In fact, there were an astonishing number of drinking establishments,* more than 100, and few activities in the town strayed far from the tavern, bawdy house or cockpit. Sir Henry Morgan had been deposed from his official positions in 1682 (with Peter Beckford taking his role as commander of Fort Charles, and, it appears, living with his young family in Port Royal),† but Morgan continued to stir up trouble in Port Royal. 'In his debauches, which go on every day and night, he is much magnified', complained Governor Lynch. Morgan had a brief return to favour under the governorship of the second Duke of Albermarle, a fellow fast-liver who was more interested in sunken Spanish treasure than good government; both, however, drank themselves to death. Sir Hans Sloane treated Morgan shortly before his demise in 1688, aged 53: the doctor

---

* A small number of their names have survived, their signs uncovered by archaeologists: Black Dogg, Blue Anchor, Catt & Fiddle, Sign of Bacchus.

† Peter Beckford's portrait has him standing by an open window with a fort in the background, probably Fort Charles, wearing a magnificently embroidered coat that reaches to his knees. On the windowsill is an enormous hat, with ostrich plumes.

found him 'Lean, sallow coloured, his eyes a little yellowish, and belly a little jutting out or prominent. Not being able to abstain from company, much given to drinking and sitting up late.' Morgan rejected Sloane's treatment, instead turning to a black doctor who gave him injections of urine and plastered him all over with wet clay. He died soon afterwards.

But even with Morgan gone, his lawless, violent and self-destructive spirit lived on in Port Royal. John Taylor described the town as 'very loose . . . by reason of privateers and debauched wild blades which come hither'. The favourite activity of the buccaneers, still operating as official, and sometimes unlicensed, privateers (in spite of constant orders from London for the suppression of their 'mischief'), was to buy a pipe of wine or a barrel of beer, place it in the street, and force all the onlookers at pistol point to drink. A buccaneer might spend 2,000-3,000 pieces of eight in one wild Port Royal bacchanalia 'in Taverns and Stews [brothels] . . . by giving themselves to all manner of debauchery, with Strumpets and Wine'. Taylor warned that the town, 'fill'd with all manner of debauchery', was 'now more rude and antic than 'ere was Sodom' and might well share that city's fate.

Then came what seemed like Judgement Day. On 7 June 1692, the Rector of Port Royal, Emmanuel Heath, having been at church reading prayers 'to keep up some show of religion among a most ungodly and debauched people', was partaking of a glass of wormwood wine with the president of the council, John White, 'as a whet before dinner'. He was sitting smoking his pipe when the catastrophe started. 'I found the ground rolling and moving under my feet, upon which I said to him [the President] "Lord, Sir, what is that?" He replied, being a very grave man, "It is an earthquake; be not afraid, it will soon be over." But it increased, and we heard the church and tower fall, upon which we ran to save ourselves.'

Outside was a scene from the end of the world: 'I saw the earth open and swallow up a multitude of people', wrote Heath, 'and the sea mounting in upon them over the fortifications.' A Captain Crocket, another eyewitness, saw 'whole streets sinking under Water, with Men, Women and Children in them . . . such Crying, such Shrieking and Mourning I never heard . . . a whole Street Tumbling down . . . this Town is become a heap of Ruins'. According to a later report by the council, 'a great part of the inhabitants [were] miserably knocked on the head or drowned'. Within three minutes the earthquake had plunged half the town into the harbour. Two more shocks followed, each more violent than the last, until much of the town was underwater, with only the tops of houses and the masts of vessels sunk at the same time showing above the surface. One man, a Dr Trapham, survived by 'hanging by the hands upon the Rack of Chimney, and one of his Children hanging about his Neck', but his wife and the rest of his family perished. Others had miraculous escapes, 'swallowed up in one place, and by the rushing of Waters to and fro by reason of the agitation of the Earth at that time, were cast up again by another Chasm at places far distant'.

The rector found an open street and led a group of citizens in prayer for nearly an hour – 'the Earth working all the while with new motions, and tremblings, like the rowlings of the Sea . . . I could hardly keep myself on my knees' – before being rescued by boat.

The violent tremors had the effect of liquefying much of the sand on which the town was built. The horror for anyone alive caught in this soupy mix was that it solidified rapidly: 'some inhabitants were swallowed up to the Neck, and then the Earth shut upon them; and squeezed them to death', wrote the rector, Emmanuel Heath. 'And in that manner several are left buried with their heads above ground.' One so trapped was Colonel Peter Beckford; fortunately there was someone nearby to dig him out in time.

The next day saw the harbour choked with perhaps 1,000 bodies, bobbing up and down, causing an 'intolerable stench'. Included among the dead, noted Captain Crocket, were 'Mr Beckford's two daughters', Priscilla aged 17, and 14-year-old Elizabeth. Joining those killed by the earthquake and now floating in the harbour was a large number of corpses washed from their sandy graves on the nearby Pallisades.

Many saw the dreadful hand of God's punishment on the city, that 'the Lord spoke terrible things in righteousness . . . as a Fore-runner of the Terrible Day of the Lord'. The council reported the disaster as 'an instance of God Almighty's severe judgment' and vowed thereafter to better enforce laws relating to piety. Everyone could agree that the wicked city, and the most 'ungodly people on the Face of the Earth', had got what they deserved.

Crocket observed that in the immediate aftermath of the disaster, 'many of the old Reprobates are become New Converts; those that use to Mock at Sin, Now Weep bitterly for it'. But he also noted that in no time, some were 'at their old Trade of Drinking, Swearing and Whoreing; breaking up Ware-houses; pillaging and Stealing from their Neighbours'. Indeed, even before the tremors had ceased, men were at work robbing the dead, emptying their pockets or cutting off fingers to get at rings, while dogs gnawed at the heads sticking out of the ground.

The earthquake, which also 'threw down all the churches, dwelling houses and sugar works in the island', was followed by widespread looting, and unsurprisingly, considering the gruesome scene, severe attacks of disease, including malaria, attributed at the time to 'the hurtful Vapours belch'd from the many openings of the earth'. At least another 1,000 died in the aftermath from the general lawlessness and sickness. The large number rendered homeless attempted to build crude shelters on the mainland on the site of what is now Kingston, but 'lying wet, and wanting medicines . . . they died miserably in heaps'.

The wrecking of Port Royal destroyed forever the playground of the buccaneers, contributing to their final eclipse by the planter interest.* Most immediately, the destruction of the strongest defensive position on the island, as well as some 2,000 inhabitants, left the entire island in a chronically vulnerable condition. 'Our first Fears', wrote a Jamaican to London at the end of June, 'are concerning our Slaves, those Irreconcilable and yet Intestine Enemies of ours, who are no otherwise our Subjects than as the Whip makes them; who seeing our strongest Houses demolisht, our Arms broken . . . might be stirred up to rise in Rebellion against us.' Almost as bad was what now seemed like an inevitable 'forcible Invasion of the Barbarous French'. For by now, Britain and France were once again at war.

---

* A subsequent fire in 1704 completed the work of the earthquake, although the remaining tiny spit of land remained a Royal Navy base for many years.

15

THE PLANTER AT WAR:
CODRINGTON IN THE LEEWARD ISLANDS

'[These colonies'] whole past history ... presents only a succession of wars, usurp-
ations, crimes, misery, and vice ... all is one revolting scene of infamy, bloodshed,
and unmitigated woe, of insecure peace and open disturbance, of the abuse of power,
and of the reaction of misery against oppression.'

James Phillippo, a Baptist minister who worked in Jamaica, 1843

News of William of Orange's invasion of England and dethroning of James
II, the so-called 'Glorious Revolution', reached England's American colonies
in January 1689. The Jacobite Governor of the Leewards, Sir Nathaniel
Johnson, told the new King, William III, in May that he could not accept
the revolution. The uncertainty allowed the long-bubbling tensions on St
Kitts to explode into war and destruction. The following month, 130 armed
Irish servants rose up in the name of the deposed King James and sacked the
English plantations on the windward side of St Kitts, carrying their loot over
the border to the French parts of the island, where they were given sanctuary in the name of their shared Roman Catholic religion. Although disowned
by their governor, a number of French inhabitants joined in the 'burning and
ravaging'. Unwilling to provoke the numerically superior French into open
war, the English evacuated their women and children to nearby Nevis and,
some 450-strong, sheltered behind the walls of their redoubt, Fort Charles,
having sent a small boat to Barbados to plead for reinforcements.

But open war was not long in coming. To help check the ambitions of
Louis XIV, which included returning James II to the throne, England
joined the 'Grand Alliance', declaring war on France in May 1689.* On

---

* The War of the Grand Alliance (1688–97) is also known as the Nine Years War, and King William's
War. Across the Americas, France fought against England, Spain and the Dutch.

18 July, before news of the declaration had reached the English American colonists, an 18-ship French fleet was spotted heading for St Kitts. Soon a 3,000-strong, well-armed force was marching on Fort Charles. Shortly afterwards, Sir Nathaniel Johnson voluntarily resigned and boarded a vessel for South Carolina,* but not before nominating a new commander, Christopher Codrington, a man, he wrote to London from Antigua (now the seat of government of the English Leewards), 'of great estate here and in Barbados'.

The appointment, quickly confirmed by London, would last nine years and show Codrington at his very best, and his very worst. Then nearly 50, his extraordinary energy and skilful leadership would save the English Leewards and gain him a reputation as the most effective English military commander of the seventeenth century in the West Indies; his tactlessness and shameless greed would see him disgraced and his most progressive aims come to nothing.

Whatever his private opinions, Codrington radiated confidence, writing to London on 31 July that the defences of Fort Charles were 'so strongly built and backed by so vast a thickness of earth that there is no danger of a breach from their guns'. There was no way in for the French, he said, 'so good is the spirit of the garrison'. Straight away he moved to disarm the Irish in Antigua, some 300 of them, lest they repeat the depredations of their countrymen in St Kitts; and in Nevis and Montserrat, too, potential troublemakers were imprisoned or deported. Then Codrington, using mainly his own vessels, rushed with all the men he could muster to Nevis in an attempt to draw the French away from the besieged fort on St Kitts. At the same time he sent off pleading letters to London for help: 'We are not unprofitable appendages to the Crown', he wrote. 'We contribute as much and as heartily to enrich the royal coffers as any English subjects . . . these things entitle us to protection . . .'

The spirit of the English defenders of Fort Charles was, in fact, far from good. The men were in dire need of food, clothing and arms, and the soldiers had not been properly paid for six years, while the planters were distracted by internal treachery and dissension. After holding out for three weeks, they surrendered on 5 August.

The survivors were allowed to leave for Nevis, which was now becoming crowded, hungry and fractious with so many extra mouths to feed. Soon an epidemic broke out – likely to have been smallpox – which killed 500 whites and 200 enslaved Africans. The English in the Leewards started to

* Johnson took 100 slaves with him and became a wealthy planter, serving as governor of South Carolina for six years from 1703.

panic. Attempted raids on Antigua by Caribs added to the sense of crisis. There was still no sign of an English fleet, even though Codrington assured everyone that it was expected daily, to 'turn our mourning into joy'.

Faced by a desperate situation, Codrington opted for bluff, carrying out a series of raids against the smaller French islands, largely financed out of his own pocket, while waiting for a force to arrive from England. St Martin, St Barts and Marie Galante were attacked, and Barbuda successfully defended after another joint attempt at takeover by its Irish inhabitants and a French force. To Codrington's fury, Barbados – comparatively safe in its windward, isolated location – was proving very slow in providing help; but he knew enough about the self-interest of planters to surmise that many on the populous island would welcome the ruin of the Leewards and the consequent hike in the value of their own sugar crop.

When at last a troop of soldiers came from Barbados, Codrington was compelled to use them to keep order in Nevis, whose people, he complained, were 'most turbulent and ungovernable', although he seems to have talked the Irish contingent into professing loyalty.* Codrington was also losing patience with London. 'We are greatly discouraged by the long neglect of us at home', he complained, 'it being seven months since one of these Islands was lost.' 'Had we a fleet to make us masters of the sea', he went on, 'two thousand soldiers from England would amply suffice to make us so on land in all the French Islands.'

At last on Saturday 31 May 1690, the long-awaited fleet, with 13 warships as well as transports, dropped anchor at Antigua with military stores and a British regiment on board. Without delay Codrington prepared to take the offensive on a large scale, determined to drive the French out of the Caribbean for ever. Only the wretched state of the stores and personnel dampened his enthusiasm. 'I have inspected the muskets and think them as bad as ever came to these parts', he commented. He also preferred local, seasoned men, 'fittest for marching and accustomed to rugged paths', to the sickly soldiers from England, and used all of his charisma and energy to raise a force from Antigua, Nevis and Montserrat that soon numbered 2,300. Willoughby Byam, son of William, the former governor of Surinam and then Antigua, commanded 200 men from Antigua to be Codrington's personal guard.

On 19 June, the fleet set out for the recapture of St Kitts. They anchored

---

* Like most Englishman of his time, Codrington hated and despised the Irish, but would admit, in a letter to the Governor of Montserrat, that 'the Irish have never had any great kindness from the English ... witness Ireland itself ... they have a grievance against you, and doubtless hope for revenge'.

in Frigate Bay. The French were ready, with more than 1,000 men in well-prepared trenches, but Codrington deployed his ships as a decoy while sending a force of 500 or so of his best men, 'mostly natives', to land at between two and three in the morning at an unguarded part of the coast below 'an almost inaccessible hill'.

There was, however, a path, according to one of the soldiers on the spot, 'frequented by none but wild Goats', and the men clambered forward in the darkness, 'forced to use our Hands as well as our Feet in climbing up', 'pulling themselves forward by the bushes'. At the top they were met with a 'Volly of about seven or eight Shot, from some Scouts there placed, (who immediately upon their firing retreated) which wounded our two brisk Commanders [including Byam, who was hit in the neck], one of which died of his Wounds soon after'. But the approach allowed the attackers to charge the French trenches from the rear, and as the defenders retreated, Codrington landed 600 men to attack from the front. After two hours' fighting, the French were in full retreat as the English marched in a pincer movement on the French capital of Basseterre. A mile outside the town, there was another engagement, but soon the French 'made all the heels they could', some into the mountains, others to a fort in what had been the English part of the island. Having first ordered that all 'Liquors' be 'secured in a convenient storehouse', Codrington released his men to plunder the French town, while artillery was landed to reduce the fort into which the enemy had retreated.

The fort was overlooked by high ground known as Brimstone Hill. On 4 July, Codrington reported to London that morale in his force was excellent and that he had managed to drag two guns of 2,400 lb up Brimstone Hill, and was now pouring fire into the fort, 'riddling the houses like sieves', while his fleet pounded the French from the sea, and sappers dug trenches to within pistol shot of the fort. 'I have fully resolved', he went on, 'to find a grave in this Island or make it an entirely English Colony, which will be some reparation for lives lost and families ruined in the several wars.'

On 14 July, the French surrendered. 'The King and Queen's healths were drank', wrote an eye-witness, 'and the great guns three times fired, three vollies being also made by the whole army.' Codrington, in reporting the victory, urged London to press on with driving the French out of the West Indies, and started preparations for an attack on Martinique or Guadeloupe. He also warned against returning the formerly French part of St Kitts to its previous inhabitants. 'No Englishmen will ever settle there again', he wrote, 'having been twice ruined by the French neighbours within twenty-two years' and settlement on nearby Nevis would also be deterred. He also pointed out that he had 'disbursed large sums for the public service and am ready still to do so cheerfully, not doubting of repayment from the King'.

Codrington's actions after the victory at St Kitts in part recall the best of his period of governorship of Barbados 20 years earlier. He was careful to control his troops, who were at one point set on pillaging everything, including the property of the dispossessed English settlers. Although many in the other islands would happily have seen St Kitts laid waste to raise the price of their own sugar, Codrington set about resettling the entire island. He urged the creation of a stable fiscal structure to pay for government, and the establishment of schools, churches and hospitals; furthermore, he reserved 15,000 acres for small farmers with 10 acres apiece so as to guarantee an adequate white militia and 'middle class'. Invitations were sent to New York and New England for settlers to come.

But there was another side to the story. Like so many victorious armies, the English quickly fell out over the division of the spoils, with Codrington himself earning the greatest criticism. Certainly, he was careful to lay out for himself a lavish St Kitts plantation of nearly 800 acres, manned by slaves taken from the French, as his 'share' of the plunder. For some, this was just reward for his vigorous and effective leadership during the campaign. But as Codrington pressed the islands to provide forces and provisions for his planned, and strategically sound, campaign to drive the French for ever from the Leewards, he encountered increasing resistance – no planter wanted the production of the French islands to swamp the English sugar market – and growing criticism of his own behaviour. As early as August 1690, he was referring in letters to 'mutinous practices' and 'lies' being told about him on Nevis. He had been too kind to the French, it was alleged, and had defrauded the army for his own profit.

Codrington's response was to write to London that he was being unjustly slandered. Rather than personally profiting, he said, the campaign had led to the neglect of his own interests, and great expense from his own pocket. He had found it impossible to please everyone, and his best efforts had been 'repaid only by murmuring and discontent'.

In spite of his fading popularity, Codrington did manage to raise a substantial force to attack the French in the spring of 1691. On 21 April, with Codrington himself in the vanguard, the English descended on Guadeloupe, supported by a naval force under Commodore Lawrence Wright. Carrying all before them, the English soon had the remnants of the French forces holed up in the island's principal fort. Codrington called for reinforcements from Barbados to complete the conquest, but while waiting for their arrival, news came that a French fleet had appeared nearby. At this point the naval commander Wright took fright and withdrew his supporting fleet. Codrington was incensed, but had no option than to abandon the conquest of the island. Part of the failure was caused by the perennial problem of combined operations, that of mixed command of naval and land forces, but also to blame was the frank cowardice of Wright, for which he was arrested on his return to England.

After the Guadeloupe debacle, the trickle of complaints against Codrington became a flood. Before the start of the war, Codrington was already the richest and most influential planter in the Leewards. Clearly this wealth and power, rather than satisfying him, instead increased his greed and his feeling that he was above the law of which he himself was now supposed to be the guardian. Even his right-hand man in the conquest of St Kitts now turned against him. In July 1691, Sir Timothy Thornhill, who had commanded the Barbados contingent of the army on St Kitts (and fought with great bravery), made a series of detailed charges against his commander-in-chief. 'At the taking of St Christophers', wrote Thornhill, Codrington had seized all stocks of sugar and promptly dispatched them for sale at the Dutch islands of St Thomas and Curaçao. Thornhill reminded him of the rules of the Navigation Acts and was told to 'mind his own business'. The army was charged by Codrington for clothing that he then sold privately in Antigua. He also employed an agent (who subsequently denounced him) to round up runaway slaves, brand them with his mark, and secretly ship them, as well as further plunder, to his Antigua plantations. Even more shameless was the fact that all this was carried on in sloops for whose use in the national interest Codrington promptly charged the English government nearly £5,000. Anyone on the islands who stood up to him faced arbitrary arrest and imprisonment. Now, wrote Thornhill, the soldiers of the Barbados regiment 'would die sooner than serve under his command'. The failure at Guadeloupe, Thornhill alleged, was not just Wright's fault; Codrington had 'run off in distraction at midnight, leaving his mortar, shells and wounded men behind him' and his 'grasping and avaricious disposition [had] alienated officers and men'.

Thornhill had his own agenda, of course. He wanted the post of governor for himself. And few of the most powerful Englishmen in the West Indies did not indulge in illegal trade. Thornhill accused Codrington also of 'unseasonable devotion to the French ladies'. Certainly this licentiousness had become a great weakness of the Lieutenant-Governor, but, again, few restrained themselves who had the power to satisfy their appetites at will.

Nonetheless, even disinterested English leaders in the Caribbean were now predicting that Codrington would have to go, 'in consequence of the heavy complaint against him'. The 25-year-old conscientious idealist had, at 51, become utterly corrupted, crooked and tyrannical. But somehow he held on, bribing and bullying his way round his accusers (even, ironically, prosecuting people for violating the Navigation Acts), while writing self-congratulatory epistles to London.

All the time, anxiety in the islands about the French threat was increasing. As Codrington himself wrote: 'All turns on mastery of the sea.' In January 1692, alarming reports were received in Antigua that a powerful French fleet had arrived at Martinique. In the same month an English fleet turned up at Barbados, and there was a brief skirmish between the two forces. Both then were forced to retreat from the Caribbean theatre, as was the pattern, when disease decimated their crews, who, fresh from Europe, had no immunity to yellow fever.

For the rest of the year it was a stalemate, with the opposing naval forces effectively cancelling each other out. But in early 1693, what looked like a decisively superior English force of 13 men-of-war, three fire ships and 28 transports, capable of carrying 2,000 troops, dropped anchor at Barbados. In command was Sir Francis Wheeler. Using 1,500 English regulars and as many local men as could be raised, the orders were to conquer Martinique, Guadeloupe and the French settlements in Hispaniola – thereby wiping out the French in the Caribbean – before proceeding to New England to drive the enemy from Canada. With the fleet was a returner to the land of his birth for almost certainly the first time since leaving as a 12-year-old: Codrington's son and heir, who would become the most famous of all the Codringtons, Christopher the third.

Christopher Codrington the third was later described by Edmund Burke as 'far the richest production and most shining ornament [Barbados] ever had'. An intelligent child, particularly in contrast to his unfortunate 'idiot' younger brother, he would from the moment he could speak have had the family's slaves do his every bidding. 'Children, in these West India Islands are, from their infancy, waited upon by Numbers of Slaves, who . . . are obliged to pay them unlimited Obedience', reported a later writer on Barbados. Their 'favourite Passions', he went on, were 'nourished with such indulgent Care'.

There are hints, too, that he was indulged by his schoolmasters once he left Barbados to attend Dr Weadle's private school at Enfield. (He was probably looked after in the holidays by the Gloucestershire Codringtons.)

Nevertheless, he clearly had great academic ability, and finishing school, excelled himself at Christ Church, Oxford, at the time famous for its brilliant and exclusive circle of wits, into whose company Codrington was welcomed. At the university he studied the classics, philosophy, early Church history and contemporary European literature, while at the same time becoming an accomplished horseman and dancer and fluent in French, Spanish and Italian.

He was not only very rich and handsome, but also extremely clever, and he knew it. 'No spark had walk'd up High Street bolder', wrote a contemporary. According to an otherwise admiring biographer, 'So early and so continued a pre-eminence bred in him a certain arrogance and contempt for men less gifted than himself . . . subsequently this defect of his was the cause of much suffering and humiliation.'

While still at Oxford he was in July 1687 admitted a member of the Middle Temple, where he befriended the most eminent lawyers of the day, and acquired what would be very valuable legal knowledge. In 1690 he was elected to All Souls, Oxford, the elite of the elite in English academia, where he established friendships with such luminaries of the age as Joseph Addison and Charles Boyle. He also started collecting books in large numbers, and moving in circles that included the philosopher John Locke. The rough-and-ready life of his father in the West Indies must have seemed a long way away.

But in late 1692, he heard of a new expedition preparing for battle against the French in the Caribbean, and persuaded the college authorities to hold open his fellowship while he returned to the land of his birth. When in early January 1693 Sir Francis Wheeler's powerful fleet started out from England, the younger Codrington was on board, attached to one of the two regiments.

Some seven weeks later, Wheeler's force weighed anchor in Carlisle Bay, where they were met by a well-armed and well-equipped Barbados troop of nearly 1,000 men, as well as numerous ships, and word was sent to Governor Codrington in the Leewards to prepare to join the campaign. Codrington had been busy, pressing men into service and repairing forts, and had 1,300 troops ready to rendezvous with Wheeler's force at Martinique. The armada from Barbados arrived first, now some 45 sail, a frightening prospect for the French defenders watching from Fort Royal (present-day Fort de France). But rather than attack the well-defended capital, Wheeler sailed to the south of the island, where he put ashore a party of three to reconnoitre: the commander of the English regulars, Colonel Foulke, another local officer, and the younger Codrington. They came under fire, with Foulke being wounded, but they found a convenient landing place, and the next day, 12 April, almost unopposed, 2,500 men were landed and started marching northwards, to take the enemy's strong forts from their weaker landward side. Along the way, churches and other buildings were burned, plunder, including slaves, collected, and crops destroyed.

Eight days later, the army of Codrington senior arrived, landed, and joined in the marauding. (It must have been at this point, on the battlefield or on a man-of-war off the coast, that the two Codringtons met for the first time in 11 years.) But the key defences of Fort Royal and St Pierre proved much harder nuts to crack. A fierce French counter-attack by cavalry stopped a landing near the latter, and with losses and exhaustion among the men mounting – from the scorching sun, the harsh terrain and fever – and the Irish contingent of the force growing restless, the invasion was abandoned on 29 April, in favour of an assault on weaker Guadeloupe. But before this was undertaken, the English, with nearly 1,000 men killed, wounded or incapacitated by sickness, lost heart, and split up to return to Barbados or the Leewards. Most of the army ended up at St Kitts, where it was soon impossible to find accommodation for the sick, who now numbered something like half the army's original number.

At the end of May, the remnants of Wheeler's force sailed north, reaching Boston two weeks later. (It would leave in September, its numbers further thinned, having achieved precisely nothing.) In the meantime, Codrington took his son on an extensive tour of his domain, visiting Antigua, Nevis and St Kitts, inspecting fortifications, meeting people, getting a feel for the place. What made the greatest impression on the younger Christopher, however, was the treatment of the enslaved Africans, half starved and brutalised. 'I have always thought it very barbarous that so little care should be taken of the bodies and so much less of the souls of our slaves', he wrote before his return to the West Indies seven years later. Back in England, this caused him, he said, 'many a mortifying reflection'. He determined, should he have the opportunity, to do something about the unhappy situation.

His father also seems to have apprised his son of the identities of his growing number of bitter enemies, and also inducted him into his own freewheeling sexual behaviour. It was during this visit that the 24-year-old Codrington the Younger met the mother of his illegitimate son, William. All that is known of her is from the two men's wills: Codrington senior in his will of 1698 called her Maudlin Marianus, and bequeathed her her freedom – indicating that she was a black slave – and her son 'his freedom & £500 at 21, he to be sent to school in England & to have £50 a year'.

Christopher the Younger in his will of 1703 called her Maudline Morange, and repeated the bequest of £500 for William, but stipulated 'he is to be brought up for the sea'. In fact, William, having started in Antigua, ended up a plantation- and slave-owner in Jamaica.

Whatever the attractions of his relationship with Maudline Morange or of his father's lifestyle, and in spite of his obvious admiration for him, Codrington the Younger did not linger in the West Indies with his father. Instead, he returned to Oxford, taking his Master of Arts in January 1694. Clearly he had acquired a taste for the martial, for that spring he joined King William's army in Flanders as a captain. There he gained what would prove useful experience in siege warfare. A year later, having distinguished himself during the siege of Namur, he was promoted to lieutenant-colonel, commanding the second battalion of the First Foot Guards – a brilliant achievement for a man of 27 – and caught the eye of King William. Codrington's friend Addison wrote a poem about the heroic episode, deducing that it was the 'fierce sun' of the land of his birth that had created 'This heart ablaze, this spirit's surging foam'.

For the next four years, Codrington the Younger divided his time between campaigning in Europe and studying at Oxford, where his star continued to rise. At the same time, he became a London society wit, writing verses for the theatre and enjoying in coffee shops and clubs the company of the likes of Richard Steele and John Dryden. When the war ended, he visited Paris with the rest of London's most fashionable young men.

In the West Indies, in contrast, his father was struggling. After 1693, the English government, inefficient, corrupt and nearing bankruptcy, could ill support sending fleets and armies to the West Indies. In the six months after the departure of Wheeler's fleet, the French captured no fewer than 30 vessels bound for the Leewards. Its regiment of regulars, without pay and almost starving, were soon on the verge of mutiny. Codrington toured the islands, urging the repair of forts and trying to restore morale, but nerves remained stretched. (Codrington's own pay stopped arriving the following year.)

In December 1695, Codrington wrote to London from Antigua that his islands had enjoyed a bumper sugar crop, but had not the ships to carry it home securely. He also repeated his requests for settlers from the northern colonies for St Kitts, but it appears that few were forthcoming. At last, in 1696, pay and clothing arrived for the soldiers, and a fleet was sent out under the command of Rear Admiral John Nevill. There were grand plans for him to join with Spanish naval forces, but such was the local mistrust between the two countries – in theory allied against France – that this came to nothing. The French in the meantime, who had been fighting the Spanish in Hispaniola, had attacked and looted Cartagena. Nevill attempted to intercept the French fleet as it returned home laden with plunder, but only succeeded in capturing the enemy's hospital ship, from which his men promptly caught yellow fever.

At last, more through mutual exhaustion and bankruptcy than because anything had been resolved, peace was made between France and England at the Treaty of Ryswick in September 1697, thus ending the War of the Grand Alliance. For many Leeward Islanders, the coming of peace removed any qualms they might have had about criticising the Governor, and the following year a torrent of allegations about Codrington reached London. His plantation in St Kitts had been illegally seized, complained its former owner. Codrington had promoted the worst sort on the island – Jacobites, Papists and Irish. He had traded illegally with the French and Dutch, even during the war, and this had continued since, it was said. In fact, the failures at Guadeloupe and Martinique were Codrington's fault, as he 'minded nothing but plunder'. He had also, it was alleged, taken for himself or his cronies estates of those who had died intestate or with complicated wills; on one occasion he 'threatened to break ye head of any one that should offer to prove ye will'. Those who opposed him found themselves arbitrarily arrested and imprisoned; letters of complaint were intercepted and opened. The story of Consetts reared its head again: 'In Barbadoes', an anonymous letter that reached London accused, 'he raised himself above ye Levells of ordinary planters by most wicked practice well known to every Barbadoes Gentleman.' 'Extremly Coveteous and wicked', 'He is hated beyond Imagination', the letter continued. 'From a Governour, planter, trader without breeding, word, honour, and religion, good Lord deliver us.'

Governor Codrington had clearly provoked violent passions. During his term, two lieutenant-governors were murdered, one in Nevis and one in St Kitts. Both the killings seem to have been provoked by trouble arising out of the allegation that Codrington had been trying to get hold of someone else's estate. According to the largely admiring Codrington family historian, by the end of his life, 'the exercise of almost unlimited authority over a turbulent community turned his head'.

Codrington did get his friends to write to London in his defence: 'we are not sensible of any mismanagement or irregularities', they said, pleading ignorance, but such was the weight of complaints that the Board of Trade in London, usually careful to take into account the fractious and feud-riven nature of the islands, was moved to publicly chastise Codrington.

Just before what seemed like his inevitable recall and disgrace, Codrington died, aged 58, on 30 July 1698.

Codrington's greatest regret at the terms of the Treaty of Ryswick had been the return of the formerly French parts of St Kitts. This inevitably caused friction and ongoing arguments, and it left the English on the island vulnerable to yet another destructive attack (the French were also ceded by Spain the western part of Hispaniola, which they quickly converted into the world's most productive sugar factory). So within only a couple of years, war threatened again. This time, the 'dapper', scholarly Christopher Codrington the Younger would be in charge.

16

THE FRENCH INVASION OF JAMAICA

'War: first, one hopes to win; then one expects the enemy to lose; then, one is satis-
fied that he too is suffering; in the end, one is surprised that everyone has lost.'

Karl Krauss

Fortunately for Jamaica, in the immediate aftermath of the catastrophic earthquake of June 1692, the French were distracted by their struggle against the Spanish on Hispaniola. Nonetheless, a small French force had to be expelled from the north coast later in the year. The arrival of Wheeler's fleet in the theatre in early 1693 deterred any major attack on Jamaica, but with his departure, raids became more frequent. In October 1693, the Governor, Sir William Beeston, reported that 'the enemy daily infests our coasts'. Many abandoned their plantations on the north coast, as raids by French privateers from nearby Hispaniola increased relentlessly in size and frequency. English settlers were carried away, sometimes to be ransomed, often tortured, and always robbed of all they had. Governor Beeston even took the extraordinary step of sending a protest to the French governor in Hispaniola in a ship under a flag of truce, but his envoys were imprisoned and their vessel seized.

The French-controlled part of Hispaniola was under the command of Captain Jean-Baptiste Du Casse, a notorious former privateer. According to Beeston, he had spies everywhere in Jamaica, particularly among its Irish inhabitants, and they now reported to Du Casse that the 'island was easily taken; the fortifications at Port Royal were out of order and few men there, so that two hundred men would take that place, and two hundred more would march in any part of the country the people were so thin and so little used to arms'. Then, on the evening of 31 May 1694, Beeston was sitting in his house with a small group of friends when they were disturbed by the entrance of an Englishman, 'in a very mean habit, and with a meagre weather-beaten countenance'. The man identified himself as a Captain Stephen Elliot. Some months before, he had been taken prisoner by a French privateer and had been held in prison at Petit Goave on the west coast of Hispaniola. But he had escaped from captivity, and with two companions in a small canoe had succeeded in crossing the 300-mile stretch of water between Hispaniola and Jamaica. He now carried an urgent warning: the French had assembled a force of 20 ships and more than 3,000 men, mostly buccaneers; an attack on Jamaica was imminent.

Beeston immediately declared martial law and quickly weighed up his tactical options. Although he had command of some 4,000 men in seven militia regiments, they were currently strung out over more than 100 miles of coast and thus would be unable to stop a determined landing force. He had faith, however, in the defences of Fort Charles. During the chaotic governorship of the second Duke of Albemarle, Colonel Peter Beckford had lost his position as commander of the fort. Along with other ousted and disgruntled planters, Beckford had withdrawn to England, but after the Duke's death, he had returned and resumed his position. According to his friend Beeston, Beckford had got the fort 'into excellent order'. Using pressed labour, he had rebuilt the bastion, laid a gun platform, and mounted powerful cannon. He now prepared a fire ship to defend the harbour, and built barricades to protect the fort from the landward side.

Beeston decided that the only way to save Jamaica was to concentrate his forces. He thus ordered the abandonment of the eastern part of the island, where, given the prevailing wind, the landing was likely to take place. A system of beacons was established to warn of an approaching fleet, and Beeston announced that any slave who killed a Frenchman would earn his freedom. Free inhabitants, provisions and slaves were now withdrawn into the area around Spanish Town, Kingston and Port Royal.

On Sunday morning, 17 June, lookouts reported the French fleet 'coming into sight with a fresh gale'. They landed unopposed in the easternmost parish of the island, and marched inland, plundering, burning and destroying all in their path. Cattle and sheep were killed, crops burnt, fruit trees hacked down. 'Some of the straggling people that were left behind they tortured', Beeston later reported, 'particularly Charles Barber; and James Newcastle they murdered in cold blood after a day's quarter: Some women they suffered the negroes to violate, and dug some out of their graves.' After a month or so, the French re-embarked and cruised west-wards, before landing at Carlisle Bay, about 35 miles west of Port Royal, with a view to attacking Spanish Town from the south. The English forces were quickly on the defensive. Reinforcements were sent from the Port Royal area, and after a forced march of 36 miles, they arrived just in time to hold a number of fortified estate houses. The buccaneers among the French force, happier looting than taking casualties, withdrew, and on 3 August 1764, the French re-embarked and sailed back to Hispaniola. Slaves, pressed into service, fought for the English, and at least 14 were subsequently freed for their bravery.

The French had caused immense damage, destroying more than 50 sugar works, and carrying off nearly 2,000 slaves.* In the process, however, they had lost something like half their number to sickness. Learning nothing from this experience, or, indeed from that of previous military adventures in the islands, within a year the English were preparing a revenge attack. Led by an 1,800-strong force from home, the English linked up with the Spanish to attack the French in Hispaniola. In charge of a corps of volunteers from Jamaica – and paying for them out of his own pocket – was Peter Beckford, now a colonel in the Jamaica militia. The French were heavily outnumbered, and soon several of their towns had fallen. But as Colonel Beckford reported, 'here I reckon that our misfortunes began'. Naval personnel had been the first into a captured town, and had laid their hands on everything worth taking. 'As soon as the land forces came in', wrote Beckford, 'they were for taking all from the seamen and threatening to shoot all of them that carried off anything.' A full-scale battle was narrowly avoided, but soon the Spanish fell out with their English allies, and on all sides disease began to take a heavy toll. Once again, the English naval and army commanders squabbled with each other, no decisive victory was obtained, and the port of Petit Goave, whence all the troublesome privateers had emanated, was left undisturbed. By the time the English left the island, they had achieved nothing and had lost more than half their number to sickness. Colonel Beckford himself was ill as well, though he recovered within a few months.

The sorry coda to the war in this part of the West Indies involved another English attack on Hispaniola in mid-1697, the year that peace was made at the Treaty of Ryswick. This time a squadron under Rear Admiral George Mees succeeded in surprising the defences of Petit Goave, and by 8 July the town was in English hands. But at that point the men of the landing party found a large quantity of liquor in a dockside warehouse. Within a short time, they were out of control, and were in no fit state to repel a French counter-attack led by Du Casse. After heavy losses, they set fire to the town and re-embarked.

*   *   *

---

* This was the moment that Ned Ward visited Jamaica – when it was at its most wretched.

For Jamaica, the fighting during the 1690s would have a side effect more devastating than any of the burning and looting of the French. When Du Casse's men gave up their attempt to conquer the island, they left behind a deadly virus. Until this time Jamaica had been relatively free of yellow fever. Now it struck the island with such ferocity that the white population came close to demographic collapse.

Even before the French invasion, early mortality was common in Jamaica. In 1691 the Governor wrote to London that 'people die here very fast and suddenly, I know not how soon it may be my turn'. In the same year, Peter Beckford's wife Bridget died, presumably of disease (he remarried the following year to Anne Ballard, from another wealthy planter family). The aftermath of the invasion, however, saw the death rate at its worst in Jamaican history. In Kingston, a quarter of the population perished, and it has been estimated that as many as 200 per thousand of the town's population died every year during the first decades of the eighteenth century. (Comparable rates for England and New England respectively were 25 to 30 and 15 to 20 per thousand.) While on active service in Hispaniola, Colonel Peter Beckford received a letter from his friend Governor Beeston: 'Mrs Beckford has been ill but is recovered, and pretty well again and longs to see you.' But soon she was ill again, and died in 1696. Thus Colonel Beckford had lost two wives and two daughters in the space of only five years. Beeston himself wrote to London that he had lost his entire family save his wife and one child, and of his servants, only his cook survived. By 1699, there had been no let-up in the epidemics: 'the sickness is still there after nine to ten years', wrote Beeston, 'and the Country is soe reduced that it is difficult to fill posts. There are so many dead that it is hard to bury them.' Beeston pleaded to be allowed home, 'finding a great decay in his health', a request eventually granted in January 1702. His replacement wrote on 30 March that year that the island was still 'at present sickly.' To blame was 'that mortal distemper called the bleeding fever' – yellow fever. The new governor was unable to finish the letter and was himself dead six days later.

Indeed, the biggest killers were malaria and yellow fever, both carried by mosquitoes that now thrived as never before. Forest clearances to grow sugar had reduced the bird population that ate the insects; discarded clay pots needed for the sugar industry provided an ideal breeding ground for the yellow-fever-carrying mosquito *Aëdes aegypti*, which, with its sweet tooth, gorged itself on sugar. Both Port Royal and Kingston had nearby swamps, which provided breeding grounds for the *Anopheles*, malaria-carrying mosquito.

As in Barbados a generation earlier, the yellow fever virus thrived because it found in Jamaica a European population with no immunity. This was exacerbated by the arrival during the war – in the form of soldiers and sailors – of large numbers of fresh un-immune victims.* A report to London in 1702 confirmed that 'the mortality reigns chiefly over the new-comers'. In addition, the white population was hemmed in by the effective maroon control of the island's hinterland. Thus some 3,000 whites died during the epidemic, reducing Jamaica's white population to 7,000 by 1700, where it remained for the next decade, further worsening the proportion of whites to black slaves, whose population continued to grow sharply, reaching 42,000 by 1700. In fact, it was only the arrival of so many Africans, most of whom had some immunity to yellow fever, that eventually checked the disease. The only consolation for Jamaicans was that in 1701–2, their enemies in the nearby islands were suffering just as much, as war with France loomed again.

---

* The worst periods for disease would always coincide with military expeditions from Europe, for example 1693, 1703–4, 1732 and 1745.

17

CODRINGTON THE YOUNGER
IN THE WEST INDIES

'A British Muse disdains
Lo! Torture racks, whips, famine, gibbets, chains,
Rise on my mind, appall my tear-stain'd eye,
Attract my rage, and draw a soul-felt sigh:
I blush, I shudder at the bloody theme.'

Anon, 'Jamaica: A Poem in Three Parts'

Amongst the many accusations levelled against Christopher Codrington senior had been that he was uneducated and inexperienced as a military commander. Neither of these could be said of his son Christopher the Younger, appointed as Lieutenant-General of the Leeward Islands in February 1699, in recognition of his service in Flanders during the war. On paper he was an ideal man to govern this part of the empire: at 31, old enough to be able to manage his appetites, but young enough to be uncynical and energetic; of independent means, so not under the power of any assembly for his income; knowledgeable about the West Indies and born there, but not corrupted by long residence in the tropics; highly educated, trained in the law and multilingual, but also a battle-proven soldier.

Codrington also had ambitions to reform what had shocked him so much on his brief visit to the islands seven years earlier – the brutal treatment of the black slaves. (Like all other seventeenth-century Englishmen, the idea that slavery itself was wrong did not occur to him). He aimed, he wrote while still in England, 'to endeavour to get a law restraining inhuman severities and punishing the wilful killing of Indians and Negroes with death'. But at the same time, he knew enough about the West Indies to be realistic about what would actually be possible, that he would 'certainly be opposed by all the planters,' if he tried to pass a law protecting the slaves' 'limbs and lives'. Nonetheless, he wrote, 'I will certainly recommend something of the kind', and failing that, at least make sure his own slaves were properly fed. He was also determined to promote the baptising of the slaves, but again was realistic enough to point out that the necessary education was not achievable with the islands' 'few and ill-qualified clergymen', but would require a large influx of clergy from England 'under vows of poverty and obedience'. Although he knew that this, too, would be fiercely opposed by the planters, he wrote: 'Nothing will hinder me from promoting boldly and impartially a design so pleasing to God and truly beneficial to my fellow-creatures.'

The issue of slavery aside, it is easy with hindsight to detect from the beginning weaknesses that would be his undoing. Codrington flatly refused to travel out to take up his new position until the Treasury paid up the wages owed to his father. He was well within his rights, of course, but this does betray a certain hauteur and sense of entitlement; more practically, he wrote to the Lords of Plantations in February 1700 that he had suffered 'a long fit of sickness' (he had been seriously ill since the previous November). As we have seen, survival in the West Indies required almost supernatural physical hardiness. If Codrington was poorly in England, it did not bode well for his sojourn in the deadly tropics.

For a year and a half Codrington wrangled with the Treasury, and in the meantime he continued to mix with the wits of Drury Lane, writing verses for the theatre and engaging in entertaining literary feuds. Having inherited his father's fortune, he also took the opportunity to purchase Dodington Hall in Gloucestershire from Samuel Codrington, a distant cousin, thereby acquiring amongst his London circle the nickname 'the dapper squire'.

At last he set sail for the West Indies, leaving Gravesend on 17 August 1700. His hopes were to put the family plantations in order, bring good government to the islands, win glory against the French, and then return as quickly as possible to England to divide his time between his glittering London circle and his new estate at Dodington.

He arrived at the Leewards in September 1700 to be met by a scene of confusion. Everyone, it seemed, was engaged in illegal trade in defiance of the Navigation Acts. The French, re-established on St Kitts, were a constant source of worry and threat. Everywhere there was demoralisation and corruption.

Continual war, or threat of war, had meant that there was little point in building smart houses like those now seen in Barbados. In 1650 the churches in St Kitts had been 'very fair . . . well furnish'd within with Pulpits, and Seats, or excellent Joyners work, of precious wood'. But the colonists had tired of rebuilding them after every war and so by Codrington the Younger's time, they were primitive and cheap, valued at only £250. Even the richest man in St Kitts lived in a house only 90 by 16 feet, with four rooms. Many smaller farmers lived in flimsy huts built of little more than cane trash. There were few luxuries and almost no books. It was a long way from All Souls, Oxford.

Codrington established his headquarters at Antigua and then toured the islands, everywhere receiving flattering, what he called 'too fulsome', addresses. At once, he set about reforming the chaotic judicial system. At Nevis, for example, it was said he had 'dispatcht more business and done more justice in three weeks than had been done in thirty years before'. According to a contemporary, justice on the islands was characterised by 'universal corruption'; 'if a man goes over never so honest to the Plantations, yet the very air does change him in a short time'. As well as corrupt, the system was inefficient: each tiny island had its own peculiar mode of procedure, and there was a chronic shortage of competent personnel. Codrington made standardising the islands' laws one of his first priorities.

He also quickly noticed the great weakness caused by the disappearance of poor whites from the islands, and introduced measures to distribute land in parcels of 10 acres 'for the Encouragement of poor settlers'. This included a tax on the great swathes of land that had been bought up through 'the Avarice of some Men' and left undeveloped. (Ironically this included his own inheritance: his father had purchased more than 500 acres in St Mary, Antigua and done nothing with it.) 'I have refused all presents, public and private', Codrington wrote to London, 'I have defended the poor against ye rich, and done justice to servants against their masters.'*

Codrington also attempted to take on the endemic illegal trading, in reality an impossible task, and one that only won him enemies. As Codrington pointed out to his superiors, in nine out of ten cases local officials, poorly paid if paid at all, supplemented their income by 'winking' at clandestine trade. To be an honest governor, he calculated, was costing him £1,500 a year. Indeed, soon the first signs of discouragement become evident. 'I'm sure if your Lordships knew all the folly and Knavery I have to struggle with, you would pity me', he reported back to his superiors in May 1701. 'There is so much Ignorance, laziness and Corruption.'† Soldiers that he had settled with land in Antigua quickly proved

---

* That said, he did find a lucrative job for his cousin William, his uncle John's son, then aged 21, according to his uncle 'a young gentleman of great virtue and efforts'.

† Codrington would later write of the people of St Kitts that 'They are a parcell of Banditts, and wd willingly be without government, religion, or any appearance of order.'

to be 'idle and vagrant fellows'. Efforts at persuading the islands to cooperate with each other on defence or justice were getting nowhere. And
to his great fury, a serious accusation from an old enemy of his father
about his behaviour – that he had improperly interfered in a criminal
trial for his own gain – had been put before the Council of Trade back
home. (This charge, of which, after much delay, Codrington would be
entirely cleared, baffled George Larkin, a commissioner for the Board
of Trade visiting the West Indies, who wrote that Codrington was 'the
only Governor that I have met withall since my coming into America
that can be called a Good Governor'.)

There was an element in Codrington that we would probably now call
manic depression. Just as he had two contrasting sides to his character –
the reflective man of learning and the man of action – so he seemed to
have veered between energetic enthusiasm and despondent lethargy. In
many ways his father had been the same. A later perceptive witness of the
West Indian 'planter type' would notice this trait as a characteristic of the
typical sugar baron: 'his spirits will sometimes lead him to the highest
flights of extravagance, yet will reflection often sink him to the lowest
despair. His disposition is, in some instances, not unlike that of a Frenchman,
who is as easily elevated, as soon depressed.'

Furthermore, the task to which, Codrington had written, he was 'most
inclined', the improvement of justice for the slaves, also seems to have run
into trouble. On 27 December 1701 occurred the lurid murder of a planter,
a Major Martin, who owned 500 acres and 114 slaves, and, like the Byams,
had come to Antigua from Surinam in 1667. At about eight o'clock in the
morning, some 15 of his slaves entered his bedroom and fell on him with
knives and bills in the presence of his wife. Despite his wife's gallant intervention, Martin was killed, the assailants cutting off his head, 'which we
afterwards took up in the grass, where they had washed it with rum and
triumphed over it'. Codrington's explanation to London of the event is
extraordinary: although he wrote that 'we have lost a very useful man in
Maj. Martin', in effect he blamed the planter for his own murder, for
Martin, he wrote, was 'guilty of some unusual act of severity or rather
some indignity towards ye Corramantees'.

Thus it is surprising that the 'Act for the better Government of Slaves
and free Negroes', passed in Antigua on Codrington's watch the following
June, did not reflect this sympathy, nor did it include measures, as per the
Governor's stated earlier ambition, for 'restraining inhuman severities and
punishing the wilful killing of Indians and Negroes'. Rather, the Act
followed almost exactly the brutal rules and punishments of the Barbados

code of 1661, including the latitude for just two Justices of Peace to sentence a slave to death. It was also clearly stated that 'if a slave lose life or Limb by Punishment for a crime, no person shall be liable to the law'. The only hint of amelioration came with the revoking of an earlier Act that stipulated the death sentence for a runaway of more than three months, which was 'sometimes found too severe, by reason of new ignorant slaves'. (Nonetheless a capital punishment could still be imposed 'at the Discretion of two Justices of the Peace'.)

It is impossible to say exactly why Codrington's ambition to protect the slaves came to nothing. Perhaps the assembly dug its heels in; maybe the whites had taken fright at the murder of Major Martin. Or maybe Codrington, in a very short time, came to understand the brutal realities of the garrison society that slavery had created, where violence and fear were crucial weapons to protect the numerically inferior planters. Perhaps, like so many others, his journey from England to the West Indian empire involved entering a different moral universe.

To be fair, he also had his hands full preparing the woefully ill-equipped islands for what seemed like the inevitable resumption of war with imperial rival France. Codrington, who now held the rank of general, correctly identified St Kitts, still uneasily divided between English and French, as key: 'The first blow must be struck here', he wrote in late 1701. On his first visit he found the planters too busy quarrelling amongst themselves to have taken defensive measures, and not a single pound of gunpowder on the island, the little there had been having been fired by the Lieutenant-Governor, Colonel Norton, 'When He and His Council and Assembly after falling out got drunk together and grew Friends agen'.

Codrington appealed to Barbados for help, but apart from a few barrels of gunpowder got nothing. As he reported to London, 'Barbadoes has noe inclination to serve or save these Islands. Nor have one of these Ilands to help Another; because if a Sugar Iland is lost, So much ye les of ye Commodity is made, and consequently ye price is rais'd.' Appeals to Nevis and Antigua were similarly unsuccessful, and Montserrat, containing mostly Irish Roman Catholics, also refused to help. In fact, the rumours were that the Irish were preparing to hand the island over to the French.

Undeterred, Codrington spent most of his time in St Kitts, drilling, organising, repairing forts and above all inspiring. 'I have done all yt it wd. have been possible for any to have done in ye same circumstances', he declared. 'I can safely tell you I have been no onely General but Engineer, Serjt. and Corporall.'

Considering the circumstances, Codrington did a commendable job preparing for the war. As the French arrived in force, still in command of the sea, he rejected their offer of neutrality for the English at St Kitts, telling them that 'the English would take care to meet their Enemys with their Eyes open and their Swords in their hands'. In late 1701, as both sides made preparations for the coming conflict, Codrington met Father Labat, the French priest-spy-military-engineer, at a dinner in St Kitts. Labat, who would distinguish himself in the battle to come, left a fascinating account of the encounter, which gives us a rare eye-witness glimpse of the younger Codrington at this time.

Codrington arrived at the home of an English planter with a large entourage, which included a number of trumpeters, who signalled his advent with a loud blast. Among those at the dinner party was a M. Lambert, a prominent French privateer. Lambert, who, according to Labat, 'had very nearly captured the General one night in a raid', during Codrington's previous visit back in 1693, was treated to some good-natured ribbing by Codrington, who 'was very pleased to have this opportunity to make his peace with him, as he had wished every possible ill to befall him in the last war for spoiling his sleep so often'.

The debonair banter continued. Codrington gave his opinion that war would soon be declared, and 'that then he would see himself master of all St Kitts', Labat wrote. 'I smiled and told him that such a conquest was unworthy of him and I believed that he was really thinking of Martinique. "No, no," he said, "that is too much of a mouthful to start with. I mean to seize the French quarters of St Kitts first, and then I will pay you a visit in Guadeloupe."'

Labat was impressed that Codrington spoke fluent French throughout, and declared the general 'far more sober than are most of his nation as a rule'. Beneath the bonhomie, both sides attempted to prise information from the other. 'General Codrington asked a hundred questions about my voyage to San Domingo', says Labat, 'and about many other things. But he spoke so quickly that he asked two or three questions before I had time to answer.' However charming Labat found Codrington, he added an interesting criticism: 'I could not help observing how very vain are the English, and in what little esteem they hold other nations'.

Certainly Codrington's entourage was revealing of a man with a very high opinion of his own grandeur and position. When he left, 'two trumpeters rode in front of him and he was accompanied by eight persons who appeared to be servants'. He also had a chaplain and a soldier, a major general, in his party. 'Nine or ten negroes ran in front of the trumpeters although their horses always travel at a canter', says Labat. 'I felt sorry for a small negro about fifteen years old who was being taught to be a runner. He only wore a pair of pants without a seat, but was made to take off even this garment and run naked in front of everyone. He was followed by a negro with a whip which was applied every time he came within range.'

Not all of Codrington's confidence was bravado. When he received orders to attack the French in St Kitts in the event of war, he replied to London with a scheme for capturing all of the French islands. And at last he managed to line up some militia fighters from Nevis and Antigua to be ready to reinforce the English on St Kitts. During the spring, everyone waited. Out at sea, warships stopped vessels from Europe to see if war had begun.

War was declared by Queen Anne on 4 May 1702 (William III had died in March), but confirmation of the news did not reach Codrington in Antigua until 28 June. By now, the Governor had fallen sick. He also remained furious at the accusations made about him to the Council of Trade the previous winter (still being laboriously scrutinised), writing, rather pompously, that 'My honour is much dearer to me than an employ more valuable than mine is.' In May he had asked for a furlough of six months to come to London to clear his name, which was refused, but clearly his private thoughts were about returning home. In June, just before he received the news of war, he wrote to a friend how he was looking forward, 'If ever I return from the Indies', to touring Europe looking for books for his library, which he wanted to make 'as curious as any private one in Europe'.

As soon as he heard of the declaration of war, Codrington dashed off a letter to London. 'I am so weak and spiritless that I am not able to hold up my head', he wrote, in a markedly more shaky hand than usual. 'I am much fitter for my bed than the field, but we are not to sleep now at St Kitts; the cause must be decided and our people won't go where I don't lead.' 'If I dye in the action, my Lords', he ended, 'believe I dye an honest man. If I live, I'le satisfy the world I am so.'

As good as his word, Codrington mustered all his available forces and rushed to St Kitts, straight away sending 20 vessels full of troops to bombard French settlements and demand their surrender. A force was also sent overland to advance against enemy positions. After only a brief skirmish, the French commander (later court-martialled for cowardice) capitulated on 5 July 1702.

'Her [Majesty's] Flag is now flying on ye French fort . . . better success than I could have wished for', reported a triumphant Codrington the next day. The French were cleared out of St Kitts for the last time, as it later transpired; thus Codrington fulfilled his father's thwarted ambition.

But this was the high point for the English in the Leewards. For the rest of the War of Spanish Succession (1702–13), the familiar litany of incompetence, wanton destruction, greed and crippling losses from disease took hold. The English on St Kitts quickly fell out over distribution of the spoils. Codrington, a little recovered from his sickness, turned his thoughts once more to peace and a return to England, writing, 'When this is over, I shall deserve to come home, for I am unalterably determined to return . . . if I live to see England, I will pass my life in my Library and be buryed in my garden . . . please to let one of your under-gardiners plant me some fruit trees and vines at Dodington.'

The course of the War of Spanish Succession would be decided in Europe, in particular by the victories of the Duke of Marlborough, but in the West Indies, fortunes fluctuated depending on who had command of the sea. Island colonies from both sides looked anxiously at the comings and goings of rival fleets, while their respective privateers took a heavy toll on shipping and trade, causing hunger and dissatisfaction everywhere. In October 1702, naval power shifted sharply after the rout by English and Dutch warships of the combined Spanish and French fleets in Vigo Bay in northern Spain. The chance to drive the French out of the West Indies, as Codrington had urged, had arrived. Before the end of the year, a powerful fleet under Rear Admiral Sir Hovenden Walker was dispatched from England boasting six men-of-war and 10 transports carrying no fewer than 4,000 men.

As before, in the tradition of the wild optimism experienced by the likes of Wheeler, Penn and Venables, there were great hopes for the expedition – it was to meet up with a further force of English and Dutch, and having destroyed French settlements on Guadeloupe and Martinique, proceed via Jamaica to attack Havana and Cartagena to induce the Spanish to break their alliance with France. Thereafter it was to deliver a blow against the French in Newfoundland and, some even suggested, with the help of the New Englanders it could take Quebec and drive the French out of Canada.

But even before they reached the West Indies many of the soldiers were sick, and there were hardly enough seamen fit to man the boats. On Walker's own ship, 100 men were buried at sea, and another 100 sick when they reached Bridgetown on 5 December. There, the situation worsened. To Walker's fury, the Englishmen of Barbados did not seem to care about the larger, grandiose imperial picture, refusing to quarter many of the men (who thus remained on their stinking, crowded ships), instead concentrating on blatant illegal trade with the French enemy. They did, however, sell the troops copious amounts of rum (against official orders), with disastrous consequences. As Codrington later wrote, they 'murdered them with Drinking'. Old West Indian hands might have 'bodies like Egyptian mummys', said Codrington, but for 'a New-Comer', such rivers of rum 'must certainly dispatch [them] to the other World'.

Speed was of the essence: Martinique, the key French bastion in the Leewards, was denuded of men, as most were at sea as privateers, and as vulnerable as it had ever been. It was imperative that Codrington be informed of Walker's arrival in Barbados and plans made to strike quickly. This necessitated sending a fast sloop to Codrington, but the Barbados assembly owed money to the owner of the usual vessel, and the treasurer refused to release the necessary funds. Unbeknownst to Walker (now ill himself), no message was sent for weeks; meanwhile, about a quarter of his force – 1,000 men – were lost in Barbados to sickness, drink and desertion, and the alerted French called in their men, numbering some 1,800, to defend Martinique. A great chance was thus lost.

Eventually, on 20 January 1703, word of Walker's arrival got to Codrington, who had, with great difficulty, raised a force of ships and men from his islands. As Martinique was now too hard a nut to crack, it was decided instead to descend on Guadeloupe.

Before he set sail from Antigua with his forces, Codrington, with signs of his illness returning and facing dangerous battles ahead, made what would turn out to be the most extraordinary will of any of the sugar barons.

The will, dated 22 February 1703, strikingly revealed how immensely rich he was; it is no surprise that he was considered the wealthiest man in the West Indies, with sugar plantations in Barbados, Antigua and St Kitts, as well as ownership of the entire island of Barbuda and the valuable estate of Dodington back in England. In his will he doled out huge sums, in the hundreds of pounds, to cousins; in England, the Codringtons from the previously dominant line of the family were, in contrast, writing wills bequeathing £5 here and £10 there. The largest single beneficiary of the will was to be Christopher's cousin William, his 'neirest kinsman', who was to inherit Dodington, the main Antigua estate at Betty's Hope (which now included the next-door Cotton plantation, so totalling just over 800 well-developed acres), the lands in St Kitts and most of the island of Barbuda.

Christopher's illegitimate son William was to get an allowance and £500 at the age of 21, paid out of the proceeds of another Antigua plantation in St John's left to two local friends. The scanty evidence available suggests that this William, then aged 10, was living in Antigua, presumably at Betty's Hope, but nothing about the nature of his relationship with his father, or the whereabouts of his mother, the mysterious Maudlin Morange, has come to light.

From cousin William's lavish inheritance was to be paid £10,000, in £2,000 annual instalments, to All Soul's College Oxford; £6,000 for the building of a library, with the rest for the purchase of books. Codrington the Younger's own book collection, now numbering more than 12,000 volumes and one of the finest in the world, valued at £6,000, was to provide the nucleus of the library, designed by Nicholas Hawksmoor, which even today remains second in Oxford only to the Bodleian. This donation was utterly unprecedented for the sugar barons, but an even more surprising legacy followed: the valuable Barbados estates, comprising two highly profitable plantations on the east coast – Consetts and Didmartins – 'I give to the Society for the Propagation of the Christian Religion in Foreign Parts.' Part of the value of the island of Barbuda was included as well. This society had been founded two years before by King William to improve the calibre of the clergy in the English Americas in order to convert 'heathens and infidels', including black West Indian slaves. Codrington stipulated that the two plantations should be kept up and running, with at least 300 slaves, to provide money for the construction and maintenance of a new Codrington College. Here, a convenient number of professors and scholars, under vows of 'poverty, chastity and obedience' (this phrase, considered 'popish', was later quietly removed by the Society), were to 'study and practice physic and chirurgery, as well as divinity', so that they would be able to minister to the 'souls', as well as 'care for the bodies' of the island's 'Heathens'.

Codrington had failed the previous summer to persuade the planters to improve the slaves' legal rights, but now, perhaps, he had his revenge. He was no abolitionist; part of the aim of conversion and better medical care was to improve the slaves' efficiency as workers and obedience to their masters. In this respect, he was the inheritor of the ideas of the likes of Godwyn, Baxter and Fox. Like them, he was compassionate, sensitive and appalled by the cruelties meted out to the slaves, without quite making the leap to turning against the institution of slavery itself. But he must have known how hated this innovation would be by the planters, for whom slave conversion – treating enslaved Africans as people, rather than property – was a dangerous anathema that undermined the whole foundation of their society and prosperity. In this respect Christopher showed himself to be an expatriate Englishman, rather than a proper West Indian Creole like his father, one of the few differences between them.

The Society (correctly, the Society for the Propagation of the Gospel Overseas) would, in coming into its inheritance, find itself in a very difficult, and subsequently embarrassing, position. Every effort was made, including by Codrington's heir, to thwart his vision, and for some, the Church of England becoming a substantial slave-owner – branding its slaves 'Society' – would be unforgivable. But the radical experiment of Codrington College would serve as a laboratory for the later crusade for the Christianisation of native peoples in India, Australia and elsewhere, and it gave a toehold in the mother of the slave colonies, Barbados, to an organisation that was firmly opposed to the vicious world that the planters had created. In 1711, the year after Codrington's will was proved, the preacher of the Society's Annual Sermon would declare that 'Negroes were equally the Workmanship of God with themselves [the planters]; endowed with the same faculties and intellectual powers; Bodies of the same Flesh and Blood, and Souls certainly immortal.' The sermon would be distributed widely, with 2,000 copies sent to the West Indies. The slaves on the Codrington plantations had to be instructed in the Faith of Christ (and therefore educated to a degree) and brought to baptism, the preacher declared. 'This will be preaching by Example', he went on, 'the most effectual way of recommending Doctrines, to a hard and unbelieving World, blinded by Interest, and other Prepossessions.' It would, of course, be more than 100 years before the logical outcome of this approach – abolition – would occur; but Christopher Codrington, writing his will in Antigua in 1703, while ill and facing battle, had, however unwittingly, radically undermined the system on which his family had built their fortune.

On 5 March 1703, the English armada, consisting of Walker's much-reduced force and Codrington's Leewards militias, sailed from Antigua. At noon the next day they sighted the tall, vividly green mountains of Guadeloupe. For a number of days they reconnoitred the coastline, looking for unfortified landing spots. But the French engineer Labat had been busy, throwing up defences, including tall towers, and the French commander did a skilful job of moving his forces around to demonstrate strength that he really did not have. The first landing by some 500 troops was quickly driven off. But then the English went ashore in three different places simultaneously and were soon advancing on the fortified town of Basse Terre. By 2 April, Codrington, leading from the front, had taken the outer trenches and established batteries to open fire on the French walls.

Marches and counter-marches by both sides followed, as the English soldiery extensively burned and looted the plantations of much of the island. Soon the French would abandon their redoubt and take refuge in the hills, but not before Codrington had fallen out with his naval commander, Walker, and become seriously ill again. It might have been malaria, which is recurring and often leads to depression, or a form of rheumatic fever. Codrington reported that he was 'afflicted with terrible pains', lost the use of his limbs, and was blinded from the huge quantities of laudanum he took to relieve the agony. As he was invalided off the battlefield, the French managed to bypass Walker's cumbersome armada and land reinforcements from Martinique. On 5 May, the English, suffering widespread sickness, decided that they did not have the provisions to stay on the island any longer, and abandoned the conquest.

For Codrington, reporting to London some time later, the fault for the failure could be attributed to the lack of light frigates to prevent French reinforcements being landed, the paucity of artillery and siege equipment and the poor standard of the troops and their leadership – 'no one to take care of them . . . save one drunken Major who soon dispatcht himself'. Also at fault, yet again, was the divided leadership. Walker had cut and run, Codrington alleged, 'just when we were to reap the fruit of our hazards & fatigues'. Walker, for his part, blamed the Creole contingent for a lack of fighting spirit.

After Guadeloupe, both sides in the war relegated the West Indies to a low priority compared to Europe, although privateers continued to wreck trade in the region. In one month the following year, out of 108 ships that left Barbados and the Leewards for England, only 61 arrived at their destination, with 43 taken as prizes into French ports. During the summer of 1703, Codrington remained desperately ill, disappointed and depressed, writing to his superiors in August that 'I still continue so wretchedly weak and my head so dizzey that I can scarce read your Lordships' letters, much less answer them as I should . . . I expected a Furlow by this ordinary, but find myself abandon'd by all my friends. Never man who liv'd was ever reduc't to so low a condition as I have been; having lost every drop of blood in my veins, my eyesight and the use of my limbs. I believe I cannot perfectly recover without a voyage to Europe.'

Hearing nothing more from Codrington, and receiving no replies to their further letters, the authorities in London agreed in October that he should be allowed to return home. However, for the 'security of those Islands', they appointed a new governor, Sir William Mathew. As soon as Codrington discovered that he had, in effect, been dismissed, he was mortified, and found his considerable pride severely affronted. In February 1704, with this health seemingly restored, he wrote to London that if a deputy governor was deemed inadequate to hold the fort during his 'furlow', then he was happy to stay on in his post. But the decision had been made; the new governor arrived soon after. Writing to London at this time, Codrington struck a heroic but aggrieved pose, while stressing that his earlier physical weakness was a thing of the past: 'Thank God I have perfectly recovered my limbs & strength', he said, 'and will serve the Queen somewhere or other during the War, tho it be with a Muskett on my shoulder.'

As it turned out, Sir William Mathew would join the crowded ranks of those swiftly undone by the mortal dangers of the tropics. In November he wrote to London that he, his wife and his secretary, as well as most of his family, were seriously ill. The following month, on 4 December, he died. Codrington saw his chance, and two days later wrote to the Council of Trade begging to be reinstated to his old position, one that he seems to have considered his by right of birth and merit: 'Since I am upon the place and now season'd', he said, 'I shall be willing to serve her [the Queen] here during the war, and beleive I may serve Her better than an another at present.'

But 'an another' was about to be appointed, leading to a tragic and bloody series of events. The Lords of Trade supported Codrington's application, but to the former governor's bitter disappointment, it was not to be. After the Battle of Blenheim, the news of Marlborough's great victory had been carried to London and delivered to the Queen by Daniel Parke, a 35-year-old lieutenant-colonel, described as of 'fine appearance and handsome bearing'. Parke's reward for being the bearer of such good tidings was 1,000 guineas, a miniature portrait of the Queen and, in due course, the governorship of the Leeward Islands.

Parke was a Virginian; he had sat on the colony's assembly and council in the 1690s before relocating to England, where he stood unsuccessfully for Parliament. Joining Marlborough's army, he caught the eye of the Duke and served as his aide-de-camp.

Although he was appointed in March 1705, Parke took his time before taking up his new position. In the interim, the islands were run by John Johnson, previously Lieutenant-Governor of Nevis. Johnson, who was from humble origins, owed his promotion entirely to Codrington; one of his first acts was to give his former patron a further grant for Barbuda for 99 years at the rent of a fat sheep yearly. He also backed Codrington in a dispute over the highly contentious estate at Godwin in St Kitts. Johnson made a commendable attempt to improve the islands' defences, but lacked the authority to have his instructions carried out, particularly in St Kitts, where a dispute led to soldiers being turfed out of their indifferent quarters into open fields. 'I heartily wish for Col. Park's arrival', wrote Johnson in July 1705, 'for I have such ill-natured and troublesome people to deal with, that I am already weary of my Command.'

In early 1706, the French found themselves in a position to exact revenge for the depredations carried out in Guadeloupe. On 4 February, a fleet of 30 ships, including seven men-of-war, appeared off the Antiguan coast. A strong northerly gale prevented the French vessels from beating in close to shore, so they bore away to Nevis, anchoring in front of the main port of Charlestown. For five days the French exchanged fire with the forts of the town, before pulling away towards St Kitts. Here, as Johnson had warned in vain, the defences were much less potent. Three columns were landed in different parts of the island, with the English, outnumbered 2,300 to 700, retreating in panic to the redoubt at Brimstone Hill. The French lacked the heavy guns needed to reduce the fort, but for several days they devastated the island at will, wrecking every plantation and mill and carrying away 600 slaves and huge quantities of sugar-making equipment.

The following month, they tried again at Nevis, which up until now had escaped the regular depredations suffered by nearby St Kitts, and was for this reason the wealthiest of the English Leewards. Having tricked the English commander into posting his troops – only about 200 strong – in the north of the island, the French successfully landed 2,000 men in the south. After brief resistance in the island's mountain stronghold, the planters surrendered. Half of the island's slaves, just over 3,000, were taken away, and every building except 20 destroyed. The Nevis planters estimated the loss at more than a million pounds sterling. An epidemic of smallpox then ravaged the survivors of the attack.

The defeat at Nevis sent shock waves through English America. While the nearby islands of Montserrat and Antigua swirled with rumours of further attacks, as far away as Newport in Rhode Island, batteries were hastily constructed to improve the defences against the French threat.

18

THE MURDER OF DANIEL PARKE

'It will be very hard with this Island for we have stain'd the Land with so much Blood . . . I fear a scurge is over our heads.'

Quaker Abraham Redwood, Antigua, February 1711

On 14 July 1705, Daniel Parke arrived at last in Antigua. The people of the Leewards, fearful of another French attack, gave the glamorous new governor – known as a favourite of the Queen – a warm welcome; the Antigua assembly 'furnish'd his Cellars with Wine & liquors'. But Parke soon regretted his appointment. Of no independent wealth, he had hoped for the more lucrative governorship of Virginia, and found the Leewards, devastated by war and disease, a poor place to make his fortune. A fierce hurricane at the end of August and an ongoing drought further impoverished the islands. His salary of £1,100, which had not even been paid, would have been insufficient, Parke complained, had it been three times the amount.

Parke had a regiment of 928 men at his disposal, which he considered quite inadequate to defend the islands. When he visited recently ravaged Nevis, he took troops with him for his own protection, lest 'I have my brains knock't out, [and] the Queen must send some other unfortunate devil here to be roasted in the sun'. He begged London to send 'some nimble frigots to protect us from the privateers', who seemed to take every vessel headed to the islands. 'We are so frighted, every two or three sloops, we believe is another French fleet', he wrote. 'I am deservedly punished for desiring to be a Governor.'

To make matters worse, soon he and his household were ill. Of the 26 who had come out with him, after a few months only four remained. Five had quickly returned to England, but the rest were dead. Parke himself wrote that he had suffered 'the plague, the pestilence and bloody flux, and have been out of my bed but four days of a malignant feavour; I am so weak I can hardly write to your lordships'.

To his credit, Parke quickly identified what needed to be done to improve the security and government of the islands, coming to the same conclusions reached by both the Codringtons. He first attempted to bring the four islands under one unitary government; he tried to force the colonists to provide quarters to the troops; and he stopped the big planters buying out the smallholders by fixing land auctions. Martinique had to be conquered, he argued, to vanquish the French threat; could 10,000 Scots soldiers be sent out to perform the task? He even suggested that Porto Rico be taken from the Spanish and the entire populations of the islands moved there. The problem of defence was the same as ever: about Nevis, Parke wrote that it was 'a rich little Island, but here are but few people, the Island was divided amongst a few rich men that had a vast number of slaves, and hardly any common people'. Parke, according to his own accounts, also worked very hard at stopping the illegal trade, particularly the buying of European goods at the nearby Dutch islands, where they were considerably cheaper. But everywhere he turned he met resistance, lethargy and self-interest. He also quickly acquired a powerful enemy: 'To the rest of my afflictions', he wrote home, 'I would have added Colonel Codrington.'

From the very start, the two men were bitter foes. Shortly after his arrival, Parke wrote to his superiors: 'I think I have the good fortune to please the people, except Colonel Codrington. He has opposed everything and is just as much troublesome as I told you he would be.' Parke was convinced that Codrington, whose hauteur he detested, was plotting to recover his governorship. According to a friend of Parke, Codrington was 'enraged with Envy, at Colonel Parke's being preferr'd before him', and was 'excited by the wild Starts of a crazy Brain, that much about that Time began to affect him'. This is, of course, a partisan account, but given the family's history of mental illness and Codrington's own manic depressive temperament, it might contain an element of truth. For his part, Codrington wrote to a friend in England in September 1706: 'I continue my resolution of leaving the Indies ye beginning of January. It is impossible for me to live with our brute of a General – he is a perfect frenzy of avarice.'

Clearly Antigua was not big enough for both of them, and Parke was not the sort of man to back down. He quickly went after his rival, bringing a suit to recover prize money the Codrington family had accumulated during the wars against the French. He confiscated the Codrington estate in St Kitts, and then questioned the family's rights to Barbuda. In response, Codrington 'infused Fears and jealousises into the Minds of the People, and stirr'd them up to Division', according to a later defender of Parke.

If that was indeed Codrington's aim, it was spectacularly successful. The initial glamour of Parke as confidant of the Queen quickly faded as he took on the planters used to getting their own way. He also won enemies by 'attempting to debauch some of the Chief women of the Island'. This was, it seems, nothing unusual in Antigua: it was 'not much taken notice of, but looked upon to be a frolick & passed over', until Parke started a relationship with a Mrs Chester, wife of one of the richest men on the island and a member of the assembly.* The cuckolded husband, admittedly a major smuggler, found himself locked up in prison.

There now developed a state of mutual loathing between Parke and his circle, called by a detractor his 'vulgar associates', and the majority of the white Leeward Islanders rallying around Codrington. Parke complained to London that the West Indians 'expect the Queen should do everything for them, though they do not endeavour to help themselves'. The more Parke was criticised for being a 'great debauch', the more he reported to London of the Leeward Islanders' own sexual depravity, 'a mungrill race [of mulattoes] liveing witnesses of their unnaturall and monstrous lusts'. There were, Parke alleged, 'a succession of Codringtons ... among the slaveish sooty race [of mulattoes]'.† Christopher Codrington himself, Parke reported, had an Irish 'wench', a Kate Sullivan, who 'layd two bastards to him, but she giving him the pox, he turned her off'. To gain ammunition against his enemies, and intelligence about smuggling operations, Parke now took to patrolling around at night in disguise in St John's, armed with 'pocket-pistoles'. 'You may easily imagine', he reported to London, 'that a sea-port town in the West Indies, full of punch-houses and taverns, cramm'd with soldiers and privateers to be very licentious.' The islanders complained in reply that this sneaking about only brought 'his person and authority in contempt'.

In August 1707, Codrington left his home at Betty's Hope, Antigua, and retreated to his estates in Barbados. It seems he intended to at last fulfil his ambition of returning home to his English garden and library, but either

---

* Parke and Mrs Chester had a daughter, Lucy. In his will, Parke requested that she change her name to his, and that anyone marrying her also become a Parke.

† William Codrington, Chistopher's nephew and heir, would father a number of mulatto children, whom he cheerfully acknowledged and took with him to England when he became an absentee sugar baron.

a recurrence of poor health (possibly a sexually transmitted infection, as Parke alleged) or a continued engagement in local politics prevented him making the long and arduous voyage. According to his funeral oration, given by his friend the Reverend William Gordon, he spent the last three years of his life in quiet contemplation and academic study. But another account had it that 'from [Barbados], by an uninterrupted Correspondence [with Antigua], he continu'd to refresh the Dissensions he had sown'. The Reverend Gordon himself was a scoundrel of the first order, 'insidious, restless, meddling', addicted to gambling, so it is likelier that Codrington continued to seethe with anger and jealousy, and to conspire to regain his Leewards fiefdom. Like his father, in the corrupting heat of the tropics, 'beyond the line', he had made a journey from conscientious, idealistic reformer to a man of faction, self-interest and bitterness.

Encouraged by Codrington or not, soon the Leeward Islanders had prepared extensive complaints against Governor Parke: there was his personal conduct; in addition, he had seized vessels and 'made prizes of them contrary to Law'; he had concealed wills to buy up for himself supposedly intestate estates; while professing to counter illegal trading, he had sent vessels to Martinique; he had bought land, slaves and cattle for a low price and 'if any other Gentleman bid higher or nearer the value they were sure to feel his resentments'. Helped by money from Codrington, these complaints were sent to London in March 1709, and every effort made to turn the home authorities against Parke.

Codrington would not live to see the grisly fate of his great enemy. On 7 April 1710, having never really recovered his health since Guadeloupe, he died aged just 42. According to the perhaps unreliable testimony of Parke, 'he was in great perplexity before he died to alter his will and according sent 6 times for one to do it, but those about him prevented the messengers going . . . and a vollpony will he made takes place, so that ye most of his estate goes to those he mortally hated before he died'. Thus the extraordinary will of 1703 stood, with the Society for the Propagation of the Gospel Overseas getting the Barbados estates (at that time clearing a huge annual profit of £2,000), and cousin William coming into most of the rest. If Parke's story about changing the will is to be believed, it is more likely that Codrington would have wanted to disinherit William, a slippery character who at one point sided with Parke, than the Society, though it is not impossible that he had changed his mind about that as well.

Parke was jubilant that 'the author and contriver of all this vilany against me is now answering for it'. 'They say he broke his heart', Parke went on, 'not being able to get the better of me.' But the Governor's own days were numbered. As indications came from London that Parke's star was on the wane, the Leeward Islanders responded with growing violence and lawlessness. A riot in St Kitts saw the murder of the former Acting Governor John Johnson. In Antigua, Parke narrowly survived two assassination attempts. He reacted with a further escalation of violence, taking personal charge of the garrison and ordering them to attack and harass his enemies. At last he was recalled by the authorities in London, more through sheer weight of complaints than any decision against his conduct, but he ignored the order, instead becoming ever more reckless and paranoid.

The Antigua assembly was now dissolved by Parke, but it continued to meet in the island's capital, St John's, refusing to recognise his authority. Rumours started circulating that the Governor was preparing to surrender the island to the French. Refusing to back down, on 7 December Parke sent a detachment of troops to an assembly meeting, and dispersed the men at gunpoint. Within a short time, some 300 armed planters had poured in from surrounding area to support the assembly members. Parke retreated to his St John's house, with about 70 loyal soldiers, and deployed five field guns to cover the main approaches.

Deputations from the council and from the assembly approached to try to persuade Parke to leave the island while he still could, but in the meantime, the house was surrounded. Parke would not hear of surrender, and as tempers flared out of control, the two sides opened fire. Parke himself fired his cannon at the throng, who then charged the house. One of the rebel leaders was personally shot down by Parke, but then the Governor was hit in the thigh. An eye-witness reports that 'they then broke in upon him, tore off his cloathes, dragged him by his members about his house, bruised his head, and broke his back with the butt end of the pieces'. The wounded Governor was then dragged from his house and brutally treated as he lay dying; when he asked for water, they spat in his face. Of his 70 guards, 11 were killed and 35 wounded; four rioters were killed and eight wounded. Parke's house was ransacked, the mob stealing everything they could lay their hands on, including (apparently by 'One Turnor a farrier') the miniature of Queen Anne that had hung around Parke's neck.

Parke's brutal murder was outrageous and shocking even by the standards of the 'beyond the line' West Indies. But no one was ever punished. A new governor, Walter Douglas, was sent out, but found no one willing to testify against the ringleaders; after all, you could hardly prosecute the entire Antigua white population. Douglas decided instead that it was safer to accept bribes to clear those implicated in the crime. For this, and other misdemeanours, which included stealing the communion plate from St John's church, he was recalled, tried and imprisoned.

Thus the colonists had proved themselves almost ungovernable. (In this light, the efforts of the Codringtons, however severely tainted by self-interest and personal psychological issues, look all the more commendable.) But while some Antiguans celebrated their deliverance from the interfering Parke, others never recovered their belief in the happy future of the colony.

Abraham Redwood was one of those horrified and sickened by what had occurred. Originally from Bristol, Redwood had worked as a slave trader and mariner on the West India route, before marrying the daughter of the wealthy Antiguan planter and Quaker pioneer Jonas Langford and settling on the island. Redwood himself was by now a Quaker, and as well as looking after land in his own name worked as a partner in Langford's extensive sugar business. In 1709, shortly before Parke's murder, his third son, another Abraham, was born. Following the early deaths of his elder brothers, this Abraham would turn out to be the inheritor of a great sugar estate in Antigua, and subsequently, based in Newport, Rhode Island, one of the richest men in North America.

Abraham senior's thoughts seem to have turned for a while towards the northern American colonies. For him, Antigua was just a stepping stone to a future for his family in the distinctly more God-fearing, calm and law-abiding mainland. We know that he and his wife had travelled to Newport, probably on business for his father-in-law (his eldest daughter, Mary, was born in Newport in 1698). He had sent his eldest children to school in Quaker-friendly Philadelphia, and was in correspondence with Jonathan Dickinson, an old West India hand fast establishing himself in that city.

On 11 February 1711, only six weeks after Parke's murder, Redwood wrote to Dickinson that he would himself have been in Philadelphia by now, had not the sloop due to carry him there been 'Taken'. He had received, he reported, 'the 3 barrels of bread and 3 barrels of beer' sent to him to pass on to Langford, and urgently requested news of his children, of whom he had heard nothing for too long. The gloomy letter also reported the 'miserly Dry Dry Times' and expressed a hope for a 'speedy peace' with France, after so much destruction: 'We are now daily expecting the French by good Intelligence if not for this Islands for another of the Leeward Islands.' All this worry caused Abraham great 'discomposure of mind'.

On the morning of his death, Parke had written a codicil to his will, appointing a new executor after the death of a previous nominee. That new man was Abraham Redwood. His take on the murder that day is therefore informed by this loyalty, as well as by his growing distaste for life in Antigua. I have 'much fear', he wrote to Dickinson, that 'it will be very hard with this Island for we have stain'd the Land with so much Blood that wee Can expect nothing but Banness [destruction] on this Island and I fear a scurge is over our heads'. 'I desire to settle in Philadelphia', he went on, 'for I see nothing good here for I much fear our Distruction by Drawing god's Judgemt On Us that So wee are a miserable people ... Pride goes before Distruction which is our Miserable Case.'

Abraham Redwood would remove his family from seemingly tainted Antigua within a couple of years, with fairly tragic results; the predicted retribution came sooner than that, with further misery heaped on the heads of the English Leeward Islanders. In July 1712, a French force, having attacked Antigua unsuccessfully, descended on Montserrat and laid waste the island for several days, carrying away 1,200 slaves and a booty worth an estimated £180,000.

By then, unknown to the distant West Indies, negotiations were already under way in Europe to end the war. What would eventually become known as the Treaty of Utrecht, signed the following year, for once did not entirely reconstitute the pre-war situation in the West Indies. The French parts of St Kitts were at last permanently ceded to Britain (as it now was called, after the union with Scotland). Although concerning only a tiny amount of land (and of minor international signficance compared to the gaining by Britain of Gibraltar, Novia Scotia and other territories), this was hugely helpful in ending the awkward sharing arrangement – made in the face of Carib and Spanish threats many years before – that had caused so much friction and conflict between France and England in the Leewards.

Long before the end of the war, the conflict in the West Indies had deteriorated into simple vandalism and looting. Neither side really wanted to flood their home markets by actually conquering more sugar acreage – the English had all they could use in Jamaica, and the French in Hispaniola. With the land everywhere in the hands of a tiny elite, the chance to plunder presented by the conflict had provided perhaps the best hope for the poor whites of either side to gain a quick fortune, but in the medium and long term they were losers in the war, and not just because they made up the cannon fodder. Lands left empty were snapped up by the big sugar barons, and many of the smallholders who left their home islands during the periodic expulsions never returned, giving up on cultivation in favour of privateering or emigration elsewhere. This left the islands more socially divided among the whites, and ever more polarised, with a tiny planter elite precariously perched on the top of a growing slave population.

A census carried out by Governor Parke in 1708 shows that the white population of all the English Leeward islands, bar one, had shrunk since the previous census 30 years earlier, most markedly in Nevis, where it was less than a third of its 3,500 earlier population. The exception was Antigua, almost totally undeveloped in 1678, whose white population had grown by 500 to 2,892. Having, uniquely in the Leewards, escaped French invasion, Antigua was now the most important sugar island in the group, and had a slave population just short of 13,000. No one at the beginning of the eighteenth century could call the Leewards settler communities. As in Barbados 20 years before, the gradual transformation to slave society was complete.

Amazingly, in spite of the destruction, sugar production had doubled in the Leewards during the war, from around 5,000 tons in 1689 to 10,000 in 1713. Worse wars against the French were still to come, but after the Treaty of Utrecht, the Leewards enjoyed a generation of peace. For the islands' surviving sugar baron families – the Byams, Martins, Gunthorpes, Fryes and, of course, Codringtons – the chance was there to become a colonial sugar aristocracy on the Barbados model.

19

THE BECKFORDS: THE NEXT GENERATION

'The Passions of the Mind have a very great power on Mankind here.'
Sir Hans Sloane on Jamaica, 1707

In Jamaica, the creation of the most powerful and spectacular sugar dynasty of all was already well under way. By the end of the seventeenth century, Colonel Peter Beckford had upwards of 4,000 acres, he was the factor for the Royal African Company, had widespread shipping and trading interests and, like the Codringtons, looked to combine wealth with political power to the benefit of both. By the late 1690s, Colonel Beckford was President of the Council; furthermore, Governor Beeston, some five years before he left Jamaica in 1702, had obtained for his friend Beckford a commission 'to succeed to the Government of Jamaica' should the post become vacant.

But in the intervening period an incident had occurred that severely damaged the family's reputation. Beckford's eldest son Peter, having been educated at Oxford, returned to Jamaica in around 1692, when he was about 19 years old. Nothing is known of his time in England – he made no great impression, as the younger Codrington had done – and he arrived back in Jamaica an unvarnished chip off the old block – headstrong, violent and, as would subsequently be shown, a shrewd and skilful businessman.

By virtue of his father's wealth and political power, Peter the Younger quickly assumed a civil position, sworn in as Receiver General in October 1696 'on giving the usual security'. But at the end of the following year, on 9 December 1697, Governor Beeston was forced to add an unusual footnote to his customary report to London: 'This Eve Mr Lewis [the Deputy Judge Advocate] was unfortunately killed by Mr Beckford the Reciever Generall, by which both these offices are at present void but I will endeavour to fill them with the most capable men I can find for them.'

Lewis had been nearly 60, a venerable age for a white Jamaican. He was a respected and senior member of the establishment, and was not without his own political contacts and influence. Peter the Younger quickly fled Jamaica, first to Hispaniola, then France. According to Lewis's son-in-law in England, who was soon appealing for justice from the Lords of the Plantations, the murder was 'barbarous, wilful and forethought'. It had occurred after a quarrel on board one of HM's ships at anchor in Kingston harbour. Peter had stabbed Lewis, who had 'immediately dyed (his sword not being drawn out of the scabbard)'. The Beckford family, in turn, was quickly using its influential friends in England to try to downgrade the case to manslaughter. Colonel Beckford even travelled to England in early 1698, in an effort to clear his son's name.

In the end, the Lords of the Plantations decided that the case should come to trial in Jamaica. Peter returned to the island, and there was, apparently, a lengthy court case. Details have not survived, but as a writer in Jamaica reported a few years later, 'To say the Truth, our young Squires are not much afraid of the Courts of Justice.' Peter seems to have entirely escaped punishment, and was soon back on the rise in Jamaican politics. Clearly the Beckfords were big enough in Jamaica to be above the law. Shortly afterwards, if a subsequent report is to be believed, Colonel Beckford's other son, Thomas, was also tried for murder, but 'by the interest that was made he . . . came off too without damage'.

Yet some of the mud must have stuck. When Governor Beeston returned to England in January 1702, he was replaced not by Colonel Beckford, but by an appointee sent out from England. Having struggled for a short time with the locals, 'a people very capricious, jealous, and difficult to manage', this new governor succumbed to fever, and Colonel Beckford had his chance at last.

On 5 April 1702, Colonel Beckford activated his five-year-old commission and, as curmudgeonly as ever, 'caused himself to be proclaimed [Lieutenant-Governor of Jamaica], saying to the Assembly "I have gone through most of the offices of this Island, though with no great applause, yet without complaint"'. According to his subsequent report to London, the announcement was met 'without any reluctancye of the people'.

Others tell a different story. The new Governor and his two violent, firebrand sons were clearly widely feared and, according to one note written to London, 'generally disliked'. A military commander who was in Jamaica at this time wrote of Colonel Beckford: 'I have not heard one man speak well of him since I came to the Island.'

Colonel Beckford served as lieutenant-governor for some eight months, during which his official correspondence reflects the anxieties of the island as a whole: attacks by maroons on isolated settlements; the resumption of war with France, news of which reached Jamaica in July 1702; the lack of troops and ships to defend the island; disruption of trade caused by the swarm of privateers unleashed by the war. He also offered, if reinforcements from England were forthcoming, to lead attacks on the isthmus of Panama and elsewhere (he implied that he had been part of the famous attack by Morgan 30 years earlier). His fellow governor in the Leewards, Christopher Codrington, came in for particular criticism for shipping his French prisoners from St Kitts to nearby Hispaniola: 'we were served so the last war and felt the unhappy consequence of it', Beckford wrote to London. In September 1702, Beckford offered to 'maintain things in a quiet and good posture till H.M. shall be graciously pleased to send over a new Governor, or further powers'.

But the Lords of the Plantations were already lining up a new permanent governor, perhaps influenced by the letters they had received from Admiral Benbow, the supreme commander in the Caribbean during the early part of the war. According to Benbow, Beckford was doing nothing for the national interest, but everything for his own benefit and that of his fellow sugar barons. Under Beckford, the Admiral wrote, 'the Government of this Island now is entirely in the hands of the Planters who mind nothing but getting Estates . . . having no regard to the King's Interest or Subjects'. 'The Inhabitants are grown very rich', Benbow continued, 'they doe whatever the desire of Gain leads them to without any regard to the Laws of our Country.' Benbow blamed this in part on the increasing desire of young planters to make a quick fortune and retire back to England or New England while they still had their mental and physical health – their 'constitutions' – in one piece.

On 4 December 1702, Colonel Beckford reluctantly handed over the governorship to Colonel Thomas Handasyd, 'a brave and resolute officer', who was deputising for an English earl appointed to the post who declined to take it up. Beckford, promising to be 'ready . . . on all occasions to express my duty to her majesty', returned to the council.

The loss of the supreme office in the island seems, if anything, to have given a spur to Beckford's desire for power for his family. In 1704, he arranged for his son Peter to be elected to the assembly for Port Royal; the following year, Peter the Younger was returned by no fewer than three different parishes, choosing to sit for St Elizabeth. His younger brother Thomas soon joined him in the assembly, for which Peter was chosen Speaker in 1707. By this time, his father had brokered a highly advantageous marriage for Peter, to Bathshua, daughter and co-heiress of Colonel Julines Herring, who had settled in Jamaica soon after the English invasion. Their first child was born around 1705–6. By now Peter the Younger was, amongst other public roles, Customs Collector for the island, a position of great influence. His brother Thomas also married an heiress, Mary Ballard, at about this time.

Their father, the Colonel, was now in his sixties, and in 1705, 'thro' the infirmity of his age', retired from one of his civil positions, Chief Justice of the Island. He remained, though, on the council, much to the exasperation of the Governor, who was fighting a long battle with the islanders to establish his authority and to make them pay for some of their defence. In August 1705, Governor Handasyd wrote a long, despairing letter to London that draws a vivid picture of the Beckfords' power and methods: 'I am of opinion I have had a snake in my bosom all this while,' he wrote, 'for I do believe all the disturbances that have happened proceeded from Col. Beckford's family, which has always kept a handkerchief over my eys, under the pretence of friendship, but I have now discovered the deceit.' But there was little he could do about the influence of the Beckford family. At the end of the following year, complaining once more that the assembly 'cannot bear English Government, but are still contriving to entrench on H.M. prerogative', he again identified 'The chief ffomenters of all this work' as 'Col. Beckford and his two sons, whom he has got into the House; they have been both tried for murder, and, I am of opinion, both were guilty, tho the Jury would not find it so'. To the fury of the Governor, the assembly kept electing Peter the Younger as Speaker, and influential friends of the Beckfords in London even had him nominated for the council in early 1709.

The governor succeeded in blocking Peter the Younger's rise to the council, but Beckford remained the leading force in the assembly, and, according to the hard-pressed Governor, 'the chief contriver and promoter of faction and discord'.

Often this 'faction and discord' spilled over into duels and violent armed quarrels, even in the House of Assembly itself. During a late-night session in the assembly on 3 April 1710, Peter Beckford the Younger, then Speaker, was kept by force from adjourning the chamber. The doors were barred and swords drawn. According to the Governor, who was nearby, the assembly members 'fell into such warm debates . . . that they put the whole Town into an uproar and murder was cryed out in severall places'. Governor Handasyd then ran 'with all speed' towards the Assembly House, encountering on the way the Speaker's father, Colonel Beckford, who from the nearby council chamber had recognised the voice of his son shouting for help. Colonel Beckford cried out that his son was about to be murdered. Handasyd might not, in truth, have minded such an outcome, but he reassured the old man that he 'hop't to God I should come time enough to prevent it'. At that point there was an enormous crash. Sixty-seven-year-old Colonel Beckford had tripped and fallen heavily – possibly down some stairs – 'by which he dy'd in 2 or 3 minutes, notwithstanding there was severall hundreds of people abt. him, and endeavour'd all they could to bring him to life again, but nothing to the purpose'.

It is perhaps fitting that Colonel Beckford died during a violent uproar. Nonetheless, he had enjoyed an extremely long life. In the English West Indies at this time, only about three in a hundred of the white population survived beyond the age of 60. He had used this time to amass spectacular wealth, even for a West Indian sugar baron. Reports vary, but he appears to have owned more than 1,000 slaves, had a share in 20 estates and possessed considerable bank stock as well.

How was such a huge fortune created by one man from virtually nothing? People made money in the West Indies through growing, processing and exporting sugar, of course, but also from marriage alliances, buccaneering, importing wine, spirits and luxury goods, slave-trading, moneylending, raising provisions and livestock, from speculation in land or through lucrative public offices. Several prominent Jamaicans combined three or even four of these activities. But Colonel Peter Beckford did them all. Furthermore, having made his living in his early years on horseback or in a ship's crew, he had remained 'very active' for his whole life, and although he dealt in huge quantities of liquor, he remained, unlike many of his contemporaries, 'sober', hard-working and 'fit'. 'They who have attained to the greatest age here', as a commentator on Jamaica wrote some years later, 'were always early risers, temperate livers in general, inured to moderate exercise, and avoiders of excess in eating.' This behaviour made Colonel Beckford an exception among West Indian planters.

Most of the inheritance went to Peter the Younger, who had survived the uproar in the House thanks to the intervention of the Governor, who forced the doors and declared the assembly dissolved in the Queen's name. Peter did not sit back on top of this fortune, nor retreat to England to mimic the life of a country squire, as some of his contemporaries were starting to do. Like in his father, in Peter the Younger were combined the business acumen of the Draxes and the political opportunism of the Codringtons, together with a violent ruthlessness that was all the Beckfords' own. Over the years after his father's death, Peter acquired a further

3,593 acres in his own name, including, in 1715, nearly 1,000 acres of the wonderfully fertile and well-watered Drax plantation on the north coast.

The male Drax line had died out in Barbados. Now the Jamaica Draxes saw themselves eclipsed by the unstoppable rise of the Beckfords. Charles Drax, who had inherited the excellent plantation in 1697 and built a Great House, died in 1721, leaving an estate worth about £8,000. Two thirds of this was accounted for by the value of his 300-strong slave force. Like his uncle Henry, he was without a male heir,* and although his successor would still hold a similar number of slaves in the 1750s, this was a family now on the wane. The rest of the estate was sold to Peter Beckford's main heir, 'Alderman'† William Beckford, in the early 1760s, and would form a super-profitable part of the Beckford sugar empire for Alderman William's heir, the extraordinary William of Fonthill.

That the Beckfords, rather than the Draxes (founder barons of the sugar empire), were triumphant in the West Indies offers insights into both lineages. The Drax family, over the generations following the remarkable Sir James, produced less able or ruthless leading sons, whereas from old Colonel Peter Beckford through to his grandson Alderman William and until the disastrous fourth generation born in the mid-eighteenth century, the Beckfords consistently produced sons even more capable and remorseless than their fathers.

Several aspects of Charles Drax's will are striking. The Jamaican Drax Hall, from what we know from archaeology, was certainly grandiose for the island, but the household goods and furniture inside the mansion were valued after Charles's death at only £213; compared to the Beckfords, this was distinctly frugal and safe. Whether this was from necessity or choice is impossible to say, though the fact that Charles was forced to sell so much land in 1715 points to the former. Drax also had an unusually high percentage of unproductive slaves among his 300-strong inventory – 17 'old and lame negro men . . . eleven old women'. He had 41 'boys and girls' – admittedly 'hardy' and therefore working – but no fewer than 77 'children'.

In later years, when the supply of enslaved Africans became much more expensive and problematic, some planters made an effort to encourage their slaves to produce children – who would be born as slaves and belong to their mother's master – as a way of replenishing their labour force. But in

* The plantation went to his sister and brother-in-law Samuel Reynold.
† William Beckford became an alderman of London in 1752; he is known as Alderman William distinguish him from his son, William Beckford of Fonthill.

the first decades of the eighteenth century, the opposite was the case. Hard work, cruel treatment, disease and malnutrition among the enslaved women resulted in a very low birth rate. For the typical planter, women were more useful as workers than breeders: small children were considered useless mouths to feed, and the whole business a distraction from the important labouring role of the women. So mothers were forced to work almost right up to full term and driven back to the fields within days of giving birth, where they toiled with their infants strapped to their backs or lying 'in a furrow, near her, generally to the sun and rain, on a kid skin, or such rags as she can procure'. Very few of the babies survived for long. Tetanus alone, often exacerbated by unhygienic delivery, killed about half of them. Such a 'young' community among Drax's slaves was therefore unusual for his time. In the same way, the proportion of elderly slaves stands out: most rendered unproductive by old age or infirmity were simply worked to death. A slave-trader was told by an Antiguan planter that it was cheaper to drive slaves to the utmost, and by 'little relaxation, hard fare, and hard usage, to wear them out before they became useless, and unable to do service; and then to buy new ones to fill up their places'.

It may be too much to conclude from the make-up of Charles Drax's household that he was entirely atypical in his treatment of his slaves. After all, the inventory also includes three 'great guns', seven small arms and four blunderbusses – weapons on site essentially for the white overseers to defend themselves against furious vengeance from the blacks. But there is also a curious bequest in Charles's will. He designated that a school be established on part of his land, operated out of proceeds of the estate, and ordered that eight poor boys and four poor white girls from St Ann parish were to be taught reading, writing, arithmetic, and the 'principals and doctrine of the Church of England'. He also specifically requested that a slave named Robinson, from his plantation, was to be admitted into the free school and to be brought up and placed out as 'one of them'. Upon completion of school, Robinson was to be a free man. If matters had been carried out as specified in his will, it would have been the first free school in Jamaica and most assuredly the first to turn out a free black with a formal education. Over 70 years later, legal action against the later owner of the estate, William Beckford of Fonthill, successfully obtained the necessary funds for the school however, aspects of Drax's bequest were eliminated. For one thing, its charter formally forbade the admission of blacks.

While the Jamaican Drax family line came to an end, the Beckfords' bloomed. Peter Beckford the Younger had 12 legitimate children, six of whom were sons who survived into adulthood. No expense was spared on the boys' education, all being sent to first Westminster, then Oxford – Balliol College in the main. By the late 1720s, the eldest was installed as assembly member for Westmoreland parish, in Jamaica's isolated but highly fertile extreme western region, where the Beckfords had been dramatically increasing their holdings.

Peter Beckford the Younger, now the leader of the extended family, held court at his lavish mansion in central Spanish Town. Here he indulged his new-found taste for beautiful *objets* and furniture. By the 1730s, the contents of his main home were valued at over £5,500, more than 20 times that of Charles Drax's Great House. Like his father, Peter Beckford had wide-ranging commercial interests. But most of this mammoth expenditure was from the profits of sugar.

By 1700, the Portuguese sugar estates in Brazil were in sharp decline, outproduced and undercut by the British West Indian planters. Fifty times as much sugar was being imported into Britain than in 1660, about a quarter of which was re-exported to western Europe, providing about half their total consumption. In the three years after the coming of peace in 1713, the Leeward Islands, Barbados and Jamaica each exported to the United Kingdom more than, or nearly as much as, all the mainland colonies of North America put together.

No one benefited more than Peter Beckford, who by the 1730s owned 11 plantations in his own right, and had substantial shares in at least the same number again. To work this acreage, he owned 1,737 slaves outright and had part-ownership in another 577. He also now had £20,000 of property in England, but he remained nonetheless focused on Jamaica. Beckford's plantations were spread out over almost the entire island. To manage the far-flung overseers and managers would have required a very firm hand, as other weaker owners found to their cost.

In the political sphere, the island's successive governors all but gave up with taking on the local power of the Beckfords. Governor Lord Archibald Hamilton, in letters to London in 1716, described Peter as the 'chief actor in all the unhappy differences in the country' and 'the chief, and allmost absolute Leader'. Hamilton alleged that the Beckfords, Peter and his brother Thomas, controlled the elections to the assembly, through 'influence, threats and unfair unproceedings'; men were being chosen, he went on, 'of most violent and pernishious principalls'. The Governor tried to have Peter stripped of his customs-collecting role, but instead saw him reappointed by London.

Hamilton had crossed swords with Thomas already. In November 1712, the Governor wrote to London that 'ye younger Beckford just at ye close of ye Assembly, had like to have murdered Mr Tho. Wood'. The argument had started in an assembly committee. When the killing was discovered, the Governor immediately sent for 'Mr Beckford', who 'before us all own'd ye matter charg'd upon him, and with very indecent carriage justifyed it as a matter of gallantry'. The Governor insisted that he give securities for his good behaviour, which Thomas swaggeringly refused, threatening to complain about the Governor in England. Hamilton looked for support from London against this menace, but received in reply only a recommendation that Thomas's brother Peter Beckford be given his 'protection and favour'. When Hamilton crossed Peter four years later, blocking his appointment as the island's deputy secretary, he found himself the same year on the boat home accused of profiting from secret links to local pirates.

Further governors fared no better. One complained that Peter Beckford was the 'chief instrument of all our misfortunes', and the leader of the opposition to the rule of the King. 'He boasts himself in his riches by means of which he has many dependants', wrote Governor Sir Nicholas Lawes in May 1718. This gave Beckford great 'sway' in the assembly; he used his position as Customs Collector, wrote Lawes, 'as a cloak to do mischief'.

Demanding that Beckford be stripped of his position, Lawes found instead that someone had taken copies of his letters of complaint and passed them to Beckford, who then waved them in the Governor's face, along with his re-appointment from London as Customs Collector. Beckford soon had his revenge, reporting Lawes for illegal trading.

Thomas, who by the late 1720s had followed his brother to the position of Speaker of the assembly, eventually had his comeuppance. In 1731 he was killed in a violent fracas – fighting a duel with Richard Cargill, an assembly member for Vere parish. According to a contemporary account, Cargill had been 'justly provoked' to defend his honour.

By the time of his brother's violent death, Peter Beckford was the richest man in the British Caribbean. As well as his sugar fortune, he had made money from his dozen or so provision plantations, and from moneylending: by the 1730s he was owed £135,000 by 128 other planters. It was a frequent complaint of incomers that the Jamaica plantocracy at its highest level was indolent and useless. Not so Peter Beckford, who also found time to operate as a leading wine shipper, factor and slave-trader.

For merchants of the Caribbean, the years following the Treaty of Utrecht in 1713 were a golden time. Part of the treaty had given Britain the *asiento*, the monopoly contract, previously held by Portugal and then France, to supply slaves to the Spanish American empire (Spain herself had no forts or factories on the African coast). Along with this deal came the right to send a 500-ton galleon of trade goods to the great annual fair at Porto Bello in Panama. Most importantly, the contract provided a host of loop-holes through which a far wider trade could be established with the Spanish settlements. Both Jamaica and Barbados soon became flourishing entre-pôts, thanks to this trade.

As was usual practice, the *asiento* was passed on to a private syndicate. The South Sea Company, founded recently, now took on the contract in return for shouldering nearly £10 million of Britain's national debt, accu-mulated during the recent war. The government promised to pay annual interest on this debt of about 6 per cent, money it planned to raise by a new duty on goods imported from the Spanish empire.

The scheme was met with open arms by a public aroused by the seem-ingly unlimited potential of the Americas, and who saw the capture of the *asiento* as the greatest achievement of what had been a less than spectacu-larly successful war. The great and good all piled their savings into shares in the company, which soon soared. Isaac Newton, Daniel Defoe, John Gay, Alexander Pope, most of the House of Lords and the entire royal family were among the investors.

Amid widespread speculation and fraud, the shares crashed suddenly in August 1720. Many great fortunes were wiped out. A small number made a killing, among them speculator Thomas Guy, who gave his profits to found a hospital in his name in London. Most lost heavily – Isaac Newton found himself down £20,000.

But the bubble was more about English domestic politics, finance and corruption than about the company's undertaking in the West Indies. The contract specified that the company deliver 4,800 slaves a year to the Spanish American colonies. At this they were relatively successful, shipping thou-sands from West Africa to Barbados or Jamaica. Here the strongest and most valuable were 'refreshed' – fattened up with two meals a day, bathed in water in which herbs had been soaked, given rum or even a pipe to smoke – then sent off to the Spanish colonies on the mainland to fetch the highest prices. The company also bought slaves from independent traders, allowed to operate freely after 1713, and then sold them on to the Spanish.

By 1720, there were nearly 150 British ships engaged in the slave trade, mostly from London and Bristol, but also Liverpool, and lesser ports such as Whitehaven, Lancaster, Chester and Glasgow. During the following decade, the British shipped more than 100,000 enslaved Africans to the Americas, about a tenth of whom ended up in the North

American mainland colonies, and a great number in Cuba. But the English Caribbean also maintained a seemingly inexhaustible demand for new slaves.

Sugar production was being expanded, particularly in Jamaica, whose slave force grew to 80,000 by 1730 (with only 7,500 whites), but the need for such huge regular replenishment was in the greatest part caused by the appalling mortality rate on the plantations.

According to the Reverend William Robertson, a clergyman-planter from Nevis writing in the early 1730s, about two fifths of the imported slaves died in the first two or three years, while in theory they were being 'seasoned' – kept from the hardest jobs – until accustomed to the climate. The others, he wrote, died at a rate of about one in 15 each year, rising to one in seven during dry years when provisions were scarce, or in 'sickly seasons; and when the small pox . . . happens to be imported, it is incredible what havock it makes among the Blacks'. Mortality actually worsened during the early eighteenth century, at which time a slave would have a life expectancy after arrival of only seven years. To blame, along with smallpox, were parasites such as hookworm, yellow fever, colds, elephantiasis, yaws (similar to syphilis) and other venereal diseases, leprosy and tetanus, all worsened by malnutrition, alcoholism, overwork and cruel treatment together with the unhealthy psychological state caused by captivity. Thus traders found that new slaves were always needed. For example, between 1708 and 1735, the Barbados planters imported 85,000 new slaves in order to lift the black population on the island from 42,000 to 46,000.

The large numbers dying soon after arrival in the Caribbean were in part the result of their exposure to unfamiliar diseases, but also because of how they were transported. The horrific details of the infamous 'Middle Passage' remain profoundly shocking. Even before being chained up in the filthy hold of a ship, the typical slave would already have been weakened by the trauma of his or her original capture and the often long and hungry journey to the coast. Most slave ships were small – perhaps 80 feet long and 20 feet wide, so that they could negotiate the river mouths of West Africa. Crewed by about 30 whites, the majority carried between 200 and 400 slaves, and never anything like the water required to prevent severe dehydration. According to a famous account by Olaudah Equiano, the male slaves chained below deck 'scarcely had room to turn' themselves, and almost suffocated in the intense heat. 'The wretched situation' was made worse 'by the galling of the chains, now become insupportable; and the filth of the necessary tubs, into which the children often fell, and were almost suffocated. The shrieks of the women, and the groans of the dying, rendered the whole a scene of horror almost inconceivable.'

Dysentery was commonplace, and in the fetid and enclosed conditions of the ship, many other illnesses thrived. One white sailor likened a slave ship to 'a slaughterhouse, Blood, filth, misery, and diseases'. On average, 11 to 12 per cent of all slaves taken from Africa died during the voyage. Many more, of course, were so weakened and demoralised that they died shortly afterwards. (The white crews, often men or boys press-ganged in Liverpool or Bristol, proportionately fared even worse, losing on average a fifth of their complement each voyage, sometimes much more. This was largely due to spending longer on board ship and exposure to West Africa – the only place in the world more deadly to Europeans than the Caribbean.)

The distinguished investors in the South Sea Company may have had little idea of the reality of the trade they supported. Most would have concurred with the views of a majority of the slave ship captains: that 'these poor wretches' they took on board would be happier as slaves in the West Indies than slaves in their own countries, 'subject to the caprices of their native princes'. To remove them was 'an act of humanity'. Some even claimed that a West Indian slave was, in fact, better off than a free man at the bottom of the pile back in Europe – 'Think of the miserable beings employed in our coal-pits . . . Think of the wretched Irish peasantry! Think of the crowded workhouses!' one wrote.

This dominant view was challenged by John Atkins, a 36-year-old naval surgeon who saw the trade face to face and wrote an account of his experience. Atkins had been at sea – though never before to Africa – since the age of 18, but was widely read, knowing Pope, Milton, Horace and Juvenal among others. He sailed in early 1721 in the *Swallow*, one of two warships protecting a convoy of slave-traders making the journey from England to the West Indies via West Africa. From the beginning of April, and for several months thereafter, his convoy cruised along the coast from Sierra Leone to Elmina, and as far as Whydah and the Gabon.

Braced by tales of savagery and cannibalism among the Africans on the coast, he was surprised to find that they were actually in the main a 'civilized people'. Rumours of cannibalism were caused by 'the credulity of the Whites', he wrote. The defence of the slave trade was that the savage Africans would be conveyed 'to a Land flowing with more Milk and Honey, to a better Living, better Manners, Virtue and Religion . . . a better state both of Temporals and Spirituals'. But by the time he wrote his book, Atkins had seen the West Indian plantations and societies: as for the spiritual side, 'few have the Hypocrity to own', he wrote, and the temporal side was far from being an improvement: 'hard Labour, corporal Punishment'. Africans at home might be poor, but they were, Atkins decided, 'happily ignorant of any thing more desirable'. He concluded that 'to remove Negroes from their Homes and Friends, where they are at ease, to a strange Country, People and Language, must be highly offending against the laws of natural Justice and Humanity'.

There was a flutter of concern at the head offices of the South Sea Company, which in 1721 ordered an investigation asking how slaves were obtained – whether they were genuine prisoners of war and criminals, or else volunteers who had sold themselves into slavery to pay a debt or prevent ruin, as defenders of the trade argued, or, as some complaints alleged, innocent victims of kidnap. But it was almost impossible to establish the truth. By the time the captives reached the coast, they had sometimes covered as much as 1,000 kilometres on their forced march from villages deep in the interior, driven from market to market and sold on many times.

Atkins found highly suspect the idea that the slaves being sold were facing a just punishment for a crime, as those in charge of them seldom had jurisdiction beyond their own town. Nor did he believe that they were legitimate prisoners of war, as 'By War for the most part is meant Robbery of inland, defenceless Creatures, who are hurried down to the Coast with the greatest Cruelty'. Slaves were procured by 'Villanies and Robberies upon one another'. Atkins remarked that 'it is not unfrequent for him who sells you Slaves to-day, to be a few days hence sold himself at some neighbouring Town'.

The trade did, indeed, provide a disastrously destablising influence on the region for hundreds of miles inland from the long coast. As early as 1703, reported a Dutch official, the Gold Coast had 'completely changed into the Slave Coast', where 'the natives no longer occupy themselves with the search for gold, but rather make war on each other in order to furnish slaves'. It was not just the demand for captives, but also what the European traders brought in return: Atkins reported them selling iron, linen and tools, but most popular were guns and gunpowder and 'strong English spirits, whiskey and gin'. By 1730, it is estimated that 180,000 guns had been sold into the Gold Coast and Bight of Benin areas, creating a vicious circle whereby captives were sold for guns to procure more captives. Atkins concluded that the slave trade was 'illegal and unjust', 'an extensive Evil, obvious to those who can see how Fraud, Thieving, and Executions have kept pace with it'. At fault, for Atkins, was the very idea of empire: 'the

Settlement of Colonies are Infringements on the Peace and Happiness of Mankind', he wrote.

Throughout his voyage, Atkins made careful notes not just about the Africans he encountered, including their languages, diets and spiritual practices, but also about wildlife, topography and the currents of the coast. He was kept busy, as well, nursing the crew; during an attack of fever, three or four were dying each day for six weeks. To keep the ship sailing, it became necessary to 'impress Men from the Merchant-Ships'.

Near the Sierra Leone river, they had encountered the *Robert* of Bristol, taking on 30 slaves before heading further along the coast. A short time later, the *Swallow* met the Bristol ship again, and heard from its Captain Harding that there had been a slave uprising on board.

Among the 30 slaves transported from their last stop had been a Captain Tomba. Beforehand, Tomba had led an effort to unite a group of inland villages against the raids of the slave-traders. But after early successes, the traders had found Tomba and 'surprised and bound him in the night . . . he having killed two in his defence before they could secure him'. Tomba had been himself enslaved and then sold to Captain Harding. Keen to strike while they were still in sight of their homeland, Tomba 'combined with three or four of the stoutest of his Country-men to kill the Ship's Company, and attempt their Escapes'. A female slave, given more freedom on board, was recruited to pass them hammers and give the signal when the crew was at its weakest. Breaking out of their shackles, Tomba's party urged the other slaves to join them, but procured only one further recruit. The first guards encountered, however, were fast asleep, and two were quickly 'dispatched, with single Strokes upon the Temple'. The third roused himself enough to seize one of the escapees, but was then similarly 'dispatched' by Tomba. 'Upon the confusion', however, the other guards were alerted, and grappled with the handful of slaves. According to Atkins (or, more precisely, Harding's own account), the ship's captain saved the day by rushing into the melee, seizing a 'Hand-spike, the first thing he met with in the Surprize, and redoubling his Strokes home upon Tomba, laid him at length flat upon the Deck, securing them all in Irons'.

Harding went on to describe his resulting vengeance. Tomba and the other main leader were too strong and valuable to be killed, so escaped with a severe whipping. The three others, 'Abettors, but not Actors, nor of Strength for it', looked less valuable and so were sentenced to death. After the first was killed, the other two were forced to eat his heart and liver (the only case of cannibalism Atkins came across during his time on the African coast) and then executed. 'The Woman he hoisted up by the Thumbs, whipp'd, and slashed her with Knives, before the other Slaves till she died.'

Atkins commented that 'there has not been wanting Examples of rising and killing a Ship's Company'. The slaves, he wrote, thought themselves 'bought to eat' – that the cannibals were the Europeans. Moreover they believed that 'Death will send them into their own Country'. With seemingly nothing to lose, at least one in ten slave voyages saw a major rebellion, along with frequent fights and brawls. Most took place while the ship was still close to the African coast. A small number were successful, but most were bloodily suppressed, often with the aid of other European ships nearby.

20

PIRACY AND RUM

'I pity them greatly, but I must be mum,
For how could we do without sugar and rum?'

William Cowper, 'Pity for Poor Africans'

Dealing with slave rebellions was not, however, the primary purpose of Atkins's warship the *Swallow* and her sister ship the *Weymouth* as they cruised off the coast of West Africa in 1721. Instead they were an anti-pirate force, protecting the slave trade. Some three months after arriving off the coast of Africa, Atkins heard that notorious pirates 'under the Command of Roberts' were in the area, causing 'great Ravages upon the Merchant Ships'. Local traders were panicking. Thereafter, the Royal Navy vessels played cat-and-mouse with Bartholomew Roberts's pirate flotilla; several times they were told the pirates were windward of them, 'which kept us Plying'. But soon afterwards they would hear a contradictory rumour. Then at Whydah they missed Roberts by only 48 hours; the pirates had 'plundered and ransomed 11 Sail of Ships', but on hearing they were being pursued, quickly left the harbour. At last Atkins's ship, minus its leaking sister ship the *Weymouth*, encountered Roberts's three vessels at anchor near Cape Lopez, south of the Gabon river. Straight away, battle was joined.

As in the West Indies, pirates and state-sponsored privateers had infested the West African coast and far beyond since almost the very earliest European voyages. The growth of the slave trade had increased the traffic and number of targets. Some years before Atkins's visit, a ship called the *Beck-ford* – 200 tons, 24 guns, 30 men – had been taken by pirates while loading slaves at Madagascar. Apparently while the master was on shore, men under

'Ryder the Pirate' had boarded the vessel, 'turned' nearly half the crew, and put the rest ashore before sailing off with their prize. The seven owners of the vessel, with old Colonel Peter Beckford at their head, had appealed to the Council of Trade and Plantations for the capture of Ryder, 'a middle-sized man, of a swarthy complexion, inclinable by his aspect to be of a churlish constitution; his own hair short and brown, and apt, when in drink, to utter some Portuguese or Moorish words'.

At the end of the war in 1713, a large number of Anglo-American sailors, previously engaged in privateering or on naval vessels, found themselves unemployed. They turned en masse to piracy, attacking vessels whatever their nationality in the Caribbean, the American eastern seaboard, the West African coast and the Indian Ocean.* This launched the climax of the 'Golden Age of Piracy', during which English island governors complained endlessly about the dangers of the sea routes and of the daily increase of 'pyrates'. Charismatic pirate leaders such as 'Blackbeard' (Edward Teach), 'Calico Jack' Rackham and Charles Vane became well-known names, even in England.

The disruption to the hugely profitable sugar and slave trades was such that the European governments were forced to take action. A Royal Proclamation by George I of Britain in 1717 promised amnesty to those pirates who gave themselves up, and a number surrendered in Jamaica and Bermuda, several on more than one occasion. But hundreds remained at large, based in the Bahamas and elsewhere. The Royal Navy, helped by local auxiliaries, waged a determined campaign against the pirates during the early 1720s. Teach was killed during a fight on the high seas in 1718. Rackham and Vane were captured, hanged and then gibbeted outside Port Royal shortly afterwards, along with 20 of their crews. (Female pirates Anne Bonney and Mary Read were also sentenced to death but were spared execution on the grounds they were 'quick with child'.) Others were executed in Barbados and the Leewards.

But of all of them, Bartholemew Roberts was perhaps the most successful and thereby infamous. It has been estimated that he captured as many as 470 vessels during a spectacular career that lasted less than three years. Roberts, a Welshman born in 1682, had been serving as a mate on a slaving ship when in 1719 it was captured by pirates off the Gold Coast. He was forced to join the pirates' crew, but took to it, pledging himself to a short but merry life, and was soon afterwards elected captain of the band. He

---

* It was not just Anglo-Americans; all nationalities engaged in piracy. One of the worst was a Spaniard, Miguel Enriquez, who was based in Puerto Rico, and whose favourite tactic was to maroon the crews of the ships he attacked on deserted islands to die of hunger or thirst.

adopted an outfit consisting of a rich crimson damask waistcoat and breeches, a red feather in his hat, a gold chain with a diamond cross round his neck and two pairs of pistols slung over his shoulders.

Roberts's leadership saw successes off Barbados and Martinique before he headed north to Newfoundland in search of fresh victims. Each time a bigger vessel was taken, Roberts would 'trade up' his flagship for a new model, while most of the time keeping a 'fleet' of two or three captured ships under his command. In late 1720 he returned to the Caribbean, where he took vessels in the roadstead of Basseterre, St Kitts, and a month later, seized 16 French sloops off Dominica and Martinique, capturing the Governor of Martinique in the process and unceremoniously hanging him from the yardarm, as well as torturing other prisoners.

By the spring of 1721, Roberts's depredations had almost brought seaborne trade in the West Indies to a standstill, so with potential victims few in number, he headed to West Africa. He soon heard about the presence in the region of the Royal Navy vessels the *Weymouth* and *Swallow*, but continued his attacks with his three ships the *Royal Fortune*, the *Ranger* and the *Little Ranger*, capturing a number of vessels before his successful descent on Whydah in January 1722. Thereafter he proceeded south to Cape Lopez for repairs.

On 5 February the crew of HMS *Swallow*, with Atkins on board, spotted the three pirate ships. But on her approach to engage, the *Swallow* was forced to veer away to avoid a shoal. This unwittingly deceived the pirates into thinking she was a merchant ship fleeing at the sight of them. One of Roberts's flotilla, the *Ranger*, raced off in pursuit. Once out of sight of the other pirates, the *Swallow* opened fire, and after a short engagement, the *Ranger* surrendered.

The *Swallow* returned five days later and found the two other pirate ships still at anchor at Cape Lopez. In fact, they had just captured an English ship, the *Neptune*, and were celebrating hard in true pirate fashion. At first the pirates thought that she was the *Ranger* returning, but a deserter from the *Swallow* alerted them. Roberts donned his finest outfit, and ordered a daring break for freedom. But at the crucial moment, his crew proved too drunk and disorderly to carry out his commands (Roberts himself is said to have preferred tea to rum). The *Royal Fortune* lost its course and came under sustained broadsides from the *Swallow*. Roberts was killed – hit in the throat by grapeshot while standing on his deck – and his crew surrendered soon after.

'The Pyrates, tho' singly Fellows of Courage', concluded Atkins, had been undone by their 'Drunkenness, Inadvertency, and Disorder'. The

death of Roberts, previously considered by many to be invincible, is now
seen as the end of the golden age of piracy.

Roberts's third ship was soon afterwards captured, and the prizes and
prisoners taken to the English castle at Cape Coast. According to Atkins,
'the pyrates in this Passage were very troublesome to us, from a Project
or two they had formed for their Deliverance', but they were delivered
safely to justice. The captured crews, totalling 272 men, turned out to
consist of 75 blacks, who were quickly sold to slaving ships, a large number
of West Country Englishman, and a mix of Londoners, Irish and Scots,
together with Dutch and Greeks. More than 50 were hanged; 20 were
allowed to take on indentures with the Royal African Company, by reputation 'a lingering death', 20 were sent to London for trial, and about a
third were released.

The captain of the *Swallow*, Challenor Ogle, was rewarded with fast
promotion and a knighthood, the only British naval officer to be honoured
specifically for his actions against pirates. He also became instantly a very
rich man. According to Atkins, on board the ships was 'great plenty of
trading Goods, and, what more attracted the Eye, a large quantity of Gold
Dust, by computation, 8 or 10,000*l.*' The gold disappeared into Challenor's
pockets. In the division of the spoils, Atkins got only £26.

The *Swallow*, with its prize the *Royal Fortune* in attendance, now left
Africa for Brazil, Barbados and Jamaica, accompanying English slave-
traders, who would then return to England with sugar and other tropical
products, completing the famous trade triangle.

Atkins was impressed with a lot of what he found in Jamaica: the wide
streets of Kingston, open to the sea breeze; the 'Magnificence of Living'
of the 'Gentlemen', whom he described as 'true Republicans in Disposition'. But the slavery he saw – men, women and children treated as 'beasts
of burthen' – confirmed him in his view that the Africans were not, as had
been suggested, better off in the West Indies. He was also concerned about
the ratio of blacks to whites, now in the region of eight to one: 'a Disproportion, that together with the Severity of their Patrons, renders the whole
Colony unsafe'. Maroons, he wrote, 'daily increase'.

There was to be a more immediate danger, however. A week after his
arrival in Jamaica, Atkins had first-hand experience of a hurricane. The
island had been hit 10 years before, but this one was worse. For 48 hours
the storm gave warnings of its imminent arrival: waves crashed noisily
against the wharfs and the nights saw 'prodigious lightnings and thunder'.

When the hurricane started on 28 August 1722, Atkins found himself 'left alone proprietor of a shaking old house, the streets full of water and drift, with shingles flying about like arrows'. Most of the population of Kingston took shelter in the church, as the two blocks nearest the sea 'were undermined and leveled with the Torrent'. But the flimsy church then collapsed too, killing 300–400 people in the ruins.

Only six of the 50 vessels in the harbour survived, (including the *Swallow*, though not her prize), but all had their masts and booms blown away. Wrecks and drowned men were everywhere to be seen along the shore, 'a melancholy scene'. Left behind were pools of stagnating water, which 'brought on a contagious distemper, fatal for some months through the island'.

Along with epidemics of disease, natural disasters remained a fact of life in the West Indies, contributing to the colonies' pervading sense of crisis and impermanence. Jamaica would be hit once more by a hurricane four years later, then again in 1734. The French settlements, where sugar production was now rising sharply, were just as vulnerable. Guadeloupe, for one, was visited by hurricanes in 1713, 1714 and 1738. Antigua was now, in terms of production, the fastest-growing British Leeward sugar island, but this was in spite of losing a sixth of its inhabitants to a fever epidemic in 1725, followed by a severe drought and then a hurricane in 1728.

Bristol-born Quaker Abraham Redwood, who had written to a friend in Philadelphia after Parke's murder in 1710 that Antigua had called down God's judgement on itself, inherited, together with his sons, substantial estates on the island on the death in 1712 of his father-in-law, the ancient Quaker Jonas Langford (all of whose sons had predeceased him). Almost immediately, Redwood removed his family – now consisting of four or five children – north to Newport, Rhode Island, safe, he must have hoped, from the threats of war and disease in Antigua.

But by the spring of 1714, Redwood was preparing to return to Antigua. His family, it seems, had not taken to the New England winter. It is 'too Cold in this place', he wrote to John Dickinson from Newport in January 1714. The whole family had been ill, and his eldest son, 16-year-old William, had died in October 1712. William's three-year-old brother John died the following year.

However, the return was not a success. Abraham's wife Mehitable died in 1715, and, leaving his estates in the hands of an attorney, Redwood relocated north again, to Salem, Massachusetts, where he remarried. Although by now 51, he went on to have a further five surviving children with his new wife, Patience, including one son, William. Nonetheless, there would be further tragedy: in October 1724, Redwood's eldest son, Jonas, aged 18, died after a fall from a horse. This meant that his third son, another Abraham, was now set to inherit the Antigua plantations.

Abraham junior rose to the challenge. From 1726, although only 17, he based himself in Newport and, using his family's Quaker business contacts, started selling the Antigua produce there – sugar, rum, molasses and cotton – shipping out to the West Indies in return peas, beans, candles and horses, as well as occasional gifts of fruits and cheese, and corresponding with his family's agent in Antigua, at that time Edward Byam.

The young Redwood was part of a Rhode Island colony that had found its role in the imperial system. The overriding purpose of the commercial economy of colonial New England was to obtain the means with which to purchase English manufactures (an objective the Virginia planter accomplished by the simple expedient of exporting tobacco). Rhode Island had turned out to be too barren to compete on agricultural production and had no access to fisheries. What it did have was excellent ports and an enterprising population. The answer was to build ships and to trade. Hundreds of vessels of all sizes were constructed in the colony during the early decades of the eighteenth century, during which time New England came to dominate the supply of provisions, horses and lumber to its key market – the West Indian sugar colonies.

Self-assured, decisive, and independent-minded, Redwood was an able but headstrong young man, a great contrast to his gloomy and God-fearing father. Certainly Abraham junior felt no compulsion to follow in his parents' devout Quaker tradition, as evidenced by his marriage, aged just short of 18, to Martha Coggeshall, from an old but far from wealthy Rhode Island family. To the shock of the Newport Quaker community, the youngsters married outside the Society of Friends. A marker had been laid down: Abraham would pay scant regard to the Friends' distaste for luxury and, in time, slavery.

By the time of his father's death in January 1729, Abraham Redwood junior, although remaining in Newport, had acquired solid experience of managing the family's interests in Antigua, centred on the Cassada Gardens plantation, now bringing in £2,000–3,000 a year profit on the back of the work of more than 200 slaves. By this time, he had laid down firm roots in North America, having acquired an elegant house with a large garden on the Newport wharf at Thames Street, as well as warehouses and loading facilities on the docks, and another house in Spring Street. To compete with the showiness of his neighbours, the pre-eminent Newport merchants, the Malbones, he had imported gates and bricks from England for the entrance to his mansion, as well as specially commissioned carved stone pineapples to top the gates (the English West Indian symbol of welcome that is today everywhere to be seen in the older parts of Newport).

From as early as 1727, Redwood was also importing enslaved Africans from Antigua to Newport. This was in part, like the mansion gates, a question of status – it was suddenly the thing to have in attendance a black child as a page or maid. There is voluminous correspondence about 'negro' boys and girls requested by Redwood ('I have bought you a negro Girle of about nine or ten years of age . . .') and sent to him by his Antigua agents. Sometimes this was tricky: on 20 July 1728, Byam wrote: 'I would have sent ye girle you desired but . . . those on your plantation who are in family are very unwilling to part with their children.' In the same letter, Byam congratulated Redwood on the birth of his first child.

But slaves in Newport were not just ornaments. By the 1730s, they were doing a lot of the hard physical work of a trading and shipbuilding colony, and made up 10 per cent of the population of Newport. Most were imported from Barbados, some 30 a year, and it seems that unlike in the West Indies, the slave owners were 'supplied by the offspring of those they have already, which increase daily'. (In contrast, the Carolinas at this time were importing about 1,000 slaves a year; by 1732, the population of South Carolina was 14,000 whites and 32,000 blacks.)

More significantly, a number of North Americans were now involving themselves directly in the slave trade from Africa. As early as 1700, Rhode Island and Boston ships were to be found on the West African coast, picking up slaves who were then sold in Barbados or the other West Indian islands, with perhaps one or two brought back to North America. But in the 1720s, this trade surged.

The key to this was rum. Places like Newport and Boston had been distilling since the 1690s, but most of the resulting spirit had been for local consumption, or for sale to the 'Indians' in return for furs, and, according to later complaints, to 'debauch them'. But from the 1720s onward, about a third of Rhode Island's rum production was loaded on to ships for Africa, where it was traded for slaves. Rum was perfect: cheap to produce; easy to transport; it did not deteriorate with age; and it lent itself to adulteration by clever North American traders. Most importantly, the super-proof 'Guinea' rum produced by the New England distilleries was massively popular in West Africa, much preferred to its rivals, West Indian rum, English spirits or French brandy. Soon the New England rum was a de facto currency of the Slave Coast. Adult male slaves could be bought for as little as 80 gallons, which cost only five pence per gallon to produce. Within a short time, there were as many as 20 vessels from Newport alone making the voyage every year, carrying about 1,800 hogsheads of rum. Slaves were sold on in the Caribbean or in New England for between £30 and £80.

The highly profitable trade was not without its risks. The journey from Newport to Africa took 40 to 50 days – plenty of time for shipwreck, pirate attack* or other disasters – and the diseases of the West African coast remained deadly to outsider whites.

The demand for the raw material of rum – molasses – also threatened to cause severe long-term problems. In the late 1720s and early 1730s, a gallon of molasses from Barbados cost 9–10d; in French Martinique the same quantity could be had for as little as 4d. Inevitably, the French islands secured the new market and benefited from the increased demand from New England. Furthermore, the French, by trading with the New Englanders, pushed up the prices of the goods supplied by the northern colonies to their sister settlements on the British islands.

The British sugar planters were not prepared to put up with this for long. Starting in 1730, they complained of penury, and lobbied Whitehall to impose a heavy duty on all foreign sugar, molasses and rum imported into the northern colonies. New Englanders mocked the claims to poverty, pointing out that the sugar barons still 'live like Lords, and ride in a Coach and Six'. But it was the sugar interest that prevailed in London, where trading with a rival power was seen as against the national interest and the prevailing mercantilist economic orthodoxy. In 1733 the Molasses Act was passed, imposing a duty of sixpence per gallon on molasses imported from non-British territories. This was not a revenue bill, it was effective prohibition, doubling the cost of French molasses for the New England distiller.

The Act represents a turning point in the history of Britain's first western empire. As John Adams would later write: 'Molasses was an essential ingredient in American Independence.' Crucially, the legislation clearly favoured the interests of one set of colonies over another. North Americans complained vociferously that the duty was contrary to their rights as 'ye King's natural born subjects and English men in levying subsidies upon them against their consent when they . . . have no Representatives in Parliament'.

Such dangerous words should, with hindsight, have caused alarm in London, but just as worrying was the subsequent carrying-out of the

---

* A slaver owned by the Malbones of Newport was attacked by pirates, whereupon the captain offered freedom to all the slaves who would join in defending the vessel. The enemy was repulsed and the freed slaves settled on the Malbone estate in Pomfret, Connecticut.

Molasses Act. In short, it was a dead letter. Rhode Island traders such as James Brown, the founder of the dynasty that would establish Brown University in Providence, quickly sent messages to their captains to bring their molasses, picked up in Martinique, into one of the many quiet bays around the island, out of sight of British patrols.* Some made even less effort, simply paying off officials who realised that a port without commerce benefited nobody but the distant planter interest in the islands. Thus the flagrant violation of the Molasses Act indicated that North American colonial merchants would not observe, nor would local British officials enforce, a law that would seriously disrupt trade.

So New England's transatlantic activities continued, with Barbadians complaining in 1736 that the New Englanders sold their slaves in the English islands for cash, which they then spent in the Dutch enclave of St Eustatius on imported goods or on molasses from the French islands. In the same year, the first slaver set sail from Providence, Rhode Island – the *Mary*, owned by the Brown family and with Obadiah Brown, James's younger brother, in charge of the cargo. (A ledger of James's accounts shows a bill from a blacksmith for '35 pare of handcoofs', which indicates they were aiming to take on 70 male slaves.) In Newport, the slave population continued to grow.

Many of the Rhode Islanders growing rich on the West Indies–Guinea trade (such as the Malbones, Godfreys, Vernons, de Wolfs, and Simeon Potter, 'the father of slaving at Bristol, Rhode Island') invested their money in sugar estates in the Caribbean. Further afield, the Dickinsons of Philadelphia continued to hold land in the English West Indies, as did a number of other elite North American families. By 1720, Philip Livingstone, whose son would be one of the signatories of the Declaration of Independence, was a well-established New York merchant shipping rum, tobacco and cheese to England, where he picked up guns and cloth. From there he sailed to West Africa, trading for slaves. With the proceeds he bought up and ran plantations in Jamaica.

For Abraham Redwood, the ownership of estates in Antigua seems to have provided him with a particular hold over his slave workforce in Newport: if you displeased the master, you were sent to join the toilers at Cassada Gardens in Antigua. Redwood's correspondence tracks the case of one such unfortunate, named only as 'John'. Clearly, life as a slave in

* On 6 March, James Brown wrote to Captain Fields: 'it is ticklish times here my neighbors threaten to inform against us, so I hope you will not be too bold when you come home, enter in the West Indias [western inlet] if you can, and if you cannot bring too down the River and send your cargo some to Rhode Island and some up here in boats, so as not to bring but a few hhds. up to Wharff'.

Antigua was considerably harder than in Rhode Island. 'I fear he will hardly be able to endure such coarse dyet & hard labour as our slaves are put to in this place', reported Redwood's agent Edward Byam shortly after John's arrival in Antigua. Less than a year later, Redwood was told that John was on his way back north, having 'promised a great amendment'.

The lengthy correspondence of Abraham Redwood also gives a vivid picture of the everyday running of a sugar business by an Anglo-American. What is immediately striking is how difficult and uncertain tropical agriculture was, particularly as monoculture took over, with its attendant problems of pests and soil deprivation. 'Cane blast' – infestation by aphids – was a particular menace, as it destroyed acres of crop and required a huge amount of extra work to get rid of. Drought was a constant worry in Antigua – at one point in the late 1720s, water had to be imported at 15 shillings a hogshead. The quality, and therefore marketability, of the sugar varied dramatically, as did its price in Europe, and there never seemed to be enough hands to run the estates to their full potential. Constant rumours of war through the late 1720s and 1730s further destabilised the efforts of Redwood's managers.

Also noticeable is that a very small coterie of families dominated business on the island, which by the 1720s had a white population of about 5,000 (with some 18,000 black slaves). A tiny handful of names – Langford, Byam, Gunthorpe, Martin, Tomlinson – occur again and again, as fathers and sons, cousins, and often people linked by marriage to each other. The same families led the government and militia on the island.

Between his merchant business and estates in Rhode Island, his plantations in Antigua, and his sugar factor in London (another Tomlinson), Redwood's operations were complicated and far-flung. He also dealt with merchants in Boston and Bristol, all in a time when letters took months to arrive, and were often lost (the practice emerged of sending the same letter two or even three times to ensure its arrival). To succeed at this was, on its own terms, immensely impressive.

Even before his father's death, the attorneys running the Redwood core business in Antigua – Byam, then Redwood's cousin Jonas Langford – had written that Abraham junior should come to 'look into his affairs'. There were warnings, however, that 'our Island is very sickly', 'especially to strangers'. In the event, it appears that Redwood, on his own, visited Antigua during 1730 for not more than six or eight months. From the subsequent letters, he seems to have been a vigorous presence, suggesting all sorts of improvements, including building work and taking into direct management land on his estate currently rented out to smallholders.

But instead of expansion and improvements, the 1730s would see hard times on the Redwood Antigua estates, as elsewhere in the sugar-producing Caribbean. Expanded French production, particularly in spacious and fertile St Domingue, saw a significant fall in the international price of sugar, and other factors in Antigua contributed to the recession there during the decade. In May 1731, Redwood received a letter from Jonas Langford warning him that the lack of rain meant that income from the crop was insufficient to cover provisions and clothing for the slaves. Shortly after-wards he heard that 'a most destructive blast' had ruined his latest sugar and that his London agent was warning that 'all the merchants refused to advance anything for the West India correspondents; sugars being then so low and the Islands in so declining a condition'. On Antigua, as elsewhere, debts became suddenly much more difficult to collect.

The lack of credit, combined with plagues of insects and droughts, led to an island-wide shortage of provisions in Antigua. Of course this hit the slave population first, and towards the middle of the decade the Redwood letters show unmistakable signs of the troubles to come, with hungry slaves stealing or fighting among themselves for ever more scarce food. In May 1735, Redwood heard that one of his slaves – Jaffrey – had 'barbarously' killed another slave, 'of Mr French, Barbados, valued at seventy pounds'. Jaffrey was hanged and Redwood was forced to pay compensation to French for the value of his property.

The Antigua planters had been severely rattled by the gruesome murder of Major Martin in 1701, but since then they had become distracted by their own feuds and complacent about the threat the ever-growing slave population presented. In 1729 a plot was uncovered involving some of the island's most trusted Negroes (one was a chief slave of Samuel Martin, son of the murdered major, another a senior slave owned by William Codrington, who had retired to England to act the role of absentee land-lord). As always, the response was brutal, with three conspirators burned, one hanged, drawn and quartered and 10 others banished. But in fact the conspiracy had been much more widespread than the planters realised, and continued to simmer thereafter.

In 1736 a further, even more extensive slave uprising plot was uncov-ered in Antigua. Sophisticated plans had been laid for an enormous and deadly explosion to strike at the entire white leadership. One of the plot-ters had obtained the job of installing the seating for a lavish ball being held to celebrate the anniversary of the King's coronation. This man was to plant enough gunpowder to blow up the island's elite in one go, where-upon the slaves would seize the forts and the ships in the harbour and thereby take control. But the grand ball was delayed by two weeks due to the illness of the Governor's son, and in the meantime the plot was betrayed. Six offenders were hanged (or, possibly, gibbeted alive), five broken on the wheel, 42 banished, and no fewer than 77 burnt alive. Nearly 50 of those put to death were skilled artisans. The killing only stopped when the treasury ran out of money to compensate the owners. Two of the slaves burnt at the stake – Oliver and Scipio – had come from Abraham Redwood's labour force at Cassada Gardens. At last, at the end of 1736, Redwood decided to return to Antigua to put his affairs in order.

In spite of the severe difficulties faced by his plantation business, and by the island as a whole, the 26-year-old Redwood, having left his young family behind in Newport, appears to have had a highly enjoyable time in the unbuttoned atmosphere of Antigua. It may have been a relief to escape from what must have been a grief-stricken and gloomy Redwood household in Newport. In 1735 a daughter, Elizabeth, had been born, but she died within months. The following year, their eldest son, eight-year-old Abraham, also died.

Redwood, young, rich and with lucrative jobs in his gift, was given a warm welcome by the coterie of young Byams, Langfords, Martins and the handful of others who made up his generation of the Antigua planter elite. There was an almost continual round of dinners and dances. Redwood was soon writing to his friend David Cheeseborough, left in charge of his affairs in Newport, to send out some dancing 'pumps'. Cheeseborough complied with '4 paire of fine Pumps', but with a slight warning: 'we are concerned least [you] should stay to Dance out the fine Pumps. Your spouse was very unwilling they should be sent.'

Abraham Redwood was now also launching himself into the slave trade, ordering the fitting out of a Newport sloop, the *Martha and Jane*, and sending her to Africa to bring him slaves direct to Antigua. It appears that the first voyage was not a success. Cheeseborough wrote to him soon afterwards, urging him not to take on another 'Guinea voyage', as the proceeds had not covered the cost of fitting out the vessel. The *Martha and Jane*, he wrote, 'was an Unlucky Changeable Beast'. Instead Redwood should load the boat with his plantation produce and return home: 'it would be to our satisfaction who all long to See you once more', he said. 'Her Load would doubtless pay all your debts and put a good Sum in your pocket which I know you are determined upon.'

Redwood ignored this advice and persisted with the trade. But his wife was determined to get him back to Newport. In early February 1739,

Redwood's father-in-law wrote to him that 'thy wife has beene very much out of order . . . I would have the consider to they selfe what a vast deale of troble she must needs meat with in living without a husband three years . . . thy wife cant compose her selfe to write at present'. Abraham relented and promised to return in the spring. 'You have raised our Expectations of Seeing you by your promises pray let them not faile at last', pleaded a letter soon afterwards from Cheeseborough. Redwood's wife, he said, 'is got pretty well . . . but thinks her Self not able to write to you'.

After fond farewells, Redwood left Antigua for the last time in April 1739. Shortly afterwards he received a letter from John Tomlinson on the island, which gives an indication of the sort of social life he was leaving behind: after masculine banter about Redwood receiving 'pleasure & delight' from 'a Fond Wife, after a long absence', he continued, 'Last night Major Byam, your cousin Jonas, Samll Martin, Warner Tempest and self tasted your Burgundy and Champaigne, not forgetting the Founder . . . your cousin I think was never drunker in his life.'

Abraham Redwood continued his slave-trading operations after his return to Newport. Correspondence in 1740 indicates that Francis Pope, the man entrusted by Redwood to skipper his ship, buy slaves on the African coast and then sell them in Antigua, was poor as a salesman and a sailor. On 23 April 1740 he arrived in Antigua with 76 slaves, which would have been a fairly full cargo for a vessel the size of the *Martha and Jane*. But 21 of them, Redwood's friend Tomlinson reported, were 'in the Old Condition, Carted up to your Estate, the rest ordinary enough'. More than half remained unsold. 'For God's sake think no more of Guinny', wrote Tomlinson. Another friend made in Antigua, Thomas Gunthorpe, wrote to Redwood in July, 'I am heartilly sorry Pope has againe made you so bad a voyage too and from the Coast of Guinea Especially as I am given to understand you have made a considerable purchase of lands in Rhode Island and depend in a greater measure upon the returns of your Guinea cargo to fulfil your engagements therein . . . pursue the Guinea trade no further, under the direction of Capt. Pope.'

A month after landing, Pope still had 'nineteen slaves unsold'. By the end of June they were all at last sold, but there was still a problem: 'the people hear in General is very Backward in paying there debts . . . I meat with a great dile of troble and dissapointment in getting my money.' Indeed, the planters were notoriously bad payers. Earlier, the Company of Royal Adventures Trading to Africa decided to offer its Caribbean debts to the highest bidder, but they were so toxic they had few takers.

Redwood seems to have thereafter avoided the trade, buying his slaves in Antigua or in Rhode Island. In the 1750s, however, the business would be reactivated, under the management of his sons. In the meantime, Redwood concentrated instead on giving directions for the improvement of Cassada Gardens, and on flaunting his wealth in Newport. Happily for him, the slump in sugar price ended in about 1740, and over much of the sugar-producing Caribbean the rich times returned.

21

THE MAROON WAR IN JAMAICA AND
THE WAR OF JENKINS'S EAR

'That the Negros here use Naturall (or Diabolical) Magick no planter in Barbados doubts, but how they doe it none of us knows.'

Letter from a white farmer in Barbados, 1712

Jamaica had suffered during the slump of the 1730s, but because of its greater space for growing provisions and heavier rainfall, it experienced nothing like the hunger of Antigua. But it had its own severe problem with its slave workforce.

This centred on the continuing existence of the maroons, communities in the interior of Jamaica originally composed of runaway slaves and surviving 'Indians' from the Spanish era, but now largely made up of those who had escaped from slavery on the English plantations. On the western, leeward side of the island, a permanent settlement had grown up in the isolated and inaccessible 'cockpit country' on the border of Trelawny parish and St James. This had become known as Cudjoe's Town, after the leader of the main band. Cudjoe himself seems to have been a pragmatist – he had no interest in attracting the attention of the heavily armed white population of the coastal regions, and for a long time kept his 500 or so followers under strict control, concentrating on expelling rival groups rather than antagonising the plantation owners.

On the eastern, windward side, another concentration of maroons had been formed from a nucleus of those who had taken part in the rebellion of 1690 and had fled to the high mountains above Kingston. The chaos caused by the French invasion of a few years later had swelled their numbers. Their base was Nanny Town, a mountain fastness like that of the leeward maroons, although surrounded by 100 acres of land 'well planted with provisions'. The town was named after a near-mythological figure – Nanny, a black woman who was credited with supernatural powers, including the ability to catch the bullets fired at her by British troops in her buttocks and then fart them back at her enemies.

This group, led by Captain Quao, was much more troublesome. As early as 1702, Lieutenant-Governor Colonel Beckford was writing to London that 'rebellious negroes . . . have been so bold to come down armed and attack our out settlements to Windward'. Colonel Beckford had sent out four parties, one of which, consisting of only 20 men, had fought for six hours against 300 maroons: 'the negroes faced our men so long as they had any ammunition left, and wounded three of our party. We killed and took several.' Outlying maroon settlements were burned, but the threat was far from extinguished.

By the mid-1720s, the maroons numbered in their thousands rather than hundreds: travel on the north coast had become hazardous; St George and St James parishes were almost deserted. In 1730, after a raid on a plantation saw six female slaves carried off, three major militia expeditions were launched against the more troublesome windward maroons and a bounty of £10 was placed on the head of any rebel captured, who would be tortured and executed and their children sold into slavery to other islands. But the maroons had an effective network of spies as well as supplies of guns and powder. All efforts by the whites ended in disaster: one expedition was ambushed, a second driven back to the coast, and another got lost in the swamps and a quarter of the men drowned or died of fever.

The following year, two regiments of foot were relieved of guard duty in Gibraltar and sent to Jamaica to deal with the maroons once and for all. In May 1731, the Governor of Jamaica reported that the newly arrived troops were 'pretty healthy and might be kept so were it not for rumm'. But six months later, the troops were in a 'wofull state, some companys having lost more than half their compliment chiefly owing to drunkenness'.

Nonetheless, they were sent into action to support the militia, who had some success in November, surprising Quao's maroons in their chief settlement of Nanny Town. The maroons were driven out and the town held for three days, before the isolated English soldiers were forced to withdraw. For the next two years, both sides had victories and setbacks in what amounted to a stalemate, exhausting for both sides. Then, in April 1734, Nanny Town was captured again after light artillery pieces had been dragged up the mountains to bombard the settlement. The town was destroyed and its inhabitants dispersed for good, although many of them slipped westwards to join up with Cudjoe's leeward maroons.

This was now the new focus of British efforts; several deserters from Cudjoe's community served as guides for the militia and regulars who now looked to end the maroon threat for good. Small artillery pieces were used with good effect, as well as imported dogs and Moskito Indians from the Honduran coast, accomplished trackers. But it was an unwinnable war for the British: there were endless ambushes; settlements could be destroyed, but new ones were continually established in even more remote locations. An exasperated Governor Trelawny reported that 'The service here is not like that in Flanders or any part of Europe. Here the greatest difficulty is not to beat, but to see the enemy.' Troops were forced to march up the currents of rivers, over steep trackless mountains and precipices, or through woods so thick that they were obliged to cut their way at almost every step. 'In short', said Trelawny, 'nothing can be done in strict conformity to the usual military preparations and according to a regular manner, bushfighting as they call it being a thing peculiar to itself.'

As early as 1734 there had been efforts from the British to come to some sort of terms with the maroons. Neither side could survive a state of constant war. But only in 1738 was a negotiator appointed whom the maroons felt they could trust. Eventually, in March 1739, Cudjoe agreed a peace treaty: his band were to be declared free men and have 1,500 acres to grow provisions (though not sugar); in return, he was to build and maintain roads from his settlements to the white areas (thereby ensuring easy access for British troops) and to promise to return any further runaway slaves from the plantations and to help the British in the event of a foreign invasion. Two white men were to be stationed permanently in the maroon towns, whose leaders would have to report to the Governor once a year. A similar treaty was made later in the year with the remnants of the windward maroons.

In 1735, before the end of the Maroon War, Peter Beckford the Younger had died. Uncharacteristically for his family, it was peacefully in bed. He was 61, a great age for a planter, though not quite that achieved by his father.

The inventory of his possessions made after his death, preserved in the archive in Spanish Town, gives a vivid indication of his eye-popping wealth: plantation after plantation; pages and pages of slaves, all individually listed and named, many hundreds of lives owned by this one man. In all, he was worth in the region of £300,000.

Property in England was left to the eldest son, but he died unmarried two years later, and his inheritance went to the second son, William, who was also left the greatest part of the Jamaica property. The third son, Richard, who was in England training as a lawyer, received two plantations, and the other brothers, Nathaniel, Julines and Francis, seem to have inherited one plantation each.

William, later known as 'Alderman Beckford', was born in Jamaica in 1709, the year before Abraham Redwood, and had been sent to England for schooling at the age of 14. At Westminster, he was reportedly one of the best scholars the school had ever had, although he was criticised and ridiculed for his poor grammar and Jamaican accent. It is said he 'possessed few of the external graces as far as expression and manner were concerned'. In short, he did not really fit in. Like other Creole (that is, born in the West Indies) whites, he would have thought of himself as European. It was only on visiting England that people like him were confronted with the realisation that they thought, spoke and reacted differently from Europeans. Eating habits, mannerisms and emotional reactions marked them as aliens.

After Balliol College, Oxford, William Beckford studied medicine in Leyden, where, the story goes, he fell in love with an unsuitable girl, the daughter of a shopkeeper. They had a child, Richard (the first of a huge number of illegitimate children Beckford would sire), who was kept secret from his irascible grandfather. Beckford moved the mother and child to London, and put them up in a flat, with a mulatto servant, presumably shipped over from Jamaica. To Beckford's horror, this page boy, only 16 years old, then fathered a child with the woman. William was reportedly heartbroken; the woman was shipped off with an annuity back to Holland.

On the death of his father, then his elder brother, William returned to Jamaica, where he remained for the next seven years, before returning to England in 1744. It is fascinating to speculate whether, after his time in England and Europe, he saw Jamaica as home. Many years later he would request that his heart be sent to the island after his death to be buried there; yet very soon after coming into his inheritance he started putting down roots in England, purchasing a grand manor with 5,000 acres at Fonthill in Wiltshire. To his contemporaries he seemed a 'strange and contradictory character'. It is likely that he, like others born in the West Indies but educated elsewhere, did not feel that he really belonged anywhere.

According to his later account, while in Jamaica William Beckford served as 'a common soldier' in the island's militia. When war was declared in 1739, he volunteered to join an expedition from the island.

The enemy was Spain. In spite of the partnership implied by the granting of the *asiento* after the Treaty of Utrecht in 1713, tensions had remained high, with Spanish *guarda costas* – freelance customs inspectors, effectively privateers – seizing a large number of English vessels, including legitimate traders. The government in London was besieged by complaints. One petition, demanding protection from the 'insults on persons and properties' being carried out by the Spanish, was signed by William Beckford's brother Richard, as well as his cousin Thomas Beckford, who acted as a sugar factor for the family in London. Among the other signatories were almost all the 'sugar names' – Frye, Tomlinson, Warner and others.

It was effectively a state of undeclared war, and to be fair, the English gave as good as they got. South Sea Company directors in Jamaica as well as naval commanders were active in the illegal trade, in defiance of all regulations. As Rear Admiral Charles Stewart wrote to London from Jamaica in 1731, 'you only hear one side of the question; and I can assure you the sloops that sail from this island, manned and armed on that illicit trade, have more than once bragged to me of their having murdered seven or eight Spaniards'. 'Villainy is inherent to this climate,' he concluded.

In the same year, Captain Robert Jenkins's vessel, the *Rebecca*, was boarded by *guarda costas* while off Havana. Jenkins had his ear cut off and was told to present it to the King of England. (Although he wasn't then forced to eat it, this was the sort of mutilation afforded to a slave, not a Briton.) When the case came to light, it provided a rallying point for a 'Patriot Party' – driven by William Pitt, and gathered around the Prince of Wales – that demanded war. Prime Minister Sir Robert Walpole did what he could to preserve the peace, but the country was full of bellicose talk of British naval supremacy and the weakness and effeminacy of Spain. On 13 October 1739, Abraham Redwood's London agent wrote to him: 'At present we have nothing but Rumours of War & daily advices of ye Spaniards taking our Ships hope we may soon have an oppo. of banging 'em heartily for without it they will not be brought to reason.' The same month, war was declared.

In some respects 'the War of Jenkins's Ear', which merged into the War of Austrian Succession, otherwise known as King George's War, was different from a lot of what had gone before. This was not about European balance of power or dynastic squabbles, but about imperial trade, empire. It was also started in the West Indies. But in other respects, for the Caribbean theatre it followed the depressing course of previous conflicts. Initially the British had a great success. In November 1739, Vice Admiral Edward Vernon, with only six ships, launched a skilfully planned and well-executed attack on Porto Bello in Panama. The city surrendered in 24 hours, and Vernon stayed three weeks, destroying fortifications and the port facilities that had been used to fit out the *guarda costas*.

Vernon became a national hero overnight (it helped that he was identified with the opposition to the unpopular Walpole), and streets and villages in England were renamed Portobello in honour of his feat. Victory celebrations the following year in London saw the first performance of 'Rule Britannia'.

But now the government found it could not resist the popular clamour for further military adventures in the West Indies. So in January 1741, a force of 8,000 regular troops, with a substantial squadron under Rear Admiral Sir Challenor Ogle (Atkins's former captain on the *Swallow*), was dispatched to the Caribbean. Reinforced with colonial troops (including 200 men from Rhode Island and a Virginia contingent that included George Washington's brother Lawrence), new recruits, and a host of troop transports, merchant and naval ships, this force was then launched against the important Spanish city of Cartagena.

Here, the unhappy precedent of Hispaniola asserted itself once again: disagreements between land and sea commanders and crippling disease, mainly yellow fever, hampered the British as much as did the strong Spanish defences, and the attack was abandoned. Next the force was sent against Santiago de Cuba, with a similar result. By the time the armada returned to Jamaica at the end of November, three quarters of the men had been lost, mainly to yellow fever. Of the original 28,000 soldiers and seamen, 22,000 were dead within a year, and only 1,000 of those through combat. Mosquitoes claimed the rest. 'Universal dejection prevailed', wrote novelist Tobias Smollett, who served as a surgeon's mate on one of Ogle's vessels. 'The distemper which then raged among the English was the bilious fever', he explained, 'attended with such a putrefaction of the juices that the colour of the skin, which at first is yellow, adopts a sooty hue in the progress of the disease, and the patient generally dies about the third day, with violent atrabilious discharges upwards and downwards.' By comparison, during the fighting in Europe at the same time, the British army lost just 8 per cent of its strength to fighting and disease.

William Beckford would later write to Pitt that in the West Indies, 'whatever is attempted in that climate must be done *uno impetu*; a general must fight his men off directly, and not give them time to die by drink and disease; which has been the case in all our southern expeditions, as I can testify by my own experience'. Vernon's attack on Porto Bello had met these criteria for success; the later disasters, which presumably included Beckford as a volunteer, did not.

The 'damage and disgrace' led to the fall of Prime Minister Walpole in 1742, and little more was attempted against the Spanish in the Caribbean. In March 1744, the French joined the war against the British, but neither side was keen on conquering each other's sugar acreage. Instead, the war was fought on the seas, largely by privateers from all sides.

The English islands benefited: a report from St Kitts told of 10 privateers already at sea, with four more being fitted out – 'We flow in Money'. A recent split of a couple of prize cargoes had seen the lowliest crew member receiving £200. In Jamaica, a contemporary account reported, 'the People of this Island were intent on nothing so much as encouraging Privateers; and tho' sometimes they suffered considerable Losses, yet . . . many rich Prizes . . . were daily brought in'. But for the maritime economy of Rhode Island, the war was a godsend. On Tuesday 22 April 1740, His Majesty's Declaration of War against Spain was publicly read at Newport before an assemblage of civil and military officers. A number of gentlemen with drawn swords attended the solemnities and at the conclusion gave three rousing huzzas. Already the Rhode Island assembly had authorised the Governor to grant commissions to privateers to act against Spain. Immediately upon the receipt of the 'so long wish'd for news', armed vessels started pouring out of Newport harbour.

In contrast with the War of Spanish Succession 20 years earlier, these were not irresponsible wandering sea captains, vulnerable to accusations of piracy. This time the privateers were owned by the wealthiest and most respected citizens of Newport, such as the Malbones and the Wantons. Much of the colony's small arms, pistols and cutlasses were lent to the ships, and about a third of the colony's male workforce, enslaved and free, were now on the seas.

The news of the declaration of war by France was greeted with similar glee. A French spy in Newport suggested, 'Perhaps we had better burn it, as a pernicious hole, from the number of privateers there fitted out.' Soon there were 21 Rhode Island privateers at sea. A visitor to Newport in 1744 attended a meeting of the Philosophical Club. 'But I was surprised to find that no matters of philosophy were brought upon the carpet. They talked of privateering and building of vessels', he wrote.

With the fitting-out of the *Reprisal* in the same year, Providence entered the field of privateering. The 90-ton *Reprisal* had 12 carriage guns and 16 swivel guns. It was captained by John Hopkins, brother of Stephen, who was a part-owner. Stephen Hopkins was then Speaker of the Assembly, and would later be Governor of Rhode Island and a signatory of the Declaration of Independence. The vessel's first success was in capturing a small

French merchantman carrying sugar, cocoa, cotton and coffee to France, although in the skirmish it lost one of its 90-man crew. A second ship was taken soon afterwards, then, with another privateer, the *Reprisal* took on a Spanish ship of 36 guns. Hopkins was killed and the Spaniard escaped.

Captain James Brown of Providence had died suddenly in 1739, having injured himself, with typical machismo, in a weightlifting contest. His more pragmatic younger brother Obadiah took over the family business, and the raising of his five sons, James, Nicholas, Joseph, John and Moses. From 1747, this business included privateering – most noticably with the brigantine *Providence* – sometimes in partnership with Stephen Hopkins.

But there were other, even more dubious ways that the Americans could make fortunes in the West Indies, particularly in times of war. During the previous conflict, there had been extensive trade with the enemy. Colonel Peter Beckford, while briefly governor of Jamaica, had complained about ships from 'our Northern Plantations' supplying the Spanish. In the intervening peacetime, Rhode Islanders had profited from illegally supplying their tobacco (an enumerated commodity, according to the Navigation Acts) to Surinam and elsewhere. Obadiah Brown in the *Rainbow* had been seized by a British warship and prosecuted in 1738 for landing tobacco at St Eustatius. But the coming of war meant boomtime for smugglers, as supplies to Spanish and then French colonies were disrupted and demand and prices soared.

Trade with the enemy was conducted directly and indirectly. Direct trade sometimes involved French or Spanish governors issuing licences, but more frequently it was carried out under a huge scam known as 'flags of truce'. Passes were issued by colonial governors, allowing vessels to sail to enemy colonies for the ostensible purpose of exchanging prisoners. Obadiah Brown ran several of these 'flags of truce' out of Providence, Rhode Island, during the war, as did the Newport grandees. Alternatively, there was indirect trade, carried out through the neutral islands, particularly the Dutch enclave of St Eustatius, which acted as a 'middle man' between the New England traders and the French colonies who needed their plantation supplies – particularly horses and lumber – and in return sold cheap sugar products they could not ship home to Europe.

As the war progressed, this trade became ever more extensive, shameless and, according to the British, detrimental to the wider imperial interest. The British sugar islands suffered as New Englanders started demanding cash rather than sugar products in return for their supplies of lumber. This money was then taken to St Eustatius or the French islands, where it was used to purchase cheaper sugar or molasses. Thus islands like

Barbados were stripped of specie as well as losing out to the French in selling their sugar products.

Charles Knowles, later a governor of Jamaica, but during the war a navy admiral, reported at an inquiry after the end of the conflict in 1748 that at the beginning of the war he had seen 16 or 17 vessels from the North American colonies brazenly loading and unloading at St Eustatius. The inquiry also heard how a practice had developed of taking on hogsheads in Barbados, which were filled with water, cleared out of port as English rum, and then refilled with cheaper French rum direct from Martinique or through one of the neutral entrepôts. Asked how to deal with this, the witness at the inquiry suggested that 'one or two men-of-war stationed at Rhode Island would be sufficient'.

It appears that the Rhode Islanders were the worst offenders. 'Smuggling is practiced over all the Northern colonies particularly at Rhode Island', another witness reported. 'Goods are landed and exported again as English.' Indeed, rum made from French molasses was even imported into Ireland and England. Rhode Island was also a leader, along with Philadelphia, in the 'flag of truce' trick. According to Knowles, by the end of the war the Governor of Rhode Island was sending 40 or 50 'flags of truce' every year to enemy ports in the Caribbean. Many had only one or two actual French prisoners on board. Indeed, a market grew up in which such valuable prisoners were actually traded for large prices between the northern colonies. Each time, the 'flag of truce' would sail 'laden with provisions and Naval Stores, who bring back French Rum and Molasses'. At one time, there were at Hispaniola no fewer than 42 British colonial vessels 'with fictitious flags of truce'.

For the Lords of Trade and Plantations, hearing evidence back in London, this was more than just illegality – it was treasonous disloyalty during a time of war. Knowles reckoned that without the provisions and plantation supplies received from New Englanders, 'he should certainly have taken Martinique'. These practices, said another witness, meant 'the prosperity of the French Islands and the ruin of our own'.

Sometimes the New Englanders were caught. The proceedings in the Court of Admiralty at Boston tell the story of the *Victory* brigantine, which sailed as a flag of truce from Newport on 12 January 1747 with five French prisoners to Cap François in Hispaniola; she carried, it turned out, 'a cargo of 300 quintals of codfish, some onions', and other goods. With the profits from these she 'bought 174 casks of molasses of different sizes which were to have been delivered to Joseph Whipple, Esquire, of Newport, her owner'. The *Victory* was taken by the Royal Navy off Lock Island, and her cargo confiscated. Whipple, a substantial Newport merchant, was Abraham Redwood's brother-in-law.

Each case caused uproar in England, where the public saw the Americans as guilty of breaking a blockade that would have meant the capitulation of all the enemy islands in the West Indies. In terms of the 'imperial family', the New Englanders were increasingly seen as ungrateful children of a parent whose tolerance was fast running out. Just as ominously, the New Englanders, in turn, had demonstrated that allegiance to the interests of the mother country counted for next to nothing compared to the lure of molasses, rum and sugar-fuelled profits.

Not all Newport interests were entirely served by the war. Abraham Redwood's Antigua agent John Tomlinson complained in 1744 that he was having difficulties getting his sugar crop harvested and processed because so much of his labour force had been pressed into 'building Batteries & throwing up entrenchments'. Two years later, Tomlinson reported that 'We are now in the utmost distress for want of provisions & Lumber of all sorts.' He had 60 hogsheads of sugar to ship, '& no vessel to take them in'.

Nonetheless, Redwood was clearly enjoying immense profits from Cassada Gardens, helped by a rise in the sugar price from the beginning of the war onwards. Soon after his return from Antigua, he had imported from England a coach and horses (and tried without success to import an English coachman as well). An agent in Madeira now sent him his own special pipes of wine. It had become the practice of Newport grandees to establish elegant country estates outside the town: in 1741, Godfrey Malbone built a country seat that was declared 'the largest and most magnificent dwelling' in America. Redwood seems to have been piqued by this, as he was richer even than Malbone, and two years later he spent £6,500 on a 140-acre estate in Portsmouth, Rhode Island. Here he built a house and, with the help of an expert gardener imported from Britain, laid out lavish grounds. These included a huge greenhouse and various hothouses. A visitor in the 1760s described it as 'one of the finest gardens I ever saw in my life. In it grows all sorts of West Indian fruits, viz: Orange, Lemons, Limes, Pineapples and Tamarinds and other sorts. It has also West India flowers – very pretty ones.'

Elected to the assembly in 1746 and 1747, Redwood had now also become Newport's leading philanthropist. He gave £500 towards the founding of a Quaker school, and offered another £500 if the mooted Rhode Island university be situated at Newport (he would lose this battle to the Browns of Providence). In 1747 he began the process of establishing what would open in 1750 as the Redwood Library, the oldest lending library in North America, and the continent's first classical-style building, chartered to promote 'virtue, knowledge and learning . . . having nothing in view but the good of mankind . . .'* He had his agent in London send over hundreds of pounds' worth of books, paid for from the proceeds of his Antigua sugar.

By the 1750s, Newport rivalled New York, Boston and Philadelphia as a shipping centre. These ports now dominated the supply of provisions, lumber and other goods to the West Indian islands. A visitor to Antigua in 1756 commented that 'almost every thing' was brought 'in the lumber vessels from America'.

This vibrant sector fuelled a wider trade throughout the Atlantic, as well as providing capital and markets for new industries in the colony. By the mid-century there were 30 distilleries in Newport alone. In Providence, Obadiah Brown and his nephews had established a distillery, and also chocolate and candle factories. An iron furnace would follow soon after. The family was now trading directly with London (bypassing Newport and Boston), and owned outright or jointly more than 60 vessels. In 1759, they dabbled again in the slave trade, although the vessel, the *Wheel of Fortune*, was 'taken' by privateers off the African coast. By this time, however, they were once more making wild profits in privateering and illegal trade in the West Indies, thanks to the mother country's new war with France.

---

* The style of the library would be hugely influential: it was much admired by Thomas Jefferson, when he visited Newport in 1790. Thereafter Jefferson began championing classical architecture as the model for public building in the new republic.

22

BARBADOS, THE 'CIVILISED ISLE'

'In the slave society, where self-fulfilment came so easily, this liveliness began to be perverted and then to fade, and the English saw their pre-eminence, more simply, as a type of racial magic.'

V. S. Naipaul, *The Loss of El Dorado*

Barbados, for so long the leading sugar colony and the jewel in the crown of England's western empire, had by the 1720s been surpassed in sugar production by Jamaica and the Leewards and thereafter acquired the reputation of a place in slow but irreversible decline. Naval surgeon John Atkins was briefly there in the 1720s on his way to Jamaica. He found the white women in Bridgetown to be 'most Scotch and Irish, very homely and great Swearers', was impressed with the men's 'magnificent way of living', but observed that 'the Crops of late years have very much failed . . . The Soil fertile in the Age past, seems now growing old, and past its teeming time.'

The slump of the 1730s hit the island hard, not helped by a destructive hurricane in 1731 and a subsequent drought that left the soil 'a dry crust, burnt up and gaping'. But even more seriously, after 60 years of intensive sugar monoculture, the soil of the island was stripped. This meant that ever more labour – manuring and replanting – was needed to produce the same amount of sugar. During the eighteenth century, then, production fell by some 20 per cent, even though the slave population increased by nearly a third. In the 1760s, soil exhaustion became such a problem that the desperate measure was undertaken of importing soil from Surinam. But this was not a success: wood ants made such ravages in the hull of the ship that the experiment was abandoned.

It was not just the soil: there was also a feeling that the energy and spirit of the planters were failing. 'The industry & integrity of its first founders is lost', one Barbadian wrote of his island. The planters were now merely reaping the benefit of the 'hardship, sweat, and toil of their forefathers', reported another. Where the first generations of sugar barons had channelled their 'fiery, restless tempers' into the hard work of creating the first sugar plantations, their successors had degenerated into luxury, faction, decadence and drunkenness. 'Vain and shewy', many were living way beyond their reduced means, and falling into debt.

'There is no Recreation out of Business, but in Drinking or Gaming', reported Atkins. It was too hot for the English gentry pursuits of hunting or hawking, wrote a visitor in 1747; instead the Barbadians were 'oblig'd, for the most part, to sedentary Diversions at Home; as Cards, Dice, Tables, Quoits, Bowling . . . There are some good Fellows here, who, 'tis said, will drink five or six Bottles of Madera Wine, to their share, every Day, for which they find sweating the best Relief.'

It was not entirely sedentary: riding in the cool of the morning was popular; there was some shooting of migratory birds from July to December. Towards the end of the century sea bathing at last became fashionable, and there were always visitors to be taken on trips round the island, and to the impressive limestone caves.

Above all, there were dances. At every social gathering, even lectures, the evening would always end with dancing. Every assembly meeting in Bridgetown was accompanied by a succession of balls. 'Though a Creole was languishing on his death bed', wrote an islander later in the century, 'I believe the sound of the gumbay or violin would induce him to get up and dance till he killed himself.' Indeed, William Hillary, a respected doctor who wrote about the illnesses of Barbados, even warned: 'Dancing is too violent an Exercise in this hot Climate, and many do greatly injure their Health by it, and I have known it fatal to some . . . But most of the Ladies are so excessive fond of it, that say what I will they will dance on.'

By the 1730s, a number of the leading proprietors had followed the example of Henry Drax and become resident in England. In their place at the top of Barbados society came a new breed: merchants with juicy government contracts; moneylenders; beneficiaries of official positions. Never entirely honest, civic life now became further mired in corruption. The first half of the eighteenth century saw a procession of crooked governors; assembly elections were frequently fixed; judges were appointed who were illiterate or corrupt (in 1716, a man got himself appointed a judge for one of the districts of Barbados where a case against him was to be tried). Lucrative official positions were bought and sold regardless of honesty or competence: in 1728, one man held eight civil and military posts.

In around 1715, the founder of one of the greatest Barbados fortunes, Henry Lascelles, was appointed Collector of Customs for the port of Bridgetown, amongst the most valuable revenue posts in the British customs service. Henry's father Daniel had married the daughter of Edward Lascelles, from another branch of the family. This Edward had been in Barbados in 1648, when he had bought a small sugar estate called Frames. The following year he had purchased a further 100 acres in an adjoining parish, and in partnership with his brothers had built a valuable sugar and trading business, before returning to England in 1701 having lost three young children to the Barbados climate. Two further sons were produced, but both died childless, the elder drinking himself to death, so most of his property descended through his daughter to Daniel's branch of the Lascelles family.

Daniel Lascelles' eldest sons, George and Henry, were trading in Barbados by the 1710s, shipping as well as planting. Soon afterwards their half-brother Edward (credited with introducing the mango to Barbados) joined them on the island; in 1730 he would succeed Henry in the post of Collector of Customs (George died in 1729).

Henry became a force to be reckoned with in Barbados politics and, partly thanks to his official position, immensely wealthy. According to accusations made against him, he submitted fraudulent accounts concerning the 4½ per cent duty on sugars shipped from the island. In 1720 he was summoned to London to answer the charges, but was cleared. Soon afterwards he was accused of importing cheaper French sugar from Martinique and sending it to London to benefit from the higher price arising from the monopoly. Again he held on to his job. His brother faced similar charges in 1744, which led to his suspension and a surcharge against Henry of just under £40,000. But Henry and his second son Daniel became MPs the following year, and also gave financial support to the Hanoverian regime. The nasty fine went away.

In 1730, Henry returned to London, leaving Edward in charge in Barbados. From London Henry became victualler to the armed forces and a substantial slave-trader, taking over forts on the West African coast. With a partner, George Maxwell, he established a banking house and started lending large amounts of money to planters – £85,154 by 1753 – while selling his own land in the West Indies.

By the time of his death in 1753, Henry Lascelles had installed his eldest son Edwin as Lord of the Manor of Gawthorpe and Harewood, estates that Henry purchased in 1739 for just under £64,000. (His second son, Daniel, was by now established as a partner in Lascelles and Maxwell.) In spite of this outlay, Henry was still worth around half a million pounds; without doubt, he died one of the richest men in Britain.

Independently of Henry, his half-brother Edward had prospered. His son would purchase an estate at Darrington, commissioning John Carr to build Stapleton Park. The manner of Henry's death is a mystery. He is reported 'to have cut his throat and arms and across his belly'. The reason for his suicide remains unknown.

Much of the money Henry lent went to New Englander Gedney Clarke, a close trading partner based in Barbados. Back in 1637, John Gedney, a Norwich weaver, had sailed from Yarmouth to New England on the *Mary Ann* with his wife and three children. After his wife's death he had married a wealthy widow, Callie Clarke, and had taken over a tavern and small farm on the border of the townships of Salem and Lynn. The family grew rich through trading, shipbuilding and marriage, and during the eighteenth century the Gedney Clarkes dispersed along the eastern seaboard and overseas to the Caribbean. John Gedney's great-grandson Gedney Clarke migrated to Barbados in 1733, aged 22. Having forged links with international trading networks that took in London, New England, Virginia, Barbados, Lisbon and Bilbao, a decade later the New Englander was one of Bridgetown's leading merchants. In the 1740s he moved into land, acquiring huge tracts of Virginia as well as estates in Barbados and new investments in Dutch Guiana and Demerara (one such investment is said to have recouped the £12,000 outlay in just one year). By now he was in close partnership with Henry Lascelles' operation.

Lascelles and Maxwell were Gedney Clarke's London bankers, and they had many shared interests in slave-trading vessels. Clarke illicitly sold slaves in the Dutch colonies and even smuggled slaves into New York itself, making use of the coves and inlets of Long Island, where happily the Gedney family owned 200 acres astride a fine natural harbour. He also supplied slaves to Henry Laurens in Charleston, who on one occasion was requested to send back in return a number of deer to grace the Gedney Clarke lawns in Barbados.

As his family had done in New England, Gedney Clarke combined commercial interests with military and public service. In 1748, he succeeded Edward Lascelles as customs collector for Bridgetown. The position would stay in the Clarke family for the next 30 years, despite allegations of bribery and other misconduct. When, on one occasion, he was suspended from his post, such was his influence in England that orders came by return packet for him to be restored.

Naval power was crucial to the security of the plantations and the defence

A brilliant soldier, academic and wit, Christopher Codrington the Younger started his West Indian career appalled by the realities of the sugar–slave societies, but ended up consumed and corrupted by their values

A drawing of Codrington College in Barbados from the 1720s. A is the college, B, Consetts Great House, C, the windmill, D, the boiling house, E, the Curing House and F, Consetts Bay.

A PROSPECT OF CODRINGTON COLLEGE &c.

The College today, now part of the University of the West Indies. Founded by Codrington the Younger, the college's mission to educate and convert Barbados' black slaves was bitterly resisted by the island's planter elite.

A typical West Indian planter, with slave girl in attendance. Many planters led lives of luxury, indulgence and intoxication.

Bartholomew Roberts, notorious pirate, who in the early 1720s brought trade in the West Indies to a near standstill

In this parodic cosmological diagram, the luxuries of life for the planters of Jamaica are shown resting on death's scythe, held here by the beast of yellow fever. The angel above holds a bottle of opium. The close proximity of death dominated every aspect of the societies of the sugar empire.

The Jamaican Drax Hall on the north coast.
By the mid-eighteenth century the highly profitable estate
had fallen into the hands of the Beckford family.

A miniature of William Beckford of Somerly,
painted just before he and his wife left for
their calamitous adventure in Jamaica

An idealised prospect of Beckford of Somerly's Roaring River Estate, Westmoreland,
engraved from a painting by George Robertson. This was almost certainly among the
prints given by Somerly to Thomas Thistlewood.

'Alderman' William Beckford: Member of Parliament for the City, twice Lord Mayor and close confidant of Pitt the Elder, he represented the pinnacle of power and influence for the Beckford family and the sugar lobby.

'Fonthill Splendens', 'Alderman' Beckford's lavish Palladian mansion at Fonthill in Wiltshire. Beckford was never accepted by the local gentry, who disliked his Jamaican accent and 'tawdry' ostentation.

William Beckford of Fonthill. As soon as he inherited a vast fortune from his father 'Alderman' Beckford, his life descended into decadence and disgrace.

The ruins of Fonthill Abbey, the epic folly that consumed the Beckford fortune within a generation

The Battle of the Saintes, 12 April, 1782, by Thomas Luny.

A shift of wind enabled the British to break the French line in several places with decisive results. In the centre foreground the *Ville de Paris* is shown in the act of striking. The British *Formidable* is firing her last broadside into her. British victory in the battle saved Jamaica from invasion. ©NMM

A wooden model of the Liverpool slave ship 'Brookes', used by William Wilberforce in the House of Commons around 1790, to illustrate the method in which enslaved Africans were transported in the Middle Passage

Slaves on a ship, 'so many and so close together, that we can hardly breathe … suffocated, stewed and parboyled altogether in a Crowd, till we almost rot each other and our selves.'

An insurrection aboard a slave ship, one of the many hazards of the 'unrighteous' trade

A slave hung by the ribs and left to die. Slave owners in the West Indies constantly surpassed themselves at the invention of ever more brutal tortures.

'Revenge taken by the black Army [in the Haitian Revolution] for Cruelties practiced on them by the French', from a book published in London in 1805

The Haitian Revolution as imagined by a German artist. Fear of retribution by the blacks dominated the lives of the whites in the slave societies of the West Indies.

A Gillray cartoon from 1791 showing a plantation overseer using a whip to stir a black body into a vat of boiling sugar. Opposition in Britain to slavery saw tea being labelled a 'blood-sweetened beverage' and led to a consumer boycott of slave-grown West Indian products.

The anti-slavery convention of 1840 in London. In full oratorical flow is Thomas Clarkson. In the foreground can be seen Henry Beckford, a freed slave and delegate from Jamaica. From being the world's greatest slave trader, Britain now led the campaign against slavery.

of colonial trade. The Clarkes' influence in this area was, therefore, of paramount importance to the family's commercial interests, and Clarke's house was famously welcoming of military and colonial officials. As well as wining and dining at his lavish Belle plantation those who might prove useful, Clarke also went into partnership with a number of naval officers in order to prosecute the slave trade and to profit from victualling and privateering. The delivery of slaves to Charleston, for instance, was a venture he conducted jointly with Admiral Thomas Frankland. In the wars of the early 1740s, Clarke took prize cargoes in partnership with Edward Lascelles and, again, Admiral Frankland.

Such arrangements between traders and the military were not exceptional, nor were they illegal, although they could frequently involve participants in conflicts of interest. The influence wielded by the Clarkes, however, exceeded the norm and, on occasion, obliterated the distinction between private and public interest.

In 1755, Clarke's son, Gedney Clarke Jr, was sent, aged 20, to Amsterdam to learn Dutch and become naturalised, so that restrictions on the Clarkes' property ownership in the Dutch South American colonies could be avoided. In 1762, Gedney Clarke Jr married Frances Lascelles, daughter of Henry's half-brother Edward, cementing the close business relationship between the two families.

As the Seven Years War got underway in 1756, a naval lieutenant, Edward Thompson, wrote a series of intriguing letters from various outposts around the far-flung empire. By the time he got to the West Indies, he had seen it all, from Europe to the Far East. From Antigua he reported, 'I am sorry I cannot say any thing pleasant about this place.' Barbados was the next stop, and he was optimistic that from there he could 'entertain' his correspondent 'with more pleasing accounts'. Arriving in Barbados in early December 1756, he found that 'This island looks more like a Christian country, than any of the Caribbees.'

Barbados was indeed different from the other islands in important ways that in the eyes of European visitors and white Barbadians alike made it, in comparison, 'the civilised island'. For one thing, the ratio of blacks to whites was in the region of four to one, rather than the 10 to one in Jamaica, and 18 to one in Antigua. This proportionally larger white population, unlike the tiny garrison communities in the other islands, was substantial enough to exhibit rigid class distinctions reassuringly similar to England. The early arrival of the Sugar Revolution in Barbados might have wrecked the island's soil, but it also meant that a number of families had now been there for four or even five generations: a small number even began to think of themselves as Barbadian or Bajan rather than English. There were, indeed, high-profile absentee owners, but because of the falling yields, only those with the best and most substantial estates could actually afford to retire to England. This kept many of the planters physically on the island and emotionally connected to its future.

In the same way, because widespread African slavery had started so much earlier in Barbados, there were, in spite of the ferocious infant mortality, a large number of Creole slaves, those born on the island: as many as 50 per cent of the black population. Together with other factors, this contributed to the lack of a major slave revolt in Barbados for the duration of the eighteenth century.

Barbados was less 'Africanised' than the other islands: for instance, Bajan Creole is much closer to English than, for example, Jamaican patois. People even called Barbados 'Little England', not a term that was ever applied to Jamaica. Edward Thompson commented on Antigua that most of the estates were run by newly arrived Scotsmen. In Barbados, everything was more settled, and less transient: the vast majority of the plantation managers were island-born, rather than fortune-hunters from Europe.

A spur to the creation of a Creole Barbadian identity came with the launch of the island's first newspaper, the *Barbados Gazette*, in 1731. This gave a forum for the white population to talk to each other as fellow islanders. Theatre productions seem to have started about this time. Although Codrington's bequest to establish a college on the island still languished under repeated attacks from his heir and others, the 1730s saw the establishment of a number of good-quality schools. Those few who could afford it still sent their children to England to be educated, but an increasing number of white children were not only born on the island, but schooled there. They even started talking in a recognisably Bajan accent, 'the languid syllables . . . drawled out as if it were a great fatigue to utter them', as an English visitor complained.

The visiting Royal Navy lieutenant Edward Thompson found Barbadians 'more easy, hospitable and kind, than those on the other islands'. He also admired Bridgetown: 'extensive and well built, and the merchants' houses elegant'. The port remained an important entrepôt, rivalled in the British Americas only by Boston.

Links between the West Indian islands and the northern colonies continued to grow, in spite of suspicions on the part of the Americans of the decadence of the sugar islands: 'We do not live so flash and fast', wrote one New Englander, 'yett wee live well and enjoy life with a better gust.'

As well as commercial and educational links, there were itinerant artists, entertainers and theatrical companies who toured the mainland colonies and the islands.

Visits were exchanged, often by those seeking the better health conditions of the north. Barbados sent Philadelphia her hard drinkers, with their 'carbuncled faces, slender legs and thighs, and large, prominent bellies', as a later account relates. It was jokily suggested that a house be set up in the city called the 'Barbados Hotel, putting up for a sign, the worn-out West Indian, dying of a dropsy from intemperate living'.

The traffic also went in reverse. Barbados, in particular, had a reputation as a place good for easing respiratory diseases. Thus in September 1751, future first president of the United States George Washington set sail for the island with his elder half-brother, Lawrence, who was suffering from tuberculosis. His doctor had recommended a stint in the tropics to relieve the disease.

They left the Potomac river on 28 September 1751. Their vessel was probably the *Success*, a square-sterned sloop of 40 tons. As well as the passengers, the ship carried nearly 5,000 barrel staves, just under 1,000 bushels of corn and 31 barrels of herring. Having spent six weeks on what George Washington called the 'fickle & Merciliss Ocean', they landed at Bridgetown on 2 November.

The 19-year-old George Washington kept a diary during the seven weeks he spent on the island, the only time in his life that he left North America. Unfortunately the pages that might have recorded his first impressions of Barbados are missing or damaged, but we can assume that Bridgetown, a cosmopolitan port city totally unlike anything he had experienced at home in rural Virginia, must have made a considerable impact. For the first couple of nights the brothers lodged in a tavern in the city, but were soon invited to the house of Gedney Clarke. The Washingtons had family links with the Clarkes through Lawrence's wife Anne, and Clarke himself owned 3,000 acres in Virginia at Goose Creek. This connection must have influenced the decision to go to Barbados, and presumably the brothers expected to stay at the Clarkes' house.

But there was a snag. Clarke's wife had smallpox; Lawrence had had the disease, so was immune, but George had not. It was not possible, then, to stay at the Clarkes' although, 'with some reluctance', the brothers accepted the invitation to dinner.

Soon after their arrival, Lawrence was visited by Dr Hillary, who recommended that they find lodging in the country. Accompanied by a high-ranking local, they rode out of town seeking a house to rent. Washington recorded that he was 'perfectly enraptured' by the beauty of the island, 'the fields of cane, corn, Fruit Trees &c in a delightful Green' and the abundance and richness of the vegetation. 'How wonderful that such people shou'd be in debt!' he exclaimed.

After a couple of days, they found a house to rent in the swampy Garrison area, now on the outskirts of Bridgetown (where the house still stands), but then surrounded by canefields. It was owned by Richard Crofton, a captain in the British army. Crofton asked for £15 a month rent, which Lawrence found 'extravagantly dear' (it was three times what Crofton had recently charged the Barbados council for use of the house), but felt 'oblig'd' to give the asking price. The house was small, but pleasantly situated: 'the prospect is extensive by Land and pleasant by Sea', wrote George. 'We command the prospect of Carlyle Bay & all the shipping in such manner that none can go in or out without being open to our view.'

Young George's days were thereafter spent riding around the island, where he carefully noted the intensive plantation agriculture, and enjoyed the hospitality of the local elite at leisurely afternoon dinners. Everywhere, he wrote, he was 'Genteely receiv'd and agreeably entertain'd'. Like all small, isolated communities, the Barbados gentry were fond of new faces. For George, it was a definite step up from his status in Virginia. On one occasion, he was given a ticket to a play; it seems to have been the first time he had been to a theatre. One night he was invited to dine with the gentlemen's 'Beefstake and Tripe Club', where 'After Dinner was the greatest Collection of Fruits I have yet seen on the Table'. He enjoyed the new experience of an avocado pear, but like most visitors, was most enraptured by 'the Pine'.

The visit was full of new experiences. Perhaps most importantly, he toured the island's fortifications, taking on a new passionate interest in military matters. He also contracted and survived smallpox – almost certainly from his visit to the Clarkes' on 4 November. His subsequent immunity to the disease would be of huge importance, since smallpox would kill more Continental soldiers during the American Revolution than would the British.

His brother, however, did not get better. George left for Virginia on 22 December, and his brother sailed to Bermuda, which does not seem to have helped much either. Lawrence returned home and died in July 1752.

George commented about the white population of Barbados that there were 'very few who may be called middling people they are either very rich or very poor'. (In fact, compared to the other sugar islands, Barbados had a fair number of 'middling people'.) But there is hardly any reference in his diary to the enslaved Africans who made up three quarters of

Barbados's population. George commented about the young white ladies of the island that they were 'Generally very agreeable, but by ill custom . . . affect the Negro Style'. Apart from this one mention, the black population seems to have been totally invisible or unworthy of comment to the young Virginian.

However much Barbados was admired as a comparatively 'civilised isle' for the West Indies, other visitors could not help but comment on the realities of the slave society there. 'The planters at Barbadoes are cruel to their unhappy slaves, who are condemned to servile labour and scanty fare', wrote a Rhode Islander, John Benson, in the 1760s. Benson was shocked to see 'the heads of slaves, fixed upon sharp pointed stakes, while their unburied carcases were exposed to be torn by dogs and vultures on the sandy beach'. Lieutenant Edward Thompson would have been witness to the habitual extreme violence – whippings and executions – used at that time to enforce discipline in the Royal Navy, but he was still deeply shocked to see in Barbados (which he pronounced 'kinder' than the other islands) a young slave girl tortured to death for 'some trivial domestic error'.

Thompson ascribed this cruelty to the way Barbadians were 'taught in their very infancy to flog with a whip the slave that offends them'. Other writers agree that a habit of cruelty to the enslaved population was taken in almost with the mother's milk. A later visitor reported that he had seen children as young as five or six 'knocking the poor Negroes about the cheeks with all the passion and the cruelty possible . . . never checked by their parents'. In return, the domestic slaves were expected to indulge every whim of the young Creoles, whose strange characteristics were of increasing interest to the British reading public. Barbadians and other West Indians responded that they were simply 'of a more volatile and lively Disposition' than Englishmen who had remained at home; warm temperatures, they said, had put their 'Animal Spirits . . . in a high Flow'.

The majority of those arriving in the West Indies fresh from Britain or the northern colonies became 'Creolised' in various ways after a series of changes that often started with a sense of overwhelmed bewilderment. 'Here I find every Thing alter'd . . . amidst all the Variety which crouds upon my Sight', wrote one immigrant on his first arrival in Jamaica in the 1730s. In a book of advice for a newcomer to Jamaica, published later in the century, an old planter hand warned that 'When you get to Kingston, if you had five more senses, they would be all engaged; the compounded stench . . . the intense heat, and the horrid scene of poor Africans, male and female, busy at their labour with hardly rags sufficient to secret their nakedness, will affect you not a little.'

In Jean Rhys's *Wide Sargasso Sea*, Mr Rochester, riding out into the country for the first time, finds himself overwhelmed by the sheer energy and strangeness of the lush tropical vegetation. 'Everything is too much', he thinks. 'Too much blue, too much purple, too much green. The flowers too red, the mountains too high, the hills too near.' In Jamaican writer Henry de Lisser's *White Witch of Rose Hall*, his hero, Rutherford, fresh from England, is similarly overcome by the foreignness, teeming insects and violent heat. Don't worry, he is told, in a month you'll be used to it.

In no time he is taken to bed by a slave girl and 'hardened to the callous frankness of a Jamaica liaison'. 'He was secretly startled', wrote de Lisser, 'that he had so quickly succumbed to what he had heard at home were the manners and customs of this country . . . however flagrantly might be violated every principle of circumspect conduct.' His fellow bookkeeper tells him that he 'had seen many a young man arrive from England with the noblest resolves and the highest ideals, and sometimes in a week these all seemed to disappear as completely as if they had never existed'. Rutherford starts drinking heavily. 'This was Jamaica', he says to himself, 'to be a model of virtue here would be merely to make oneself ridiculous.'

Most disorientating of all was the sudden introduction to the violent cruelties of slavery. One of the first sights on arrival at a West Indian island was often a gibbeted slave, starving to death, sometimes with a loaf hanging just out of reach in front of him. 'I have seen these unfortunate Wretches gnaw the Flesh off their own Shoulders, and expire in all the frightful Agonies', wrote one shocked newcomer. In 1745, a young man recently arrived in Barbados wrote to George Maxwell, the partner of Henry Lascelles. Maxwell was Barbados born, and seemed to miss the island from his chilly exile in London. The young man, John Braithwaite, reported that he was finding the task of acting as a slave master unpleasant. Maxwell confessed that he had feared the job 'would ill suit a gentleman of your nature', but he reassured Braithwaite that experience would eventually inure him to the harsh realities of life on a sugar plantation: 'It was become familiar to me by use', he wrote. 'I was once owner of above 100 [slaves], and perhaps was one of the mildest masters. None clothed or fed better, yet they are by nature so stupid that I found none so ill served as I was; and therefore some correction is necessary. I used to pity their abject state at first, but afterwards found they were just as happy as their nature was capable of being.' But like his partner Henry Lascelles, who would commit suicide eight years later, there was something anguished about George

Maxwell. 'My mind is in Continual Agitation', he went on, 'I have as little enjoyment of life as anyone. Most people here have real or imaginary Crosses, which are the same in effect.'

John Newton, a slave-trader who turned abolitionist, described the process whereby his crews on the Middle Passage experienced a ruination of their sensitivities: 'The real or supposed necessity of treating the Negroes with rigour gradually brings a numbness upon the heart and renders those who are engaged in it too indifferent to the sufferings of their fellow-creatures.' The old Jamaica hand, writing a book of advice to newcomers, explained the process of getting used to slavery on a West Indian plantation. 'Like wax softened by the heat', he wrote, men from other countries 'melt into [West Indian] manners and customs'. 'Men from their first entrance into the West Indies are taught to practice severities to the slaves', he went on, 'their minds are impressed by their brother book-keepers, or others, with strange and cruel ideas of the nature of blacks, so that in time their hearts become callous to all tender feelings which soften and dignify our nature; the most insignificant Connaught savage bumpkin, or silly Highland gauky, will soon learn to flog without mercy to shew his authority.'

For many eighteenth-century writers on the West Indies, and on the nature of the 'Creole' whites, the institution of slavery seemed to have ruined everything and everybody – slave and master. The 'despotick government over their poor slaves', wrote Lieutenant Thompson, had made the planters 'haughty, ignorant and cruel'. The violence that lubricated the whole system had turned the men who wielded it into sadists: one visitor reported that he had seen 'terrible Whippings . . . for no other Reason, but to satisfy the brutish Pleasure of an Overseer'.

This 'brutish Pleasure' is nowhere better illustrated than in the diaries of the violent and sadistic Thomas Thistlewood, an associate of the Beckfords, who worked as an overseer for many years in Jamaica from 1750 onwards. Thistlewood tells us a lot about the unspeakably cruel day-to-day 'ground-floor' management of a provision or sugar estate in mid-century Jamaica. Most striking, however, is what emerges in these particular diaries from the human wreckage of slavery: perhaps the eighteenth century's most unlikely love story.

23

THOMAS THISTLEWOOD IN JAMAICA: 'TONIGHT VERY LONELY AND MELANCHOLY AGAIN'

'Would to heaven I had been dropped upon the snows of Lapland, and never felt the blessed influence of the sun, so had I never burnt with these inflammatory passions.'
Jamaica planter Belcour, in Richard Cumberland's *The West Indian*, 1771

Thomas Thistlewood landed at Jamaica in April 1750, aged 29. Like Ned Ward, Richard Ligon, John Taylor and so many others, he came out at a time of personal crisis, to 'mend his fortune'. He would live in Jamaica for the rest of his life.

Thistlewood was born in Tupholme, Lincolnshire, a second son. His father died when he was six, leaving him a small inheritance of £200 – enough for a good education and a reasonably comfortable childhood, but not sufficient thereafter to set him up in business or property. He had spent his twenties drifting between agricultural jobs, and at one time, after a scandal when he got a young local girl pregnant, he spent two years travelling to India with the East India Company. But the end of his twenties saw him unemployed and penniless.

He was also heartbroken: the family of the woman he loved had refused to let her marry a man with such meagre prospects. At this point, he decided, after a visit to the Jamaica Coffee House in the City in October 1749, to try his luck in the West Indies.

He collected some letters of introduction from local Lincolnshire gentry with Jamaican connections, one of whom recommended he contact Alderman William Beckford. In November he took a letter of introduction to Little Grosvenor Street, near Grosvenor Square, 'to enquire for Mr Beckford Esqr . . . but was informed he is now in Jamaica'. Other contacts proved more rewarding, in particular William Dorrill of Westmoreland parish, in the underdeveloped extreme west of the island, near where Richard Beckford, William's younger brother, held his substantial sugar acreage. Dorrill, who lived openly with his wife and coloured mistress, put Thistlewood up on his arrival, and promised a job when one became available.

In the meantime, Thistlewood took up an offer from Florentius Vassall, scion of the Anglo-American family whose interests stretched across the Atlantic. Thus, a month after his arrival, he found himself in charge of 42 slaves as an overseer of the Vineyard Pen in the parish of St Elizabeth. Here, in one of the hottest parts of the island, cattle and provisions were raised and logwood harvested. Vassall paid Thistlewood an annual wage of £50, together with an allowance of rum, sugar and beef. After a year, Thistlewood had fallen out with Vassall and accepted a more lucrative position as head overseer on a sugar plantation called Egypt, owned by William Dorrill and manned by about 60 slaves and a handful of more junior white employees. Egypt was distinctly undercapitalised and had insufficient slaves, a tough place to make a success of.

While running the sugar plantation, Thistlewood branched out into slave ownership, investing his wages in a young Ibo boy, Lincoln, in 1756, and three further slaves in 1758. All were branded with his TT mark on their right shoulder, using a silver branding iron purchased on 3 January that year. These slaves were then rented to other planters and provided a steady supplementary income. At other times they helped Thistlewood with small-scale trading of vegetables and fruits he grew on his own initiative. Profits were reinvested in further slaves and by 1767, he had accumulated some 20 workers and enough capital to take on a small plot of land himself, where he grew provisions and experimented with horticulture.

Thistlewood was not a typical Jamaican white overseer: he was older and more highly educated. He arrived with Chaucer, Milton, Pope and Addison in his luggage (along with a Bible and Book of Common Prayer). He was also soberer and more careful with his money than the typical, younger white employee. His greatest extravagance was books: throughout his time in Jamaica, he ordered numerous volumes from London or elsewhere (in 1763 he got Benjamin Franklin's book on electricity), often on publication, and received a number of periodicals. He read mathematics, botany and horticulture, as well as Hume, Gibbon and Adam Smith. In Westmoreland he found a small circle of white planters – all fellow slave-owners – keen to exchange and talk about books from these and other Enlightenment thinkers. No doubt Thistlewood saw himself as a harbinger, in a modest way, of the Enlightenment in the tropics, a scholar and perhaps even gentleman, loyal friend and respectable imperial subject, a man of principle and integrity, a better-than-ordinary Englishman. But for a modern reader of his diary, he is a monster: a rapist and a brutal sociopath.

Thistlewood's acclimatisation was rapid. On the way to Jamaica, his boat stopped briefly at Antigua, where he was propositioned by black prostitutes and met an 81-year-old planter who cheerfully discussed his 'kept' young mulatto mistress. During his first days in Jamaica, he saw a slave whipped and then his wounds marinated in salt, pepper and lime juice, as well as another decapitated and his body burned for the crime of running away. His first boss, Florentius Vassall, seems to have possessed the common white Creole attribute of a steady, simmering rage, which would occasionally explode into violence, particularly after drinking. Only days after starting work at Vineyard Pen, Thistlewood witnessed a senior driver slave being given 300 lashes on the orders of Vassall. Shortly afterwards, Thistlewood himself ordered another high-ranking slave be given 150 lashes, thus imposing his own authority. He had hardly arrived at Egypt plantation before he was sent the severed head of a runaway slave to display to his workforce. Thistlewood, as instructed, 'Put it upon a pole and stuck it up just at the angle of the road in the home pasture', where it stayed for four months.

Soon after his arrival in Jamaica, Thistlewood got hold of a series of instructions, written by Richard Beckford, about the best management of a plantation workforce. Beckford owned nearly 1,000 slaves and the largest and most fertile estates in Thistlewood's parish of Westmoreland. 'The Unhappy situation of a Slave is a Circumstance that will touch every Generous Breast with a Sentiment of Compassion', he wrote. Slaves should be treated with 'Justice and Benevolence', so that 'their lives may be render'd as cosy as their Condition will permit'. Beckford, like Henry Drax, whose own 'Instructions' were also procured by Thistlewood, gave detailed advice on feeding and care of slaves, and a warning that although they were un-educated, this was no reason for not 'treating them as Rational Beings', lest they should have a 'Sense of Injury which will dispose them to Revenge that may produce more fatal Consequence than desertion'.

Thistlewood took on board many of Richard Beckford's recommenda-tions, including the care of sick Africans, and thereby suffered a slightly less brutal mortality rate than other estates. But the 'Revenge' threat really struck home. Having laboriously transcribed the 'Instructions' into his diary, he followed them with a poem in which slaves turn on whites in a 'Bacchanalian Frenzy' with 'Full Acts of Blood and Vengeance'. It did not take long for Thistlewood to realise that the slaves hated him and wanted him dead.

This was no idle fear. The west of the island, where Thistlewood lived and worked, was more recently settled than elsewhere, and had even fewer whites, outnumbered by the enslaved Africans by as many as 16 to one. At Vineyard Pen, he went for weeks on end without seeing another white person. The move to the sugar plantation meant that a handful of lower-ranking whites were present, but it was also a much harder and more brutal establishment, with many more slaves. Soon after moving to Egypt, Thistlewood had a narrow escape.

In December 1752, he came across a runaway slave, Congo Sam. Attempting to seize him, Thistlewood was attacked with an axe the slave carried, as Congo Sam shouted 'in the Negro manner, "I will kill you, I will kill you now"'. Although Thistlewood parried most of the blows with a stick he was carrying, several times Congo Sam hit Thistlewood's coat, but 'the bill being new was not very sharp', and the white man 'received no harm'. Thistlewood was by now shouting at the top of his voice, 'Murder!' and 'Help! For God's sake!' 'but no assistance came'. Thistlewood, fearing he had 'no prospect but to lose [his] life', threw himself at the African and succeeded in grabbing the end of the axe, and dragging Congo Sam back towards his plantation. But at the watch hut by a bridge that marked Egypt's boundary, 'he would get no further. Bella and Abigail were there, but would not assist me. (He spoke to them in his language and I was much afraid of them)', Thistlewood wrote in his diary. Sam took the chance to shake his captor free and throw himself in the river. Thistlewood jumped in after him, and the two men wrestled for possession of the axe. During the course of the struggle, five 'Negro' men and three women, none known to Thistlewood, crossed the bridge and observed the battle. Thistlewood called out for help with capturing the runaway, but they 'would by no means assist me, neither for threats nor promises; one saying he was sick, the others that they were in a hurry'. Eventually one of Thistlewood's slaves, London, came to his assistance, and Congo Sam was captured. (London subsequently attempted to let Congo Sam escape, and then refused to testify against him). For Thistlewood, it was a close-run thing.

Thistlewood perceived that he was a marked man, and noted the murderous mutterings against him. His response was to attempt to demean, demoralise and traumatise the slaves into obedience and passivity. 'The first thing you learn is discipline', he wrote of his acclimatisation. During his year at Vineyard, he whipped almost two thirds of the men and half of the women. At Egypt, the regime was even worse, particularly when the Seven Years War made provisions scarce and the slaves hungry. At one point Thistlewood reported in his diary, 'My pocket Whip is broke and

Wore out.' For those caught eating cane from the fields, Thistlewood developed his own particular punishment, which was repulsive even by the standards of the time and place. On Wednesday 28 January 1756, he noted in
his diary that one of his charges had been caught foraging among the canes:
'Had Derby well whipped, and made Egypt shit in his mouth.' This
disgusting punishment, which became known as 'Derby's Dose', did not
even work. Derby continued to eat cane and then ran away.

This punishment for eating cane was repeated numerous times during
the year, sometimes with even crueller modifications. In July, one slave
who had run away was given a 'moderate whipping', but was then 'well'
'pickled', 'made Hector shit in his mouth, immediately put in a gag whilst
his mouth was full & made him wear it 4 or 5 hours'. On another occasion a slave was made to urinate into another slave's mouth. Cuttings and
mutilations were also deployed. When Derby continued to run away, he
had his face chopped with a machete so that his right ear, cheek and jaw
were almost cut off. Thistlewood also used stocks and 'picketing', where
the victim was hung by the hands with only a toe taking the weight of the
body. Once, he punished a female slave, Cubbah, for leaving the property
by having her 'picketed' on 'a quart bottle neck till she begged hard'.

In spite of this reign of terror, Thistlewood's diary shows how the
enslaved workforce continued to resist the total dominance of their masters
– by working slowly or deliberately incompetently, through pretending
illness, by constantly wandering off the plantation, or by plotting the overthrow of the whites.

This was the case throughout the island, as the dramatic events of 1760
illustrated. On 7 April, more than 100 slaves, under the leadership of a
charismatic young Akan or Coromantee called Tacky, left their estates in
St Mary parish and raided an arsenal in Port Maria, on Jamaica's north-
eastern coast. They then swept southwards, killing whites they came across,
burning crops and buildings, and gathering recruits. Soon they were 1,000
strong, as rebellions started flaring up all over Jamaica. It was the most
significant slave revolt in the West Indies until the Haitian revolution. A
Jamaican writing less than 15 years later claimed that the aim of 'Tacky's
Revolt' was 'the entire extirpation of the white inhabitants'. Africans who
refused to join would become slaves of the new regime of small princi-
palities throughout the island.

In May, the rebellion flared up in Westmoreland, and at Egypt plantation news of massacres of nearby whites combined with sightings of rebels
in the morass to bring a feeling of embattled crisis to Thistlewood's plantation. On one occasion Thistlewood heard that the adjacent estate had

been overrun. Soon he could see nearby buildings burning. He armed his most trusted slaves and guarded his property carefully, as rumours swirled around – 'strange various reports with torment & confusion'. There was a constant stream of militia and regular troops passing though, whom Thistlewood fed, lodged and watered, as Egypt became a staging post for operations against the rebels.

One night, one of the junior overseers at Egypt panicked and started shooting at all blacks he saw, for which he received a severe reprimand from Thistlewood. But the fear was well justified. Thistlewood, in the end, was reliant on his slaves to remain loyal to him. The Egypt slaves could easily have turned on the handful of whites and made themselves masters of the plantation. But although a number, to Thistlewood's alarm, shaved their heads, the motif of the rebellion, and a couple ran away, they did not revolt, but instead faithfully guarded the borders of the property.

This loyalty was about more than the terrible punishments rebels could expect if the revolt was unsuccessful, or the demeaning slave regime that deliberately 'demanned' its victims. Many of the slaves actually had a small stake in the status quo – possessions, livestock, other articles of property, family. Enough were prepared to stick with the 'devil you know' to render the revolt at last unsuccessful.

Another key factor was the maroons. Ironically, the free maroons were an inspiration for the rebellion. One account reported the rebellious slaves planning 'to fire all the plantation they can, til they force the whites to give them free like Cudjoe's Negroes'. But Cudjoe stuck by his deal made at the end of the war of the 1730s, and sent his men to support the whites against the rebellious slaves.* Ultimately a maroon tracked down, shot and killed Tacky, which was the beginning of the end of the rebellion, and maroons were used to mop up resistance, which simmered on until the following year.

Along with several hundred black slaves, some 60 whites were killed before order was restored. The retribution enacted illustrates the white community's sense of shock and fear. Five hundred slaves were transported, in the main to Honduras, and 100 executed, mostly in slow and painful ways. One 'was made to sit on the ground, and his body being chained to an iron stake, the fire was applied to his feet. He uttered not a groan, and saw his legs reduced to ashes with the utmost firmness and

---

* Thistlewood had met Cudjoe back in 1750, and found his men a reassuring presence: 'He Shook me by ye hand and Begg'd a Dram of us, which we gave him – he had on a feather'd hatt, Swords at his Side – gun upon his Shoulder &c Bare foot and Bare legg'd, Somewhat a Majestick look – he brought to my Memory ye picture of Robinson Crusoe.'

composure, after which, one of his arms by some means getting loose, he snatched a brand from the fire that was consuming him, and flung it in the face of the executioner.' In addition, far stricter rules were introduced, mainly to control the wanderings of slaves off their plantations, and dividing lines between whites and non-whites became much more rigid.

As well as dispassionately noting the brutal punishments dealt out under his rule, Thistlewood's diary also details his voracious and predatory sexual behaviour. Using schoolboy Latin, he lists all of his 'conquests': '*Sup. lect. cum Marina*' (on the bed with Marina), '*Cum* Flora, a congo, *Super Terram*, [on the ground] among the canes'. Everywhere on the estate – the fields, the boiling house, the Negro shacks – Thistlewood took his pleasure with the slave women, not caring who saw. In his first year in Jamaica he had sex with 13 different women on 59 occasions. Hardly any of the available female slaves escaped his attentions. On average he had 14 different part-ners in a year, and overall slept with nearly 140 different women, almost all black slaves, while in Jamaica.

Very soon after his arrival, he contracted a venereal infection, writing in his diary in September 1751, 'Perceived a small redness, but did not regard it.' Two days later he was 'last night *Cum* Dido', but had 'A greater redness, with soreness, and scalding water. About 9 a.m., a running begin, of a yellowish greenish matter.' This was followed a subsequent night by 'painful erections, and sharp pricking, great torment, forced to get up and walk about'. Worse symptoms followed, then the following week he recorded: 'Spoke to Dr Joseph Horlock. A rank infection.'

Horlock charged him nearly £3 for the treatment, which consisted of bleeding, mercury pills, salts and 'cooling powders', together with instruc-tions that had Thistlewood 'bathing the penis a long time in new milk night and morning'. None of this, however, stopped his amorous advances. The next day he was '*cum*' Nago Jenny.

Thistlewood was unusual in noting his sexual encounters, but entirely typical in his behaviour. At the beginning of the same year, he casually noted in his diary that 'ye Barb[ados] woman that was rap'd by three of them (at Kingston) in a short space' had produced a bastard child, to the consternation of the white men. It was the complication of the child, rather than the triple rape, that made the story noteworthy for Thistlewood. All the white bookkeepers at Egypt took slave 'wives', and many came down with venereal disease. On one occasion, in March 1753, Thistlewood acted to stop a rape at the plantation: 'At Night Mr Paul Stevens and Thomas Adams going to tear old Sarah to pieces in her hutt', he wrote, 'had a quarrel with both of them. They burnt her and would fire the hutt Note they both drunk.' The concern, though, seems to be more with damage to property than to the unfortunate victim.

At the end of 1754, William Dorrill died and the ownership of Egypt passed to John Cope, from a local gentry family, who had married Dorrill's young daughter Molly. Cope's speciality was turning up at Egypt, getting drunk, then summoning a slave woman to his bed. In March 1755 he arrived with a party of six, four of whom 'being heartily drunk, haw'led Eve separately into the Water Room and were Concern'd with her[.] Weech 2cd. First and last.' Thistlewood did nothing to stop the rape, but did not punish Eve when she subsequently ran away for a few days.

On another occasion Cope, following a drinking session with Mr MacDonald ('who had Eve to whom he gave 6 bitts'), ordered 'Tom fetch Beck from the Negroe's house for himself with whom he was with till morning'. But Beck had not been the first choice, as the next Monday Cope ordered 'Egypt Susannah and Mazerine whipped for refusal'. In revenge, 'Little Phibbah told Mrs Cope last Saturday's affair. Mrs Cope also examined the sheets and found them amiss.'

But Cope continued the same behaviour, which became increasingly drunken, erratic and angry. In October 1756, Thistlewood noted, 'Mr C. in his tantrums last night. Forced Egypt Susanah in the cookroom; was like a madman most part of the night, &c. Mrs Cope very ill today.' Cope made no effort to hide his behaviour, and his young wife Molly was forced to turn a blind eye; nor did it stop Cope becoming an assemblyman and custos of the parish.

Thistlewood hardly ever condemned any of this behaviour, except for when Cope forced himself on girls as young as nine. Men like Thistlewood and Cope expected white men to have sex with enslaved black women, whom they thought of as the embodiment of earthiness, sexuality and physical strength. Attractive female slaves, 'young and full-breasted', always fetched a premium at slave auctions. White bookkeepers were even encouraged to take on black 'wives', in the hope that their concubines might betray an incipient Negro plot. The resulting stream of mulatto children, some 10 per cent of all births in Jamaica, were, for visitors, evidence of the planters' 'licentious and even unnatural amours . . . a crime that seems to have gained sanction from custom'. From the highest to the lowest, almost all white men, 'of every rank, quality and degree', chose to 'riot in these goatish embraces', as an eighteenth-century historian of Jamaica put it.

Indeed, many planters, managers and overseers, even some whose wives and children were with them, lived openly with black mistresses. When they died, many who could afford it, like Codrington, made provision for them in their wills. Typical was one Jamaican planter, who died in 1714, having fathered four mulatto children. He freed their mothers and bequeathed the children 100 acres of his best land together with 20 of his black slaves. Others, however, for reasons of poverty or indifference, abandoned their own mulatto children to slavery.

According to a later writer, J. B. Moreton, who worked as a bookkeeper in Jamaica, attorneys managing plantations for absentee owners would 'keep a favourite black or mulatta girl on every estate'. He complained that these women 'are often intolerably insolent to subordinate white men'. Alternatively, as Moreton explained, an attorney would come with 'a few dissipated gentlemen' and then order the manager to 'procure some of the finest young wenches for the gentlemen'. At sunset, the girls were called from the fields; 'these poor wretches wash themselves in some river or pond, brace up their breasts, and meet at the Great House'. There, they danced for the white men, and then were taken to bed. 'Their black husbands', Moreton continued, 'being neglected, silently pass those nights in disagreeable slumbers, wrecked with jealousy and torture.'

Sometimes, it seems, revenge was had. Henry McCormick, who worked for Thistlewood at Egypt, was killed by a tree being felled by slaves. Thistlewood noted that the slaves, who were now runaways, had 'murdered him for meddling with their women'.

In early 1764, Thistlewood's nephew John came out to Jamaica. The nephew kept his own diary, reporting on 25 February 1764 after a welcoming reception from his uncle: 'Things seemed odd, but yet very pleasant.' John Thistlewood wasted no time in partaking of the slave women at Egypt, in particular Little Mimber, who had previously been a favourite of both his uncle and John Cope, but was now the wife of Johnnie, the driver on the Egypt estate and therefore a highly valued and important slave. Johnnie complained vociferously to Thomas Thistlewood, who took his side, chastising his nephew and punishing the woman. But John Thistlewood went ahead and slept with Little Mimber anyway.

Shortly afterwards, he died while out fishing. His drowned body – 'how strangely he looked', his uncle noted – was found by one of the white drivers. The slaves celebrated 'with load Huzzas', Thistlewood wrote, 'for joy that my kinsman is dead, I imagine. Strange impudence.'

Sexual encounters between white masters and black slaves were, in the main, about domination, violence and power. Ironically, though, while reaffirming the degraded state of slave women, they often at the same time went some way towards undermining the presumptions under which slavery operated. Most white men settled on a favourite black woman, and although they were obviously wildly unequal relationships, they were nonetheless intimate in a way that softened and disturbed racial boundaries; and their mixed-race progeny, of course, were a highly visible affront to the racial certainties that were so important to the institution of slavery in the Americas.

Indeed, Thistlewood's diary gives us a picture of slavery that is much more subtle and nuanced than the popular perception. For all his brutality, Thistlewood often broke the laws governing management of slaves: he gave them alcohol and firearms, allowed them, if in his good books, to travel off the plantation to visit friends or relations or to sell produce at the Sunday markets. Thistlewood's slaves were not just his livelihood, but his life: he existed intimately among them, and noted every coupling, fight, theft or illness. They used him to settle disputes among themselves, and he, in turn, was forced, at times like Tacky's Revolt, to trust them with his life. While still fundamentally conflicted, slave and master also co-operated when their interests coincided, for example when faced with a shortage of provisions or an outside threat. In the same way, the sexual relations depicted in the diary show that the intimacy of man and woman could challenge the most fundamental presumptions of slavery.

William Crookshanks was Thistlewood's subordinate at Egypt in 1754. Within a month of arrival he had contracted his first bout of venereal disease, but soon he was drawn to one slave, Myrtilla, who belonged to Elizabeth Mould, the coloured mistress of the recently deceased William Dorrill. By February the next year, Myrtilla was heavily pregnant and dangerously sick. Crookshanks was distraught. 'Mirtilla is very ill, it is thought going to miscarry', wrote Thistlewood. 'William cries sadly, the more fool he, as it is probably for Salt River Quaw', he added.

Myrtilla lost the baby, but not the affections of Crookshanks, who persuaded her owner to rent her to him for £20 a year. Crookshanks still made her work, but made a loss of about £5. Then, after 12 months, with Myrtilla pregnant again, Mould demanded her back. When she was returned, she was punished by having her head put in a yoke. Learning of this, Crookshanks exploded: according to Thistlewood, he 'abused Mr and Mrs Mould in an extraordinary manner, at their own house'. Afterwards, perhaps realising that he had overstepped the mark by implicitly questioning the 'master's' right to ownership, he became 'crazed [and] went down [on] his knees & begged their pardons'.

Thistlewood, as well as continuing to rape his slaves at will, also had favourites, the first, Marina, in the year of his arrival in Jamaica. Marina

was lavished with gifts – sugar, rum, clothes and food. After her, he transferred his affections, and presents, to Jenny, but this caused problems, as
Jenny had little status among the other slaves, who resented the airs and
graces she assumed once installed as the master's favourite concubine.
Then Thistlewood made a happier match, to a woman like him in her early
thirties, who was already an important matriarchal figure amongst the
enslaved community. Her name was Phibbah.

Phibbah was the senior house slave in charge of the kitchen at Egypt
plantation when Thistlewood started work there in 1751. She was owned
by William Dorrill, who bequeathed her to Elizabeth Mould, who in turn
left her to Molly Dorrill, the long-suffering wife of John Cope (Molly may
well have been Elizabeth's daughter). Phibbah had a daughter, Coobah. At
the beginning of 1752, Thistlewood had Phibbah flogged for a minor infrac-
tion, and after Congo Sam's attempt on his life, he suspected her of
complicity in the attack. But at the end of the following year he took her
to bed, and she became his 'wife', supplanting Jenny, in February 1754.
Thistlewood did not stop his predatory philandering with the other slave
women, but Phibbah shared his bed more than all the others put together
(Phibbah herself was sometimes suspected of sleeping with others as well).
In their first year, they had sex 234 times, and continued a vigorous sex
life thereafter. The relationship lasted for the rest of Thistlewood's life –
more than 30 years.

Phibbah had managed to acquire cash and property even before she met
Thistlewood, selling food and animals in the informal trading networks,
and through her skills as a seamstress and baker; she would in time save
enough money to buy the freedom of her sister, Jenny, who lived on a
neighbouring plantation. Thistlewood looked after her money, and helped
buy cloth, and she even lent him quite a substantial sum early in his career.
They nursed each other when either one was sick.

In 1757, Thistlewood fell out with the odious John Cope, mainly over
unpaid wages, and in late June took up a job as overseer of an estate a few
miles north of Egypt called Kendal. Separation from Phibbah seems to
have pained them both. 'Phibbah grieves very much', Thistlewood wrote
of her receiving the news of his move. For his part, 'I could not sleep, but
vastly uneasy.' He 'begged hard of Mrs Cope to sell or hire Phibbah to
me, but she would not'. On their parting, he gave Phibbah money, cloth
and soap, and she gave him a gold ring 'to keep for her sake'. Installed at
Kendal, Thistlewood noted he was 'mighty lonesome'.

Phibbah made sure she was not forgotten, sending numerous gifts – of
biscuits, cheese, fish – usually carried to Thistlewood by his slave Lincoln.

She also made regular trips, staying overnight at weekends. After one such visit in early July, Thistlewood wrote in his diary, 'I wish they would sell her to me . . . Tonight very lonely and melancholy again. No person sleep in the house but myself, and Phibbah's being gone this morning is fresh in my mind.' Later in the month, he heard that she was ill, which prompted Thistlewood's only comment on slavery, and a strikingly rare expression of sympathy and humanity: 'for which I am really very sorry. Poor girl, I pity her, she is in miserable slavery.'

Phibbah, acting as a go-between for Thistlewood and Cope, was instrumental in getting their disagreement resolved and Thistlewood returned to Egypt after just under a year at Kendal. Here he remained a further 10 years or so, with Phibbah as his 'wife' throughout. When in 1767 he moved with his slaves to his own 'Pen' called Breadnut Island, Phibbah, now probably in her forties, went with him; the Copes had at last agreed to rent her to Thistlewood for £18 a year.

Naturally, her close relationship with Thistlewood gave Phibbah great advantages among the enslaved community. On the basic level, she was not short of food and escaped the lash. Apart from noting a 'correction' he gave her early in their relationship, probably connected to some infidelity on her part, there is no other violence against her recorded in Thistlewood's diaries. (That said, many of the other owner–slave relationships that are mentioned seem to have been violent, so this may have been a particular, rather than general case.)

Phibbah's daughter Coobah also benefited from the arrangement. Thistlewood took to treating her almost as his own, giving her presents and reasonably well-paid work. In 1758, against his usual practice, he intervened to stop the rape of Coobah (probably still a child) by a white bookkeeper, who 'Attempted to Ravish her' in the boiler house, having 'Stopp'd a handkerchief into her mouth'.

Phibbah retained the status she had achieved as a house slave, and, like most 'wives', was spared the gruelling and often fatal labour in the canefields. Indeed, she had time to perform paid work for herself, and in partnership with Thistlewood. By 1761, Thistlewood held nearly £70 for her, the equivalent of two years' wages for a white underling. Like many slave mistresses, such as Codrington's Maudlin Morange, Phibbah was freed by a clause in Thistlewood's will (so long as she did not cost more than £80), and given £100 to buy land and build a house.

But to a degree, Phibbah had already 'transcended' her state of 'miserable slavery', particularly after being rented by Thistlewood from the Copes. She was friends with free people, including whites, exchanging gifts all over the local area. When she was ill in 1760, 'with a bad loose-ness', Mrs Cope sent flour, wine and cinnamon. On one occasion in 1779, she even entertained the white wives of two local grandees to tea 'under ye guinep trees in ye garden at Breadout blood Pen'. Most strikingly, perhaps, she even owned slaves herself. In 1765 she was given Bess, an 11-year-old girl, heavily scarred from yaws, as a present from Sarah Bennett, a free coloured woman, although legally Phibbah could not possess slaves. Bess subsequently had a child, Sam, who thus also belonged to Phibbah. Phibbah on occasion punished other slaves. She had effec-tive jurisdiction in the kitchen, and when a slave named Sally was caught stealing there, Phibbah had her tied up outside, 'naked for the mosqui-toes to bite here tonight'.

Thus the role of black mistresses, particularly those like Phibbah who were resourceful and accomplished, blurred the rigid distinctions of race and slavery. Most remarkably perhaps, Phibbah retained the affection and respect of the rest of Thistlewood's slave community, despite her 'halfway' position.

In addition, almost all the slave women had direct experience of how it was impossible to reject the attentions of Thistlewood. Most would also have accepted the reality that using their bodies was pretty much the only way they would achieve any sort of agency, and in some circumstances even freedom. A white visitor to Barbados during the late eighteenth century noted at length the availability of young black prostitutes in the bars and hotels of Bridgetown. He added, 'this offers the only hope they have of procuring a sum of money, wherewith to purchase their freedom; and the resource among them is so common, that neither shame nor disgrace attaches to it; but, on the contrary, she who is most sought, becomes an object of envy, and is proud of the distinction shewn her'.

Other slaves found that having Phibbah in a 'halfway' position, between them and the master, was to their interest. Phibbah no doubt kept Thistle-wood informed of the ins and outs of the slave dwellings. But she also interceded with him on the side of the slaves.* On at least three occasions, Thistlewood actually reprimanded her for pushing too far on behalf of the field slaves, which he considered outside her jurisdiction. Nonetheless, the regime notably softened. Writers on Thistlewood all agree that Phibbah 'civilised' him.

---

*During Tacky's Revolt, a group of rebels shot the three white people they found on an estate, then raped and prepared to kill the white overseer's mulatto mistress. She was spared after the interces-sion of the plantation's slaves, who saw her as their friend.

A major incentive for slave women to become 'wives' of whites was to do with their children. The child of a slave was automatically a slave him- or herself, and thus could be sold to other distant plantations or even off the island entirely. Hans Sloane, who was in Jamaica 70 years earlier, advised against this, as it often led to the suicide of the parents – but the practice was nonetheless widespread. This outcome was much less likely for mulatto children, who often enjoyed other substantial benefits.

After a difficult pregnancy, Thistlewood and Phibbah had a child, John, in 1760. When born, Thistlewood's child belonged to another white – Phibbah's mistress, Molly Cope. After a struggle, Thistlewood bought his son's freedom when the boy was two years old. From the age of five he was educated at the local school. Thistlewood added children's books such as 'History of Jack the Giant Killer in 2 parts' to his regular orders from London. As a teen, John was apprenticed to a carpenter. Thistlewood reported regular battles with his son: he was caught lying; he was indolent. But Phibbah adored him, and according to Thistlewood, spoilt him rotten.

Had John survived, he would have inherited his father's estate, as well as the not insubstantial property amassed by his mother. He would then have gone on to 'become a member of Jamaica's brown elite'. But it was not to be.

In August 1780, John was spending a lot of time at a neighbouring plantation where he had become friendly with a slave girl, Mimber. On 1 September, Thistlewood received word that his son was 'very ill'. He was too sick to return home, so Phibbah, on foot, went to nurse him. While she was away, Thistlewood had Sally in his bed.

Phibbah got her son as far as Egypt, whence Thistlewood rode from Breadnut Island Pen to see him. The next day John was brought home, 'very weak indeed & not in his right senses'. A doctor summoned from a nearby estate pronounced him in very great danger, recommending doses of bark and rhubarb to curb his fever. Another doctor arrived 'much in liquor' and 'laid blisters inside each thigh; but he continued light headed'. Two days later, 'burning with the fever', he died. Phibbah was devastated, 'almost out of her senses'. Thistlewood, in his grief, made wild accusations that his son had been poisoned, but the doctors confirmed the cause of death as 'putrid fever'.

John was buried on the day of his death, Thursday 7 September 1780, 'in the old garden, between the pimento tree and the bee houses'. Gathered at his graveside was an extraordinary cross-section of Jamaican society: planter friends of Thistlewood, free fellow-apprentice friends of John, enslaved friends of his mother – the entire radical diversity through which, had he survived, John Thistlewood would have had to negotiate.

24

JAMAICA: RICH AND POOR

'Franklin gripped the bridge-stanchions with a hand
Trembling from fever. Each spring, memories
Of his own country where he could not die
Assaulted him. He watched the malarial light
Shiver the canes.'

Derek Walcott, 'Tales of the Islands'

Thistlewood never had the capital or manpower to go into sugar on his own account. Nonetheless, he did much better in Jamaica than he ever would have done at home, achieving in the West Indies his dream of landed independence. He was even financially secure enough to have time for reading, gardening and socialising. In spite of severe setbacks late in his life, he was worth nearly £3,000 at the time of his death. By comparison, the average holder of wealth in England was worth only a little more than £200. In the northern colonies it was about £300. By far the most valuable asset Thistlewood owned when he died was his slave force – some 35, worth more than £1,500.

But Thistlewood, judging from his diaries, was something of an exception among the more 'middling' whites of Jamaica. During a five-year period at Egypt, he had 18 different white men working for him. Only one stayed more than a year, some lasted only days. Those not dismissed for indolence, drunkenness or excessive violence against the slaves sickened and died.

On most sugar plantations, below a head overseer like Thistlewood would be found two or three white 'bookkeepers'. By the mid-eighteenth century, many were young Scots (Robert Burns was appointed a bookkeeper in Jamaica, and was ready to depart for the island when halted by the news of the success of his first volume of poetry). The work included driving the slaves, as well as managing the planting, harvesting and processing of the cane.

This undertaking remained as hectic as in the seventeenth century. The technology had barely changed since the days of Sir James Drax. The cut canes still had to be ground and the juice boiled on a fiercely rapid and potentially problem-strewn schedule: mills still broke down, particularly in undercapitalised estates where a new set of rollers or machinery was unaffordable. The boiling went wrong (expert boilers, the vast majority now the most valued slaves, were in great demand, and were lent out to other plantations at considerable expense). Bookkeeper J. B. Moreton complained that during the harvest, he only got three or four hours' sleep out of 24.

As well as hard work, it was isolated, poorly paid, 'a dull, cheerless, drudging life', as one bookkeeper later complained. Unless armed with an introduction, the young men were shunned by 'smart' white society. It was, the bookkeeper wrote, 'A line of life where, to his first conception, everything wears the appearance of barbarity and slavish oppression.' The consolations of plentiful alcohol and sex often contributed to the young men's downfall.

A string of casualties from this cadre of rootless, dispirited young men process across the pages of Thistlewood's diary. John Hartnole, only 19 years old, who took over at Egypt plantation, was called 'Crakka Juba', 'Crazy Somebody', by the slaves. Thistlewood reported him as overindulging in food and alcohol to the extent that he soiled himself. Another underling of Thistlewood, Patrick May, was said to be 'in his house all day, drunk'. He was quickly dismissed after violently assaulting his slave lover.

In 1761, a bookkeeper called John Groves was taken on at Egypt. He had come from nearby Roaring River plantation, owned by the estate of Richard Beckford, having been fired for excessive brutality. Soon after his start, Thistlewood noted, 'Yesterday afternoon John Groves like a madman amongst the Negroes, flogging Dago, Primus, &c. without much occasion.' Thistlewood reprimanded him, and Groves left the estate. His replacement, Thistlewood complained, did nothing but eat. He died four months later. In November 1761, another bookkeeper was fired for attacking the slaves in the fields when he was drunk.

The chance was still there for a first-generation immigrant, who worked hard and avoided an early death from disease or drinking, to put together enough property to pass on at least the germ of a great Jamaican sugar estate to the next generation. By the end of the eighteenth century, a high proportion of Jamaican wealth was held by Scots – in the main the sons or grandsons of young bookkeepers who had come out at the beginning of the century, survived and prospered. Nonetheless, from the lower-ranking whites there must have been more than a few envious glances at the vigorously displayed riches of the Jamaica sugar barons.

By mid-century, inequality of wealth was extraordinary in Jamaica; Barbados looked almost egalitarian in comparison. Ten per cent of those who held wealth owned two thirds of the island's total. At the other end of the scale from the slaves and their young white drivers, the owners of large Jamaican sugar plantations were thriving spectacularly.

Against a climbing sugar price – from 17 shillings per hundredweight in 1733 to 43 shillings in 1747 – Jamaica had dramatically increased output as new plantations were established and consolidated. By 1750, nearly half of the sugar imported into the UK came from Jamaica, which also had the most productive mills.

The total wealth of the island had risen fivefold between 1700 and 1750 and would triple again up to 1774 as Jamaica experienced extraordinary economic growth. This was based partly on trade with Spanish America, but mainly on rum and sugar. Between 1740 and 1790, the plantations marched along the north coast, through Llandovery, Rose Hall and Tryall, and southward on to the Westmoreland plain by way of Friendship and the Roaring River and Williamsfield estates. There had been about 400 sugar mills on the island in 1740; by 1786 there would be more than 1,000.

This sugar production made the colony 'not only the richest but the most considerable colony at this time under the government of Great Britain', and its inhabitants the wealthiest. In spite of the radical inequalities, the average Jamaican white was worth between 20 and 30 times as much as the same man in Britain or North America. In 1774, per capita wealth in England was around £42; in Jamaica for a white man it was more than £1,000. While in Chesapeake only the richest planters had more than 30 slaves, in Jamaica the average sugar plantation in 1750 had some 200. Over the following 25 years, some 177,600 further slaves would be imported.

Major beneficiaries of this sugar bounty were the Beckford family. On one occasion, it was suggested to Alderman William Beckford that he invest in a putative silver mine in Jamaica. Pointing to his fields of cane he said, 'While we have so profitable a mine above ground we will not trouble for hunting for one underground.' All the Beckfords had been using sugar profits to add to their inheritances: Richard had acquired three more plantations, Julines two, Francis one. Most aggressive was William, who had

22,000 acres in Jamaica by 1754, with his brothers and cousin Ballard (son of Peter's brother, Thomas Beckford, killed in a duel) together owning about the same again, spread across 12 of Jamaica's parishes. All had increased their slave holdings at the same time, William to some 2,000.

The Price dynasty, founded by Francis, a soldier in Cromwell's invasion force who had acquired more than 1,000 acres in his own lifetime, also prospered. Francis's son Charles developed the huge, rich sugar estate at Worthy Park, which by the time of his death in 1730 was the most envied on the island. Of his nine children, only three outlived him, and only one for any length of time. This was another Charles, who had been sent back to England to attend Eton and Oxford. Sir Charles, as he soon became, owned in his prime about 26,000 acres and some 1,300 slaves, located in 11 of Jamaica's parishes. This bloated portfolio came partly from canny dynastic marriages and successful speculations during Jamaica's most expansive era, but mainly through Charles's unashamed manipulation of his political power as close friend of the Governor, Edward Trelawny, and perennial Speaker of the assembly, a position he held almost continuously for 18 years, despite the accusations of his enemies that he was a man 'of no abilities or experience' who 'frequently Lyes with Black women'. This political power enabled him to bypass rules about the size of patents that could be granted, and gave him first refusal when Crown lands came up for sale.

In 1760, Price built the most grandiose surviving Jamaican Great House, Rose Hall, on the north coast of the island, at the staggering cost of £30,000, even though he was already being described as 'rich a man as William Beckford, for possessions but in debt'. Eight years later he became Sir Charles, Baronet of Rose Hall. But this was only part of his empire: his house in Spanish Town occupied a whole block, and the mansion at Worthy Park had a staff of at least 20 individuals: a butler, two footmen, a coachman, a postillion, an assistant, first and second cooks, a storekeeper, a waiting maid, three house cleaners, three washerwomen and four seamstresses. Each of the children in the family was provided with a nurse and a boy or girl helper. When Price left his broad acres, he was accompanied by a handyman who made the trip on foot, holding on to the tail of his master's horse.

Sir Charles was a leading light in the Jamaica Association, formed at his Spanish Town mansion in 1751 by the island's most powerful planters to check the power of the London-appointed governor and advance their own interests. With him in a triumvirate at the top of Jamaican politics was Richard Beckford, brother of Alderman William, and another man, Sussex-born Rose Fuller.

The Fullers, originally gun makers ('JF'-marked cannons are still to be seen in the Tower of London), were beneficiaries of a very lucrative marriage. In 1703, John Fuller had married Elizabeth Rose, the daughter of Fulke Rose and heir to his fortune, built up since the earliest days of English settlement in Jamaica, which now amounted to more than 15,000 acres.* John Fuller renamed his family house, Brightling Park in Sussex, Rose Hall, and his second son, born in 1708, was named Rose in honour of the Jamaica fortune. The Fullers were also linked to the Price family through the Rose connection.

Rose Fuller was educated at Cambridge, then trained as a doctor at Leyden, under the same tutor as Alderman William Beckford. He sailed to Jamaica on 11 December 1732 after the management of the inherited estates by attorneys had come in for criticism and, during the difficult 1730s, profits were slipping.

Rose Fuller was a loud and rough-spoken man, hearty and genial, but prone to towering rages. Enemies said he was not malicious, but marked by a considerable lust for power. His first years in Jamaica, though, were scarred by money worries, homesickness and tragedy. Six or seven years after his arrival, he married a 17-year-old girl, Ithamar Mill, daughter of the island's receiver general, and possibly a relative of both the Beckfords and the Vassalls. But the letter of congratulation from his father, John, had not even reached him from England before both his wife and her unborn child were dead from disease. Thereafter John constantly nagged his son to make provision for the properties should he die as well, while warning him to avoid the 'High Living' he had heard about in Jamaica. Rose did not marry again, although in his will he left a £100 legacy to 'Mary Johnson Rose of J'ca a free mulatto woman formerly my housekeeper'.

Rose was fortunate in having a lucrative sideline as a doctor, where, helped by the Sloane connection and a valuable contract to minister to the regular troops, he soon had an 'Abundance of Business'. Meanwhile, he worked tirelessly to turn round a failing concern. When sugar prices rose at the end of the 1730s, so did his fortune, and in 1742, his younger brother Thomas started work as his sugar merchant in London. By 1745, Rose had inherited in full the Jamaica estates, was rich enough to be lending money to Richard Beckford, and was to be found in the thick of Jamaican politics – which, as with the Beckfords, in large part revolved around getting supporters in England to block anything the Governor proposed

---

* It was a double wedding, with Rose's widow marrying the distinguished Sir Hans Sloane, who would thereafter be looked upon by the Fuller boys as their true grandfather. The links between the two families strengthened further when Rose's sister Elizabeth married Sloane's son William in 1733.

that undermined the interests of the planters, and seeing off the attacks of Jamaica's merchant faction in Kingston, whose interests did not always coincide with those of the planters.

When the likes of the Fullers, Beckfords and Prices descended – for assembly meetings or social events – Spanish Town came to life. It was 'surprising to see the number of Coaches and Chariots which are perpetually plying', one visitor reported. Gentlemen sailed past, 'very gay in silk Coats, and Vests trimmed with silver', waited on by blacks in the smartest livery, 'tho' 'tis the utmost Pain to the uneasy slave'. The inventory of a merchant tailor who died in 1756, with a client list that encompassed many of the sugar baron families, included black silk breeches, silver spurs, coats with silver or gold lace, Dresden ruffles, silver buckles and expensive belts and swords.

The ladies, for their part, were dressed 'as richly' as anywhere in Europe, 'and appear with as good a Grace'. They wore the latest fashions from London or Paris – imported through Martinique – even if it was winter in Europe and the clothes were totally unsuited to the tropics.

A visitor in the first part of the eighteenth century reported that at Spanish Town they 'lately have got a Playhouse, where they retain a Set of extraordinary good Actors'. As in Barbados, there were frequent dances. The Governor's Ball was the social occasion of the year, the best chance for show and one-upmanship. A governor's residence, known as the King's House, was completed in 1762 at a cost of £30,000 to the island. With Doric pillars in the grand style, it took up an entire 200-foot side of the main square of Spanish Town. It was, a writer on Jamaica in the 1770s declared, 'the noblest and best edifice of the kind, either in North-America or any of the British colonies in the West-Indies'. (It is now, following fire, earthquake and neglect, a ghostly ruin, with only the façade surviving.)

Most of the rest of Spanish Town, usually home to about 500 whites and some 800 slaves, free blacks and coloureds, was less impressive. Visitors could not help remarking that its most elegant days seemed to have passed with the departure of the Spanish, and the wrecking of the town by the Cromwellian soldiers. Those buildings that had survived had been 'suffered to decay', and many existed only as broken columns.

Spanish Town was very much the planter capital, but most of the grandees only made brief visits before retreating to the relative cool of their upland plantations. Kingston was the merchant centre, and a much more vibrant and seemingly prosperous place, with about 5,000 each of whites and slaves, and some 1,200 free blacks or mulattoes. Here were superior brick-built houses of two or three storeys, their fronts shaded with a piazza below and a covered gallery above. With nearly 2,000 buildings by the 1770s, Kingston had grown beyond its original grid and straggled out into the hills behind.

Beneath the civilised veneer of planters and merchants plying the streets in their smart carriages, both Jamaican towns featured many less salubrious activities. Gaming was the island's favourite vice – dice, shovelboard, faro, ace of hearts, passage and hazard were all played. Prostitutes, including barely pubescent mulatto girls, touted openly for business, and in Kingston in particular there exisited an 'incredible number of . . . grog shops, occupied by people of the vilest characters (rogues and whores) who . . . in those dens of infamy, riot away days and nights drinking new rum'.

An eighteenth-century visitor to Jamaica was shocked by the appearance of passers-by in the streets. 'The People seem all sickly', he wrote, 'their Complection is muddy, their Colour wan, and their Bodies meagre; they look like a Corpse . . . Death deals more in this Place than another.'

Few children born to slaves survived. Thomas Thistlewood recorded in his diary 153 pregnancies, which produced 121 live births. Of the 66 whose fate is known, only 15 survived beyond seven years of age. In contrast, slave women in the Chesapeake were each bearing between six and eight children, of whom about four survived into adulthood. A 1757 letter to Abraham Redwood from his Antigua manager, 'An Account of negroes and Stock dead on the Casada Garden Estate since our last Account', gives a vivid picture of how death arrived to all ages: 'Nestor a woman superannuated 80 years died with the timpani Hatty a man aged 40 Year died with the Dropsy constant runaway. Sombah a man aged 30 Years died with a disorder in his head and dropsy a constant runaway. Sarah a Girl aged 6 Years died with the Kings evil and small pox. Hannah a new negroe woman aged 20 Years died with the pox. Sarah a new negroe woman aged 22 years died being obstructed. Mary a woman aged 90 years died with old Age. Puthena a woman aged 22 years died a sudden death Oct. 4th. Gritta a Girl aged 7 Years died a sudden death Octob. 27th. Nanny aged 60 Years died with the Cax and flux, 15th Nov. Cudjoe a man aged 30 Years died with the pleurisy 5th January. Scipio a man aged 60 Years died with the Dropsy a constant runaway.'

But in the streets of Kingston, this song was sung:

> 'One, two, tree,
> All de same;
> Black, white, brown,

All de same:
All de same.
One, two, &c.'

Indeed, in Jamaica, the ever-present shadow of an early death, like the inti-macy of sex, was a great leveller. In fact the proportionately few whites died at an even greater rate than the overworked, half-starved and brutally treated black slaves. Africans often had some immunity to yellow fever and malaria, but for white Europeans, Jamaica was the most deadly place in the world after West Africa. Kingston had the worst death rate, with as much as 20 per cent of the town's population dying every year in the 1740s and 1750s. This is a similar rate to that suffered by London during the Great Plague; but in Kingston it continued every year. This was partly accounted for by the presence of vulnerable newcomers, seamen and tran-sients, but elsewhere was bad too, with mortality at about 10 per cent per year. This was a worse rate even than South Carolina and Chesapeake during the seventeenth century, famously described as a 'great charnel house'. Infant mortality in Jamaica even increased from the seventeenth to the eighteenth century. Before 1700, 46 per cent died before the age of five. After 1700 it was 60 per cent, as Jamaica's commercial success made it a hub for new and more virulent strains of fever and smallpox. Surviving infancy was no guarantee of a long life: a third of 20-year-olds did not get to their thirtieth birthday, and half of 30-year olds were dead before reaching 40. John Taylor commented that the 'Creolians . . . seldom live to be above five and thirty years, for as soon as they are twenty they begin to decline.'

The contrast with the northern mainland colonies is striking. There had been similar emigration from Europe to the Caribbean and to North America – about half a million; but in 1776 there were only 50,000 whites in the British Caribbean compared to two million in the Thirteen Colonies. Although the white population of Jamaica did grow to nearly 20,000 by the 1770s, in the same time the population of some of the North Amer-ican colonies had increased tenfold.

Eighteenth-century writers on Jamaica, hoping to promote white migra-tion to the colony, could not deny the fearsome death rate. One even wrote that although Jamaicans 'declined sooner', 'They console themselves, however, that they can enjoy more of the real existence here in one hour, than the fair inhabitants of the frozen, foggy regions do in two.' Most, though, like earlier promoters of Barbados, blamed the habits of the Creoles for contributing to their own downfall. Too many, wrote one, 'keep late hours at night: lounges a-bed in the morning; gormandizes at dinner and supper on loads of flesh, fish, and fruits; loves poignant sauces; dilutes with ale, porter, punch, claret, and Madeira, frequently jumbling all together; and continues this mode of living till, by constantly manuring his stomach with such an heterogeneous compost, he had laid the foundation for a plentiful crop of ailments'. Everyone agreed that rum, or 'Kill Devil', had accounted for thousands.

Certainly the diet and alcohol consumption of the typical planter was far from healthy; it has been estimated that Jamaica in the late eighteenth century imported as much alcohol per white as was consumed per capita in the United States in 1974. This doesn't even include home-produced rum. But the sober sickened and died as well. One visitor remarked at being shocked at seeing 'three English ladies, wives to some of the officers here, who only three months ago had come to this country as fair as lilies, blooming as roses, now pallid, sallow and sickly, with the appearance of being ten years older than they really are'. An old planter who had headed a respectable family wrote to a friend at the end of his life that he had lost to disease two wives and 16 children out of 21.

So death, rather than reproduction, dominated Jamaican life. Family life, which underpinned society in England and in northern America, was virtually non-existent. Marriages only lasted an average of eight years before one of the partners died, and few left surviving children. As in Barbados, those youngsters who did reach adulthood would seldom have parents still alive. Lack of parental supervision and early inheritance of property contributed to the 'anarchic individualism' of the West Indies.

'The frequent occurrence' of death, one visitor to Jamaica noted, 'renders it an object of far less solemnity than in England. The victims are almost immediately forgotten: another fills their office, and their place knows them no more for ever.' When Thomas Thistlewood arrived in Jamaica in 1750, he was told that of the 136 who had arrived on a ship 16 months earlier, 122 were dead. He reacted fearfully, worrying about diseases and trying to ascertain treatments that worked. But this only lasted a year; thereafter he assumed a more fatalistic attitude to death. In the same way, his early days see him shocked at the cursoriness of a slave's burial, and noting with alarm the deaths of the people he knows. But soon the frequent deaths, even of his own family, elicit little emotion. In contrast, New Englanders, in a much healthier climate, thought about death all the time.

'No Sett of Men are more unconcerned at [death's] Approach', wrote an observer of the Jamaica Creoles. 'They live well, enjoy their Friends, drink heartily, make Money, and are quite careless of Futurity.' Indeed, the imminence of death contributed to the sense of impermanence, the narrow hedonism and the absence of the preserving spirit found in North American colonies. There was, one writer complained, a 'lack of public spirit' in Jamaica: there were hardly any bridges, fords or roads. Schools were thin on the ground, and universities and libraries non-existent. While the North Americans had Harvard and Yale, Jamaicans who could afford it almost all sent their sons to England to be educated (the number of West Indian boys attending Eton increased sixfold in the second half of the eighteenth century, dwarfing the number of boys from North America by a factor of about seven). Only in 1721 did Jamaica get its first printing press, nearly 100 years after Massachusetts. Few people went to church or read books (Thistlewood being an exception), preferring 'gaming' to 'the Belles Letteres' and 'a Pack of Cards' to 'the Bible'.

So the West Indies had none of the things that sustained and nourished the northern colonies: a stable and rising population, family, long lives, and even religion. Instead there was money, alcohol, sex and death. A later writer, contrasting the life of colonists in the North American settlements with the comparative luxury of the West Indian plantations, commented that emigrants to North America had brought with them the tools of culture, religion and settlement. But in the West Indian world, the founders 'carried no Gods with them', going instead into 'the wilderness of mere materialism'. A later visitor would complain that Kingston, by then the largest English town in the Caribbean, had 'not one fine building in it', whereas Spanish Havana in Cuba was a 'city of palaces, a city of streets, of colonnades and towers, and churches and monasteries'. 'We English', he ended, 'have built in those islands as if we were but passing visitors.'

Most were, indeed, sojourners, incomers, transients, looking not to belong in Jamaica or to be part of a viable settler society, but to make money fast and get out while still alive. This feeling was shared by almost all parts of white Jamaican society. 'It is to Great Britain alone that our West India planters consider themselves as belonging', wrote a historian of the West Indies at the end of the eighteenth century. 'Even such of them as have resided in the West Indies from their birth, look on the islands as their temporary abode only, and the fond notion of being able to go home (as they emphatically term a visit to England) year after year animates their industry and alleviates their misfortune.' Although Barbados, uniquely, developed a real Creole identity of its own, elsewhere the whites in the British West Indies were exiles who, a Nevis planter wrote, 'incessantly sigh for a return'.

Increasing numbers did, indeed, return to Britain, becoming absentee landlords. One third of Jamaican plantation owners were absentees by the

1740s, two thirds by 1800. Absenteeism was rare in the Leewards in the 1730s, William Codrington being an exception, but was at chronic levels less than 20 years later. In St Kitts, half the property was owned by absentees by 1745. This trend would constitute one of the greatest factors in the sugar empire's rapid decline.

25

THE SUGAR LOBBY

'*[The West India interest] have frequently . . . shown themselves above parliament
. . . Lord North used to say that they were the only masters he ever had.*'
                                                    Herald newspaper, 23 August 1797

The story goes that George III was out riding with the Earl of Chatham, William Pitt the Elder, near Weymouth when they passed a very pretentious equipage with numerous outriders in grand liveries. To the King's fury, it made his own carriage look rather meagre. When he learnt that it belonged to a Jamaican, he exclaimed, 'Sugar, sugar, hey? – all *that* sugar! How are the duties, hey, Pitt, how are the duties?'

Sugar was king. Imports to England, having already quadrupled in the last four decades of the seventeenth century, trebled between 1700 and 1740, and had doubled again by 1770. By then, sugar had achieved a revolution in eating habits in England. Along with coffee, tea and cocoa, jams, processed foods, chocolate and confectionery were now being consumed in much greater quantities. Treacle was spread on bread and put on porridge. Breakfast became sweet, rather than savoury. Pudding, hitherto made of fish or light meat, now embarked on its unhealthy history as a separate sweet course.

In Hannah Glasse's famous 1747 book, *The Art of Cookery Made Plain and Easy*, which was the first recipe book in English aimed at the middle classes, she assumed they would have plenty of sugar. (Jane Austen's *Sense and Sensibility* records a moment of anxiety when impending poverty threatens the heroine's family's purchase of sugar.) Glasse's recipe for 'cake in the Spanish way' required three pounds of 'best moist sugar'. Marmalade, as invented by Rebecca Price, required a pound of sugar for every four oranges. Use of sugar can also be seen in the fat faces of contemporary monarchs, beauties and actresses.

Once a luxury, sugar became an essential. The tea break had arrived, with even the poorest labourer taking sustenance from the combination of stimulant and calorie hit. 'Sugar is so generally in use, by the assistance of tea', read a 1774 report, 'that even the poor wretches living in almshouses will not be without it.' A contemporary recommended that 12 to 16 pounds of sugar be used with every pound of tea. Indeed, one of the attractions of tea, and a secret of its success, was that it could carry a large amount of sweet calories. In all, by the end of the eighteenth century, a typical poor family in England would give as much as 6 per cent of its income to sugar.

By this time, sugar, along with other New World luxuries such as chocolate, coffee, tea, rum and tobacco, had helped shape a consumer mentality among ordinary people, more pliant and willing to accept factory discipline in order to afford their luxury stimulants.

Some saw the expenditure on tea and sugar – brought from so far away – as a diversion of wealth; but many others saw it as an incentive for extra effort: a cotton manufacturer observed: 'Among the lower orders . . . industry can only be found, where artificial wants have crept in, and have acquired the character of necessities.'

In sugar consumption Britain now led the world by a large margin, importing more than twice the amount as much more populous France, where tea was shunned in favour of wine. Sugar's ugly sister rum also failed to catch on in France, where brandy reigned supreme, but in Britain and Ireland it was another story.

Wine and brandy consumption had fallen off in England when, at the outbreak of war in 1689, commerce with France had been banned. Thereafter distillers of malt and molasses spirits benefited from legal restrictions on French spirits. This led to a boom in new types of distilling, and, from about 1713, what became known as the 'Gin Craze'. When this turned ugly and gin-making was curbed by the government, the British consumer, now used to drinking spirits, looked for an alternative. The West India lobby was ready with a pamphlet campaign that extolled the health benefits of rum and reminded the consumer that British livelihoods in the West Indies colonies depended on it. It was a patriotic tipple. The fashionable served it as punch in elaborately decorated bowls. A contemporary observer wrote of the merchants of Liverpool: 'their rum is excellent of which they consume large quantities in punch, made when the West India fleets come in mostly with limes, which are very cooling, and afford a delicious flavour'.

Rum consumption, like that of sugar, grew almost exponentially. Soon 'Kill Devil' had invaded almost all areas of English social life. Eighteenth-century elections, notorious for their bribery and drunkenness, saw rum freely distributed, so much so that at election time the price went up. From 2,000 gallons a year in 1700, by 1773 rum imports into England and Wales had risen to two million gallons, further swelling the coffers of the sugar barons.

The sugar empire was now undisputedly Britain's most important possession. Sugar was the most valuable import into Britain, worth more than the total exports of all the North American mainland colonies combined. Towards the end of the century, the younger Pitt estimated that four fifths of British incomes derived from overseas came from the West Indies. The islands also took far more English-manufactured goods than the North Americans, even though there were many fewer settlers there. Jamaica was described as 'a constant Mine whence Britain draws prodigious Riches', and as a 'necessary appendage to our present refined manner of living'.

One economist concluded that the labours of the people settled in the West Indies doubled and perhaps trebled the activity of all Europe. 'They may be considered', he wrote, 'as the principal cause of the rapid motion which now agitates the universe.' Sugar was a driving force and an important part of Britain's rapidly expanding and now global commerce. Its sister trade, of course, was in slaves.

By the 1750s, the English were pre-eminent in the slave trade, shipping some 200,000 during the decade. Bristol had boomed on the back of slavery during the first decades of the eighteenth century, as its rich, elegant architecture of that time testifies. But after about 1740, Liverpool, with its superior port facilities and easy access to the manufacturing heartlands of the country, reigned supreme. The population of Liverpool, only 5,000 in 1700, had grown to 34,000 by 1773, by which time it was sending 100 ships a year to Africa.

Banks, insurance companies, shipbuilders and brokers all participated in and benefited from the trade, and profits were invested in manufacturing. Manchester, in particular, thrived, producing textiles that the Liverpool shippers took to Africa to pay for the slaves. Manufacturers of tools and guns also found a ready market.

The operation on the Slave Coast became more efficient, with one planter partnership with Scottish roots even buying an island (Bunce Island) off the coast of Sierra Leone to act as a collection point (for the whites there was a golf course with African caddies in kilts). After 1750, an organisation was formed of British slave traders, which maintained the forts on the coast.

The huge demand for slaves – and the importation of tens of thousands of guns a year – led to constant war over large areas of West Africa. When prisoners could not be acquired this way, West Africans started looking for new excuses to condemn someone to slavery, including twins and mothers of twins.

In England, it was fashionable for aristocratic women to be accompanied by a black boy, who was treated as a sort of toy (when he outgrew this role, he was usually sent to the Caribbean). Blacks started appearing in art and caricature by, for instance, Hogarth and Cruikshank. In other ways the West Indies was becoming more highly visible in English society. The ample sugar profits could now fund absentee proprietorship on an ever-increasing scale. Many of the sugar barons were back in England, spending money ostentatiously.

Alderman William Beckford would continue to expand his interests in Jamaica: in 1762 he bought Drax Hall, in a manner, reported some, 'that excited the indignation of every honest man who became acquainted with the transaction'. Apparently Beckford obtained the estate for far below its value by calling in a loan, or possibly a gambling debt. This appears to have been a favourite tactic of his. (Drax Hall would make a great deal of money for the Beckfords.) But after about 1744, he was mostly in England, expanding his merchant interests and investing in the cloth industry, property, moneylending and government bonds.

While becoming a big name in the City of London, Beckford was first a local magistrate for the area near his manor at Fonthill in Wiltshire, then, in 1747, MP for Shaftesbury. Five years later he was admitted to the Iron-mongers' Livery company, and became alderman of the Billingsgate ward in the City. The following year he was Master of the Ironmongers, then, in spring 1754, he was returned as MP for the City of London.

William's generation of Beckfords represented the pinnacle of the sugar planters' power and wealth. With the help of his elder brother, Richard Beckford secured election as MP for Bristol in 1754, which took considerable effort, as he was in Jamaica at the time. Richard also acquired property in England before his death in 1756. His estate was held by his younger brother Julines in trust for his 'natural son' William, known, to differentiate him from other William Beckfords, as 'William of Somerly'. Somerly was only 12 at the time, and still at school in England, where he had been sent from Jamaica at the age of five.

Julines Beckford was by the 1750s established as a West India merchant in London. In 1754 he became MP for Salisbury. Their sister Elizabeth married the second Earl of Effingham, and their younger brother Francis married a daughter of the Duke of Ancaster. By the time of his death in

1768, Francis owned lands in Hampshire and Surrey, as well as a house in Albermarle Street, London.

The West India planters who returned home were the most conspicuous rich men of their time. 'As wealthy as a West Indian' was proverbial. They soon acquired a reputation for hospitality, extraordinary consumption and slavish imitation of the landed aristocracy. They were mocked in some quarters as vulgar Creoles, or 'pepperpots', nonetheless their conspicuous success helped give an impression that empire was worth creating and defending.

Having made their fortunes, the planters now wanted landed aristocrat status: it was boom time for the designers and builders of stately homes. Among those families purchasing great estates and building vast new mansions were the Lascelles. Henry's heir Edwin built the enormous Harewood House in Yorkshire, designed by John Carr, with interiors by John Adam and furniture by Thomas Chippendale. The mansion also contained a 70-foot-long gallery to display family portraits of the Lascelles by Sir Joshua Reynolds. Edwin would subsequently become the first Baron Harewood. At Dodington in Gloucestershire, the Codrington family seat, a new garden was laid out by Capability Brown, and James Wyatt constructed a lavish mansion with a huge Corinthian portico.

Many other returning West India nabobs followed suit. By the late 1770s 'there were scarcely ten miles together throughout the country where the house and estate of a rich West Indian was not to be seen', as Lord Shelburne, later Prime Minister, declared in the House of Commons. Most had a London residence as well, with many buying up houses in the fashionable new development around Marylebone, particularly on Wimpole Street.

In 1755, William Beckford's expensively refurbished mansion, Fonthill, burnt to the ground. Beckford is reported as announcing, 'I have an odd fifty thousand pounds in a drawer. I will build it up again!' The result became known as Fonthill Splendens, a lavish stately pile designed in the Palladian style, stocked with the best furniture, objects and paintings that money could buy. On the ground floor was an immense Egyptian Hall, from which radiated numerous vaulted corridors. Upstairs was a suite of stately apartments, all with marble floors, and further up were found galleries filled with precious art and furniture. It was, said one visitor, a place 'where expense has reached its utmost limits in furniture and ornaments, where every room is a gold mine and every apartment a picture gallery'. Descriptions of Splendens by contemporaries paid tribute to its lavishness while hinting at touches of vulgarity. One referred to the 'utmost profusion of magnificence' of the *piano nobile*, 'with the appearance of immense riches, almost too tawdrily exhibited'. In fact, there were few visitors: local gentry considered Beckford a nouveau riche 'radical', and were unimpressed by his morals, as evidenced by his huge brood of illegitimate children.

The house lay at the foot of a wooded valley on the western margin of an artificial lake, complete with bridge, grotto and boathouse, designed to look like a rococo basilica in miniature. Beckford also rebuilt the local church, replacing it with an ugly and pretentious building that resembled an ill-proportioned Grecian temple. Villagers were unimpressed with the new building, and regarded the fact that ancient monumental inscriptions from the previous church had been buried as an ill omen.

The Beckfords were not the only West Indians entering Parliament. By mid-century, most of the biggest sugar names had at least one family member as an MP, including the Lascelles, the Tomlinsons and the Martins from Antigua, the Dawkins and Dickinsons from Jamaica, the Pinneys and Stapletons from Nevis, and many others. Christopher Codrington's heir, Sir William, baronet, who had been steadily increasing his acreage in Antigua, was MP for Minehead until his death in 1738. His brother-in-law, Slingsby Bethell, managed the Codrington plantations in Antigua as a young man and then moved to London to establish a sugar factorage business, acting as a commission agent for the Byams, Martins and Tomlinsons. He was Lord Mayor of London in 1756 and represented the City in Parliament. Sir William's son represented Tewkesbury. The Draxes of Barbados were also now English MPs, a tradition that has continued to this day.

In 1767, Lord Chesterfield's offer of £2,500 for a seat in Northampton was disdainfully refused by a borough jobber. His lordship was told that 'there was no such thing as a borough to be had now, for the rich East and West Indians had secured them all, at the rate of three thousand pounds at least, and two or three that he knew at five thousand'. 'The landed interest is beat out', wrote another member of the aristocracy in 1768. 'Merchants, nabobs, and those who have gathered riches from the East and West Indies stand the best chance of governing this country.'

Indeed, in 1765 it was estimated that there were more than 40 MPs who were 'West Indians', able to 'turn the balance on which side they please', as the agent for Massachusetts Bay complained. In contrast, the North Americans had no comparable lobby, causing Benjamin Franklin to bemoan that in Britain, the 'West Indies vastly outweigh us of the Northern Colonies'.

In 1754, Rose Fuller returned to England from Jamaica and the next year became MP for Rye. In 1764, his younger brother Stephen became Jamaica's agent in London, a post he held for 30 years, praised above all his predecessors in the role for his 'vigilance to the welfare of the colony represented' and his 'intelligent and perfect' 'comprehension of its essential interest'. Perhaps Stephen Fuller's greatest coup came when he persuaded the Royal Navy to adopt rum in place of brandy. He also organised the purchase by the government of vast amounts of molasses to be distributed to Poor Houses.

The West Indian lobby now held very considerable sway over national policy, able to persuade the government that what was good for the sugar interest was good for the empire. Congregating in the King's Arms Tavern in Cornhill, the Mitre Coffee House in Fleet Street, or the London Tavern in Bishopsgate Street, the absentee planters planned their lobbying and wove their webs of influence. Any attempt to raise the import duty on sugar to a level nearer that for other imported products, or to open the huge British market to cheaper foreign-grown sugar, was fought tooth and nail. Efforts by sugar refiners in England to combine to fix prices, or to demand that more land in Jamaica be planted in sugar to lower the price, were successfully brushed aside, with Alderman William Beckford leading the lobby in the House.

In spite of his influence, Beckford had a reputation in Parliament as brash, irascible and long-winded. In smart society, he was 'loud, voluble' and 'self-sufficient', but would sometimes be the butt of jokes, 'which he could not parry'. Nonetheless, he was re-elected for the City in 1761, and the following year was made Lord Mayor of London. Following his swearing-in, he gave four entertainments, reportedly unrivalled in 'splendour and hospitality' since those of Henry VIII. One cost an amazing £10,000. Guests included the Emperor of Germany, the King of Denmark, and the Dukes of Cambridge and York. 'The costly magnificence he displayed astonished the public', wrote a contemporary, although Beckford himself was 'remarkably moderate in eating and drinking, always living with great temperance, and hence somewhat out of place in City epicurism'.

Beckford had married for the second time in 1756, to Maria, a member of the family of the powerful Duke of Hamilton. William was 47, Maria was 32, much more religious than him and very proud of her superior blood. Beckford already had a large number of illegitimate children, possibly as many as 30, but in 1760 his son and heir, another William, was born.

As a babe in arms, this young Beckford was carried by a paternal aunt, who was a Lady of the Bedchamber, into the royal presence at St James's

Court. This set the tone for a gilded childhood. William Pitt the Elder was one of his godfathers, and at the age of five, William Beckford received piano tuition from Mozart (himself aged only nine). Beckford of Fonthill (as the younger William Beckford is commonly known) was also amazingly precocious: he was speaking and reading French by the age of three or four, and had mastered Latin by the time he was seven. Eventually he would also speak Italian, Portuguese, German, Spanish, Persian and Arabic. His tutor recorded of him at seven years old: 'He is of a very agreeable disposition, but begins already to think of being master of a great fortune.' He was not sent to school, so led an isolated life with no friends of his own age.

His father was often absent. Alderman Beckford did not like the local country gentry who looked down on him as nouveau riche, and spent most of his time at his London base at 22 Soho Square. In the city he threw himself into politics, becoming a key supporter and ally of William Pitt against the power of the court party. This would be useful for Pitt: he used the commercial expertise of Beckford to win battles in the Commons over foreign policy; during the coming war, Beckford was tireless in raising money to pay for the military. But it was also helpful to Beckford and the sugar interest; enemies accused him of promoting expeditions – such as that of 1758 against French slave forts in Africa – for his own rather than the national interest.

The Seven Years War (known in North America as the French and Indian War) was blundered into by France and Britain after skirmishing in North America and at sea. The conflict, from 1756 to 1763, saw fighting in Europe, India, North America and the West Indies, where it was the most severe struggle yet.

The war started with the loss by Britain of Minorca, and the famous execution of Vice Admiral John Byng, 'pour encourager les autres'. This led to the fall of the government and a new ministry being formed, led by the aggressive imperialist William Pitt.

In Jamaica, invasion fears at the beginning of the war saw the imposition of martial law. Thistlewood recorded in his diary hearing 'great guns fired out at sea', and several attacks on coastal estates by enemy privateers. On one occasion, he wrote, raiders 'plundered Mr Thos. White's house [at nearby Bluefields] . . . of his plate, furniture, wearing apparel, &c; the girl he kept &c., even made him help carry his own things down to their canoe, stripped him naked except an old dirty check shirt they gave him'.

But in late 1758 a powerful fleet and reinforcements arrived, freed up after victory at Louisburg in North America, and the British were in a position to launch offensives. French privateers based in Martinique had been causing havoc, so in January 1759 a force of 6,000 troops and 10 ships of the line launched an attack. But Martinique had strong defences, and three days later the British withdrew, and landed at Guadeloupe instead. Although there were soon 2,000 men down with sickness, the French capitulated on 1 May.

Victory in Canada by September 1760, and the earlier defeat of the French fleet at Quiberon Bay, gave Britain command of the seas, and freedom to concentrate on the West Indies. Dominica was captured by a North American force in June 1761, and in January 1762 some 16,000 troops, including nearly 600 men from Barbados, descended once more on Martinique. Well led by Rear Admiral George Rodney, and with massive superiority in numbers, the British were at last successful, although the capitulation of the French on 16 January might have been motivated in part by what they had seen happening in Guadeloupe. Since its British capture, the island had been doing rather well selling its sugar into the British market and buying thousands of slaves from Liverpool traders. St Lucia and Grenada were captured soon afterwards, leaving only the hugely valuable St Domingue still in French hands.

Spain, under the new leadership of Charles III, who had a deep hatred of the British, joined the war in January 1762. Britain responded with a decision to attack Havana, the heart of Spanish power in the Caribbean. A bold approach through the Old Bahama passage along the north coast of Cuba, together with complacency and incompetence on the part of the Spanish governor of the city, allowed a successful landing on 7 June. But a drawn-out siege followed, and by the time the city surrendered on 13 August, the British force had suffered appallingly from yellow fever, with only 3,000 men still in action out of an original force of nearly 15,000. Spain's best defender against attack from European rivals, the mosquito, had almost succeeded again. The losses contributed to Britain's decision to return Havana to Spain at the end of the war the following year.

Britain gained Florida from Spain in return, and Martinique was given back to France in exchange for Minorca. Britain also acquired St Vincent, Dominica, Tobago and Grenada. When it came to the fate of Guadeloupe, the sugar lobby, led by William Beckford and Rose Fuller, intervened. Since its capture, the huge sugar production of Guadeloupe – at 80,000 hogsheads a year more than all the British Leewards combined – had arrived on the English market. This jump in supply saw the sugar price fall by over nine shillings per hundredweight, to the horror of the British planters. Pitt stayed loyal to his friend Beckford, and at the negotiations for the Treaty of Paris, the French were given the choice of retaining Guadeloupe or ceding large parts of Canada; they did not hesitate to hand over the undeveloped and relatively worthless wastes of the north.

From the beginning of the war, West Indians and North Americans had launched themselves with gusto into privateering and illegal trade. As in the previous conflict in the 1740s, the 'flag of truce' scam, where vessels sailed to enemy ports ostensibly to exchange prisoners, was widely deployed. Rhode Island alone sent 32 in the first four years of the war. This kept the French privateers manned, to the fury of the Royal Navy, who complained that several prisoners had been taken by their cruisers four times in less than two months.

The Brown family, Obadiah and his four nephews, John, Moses, Nicholas and Joseph (the eldest brother, James, had died in his twenties), invested in privateers and flags of truce. The records show that they lost at least three vessels to the 'enemy' – that is, the Royal Navy – but such were the profits of the trade that these setbacks could be borne.

A year into the war, a committee was established in Rhode Island to investigate allegations of trade with the enemy. Obadiah Brown had himself appointed a member. A year later, at the urging of the Board of Trade in London, the colony appointed a committee to inspect the holds of flag-of-truce ships to ensure they carried no trading goods. The committee consisted of Elisha Brown, the four brothers' uncle, and family friend Daniel Jenckes. They were happy to sign off the paperwork promising that the ships only had on board enough victuals for the crew and prisoners, without checking what the vessels actually left port carrying.

French officials ordered their men-of-war and privateers not to tamper with American vessels trading with French islands. Some even sent agents to the English colonies selling safe-passage passes for $200. One such pass was found concealed on the person of William Carlisle of New York, master of the sloop *Dove*, 'sewed in the hinder part of his britches or drawers'.

As had occurred earlier, neutral Caribbean ports such as St Eustatius, St Thomas and St Croix were used by American and West Indian traders to supply the French indirectly. Until the entry of Spain into the war, the most popular port for the North Americans, though, was Monte Christi, just inside the border between Spanish and French Hispaniola, and near the important French sugar port of Cap François. Dealing through Spanish middlemen, or direct with French merchants at Monte Christi, the North Americans delivered provisions and lumber, and loaded up sugar. Until

condemned by London in 1760 as traitorous (with the charter colonies of
Rhode Island and Connecticut deemed the worst offenders), this was tech-
nically legal, but only if the sugar was Spanish. In fact Spanish Hispaniola neither grew nor processed sugar. The Spanish governor even erected
a sugar mill in his province to make the chicanery a bit less blatant.

In August 1760, Pitt, having been told by his commander in North
America that the Rhode Islanders were 'a lawless set of smugglers', wrote
a circular letter to all the American governors railing against the 'illegal
and most pernicious trade . . . by which the enemy is . . . supplyed with
Provisions and other Necessaries whereby they are principally, if not alone,
enabled to sustain, and protract, this long and expensive war'. He urged
that offenders be severely punished. But although some states passed new
laws against the trade, this had little effect. The following year, while Royal
Navy ships languished in port for want of victuals, the French were plen-
tifully supplied. Indeed, flour was 50 per cent cheaper in Hispaniola than
in Jamaica.

It was immensely frustrating for British naval commanders, who could
see that the illegal trade had effectively negated important advantages of
their supremacy at sea. In 1762, Admiral Augustus Keppel complained
that the French fleet and garrison at St Domingue were not likely to want
for food, because of 'the large supplies they have lately received from their
good friends the New England flag of truce vessels'. During the siege of
Havana, the British naval contingent found that they had to 'guard as much
against' North American vessels supplying the Spanish garrison 'as our
professed enemies'.

Not all North Americans showed so little imperial sentiment. On 12
August, the brigantine *Prudent Hannah*, owned by Obadiah Brown and his
four nephews, and captained as a flag of truce by Paul Tew, was seized by
a British man-of-war off the coast of Virginia. Tew urged the British captain
to take him to a northern port, but instead he was taken to Williamsburg.
Paperwork signed off by Elisha Brown stated that he had five barrels of
pork or beef and 30 of flour. In fact the *Prudent Hannah* carried 47 barrels
of flour, 37 of beef and pork, 213 barrels and hogsheads of fish and firkins
of butter, as well as bread, and 1,000 bunches of onions. When he got to
shore, Tew wrote to the Browns, 'they Looked on me as an Enemy and
Trator to my Country'.

This was certainly the view in England, and the illegal trade in sugar
and molasses by the North Americans would have some very important
consequences. More than ever, the colonials were seen in Britain as corrupt
and self-serving, having preferred to trade with the enemy rather than

support the war effort. Measures taken by the Royal Navy against this traffic led to a review of the whole system of enforcing trade and revenue laws in America, and the use of the Royal Navy to suppress smuggling found a ready place in George Grenville and Charles Townsend's plans for a new imperial system.

In many ways the decade after the end of the war in 1763 represents the high-water mark of the 'first' British empire. Peace brought a further expansion of trade in tropical and subtropical commodities: not only sugar, but also tea and spices from India and China, tobacco, rice and indigo from the southern mainland colonies of North America, rum, coffee, cotton and dye woods from the West Indies flowed into the mother country to raise standards of material welfare, pay for the reverse flow of British manufactures and employ ships and seamen for the Royal Navy, which provided global security for the system.

But in other ways, it was the beginning of the end. There were danger signs in the disloyalty and lack of respect for the law shown by the illegal traders, particularly now that France had been expelled from North America, removing the threat that had kept the Americans close to the British. Furthermore, the war had left Britain with a colossal debt of £140 million and vastly enlarged imperial responsibilities, problems and expenses. Difficulties with hostile Native Americans meant that 8,000 soldiers were to be stationed in America, twice as many as in 1754, and a North American squadron maintained of 26 ships and 3,290 men, the largest in the Royal Navy apart from the Home Fleet. British taxpayers thought the ungrateful colonials should start to share the expense.

Meanwhile, in the West Indies, the expansion of the empire achieved at the Peace of Paris was to have unforeseen and unfortunate consequences.

PART THREE

The Inheritors

26

LUXURY AND DEBT

'Sugar, sugar, is the incessant cry of luxury, and of debt.'
Reverend James Ramsay

Gedney Clarke, the Barbados-based trader, customs collector, planter and friend of George Washington, had not had a good war. It appears that the government victualling contracts that he had secured had not been as profitable as expected, and a loan of £15,000 from the Lascelles was needed to keep the operation going. In 1763, the London money market took a sharp downturn, and speculators were badly burned, Clarke among them.

The same year, a huge slave revolt broke out in the Dutch colony of Berbice, where the white population had been decimated by an 'epidemical disorder', and where Clarke had substantial estates. As soon as he heard, Clarke, at huge expense, dispatched four armed vessels to Berbice. On board were 50 Barbados militiamen, whom Clarke had persuaded to come with 'Threats, Arguments & the force of money'. This body was augmented by 100 marines and sailors aboard HMS *Pembroke*, lent to Clarke by his friends in the Royal Navy, even though there was no official sanction for the task force, whose role was clearly to protect the property of Gedney Clarke. Other recruits made the force up to 300, and its contribution to the defeat of the rebellion was crucial.

But in August 1764, Gedney Clarke junior, who had settled in London and recently succeeded George Maxwell as a partner in the Lascelles firm, heard news 'of the Extream Illness of Col. Clarke'. Due to the 'severity of his Feaver and other disorders', Gedney Clarke Sr was dying. What was more, his business affairs were in turmoil. 'Thus I am placed in his shoes', his son wrote soon afterwards. Clarke Jr had been enjoying establishing himself in London, but he now had to return to Barbados to sort out the mess and to take over the family customs position.

In the 10 years after 1744, Henry Lascelles had lent Clarke around £30,000. After Henry's death in 1753, his sons had continued to proffer assistance. Now the debts were out of control. Clarke Jr's first move was to sell his holdings in the Dutch colonies. It was good timing, but he simply exchanged one imminent disaster for another. With the proceeds he purchased four new plantations in the recently-ceded territories of Grenada and Tobago. In Tobago alone he bought more than 2,000 acres on his own account or in partnership.

After the end of the Seven Years War, many others, a lot of them Scots, rushed to plant the newly British and relatively undeveloped islands of Dominica, St Vincent, Grenada and Tobago with sugar. The lure of sugar profits led to a wave of speculation in land, with prices rising to ridiculous levels. Thus Gedney Clarke paid inflated prices for the land in Tobago, using mortgages that could be financed only for as long as sugar prices remained high and interest charges stayed low. But profits were disappointing. The new plantations in the ceded islands, together with an increase in production from the Dutch in Surinam and the French in St Domingue, saw the world sugar price start to slide.* There was also a great increase in demand for slaves, pushing up the price considerably. A field worker who had cost £25 in 1755 went for £60 in 1770.

Income from the new estates and those on Barbados hardly covered Gedney Clarke's current account with the London Lascelles company, and so interest on the overall debt kept rising. In desperation, Clarke took to embezzling customs revenue. In 1771 this was spotted, and a commission of inquiry was dispatched to Barbados. Clarke, it emerged, had taken more than £15,000, plus large balances in kind. He was suspended, but amazingly had the political contacts to get himself reinstated, just as his father had done, and the Lascelles brothers before him.

But a credit crisis and a sharp fall in the price of sugar in 1772–3 saw the end for Gedney Clarke. By now the Lascelles were owed some £130,000. It seems from their books that they had been illegally charging compound interest. Either Clarke did not know about this, or he was so desperate that he was forced to agree to the terms. Worried about competition from other creditors, the Lascelles family took over the Gedney Clarke property. It was the most spectacular bankruptcy the West Indies had seen so far, described in a letter of 1774 as 'the greatest failure that ever happened

---

* By 1767, there were nearly 600 sugar works in St Domingue, producing, with the labour of more than 200,000 slaves, some 60,000 tons of sugar, about twice the production of Jamaica.

here'. In all, Clarke was in the red to the tune of about £200,000. Four years later and now paupers, Gedney Clarke and his wife both died on Barbados.

Although none were quite so noteworthy, there were many other early failures in the ceded islands, where planting was often hindered by difficulties with the terrain, with slaves who had escaped during the capture of the islands, and with the Caribs who still lived on several of the islands, most notably Dominica and St Vincent. Among those going under was the Attorney General of Grenada, Joseph Baker, who ended up arrested and imprisoned for debt in England.

Sugar planters had always borrowed money. Many plantation operations were carried on essentially by credit based upon anticipated income from the next crop. Huge advances had been secured with ease, and this often led to great extravagance, and the brushing aside of natural caution in financial matters, engendering a spirit of speculation without due regard for the actual risk involved.

But by the 1770s, planters in Grenada alone owed something like £2,000,000, a vast amount of money. In all, the ceded islands were a huge drain on capital and credit, and this contributed to the 1772 collapse of a large Scottish bank and the ensuing credit crisis.

There were also huge debts in Jamaica. Sir Charles Price, an almost pre-eminent figure in Jamaican politics since the 1740s, had by the 1770s accumulated more than 26,000 acres across 11 parishes. But such expansion was more a symptom of megalomania than sound business sense. The plantations were severely burdened by debt, and on the cusp of reclamation by mortgage holders. Sir Charles now preferred to live at the Decoy, a mansion 2,000 feet up in the hills of St Mary parish. Here he entertained visitors from England, who could enjoy the surrounding park, grazed by imported fallow deer, in a weird, totally inappropriate mimic of the aristocracy at home. In front of the house was 'a very fine piece of water, which in winter is commonly stocked with wild-duck and teal', a visitor reported. Behind was an elegant garden, with numerous richly ornamented buildings and a triumphal arch. Here at the Decoy, Sir Charles would live out his final years before his death in 1772, shielded from the world and his collapsing fortune.

His son, the second baronet, also Charles, moved to England in 1775, intending never to return to Jamaica. But the financial difficulties of the Jamaica plantations brought him back, and he died on the island in 1788. Eight years later, a Kingston magazine described the Prices as 'that respectable but unfortunate family'.

In other ways the sugar barons were losing their lustre. In 1776, the Scottish economist and philosopher Adam Smith published his hugely influential *The Wealth of Nations*, in which he argued in favour of free trade and against mercantilism, the policy whereby British sugar was given an effective monopoly on the home market in return for using British ships and buying British manufactures. The first sugar barons had hated the Navigation Acts, but by the middle of the eighteenth century, the protected British market that was part of the original deal was of overwhelming importance to the British sugar producers. Because of soil exhaustion and a failure to invest in new technologies, the British islands now needed four times the labour to produce the same sugar as the newer French possessions, led in production by St Domingue. This, of course, made British sugar more expensive, thus the British consumer paid up to 30 per cent more for his sugar than customers in other parts of Europe. A pamphleteer of 1761 estimated that what he called the 'fraudulent Trading of the Sugar Planters' had deprived the kingdom of 'over and above Twelve Million Pounds Sterling'.

In some ways, the mercantilist policy had undoubted benefits for the nation. The system guaranteed supply of the commodity and profits at home from processing and, until the European market was lost to the French, re-exporting it. An overseas market was secured for finished British goods (exports to all the American colonies expanded by over 2,000 per cent during the eighteenth century); and it supported the growth of the civil (and military) marine. Substantial duties were paid when the sugar arrived at a British port, even if they were much lower than for other tropical products.

But the cost of the preferential duties was paid by the British consumer, and the costs of administration and defence of the colonies by the British taxpayer. The mercantilist policy might have tied the colonies to the mother country, but in the final reckoning economically it did little more than provide income for the government and enrich a special interest group. Adam Smith declared that 'the interest of the home-consumer has been sacrificed to that of the producer with a more extravagant profusion than in all our other commercial regulations'.

The system had also, of course, severely limited the development of the West Indian islands. Industry was strongly discouraged as part of the mercantile system. Market towns and ports were all that could develop. Jamaica had to import processed white sugar from England, as its two tiny refineries could not even satisfy domestic demand. Cushioned by the ever-rising demand for their product and by the home market monopoly, those planters still on the islands, rather than the absentees, stagnated, and the energy and verve of their fathers and grandfathers ebbed and slipped away. If the market for sugar was 'unreal', so were the islands' economies, now an artificial creation, sustained by political intervention rather than the true market price for their product. But still sugar monoculture expanded. By the late eighteenth century, sugar accounted for 93 per cent of Barbados's exports.

Adam Smith also argued in favour of free labour. To increase the productivity of their workers, slave-owners could not sack them or lower their wages, but could only whip them. With no property, Smith wrote, the only impulse is to eat as much as possible and do as little work as possible. 'From the experience of all ages and nations', he concluded, 'I believe that the work done by slaves is in the end the dearest of any.' This argument would provide ammunition to the abolitionists, emerging by the time of Adam Smith's book as the greatest threat to the sugar barons.

The first half of the eighteenth century in Britain, like the 30 years before, saw only isolated and unrepresentative voices raised in opposition to slavery. The London yearly meeting of the Society of Friends in 1727 produced a resolution that condemned the slave trade and censured Quakers who participated in it. The effects were negligible, but for the Friends a course had been set. After 1761, British Quakers who persisted in the trade were excluded from the Society, and in 1768, Quakers unsuccessfully petitioned Parliament to abolish the slave trade.

The mid-eighteenth century was a period of rising material wealth and improved education for the middle class, who now had time to read philosophy, politics and travel literature, as well as the burgeoning new magazines and newspapers. Broadly speaking, 'Enlightenment' writers and thinkers were opposed to slavery. Montesquieu wrote in 1748: 'The State of Slavery is in its own nature bad. It is neither useful to the master nor to the slave.' Rousseau condemned slavery in a work of 1755, and in his *Social Contract* of 1762. Diderot's *Encylopedia*, in the volume published in 1765, condemned slavery as 'a business which violates religion, morality, natural law, and all human rights'. In Voltaire's *Candide* (1759), his hero observes a young slave who had an arm and a leg cut off as the price demanded for the sugar sent to Europe. (Quite rightly, slavery was associated with sugar: two thirds of all American slaves worked for the sugar barons.)

One of the most popular plays of the eighteenth century was a dramatisation of Aphra Behn's novel *Oroonoko*. First published in 1696, it tells of the capture of an African prince and his brutal treatment as a slave in Surinam. Sweetened with a sensational and tragic love story, the piece fascinated audiences for 100 years and prepared literary types for humanitarian opposition to slavery. The author of 'Rule Britannia', the Scottish poet James Thomson, would publish in his *Seasons* in 1730 a poem describing a slave ship being followed by a shark, waiting for the inevitable casting overboard of dead meat. Pope, in his 'Essay on Man', imagined 'Some happier island . . . Where slaves once more their native land behold.' Laurence Sterne and Sir Richard Steele also condemned slavery in their widely read works.

Perhaps most famously, Dr Samuel Johnson, a giant of the British literary scene, had a lifelong hatred of slavery. In 1756, in the first issue of his new *Literary Magazine*, he denounced eighteenth-century Jamaica as 'a place of great wealth and dreadful wickedness, a den of tyrants, and a dungeon of slaves'. In 1759, he wrote a tract attacking the slave trade, and at a 'grave' dinner at an Oxford college, he shocked all and sundry by proposing a toast to the 'success to the next revolt of the negroes in the West Indies'.

Such gestures were not about to end chattel slavery on the plantations of the sugar barons. Nor, of course, were poems and plays. Furthermore, many of those thinkers condemning slavery offered few ideas as to what to do about it. But they did create a soil in which later movements could grow.

The absentee West India nabobs had never been accepted as proper English gentry. Now, increasingly, there seemed something about their money that just did not smell right. In 1769, press references started appearing referring to the new Lord Mayor as 'negro whipping Beckford'. William Beckford had strongly supported John Wilkes's battle against the King, fought on the slogan 'Wilkes and Liberty!', and founded the radical *Middlesex Journal: or chronicle of liberty*. The irony was not lost on a satirist writing for the *Public Advertiser* in November 1769:

> 'For B . . . f . . . d he was chosen May'r,
> A Wight of high Renown,
> To see a slave he could not bear,
> Unless it were his own.'

Johnson mocked Wilkes for being supported by Beckford, whose attachment to 'Liberty' encapsulated the irony that Britain, the freest nation in Europe, was also the world's biggest slave-trader. Gradually a feeling was growing that the slave societies of the Americas were out of date, 'made in less enlightened times than our own', as one early abolitionist put it.

In 1765, Granville Sharp, a junior clerk in the Ordnance office, had come across a slave, Jonathan Strong, in the streets of London and befriended him. Strong had been badly injured by his master, a David Lisle of Barbados, so much so that Lisle had thrown him out as useless. Sharp restored Strong to health, and got him a job. But Lisle spotted his former slave in the street, had him imprisoned in a private jail, and sold him to a planter in Jamaica for £30. Sharp got him released, but then found himself being sued by the Jamaican planter and challenged to a duel by Lisle. When the case came to court, Sharp successfully persuaded the judge that in England, a slave had to have willingly, in writing, bound himself to his master, and Strong was freed. This victory brought Sharp other similar cases. In 1772, he acted in the same way on behalf of a slave, James Somerset, who had been brought from Jamaica to England by his owner, Charles Stewart of Boston. Somerset escaped, then was recaptured and put on a ship bound for Jamaica, where he was to be sold. Sharp managed to have the case transferred to the King's Bench, where the presiding judge was Lord Chief Justice Mansfield. Mansfield had in his household a mulatto girl, Dido, daughter of his nephew, Rear Admiral Sir John Lindsay, by a slave mother whom Lindsay had captured during the siege of Havana. After a long trial, Mansfield freed Somerset, declaring 'The status of slavery is so odious that nothing can be suffered to support it but positive law.' It was a great victory, interpreted by the public as the prohibition of slavery in Britain. A court in Scotland came to the same verdict six years later.

John Wesley, who had seen slavery in action in South Carolina, published *Thoughts on Slavery* in 1774, which had a huge circulation. 'I absolutely deny all Slave-holding to be consistent with any degree of even natural Justice', he wrote. Better that the islands be 'altogether sunk in the depth of the sea, than that they should be cultivated at so high a price as the violation of justice, mercy and truth; and . . . that myriads of innocent men should be murdered and myriads more dragged into the basest slavery'. Because of the wide appeal of Methodism, with its numbers already far outstripping those of the Quakers, Wesley's pamphlet constituted the most severe attack yet on slavery.

In North America, the anti-slavery movement was similarly nurtured by Nonconformist Christians. As early as 1696, Quakers in Pennsylvania advised their members against the slave trade and urged them to bring their blacks to meetings for religious instruction. Nevertheless, prominent Quakers such as Jonathan Dickinson continued to own and trade in slaves.

John Woolman, a New Jersey Quaker, published his first anti-slavery tract in 1754, and then travelled round the country, including the slave trade centre of Newport, addressing his fellow Quakers, and trying to persuade them of 'the inconsistency of holding slaves'; the same year came the first of a number of resolutions from Quakers in Pennsylvania condemning the slave trade. In 1764, Anthony Benezet, a Pennsylvania Quaker, published his first propaganda tract against the Atlantic slave trade.

Benezet liked quoting Montesquieu, and also a visitor to the West Indies who wrote 'it is a matter of astonishment how a people [the English] who, as a nation are looked upon as generous and humane . . . can live in the practice of such extreme oppression and inhumanity without seeing the inconsistency of such conduct'. The Quakers, as a movement, were now decided, declaring that it was impossible to be a Friend and a slave-trader or slave-owner. One high-profile casualty of this stand was Abraham Redwood in Newport. On 26 September 1775, they demanded that he free his slaves in Rhode Island and in Antigua. As this would have ended his operation at Cassada Gardens, Redwood refused. 'Wherefore we', the Newport Quakers resolved, 'on that account do Disown him to be any longer a member of our Society.' Redwood appears to have borne no grudge, bequeathing a substantial sum in his will for the foundation of a Quaker school in Newport.

Elsewhere, as in Britain, momentum was growing against the trade, and not just among Quakers. In 1774, Benjamin Franklin and Benjamin Rush, a friend of Tom Paine, founded America's first anti-slavery society. The motives for the change of heart were varied: some were driven by what they interpreted as Christian teachings; others by the economic arguments of the likes of Adam Smith, or by fear that slave societies could only result in a bloodbath of revenge and rebellion. For a number, it was personal experience of the trade that turned them against it.

Like many in New England, the Brown family from Providence had made a fortune in the West India trade, a lot of it illegal, and in sponsoring privateers during the intermittent warfare between England and Spain or France. Not until 1764, on the prompting of a slave-hungry customer in Virginia, did the brothers, led by John and Moses (Obadiah had died in 1762), invest in their first slave ship, the *Sally*, a square-rigged brigantine, larger than the sloops and schooners that made up the rest of the family fleet. The vessel was stocked with 17,000 gallons of rum and was captained by Esek Hopkins, later first commodore of the United States Navy and brother to Stephen Hopkins, Rhode Island's great revolutionary leader and theorist. Esek Hopkins was an experienced mariner, but knew nothing of the delicate processes of bribery and negotiation that were required in West Africa. He spent far too long searching for slaves to buy – more than nine months. All the time he remained on the coast he was at risk from disease and slave insurrections, and by the time he left, he had already lost two crew members and 20 slaves, several of whom hanged themselves from the rigging.

During the course of the 'Middle Passage' to their destination at Antigua, there were deaths almost daily. '1 boye slave Dyed', Hopkins wrote on 25 August in a typical entry in the vessel's account book. Partly at fault were the filthy conditions on the *Sally*. The women, mostly naked, lived unchained on the quarterdeck. The males, chained together in pairs, were kept below deck, where they struggled for air in the dark, humid hold. Their spaces were so cramped they were unable to sit up. In good weather, Hopkins and his crew exercised the more than 100 African slaves on deck and had their filthy quarters scrubbed with water and vinegar. Then, eight days after leaving the coast of Africa, Hopkins unchained some of the male slaves to help with the chores. Instead, they freed other slaves and turned on what was left of his crew. Outnumbered, the sailors grabbed some of the weapons aboard the *Sally*: four pistols, seven swivel guns, 13 cutlasses and two blunderbusses. The curved cutlass blades and short-barrelled blunderbusses, favoured by pirates and highwaymen, were ideal weapons for killing enemies at close quarters. According to a report in the *Newport Mercury*, 'by letters from Capt. Hopkins', the slaves were 'happily prevented' from getting possession of the vessel 'by the captain, who killed, wounded and forced overboard eighty of them which obliged the rest to submit'.

After the failure of the revolt, the survivors, Hopkins wrote, 'were so dispirited that some drowned themselves, some starved and others sickened and died'. Those still alive by the time the *Sally* reached Antigua were so emaciated that they only fetched about £5 each.

Slave-traders were used to losing up to 15 per cent of their human cargo, but Hopkins had lost more than half. The venture cost the Brown brothers a fortune. Neither the grisly death toll nor the financial loss deterred John Brown from further involvement in slave-trading. But for Moses, always the more sensitive and thoughtful of the two, it was an epiphany. Thereafter, he refused to play any part in the trade, joined the Quakers, and in 1773 freed his own six slaves with generous pay-offs, including use of his land. He also launched himself into campaigning to outlaw slavery in Rhode Island.

By the time of Moses Brown's conversion, the North American colonies were in turmoil. Towards the end of the Seven Years War, with North

American trade with the French so blatant that insurance rates for voyages
to St Domingue were openly quoted in Rhode Island and elsewhere, the
British sought to resurrect the largely defunct Molasses Act. The entire
customs operation in North America was strengthened and overhauled,
with informants richly rewarded, smuggling loopholes closed, and new
provisions made for search and seizure. These measures, wrote the Governor
of Massachusetts to an official in London, 'caused a greater alarm in this
Country than the taking of Fort William Henry did in 1757'.

The aim of the Molasses Act of 1733 had been to make foreign molasses
prohibitively expensive for the rum distillers of New England. Now it was
proposed by the indebted government in London to put through a new
Sugar Act, designed instead to raise revenue. Duty on foreign molasses
would be reduced from six pence a gallon to three pence, but the collection would now be rigorously enforced, with fresh regulations imposed,
including new procedures in the vice-admiralty courts, which removed the
right to trial by jury.

News of the planned Act reached Rhode Island and elsewhere in North
America in September 1763. In the same month, the Browns' agent in
Philadelphia, Tench Francis, wrote to Nicholas Brown, who ran the family's
distillery, 'What are the people of England now going to do with us? Nothing
but Ruine seems to hang over our heads', and then listed the 27 men-of-
war assigned to enforce the trade laws. The following month Elisha Brown,
the four brothers' uncle, wrote to Nicholas that the merchants of Providence should meet to plan 'What method will be best for us to Take when
any of our Vessils Arrives which is Liable to Pay Duties – So as wee may
Stand by Each other.' Others colonies were now doing the same thing,
most notably New York and Massachusetts, where a memorial was prepared
in December and circulated to merchants in other colonies – including
two prominent traders in Newport – as well as to colonial agents in London.
In the *Boston Evening Post*, it was suggested that the city 'open a correspondence with the principal merchants in all our sister colonies, endeav-
ouring to promote a union, and coalition of all their councils'. From
Providence, Nicholas Brown wrote to a merchant in New York that the
Governor of Rhode Island, Stephen Hopkins, had convened the colony's
assembly 'in order to . . . Join with Those of the other Colonys . . . to
prevent if Possible the Continuance of the Sugar Act'.

This meeting produced the Rhode Island Remonstrance of 27 January
1764, making the colony the first to lodge an official protest against the
Sugar Act. Up to 30 distilleries, 'the main hinge upon which the trade of
the colony turns', faced ruin, it was alleged, if the duty on foreign molasses

were to be enforced. Rhode Island imported £120,000 of British manufacture annually and only exported £5,000 of native products, the difference being made up by the molasses and rum trade. Of the 14,000 hogsheads
of molasses imported annually, only 2,500 were British Caribbean in origin.
Collecting the threepence a gallon on the rest would wreck the colony's
economy and make it unable to afford imported British goods. How could
this be in Britain's interest? Instead, Governor Hopkins argued in an article
for the *Providence Gazette*, it only favoured the 'rich, proud, and overbearing Planters of the West Indies'.

Trouble had been expected from Rhode Island. In 1763, the London
Customs Board had requested the Admiralty to station a 'competent number
'of ships to halt the 'excessive contraband Trade carried on at Rhode Island'.
The 20-gun *Squirrel* was ordered to winter at Newport, but for various
reasons it did not arrive, and even if it had, one stationed ship could not
possibly cover the three mouths of Narragansett Bay. In the meantime, the
smugglers of Rhode Island made the most of it, with only about half of
their imported molasses troubling the customs service. In the meantime,
the *Providence Gazette* announced to the world that Rhode Island could
handle her own affairs 'without the concurrent Assistance of *Swaggering
Soldiers* or insulting *Captain Bashaws*, I mean Captains of War Ships'.
Laws cannot be 'wholesome, or for the general Good', the paper argued,
if they could only be enforced by 'Intimidation'.

The *Squirrel* finally arrived in April 1764 and was made less than
welcome. A rumour was started that it was about to impress men to
replenish its crew, and provision boats that normally rowed out to sell their
wares to seagoing vessels stayed away. Eventually the captain, Richard Smith,
was forced to publish a disclaimer in the *Newport Mercury*.

Because of the sugar and molasses duties, tensions between Rhode
Islanders and the British military rose fast. In June 1764, a Royal Navy
schooner, the *St John*, appeared in Narragansett Bay and captured a ship
that was unloading by night a cargo of 93 hogsheads of sugar. But then
three sailors from the *St John* allegedly stole some pigs and chickens. The
local sheriff rowed out to make the arrests but was not allowed on board.
Then a party from the ship, which had rowed ashore to recapture a deserter,
was attacked, with the officer in charge seized and held hostage. Soon
afterwards, a sloop was filled by a mob of angry locals to board the *St
John*, but retired at the sight of the ship's ready guns. The *St John* then
anchored under the protection of the man-of-war, the *Squirrel*, but the
sheriff meanwhile had contacted two members of the Governor's council,
who then signed an order to Aniel Vaughan, ceremonial gunner at Fort

George on Goat Island, to sink the *St John* if she attempted to leave without giving up the three thieves. Vaughan almost fired the opening shot of the American Revolution, but instead kept a cool head and aimed wide. The *Squirrel* brought her broadside to bear on the Goat Island battery, but, to Captain Smith's professed sorrow, 'they ceased firing before we had convinced them of their error'.

The Sugar Act was passed in April 1764, sparking vigorous protests from the legislative bodies of Rhode Island, Massachusetts, Connecticut, New York and Pennsylvania. There was a certain amount of exaggeration, but the North American distillers were indeed hit hard by the Act's enforcement (of the 15,000 gallons of molasses imported by Massachusetts for its 60 distilleries, all but 500 came from foreign colonies in 1763). Traders suffered as well. A Rhode Island newspaper lamented that a great empire had been delivered to a 'few dirty specks, the sugar islands'. Certainly, the Sugar Act benefited the West Indies at the expense of the wider empire. John Adams would write that 'There was not a man on the continent of America who does not consider the Sugar Act, as far as it regards molasses, as a sacrifice made of the northern colonies to the superior interest in Parliament of the West Indians.'

For the wider empire, the Sugar Act was a disaster. In July 1764, Tench Francis wrote to the Browns from Philadelphia: 'every one is convinced of the Necessity of a Unanimity amongst the Colonies, to ward off any Burden that may be intended for Us'. Thanks to the Sugar Act, inter-colonial cooperation had been launched in North America. By the summer of 1764, committees of protest had been formed, and soon they were in touch with each other. On their foundations were erected the later and better-known Committees of Correspondence.

The implementation of the Act caused huge friction. Benjamin Franklin complained that English captains 'executed their Commissions with great Rudeness and Insolence'. 'All Trade and Commerce, even the most legal . . . was harass'd, vex'd & Interrupted, by perpetual Stoppings of Boats, Rummagings and Searchings, Unladings & Detainings.' In Philadelphia, a British captain reported receiving 'the most violent abuse and Insults, which is now so common, that neither myself nor any of my Officers can walk the streets without being affronted'.

In Rhode Island was heard for the first time criticism of the term 'mother country'. Ten years ahead of their time, people were beginning to advocate non-importation of British goods, and to talk about the issues of internal and external taxation.

Thus the Sugar Act, although short-lived, to an extent unified the

northern colonies, and marked the beginning of a period of strained relations with Britain. The power of the West India lobby in London had put
the New England colonies on a collision course with Britain, and set the
stage for the revolt the following year and the subsequent rebellion and
war.

In 1766, the Sugar Act was replaced by a new Act that reduced the duty
on molasses to a penny a gallon (the sugar interest, led in London by
William Beckford and Rose Fuller, was compensated with attached measures to their benefit). This deterred smuggling and would become the
single most important source of revenue collected in America. But by then,
events had moved on, with the passing of the Stamp Act in March 1765,
which firmly united all of the Thirteen Colonies against the 'mother
country' and led to violent protests all over British North America.

The North Americans wanted from the West Indians a united colonial
front against the Stamp Act. In fact, the measure, which tried to raise
further revenue by insisting that all wills, pamphlets, newspapers and
playing cards in the American colonies carry a tax stamp, affected the
islands worse than the mainland, and was unsuccessfully campaigned against
by Beckford and Fuller. But to the fury of the North American 'Patriots',
the West Indians in the islands largely complied, producing nearly 80 per
cent of Stamp Act revenue before the measure's repeal in February 1766.
Only in the Leewards, threatened with an embargo by North American
merchants, were there protests.

Divisions between London and the Thirteen Colonies were now
becoming entrenched. In February 1767, Abraham Redwood Jr, acting as
agent in London, wrote to his father in Newport. 'I was at the House of
Commons yesterday . . . Mr Grenville got up & spoke very much against
America & seemed in a great Confucion at their Disobedience as he called
it & that they ort to have ten thousand men sent over directly & to Quarter
them in the Principal Town of Every Province, his speech was received
with great applause,' the young Redwood reported, 'nothing was heard but
Hear hear, hear hear.' Although in the sugar islands there was an entire
absence of the petitions and pamplets emanating from the north, Beckford and Fuller, leading the West India lobby in London, both attacked
the policy of taxation of America, and Beckford tried to present petitions
from the agent from Massachusetts against the revenue-raising Townshend
Acts of 1767. But as a British 'patriot' with only a confused and partial
self-image as an 'American', Beckford was joining those hardening their
view of the stand-off. 'The Devil has possessed the minds of the North

Americans', Beckford wrote to Pitt in February 1767. 'George Grenville and his Stamp Act raised the foul fiend: a prudent firmness will lay him, I hope, for ever.' For his part, Rose Fuller, having previously supported the cause of the North Americans in Parliament, was so outraged by the Boston Tea Party in December 1773 that he suggested that Boston pay £20,000 compensation to the East India Company.

In North America, the Caribbean colonies were seen as a continuous extension of the mainland colonies. Joseph Galloway of Pennsylvania described the British West Indies as 'natural appendages of North America as the Isle of Man and the Orkneys are to Britain'. North Americans wanted to put pressure on the West Indians to use their power in the House of Commons unequivocally on the colonials' side. Through the summer and autumn of 1774, as measures against Britain were discussed, it was decided to include the West Indies in the threat of a trade embargo. On 1 December 1774, the First Continental Congress, a meeting in Philadelphia of delegates from 12 North American colonies, closed their ports to British Caribbean produce and threatened to ban the export of commodities starting in September 1775, if its demands were not met. It was time for the sugar barons to decide whose side they were on.

27

THE WAR AGAINST AMERICA

'A little rebellion now and then is a good thing.'
Thomas Jefferson

The threat of embargo caused huge alarm in the British West Indies; with the islands planted everywhere with sugar, they were dangerously dependent on provisions and plantation goods from the North American colonies: if they 'withhold their supplies', read a petition to London of March 1775, 'nothing will save Barbados and the Leewards from the dreadful consequences of absolute famine'.

In London, the West India lobby did everything it could to avert war, while trying to offend neither the Americans nor the British. There were warnings that outlawing trade with the rebellious colonies would bring ruin to the West Indies. 'You will starve the islands', one declared, 'and uniting them in the same cause with North America, drive them into revolt also.' But the likes of Beckford and Fuller never entertained the idea of revolt, and only warned of its possibility in order to try to jolt the British government into adopting a conciliatory policy.

The West Indian assemblies had a long tradition of defying imperial control from London, and as early as 1652 Barbados had requested representation in Parliament. The Jamaican assembly had been one of the most vigorously assertive in British America. In 1757 it was the first to be censured by the House of Commons. In December 1774, the Jamaican assembly petitioned George III in words and sentiments that were almost indistinguishable from those of the patriots in North America, including repudiating parliamentary sovereignty over the internal affairs of a colony. It even repeated the mainland conspiracy theory that there was a 'plan' to 'enslave' the colonies.

When fighting broke out at Lexington in April 1775, the Grenada assembly petitioned the King, deploring 'the horrors of a Civil War already manifested in the effusion of blood on our countrymen and friends on both sides'. The Governor immediately dissolved the assembly, but its New England-born Speaker was already on his way to Britain with a copy of the petition.

So, on the islands the sugar barons were at first divided. In St Kitts, planters fought duels over the imperial question, resulting in the deaths of two men. In March 1776, Admiral Gayton in Jamaica complained that it was impossible to persuade local courts to give judgements against North American ships, and that there were 'too many friends of America in this island'. These tended to be those 'closely connected by Relationship and trade with North America'; or to have 'formerly lived in America, & imbibed no small portion of her levelling spirit'. Anglo-American Florentius Vassall told Thomas Thistlewood that he desired 'the North Americans might beat the English else they will be enslaved and ruled with a rod of iron, and next us'. Vassall predicted a British defeat, as no army could 'keep in awe . . . 2 thousand miles' of American territory. But most Jamaicans Thistlewood knew backed Britain in the conflict, and toasted their victories.

Loyalty to 'home' was a factor: the English in the West Indies never had the attachment to the place that those in North America developed. For them, 'home' remained Britain. In addition, more practical considerations would see the West India colonies fail to join the North Americans in their struggle for self-rule. In the Caribbean, the planters lived in constant fear of attack by the French (a threat removed in North America by the events of the Seven Years War), and of being overrun by their slaves, who, unlike in the north, were in a massive majority on the islands. Both threats required the support of Britain's military. The planters were also dependent on the protected British market for their uncompetitively produced sugar.

The war brought instant hardship to the islands. To find money for its military, the British government raised the import duty on sugar, leading London merchants to withdraw credit and recall debts from the West Indies. With supplies from North America cut off and trade disrupted, plantation profits fell to their lowest levels of the century as sugar production dropped by half. Prices for essential provisions doubled during 1775, meaning that many planters could no longer pay the interest on their debts.

The greatest fear was that food shortages would lead to slave rebellion. By the end of 1775, thousands of slaves had died in Jamaica and the Leewards of malnutrition and its accompanying illnesses. The West Indians pleaded for more troops from home as a revolt broke out in Tobago in

1774, with another plot discovered in Jamaica the same year. Maroon raids on St Vincent the following year worsened the situation.

In the meantime, American privateers had been pouring into the Caribbean. There were continual losses of cargo, leading to a sharp hike in shipping and insurance costs. Against this backdrop, the popularity of the American cause waned fast. By mid-1776, most islanders were hoping for 'the total reduction of the colonies by the Administration'.

American patriots were now being arrested. One man who 'falsely imagining that he might declare his mind here as freely as he did in England, being a favourer of the Americans' was executed in Antigua. Loyal petitions were sent to the King, and the inhabitants of Nevis presented British troops with 50 hogsheads of rum 'to inspire [them] with courage to beat the Yankee Rebels'. There was a further hardening of attitudes after a slave revolt in Jamaica in 1776. For the first time on the island, skilled Creole slaves rebelled, inflamed, it was thought, by rhetoric coming out of North America, and armed by the Yankee rebels.

All the time, the North American privateers, fitted out in French West Indian ports, became more successful and bold, even launching land raids, invading Nassau in the Bahamas in 1776 and twice attacking Tobago the following year. The British responded by arming their merchant ships and attacking American trade with the neutral islands, but by February 1777 American privateers had taken some 250 British West India merchant ships, contributing to the collapse of four major West India merchant companies in London.

The situation worsened with the entry of Spain and France into the war against Britain. In September 1778, Dominica, lying between Martinique and Guadeloupe, and defended by only 46 regulars and a militia of 150 men with almost useless weapons, capitulated to a 2,000-strong expeditionary force from Martinique. The loss was compensated for by the capture by the British of St Lucia, with its matchless anchorage in what is now Rodney Bay, but in June 1779, St Vincent and then, nine days later, Grenada fell to the French.

The planters could not understand it. They regarded themselves as the source of British power and expected their defence interests to be given absolute priority. But there were something like eight times more French troops than British in the theatre. Now, it was evident that Britain had lost control of the sea. A small fleet under Admiral George Rodney reached the Caribbean two days after the surrender of Grenada, but a fresh French squadron had also arrived to restore their overwhelming superiority. After an indecisive sea battle off Grenada, the shattered British ships left to refit in St Kitts. The fleet made a shocking sight when it landed the dead and wounded. The decks of the *Grafton* were 'entirely covered with Blood' and the *Prince of Wales* had 'ninety-five Holes intirely through her Sides'. The French admiral, meanwhile, boasted that he did not intend to leave George III enough British sugar 'to sweeten his tea for breakfast by Christmas'. Every sail on the horizon was cause for new alarms. 'This island is in the utmost distress', wrote a St Vincent planter from Barbados, having fled his own island shortly before its capture, 'the necessaries of life scarce to be purchased, no credit or money, in expectation of being invaded every moment.'

In fact, the British were simply unable to match the combined forces of America, France and Spain, particularly when there were invasion fears at home. The planters may have felt abandoned, but actually the opposite was the case. George III and his ministers persisted in the war in part because of their belief that the loss of the Thirteen Colonies inevitably meant the loss of the West Indies, which were seen as essential for maintaining national wealth and greatness. (In 1773, exports from Grenada alone were worth eight times those from Canada.) The defence of Jamaica was given priority over the war in America, and when the prospect of a French war had loomed, the British government had agonised over whether to abandon the mainland effort to launch offensive operations in the Caribbean. Following the declaration of war by the French, the British had given up Philadelphia, then the largest city in the United States and the capital of the Revolution, primarily to free up 5,000 troops for the conquest of St Lucia.

In December 1780, Britain gained a new enemy, declaring war on the Netherlands, having been angered by the sheltering of American privateers in Dutch ports, and in the hope of cutting off naval supplies to France. News of this reached Rodney in the Caribbean in February the following year, along with orders to capture the Dutch island of St Eustatius, which had become a major trans-shipment point for supplies, particularly gunpowder, to Washington's army in America. The tiny island offered no resistance, and Rodney then proceeded to loot everything he could find in the crowded warehouses, regardless of whether they belonged to neutrals, or even friends.

Rodney remained at St Eustatius for three crucial months, preoccupied with the sale of the captured goods, leaving his deputy, Rear Admiral Sir Samuel Hood, to attempt to intercept a large French fleet under Vice Admiral the Comte de Grasse. When this failed, de Grasse succeeded in capturing Tobago in June.

As was usual, with the advent of the hurricane season that summer, naval operations in the West Indies came to an end. Rodney returned to England, partly because of poor health, and also to answer charges of improper conduct over the looting of St Eustatius. He sent three ships to Jamaica, and only 10, under Hood, north to the Chesapeake, where General Earl Cornwallis, the commander of the British army in the southern American colonies, had fortified himself in Yorktown and was waiting complacently for the Royal Navy to come and collect him. De Grasse, however, proceeded north with his entire fleet of 26 ships of the line.

It was a fatal miscalculation. Heavily outnumbered, even with support from the New York squadron, Hood was unable to break the French blockade of the mouth of Chesapeake Bay. A second relief force was sent from New York on 19 October, but it was too late, Cornwallis having surrendered with upwards of 6,000 men the previous day to Generals Washington and Rochambeau. When he heard the news, the British Prime Minister Lord North exclaimed, 'My God! It is all over.'

The following month, de Grasse returned to the Caribbean with the intention of sweeping the British from the West Indies. Soon he had almost achieved his mission. In January, he covered a French landing at St Kitts. After an epic siege of the redoubt at Brimstone Hill, the island surrendered on 13 February. Nevis and Montserrat fell soon afterwards. Now only Jamaica, Barbados, newly captured St Lucia and drought-stricken Antigua remained of the British West Indian empire.

The brave resistance at Brimstone Hill had, however, bought time for Rodney to return with his fleet. Sailing from England on 16 January, told by the head of the Admiralty, 'the fate of this Empire is in your hands', he reached Carlisle Bay in Barbados on 19 February. Hearing that de Grasse was at anchor at Fort Royal in Martinique, preparing for a descent on Jamaica with 5,400 men, Rodney headed for St Lucia, taking shelter in Gros Islet Bay (now Rodney Bay), from where Martinique was within sight. Rodney's men worked day and night provisioning, watering and refitting the fleet.

The inhabitants of Jamaica had learned of de Grasse's plans, which included linking up with a Spanish force from Hispaniola, and were in a state of panic. The militia had been called up, heavy taxation imposed to meet the cost of defensive preparations, and the island's roads had been rendered impassable by felling large trees across them. Trade was at a standstill. A message from a spy on St Thomas read, 'The attack on Jamaica makes more noise than all North America. Spain has told France that cost what it may they wish to have Jamaica.'

On 8 April the French fleet – 37 ships of the line and a large troop convoy – left Martinique to link up with a Spanish force at Santo Domingo to invade Jamaica. As well as siege weapons, French supplies included 50,000 sets of manacles destined for Jamaica's slaves. Rodney's fleet, evenly matched in numbers with that of de Grasse, followed in pursuit. After four days of manoeuvring in little wind, battle was joined at seven in the morning under the lee of Dominica.

As was standard in such encounters, the two lines of vessels started the battle sailing in parallel in opposite directions, blasting their cannons in a naval artillery fight. But at the height of the battle, with visibility impaired by clouds of smoke, a shift in the wind threw both sides into confusion, and a number of British vessels tacked through the French line in three places. The unintended move brought chaos and carnage to the French, with the ships around de Grasse's flagship, the massive 110-gun *Ville de Paris*, now surrounded and the main French fleet separated from their van and fired on from both sides. When the battle ended at about half past six in the evening, five French ships had been captured, including the *Ville de Paris*, one sunk, and the rest, according to a letter Rodney sent on to Jamaica, 'miserably shattered'. According to a British doctor who boarded a captured enemy ship, 'the decks were covered with the blood and mangled limbs of the dead, as well as the wounded and dying'. French naval supremacy in the theatre had been consigned to the depths, and Jamaica saved from invasion.

The 'Battle of the Saintes' was not materially as decisive as Rodney made out. The 'Breaking of the Line' had allowed much of the French fleet, previously trapped between the coast and the British, to escape to leeward. But it had a great psychological effect, with extraordinary rejoicing in England, and mutual recriminations and a series of courts martial in France. When the news reached Jamaica, the relief was immense. Church bells were rung and flags triumphantly hoisted. Two years later, Stephen Fuller would write to Rodney, now a lord, giving him the news that the Jamaica assembly had voted 'to prepare an elegant Marble Statue of your Lordship'. The florid monument, with Rodney in Roman toga, still stands in the main square in Spanish Town. Rodney replied to Fuller's letter, thanking the inhabitants of Jamaica and assuring them that 'No Man has their Interest more at Heart than myself, being convinced that Jamaica is the best Jewel in the British Diadem, and that too much care cannot be taken to preserve it.'

Jamaica had been saved, and at the Treaty of Paris in 1783, which ended the Revolutionary War, St Lucia and Tobago were surrendered, but

Britain recovered its former possessions in the Caribbean. Yet the loss of the Thirteen Colonies changed everything for the sugar planters. The West India interest in London, planters on the islands, and statesmen of the new republic of the United States all agreed that trading relations had to be restarted. Stephen Fuller, in a memorial to the government, said it was required by 'the invincible law of absolute necessity'. John Adams declared: 'They can neither do without us, not we without them. The Creator has placed us upon the globe in such a situation that we have occasion for each other, and politicians and artful contrivances cannot separate us.'

But for London, yielding to those wishing to establish the pre-war status quo would have been the death blow to the old continental system and the Navigation Acts. Many argued that the islanders' clamour to be given access to supplies from a now foreign source should be ignored while they continued to enjoy their peculiar century-and-a-quarter-old monopoly rights for the UK market. Here, for the first time, the powerful West India lobby looked like it could lose the battle.

However, for the first couple of years after the war, British naval commanders in the Caribbean turned a blind eye to continued trade with the North Americans. An exception was young Horatio Nelson, a frigate captain, appointed in March 1784 to command the 28-gun *Boreas*. Nelson had served in the Caribbean before. He was on the Jamaica squadron from 1777 to 1782, and in June 1779 had been appointed to Peter Beckford's old role as post captain in charge of the batteries at Fort Charles. But he seems to have picked up little understanding of how things were done in the West Indies. 'Our Governors and Custom-house officers pretended . . . they had a right to trade', he wrote, appalled, to his brother in England. 'I seized many of their Vessels, which brought all parties upon me; and I was persecuted from one Island to another, that I could not leave my ship.' Although ostracised for 'doing my duty by being true to the interest of Great Britain', Nelson did manage to meet and marry a rich Nevis widow, Frances Nisbet, before he left the West Indies in June 1787.

After a certain amount of debate in London, a decision was made in 1786 to definitively shut out American ships. Canada and Ireland, it was hoped, would fill the gap. As compensation, the Admiralty sent an expedition under Lieutenant William Bligh to the Pacific to bring back bread-fruit trees to feed the slaves. This effort came to grief with a mutiny on the *Bounty*, but a second expedition successfully introduced the tree to the islands. Unfortunately few slaves would eat the resulting fruit.

In the face of the new embargo, there was large-scale smuggling and

Canada massively increased its exports to the West Indies of lumber and fish, but it was not enough. Costs for essential supplies rose considerably for the planters. At the same time, the price of sugar was falling, and duties set during the war were not removed, as the increased Sugar Tax had become one of the most productive sources of national income. Further problems were now crowding in on the sugar barons, some from no fault of their own, others of their own making. Worst of all, pehaps, were the disastrous effects of absentee ownership of the sugar estates.

28

THE WEST INDIAN 'NABOBS': ABSENTEEISM, DECADENCE AND DECLINE

'Despair . . . has cut off more people in the West-Indies than plagues or famine.'
William Beckford of Somerly

In increasing numbers during the last decades of the eighteenth century, sugar planters, unable to feel that the West Indies was home, and scared of the constant war and frightening mortality rate, returned to Britain to become absentee proprietors. Their plantations almost always suffered.

The estates of absentee proprietors were managed for them by locally based 'attorneys'. Some ran 15 to 20 plantations and were 'nabobs' in their own right, but most looked after about five or six. The managers were paid a commission out of the crop, in return for running the planting, harvesting, processing and shipping of the sugar, although most of the hands-on work was organised by an overseer.

The system was wide open to abuse, and few attorneys could resist the temptation to steal from the absent planter. The Codringtons, once they had left Antigua, were repeatedly forced to fire their managers there for dishonesty. In general, short-termism dominated: improvements were seldom made because they temporarily reduced net returns; buildings and equipment were allowed to become dilapidated; fields were tilled until exhausted and then left to grow up in weeds. New lands were seldom opened up to cultivation because of the large initial outlay and great amount of supervision required. There was no incentive to experiment or improvise.

In most cases, life and conditions for the enslaved workers were even worse on absentee estates. At Drax Hall in Jamaica, the number of live births on the plantation was five times higher when locally owned than when it passed into the hands of the absentee Alderman William Beckford.

Alderman Beckford's brother Richard had died in 1756, leaving an estate worth about £120,000, which included nearly 1,000 slaves, two cattle pens and three contiguous sugar estates in Westmoreland parish, about seven miles north-east of Savannah-la-Mar, called Roaring River, Fort William and Williamsfield.

In 1765, when he was 21, his son William Beckford of Somerly graduated from Balliol College, Oxford, and came into possession of his inheritance of about 7,000 acres of prime Jamaican land. Although sugar output had declined since 1756, the estates seemed to be profitable, and Somerly was in no hurry to sail to Jamaica. Instead, with two friends, he embarked on an extensive Grand Tour of the sights of Europe.

His father had wanted him to become a politician, but having returned from Europe and married an 'uncommon beauty', his cousin Charlotte Hay, he lived the life of the gentry squire at Somerly Hall in Suffolk, giving a large dinner for locals each Sunday after church.

But when the profits from the Jamaican plantations began to fall, he made a decision to go to Jamaica 'to view the romantic wonders of his estates, and to witness the resources that might render them more valuable', as a friend later wrote of him. It was a very different manifesto to those of his Beckford forebears, who had been so hungry for political and financial dominance. Somerly had a plan to write a book, complete with illustrations, about these 'romantic wonders', and for that purpose took with him an artist he had met in Rome, Philip Wickstead, to serve as secretary and illustrator. Another artist, George Robertson, was also invited to be part of this vision of a tropical salon, and followed soon afterwards.

Charlotte, Somerly and Wickstead sailed to Jamaica in February 1774. The promise of 'romantic wonders' did not disappoint. Somerly was awestruck by the mysterious beauty of the Blue Mountains, 'covered with a sapphire haze'. He saw everything through the prism of his Grand Tour. Jamaica, he wrote, was no 'less romantic than, the most wild and beautiful situations of Frescati, Tivoli, and Albano'. His new home in Westmoreland parish was 'as agreeable as any spots in Italy, that have had the advantage of a Salvatore Rosa, or a Poussin to perpetuate their beauties'.

Somerly's part of Westmoreland is, indeed, beautiful and dramatic. Water draining from the limestone 'Cockpit Country' to the east bubbles up in deep blue springs; there is a profusion of bird and animal life, and wildly rich and almost overpoweringly green vegetation everywhere. Most days, in the early afternoon, the temperature and humidity rise sharply, the skies darken, and suddenly, with a huge rushing round, the air seems almost completely full of water as rain spouts down.

Somerly also saw great potential in his lush tropical acreage: 'the vegetation here, and the stamina of the land are of such a nature', he wrote to a friend in England, 'that it argues infatuation, or sloth in the inhabitants, that they are not in general more rich and independent'. The state of his own plantations, he wrote, 'was sufficient to convince me of the negligence of my attornies; and had I delay'd my projected voyage a few years longer the consequences might have been fatal to my properties'. The managers, he said, were 'vacant and inactive', more concerned with eating and drinking the products of the plantations than with stopping the estates falling into ruin.

Taking up the reins of business himself, he set up home at Hertford Pen, in the low mountainous region of Westmoreland parish. This afforded him and his wife a more salubrious climate than his sugar plantations on the flat plains. 'The situation of Hertford is one of the pleasantest in the country', an English visitor wrote. 'It is on very gently rising ground, nearly equally removed from the sea, and lofty mountains covered with wood, and at a short distance from a fine river.'

Somerly set about expanding the animal pens to raise cattle and horses for market (and to manure the canefields), and planted guinea grass for fodder with great success. Experiments planting English wheat, barley and oats fared less well. He also expanded the provision grounds available to the estates' slaves for growing their own food. At the same time he set about repairing or replacing the estates' sugar-processing machinery. He also built and lavishly furnished a new house for his family, costing nearly £10,000. By 1776, two years after his arrival, he was calling Jamaica 'My native country' and 'paternal soil'.

Putting the estates in order had not come cheap, but for now, William of Somerly remained optimistic. 'I have endeavor'd as far as was in my power to correct [the attorneys'] past abuses; and I shall expect to see my estates establish'd, in the course of a few years, upon an economical and an advantageous footing', he wrote in a letter of 1776. He was concerned, he said, about the very considerable increase in the money he now owed in England, but, he wrote to a friend, 'I hope to make an annual reduction of my DEBTS, and to see my properties increase as THEY diminish; and when this shall be in any degree effected, I shall carry Mrs Beckford back with tenfold satisfaction to her friends in England.'

Two months after landing in Jamaica, the Beckfords had been invited to dinner with the local Cope family, where they met Thomas Thistlewood. Thereafter, Beckford would occasionally hire out some of the slaves owned by Thistlewood. Two men of such different rank would never have socialised in England, but in June 1778, Thistlewood spent the day at Hertford Pen. In the morning they played billiards, and 'Looked over many

Folio Volumes of excellent plates of the Ruins of Rome', as Thistlewood noted in his diary. After a ride around the Pen, they were joined for dinner by a handful of local worthies, with the men then playing a game of cricket. Thistlewood, a keen horticulturalist, was sent home with 'some geranium slips, flower seeds, jonquil roots, &c'.

Beckford of Somerly was uneasy about 'the levelling principle that obtains among the white people of Jamaica', who, of course, stuck together for their mutual protection. He preferred the 'chain of subordination' prevalent in Europe, which, he wrote, 'preserves the strength of the whole'. Somerly found the lower classes of white people in Jamaica 'idle, drunken, worthless and immoral'. However, whatever else he was, Thistlewood was neither a drunk nor lazy, and he seems to have passed muster with Somerly, who was 'very affable and free' with him. A few days after his visit, Somerly sent Thistlewood six engravings made from George Robertson's paintings of the Fort William estate, and would later return the visit and be treated to a lavish feast of the very best of Thistlewood's produce and be lent some of his impressive collection of books.

Beckford had more in common, though, with Robert Charles Dallas, who arrived in Jamaica in 1779. Like Beckford, Dallas had been born in Jamaica, and his father, a Scottish doctor and plantation owner, had died while he was young. Robert was sent off the island at the age of 10 to be schooled first in Musselburgh, New Brunswick, and then at the Scottish school in Kensington run by James Elphinstone, a friend of Dr Samuel Johnson and outspoken opponent of slavery.

In his book on the island, Dallas described arriving in Jamaica as if for the first time – either for literary effect or because he had not returned since leaving as a young boy 15 years earlier. The lack of twilight, the insects and the extreme heat all seemed new to him. 'The heat becomes intolerable', he exclaimed on landing at Kingston. 'Oh! for a glass of rasp-berry ice! – I am melting away – the sun is exhaling all my juices – I feel them passing through my pores . . . The slightest action throws one into a violent perspiration.'

Like Somerly, he arrived to find that his estate had been badly mismanaged by the attorneys. It was also mired in legal actions, and now 'in the last stage of its disorder'. A small debt, less than a fifth of its value, had, since the death of his father, increased 'to almost its whole value'. The aim of the managers or trustees – 'really the locusts of the West Indies' – was to supply the plantation from their own stores and, he wrote, 'get a debt upon his estate, then, by management with the overseer, to keep down the annual produce till the debt encrease so much, that the proprietor is glad to take anything, or till a chancery suit foreclose a mortgage; and thus . . . make the property their own'.

Dallas was unimpressed with the white Jamaicans he met during his time on the island. The children were spoilt and the adults greedy and lazy, spending their time eating and drinking too much, and doing little else except playing cards and backgammon. 'With some exceptions', he concluded, 'the country is generally inhabited by rapacious agents, inhuman overseers, ignorant and cruel negro-jobbers, and usurious traders.'

One such exception was Beckford of Somerly, whom Dallas seems to have found a kindred spirit. He spent some time at Hertford Pen, engaged in 'Conversation, books, music, drawing, riding, bathing, fishing'. It was the most agreeable time he had on the island, and he described Beckford, who clearly had little in common with the Beckfords of old, as 'accomplished mild and pleasing . . . as a friend, sincere; as a husband, delicate and affectionate; as a brother, warmly attached; as a master, tender and humane; as a man of business, alas!'

Indeed, Somerly's aim to reduce his debts was not going to plan. Reading between the lines of his two books, written under very different and unfortunate circumstances, he made a series of bad mistakes, including experimenting with untried new theories about planting, and buying 'superfluous coppers, stills and stores'.

Beckford had also learnt to his cost that sugar producing itself remained, as a Barbadian planter had lamented 100 years before, 'a design full of accident'. He had endless problems with his water-powered mills: sometimes the flow was insufficient; other times it was so heavy that the dam on the mill pond was carried away. Machinery was always breaking down. The sugar cane itself, he wrote, 'is so treacherous a plant', often promising much but delivering little, so that 'the life of a planter is a continual state of uncertainty and trouble'. In 1777, he was forced to take out a mortgage of £25,000; and no money had been repaid four years later.

Dallas and Beckford, both educated in England at a time when slavery was being questioned, no doubt discussed their views on the matter. Dallas described his shock on seeing, on his first day on the island, a slave given a severe punch on the face for allowing a fly to land on his master's butter. 'My blood rebelled against the blow', he wrote. 'I felt an affection for the poor negro, and an instant detestation for his master.' Later, he detailed the callous treatment of slave women by the white overseers, and various cruel tortures inflicted on even the youngest slaves. Slavery, he concluded, was 'tyranny, cruelty, murder', and he started to worry that he was getting used to it. The mind, he wrote, underwent 'a total change' from the state in which it arrived in the West Indies. 'There is a kind of intoxication', he continued. 'I have not lost my natural abhorrence to cruelty, yet I see it practised with much less impatience than I did, and I have only to pray, that I may not feel an inclination to turn driver myself.' Before this could happen, Dallas left the island, explaining later that he 'daily sicken'd at the ills around me'.

Dallas was one of a number of Creole-born English who came out to the West Indies and found that it was not a place in which they could live. His younger brother arrived in 1781 with his wife, but also disliked Jamaica and moved to Philadelphia two years later.* Walter Pollard, from an old Barbados family, had been educated in England from a young age, and spent a friend-less and unhappy childhood longing for his parents and tropical home. But when at last he returned in 1788, he discovered it was not the bucolic para-dise of his memory. 'A well constituted mind ought not to remain happy in the West Indies', he wrote. 'I feel such repugnance . . . [for] negro slavery . . . a system cruel to the master and the slave and where a pure mind that reasons must shudder at the thoughts of residing and perhaps of marrying.' He moved away quickly, first to the United States, then back to England.

Thomas Thistlewood told the story of Robert Kenyon, who bought the Egypt plantation from the Copes in 1781. In February of the next year, Thistlewood reported a 'miff' between Kenyon and his overseer 'about flogging the Negroes. Mr K. can't bear to see them flogged.' Kenyon never got used to it, and sold up and left two years later.

Robert Dallas's book about Jamaica was published anonymously, to avoid offence to people he knew on the island. He did, however, return to Jamaica after marrying in England, and left the island again only because of his wife's health. Ten years after his first book, he wrote a history of the maroons, in which he backed away from his earlier anti-slavery sentiments. By the time he was in his forties, he was regretting ever having published his first book. It was ridiculous of him, he wrote, 'as a West Indian, to argue against that system upon which the prosperity of every West Indian is built. My answer is that I was young and intoxicated with the Utopian ideas of liberty, which I had imbibed in the course of my education in England.'

The case of Beckford of Somerly is slightly different. He wrote in detail about the lives of the slaves in Jamaica, and displayed his characteristic sensi-tivity and, it has to be said, naivety. He called the transportation of slaves from Africa a 'stream of misery . . . repugnant to our religion'; the manner of their sale once arrived 'harrowing'. He deplored the sadistic, often drunken violence of the overseers, inflicting 'excruciating bodily sufferings', and was highly crit-ical of the hard work imposed on the old, the sick and the very young. At one point he noted that many slaves were so 'desperate' that they committed suicide.

---

* This Dallas became Secretary of the US Treasury. His son, George Miflin Dallas, was Vice Pres-ident of the United States, 1845–8. The city of Dallas is named after him.

But, like Richard Ligon, and many sensitive Englishmen who followed, Somerly failed to see the obvious conclusion of the evidence he himself presented. Conditions on slave ships should be improved, he suggested, rather than the trade abolished. Discipline in the fields should be 'steady, not severe' and general treatment more carefully regulated (but only 'if it can be done without infringing upon the rights of individuals'). Small children should be employed, he wrote, 'in some light work' like hand-weeding, 'in which they may take delight'. For all his obvious and deeply felt compassion, he went on to repeat the mantras of those who were then defending slavery against its growing opponents: the lot of Africans in the West Indies 'under a kind owner' was, in fact, better than if they had stayed in Africa, and their conditions compared well with those of the 'labouring poor' in England; removed from his 'natal soil', the African had the chance 'to taste the comforts of protection, the fruits of humanity, and the blessings of religion'. Having criticised owners for forgetting the 'humanity' of the Africans, he pronounced: 'The negroes are slaves by nature.' Although clearly appalled by the practical application of slavery, he could not imagine a West Indian world without it.

In 1770, having recently become Lord Mayor of London for the second time, Alderman William Beckford died, aged 61. He was, reportedly, the first English commoner to die a millionaire. His son and heir, William of Fonthill, was nine. William Pitt, Earl of Chatham, was one of those appointed to look after his interests while a minor. Another was Thomas Wildman, who had worked for Alderman Beckford, and who, together with his two brothers, would run Beckford of Fonthill's interests in Jamaica, as well as act as his bankers in England.

Like his cousin, William Beckford of Somerly, Beckford of Fonthill was a very different creature to the bold, violent, determined Beckfords who had built their enormous fortune in Jamaica and then marched to the top of public life in England.

Beckford of Fonthill was highly strung and acutely sensitive. He refused to hunt or shoot. He was a brilliant amateur painter and talented composer and writer. He is best known today as the author of *Vathek*, a successful Gothic novel he wrote originally in French, but published in England in 1796, and for his jaw-dropping extravagance. When he turned 21 in 1781, Beckford of Fonthill came into an inheritance of more than a million pounds, together with an annual income of about £100,000. It was a staggering amount of money – 'the largest property real and personal of any subject in Europe' – and Fonthill was determined to spend it fast. The following year he travelled round Europe with such a vast entourage that he was mistaken for the Emperor of Austria and, the story goes, charged accordingly.

His father had collected art, but the son took his acquisitions to a new level, building up one of the world's largest collections of paintings, books, furniture and *objets d'art*: 20,000 books in his own binding; paintings by Titian, Bronzino, Velasquez, Rembrandt, Rubens and Canaletto – 20 of the paintings he once owned now hang in the National Gallery, London – as well as the major contemporary artists; a table from the Borghese Palace whose centre consisted of the largest onyx in the world; Jacobean coffers; Venetian glass; the largest collection of Japanese lacquer in the world; and thousands of objects of porcelain, bronze, jewellery, silver, gold and agate.

In March 1783, Beckford married Lady Margaret Gordon, the 21-year-old daughter of the Earl of Aboyne. The following year the couple were presented at court, and Beckford was elected MP for Wells. At the same time he started jockeying for a peerage, and in October his name was gazetted with others about to be made peers. He was to be Lord Beckford of Fonthill – the family's rise to the very top looked set to be completed.

But Fonthill had a guilty secret. He was predominantly homosexual, and since the age of 19 had been carrying on an affair with William Courtney, a famously beautiful boy whom he had met when Courtney was only 11. In November 1784, Beckford was staying with Courtney's family, Lord and Lady Courtney. Early one morning, Courtney's tutor, passing by his bedroom, heard a 'creeking and bustle, which raised his curiosity, & thro' the key hole he saw the operation, which it seems he did not interrupt, but informed Lord C [Courtney], & the whole was blown up', as the event was described. Beckford denied everything, but Courtney was forced to hand over to his father incriminating letters.

There was no prosecution – sodomy was at that time a capital offence – but Beckford's good name was gone for ever. The newspapers had a field day; it was the biggest sex scandal of the Georgian era.

Fonthill's wife Margaret, who was pregnant with their first daughter, advised fleeing the country, but for a while Beckford remained in England, cloistered away at Fonthill. Then, in 1785, the Beckfords retired to Switzerland. There Lady Margaret died the following year, having just given birth to their second daughter. The two baby girls were packed off to be looked after at Fonthill's mother's house in Wimpole Street, London. Beckford hardly ever saw them again. Newspapers blamed Lady Margaret's death on Beckford's behaviour. Even friends who had remained loyal now ceased to correspond.

In January 1787 Beckford returned to England, and shortly afterwards decided that he ought to visit his properties in Jamaica, now being managed by James Wildman. March that year saw him in Falmouth, writing to his mother: 'We are waiting in this most detestable town for a wind to carry us into a still more detestable situation. – the very sight of the waves gently heaving the vessels in the harbour makes me sick – so I leave you to judge what will be my sensations when on board. – However I am in for it – now – I cannot escape . . .' 'I cannot help confessing that no one ever embarked for transportation with a heavier heart', he wrote to Thomas Wildman in London. 'The more I hear of Jamaica, the more I dread the climate – which I fully expect will wither my health away.'

In the event, Beckford got as far as Madeira before leaving the ship and abandoning his Jamaica estates to the tender mercies of his attorneys. Instead he sailed to Portugal, where he stayed for about two years, in spite of being shunned by the British expatriate community. Further travel followed, until a return to Fonthill in October 1789, where he inspected expensive redecoration work being undertaken on Splendens. His sole companions were two oddballs he had picked up on his travels: Gregorio Franchi, the young son of an Italian court singer, and a Spanish dwarf, Perro. No visitors called, except his old tutor, who reported that there were three chefs and one confectioner employed in the kitchen and 10 footmen waiting at table upon three persons.

The return to England had also been prompted by concerns about the Wildmans' management in Jamaica. On one letter received from Thomas Wildman in April 1789, Beckford scrawled: 'Infernal rascal this Wildman!' In January, Beckford was complaining that his estates were not producing what they did in his father's day, and instructed the Wildmans to sell one of his smaller plantations. In the event, a large plantation known as Quebec, with 800 slaves, passed this year from Beckford to the Wildmans, possibly after the latter had threatened Beckford with calling in outstanding mortgages. Later Beckford would lament of the Wildmans that 'Between this harpy and two brothers who played in concert at proper time half my substance has been devoured.' The profits from the Quebec plantation would allow Thomas Wildman to purchase Newstead Abbey from Lord Byron in 1817 for £94,000.

Beckford wanted his money out of Jamaica to pay for his grandiose plans at Splendens. 'My Works at Fonthill Building planting etc are going on very briskly', he wrote in a letter to his Jamaica agent in August 1790. 'I have been raising Towers and digging Grottos, your Brother thinks I mean to imploy almost as many whites as Blacks very shortly.'

After further travels, Beckford returned to Fonthill in 1796, pretty much for good. He bought an additional 1,700 acres for the estate and planted hundreds of thousands of trees to shield himself from prying eyes. An enormous wall was built around the grounds, eight miles long, 12 feet high and topped with iron spikes (a wall of similiarly vast proportions surrounds the Drax estate at Charborough). Furthermore, Beckford was now bored with the classical sobriety of Splendens. He decided to raise himself a spectacular new building. 'Some people drink to forget their unhappiness', he is reported to have announced. 'I do not drink, I build.'

Although none were on the scale of Beckford of Fonthill, this generation of the sugar barons, many of whom were inheritors of huge fortunes, is characterised by furious extravagance, and, in particular, eccentric building projects.

Rose Fuller died childless in 1777, and his substantial estate passed to his brother Henry's son Jack, who was then 20 years old. Like Beckford of Fonthill, Jack could not spend the money fast enough. Soon becoming enormously fat, his great weakness was for building expensive and worthless follies in the grounds of his manor at Brightling in Sussex, earning him locally the nickname 'Mad Jack'. One was a 35-foot-high cone designed to look like a sugar loaf, built to win a bet. Even the otherwise sensible Draxes were constructing a huge tower of no discernible purpose in the grounds of their magnificent Charborough Park. But none came close to what Beckford, soon to be known as 'The Fool of Fonthill', now intended.

In Jamaica, Beckford of Somerly's fortunes continued to sink through the late 1770s as he struggled to service his debts amid mounting prices for provisions and supplies caused by the war. In 1780 came the hardest blow of all.

On Monday 2 October, his near neighbour Thomas Thistlewood noted in his diary that it was 'gloomy, dark & dismal in the south', the sea roared 'prodigiously', and the skies looked 'very wild'. The following morning came heavy rain, then, from midday, the wind picked up alarmingly.

Thistlewood ordered all his slaves to take shelter in the hall of his house. Moments later the Negro houses were all blown down, amid flashes of lightning and roars of thunder. The air 'darkened with leaves & limbs of trees &c. which flew with great violence'. Torrential rain flooded his garden, as the cookroom, store house, horse stable, sheep house, bee houses and 'even the Necessary house' were all destroyed, blown 'quite away over the hill into the morass'. A little before sunset, the wind was at its height, 'raging with the utmost violence & irresistible fury, tore in pieces the remainder of my house, dispersing it in different ways'.

The hurricane continued until midnight, by which time only one wall of the main house still stood. Here Thistlewood and the slaves 'stood all night in the rain which came like small shot'. The following morning Thistlewood surveyed his property: 'The external face of the earth, so much altered, scarce know where I am. Not a blade of grass, nor leaf left, or tree, shrub or bush.' His carefully tended garden was wrecked; his sheep were almost all dead or dying; buildings had simply disappeared.

Thistlewood set to work to rebuild his business, but the destruction had made him lose heart, and he decided to sell up. No buyer was to be found, and the following year his health began to fail. For the first time since he had arrived in Jamaica he started attending church. He died in 1786, aged 65.

The 1780 hurricane hit Barbados on Tuesday 10 October. In Bridgetown, 3,000 were killed as the city was reduced to 'a heap of ruins'. Heavy cannon were carried 100 feet from the forts. Outside the town, livestock and crops were devastated. Admiral Rodney, still on station in the West Indies, commented that 'the most Beautiful Island in the World has the appearance of a land laid waste by Fire and Sword'.

Further hurricanes in 1784, 1785 and 1786 contributed to the withering of the islands' agriculture, and led to an appalling death rate among the slave population – 15,000 dying on Jamaica alone between 1780 and 1787, and 3,000 in the Leewards.

William Beckford of Somerly was hit as hard as Thistlewood in the 1780 hurricane, with his own house wrecked and 'not a single set of works, trash-house, or other subordinate buildings . . . not greatly injured, or entirely destroyed'. The next morning, he wrote, 'the whole prospect had the appearance of a desert, over which the burning winds of Africa had lately past'.

In the aftermath, Beckford reported, Negroes and 'many white people' set about plundering and 'having made free with the rum that was floating in the inundations, began to grow insolent and unruly'. Several puncheons had to be 'immediately staved'. Scenes of riot and inebriety continued for several days, and for many weeks after the hurricane the air was full of the stench of unburied bodies, which 'occasioned a kind of pestilence, that swept away a great proportion of those who had providentially escaped the first destruction'.

By the following year, the Beckford of Somerly estates owed nearly £80,000 to the 'rapacious and unfeeling' mortgage holders. But Somerly was not uniquely incompetent, gullible or unlucky. By 1787, the greater parts of the plantations throughout the West Indies were under mortgage to merchants in London, Liverpool and Bristol. Along with the hurricanes, a succession of droughts and the ravages of the cane-borer, a moth larva, brought the islands to the verge of ruin. With foreclosing, properties ended up in the hands of people utterly unqualified to run tropical agriculture enterprises and who had never even seen the West Indies.

In September 1784, Somerly wrote from 'Black River, Jamaica' to his cousin, Beckford of Fonthill, ostensibly to congratulate him on his election as MP for Wells (the letter indicates that the two cousins had not met). 'Come not to Jamaica', he warned gloomily. Somerly added that he was 'too proud to be dependent', but hinted at the real purpose of the letter when he praised Fonthill for having a reputation for generosity. Whether his cousin helped him or not is unknown. If he did, it was not enough. (Somerly would later describe his cousin Fonthill as a man 'of no heart, no feeling'.)

In the meantime, Somerly's coterie of artists had come to grief. Wickstead had fallen victim to the prevalence of cheap rum, heat and boredom, and drunk away his talent and then his life, dying of delirium tremens in Jamaica in 1786. George Robertson suffered at Hertford from 'the plaguey climate', and died in London in 1788 less than 40 years old. Both had lost most of their Jamaican paintings and drawings during the hurricane.

Some time between 1786 and 1788, when he learnt that 'his creditors were proceeding hastily', Somerly 'determined to come to England to put his affairs into the best train he could' and 'to recover a constitution broken down by sickness and affliction'. But his carriage was intercepted by bailiffs before it reached London and he was imprisoned as a debtor in the notorious Fleet gaol.

Here he was visited by the writer Fanny Burney and her father. 'What a place – surrounded with fresh horrors! – for the habitation of such a man!' Dr Burney wrote to his daughter in October 1791. Once a week Burney's nephew visited Somerly, now suffering 'severe attacks of the gout, and alarming spasmodic complaints', and played to him 'on a miserable pianoforte'. Somerly's friends blamed his guileless and trusting nature for his predicament.

After some four and a half years in the Fleet, during which he wrote his two books about Jamaica, Beckford was released. His estates were gone, although his creditors left him a small annual income. Fanny Burney went to see him and found he had 'an air of dejection, a look, a voice, a manner, that all speak the term of his sufferings to have been too long for his spirits to recruit'. He lived for a few more years, contributing articles to the *Monthly Mirror* magazine under the name 'Recluse', but died in 1799 of an apoplectic fit.

29

PEACE AND FREEDOM

'Now lick and lock-up done wid'
Emancipation song, 1833

The French Revolution in 1789 unleashed a new wave of war and tumult in the West Indies. Perhaps most important of all for the region, it led to a sequence of extraordinary events on the island of Hispaniola. Before the revolution, St Domingue, the French half of the island, had been a highly productive sugar colony, but events in Paris threw the delicate balance between slaves, whites and free blacks and mulattoes into turmoil. In 1790, the mulattoes rose, demanding an end to the restriction of their rights. The leader of the revolt was captured, tied to a wheel and battered with hammers before being left out to die. But in August the following year the black slaves rebelled and took their revenge on their masters. Two thousand whites were killed and 180 sugar factories and 200 plantations destroyed as fighting continued. It was the almost total ruin of the previously prosperous colony.

In February 1793, France declared war on Britain, leading to a fresh round of invasions and counter-invasions. Martinique was taken by the British in March 1794, St Lucia and Guadeloupe the next month, and Port-au-Prince, capital of St Domingue, in June. But later that year, Victor Hugues, a disciple of Robespierre, arrived in the Caribbean, proclaiming the emancipation of the blacks and raising an army of former slaves. Guadeloupe was recaptured, and slave rebellions inspired and supported in Grenada and St Vincent. Both islands were wrecked. At the Alliabo plantation in St Vincent, the British manager was killed by being passed though his own sugar mill.

In Jamaica there was an unrelated rising by the maroons, triggered by

an incident involving pigs being stolen, but motivated by simmering resentments over encroachment by the planters on maroon lands. The island was
put under martial law and troops heading for St Domingue were hastily
recalled, and sent against the maroons, where they suffered heavy losses
from ambushes. But when the Jamaican government imported 100 blood-
hounds from Cuba, the maroons surrendered. Six hundred were exiled to
Nova Scotia, and then eventually Sierra Leone.

A large expedition that left England in August 1795 restored British
rule in St Vincent and Grenada, and captured St Lucia in May 1796.
Trinidad was taken from Spain the following year.

But the cost was immense. The British army was pretty much consumed
in defence of the sugar islands, and in the attempt to defeat the freed slave
armies of Toussaint L'Ouverture in St Domingue, then fighting under the
flag of revolutionary France. It is estimated that as many as 44,000 British
troops died in the West Indies between 1793 and 1801, about half of those
sent, together with about 20,000 seamen. On the biggest scale ever, it was
yet another repeat of the Hispaniola disaster of 1655.

In September 1798, the last British positions in St Domingue were
abandoned in return for an agreement from Toussaint L'Ouverture to leave
Jamaica unmolested.* Slave owners in Jamaica and elsewhere in the West
Indies remained nervous. In November 1798, Henry Wildman wrote to
Beckford of Fonthill: 'I am sorry to inform you St Domingo is totally
evacuated by our Troops . . . I do not like [it]. Black Governors, Black
Generals Etc. are very bad examples to our Plantations.'

But ironically, the 1791 revolt and destruction in Hispaniola and the
resulting collapse of sugar production on the island came to the rescue of
the British planters, albeit only for a short period. Almost overnight there
was a huge rise in the sugar price, as continental buyers previously supplied
by St Domingue looked to London to supply their needs. After 25 hard
years, the old prosperity returned, and the collapse of the old plantation
system in the British islands was delayed for 20 years. 'Tho' we lament
the principal cause of such high prices', wrote the Jamaican assembly to
the King in 1792, 'we declare to your Majesty that only such accidental
and temporary increase in the value of our Staples could have saved this
Island from absolute Bankruptcy'.

Jamaican sugar production, helped by the recent introduction of Bourbon
cane, a new variety more resistant to the ravages of pests, now soared, and

---

* Napoleon would try to re-establish slavery in St Domingue in 1802, but apart from the treacherous capture of Toussaint L'Ouverture, the expedition was a failure, with up to 40,000 French
troops succumbing to yellow fever. Independence, as the new republic of Haiti, was declared in 1804.

once again the island was considered in Britain as 'the principal source of national opulence'. The newly returned confidence of the sugar interest is evidenced in the construction of the West India Dock in London, completed in 1802, when it was the largest dock complex in the world. Its huge storage capacity, some 80,000 hogsheads, enabled sugar importers to control the supply, and therefore sustain high prices for their product.

Jamaica enjoyed something of an 'Indian summer'. Accounts by visitors to the island in the 1790s are as full of wonder at the opulence of the planters as were stories from Barbados in the seventeenth century. It was, read an account from 1793, 'no uncommon thing to find, at the country habitations of the planters, a splendid side-board loaded with plate, and the choicest wines, a table covered with the finest damask, and a dinner of perhaps sixteen or twenty covers'. The new houses of the planters, we are told, 'may vie, in the elegance of design, and excellence of the work-manship, with many of the best country seats in England . . . The mahogany work and ornaments within have been justly admired for their singular beauty, being, as I am informed, selected with great expense.' Huge sums were also spent on alcohol, by freemen of all classes – in Kingston alone there were 270 rum shops in 1787.

'Such eating and drinking I never saw!' wrote Maria Nugent, the wife of the Governor of Jamaica. Born in New Jersey in 1777 to a loyalist family, she had moved to England at the end of the War of Independence and married George Nugent. She arrived in Jamaica in 1801 and kept a detailed diary of everything she came across in her new home. She was amazed at the conspicuous consumption of the planters. 'Such loads of all sorts of high, rich, seasoned things, and really gallons of wine and mixed liquors as they drink!' she exclaimed of one meal, which included claret, Madeira and hock. And this was just breakfast. In short, she concluded, 'it was all as astounding as it was disgusting'.

Nugent gives us a rare glimpse of the lives of the white 'Creole' women in Jamaica, many of whom she found 'clumsy', 'vulgar' and 'awkward'. She mocked their accent: 'saying dis and dat and toder', 'an ignorant drawling out of their words that is very tiresome if not disgusting'. In fact, white women in the West Indies suffered from lack of jobs or access to education, and often crippling isolation on country estates. With slaves performing duties in the home and in the bedroom, there was little for them to do except be decorative. Somerly wrote that the white women of Jamaica 'suffer much, submit to much and lead a life of misery'.

Maria Nugent's diary also traced her constant concern for the health of her children and the chances of them getting off the island alive. Indeed, the West Indies remained deadly. An arresting account from around 1800 tells of the arrival of a shipload of white visitors. As soon as the vessel neared Kingston, 'a canoe, containing three or four black females, came to the side of the ship, for the purpose of selling oranges, and other fruits. When about to depart, they gazed at the passengers, whose number seemed to surprise them; and as soon as the canoe pushed off, one of them sung the following words, while the others joined in the chorus, clapping their hands regularly, while it lasted.

> New-come buckra
> He get sick;
> He tak fever,
> He be die;
> He be die.
> New-come, &c.

The song, as far as we could hear, contained nothing else, and they continued singing it, in the manner just mentioned, as long as they were within hearing.'

Two years after Maria Nugent's arrival in Jamaica, a case came to court that caught the eye of the public in Britain. In September 1781, a ship owned by a Liverpool merchant, the *Zong*, had sailed with a cargo of slaves from Africa for the Caribbean. But the vessel lost its way, water began to grow even scarcer than usual, and an epidemic started on board. Crew and slaves began to die. At this point, the captain, Luke Collingwood, called together his crew and pointed out that if the slaves died naturally, the loss would be to the ship's owners; but if, on some pretext of the safety of the crew, 'they were thrown alive into the sea, it would be the loss of the under-writers'. In spite of the objection of the first mate, a total of 133 slaves were flung overboard. The insurers refused to pay, and the shocking case went to court, thoroughly publicised by Granville Sharp.

The same year, the Quakers delivered a petition against the slave trade to Parliament, and numerous tracts started appearing condemning or defending the activities of the slavers. In 1787, the Society for Effecting the Abolition of the Slave Trade was formed in England. At its core were Quakers, but it also included Anglicans such as Granville Sharp and Thomas Clarkson. Clarkson had won a student prize for an essay he had written while at Cambridge University, published in 1786 as *An Essay on the Slavery and Commerce of the Human Species*. He now became a full-time and paid agent for the new Society, and went to Liverpool to collect evidence.

The campaigners took the tactical decision to go after the trade, rather than the institution of slavery, in the hope that if it ended, the planters would be forced to treat their slaves better and ultimately move towards emancipation. They also recognised that they needed representation in Parliament; in 1787, Clarkson called on William Wilberforce, a wealthy independent MP for Hull and evangelical Christian. He gave Wilberforce a copy of his essay, and became a regular visitor. Clarkson also toured the country, organising petitions, holding public meetings and encouraging the establishment of local chapters of the Society.

With the encouragement of William Pitt the Younger, in May 1789 Wilberforce made his first speech in the House of Commons condemning the slave trade, and in April 1791 he introduced his first Parliamentary Bill to abolish the trade, calling the 'bloody traffic' a 'scandal'. 'Posterity', he said, 'looking back to the history of these enlightened times, will scarce believe that it has been suffered to exist so long a disgrace and dishonour to this country.' But Parliament, alarmed at the radicalism of the French Revolution, defeated the Bill comfortably.

Nonetheless, Thomas Wildman, writing to his brother in Jamaica in May 1791, predicted that 'the Slave Trade will in a few years be abolished, as the party against it will never rest'. He urged the stocking of the Beckford plantations to the maximum while they still could.

In response to the defeat of the Bill, an attempt was made to effect social reform through economic pressure. Every person who consumed West Indian produce was 'guilty of the crime of murder', wrote one pamphleteer. Tea was a 'blood-sweetened beverage'. Furthermore, he went on, West Indian sugar contained the pus from sores on the bodies of blacks suffering from yaws and jiggers. As for rum, in a puncheon of the product from Jamaica ordered lately by a merchant it was said there had been found 'The whole Body of a roasted Negro'. In turn, writers sympathetic to the planters fought their corner. As this debate continued, the import of East Indian sugar increased tenfold as buyers called upon their grocers to supply them with the free-labour product from the Orient. In the United States a similar campaign was waged, which saw a huge increase in the production of sugar from maple.

Wilberforce tried again the following year, supported by more than 500 anti-slave trade or anti-slavery petitions, with the signatures of nearly 400,000 ordinary people as well as those of such parliamentary giants as Charles James Fox and William Pitt. The latter declared: 'no nation has plunged so deeply into this guilt as Great Britain'. A compromise solution – that the trade would be outlawed in four years' time – was passed, but the Bill met defeat in the House of Lords.

Wilberforce introduced further measures during the decade, but public interest was now waning, and the sugar lobby in Parliament still strong enough to keep abolition at bay. On 4 March 1795, Jamaica's agent in London, Stephen Fuller, wrote to the island's council: 'I have the great pleasure to inform you that on Thursday last we mustered up Force enough in the House of Commons to put off Mr Wilberforce's Motion for six months, by a Majority of 17.'

In the United States, individual northern states had started outlawing the importation of slaves from the 1780s onwards (with partial measures enacted even earlier). In 1787, Rhode Island became the first state to ban its citizens from any involvement in the slave trade. Moses Brown, together with the Reverend Samuel Hopkins of Newport, had led the campaign that produced this victory. Hopkins described Newport as the 'town the most guilty, respecting the slave trade, of any on this continent, as it has been, in a great measure, built up by the blood of the poor Africans'. In 1789, Moses Brown organised an abolitionist society in Providence that was instrumental in achieving passage of the federal Slave Trade Act of 1794, prohibiting ships destined to transport slaves to any foreign country from outfitting in American ports. The Abolition Society, wrote an anonymous critic in the *Providence Gazette*, was 'created not to ruin only one good citizen but to ruin many hundreds in the United States . . . these people you have called "Negro Dealers" and "kidnappers" are some of the "very best men" in Rhode Island'. The diatribe was signed 'A Citizen', but it was actually John Brown, Moses's brother. In 1797, John would be prosecuted by Moses's Society having once more fallen for the lure of the 'Guiney' trade. Although he was acquitted, his vessel, the *Hope*, was condemned.

John remained the foremost defender in Rhode Island of the slave trade, while his brother Moses emerged as one of its fiercest opponents. When in 1800 Congress passed an Act to strengthen the law of 1794, John Brown was one of only five House of Representatives members to vote against the bill, and also spoke in opposition to it.

The same year, Moses Brown wrote a letter that sought to explain his brother's behaviour. Long ago, he wrote, referring to the disastrous experience of the *Sally*, John 'Drew his Brothers with him into a Voyage in that Unrighteous Traffic . . . happily they and I may say we Lived to Regret it, and to Labour to have it Relinquished in this State; but my Brother John ... most Unhappily ... has often appeared in Support of a Trade [because of] his Love of Money and Anxiety to acquire it'.

In England, the absentee sugar barons fought a vigorous and expensive rearguard action against the march of abolition. In 1793, Thomas Wildman warned his brother James that Beckford of Fonthill was calling for 'large supplies' from his Jamaica plantations to 'exert himself to support the West India Int. in the next Parliament'. Jack Fuller, elected as a Sussex MP in the early 1800s, rushed to Parliament during an abolition debate, and there made a huge uproar, swore at the Speaker, whom he called 'the insignificant little fellow in the wig', and was publicly reprimanded for the offence. The latest Lascelles, Henry, whose family had called in their debts and were now major landholders in the West Indies, stood against Wilberforce in Hull, and lost, in spite of spending a fortune. Draxes and Codringtons were also represented in the anti-abolition group in Parliament.

After the waning of interest in the 'plight of the Negro' in the late 1790s, in 1803 the publicising of lurid accounts of the torture of blacks in Trinidad – taken over by the British in 1797 – reignited protest. In 1804, Clarkson, after a period of illness, resumed his campaigning work and the Society for Effecting the Abolition of the Slave Trade began meeting again, strengthened by prominent new members such as Zachary Macaulay.

Macaulay, father of the historian, had gone out to Jamaica in 1784, and worked as a bookkeeper. 'I was exposed not only to the sight, but also to the practice of severities over others, the very recollection of which makes my blood run cold', he later wrote. He recalled that at first, he was 'feelingly alive to the miseries of the poor slaves', but that he had resolved to 'get rid of my squeamishness as soon as I could ... And in this I had a success beyond my expectations ... now I was callous and indifferent.' He returned to England in 1794 and, under the influence of his evangelical brother-in-law, converted to abolitionism, contributing to the campaign his first-hand experience of slavery.

In June 1804, a new Bill proposed by Wilberforce to abolish the slave trade successfully passed all its stages through the House of Commons. However, it was too late in the parliamentary session for it to complete its passage through the House of Lords. On its reintroduction during the 1805 session it was defeated. But during the general election of autumn 1806, slavery was an issue, resulting in many more abolitionist MPs being returned.

William, Lord Grenville, the Prime Minister, was determined to introduce an Abolition Bill, but decided to do so in the House of Lords first, where it faced its greatest challenge. When it came to a vote, however, the measure passed by a large margin. A second reading was scheduled for the Commons on 23 February 1807. As tributes were made to Wilberforce, whose face streamed with tears, the Bill was carried by 283 votes to 16. The Slave Trade Act received royal assent on 25 March 1807, and came into force on 1 January 1808.

In the West Indies, the measure did, as had been hoped, lead to sensible planters treating their enslaved workforces better. It also pretty much ended manumission and saw the beginning of mass importation of indentured 'coolie' labour from south-east Asia. Inevitably, the costs of producing sugar rose sharply.

William Beckford of Fonthill had already seen his income from Jamaica dwindle. By 1805 it had fallen from more than £100,000 to somewhere in the region of £30,000. But almost as if it was 'dirty money', he was still spending at a colossal rate. In 1796 he had engaged the country's leading architect, James Wyatt, to build him an abbey at Fonthill to rival the grandeur of nearby Salisbury Cathedral.

Fonthill Abbey was to be vast, with a cruciform shape 312 feet from north to south, the same as Westminster Abbey, and 270 feet west to east, with an enormous tower. Soon 700 men were at work, throwing up a struc-ture the like of which had taken the cathedral builders of the Middle Ages decades to construct. The following year, the first spring gale brought the tower crashing down. But work pressed on. Wyatt told a friend that he reckoned Beckford was spending £120,000 a year, mainly on the abbey. In 1800, the tower collapsed again, Beckford's only regret reportedly being that he was not there to see it happen. By the summer of 1807, although far from finished, parts were ready for habitation, and Beckford moved into the south wing. Access was through huge oak doors, 30 feet high and weighing more than a ton. These would be opened to visitors by Beck-ford's dwarf, dressed in gold and embroidery, his tiny and somewhat grotesque figure accentuating the size of the doors.

The same year, Beckford had his father's Splendens pulled down, in spite of protests from Wyatt and others that it was a classical masterpiece. The elaborate formal gardens were also ripped up, to be replaced with landscaping more to Beckford's Gothic taste.

Fonthill Abbey was, like Jack Fuller's sugar loaf, or the Draxes' tower, a folly, but on a massively grand scale. Inside it was very uncomfortable and impractical. The kitchen was situated a huge distance from the oak parlour where Beckford took his meals. There were 18 bedrooms for the guests who seldom if ever came, only reachable by twisting staircases and corridors, and 13 were so small, poky and ill-ventilated as to be unusable. The whole structure was so cold and damp that 60 fires had to be kept burning, even in the summer.

There was also something irredeemably fake and hollow about the whole thing. If anyone looked closely at the furniture, they could see that many of Beckford's 'James I' coffers were obviously nothing of the kind. The ebony state bed that 'belonged to Henry VII' was seventeenth century; ebony chairs that had 'belonged to Cardinal Wolsey' were made in the East Indies also in the seventeenth century. A cabinet 'designed by Holbein' was clearly built a century after the artist's death. Everywhere there were 'ancestral' Beckford coats of arms – on windows, vault bosses and fabrics. An elaborate family tree had been drawn up – Beckford, it fortuitously emerged, was descended from the royal blood of Scotland, and from King Edward III of England.

By 1812, with most of the originally planned structure complete at huge expense, Beckford ordered a new wing be built, even though the Wildmans were still merrily embezzling the profits of his Jamaica plantations. Then, in 1821, he was forced to sell his Drax Hall and Harborhead estates for £62,000 to partially offset an estimated debt of £125,000 on Fonthill Abbey.

The following year, he suddenly got bored with the whole enterprise, and put Fonthill and much of his collection of art and *objets*, including 20,000 books, up for public auction. This generated huge excitement and curiosity, with 72,000 copies of the contents brochure printed by Christie's sold at a guinea each.

The Times commented in reaction that Beckford's collection marked him as 'one of the very few possessors of great wealth who have honestly tried to spend it poetically'. Essayist William Hazlitt was less complimentary, writing that Fonthill and its contents were 'a desert of magnificence, a glittering waste of laborious idleness, a cathedral turned into a toy shop, an immense museum of all that is most curious and costly and at the same time most worthless . . . the only proof of taste he has shown in the collection is his getting rid of it'.

Two days before the sale was to be held, everything was bought by a private bidder, a gullible nouveau riche East Indies trader with more money than sense. Three years after the sale, the grand tower collapsed once more, for the last time, in a cloud of cheap mortar.

However, the proceeds of the sale, some £330,000, allowed Beckford to

clear his debts – estimated at £145,000 – and to live out the rest of his days
in idleness at a grand house in Bath. He kept his favourite paintings by
Titian, Rembrandt, Bronzino, Holbein and Velasquez, as well as the portrait
of his father by Reynolds and of himself by Romney. His whim in his latter
years was to have the dinner table laid elaborately each day for a number
of guests but to dine in solitary state. He was having problems with his
teeth and his bladder, and was steadily losing his Jamaican properties through
Chancery suits to the Wildmans. When he died in 1844, lonely and eccentric, the unprecedented Beckford fortune built up by his father, grandfather
and great-grandfather, on the back of the labour of thousands of slaves
under the burning Jamaican sky, had all been frittered away.

In the West Indies, there was an almost palpable sense of decline in the
years following the abolition of the slave trade. The sugar price rose briefly
in 1814–15, but by 1822 had fallen by half, as sugar from newly exploited
territories in Cuba, Mauritius and India started flooding the market. A
visitor to Bridgetown at this time described it as 'having an antique appearance . . . what strikes the stranger's attention is the number of old women,
cats, and parrots'. A writer on Jamaica from around the same time noticed
how 'bad times and untoward events' had curbed even the planters' 'natural
tendency to extravagance'.

As the British state, at huge expense, undertook to fight the international slave trade, an organised movement for the 'Mitigation and Gradual
Abolition of Slavery' was inaugurated at the beginning of 1823. Once again,
a vigorous campaign saw Parliament flooded with petitions. In the same
year came a concerted attempt by East India traders, now importing sugar
but not enjoying the favourable duties granted to Caribbean produce, to
break the West Indians' monopoly rights. From the start there was close
cooperation between the two campaigns. The power of the West India
lobby was still strong, but not enough to face both these attacks at the
same time. A new boycott of West Indian products was launched, and the
government ordered a general registration of all slaves on the islands and
drew up rules for their treatment. Both moves were bitterly resisted by
the islands' assemblies, particularly in Jamaica.

The slaves themselves, a number of whom, thanks to the efforts of
Nonconformist ministers on the islands – Moravians, Baptists and
Methodists – could now read the newspapers, viewed these measures as a
prelude to emancipation. When at first their hopes were dashed, a number
decided to follow the example of the slaves of St Domingue. In 1816 there
was a major rebellion in previously peaceful Barbados, followed by an even

more serious disorder in Jamaica in late 1831 that saw the deaths of 1,000 slaves and damage approaching a million pounds.

To blame, most white Jamaicans decided, were the growing number of Nonconformist ministers who had been educating and converting the islands' slaves. Nine Baptist and six Methodist chapels were attacked and destroyed, and Baptist preacher William Knibb and four others were imprisoned. The ministers were later released, but the mob violence did nothing to endear the planters to the authorities at home, already angry at the resistance to their amelioration instructions and concerned that the next slave rebellion might actually succeed. Britain was now turning against its Caribbean colonists.

After intense public agitation against slavery, the election that followed the Great Reform Act in 1832 brought many more MPs into Parliament who were committed to the abolition of slavery. In May 1833, the Whig government introduced the Bill for the Abolition of Slavery. To ensure its passage, several large concessions were made: only those aged under six were to be freed straight away; other slaves would have to work out a period of unpaid 'apprenticeship' – effective slavery – for up to six years. Slave-owners would be compensated for their 'loss', the total sum allocated for this being around £20 million, a vast amount, equivalent to 40 per cent of the government's annual budget. In August, the House of Lords passed the Slavery Abolition Act, which ended slavery in the British Empire, effective from August 1834.

The system of apprenticeship was never workable and collapsed four years later. Thus it was on 1 August 1838 when the 800,000 slaves of the British Empire, the vast majority of whom were in the West Indies, were truly freed.

The Baptist minister William Knibb held a service on the night of 31 July in his church in Falmouth, Jamaica. The walls were hung with branches, flowers, and portraits of Wilberforce and fellow abolitionist Thomas Clarkson. Into a coffin inscribed 'Colonial Slavery, died July 31st, 1838, aged 276', church members placed an iron punishment collar, a whip and chains. 'The hour is at hand!' Knibb called out from his pulpit, pointing to a clock on the wall. 'The monster is dead!' The congregation burst into cheers and embraced each other. 'Never, never did I hear such a sound', Knibb wrote. 'The winds of freedom appeared to have been let loose. The very building shook at the strange yet sacred joy.'

Contrary to the hopes of Adam Smith, abolition failed to provide a willing and able free labour force in the British West Indies. Almost immediately after abolition, the survival rate for black births and the life expectancy of African West Indians shot up, but many black former sugar workers turned their backs on the plantations and toil that would for ever carry the stigma of slavery. Canefields were left untended, and soon became overgrown with weeds. Attempts to replace the workforce with indentured Asians had indifferent success. Costs for the plantation owners rose, and profits dwindled.

But the decline and fall of the planters, and of the 'first British empire', was caused by more than abolition alone. Intermittent but often devastating war had taken a heavy toll on lives and property. Relentless disease and periodic intense natural disasters had made the islands a personal and financial risk no longer worth the returns. To blame, also, was the split with the North American colonies, curtailing a trading relationship of great benefit to both sides – but not London. The agricultural system in the British islands was moribund, and too often in the hands of disinterested managers. Competition from newly exploited tropical territories, such as Java and Madagascar, along with cheaper slave-grown product from Brazil, Dutch Surinam and Cuba, drove the sugar price ever downwards. At the same time, a growing sentiment towards free trade undermined the protectionism on which the wasteful system had long relied. To cap it all, the end of the 1820s saw a burgeoning of the beet sugar industry in Europe. As decay became every day more apparent, so disillusionment and malaise set in among the British planters.

The continued resistance of the enslaved population had also contributed to the collapse of the world of the plantation, but in truth, as a society it had failed long before. Slavery, 'an inferior social and economic organisation of exploiters and exploited', had sacrificed human life and its most precious values to the pursuit of immediate gain. The sugar-and-slave business had encouraged greed, hypocrisy, fear and brutality, corrupting almost everyone it touched.

The sugar money, flashed around in England, had never smelt quite right. Now, for many in Britain, the whole West Indian imperial adventure stank, and was cause for national regret. The poet Robert Southey, brother of a naval officer stationed in tropical American waters early in the nineteenth century, expressed a view widely held in England, describing the colonies as 'perhaps as disgraceful a portion of history as the whole course of time can afford; for I know not that there is anything generous, anything ennobling, anything honorable or consolatory to human nature to relieve it, except what may relate to the missionaries'.

Instead, Britain's imperial focus, the ambitions of her brightest and best, had for a while been turning east. The West India planter, flaunting his wealth, was yesterday's man. The new grandees were the East India nabobs, and on the horizon was a more nuanced form of imperialism, which attempted to combine the sugar empire's greed and exploitation with an urge to 'civilise' – to convert, educate and thus subject in a subtler way than the overt racial slavery, the shameful and shaming imperialism, 'red in tooth and claw', of the Sugar Barons.

Epilogue

THE SINS OF THE FATHERS

'Jamaican history is characteristic of the beastliness of the true Englishman.'
Karl Marx

The first Drax Hall still stands, facing out over the gently sloping fields of St George's parish in Barbados. The house, apart from wear and tear, has suffered only minor modifications and damage, most notably the collapse of part of the top floor in one of the island's many hurricanes. House and estate are still owned by the Drax family, and the extent of the plantation today is almost exactly as it was put together by Sir James by the 1650s.

It remains a sugar plantation, although now its cane is ground and processed at a large factory some distance away; its giant mill, once the largest on the island, stopped operating in 1937. Cane is still planted right up to the edge of the ruined factory, and is looked after and harvested by a black workforce managed by a white overseer. The proprietor, H.W. Drax, comes out to inspect once a year. Sometimes his son and heir, Richard, accompanies him. The overseer, a white Barbadian with an accent almost indistinguishable from his black fellow-countrymen, lives in Drax Hall, but somehow does not inhabit it.

Standing now at Drax Hall, with the Jacobean house looming behind me as I survey the fields of cane, it is impossible not to feel a frisson of excitement, tinged with dread. Here is the exact place where it all began, with James Drax's secret sugar experiment. The impact of the success of that experiment is difficult to overstate. Barbados became the richest place in America, and spread its successful plantation system all over the region. Families rose and fell; wars were fought. Taste and diet in England were revolutionised. Towns and cities as far away as Newport and Bristol thrived as a result. And, of course, for millions of black Africans, there was 'miserabell . . . perpetuall slavery they and Thayer seed', brutal lives and early deaths.

The success of the sugar industry helped shape the modern world. After all, the landscape of Jamaica was dominated by 'dark satanic mills' long before that of England. The far-flung trading system that shifted the sugar and rum to their distant markets and supplied the islands with machinery, raw materials and luxury items, ushered in an era of global commerce, long supply chains, and ruthless exploitation of human and natural resources. The story of resistance to all this – from displaced Caribs, through enslaved Africans and Nonconformist Christian missionaries to sugar baron traders and businessmen seeking autonomy from regulation and control by the centre – is a parallel story that continues as well.

The legacy of the sugar barons for Britain is about more than just the resulting riches, largely invested at home rather than in the islands, or the national 'sweet tooth' that cheaper sugar created. The sugar empire also helped to define the country's role in the world, and what it meant to be 'British'. The power of inherited land faded as the British became the masters of industrial processes and the ruthlessly ambitious leaders of a newly created system of global maritime commerce.

At the same time, there remains something contradictory about the story of Britain's dalliance with plantation slavery. Although England led the Sugar Revolution in the West Indies and became the world's foremost slave-trader, the same country was also ahead of its rivals in the campaign for free trade and, more crucially, for an end to slavery. The celebration of the British abolition movement has been described as praising someone for putting out a fire he himself created. Nonetheless, it did turn out to be, as Richard Jobson had exclaimed in West Africa in 1618, 'unEnglish' to hold other people in slavery, as the ground-breaking triumph of the abolition movement in Britain testifies. In the interim, sensitive Englishmen like Richard Ligon, the third Christopher Codrington and Beckford of Somerly had found themselves painfully conflicted.

Both Henry Drax's heir, Thomas Shetterden-Drax, and Thomas's son Henry married extremely well, with the result that Henry's son, another Thomas, inherited three fortunes on the death of his father in 1755 – Drax, Ernle and Erle, part of which included the huge Charborough estate in Dorset. Twice in the next three generations there was no male heir, but each time the man marrying into the fortune took the name Drax, so it has survived to this day. With each successor, the plantation and Hall in Barbados has passed to a new Drax, though none have lived on the island for any length of time. One of these men, John Drax, previously Sawbridge, became an MP in 1841, as most of his Drax forebears had done. He was known as 'the silent member'; his only speech in the House was to ask if a window could be shut. In the 2010 general election in Britain, Richard Plunkett-Ernle-Erle-Drax, who prefers to be known simply as Richard Drax, became MP for South Dorset.*

Outside academic and local circles, the crucial role of Sir James Drax, the first sugar baron, is little known. His only likeness, the bust commissioned by his adoring son Henry, sits unremarked on a high, dusty shelf in the small, unexceptional City of London church of St Anne and St Agnes, almost opposite the Goldsmiths' livery hall, where Sir James's eldest son was apprenticed.

Christopher Codrington, although dying without legitimate heir, ensured the longevity of his name, as intended, through the bequests in his 'soldier's will' to create a library at All Souls, Oxford, and to build Codrington College.

The college has endured numerous vicissitudes. Codrington's heirs, along with most local planters, fiercely opposed the founding mission to educate and convert Barbadian black slaves. Clergy sent out from Britain to lead the project died at a furious rate. One who lasted longer than most was Thomas Wilkie, who reported in 1727 that he had taught five or six Negro youngsters to 'spel very prettily and repeat the Creed and Lords prayer'. He had three adults under regular instruction, and two of these he had persuaded to attend the Sunday church services. The three slaves had agreed to take 'one wife apiece, forbare working on Sundays . . . and live conformably to the laws of the Gospel to the best of their knowledge'. But Wilkie died insane six years later, and when the main building was finally opened in 1745, the priority was the education of white boys, and instruction of the blacks fell away for a time. For one thing, even the slave children were too busy working what was still an extensive functioning plantation.

In the mid-eighteenth century, the Society for the Propagation of the Gospel Overseas lost a fortune through business dealings with the spectacular bankrupt Gedney Clarke, and in 1780 the college buildings were wrecked by the hurricane. Nonetheless, by the turn of the century, the Society's slaves were the best treated on the island, and about a third were converts, helping to establish the enslaved blacks' rights to participation

* Bond villain Sir Hugo Drax was named after Ian Fleming's friend Admiral Sir Reginald Drax, Richard Drax's grandfather. As well as a distinguished Navy man, he was a pioneer of solar power, using it to heat his pool, but he failed to get the idea to catch on.

in Church society. In 1812, apart from one religious institution in Trinidad, Codrington College was the solitary school for blacks in the entire British West Indies.

The descendants of the strange and troubled Christophers, who were absentee landlords based at Dodington in Gloucestershire and MPs for the area, prospered for a while, as the family continued to expand its sugar and slave business through the eighteenth century. At the beginning of the nineteenth century, a grand Palladian mansion was completed at Dodington, designed by James Wyatt. The Codringtons still owned substantial Caribbean acreage in the mid-nineteenth century, but the business suffered alongside all other British West Indian sugar establishments. The last Codrington plantations were sold off in 1944.

By the 1970s, upkeep of the huge grey-stone pile of Dodington Hall required it to be opened to the public, with a children's adventure playground, a narrow-gauge railway and a carriage museum to draw in paying visitors. In 1978, a huge sale of family treasures raised a substantial and much-needed sum. Shortly afterwards, the archive of family papers, held in trust for a long time by the local county records office, was sold for over £100,000. Nonetheless, by 1982, Sir Simon Codrington reported that he and his wife were living in a kitchen and one bedroom with only an electric fire for heating. Planning permission to build a 'pleasure park' in the grounds was refused, and the following year Dodington was put on the market, ending more than 400 years of family occupancy. It was eventually purchased in 2003 for a reputed £20 million by British vacuum cleaner tycoon Sir James Dyson.

In contrast, of the British Beckfords there seems at first to be little modern trace, either in people or in buildings. Although his daughters married well, the main Beckford male line ended with William of Fonthill. There are a number of towns and streets in Jamaica named after the family, but travel to Somerly's old plantations in Westmoreland and all that is left is a scattering of ruins, and stones lying half buried by the vibrant vegetation. One has carved on it the Beckford family symbol of a heron; nearby lies a large iron wheel stamped with 'Sheffield'. Although sugar is still grown down on the Westmoreland plain, at Hertford Pen, as at the nearby site of Thistlewood's enterprise, the jungle and bush have largely reclaimed the land.

The National Portrait Gallery holds a number of paintings of Beckfords, but only one is on display. The subject is Henry Beckford, who appears in the foreground of a depiction of the London anti-slavery convention of 1840; at the centre of the picture, Thomas Clarkson is in full oratorical flow. But this Beckford is black, a freed slave and Jamaican delegate to the conference.

In Westmoreland, on the land that once belonged to William of Somerly, there are, indeed, a host of Beckfords. One elderly black gentleman of the name claims, gesticulating vividly, to have had 27 children. In fact the Beckford name is alive and well – among clergy, academics, sports and media stars. It is now indisputably a black Jamaican name.*

The West Indian islands have never recovered their pre-eminent global importance, achieved in an astonishingly counter-intuitive moment of world history. As early as the 1830s, their value as markets for British manufactures had started to decline. In 1846, the same year as the repeal of the protectionist Corn Laws, the prohibitive duties on imports to Britain of cheaper foreign sugars started to be lifted. Protection for the West India interest was an outdated priority. Less clear was how the massively over-populated islands were to survive.

On the majority of the British islands, sugar production slumped. From a high in 1805 of 100,000 tons, for most of the rest of the nineteenth century Jamaica only exported 20,000 tons of sugar annually, falling to a nadir of 5,000 tons in 1913. In the 60 years after 1850, the number of sugar plantations on the island shrank from over 500 to just 77. Sugar consumption in England continued to grow, allowing refiners like Sir Henry Tate to make fortunes, but little of the money was returned to Jamaica, and even less to the black workforce. Frantic belated attempts were made after 1900 to diversify the island's economy away from sugar monoculture.

Barbados stuck with sugar. When, in 1902, the price fell sharply yet again, widespread malnutrition appeared on the island, with an infant mortality rate reaching nearly half of live births in some places. When this was reported in London, Joseph Chamberlain, British Secretary of State for the Colonies, labelled the West Indian islands, formerly so prosperous, as the 'Empire's darkest slum'. An American journalist who visited Barbados at this time wrote, 'The island has always been and still is run for the whites . . . it is a heavenly place to live for the white man who can ignore the frightful misery of the negroes.'

Barbadians have improved their lot by emigration and a fierce attachment to education. The island is now relatively prosperous, although, as elsewhere in the region, many assets are in the hands of foreign interests or the tiny white minority. Other parts of what was the sugar empire are in a less happy situation. In general, throughout the smaller islands, the

* There are pages and pages of Beckfords in the Jamaican phone book, as there are of Codringtons all over what was the British West Indies. In contrast, there is only a single Drax in the Barbados phone book, a Greta Drax, who lives in Bowling Alley, St Joseph.

dominance of sugar has been replaced in modern times by a reliance on the shifting sands of tourism and offshore banking. The latter has attracted unsavoury characters and 'beyond the line' financial shenanigans, including fraud and money-laundering linked to mainland drugs cartels. Tourism, for its part, has, for some, awkward resonances with the region's history. In the large plantation-house-style hotels, the tourists are almost all white, the waiters, the cleaners the gardeners, the servants are all black.

The legacy of the sugar barons is most vividly shown in Jamaica, which was perhaps the most violently brutal of the British slave colonies. Jamaica has much to be proud of: it has world-beating sportsmen and women, and is probably the most influential place on earth in terms of modern music. But it has barely half the per capita GDP of Barbados and twice the infant mortality rate. Sadly, corruption and crime are endemic, and the island has a staggeringly high murder rate that demonstrates scant regard for life and respect over riches and status. If you venture away from the cool of the beach and the safety of the closely guarded tourist resorts, Jamaica seems chaotic, damaged, angry; still, as in the days of Ned Ward, 'Hot as Hell, and as wicked as the Devil'.

SOURCE NOTES

Abbreviations

B. Arch.	Barbados Archives, Black Rock, Bridgetown, Barbados
BL	British Library, London
Cal Col	*Calendar of State Papers, Colonial Series, America and the West Indies*
J. Arch.	Jamaica Archives, Spanish Town, Jamaica
JBMHS	*Journal of the Barbados Museum and Historical Society*
JCBL	John Carter Brown Library, Providence, Rhode Island
Journal	*Journal of the Commissioners for Trade and Plantations*
LNHA	Redwood papers, Library of the Newport Historical Association, Newport, Rhode Island
MSS Beckford	Beckford papers in the Bodleian Library, Oxford (MS Eng lett.)
PRO	Public Record Office, Kew, London
TD	Thomas Thistlewood's Diary, Lincolnshire County Archives, Monson 31/1-37. Used with permission of Lincolnshire County Archives

Introduction 'Hot as Hell, and as wicked as the Devil'

p. 1   It was January 1697: for clarity's sake, for all dates before 1752, the year is taken to start on 1 January.

p. 1   'with one Design, to patch up their Decay'd Fortune' and following quotes: Ward, *A Trip to Jamaica*.

1. White Gold, 1642

p. 9   'The great industry and more thriving genius of Sir James Drax'. Scott, 'Description of Barbados', 249.

p. 9   far from prying eyes, he planted a new crop: Southey, *History of the West Indies*, I:285, says, with no source given, that the first cane was planted in 1642 and the 'method remained a secret to the inhabitants in general for seven or eight years', an exaggeration.

p. 9   'ingenious spirit': Foster, *A Briefe relation of the late Horrid Rebellion*, 2.

p. 10   the canes . . . had rooted in seven days: Deerr, *History of Sugar*, 1:117.

p. 11   A French visitor at the beginning of the seventeenth century: ibid., 1:105.

p. 12   as the language of the sugar factory – *ingenio, muscovado* – demonstrates: Bridenbaughs, *No Peace Beyond the Line*, 89.

p. 12   'being eternall Prolers about': Thomas, *An Historical Account*, 36.

p. 13   '. . . Discovery of the Art he had to make it': ibid., 13–14.

p. 13   'Sir James Drax engaged in that great work': Scott, 'Description of Barbados', 249.

p. 13   'the disbersing of vast summes of money': Foster, *Briefe relation of the late Horrid Rebellion*, 2.

p. 13   'the Model of a Sugar Mill': Anon., *Some Memoirs of the first Settlement*, 3.

p. 13   'and by new directions from Brazil': Ligon, *A True and Exact History*, 84–5.

p. 13   £5 per hundredweight: Sheridan, *Sugar and Slavery*, 397.

2. The First Settlements, 1605–41

p. 15   'goodness of the island': quoted in Gragg, *Englishmen Transplanted*, 29.

p. 15   carrying some fifty settlers: Davis, 'Early History of Barbados', *Timehri* 5, 51.

p. 15   'a great ridge of white sand': Colt, 'Voyage of Sir Henry Colt', 64.

p. 15   On board the *William and John*: Handler, 'Father Antoine Biet's Visit', 69.

p. 15   Drax was 18 years old: MacMurray, *Records of Two City Parishes*, 315–16.

p. 15   'in a cave in the rocks': Handler, 'Father Antoine Biet's Visit', 69.

p. 16   'growne over with trees and undershrubs, without passage': White, 'A Briefe Relation', 37.

p. 16   rusted instantly in the warm damp climate: Ligon, *A True and Exact History*, 27.

p. 16   'as hard to cut as stone': Smith, *True Travels*, 55.

p. 16   'dayly showres of raine, windes, & cloudy sultry heat': Colt, 'Voyage of Sir Henry Colt', 65–7.

p. 16   'there is such a moisture': Ligon, *A True and Exact History*, 27.

p. 17   with £50 sterling in axes, bills, hoes, knives, looking-glasses and beads: Harlow, *Colonising Expeditions to the West Indies*, 115.

p. 17   'but not in any great plentie as yet': White, 'A Briefe Relation', 35.

p. 17   'grew so well that they produced an abundance': Handler, 'Father Antoine Biet's Visit', 69.

p. 17   'very ill conditioned, fowle, full of stalkes and evil coloured': Forbes, *Winthrop Papers*, 1:338.

p. 17   'much misery they have endured': Smith, *True Travels*, 55.

p. 18   in 1600 they landed on the tiny island of St Eustatius near St Kitts: Williams, *Columbus to Castro*, 79.

p. 19   'cockpit of Europe, the arena of Europe's wars, hot and cold': ibid., 69.

p. 19   'a country that hath yet her Maidenhead': quoted in Strachan, *Paradise and the Plantation*, 30.

p. 19   between £100,000 and £200,000 each year in gold, silver, pearls and sugar: Appleby, 'English Settlement', 88.

p. 22   'great tobaccoe house that stood to the windward': Harlow, *Colonising Expeditions*, 7.

p. 23   the Courteens, who had by now sunk £10,000 into their venture: Innes, 'Pre-sugar Era of European Settlement', 5.

p. 23   on the pretence of holding a conference: Davis, 'Early History of Barbados', *Timehri* 6, 344.

p. 23   'I cannot from so many variable relations give you an certainty for their orderly Government': Smith, *True Travels*, 56.

p. 24   promptly executed by firing squad. Davis, 'Early History of Barbados', *Timehri* 6, 347.

p. 24   'vntell we haue doone some thinges worthy of ourselues, or dye in yc attempt': Colt, 'Voyage of Sir Henry Colt', 91.

p. 24   'I neuer saw any man at work . . . all thinges carryinge ye face of a desolate & disorderly shew to ye beholder': ibid., 66–7.

p. 24   'a people of too subtle, bloody and dangerous inclination to be and remain here': *Cal Col* 1675–6, no. 946.

p. 25   'an Aromaticall compound of wine and strawberries': White, 'Briefe Relation', 36.

p. 25   'marvellous swiftness': Colt, 'Voyage of Sir Henry Colt', 67.

p. 25   'Slowth & negligence . . . liue long in quiett': ibid., 66, 73.

p. 25   the 40 or so men he left behind were 'servants': Harlow, *Colonising Expeditions*, 37.

p. 25   two or three servants to be sent out, bound to him for three to five years: Innes, 'Pre-sugar Era of European Settlement', 17.

p. 25   Some 30,000 indentured servants: Beckles, '"Hub of Empire"', 223.

p. 26   A visitor to Barbados in 1632: Captain John Fincham, in Campbell, *Some Early Barbadian History*, 65.

p. 27   a battered chest, a broken kettle, three books and a handful of pewter plates: Dunn, *Sugar and Slaves*, 54.

p. 27   from under 2,000 in 1630 to 6,000 by 1636: Chandler, 'Expansion of Barbados', 109.

p. 27   a density of population unrivalled anywhere in the Americas: Menard, *Sweet Negotiations*, 25.

p. 27   Seventy per cent were aged between 15 and 24: Games, 'Opportunity and Mobility in early Barbados', 171.

p. 27   incest, sodomy and bestiality prevalent on the island: Handler, 'Father Antoine Biet's Visit', 68.

p. 28   Much of the land was then sold on to William Hilliard: Beckles, 'Land Distribution and Class Formation', 138.

p. 28   'what would the Governor do for a Council?': Davis, 'Early History of Barbados', *Timehri* 6, 345–6.

p. 28   'granarie of all the Charybbies Iles': White, 'Briefe Relation', 34.

p. 29   'to buy drink all though they goe naked': quoted in Gragg, *Englishmen Transplanted*, 7.

p. 29   'Rhenish wine': Ligon, *A True and Exact History*, 31.

p. 29   bitten off by landcrabs as they lay passed out: Thomas Verney, quoted in Campbell, *Some Early Barbadian History*, 65.

p. 29   '. . . by their excessive drinking': Gragg, *Englishmen Transplanted*, 24.

p. 29   the value of the crop had surpassed tobacco by the late 1630s: Appleby, 'English Settlement in the Lesser Antilles', 95.

p. 30   He had 22 on one of his estates in 1641: Beckles, 'Economic Origins of Black Slavery', 41.

p. 30   'in a very low . . . very much indebted both to the Merchants and also to one another': Foster, *Briefe relation of the late Horrid Rebellion*, 1–2.

p. 31   'The Hollanders that are great encouragers of our Plantacions: Scott, 'Description of Barbados', 249.

3. The Sugar Revolution: 'So Noble an Undertaking'

p. 32   'if you go to Barbados you shal see': Forbes, *Winthrop Papers*, 5:43.

p. 32   the grants had been smaller, in the region of 50 to 80 acres: Games, 'Opportunity and Mobility in Early Barbados', 169.

p. 33   'up and down the Gullies', 'for the ways are such, as no Carts can pass': Ligon, *A True and Exact History*, 39.

p. 33   where the sugar commanded consistently high prices. Deerr, *History of Sugar*, 2:530.

p. 33   'as wheels in a Clock': Ligon, *A True and Exact History*, 56.

p. 34   'men of great abilities, and parts': ibid., 55.

p. 34   34 of the 254 slaves on the *Mary Bonaventure*: B. Arch. RB3/1, 436–9.

p. 34   'so much Suger or other merchantable commodities as shall amount to £726 sterling': Bridenbaughs, *No Peace Beyond the Line*, 78.

p. 35   'some have made this yeare off one acre off canes about 4000 weight of sugar, ordinarily 3000': James Parker to John Winthrop, 24 April 1646: Forbes, *Winthrop Papers*, 5:83.

p. 35   land that sold at 10s. an acre in 1640 sold at £5 in 1646, a tenfold increase: Dunn, *Sugar and Slaves*, 66.

p. 35   and more for the best situated: Beckles, *White Servitude and Black Slavery*, 156.

p. 35   'soe infinite is the proffit of sugar': Forbes, *Winthrop Papers*, 5:172.

p. 36   'set us on to work to provide shipping of our own': Hosmer, *Winthrop's Journal*, 2:23–4.

p. 36   'and were much feared to be lost': ibid., 2:73–4.

p. 36   but only after several deaths and massive damage to the ship and its cargo: ibid., 2:227.

p. 36   An ox that cost £5 in Virginia could be sold for £25 in Barbados: Ligon, *A True and Exact History*, 113.

p. 36   'necessary Hay and corn for voyage to Barbados, and Guinney': Bridenbaugh, *Fat Mutton*, 5.

p. 37   'where in all probability I can live better than in other places': Forbes, *Winthrop Papers*, 5:254,163.

p. 37   'New England friends' already operating there who might be able to give him an opening: Gragg, 'New England Migration to Barbados', 163.

p. 38   'How oft have I thought in my hearte, oh howe happie are New England people!': Forbes, *Winthrop Papers*, 5:84.

p. 38   'one of the most beautiful women ever seen': Handler, 'Father Antoine Biet's Visit', 62.

p. 39   'showed activity and forwardness to expedite the treaty for the surrender': quoted in Campbell, *Some Early Barbadian History*, 134.

p. 39   'men, victuals and all utensils fitted for a Plantation': Ligon, *A True and Exact History*, 21.

p. 40   'a stranger in my own Countrey', and, 'stript and rifled of all I had', was resolved to 'famish or fly': ibid., 1.

p. 40   'miscarry in the Voyage': ibid., 22.

p. 40   'age and gravity': ibid., 17.

p. 40   'afforded us a large proportion of delight': ibid., 21.

p. 40   'faithful obedience': ibid., 20–1.

p. 41   'if you had ever seen her, you could not but have fallen in love with her': ibid., 75.

p. 41   '45 Cattle for work, 8 Milch Cows, a dozen Horses and Mares, 16 Assinigoes [asses]': ibid., 22.

p. 42   'scorching'; 'sweaty and clammy'; 'a great failing in the vigour, and sprightliness we have in colder Climates.'; 'a pack of small beagles at a distance.'; 'of excellent shape and colour' 'like a Prince'; 'best Virginia Botargo'; 'the Nector which the Gods drunk': ibid., 9, 107, 27, 65, 34, 37, 33.

p. 42   'all the supplies to me at the best hand, and I returning him the sugars, and we both thrived on it': William Helyar, 10 July 1677, quoted in Dunn, *Sugar and Slaves*, 81.

p. 43   'many rubs and obstacles on the way': Ligon, *A True and Exact History*, 117.

p. 43   so noble an undertaking . . . Giants'; Modyford as able as any man he had ever known; 'civility'; 'fixt upon' profits; 'his friends welcom to it': ibid., 108, 57, 23, 107, 35.

4. The Sugar Revolution: 'Most inhuman and barbarous persons'

p. 44   'The conditions . . . were that the convicts should be carried beyond sea . . .' Lord Macaulay, *History of England*, 1:649–50.

p. 44   'hardly able to bury the dead': Ligon, *A True and Exact History*, 21.

p. 45   'and dyed in few hours after': ibid., 25.

p. 45   hardly any of the first pioneers had survived: ibid., 23.

p. 45   'ill dyet', and 'drinking strong waters': ibid., 21.

p. 45   'were suddenly laid in the dust': Richard Vines to John Winthrop, 29 April 1648: Forbes, *Winthrop Papers*, 5:219–20.

p. 45   'the plague' was 'still hott at Barbados': John Winthrop to his son John Jr, received 9 November 1648: Forbes, *Winthrop Papers*, 5:267.

p. 46   'a general scarcity of Victuals through the whole Island': Ligon, *A True and Exact History*, 21.

p. 46   something like a third of all whites died within three years of arriving in the Caribbean: Burnard, 'Not a Place for Whites?', 80.

p. 46   a third of marriages left surviving children: Burnard, 'A Failed Settler Society', 69.

p. 46   'wormed out of their small settlements': *Cal Col* 1661–8, no. 1657.

p. 46   'are now risen to very great and vast estates': Ligon, *A True and Exact History*, 43.

p. 46   probably a servant in Barbados by 1650: Bridenbaughs, *No Peace Beyond the Line*, 110.

p. 47   by the time of his death in 1679 owned 19 slaves: Campbell, *Some Early Barbadian History*, 93.

p. 47   By the time of his death in 1736 he owned 10 plantations: Hughes, 'Samuel Osborne 1674–1736', 158.

p. 47   'the land is now so taken up': declaration of Francis, Lord Willoughby, who in 1647 had leased the 'Caribee' islands from the Earl of Carlisle. Quoted in Bridenbaughs, *No Peace Beyond the Line*, 25.

p. 47   'fewell of daungerous insurrections', 'lewed and lasy felowes': Smith, *Colonists in Bondage*, 138.

p. 48   'cryinge and mourninge for Redemption from their Slavery': Harlow, *A History of Barbados*, 300.

p. 48   at least 8,000 Englishmen joining the sugar estates of Barbados between 1645 and 1650. Beckles, 'The "Hub of Empire"', 238.

p. 48   'the husband in one place, the wife in another': Handler, 'Father Antoine Biet's Visit', 66.

p. 48   'When they submitted, . . . the rest shipped for Barbados': Harlow, *A History of Barbados*, 294–5.

p. 48   'felons condemned to death, sturdy beggars, gipsics and other incorrigible rogues, poor and idle debauched persons': *Cal Col* 1661–8, no. 791.

p. 48   'in order that by their breeding they should replenish the white population': Sheridan, *Sugar and Slavery*, 237.

p. 48   'the Dunghill wharone England doth cast forth its rubidg': Whistler, *Journal of the West India Expedition*, 146 (9 February 1655).

p. 49   'the generality of them to most inhuman and barbarous persons': Beckles, 'English Parliamentary Debate on "White Slavery" in Barbados', 345–6.

p. 49   'As for the usage of the Servants': Ligon, *A True and Exact History*, 44.

p. 49   'diligent and painful labour'. ibid., 45.

p. 49   'extremely hated for his cruelties and oppression': Firth, *Narrative of General Venables*, xxx.

p. 49   'keeps them in such order, as there are no mutinies amongst them': Ligon, *A True and Exact History*, 55.

p. 49   'Truly, I have seen such cruelty done to servants, as I did not think one Christian could have done to another': ibid., 44.

p. 50   'had so much depress'd their spirits, as they were come to a declining and yielding condition': ibid., 41.

p. 50   like 'galley slaves': Handler, 'Father Antoine Biet's Visit', 66.

p. 50   'the use of severall joynt's'. Gragg, *Englishmen Transplanted*, 129.

5. The Plantation: Masters and Slaves

p. 52   'Slavery . . . is a weed' *Works of the Right Hon. Edmund Burke* (1841 ed.) 1:203.

p. 52   'and in short time [to] be able with good husbandry to procure Negroes': Forbes, *Winthrop Papers*, 5:43.

p. 52   'They were another kinde of people different from us': Donnan, *Documents Illustrative of the History of the Slave Trade*, 1:79.

p. 53   Soon the characteristics . . . were being applied to black Africans: Davis, *Inhuman Bondage*, 55, 62.

p. 53   the 'piteous company' of slaves: Thomas, *Slave Trade*, 21.

p. 54   and included wealthy Africans among its financial backers. Davis, *Inhuman Bondage*, 84.

p. 55   'unless one happened to be hanged, none died': Deerr, *History of Sugar*, 1:117–18.

p. 55   an African was considered worth four of the sickly Indians. Williams, *Capitalism and Slavery*, 9.

p. 55   only 1,000 whites and some 7,000 'maroons', as runaway slaves were known. ibid., 67.

p. 55   'Most Spaniards think that it is only a matter of years before this island is taken over entirely by the blacks': Deerr, *History of Sugar*, 2: 318.

p. 55   In the 15 years after 1576, as many as 50,000 were imported. Thomas, *Slave Trade*, 134.

p. 56   A number of Dominican and Jesuit friars who had seen the slave trade in action denounced it as a deadly sin. ibid., 146–7.

p. 56   'it would be detestable and call down the vengeance of Heaven upon the undertaking: Deerr, *History of Sugar*, 2:268.

p. 57   'miserabell Negros borne to perpetuall slavery they and Thayer seed': Whistler, *Journal of the West India Expedition*, 146 (9 February 1655).

p. 57   the black man was the better worker; some said he did the labour of three whites: *Cal Col* 1675–6, no. 1022.

p. 57   '(with gods blessing) as much as they cost': Forbes, *Winthrop Papers*, 5:43.

p. 59   assembled naked to be assessed by potential purchasers: Ligon, *A True and Exact History*, 46–7.

p. 59 'some mean men sell their Servants, their Children, and sometimes their Wives': ibid., 46.

p. 59 'notorious accidents': ibid., 52.

p. 59 'their own Countrey . . . hanged themselves': ibid., 51.

p. 61 the Christian Scheme of enlarging the Flock cannot well be carried on without it': Atkins, *A Voyage to Guinea*, 156.

p. 61 the Negroes were 'a happy people, whom so little contents' would become a stereotype of blacks in America. Amussen, *Caribbean Exchanges*, 62.

p. 62 'worser lives': Ligon, *A True and Exact History*, 43.

p. 62 the white servants feasted on the meat; the blacks ended up with the head, entrails and skin: ibid., 39.

p. 62 'though its true the rich live high': James Parker to John Winthrop, 24 April 1646: Forbes, *Winthrop Papers* 5:84.

p. 62 'season'd with sweet Herbs finely minc'd': Ligon, *A True and Exact History*, 38.

p. 63 'and all by this plant of Sugar': ibid., 96.

p. 63 James bought out his brother William's part of the plantation for 'five thousand pounds sterling': Lucas MS, *JBMHS* 23, 75.

p. 63 'skilful' and 'nimble': Ligon, *A True and Exact History*, 52.

p. 64 By 1650, the tiny island of Barbados: Chandler, 'Expansion of Barbados', 106.

p. 64 'flourisheth so much, that it hath more people and Commerce then all the Ilands of the Indies': Gardyner, *A Description of the New World*, 77.

p. 64 100 ships a year called at Bridgetown, the majority of them Dutch: Foster, *A Briefe relation of the late Horrid Rebellion*, 3.

p. 64 four years later, that number had doubled: Handler, 'Father Antoine Biet's Visit', 66.

p. 65 'one of the richest spots of earth under the sun': Ligon, *A True and Exact History*, 86.

p. 65 Barbados exports had reached the amazing sum of £3,097,800: Bridenbaughs, *No Peace Beyond the Line*, 81.

p. 65 friendly, hospitable attitude between the rich white planters: Handler, 'Father Antoine Biet's Visit', 62; Gunkel and Handler, 'A Swiss Medical Doctor's description of Barbados', 6.

p. 65 'many hundreds Rebell Negro Slaves in the woods': Beauchamp Plantanget, letter to Lord Edmund and others, December 1648, quoted in Harlow, *A History of Barbados*, 325.

p. 65 'to throw down upon the naked bodies of the Negroes, scalding hot': Ligon, *A True and Exact History*, 29.

p. 65 'commit some horrid massacre upon the Christians, thereby to enfranchise themselves, and become Masters of the Island': ibid., 46.

p. 66 'gripings and tortions in the bowels': ibid., 117–18.

p. 66 'that had for many dayes layn hovering about the Island': ibid., 119.

p. 66 'We have seen and suffered great things': ibid., 122.

6. The English Civil War in Barbados

p. 67   Sir Robert Schomburgk, *History of Barbados*, v.

p. 67   to provide a roast turkey dinner for everyone in hearing. Ligon, *A True and Exact History*, 57.

p. 67   'without the friendshipe of the perliment and free trade of London ships we are not able to subsist': Bell to Hay, 21 July 1645: Bridenbaughs, *No Peace Beyond the Line*, 158.

p. 68   through the cultivation of his influential wife. 'A. B.', *A Brief relation*, 2.

p. 68   'heart-burnings' 'towards those that wished the Parliament prosperity': ibid., 3.

p. 68   'by the malice and false suggestion of Sir James Drax and others': Harlow, *History of Barbados*, 47.

p. 68   'malignant': *Cal Col* 1574–1660, p. 384.

p. 68   Bermuda, which had declared for the King in late August 1649: Pestana, *English Atlantic in an Age of Revolution*, 91.

p. 68   'quietest and most peaceable wayes of sending these malignants into Exile': 'A. B.', *A Brief relation*, 3.

p. 68   better to kill than to exile the 'Independent' Roundheads, to prevent them stirring up trouble in England: Davis, *Cavaliers and Roundheads of Barbados*, 173n.

p. 69   'the worse for Liquour': ibid., 144.

p. 69   'Colonel Drax, that devout Zealot of the deeds of the Devill': Foster, *A Briefe relation of the late Horrid Rebellion*, 24.

p. 69   'sheathed my sword in [Drax's] Bowells', 'My ayme is Drax, Middleton and the rest': Davis, *Cavaliers and Roundheads of Barbados*, 148.

p. 69   'the Independent doggs' who refused to 'drink to the Figure II': Harlow, *History of Barbados*, 52.

p. 69   'That no man should take up Armes, nor act in any hostile manner upon paine of death': Foster, *A Briefe relation of the late Horrid Rebellion*, 37.

p. 70   had his 'tongue . . . bored through with a hot iron': Schomburgk, *History of Barbados*, 271.

p. 70   'vast quantities of Flesh and Fish': Davis, *Cavaliers and Roundheads of Barbados*, 169fn.

p. 70   Drax had corresponded from Barbados: BL Stowe MSS 184, fols. 124–7.

p. 70   'notorious robbers and traitors' . . . ordering a trade embargo: Bliss, *Revolution and Empire*, 61.

p. 71   'All Ships of Any Foreign Nation whatsoever': Sheridan, *Sugar and Slavery*, 39.

p. 71   'it shall cost them more than it is worth before they have it': Schomburgk, *History of Barbados*, 274.

p. 71   'In truth this would be a slavery far exceeding all that the English nation hath yet suffered': ibid., 706.

p. 71   Drax's cargo consisted of a valuable consignment of horses: *Cal Col* 1574–1660, p. 345.

p. 71   seven warships carrying 238 guns and somewhere near 1,000 men: Clarke, 'Imperial Forces in Barbados', 174.

p. 71   Roundhead refugees had reported that conquest of the island would be easy: Davis, *Cavaliers and Roundheads of Barbados*, 173.

p. 72   'so great was the repulse which they received, that they was inforced to make good their Retreat': Anon., *Bloudy Newes*, 8.

p. 72   to 'manfully fight' 'with our utmost power' for 'ye defence of this Island': Harlow, *History of Barbados*, 72.

p. 72   Drax himself was sent ashore to contact Thomas Modyford: 'A. B.', *A Brief relation*, 9.

p. 72   'want of necessary refreshment brought our men into ye scurvye': Bodleian, Oxford, Tanner MSS 55, fol. 141.

p. 73   'ye Seamen runninge in upon ye Enemye': ibid., fols. 141–2b.

p. 74   'the soldiers could scarce keep a match lighted': *Cal Col* 1574–1660, p. 375.

p. 74   'seeing that the fire is now dispersed in the bowels of the island': Willoughby to Ayscue, 9 January 1652, ibid., p. 372.

p. 74   'as great freedom of trade as ever': *Cal Col* 1675–6, 1574–1674, Addenda no. 199.

7. The Plantation: Life and Death

p. 77   '. . . since the Climate is so hot, and the labour so constant.' Tyron, *Friendly Advice*, 201–2.

p. 77   Drax Hall, built, it seems, some time in the early 1650s: a piece of copper guttering has the date 1653, although it is possible this is from an earlier structure.

p. 77   'unsatisfied spirits': Gragg, *Englishmen Transplanted*, 53.

p. 77   'more violent': *Cal Col* 1574–1660, p. 410.

p. 77   Drax and Modyford were organising petitions to Cromwell: ibid., p. 413.

p. 77   Drax sold to fellow Barbadians Robert Hooper and Martin Bentley 'one-eighth part of the Ship *Samuel* and one-eight part of Pinnace *Hope*': Brandow, *Genealogies of Barbados Families*, 339.

p. 78   James, aged about 15, Henry, about 12, and John, 11: Oliver, *History of the Island of Antigua*, 1:149.

p. 78   William (in London since at least June 1653): *Cal Col* 1574–1660, p. 451.

p. 78   A loan of £1,000 to two of Margaret's brothers: Drax will, PRO PROB/11/307.

p. 78   Margaret gave birth to a stillborn child, Bamfield, before the end of the year: MacMurray, *Records of Two City Parishes*, 332.

p. 78   James Drax started buying up land in various parts of England: PRO E/134/33Chas2/East2.

p. 78   '[On] the day of his departure': Handler, 'Father Antoine Biet's Visit', 69.

p. 79   'far better here . . . than ours do in England': Whistler, *Journal of the West India Expedition*, 145–6 (9 February 1655).

p. 79   'ladies and young women as well dressed as in Europe': Handler, 'Father Antoine Biet's Visit', 67–8.

p. 79   'many men loaded, and almost half melting': Hillary, *Observations on the Changes of the Air*, ix–x.

p. 80   'The wealth of the island consists of sugar': Handler, 'Father Antoine Biet's Visit', 66.

p. 80   By the early 1650s, England was importing 5,000 tons of Barbadian sugar annually: Menard, 'Plantation Empire', 310.

p. 80   The price of sugar in 1652 was less than half that of 1646, and it would continue to drop: Menard, *Sweet Negotiations*, 69.

p. 80   some 20,000, by 1655: ibid., 31–2.

p. 80   'like villages . . . ordinarily handsome [with] many rooms': Handler, 'Father Antoine Biet's Visit', 65.

p. 80   'very inferior wood, look[ing] almost like dog-houses': Gunkel and Handler, 'A German Indentured Servant', 92.

p. 81   'his whole body is drawn in, and he is squeez'd to pieces': Littleton, *Groans of the Plantations*, 19.

p. 81   ''tis hard to save either Limb or Life': ibid., 20.

p. 82   consumption rose as much as fourfold in the 40 years after 1640: Sheridan, *Sugar and Slavery*, 21.

p. 82   'a hott hellish and terrible liquor': 'A Briefe Discription of the ilande of Barbados', reprinted in Hutson, *English Civil War in Barbados*, 67.

p. 82   'infinitely strong, but not very pleasant to taste': Ligon, *A True and Exact History*, 33.

p. 82   the 'meaner sort': Colonel Robert Rich, quoted in Ogilby, *America*, 380.

p. 83   'wondered more that they were not all dead': quoted in Cundall, *Historic Jamaica*, 51.

p. 83   'the impoverishing (if not ruine) of many families': Gragg, *Englishmen Transplanted*, 8.

p. 83   more than 100 taverns in Bridgetown alone. Southey, *Chronological History*, 2:15.

p. 83   'debaucht': 'A Briefe Discription of the ilande of Barbados', reprinted in Hutson, *English Civil War in Barbados*, 63.

p. 83   'Drunknes is great, especially among the lower classes': Handler, 'Father Antoine Biet's Visit', 68.

p. 83   'nothing lacking in the way of meats . . .': ibid., 62.

p. 83   'After one has dined, and the table has been cleared': ibid., 62.

p. 83   'A German for his drinking . . .': 'A Briefe Discription of the ilande of Barbados', reprinted in Hutson, *English Civil War in Barbados*, 63.

p. 83   the English a tavern: Walduck, 'T. Walduck's Letters from Barbados', 35.

p. 84   'I did not always go': Handler, 'Father Antoine Biet's Visit', 62.

p. 84   'Tortions in the Bowells': Ligon, *A True and Exact History*, 27.

p. 84   'Most persons who come here from Europe will have to overcome an illness': Gunkel and Handler, 'A Swiss Medical Doctor's description of Barbados', 5–6.

p. 84   In the West Indies it was as low as 10: Burnard, '"The Countrie Continues Sicklie"', 59.

p. 84   during the 1650s and three times as many deaths as baptisms: Dunn, *Sugar and Slaves*, 77.

p. 85   'vanity, and folly, and madness': Rous, 'A warning to the Inhabitants of Barbadoes', 1–2.

p. 85   'a chaos of all Religions . . . Rogue Island': Bridenbaugh, *Fat Mutton*, 3–5.

p. 86   'trade decreased, and the king's subjects most impoverished': *Cal Col* 1675–6, no. 787.

p. 86   to just over 25,000 a decade later: McCusker and Menard, *Economy of British America*, 153.

p. 87   as many as 60 new vessels: Clarke, 'Imperial Forces in Barbados', 175.

8. Cromwell's 'Western Design': Disaster in Hispaniola

p. 88   'rascally rabble of raw and unexperienced men?': letter printed in Anon., *Interesting Tracts*, 91.

p. 88   'This wose a sad day with our maryed men': Whistler, *Journal of the West India Expedition*, 145–6 (26 December 1654).

p. 89   the 'Miserable Thraldome and bondage both Spirituall and Civill': Firth, *Narrative of General Venables*, 109.

p. 89   the navy was by now over a million and a half pounds in debt. Rodger, *Command of the Ocean*, 39.

p. 89   'I offer a New World': Gage, *English-American*, 2.

p. 90   'The Spaniards cannot oppose much': Rodger, *Command of the Ocean*, 22.

p. 90   Modyford . . . advised attacks on Guiana or Cuba. Long, *History of Jamaica*, 1: 222–3.

p. 90   'to gain an interest in that part of the West Indies in the possession of the Spaniard': 'Instructions unto Generall Robert Venables', 112.

p. 90   'wil obstruct the passing of the Spaniards Plate Fleete into Europe': ibid.

p. 91   'the unfittest man for a commissioner I ever knew employed': Firth, *Narrative of General Venables*, 60.

p. 91   'slothful and thievish servants': 'I.S.' *A brief and perfect Journal*, 513.

p. 91   'the looser sort out of hopes of plunder': Pitman, *Development of the West Indies*, 371.

p. 91   'old beaten runaways': Firth, *Narrative of General Venables*, 40.

p. 91   'A wicked army it was, and sent out without arms or provisions': ibid., xli.

p. 91   little ammunition or powder was to be found. Taylor, *Western Design*, 18.

p. 91   replacement horses and weapons: *Cal Col* 1574–1660, p. 432.

p. 92   the commanders were forced to abandon the wait: Anon., *Interesting Tracts*, 91.

p. 92   'a people that went to inhabit some country already conquered than to conquer': 'I.S.', *A brief and perfect Journal*, 515.

p. 92   'into a Great pachon': Whistler, *Journal of the West India Expedition*, 150. (10 April 1655).

p. 92   'Wee . . . Ware asharing the skin before wee had Cached the foxx': ibid.,150.

p. 92   'appear afar off like the smoke of ordnance': Rodger, *Command of the Ocean*, 22.

p. 92   warning beacons appeared in sight on the coast: Whistler, *Journal of the West India Expedition*, 151. (13 April 1655)

p. 93   'Our very feet scorched through our Shoes': Firth, *Narrative of General Venables*, 21.

p. 93 'Our horses and men (the sun being in our zenith) fell down for thirst': Anon., *Letters Concerning the English Expedition*, 128.

p. 93 In desperation, men started drinking their own urine: 'I.S'., *A brief and perfect Journal*, 515.

p. 93 'popish trumperie . . . wasted': Anon., *Letters Concerning the English Expedition*, 128–9.

p. 93 'brought forth a large statue of the Virgin Mary': ibid., 130.

p. 93 'extreamly troubled with the Flux': Firth, *Narrative of General Venables*, 34.

p. 94 'very nobelly rune behind a tree': Whistler, *Journal of the West India Expedition*, 154. (17 April 1655).

p. 94 'The great guns from the fort gawling us much': Anon., *Letters Concerning the English Expedition*, 131.

p. 94 'Lances . . . a most desperate wepon': Whistler, *Journal of the West India Expedition*, 155. (17 April 1655).

p. 94 'the ennimie with light maches': ibid., 161 (21 April 1655).

p. 95 'a uery sad condichon, 50 or 60 stouls in a day': ibid., 156–7 (19 April 1655).

p. 95 'sufficiently faint and almost choaked of thirst': 'I.S.', *A brief and perfect Journal*, 515.

p. 95 'whom the Negroes and Molattoes soon after dispatched': ibid., 517.

p. 96 'in a most sad and lamentable condition': Anon., *Letters Concerning the English Expedition*, 134.

p. 96 their army of thousands had been routed by just 200 Spaniards: Anon., *Letters Concerning the English Expedition*, 136; 'I.S.', *A brief and perfect Journal*, 518.

p. 96 'if all of like nature had been so dealt with, there would not have been many whole swords left in the army': 'I.S.,' *A brief and perfect Journal*, 518.

p. 96 'severely chastised': Long, *History of Jamaica*, 1:232.

p. 96 'so cowardly as not to be made to fight': Firth, *Narrative of General Venables*, 30.

p. 96 'the Disgrace of the army on Hispaniola': ibid., xi.

p. 96 'smaller success': ibid., 34.

9. The Invasion of Jamaica

p. 97 'wee saw Jamaica Iland, very high land afar off': Anon., *Letters Concerning the English Expedition*, 136.

p. 98 'the fairest island that eyes have beheld': Black, *History of Jamaica*, 25.

p. 98 'otherwise a paradise and worth more than gold': Cundall, *Historic Jamaica*, 271.

p. 100 the men were leaping out into the waist-deep warm waters of the bay: Anon., *Letters Concerning the English Expedition*, 136–7.

p. 100 'but must vanquish or die': Firth, *Narrative of General Venables*, 35.

p. 100 'wanting guides . . . very weak . . . with bad diet': ibid., 35.

p. 100 'divers Spaniards . . . with other large overtures, and high compliments': 'I.S.', *A brief and perfect Journal*, 520.

p. 101 The hides were collected (and later sent on a Dutch ship to New England to exchange for provisions): Anon., *Letters Concerning the English Expedition*, 138.

p. 101   'a uery sad creater' . . . afflicted with the 'French-disease'. 'I.S.', *A brief and perfect Journal*, 520.

p. 101   'if they complied, they were utterly ruined, and desired rather to expose their lives to the hazzard of warr then to condescend to such termes': Anon., *Letters Concerning the English Expedition*, 137.

p. 101   Bodies of dead English soldiers started being discovered, stripped naked and horribly mutilated: Taylor, *Western Design*, 100.

p. 102   'did more weaken and disable them in ten miles march there, than forty in their own country': 'I.S.', *A brief and perfect Journal*, 521.

p. 102   on starvation rations of half a biscuit per man a day: Long, *History of Jamaica*, 1:240.

p. 102   within 12 days of the landing, lack of food and water had halved the strengths of the companies: Whistler, *Journal of the West India Expedition*, 166.

p. 102   'dead men, just crept abroad from their graves': Long, *History of Jamaica*, 1:241.

p. 102   'which sweep them away by Ten and twenty per diem frequently': Firth, *Narrative of General Venables*, 49–50.

p. 102   'in some parts of this town a man is not able to walk': Lieut. Col. Barrington, 14 July 1655, quoted in Firth, *Narrative of General Venables*, xxxv.

p. 102   'The enemy lye still on the mountains, expecting our deserting this country': Anon., *Letters Concerning the English Expedition*, 140.

p. 102   1,000 men were killed by ambushes: Burns, *History of the British West Indies*, 254.

p. 102   'did the English spare any of the dogs, cats, colts or donkeys': Marks, *Family of the Barrett*, 23.

p. 103   a combination of 'flux' and 'fever': Firth, *Narrative of General Venables*, 103.

p. 103   which he saw as the Lord's punishment for his own iniquity: Haring, *Buccaneers in the West Indies*, 87.

p. 103   he had shut himself in his room and become ill: Hill, *God's Englishman*, 185.

p. 103   'fret, fume, grow impatient': Long, *History of Jamaica*, 1: 242.

p. 103   Tools were also required, he wrote: Firth, *Narrative of General Venables*, 63.

p. 103   'all known, idle, masterless robbers and vagabonds, male and female, and transport them to that island': *Cal Col* 1574–1660, pp. 431, 441; Long, *History of Jamaica*, 1:244.

p. 104   '. . . a chief end of our undertaking and design)': *Cal Col* 1554–1660, pp. 429–30.

p. 104   '. . . the skulking Negroes and Spaniards': Long, *History of Jamaica*, 1:258.

p. 104   'they lived more comfortably like Englishmen than any of the rest of the Plantations': Hutchinson, *History of the Colony of Massachusetts Bay*, 191n.

p. 105   '. . . to annoy and infest the Enemies of our Nation': Firth, *Narrative of General Venables*, 65.

p. 105   '. . . is not honorable for a princely navy . . . though perhaps it may be tolerated at present': *Cal Col* 1675–6, no. 236.

p. 105   'a cruel, bloody, and ruinating people . . . worse than the Spanish': Taylor, *Western Design*, 138.

p. 105 'fair beginnings of a town': ibid., 131.

p. 106 'a place which abounds in all things': Long, *History of Jamaica*, 1:256.

p. 106 '... do anything, however necessary, for their own benefit': ibid., 1:247.

p. 106 3,720 were still alive, besides 173 women and children: Firth, *Narrative of General Venables*, xxxii.

p. 106 '... out of a strange kind of spirit, desir[ing] rather to die than live': Long, *History of Jamaica*, 1:254.

p. 106 'Poore men I pitty them at the heart ... it is a very Golgotha': Anon., *Letters Concerning the English Expedition*, 142.

p. 107 'there scarce a week passeth without one or two slain': Taylor, *Western Design*, 102.

p. 107 'industry, unanimity, perseverance, and good order'. Long, *History of Jamaica*, 1:221.

p. 107 'very scum of scums, and mere dregs of corruption': 'I.S.', *A brief and perfect Journal*, 492.

p. 108 Other prominent figures in the island's early history: Dunn, *Sugar and Slaves*, 176.

p. 111 it was equipped with six cannon, each firing four-pound shot: Taylor, *Western Design*, 171.

p. 111 Three hundred Spanish soldiers were killed, against some 50 English: Long, *History of Jamaica*, 1:276.

p. 111 'extreme want and necesitie' on the island: BL Egerton MSS 2395, fol. 242.

p. 111 'All the frigates are gone': *Cal Col* 1574–1660, p. 485.

10. The Restoration

p. 115 For at least two years after his departure from Barbados, Drax remained in London: *Cal Col* 1574–1660, p. 451.

p. 115 'a Gentleman of much worth, and of great Interest in Plantations at the Barbadoes, where he formerly lived for some years': *Mercurius Politicus Compromising the Summ of All Intelligence*, 31 December 1657 (issue 397).

p. 116 'ministers that precht for the Parson': MacMurray, *Records of Two City Parishes*, 391.

p. 117 'It hath pleased the Lord of his mercy and goodnesse': Drax will, PRO Prob 11/307.

p. 117 the average annual wage at the time was about £8: Faraday, *Herefordshire Milita*, 17.

p. 117 'the greatest Dominion in the World ... win and keepe the Soveraignty of the Seas': Bridenbaughs, *No Peace Beyond the Line*, 306.

p. 118 Molesworth's petition was ordered to be 'laid aside': *Lords' Journal*, 9:297.

p. 118 'and inform themselves of the true state of the Plantations in Jamaica and New England': *Cal Col* 1661–8, no. 3.

p. 119 'ringin ye Great Bell for Sr James Drax': MacMurray, *Records of Two City Parishes*, 390.

p. 119 Henry would write down a series of instructions: Drax, 'Instructions which I would have observed'

p. 119 'adept at figures, and all the arts of economy, something of an architect, and well-skilled in mechanics', as well as 'a very skilled husbandman': Martin, *An Essay upon Plantership*, vi–vii.

p. 120   'distinguished not only by gentle birth but by many virtues': MacMurray, *Records of Two City Parishes*, 316 .

p. 120   'intelligible . . . and of no faction, which is rare in Barbados': *Cal Col* 1661–8, no. 1819.

p. 120   expanding the Drax estates as established by his father: *Cal Col* 1669–74, no. 1101ii.

p. 120   his Barbados estates yielded income: *Cal Col* 1677–80, no. 317; Lord Atkins to Lords of Trade and Plantations, 4 July 1677. PRO CO 29/2, 181

p. 120   his will, written in 1682: B. Arch. RB6/12, 358.

p. 120   'by the consent of her brother Henry Drax and her uncle William Drax esq. guardians': Foster, *London Marriage Licences*, 1222.

p. 120   'Planters and Merchants trading to Barbados': *Cal Col* 1661–8, no. 1342.

p. 120   He was 24, she was 20: Foster, *London Marriage Licences*, 419.

p. 121   scattered mentions of them in wills: Codrington wills, reprinted in Oliver, *History of the Island of Antigua*, 1:142–75.

p. 122   'being of a debonaire liberal humour': *Cal Col* 1669–74, no. 549.

p. 122   'divers goods, wares, and merchandizes . . . being of great value': Jesse, 'Barbadians Buy St Lucia', 181.

p. 122   'He is well beloved . . . and free from faction, an ingenious young gentleman': *Cal Col* 1661–8, no. 1283.

p. 122   'that fair jewell of your Majesty's Crown': *Cal Col* 1661–8, no. 1204.

p. 122   then producing more than 85 per cent of the sugar imported to England: Sheridan, *Sugar and Slavery*, 398; Dunn, *Sugar and Slaves*, 202–3.

p. 122   'worth all the rest . . . which are made by the English': Gragg, *Englishmen Transplanted*, 1.

p. 122   'the most flourishing Colony the English have': Anon., *Great Newes from the Barbadoes*, 3, 14.

p. 122   'A mean planter . . . thinks himself better than a good gentleman fellow in England': *Cal Col* 1661–8, no. 1871.

p. 122   'by a rational estimate' that the 'plates, jewels, and extraordinary household stuffs' on the island were worth about £500,000. *Cal Col* 1661–8, no. 1657.

p. 122   'splendid Planters . . .': Anon., *Great Newes from the Barbadoes*, 6.

p. 123   'The Devel was in the English-man': ibid., 6–7.

p. 123   'The Masters . . . live at the height of Pleasure': Blome, *Description of the Island of Jamaica*, 84.

p. 123   'the most inconsiderable of the . . . endeavour[ing] to outvye one the other in their entertainments': Davies, *History of the Caribby-Islands*, 198–9.

p. 123   'built after the English fashion . . . now general all over the island': *Cal Col* 1681–5, no. 136.

p. 124   'very fair and beautiful . . . like castles': *Cal Col* 1661–8, no. 1657.

p. 124   'Delightfully situated . . . pleasant Prospects to the Sea and Land': Ogilby, *America*, 379.

p. 124 'to Strangers at their first coming: [was] there scarce tolerable': Anon., *Great News from the Barbadoes*, 5.

p. 124 'abundance of well-built houses': Blome, *Description of the Island of Jamaica*, 80.

p. 124 'Costly and Stately': Anon., *Great Newes from the Barbadoes*, 5.

p. 124 'many fair, long, and spacious Streets . . . noble structures . . . well furnish'd with all sorts of Commodities': Davies, *History of the Caribby-Islands*, 9.

p. 125 'not a foot of land in Barbados that is not employed even to the very seaside': *Cal Col* 1675–6, no. 973.

p. 125 'a design full of accident': BL Sloane MSS 3984, fol. 217, quoted in Amussen, *Caribbean Exchanges*, 75.

p. 125 'strange and unusual caterpillars and worms': *Cal Col* 1661–8, no. 578.

p. 125 'The island appears very flourishing . . . what they owe in London does not appear here': *Cal Col* 1669–74, no. 549.

p. 125 by as much as half between 1652 and the end of the century: Menard, *Sweet Negotiations*, 69.

p. 125 about 20 per cent on their capital for the rest of the century: Craton, *Sinews of Empire*, 138–9.

p. 126 'the fewer the better': Drax, 'Instructions which I would have observed', 587.

p. 126 a labour force of 327 black slaves and only seven white servants. Hotten, *Original Lists of Persons of Quality*, 462.

p. 126 3,075 slaves to Barbados in the seven months after August 1663: Thomas, *Slave Trade*, 201.

p. 126 the retail price slipping from 1.25 shillings a pound . . . per capita consumption in 1650 was barely a pound: by the end of the century it was five pounds: Shamas, *Pre-Industrial Consumer*, 81.

p. 126 England was importing 23,000 tons of sugar a year: Amussen, *Caribbean Exchanges*, 40; Menard, 'Plantation Empire', 316.

p. 126 'Slavery is so vile and miserable a state of man': Locke, *Two Treatises on Government*, 1.

p. 127 nearly half of all products from the West Indies by value: Zahedieh, 'Overseas expansion', 404.

p. 127 The Crown, for one, made £300,000 a year from sugar duties by the mid-1670s: Menard, 'Plantation Empire', 315.

p. 127 some 700 by 1686: Amussen, *Caribbean Exchanges*, 40.

p. 127 consumed three times more by value than their cousins in the mainland North American colonies: ibid., 41.

p. 127 'the centre of trade . . . but also draw profits from them': Cary, *An Essay on the State of England*, 68–70.

p. 127 A street near the wharf in Bridgetown was renamed New England Street: Smith, *Slavery, Family and Gentry Capitalism*, 19.

p. 128 His letter book: Sanford, *Letter Book of Peleg Sanford*.

p. 128 'afatting of the swine': ibid., 35 (19 October 1667).

p. 128 'not be very Beeg in the head': ibid., 45 (10 January 1667).

p. 128   'Ronged onboard': ibid., 68 (21 December 1668).

p. 128   more than half of the ships entering and clearing Boston were involved with the Caribbean trade: Dunn, *Sugar and Slaves*, 336.

p. 129   'to treat with the natives . . . or if injurious or contumacious, to persecute them with fire and swords': *Cal Col* 1661–8, no. 489.

p. 130   'The Caribbeans have tasted of all the nations that frequented them': Bell, 'Caribs of Dominica', 21.

p. 130   Thereafter, Carib raids on Antigua became an almost annual affair: ibid.

p. 130   'Mrs Cardin and children': Flannigan, *Antigua and the Antiguans*, 15.

p. 130   In 1655 the Governor wrote to London that unless they were sent some servants, they would have to abandon the colony. *Cal Col* 1654–60, pp. 439, 443.

p. 130   'a reall Winthrop and truely noble to all': Dunn, *Sugar and Slaves*, 125.

p. 130   Warner, the story goes, then imprisoned his wife: ibid., 24.

p. 130   'I doe not find this country good for children': Bridenbaughs, *No Peace Beyond the Line*, 399.

p. 131   'the most beautiful and fertile part of the West Indies and perhaps of the world': Williams, *From Columbus to Castro*, 81.

p. 131   'the dispute will be whether the King of England or of France shall be monarch of the West Indies': *Cal Col* 1661–8, no. 823.

11. Expansion, War and the Rise of the Rise of the Beckfords

p. 132   'Next day, when the March began' Esquemeling, *Bucaniers of America* (1771 ed.), 203.

p. 132   'The great Tom Fuller come to me to desire a kindness for a friend of his': Pepys, *Diary*, 1:147.

p. 132   another 1,000 acres in St Elizabeth in 1673: MSS Beckford b.8, fols. 8–9.

p. 132   'singularly fit': *Cal Col* 1681–5, no. 1553.

p. 133   'burn their Canes for want of hands': BL Add. MSS 11410, fols. 19–21.

p. 133   about 18 by 1663: Bridenbaughs, *No Peace beyond the Line*, 296.

p. 133   a lighter and finer-grained sugar: Oldmixon, *British Empire*, 2:325.

p. 133   'dull tedious way of planting'. BL Add. MSS 11410, fols. 19–21.

p. 133   including Peter Beckford: *Cal Col* 1702, no. 743.

p. 133   inflamed' to 'leave planting and try their fortunes . . . [and] causes frequent Mutinies & disorders': *Cal Col* 1654–60, p. 480.

p. 133   the population tripled to 17,000 (of whom just over 9,000 were black): Long, *History of Jamaica*, 1:316.

p. 133   the abundance of building materials and the fertility of the virgin soil: BL Add. MSS 11410, fols. 19– 21.

p. 134   'no less than 1,500 lusty fellows': *Cal Col* 1661–8, no. 786.

p. 134   'unwillingly constrained to reduce them to a better understanding by the open and just practise of force': Marsden, 'Early Prize Jurisdiction', 54.

p. 134   booty that included nearly 17,000 pounds of ivory: Rodger, *Command of the Ocean*, 68.

p. 135 'a whole volley of small shott and his broade side': PRO CO 1/19, no. 50, quoted in Harlow, *Colonising Expeditions to the West Indies*, 109.

p. 135 'in the confusedest manner that possibly could be': ibid., 110.

p. 135 'to root the Dutch out of all places in the West Indies': Israel, 'Empire: The Continental Perspective', 432.

p. 136 'fell upon the English on ye windward side of this Island': Harlow, *Colonising Expeditions to the West Indies*, 21.

p. 136 'and some peeses of a ship' washed ashore at Montserrat: Harlow, *A History of Barbados*, 167.

p. 137 'Ye contention was verry smart for about ½ hour': letter of April 1667, quoted in Oliver, *History of the Island of Antigua*, 1:xxxvi.

p. 137 'place the island in such a state that the enemy can draw no sort of profit from it': ibid., 1:xxxv.

p. 138 Carden's head was then broiled, and carried back to his house and family: Flannigan, *Antigua and the Antiguans*, 37.

p. 138 'If wee prevaile ... Otherwise they will be put to trade or imploymt': Oliver, *History of the Island of Antigua*, 1:xxxvii.

p. 138 15,000 slaves and materials for 150 sugar works, worth a total of £400,000: *Cal Col 1669–74*, no. 520.

p. 138 proceeded to retake other islands previously under their control: Harlow, *Colonising Expeditions to the West Indies*, 221–2.

p. 138 'I am hewing a new fortune out of the wild woods': quoted in Sheridan, *Sugar and Slavery*, 191.

p. 139 doubled on the islands in the six years after 1672 to some 8,500: Higham, *Development of the Leeward Islands*, 154.

p. 139 'The wars here are more destructive': Jeaffreson, *A Young Squire*, 1:215.

p. 139 'the French are rampant among these islands': *Cal Col 1669–74*, no. 508.

p. 139 'bloodhounds': *Cal Col 1669–74*, no. 906.

p. 139 'are kept every night 14 files of men': Oliver, *History of the Island of Antigua* 1:lii.

p. 140 'the soule and life of all Jamaica ... and most profest immoral liver in the world': quoted in Burns, *History of the British West Indies*, 328.

p. 140 'rich and fat ... being always Springing': Blome, *Description of the Island of Jamaica*, 3.

p. 140 'independent potentate': Dunn, *Sugar and Slaves*, 155.

p. 140 Peter Beckford was granted 1,000 acres by royal patent: Alexander, *England's Wealthiest Son*, 29.

p. 140 Francis Price (frequently in partnership with Peter Beckford), and Fulke Rose: *Cal Col 1669–74*, no. 270.

p. 141 'look on us as intruders and trespassers wheresoever they find us in the Indies and use us accordingly': *Cal Col 1661–8*, no. 1265.

p. 141 'divers barbarous acts': *Cal Col 1669–74*, no. 697.

p. 141 his drinking and carousing reached new epic levels: *Cal Col 1675–6*, no. 673.

p. 141 who in 1676 took over the 1,000 acres in St Elizabeth: MSS Beckford b. 8, fols. 8–9.

p. 141   at the age of 33, Peter Beckford had 2,238 acres in sugar and cattle: Deerr, *History of Sugar*, 1:175.

p. 142   His first son, another Peter ... then, in 1682, another son, Thomas: Howard, *Records and Letters of the Family of the Longs*, 15–16.

p. 142   'a great incendiary': *Cal Col* 1689–92, no. 1699.

p. 142   'ruthless, unscrupulous and violent': Alexander, *England's Wealthiest Son*, 30.

p. 142   'great opulance ... superiority over most of the other Planters': Redding, *Memoirs of William Beckford*, 1:4.

p. 142   Custos of Kingston, a member of the assembly for St Catherine's: *Cal Col* 1675–6, nos. 521, 536.

p. 142   from 1675, Secretary of the Island: *Cal Col* 1675–6, no. 484.

p. 142   'carrying and using, too, a large stick on very trivial provocations': Redding, *Memoirs of William Beckford*, 2:101.

p. 142   1,700 white children and about 9,500 Africans, almost all enslaved: Dunn, *Sugar and Slaves*, 155.

p. 142   Thus, the second Drax Hall plantation estate came into existence: Armstrong, *The Old Village and the Great House*, 24.

p. 142   'in any of the Caribbee Islands, by reason the soil is new': 'Observations on the Present State of Jamaica', 14 December. 1675, PRO CO 138/2, p. 110.

p. 142   'renders not by two-thirds its former production by the acre; the land is almost worn out': *Cal Col* 1661–8, no. 1788.

p. 142   1.35 tons an acre in 1649 to less than a ton per acre by 1690: Menard, *Sweet Negotiations*, 78.

p. 143   'greatt Qwantaty of Dung Every year ... dunging Every holle': Drax, 'Instructions which I would have observed', 589.

p. 143   but Barbados needed two: Bridenbaughs, *No Peace Beyond the Line*, 301.

p. 143   Another planter decreed that 150 cows: Belgrove, *Treatise on Husbandry*, 32.

p. 143   some 400 windmills in operation by the 1670s: Anon., *Great Newes from the Barbadoes*, 6.

p. 143   an issue also addressed by Henry Drax in his 'Instructions': Drax, 'Instructions which I would have observed', 571.

p. 143   'like Ants or Bees': Littleton, *Groans of the Plantations*, 18.

p. 143   'not halfe so strong as in the year 1645': BL Sloane MSS 3662, fol. 54.

p. 144   'interested men' with property to protect: *Cal Col* 1671, no. 413, p. 162.

p. 144   'In 1643, [the] value [of Barbados], sugar plantations being but in their infancy': *Cal Col* 1661–8, no. 1657.

p. 144   From a high of 30,000 in 1650, the white population had shrunk: Menard, *Sweet Negotiations*, 25.

p. 144   'courage to leave the island, or are in debt and cannot go': *Cal Col* 1661–8, no. 1657.

p. 144   'Intemperance' and 'Gluttony' of the planters. At one feast, he reported, more than 1,000 bottles of wine were consumed: Tyron, *Friendly Advice to the Gentlemen-Planters*, 49–53.

p. 144   'There are hundreds of white servants in the Island who have been out of their time for many years': *Cal Col* 1693–6, no. 1783.

p. 145 'Since people have found out the convenience and cheapness of slave-labour': *Cal Col* 1677–80, no. 1558.

p. 145 '30 sometimes, 40, Christians – English, Scotch and Irish': *Cal Col* 1661–8, no. 1657.

p. 145 358 sugar works producing in the 1680s exports more valuable than those of all of North America combined: Sheridan, *Sugar and Slavery*, 137.

p. 145 'a miserable place of torment', a 'land of Misery and Beggary': Menard, *Sweet Negotiations*, 44.

p. 145 'rogues, whores, vagabonds, cheats, and rabble of all descriptions, raked from the gutter': Souden, '"Rogues, Whores and Vagabonds"?', 24.

p. 145 remaining popular with the assembly thanks to lavish dinners: PRO CO1/26 no. 6, *Cal Col* 1669–74, no. 388.

p. 145 pushing for the money raised in Barbados to be spent there as well as working for representation of the island in Parliament: *Cal Col* 1669–74, no. 236.

p. 145 'very glad to find himself so well backed': *Cal Col* 1669–74, no. 48.

p. 146 'poorer sort of this Island' . . . and laws to prevent accidental cane fires: *Acts of Assembly passed in the Island of Barbados*, nos, 114–73.

p. 146 Henry Drax . . . sent on trips to England to push the interests of the Barbadians: *Cal Col* 1669–74, no. 413.

p. 146 'the Committee for the Public Concern of Barbadoes': ibid., no. 558.

p. 146 skilled trades should be reserved for whites: ibid., no. 357.

p. 146 'The Deputy Governor is not an ordinary man': ibid., no. 55.

12. 'All slaves are enemies'

p. 147 'All slaves are enemies': Roman proverb, quoted in Davis, *Inhuman Bondage*, 46.

p. 147 'I feare our negroes will growe too hard for us': quoted in Bridenbaughs, *No Peace Beyond the Line*, 214.

p. 147 'much greater from within': *Cal Col* 1677–80, no. 969.

p. 147 more than three slaves for every white person: Eltis 'British Transatlantic Slave Trade', 48.

p. 148 'Act for the Better Ordering and Governing of Negroes': PRO CO/30/2, fols. 16–26.

p. 148 the only penalty being a fine, and this was easily evaded: Dunn, *Sugar and Slaves*, 239.

p. 148 'white' was 'the general name for Europeans': Godwyn, *Negro's and Indians Advocate*, 84.

p. 149 did not simply use their superior numbers to seize control of the island: Ligon, *A True and Exact History*, 46–7.

p. 149 that 'the safety of the plantations depends upon having Negroes from all parts': quoted in Dunn, *Sugar and Slaves*, 236.

p. 149 'passionate Lovers one of another': Davies, *History of the Caribby-Islands*, 202.

p. 149 'the whole may be endangered, for now there are many thousands of slaves that speak English': *Cal Col* 1661–8, no. 1657.

p. 149 'who had bene ane Exelentt Slawe and will I hope Continue Soe in the place he is of head owerseer': Drax, 'Instructions which I would have observed', 600.

p. 149   'brittle, gay and showy society': Dunn, *Sugar and Slaves*, 116.

p. 150   'our whole dependence is upon Negroes': 6 April 1676, PRO CO 29/2, fols. 29–36.

p. 150   'the weak hands must not be pressed': Drax, 'Instructions which I would have observed', 586.

p. 150   'The Kittchin being more usefull . . . then the Appothycaries Shopp': ibid., 583.

p. 150   'Noe man deserved a Corramante that would not treat him like a Friend rather than a Slave': PRO CO 152/4, no. 73; *Cal Col* 1701, no. 1132.

p. 151   precisely because he could control his 'passin': Drax, 'Instructions which I would have observed', 588.

p. 151   'Sugar, Molasses or Rum . . . when threatened do hang themselves': ibid., 587.

p. 151   'If some go beyond the limits . . . makes them shriek with despair': Handler, 'Father Antoine Biet's Visit', 67.

p. 151   'The drunken, unreasonable and savage overseers . . . than that of a horse': Connell, 'Father Labat's Visit to Barbados in 1700', 168–9.

p. 152   'led to a cycle of deformed human relationships which left all parties morally and aesthetically maimed': King, *West Indian Literature*, 9.

p. 152   'It is true that one must keep these kinds of people obedient': Handler, 'Father Antoine Biet's Visit', 67.

p. 152   'compelled to exceed the limits of moderation': Connell, 'Father Labat's Visit to Barbados in 1700', 169.

p. 152   called the slave trade 'barbarous': Davies, *History of the Caribby-Islands*, 20–2.

p. 152   'never smile upon them, nor speak to them': BL Add. MSS 18960, p. 38.

p. 153   'they think nothing too much to be done for them': Blome, *Description of the Island of Jamaica*, 84–5.

p. 153   Samuel Winthrop, 'being convinced, he and his Family received the Truth': Edmundson, *A Journal of the Life, Travels, Sufferings and Labour*, 61.

p. 153   Fox appealed to the planters to 'deal mildly and gently with their Negroes, and not use cruelty toward them': Nickalls, *Journal of George Fox*, 1803 ed., 97.

p. 153   'And did not Christ taste Death for every man? And are they not Men?' Fox, *To the Ministers, Teachers and Priests*, 5.

p. 154   'most false Lye': ibid., 77.

p. 154   'a thing we do utterly abhor and detest in and from our hearts': Nickalls, *Journal of George Fox*, 604.

p. 154   'reasonable Creatures, as well as you': Baxter, *A Christian Directory*, 557.

p. 155   'their Amputations of Legs, and even Dissecting them alive': Godwyn, *Negro's and Indians Advocate*, 41.

p. 155   The 'brutality' of the 'Negro': ibid., 23.

p. 155   'To tell the truth, they have almost no religion': Handler, 'Father Antoine Biet's Visit', 68.

p. 155   only 11 ministers for 20,000 Christians: Dunn, *Sugar and Slaves*, 103.

p. 155   'The disproportion of the blacks to whites . . . it would be necessary to teach them all English': *Cal Col* 1677–80, no. 1535.

p. 156 'so many and so close together, that we can hardly breathe': Tyron, *Friendly Advice to the Gentlemen-Planters*, 82–3.

p. 156 'sometimes most part of our Bodies': ibid., 89.

p. 156 'our luxurious Masters stretch themselves on their soft Beds and Couches': ibid., 122–7.

p. 156 'there is no one commodity whatever, that doth so much encourage navigation, [and] advance the Kings Customs': ibid., 183.

p. 157 'and cut their Throats . . . starv[ing] them for want of Meat and Cloathes convenient': Edmundson, *A Journal of the Life, Travels, sufferings and Labour* 86.

p. 157 'Buccararoes or White Folks': Craton, *Testing the Chains*, 109.

p. 157 'it was a great pity so good people': Anon., *Great Newes from the Barbadoes*, 11–13.

p. 157 'trumpets . . . a chair of state exquisitely wrought and carved after their mode': ibid., 6–10.

p. 158 'And such others that have more favour shown them by their masters, which adds abundantly to their crimes': Handler, 'Barbados Slave Conspiracies of 1675 and 1692', 323.

p. 159 'The white women . . . Whores Cooks & Chambermaids of Others': Craton, *Testing the Chains*, 114.

p. 159 'fully overheard . . . talking of . . . their wicked design' only ten days before the uprising was scheduled to take place. Handler, 'Barbados Slave Conspiracies of 1675 and 1692', 320.

p. 159 'Many were hang'd . . . according to the sentence of the commissioners for trial of rebellious negroes': ibid., 322.

p. 160 'these villains are but too sensible of . . . our extreme weakness': ibid., 322.

13. The Cousins Henry Drax and Christopher Codrington

p. 162 more than twice as many white people were buried than baptised in Barbados. A comparative analysis . . .: Dunn, 'Barbados Census of 1689', 71.

p. 162 'snatched away (alas!) too quickly': MacMurray, *Records of Two City Parishes*, 316.

p. 162 'Jamaca peper welle pickled in good wineger . . . green ginger and yams': Drax, 'Instructions which I would have observed' 601.

p. 162 '*Honor*, Thomas Warner commander': Hotten, *Original Lists of Persons of Quality*, 363.

p. 162 he left £2,000 for the establishment of a 'free school and college' in St Michael: Henry Drax will, B. Arch. RB6/12, 358.

p. 162 'utterly debauched both in Principallls and Morals': ibid.

p. 162 'the gaiety of their dress and equipage': Schomburgk, *History of Barbados*, 111fn.

p. 164 'fell into a violent burning of the stomach': Hughes, *Natural History of Barbados*, 55.

p. 164 'fraudulent proceedings': *Cal Col* 1677–80, no. 277.

p. 164   'needless impositions': Willoughby to Thomas Povey, 14 November 1672, BL
         Egerton MSS 2395, fol. 483.

p. 164   was also stripped of his command of one of the island's militia regiments: *Cal
         Col* 1669– 74, nos. 1104, 1054.

p. 164   'a great prejudice against Codrington . . . and has the power . . . and the will to
         ruin him': *Cal Col* 1669–74, no. 878.

p. 164   'was no fit man to be councilor': Schomburgk, *History of Barbados*, 295.

p. 165   Christopher is recorded as owning 600 acres in the parish: *Cal Col* 1669–74, no.
         1101.

p. 165   a still-house containing four large rum stills: Butler, 'Mortality and Labour', 49.

p. 165   the largest covered punch bowl ever recorded: Oliver, *History of the Island of
         Antigua*, 1:153.

p. 165   'Christopher Codrington of this Island . . . lett them come with what Authoritie
         or force they could': Donnan, *Documents Illustrative of the History of the Slave
         Trade*, 1:241.

p. 165   'guided only by his owne will': John Style letter, January 1669, PRO CO 25/1, p.2.

p. 166   influential courtiers in London: *Cal Col* 1677–80, no. 1501.

p. 166   to pay back nearly £600 of allegedly stolen money: *Cal Col* 1681–5, no. 832.

p. 166   she would later unsuccessfully try to retrieve her property: *Cal Col* 1677–80, no.
         468.

p. 166   two whites and 10 black slaves registered as living on the property in 1678: Oliver,
         History of the Island of Antigua, 1, lix.

p. 166   60-square-mile island of Barbuda, previously granted to James Winthrop in 1668:
         ibid.,1:170.

p. 166   he raised a mortgage on the Barbados properties of just over £4,000, and another
         £7,000 the next year: Harlow, *Christopher Codrington*, 15n.

p. 166   'if estate lost or taken by enemies . . .': John Codrington will, B. Arch. RB6/40,
         p. 167.

p. 167   'Keeps Continually about him a Seraglio of mulatoes and negro women and has
         by them no less than 4 or 5 bastards': PRO CO 152/2/83.

p. 167   'Mary Codrington . . . & £200 to the latter at 21': Oliver, *History of the Island of
         Antigua* 1:151.

p. 167   Antigua had a population . . .: ibid., 1:lxi.

p. 167   fewer than 70 slaves per man, while in Barbados the island's councillors had nearly
         200 each: Dunn, *Sugar and Slaves*, 128.

p. 167   'armed with guns' flee to the interior of Antigua: *Cal Col* 1685–88, no. 1175.

p. 167   'his leg cut off': ibid., no. 1189.

p. 167   'Negroe George', captured and sentenced to 'be burned to ashes': ibid., no. 1193.

p. 168   'the spawne of Newgate and Bridewell': Jeaffreson, *A Young Squire*, 1:258.

14. God's Vengeance

p. 169   'If thou didst see those great persons that are now dead upon the water': quoted
         in Dunn, *Sugar and Slaves*, 187.

p. 169   'made slaves . . . and there used with the utmost of Rigor and severity': Robertson, 'Re-writing the English Conquest of Jamaica', 834.

p. 169   'and in return receive only ingratitude': *Cal Col* 1681–85, no. 16.

p. 169   'are daily taking all ships they can master, and are very high': *Cal Col* 1675–6 , no. 735.

p. 170   'then took away with him her maiden daughter, Rachel Barrow of about 14 years': PRO CO 137/1, 193–6.

p. 170   A map drawn in 1677 shows a duel with pistols in motion: Dunn, *Sugar and Slaves*, 149.

p. 170   'had always been his friend, but the drink and other men's quarrels made them fall out': BL Add. MSS 12430, fol. 30.

p. 170   only four priests for the entire island: Bridenbaughs, *No Peace Beyond the Line*, 380.

p. 170   'As to the present state of the Island': *Cal Col* 1675–6 , no. 735.

p. 170   having increased tenfold since 1671: Dunn, *Sugar and Slaves*, 169.

p. 170   from 57 in 1671 to 246 in 1684: Bridenbaughs, *No Peace Beyond the Line*, 295.

p. 171   some £4,000 a year from his sugar plantations: 25 February 1684, *Cal Col* 1681–5, no. 1553.

p. 171   The Drax Hall estate would soon have more than 300 slaves: Armstrong, *Old Village and the Great House*, 36.

p. 172   slaves that cost £17 in Barbados, Beckford complained, were priced at £24 in Jamaica: Bridenbaughs, *No Peace Beyond the Line*, 259.

p. 172   'The Royal Company now begin to supply us well, there being two Shipps with 700 Negroes in port': ibid, 262.

p. 172   by 1680, the black population of Jamaica had surpassed that of the white: ibid., 227.

p. 172   'many families were murdered . . . destroyed most the Plantations in St Mary's parish': PRO CO 140/2, 447–9.

p. 172   'so trusty a negro . . . I would have put my life in his hands': quoted in Amussen, *Caribbean Exchanges*, 169.

p. 173   'master live at ease at full feed tables': Buisseret, *Jamaica in 1687*, 266.

p. 173   'All matters considered, I judge our husbandmen in Connecticut': Bridenbaughs, *No Peace Beyond the Line*, 218n.

p. 173   'misery of the slaves', 'whom the sun and tormenting insects in the field are like to devour': Buisseret, *Jamaica in 1687*, 247.

p. 173   castrated or had a foot or hand chopped off. Sloane, *A Voyage to the Islands*: 1:lvii.

p. 173   'the fire was upon his breast he was burning near 3 hours before he died': quoted in Amussen, *Caribbean Exchanges*, 168.

p. 174   'After they are whipped till they are raw': Sloane, *A Voyage to the Islands*, 1:lvii.

p. 174   the word 'sometimes' perhaps betraying his unease: Amussen, *Caribbean Exchanges*, 170.

p. 174   'for the wasps, merrywings and other insects to torment': Buisseret, *Jamaica in 1687*, 270.

p. 174   'unaccessible mountains and rocks': PRO CO 138/5, 87–102.

p. 174   'great troble and expence': Buisseret, *Jamaica in 1687*, 278.

p. 174   'so scandalous an Assembly was never chosen': *Cal Col* 1689–92, no. 1689.

p. 175   'the Store House or Treasury of the West Indies': Cundall, *Historic Jamaica*, 51.

p. 175   In one year in the late 1680s, 213 ships docked at Port Royal: Colley, *Ordeal of Elizabeth Marsh*, 4.

p. 175   'as dear-rented as if they stood in well-traded streets in London . . . but only made up of a hot loose Sand': Blome, *Description of the Island of Jamaica*, 31–2.

p. 175   'being sumptuously arrayed and served by their Negroa slaves': Buisseret, *Jamaica in 1687*, 238.

p. 175   'English servants to manage their chiefe affaire and supervise their Negroa slaves': ibid., 245–7.

p. 176   'live here very well, earning thrice the wages given in England': ibid., 241.

p. 176   'with a couple of Negroes at her tail': Bush, 'White "Ladies", Coloured "Favourites" and Black "Wenches"', 249.

p. 176   'many taverns, and an abundance of punchy houses, or rather may be fitly called brothel houses': Buisseret, *Jamaica in 1687*, 239.

p. 176   living with his young family in Port Royal: *Cal Col* 1681–5, no. 1311.

p. 176   'In his debauches, which go on every day and night, he is much magnified': ibid., no. 1348.

p. 176   Black Dogg, Blue Anchor, Catt & Fiddle, Sign of Bacchus: exhibition in Jamaica Institute, Kingston.

p. 177   'Lean, sallow coloured, his eyes a little yellowish . . . sitting up late': Sloane, *A Voyage to the Islands*, 1:xcviii.

p. 177   'very loose . . . by reason of privateers and debauched wild blades which come hither': Buisseret, *Jamaica in 1687*, 240.

p. 177   constant orders from London for the suppression of their 'mischief': *Cal Col* 1681–5, no. 11.

p. 177   force all the onlookers at pistol point to drink: Leslie, *A New and Exact Account of Jamaica*, 101.

p. 177   'by giving themselves to all manner of debauchery': Esquemeling, *Bucaniers of America*, 1:106.

p. 177   'now more rude and antic than 'ere was Sodom': Buisseret, *Jamaica in 1687*, 240.

p. 177   'to keep up some show of religion among a most ungodly and debauched people': Anon., *A full Account of the Late Dreadful Earthquake*, 1.

p. 177   'whole streets sinking under Water': Anon., *A True and Perfect Relation*, 1.

p. 177   'a great part of the inhabitants [were] miserably knocked on the head or drowned': June 20 1692, *Cal Col* 1689–92, no. 2278.

p. 178   'hanging by the hands upon the Rack of Chimney, and one of his Children hanging about his Neck': Anon., *A True and Perfect Relation*, 1.

p. 178   'some inhabitants were swallowed up to the Neck, and then the Earth shut upon them; and squeezed them to death': Anon., *A full Account of the Late Dreadful Earthquake*, 2.

p. 178   One so trapped was Peter Beckford: Anon., *A True and Perfect Relation*, 1.

p. 178   'intolerable stench': Anon., *The truest and largest account of the late Earthquake*, 5.

p. 178   'Mr Beckford's two daughters': Anon., *A True and Perfect Relation*, 1.

p. 178 'as a Fore-runner of the Terrible Day of the Lord': *Cal Col* 1689–92, nos. 2302, 2278.

p. 178 'many of the old Reprobates are become New Converts; those that use to Mock at Sin, Now Weep bitterly for it': Anon., *A True and Perfect Relation*, 1.

p. 178 emptying their pockets or cutting off fingers to get at rings: Anon., *The truest and largest account of the late Earthquake*, 6.

p. 178 'threw down all the churches, dwelling houses and sugar works in the island': *Cal Col* 1689–92, no. 2278.

p. 179 'the hurtful Vapours belch'd from the many openings of the earth': Cundall, *Historic Jamaica*, 150.

p. 179 'lying wet, and wanting medicines ... they died miserably in heaps': Sir Hans Sloane, quoted in Renny, *An History of Jamaica*, 229.

p. 179 'our strongest Houses demolisht, our Arms broken ... might be stirred up to rise in Rebellion against us': Anon., *The truest and largest account of the late Earthquake*, 11.

15. The Planter at War: Codrington in the Leeward Islands

p. 180 '[These colonies'] whole past history': quoted in Ragatz, *Fall*, ix.

p. 180 a number of French inhabitants joined in the 'burning and ravaging': *Cal Col* 1689–92, nos. 212, 237, 262, 312.

p. 181 'of great estate here and in Barbados': Johnson to Lords of Trade, 15 July 1689, ibid., no. 256.

p. 181 'so good is the spirit of the garrison': ibid., no. 312.

p. 181 'We are not unprofitable appendages to the Crown ... turn our mourning into joy': 31 July 1689, ibid., no. 312.

p. 182 he knew enough about the self-interest of planters ... the value of their own sugar crop: ibid., no. 789.

p. 182 'most turbulent and ungovernable': ibid., nos. 548, 789.

p. 182 'We are greatly discouraged by the long neglect of us at home': ibid., no. 789.

p. 182 'I have inspected the muskets and think them as bad as ever came to these parts': 4 June 1690, ibid., no. 927.

p. 182 'fittest for marching and accustomed to rugged paths': ibid., no. 977.

p. 182 'they have a grievance against you, and doubtless hope for revenge': 18 February, 1690, ibid., no. 789viii.

p. 183 'an almost inaccessible hill ... forced to use our Hands as well as our Feet in climbing up': Spencer, *A true and faithful relation of the proceedings of the forces*, 8.

p. 183 'pulling themselves forward by the bushes': *Cal Col* 1689–92, no. 977.

p. 183 'made all the heels they could': ibid.

p. 183 'Liquors' be 'secured in a convenient storehouse': Spencer, *A true and faithful relation of the proceedings of the forces*, 9.

p. 183 On 4 July, Codrington reported to London that morale in his force was excellent: *Cal Col* 1689–92, no. 977.

p. 183 'riddling the houses like sieves': ibid., no. 1004.

p. 183 'The King and Queen's healths were drank': Spencer, *A true and faithful relation of the proceedings of the forces*, 8.

p. 184 'disbursed large sums for the public service': *Cal Col* 1689–92, no. 1004.

p. 184 10 acres apiece so as to guarantee an adequate white militia and 'middle class': ibid., no. 1756.

p. 184 He had been too kind to the French, it was alleged: ibid., no. 1212.

p. 184 'repaid only by murmuring and discontent': ibid.

p. 185 'At the taking of St Christophers': ibid., no. 1608.

p. 185 all this was carried on in sloops for whose use in the national interest Codrington promptly charged the English government nearly £5,000: ibid., nos. 1609, 1613.

p. 185 'run off in distraction at midnight': ibid., no. 1630.

p. 186 'in consequence of the heavy complaint against him': ibid., no. 1623.

p. 186 'All turns on mastery of the sea': ibid., no. 1756.

p. 186 a powerful French fleet had arrived at Martinique: ibid., no. 1993.

p. 186 'far the richest production and most shining ornament [Barbados] ever had': quoted in Schomburgk, *History of Barbados*, 112.

p. 186 'Children, in these West India Islands are, from their infancy, waited upon by Numbers of Slaves': Hughes, *Natural History of Barbados*, 9–15.

p. 187 'No spark had walk'd up High Street bolder': quoted in Harlow, *Christopher Codrington*, 48.

p. 187 'So early and so continued a pre-eminence': ibid., 39.

p. 188 'I have always thought it very barbarous': *Cal Col* 1699, no. 458.

p. 188 'his freedom & £500 at 21, he to be sent to school in England': Oliver, *History of the Island of Antigua*, 1:150.

p. 189 'This heart ablaze, this spirit's surging foam': Harlow, *Christopher Codrington*, 81.

p. 189 He also repeated his requests for settlers from the northern colonies for St Kitts, but it appears that few were forthcoming: *Cal Col* 1693–6, no. 2193.

p. 190 He had traded illegally with the French and Dutch, even during the war, and this had continued since, it was said: PRO CO 152/2, pp.205–10.

p. 190 'minded nothing but plunder . . . From a Governour, planter, trader without breeding, word, honour, and religion, good Lord deliver us': ibid., p. 83.

p. 190 'the exercise of almost unlimited authority over a turbulent community turned his head': Harlow, *Christopher Codrington*, 36.

p. 190 'we are not sensible of any mismanagement or irregularities': PRO CO 152/2, p. 75.

p. 190 were moved to publicly chastise Codrington. *Cal Col* 1697–8, no. 817.

16. The French Invasion of Jamaica

p. 192 'the enemy daily infests our coasts': *Cal Col* 1693–6, no. 635.

p. 192 'the people were so thin and so little used to arms': ibid., no. 1236.

p. 193 'in a very mean habit, and with a meagre weather-beaten countenance': Anon., *Interesting Tracts*, 252.

p. 193   'into excellent order': ibid., 253.

p. 193   Using pressed labour: *Cal Col* 1693–6, no. 473.

p. 193   A system of beacons was established to warn of an approaching fleet, and Beeston announced: ibid., nos. 876, 1083, 1074.

p. 193   'coming into sight with a fresh gale': Anon., *Interesting Tracts*, 254.

p. 193   'Some of the straggling people . . . they suffered the negroes to violate, and dug some out of their graves': ibid., 255–7.

p. 194   and paying for them out of his own pocket: *Cal Col* 1693–6, no. 2178.

p. 194   'here I reckon that our misfortunes began': ibid., no. 1946.

p. 195   'people die here very fast and suddenly, I know not how soon it may be my turn': Amussen, *Caribbean Exchanges*, 84.

p. 195   he remarried the following year to Anne Ballard, from another wealthy planter family: Howard, *Records and Letters of the Family of the Longs*, 14.

p. 195   200 per thousand of the town's population died every year during the first decades of the eighteenth century: Burnard, '"The Countrie Continues Sicklie"', 49.

p. 195   'Mrs Beckford has been ill but is recovered': 15 May 1695, *Cal Col* 1693–6, no. 2022 ix.

p. 195   and of his servants, only his cook survived: BL Add. Mss 28878, fol. 135.

p. 195   'There are so many dead that it is hard to bury them': Burnard, 'A Failed Settler Society', 69.

p. 195   that the island was still 'at present sickly': March 30 1702, *Cal Col* 1702, no. 267.

p. 196   'the mortality reigns chiefly over the new-comers': ibid.

p. 196   reaching 42,000 by 1700: Dunn, *Sugar and Slaves*, 312; Amussen, *Caribbean Exchanges*, 94.

17. Codrington the Younger in the West Indies

p. 197   'A British Muse disdains' quoted in Krise, *Caribbeana*, 329.

p. 197   'to endeavour to get a law restraining inhuman severities': *Cal Col* 1699, no. 766.

p. 198   'Nothing will hinder me from promoting boldly': PRO CO 152/3, no. 23, fol. 100.

p. 198   'a long fit of sickness': PRO CO 152/3, no. 57.

p. 198   purchase Dodington Hall in Gloucestershire from Samuel Codrington: Codrington papers, BL RP 2616, reel 8.

p. 198   very fair . . . well furnish'd': Davies, *History of the Caribby-Islands*, 24.

p. 199   in a house only 90 by 16 feet, with four rooms: Dunn, *Sugar and Slaves*, 139.

p. 199   'too fulsome', addresses: 11 Jan 1701, PRO CO 152/4, no. 11.

p. 199   'dispatcht more business and done more justice': PRO CO 152/4, no. 36.

p. 199   'universal . . . the very air does change him in a short time': *Cal Col* 1700, no. 751.

p. 199   'for the Encouragement of poor settlers': *Acts of Assembly, Passed in the Charibbee Leeward Islands*, 111–13.

p. 199   more than 500 acres in St Mary, Antigua and done nothing with it: Dunn, *Sugar and Slaves*, 142.

p. 199   'I have defended the poor against ye rich': PRO CO 152/4, no. 36.

p. 199   attempted to take on the endemic illegal trading: *Cal Col* 1700, no. 658i.

p. 199   'There is so much Ignorance, laziness and Corruption': 5 May 1701, PRO CO 152/4, no. 21.

p. 199   'a young gentleman of great virtue and efforts': PRO CO 152/4, no. 46.

p. 199   'They are a parcell of Banditts': Codrington to Popple, 2 March 1704, PRO CO 152/5, no. 61.

p. 200   'idle and vagrant fellows': *Acts of Assembly, Passed in the Charibbee Leeward Islands*, 116.

p. 200   'the only Governor that I have met': PRO CO 152/4, no. 97.

p. 200   'not unlike that of a Frenchman, who is as easily elevated, as soon depressed': Beckford, *Descriptive Account* 2:375.

p. 200   'where they had washed it with rum and triumphed over it': PRO CO 152/4, no. 73.

p. 200   'we have lost a very useful man in Maj. Martin': ibid.; Higham, 'Negro Policy', 153.

p. 201   'got drunk together and grew Friends agen': PRO CO 152/4, no. 21.

p. 201   'So much ye les of ye Commodity is made, and consequently ye price is rais'd': ibid., nos. 44, 44i; *Cal Col* 1701, no. 744.

p. 201   rumours were that the Irish were preparing to hand the island over to the French: *Cal Col* 1701, no. 743.

p. 201   'I have done all yt it wd. have been possible . . . I have been no onely General but Engineer, Serjt. and Corporall': BL Add. Mss 34348; PRO CO 152/4, no. 30.

p. 202   'meet their Enemys with their Eyes open and their Swords in their hands': PRO CO 152/4, no. 31.

p. 202   'had very nearly captured the General one night in a raid': Eaden, *Memoirs of Père Labat*, 211ff.

p. 202   'far more sober than are most of his nation as a rule': ibid., 214.

p. 203   'My honour is much dearer to me than an employ more valuable than mine is': June 1702, *Cal Col* 1702–3 p. 654.

p. 203   'as curious as any private one in Europe': Codrington to Dr Charlett, 25 June 1702, quoted in Harlow, *Christopher Codrington*, 59.

p. 203   'I am so weak and spiritless' 28 June 1702, PRO CO 152/4, 104.

p. 203   'Her [Majesty's] Flag is now flying on ye French fort': PRO CO 152/5, no.2.

p. 204   'plant me some fruit trees and vines at Dodington': 30 November 1702, PRO CO 239/1, no. 3.

p. 204   it could take Quebec and drive the French out of Canada: *Cal Col* 1702–3, nos. 192, 193.

p. 204   there were hardly enough seamen fit to man the boats: ibid., no. 298.

p. 205   'murdered them with Drinking': 24 February 1703, PRO CO, 7/1, no. 3.

p. 205   The will, dated 22 February 1703: Oliver, *History of the Island of Antigua*, 1:150–1.

p. 207   'Negroes were equally the Workmanship of God with themselves': Klingberg, *Codrington Chronicle*, 4.

p. 208   'afflicted with terrible pains': PRO CO 152/5, no. 48.

p. 208   'just when we were to reap the fruit of our hazards & fatigues': PRO CO 152/5.

p. 208   blamed the Creole contingent for a lack of fighting spirit: Bourne, *Queen Anne's Navy in the West Indies*, 199.

p. 208   In one month the following year, out of 108 ships that left Barbados: October 1704, Oliver, *History of the Island of Antigua*, 1:lxxiv.

p. 208   'I still continue so wretchedly weak': Harlow, *Christopher Codrington*, 170.

p. 208   'security of those Islands': ibid., 172.

p. 209   'tho it be with a Muskett on my shoulder': PRO CO 152/5, no. 170.

p. 209   'I may serve Her better than an another at present': *Cal Col* 1704–5, no. 705.

p. 209   'fine appearance and handsome bearing': *Dictionary of National Biography*, 43:225.

p. 210   'I heartily wish for Col. Park's arrival': *Cal Col* 1704–5, nos. 1215, 1281.

p. 210   carrying away 600 slaves and huge quantities of sugar-making equipment. *Cal Col* 1705–6, nos. 168, 195.

p. 210   The Nevis planters estimated the loss at over a million pounds sterling: *Cal Col* 1707–08, no. 355.

18. The Murder of Daniel Parke

p. 211   'It will be very hard with this Island': Redwood Library Archive, Newport.

p. 211   'furnish'd his Cellars with Wine & liquors': Walduck, 'T. Walduck's Letters from Barbados', 139.

p. 211   'the Queen must send some other unfortunate devil here to be roasted in the sun': Parke to the Council of Trade, 28 August 1706, PRO CO 152/6, no. 63.

p. 212   'I am deservedly punished for desiring to be a Governor': Aspinall, *West Indian Tales of Old*, 29.

p. 212   'the plague, the pestilence and bloody flux': ibid., 27.

p. 212   'a rich little Island, but here are but few people': *Cal Col* 1706, no. 519.

p. 212   'I think I have the good fortune to please the people, except Colonel Codrington': Aspinall, *West Indian Tales of Old*, 29.

p. 212   was plotting to recover his governorship: *Cal Col* 1708–9, nos. 5, 116, 194.

p. 212   'enraged with Envy, at Colonel Parke's being preferr'd before him': French, *Answer to a Scurrilous Libel*, 24.

p. 212   'I continue my resolution of leaving the Indies': Harlow, *Christopher Codrington*, 191.

p. 213   'infused Fears and jealousises into the Minds of the People': French, *Answer to a Scurrilous Libel*, 24.

p. 213   'attempting to debauch some of the Chief women of the Island': Walduck, 'T. Walduck's Letters from Barbados', 139.

p. 213   'expect the Queen should do everything for them': Aspinall, *West Indian Tales of Old*, 28.

p. 213   'a mungrill race . . . among the slaveish sooty race': *Cal Col* 1710, nos. 391, 677.

p. 213   'layd two bastards to him, but she giving him the pox, he turned her off': *Cal Col* 1708– 9, no. 532.

p. 213   'pocket-pistoles' . . . 'his person and authority in contempt': Aspinall, *West Indian Tales of Old*, 36.

p. 213   Parke requested that she change her name to his, and that anyone marrying her also become a Parke. Flannigan, *Antigua and the Antiguans*, 340–1.

p. 214   'he continu'd to refresh the Dissensions he had sown': French, *Answer to a Scurrilous Libel*, 24.

p. 214   'insidious, restless, meddling', addicted to gambling: Lucas Mss, *JBMHS* 15, 190.

p. 214   'made prizes of them contrary to Law . . . sure to feel his resentments': Walduck, 'T. Walduck's Letters from Barbados', 139.

p. 214   'his estate goes to those he mortally hated before he died': *Cal Col* 1710–11, no. 228.

p. 214   'the author and contriver of all this vilany against me': Aspinall, *West Indian Tales of Old*, 41.

p. 215   'bruised his head, and broke his back with the butt end of the pieces': *Cal Col* 1710– 11, no. 783.

p. 215   'One Turnor a farrier': ibid., no. 677.

p. 216   before marrying the daughter of the wealthy Antiguan planter: Oliver, *History of the Island of Antigua*, 3:46.

p. 216   'the 3 barrels of bread and 3 barrels of beer': Redwood to Dickinson, 11 February 1711, Redwood Archive, Redwood Library, Newport, RI.

p. 218   A census carried out by Governor Parke in 1708: *Cal Col* 1706–8, nos. 1383, 1396; Oliver, *History of the Island of Antigua*, 1:lxxviii.

19. The Beckfords: The Next Generation

p. 219   'The Passions of the Mind': Sloane, *A Voyage to the Islands* 1:xxxi.

p. 219   'to succeed to the Government of Jamaica': *Cal Col* 1696–7, no. 1368.

p. 219   sworn in as Receiver General in November 1696 'on giving the usual security': ibid., no. 344.

p. 219   'This Eve Mr Lewis [the Deputy Judge Advocate] was unfortunately killed': PRO CO 134/4, p. 222.

p. 220   'immediately dyed (his sword not being drawn out of the scabbard)': *Cal Col* 1699, nos. 435, 449, 466; 1698, no. 86.

p. 220   'To say the Truth, our young Squires are not much afraid of the Courts of Justice': Leslie, *A New and Exact Account of Jamaica*, 42.

p. 220   'by the interest that was made he . . . came off too without damage': *Cal Col* 1708–9, no. 452.

p. 220   'a people very capricious, jealous, and difficult to manage': *Cal Col* 1702, no. 267.

p. 220   'caused himself to be proclaimed [Lieutenant-Governor of Jamaica], saying to the Assembly': Cundall, *Historic Jamaica*, 359.

p. 220   'without any reluctancye of the people': *Cal Col* 1702, no. 323.

p. 220   'generally disliked': *Cal Col* 1702, no. 267.

p. 220   'I have not heard one man speak well of him since I came to the Island': *Cal Col* 1693–6, no. 2021.

p. 221   news of which reached Jamaica in July 1702: *Cal Col* 1702–3, no. 743.

p. 221   he implied that he had been part of the famous attack by Morgan 30 years earlier: *Cal Col* 1702–3, no. 1056.

p. 221   'we were served so the last war and felt the unhappy consequence of it': ibid.

p. 221   'maintain things in a quiet and good posture': ibid., no. 978.

p. 221   'the Government of this Island now is entirely in the hands of the Planters': Admiral Benbow to Secretary of State James Vernon, 1 June 1702, PRO CO 137/45.

p. 221   'a brave and resolute officer': Renny, *An History of Jamaica*, 47.

p. 221   'ready . . . on all occasions to express my duty to her majesty': *Cal Col* 1702–3, no. 275.

p. 221   returned by no fewer than three different parishes, choosing to sit for St Elizabeth: Cundall, *Historic Jamaica*, 360–1.

p. 222   Thomas also married an heiress, Mary Ballard: Redding, *Memoirs of William Beckford*, 1:5.

p. 222   'thro' the infirmity of his age': *Cal Col* 1704–5, no. 1168.

p. 222   'I am of opinion I have had a snake in my bosom all this while': *Cal Col* 1704–5, no. 1303.

p. 222   'Col. Beckford and his two sons, whom he has got into the House; they have been both tried for murder': *Cal Col* 1706–8, no. 678.

p. 222   'the chief contriver and promoter of faction and discord': *Cal Col* 1720–1, no. 562.

p. 222   'fell into such warm debates . . . that they put the whole Town into an uproar': *Cal Col* 1710–11, no. 187.

p. 223   three in a hundred of the population survived beyond the age of 60: Dunn, *Sugar and Slaves*, 332.

p. 223   'sober' hard-working and 'fit': *Cal Col* 1681–5, p. 590.

p. 223   'early risers, temperate livers in general, inured to moderate exercise, and avoiders of excess in eating': Long, *History of Jamaica*, 1:375.

p. 224   a further 3,593 acres in his own name: Sheridan, 'Planter and Historian', 38.

p. 224   the household goods and furniture inside the mansion were valued after Charles's death at only £213: J. Arch. Inventories, Book 12, Charles Drax, inventory dated 7 March 1722.

p. 225   'in a furrow, near her, generally to the sun and rain, on a kid skin, or such rags as she can procure': Ramsay, *Essay on the Treatment and Conversion of African Slaves*, 89.

p. 225   'wear them out before they became useless, and unable to do service; and then to buy new ones to fill up their places': Martin and Spurrel, *Journal of a Slave Trader*, 112.

p. 226   more than 20 times that of Charles Drax's Great House: Sheridan, 'Planter and Historian', 39.

p. 226   he owned 1,737 slaves outright and had part-ownership in another 577: J.Arch. Inventories, Books 19–21; Watts, *West Indies*, 345.

p. 226   the 'chief actor in all the unhappy differences in the country': Cundall, *Historic Jamaica*, 361.

p. 226   'the chief, and allmost absolute Leader': *Cal Col* 1716–17, no. 357c.

p. 226   'of most violent and pernsihious principalls': *Cal Col* 1715, no. 302iii.

p. 226   'ye younger Beckford just at ye close of ye Assembly, had like to have murdered Mr Tho. Wood': *Cal Col* 1712–14, no. 149.

p. 227   Peter Beckford be given his 'protection and favour': *Cal Col* 1713, no. 276.

p. 227   Beckford, who now waved them in the Governor's face, along with his new appointment from London: *Cal Col* 1722–3, no. 142.

p. 227   Beckford soon had his revenge, reporting Lawes for illegal trading. *Cal Col* 1722–3, no. 256.

p. 227   Cargill had been 'justly provoked' to defend his honour: Leslie, *A New and Exact Account of Jamaica*, 298.

p. 227   by the 1730s he was owed £135,000 by 128 other planters: Sheridan, 'Planter and Historian', 39.

p. 228   By 1720, there were nearly 150 British ships engaged in the slave trade: Thomas, *Slave Trade*, 243.

p. 229   'sickly seasons; and when the small pox . . . happens to be imported': Robertson, *A Detection of the State and Situation*, 44.

p. 229   the Barbados planters imported 85,000 new slaves in order to lift the black population on the island from 42,000 to 46,000: Dunn, *Sugar and Slaves*, 314.

p. 229   'scarcely had room to turn': Equiano, *Interesting Narrative*, 55.

p. 230   'a slaughterhouse, Blood, filth, misery, and diseases': quoted in Brown, *Reaper's Garden*, 44.

p. 230   losing on average a fifth of their complement each voyage: Thomas, *Slave Trade*, 309.

p. 230   'Think of the wretched Irish peasantry! Think of the crowded workhouses!' one trader wrote: Crow, *Memoirs*, 176–7.

p. 230   'civilized people': Atkins, *A Voyage to Guinea, Brasil, and the West Indies*, 57.

p. 230   'the credulity of the Whites': ibid., 129.

p. 230   'to a Land flowing with more Milk and Honey . . . offending against the laws of natural Justice and Humanity': ibid., 176–7.

p. 231   'it is not unfrequent for him who sells you Slaves to-day': ibid., 151.

p. 231   'the natives no longer occupy themselves with the search for gold': quoted in Brown, *Reaper's Garden*, 35.

p. 231   180,000 guns had been sold into the Gold Coast and Bight of Benin areas: ibid., 35.

p. 231   'illegal and unjust': Atkins, *A Voyage to Guinea, Brasil, and the West Indies*, 121.

p. 231   'an extensive Evil . . . Infringements on the Peace and Happiness of Mankind': ibid., 149.

p. 232   to 'impress Men from the Merchant-Ships': ibid., 261.

p. 232   'surprised and bound him in the night': ibid., 72–3.

20. Piracy and Rum

p. 234   'I pity them greatly': H.S. Milford, ed., *Poetical Works of William Cowper*, OUP, 1950 (4th ed.), 375.

p. 234 'great Ravages upon the Merchant Ships': Atkins, *A Voyage to Guinea, Brasil, and the West Indies*, 186.

p. 234 'which kept us Plying': ibid., 191.

p. 235 'when in drink, to utter some Portuguese or Moorish words': *Cal Col* 1700, no. 400.

p. 235 island governors complained endlessly about the dangers of the sea routes and of the daily increase of 'pyrates': *Cal Col* 1717–8, no. 271.

p. 235 spared execution on the grounds they were 'quick with child': *Cal Col* 1720–1, no. 523.

p. 235 a spectacular career that lasted less than three years: Breverton, *Black Bart Roberts*, 272.

p. 235 whose favourite tactic was to maroon the crews of the ships he attacked on deserted islands to die of hunger or thirst: Thomas, *Slave Trade*, 240.

p. 236 'The Pyrates, tho' singly Fellows of Courage': Atkins, *A Voyage to Guinea, Brasil, and the West Indies*, 192.

p. 237 'the pyrates in this Passage were very troublesome to us': ibid., 263.

p. 237 'great plenty of trading Goods, and, what more attracted the Eye, a large quantity of Gold Dust': ibid., 193.

p. 237 'true Republicans in Disposition . . . daily increase': ibid., 243–5.

p. 237 'prodigious lightnings and thunder . . . a contagious distemper, fatal for some months through the island': ibid., 238–41.

p. 238 losing a sixth of its inhabitants to a fever epidemic in 1725: Sheridan, *Sugar and Slavery*, 426.

p. 238 'too Cold in this place', he wrote to John Dickinson from Newport in January 1714: Redwood Archive, Redwood Library, Newport.

p. 239 New England came to dominate the supply of provisions, horses and lumber to its key market – the West Indian sugar colonies: James, *Colonial Rhode Island*, 159.

p. 240 'I have bought you a negro Girle of about nine or ten years of age . . .': Byam to Redwood, 15 March 1727, LNHA.

p. 240 'I would have sent ye girle you desired but . . .' Byam to Redwood, 20 July 1728, LNHA.

p. 240 'supplied by the offspring of those they have already, which increase daily': James, *Colonial Rhode Island*, 220.

p. 240 by 1732 the population of South Carolina was 14,000 whites and 32,000 blacks: Thomas, *Slave Trade*, 259.

p. 240 to 'debauch them': Sheridan, *Sugar and Slavery*, 343.

p. 240 much preferred to its rivals, West Indian rum, English spirits or French brandy: Jones, 'Rhode Island Slave Trade', 229.

p. 240 Adult male slaves could be bought for as little as 80 gallons: ibid., 234.

p. 241 20 vessels from Newport alone making the voyage every year, carrying about 1,800 hogsheads of rum. Hedges, *Browns of Providence Plantations*, 70.

p. 241 'live like Lords, and ride in a Coach and Six': Sheridan, *Sugar and Slavery*, 430.

p. 241   'Molasses was an essential ingredient in American Independence': Adams, *Novan-gulus*, 290.

p. 241   contrary to their rights as 'ye King's natural born subjects': *Cal Col* 1733, no. 79.

p. 241   A slaver owned by the Malbones of Newport: Peterson, *History of Rhode Island*, 103.

p. 242   quickly sent messages to their captains: James Brown letter book in Rhode Island Historical Society, Providence, Box 1, Folder 2, p. 21.

p. 242   which they then spent in the Dutch enclave of St Eustatius or on molasses from the French islands: correspondent to the *Barbados Gazette* in 1736, reprinted in Oliver, *Caribbeana*, 2:129.

p. 242   '35 pare of handcoofs': Rappleye, *Sons of Providence*, 14.

p. 242   'the father of slaving at Bristol, Rhode Island': Thomas, *Slave Trade*, 292.

p. 243   'I fear he will hardly be able to endure such coarse dyet & hard labour as our slaves are put to in this place': Edward Byam to Redwood, 20 July 1728, LNHA.

p. 243   'promised a great amendment': William Hillhouse to Redwood, 4 April 1729, LNHA.

p. 243   by the 1720s had a white population of about 5,000 (with some 18,000 black slaves): Sheridan, 'Rise of a Colonial Gentry', 343; *Cal Col* 1724–5, no. 260.

p. 243   'look into his affairs': Jonas Langford 14 March 1728, LNHA.

p. 243   'our Island is very sickly' 'especially to strangers': Byam to Redwood, 17 March 1730, LNHA.

p. 244   'all the merchants refused to advance anything for the West India correspondents': Ford, *The Commerce of Rhode Island*, 38–9.

p. 244   'of Mr French, Barbados, valued at seventy pounds': Tomlinson to Redwood, 30 June 1735, LNHA.

p. 245   'Your spouse was very unwilling they should be sent': Cheeseborough to Redwood, 27 February 1738, quoted in Donnan, *Documents Illustrative of the History of the Slave Trade*, 3:134.

p. 245   'an Unlucky Changeable Beast': ibid.

p. 246   'thy wife has beene very much out of order': Coggeshall to Redwood, 3 February 1739, LNHA.

p. 246   'You have raised our Expectations of Seeing you': Cheeseborough to Redwood, 6 February 1739, LNHA.

p. 246   'your cousin I think was never drunker in his life': Tomlinson to Redwood, 26 April 1739, LNHA.

p. 246   'in the Old Condition, Carted up to your Estate, the rest ordinary enough': Tomlinson to Redwood, 1740 (n.d. fragment), LNHA.

p. 246   'I am heartily sorry Pope has againe made you so bad a voyage too and from the Coast of Guinea': Gunthorpe to Redwood, 22 July 1740, LNHA.

p. 246   'nineteen slaves unsold': Pope to Redwood, 24 May 1740, LNHA.

p. 246   'the people hear in General is very Backward in paying there debts': Pope to Redwood, 23 June 1740, LNHA.

p. 246   buying his slaves in Antigua or in Rhode Island: Donnan, *Documents Illustrative of the History of the Slave Trade*, 3:140.

p. 247   the business would be reactivated, under the management of his sons. ibid., 2:152.

21. The Maroon War in Jamaica and the War of Jenkins's Ear

p. 248   'That the Negros here use Naturall (or Diabolical) Magick no planter in Barbados doubts': Walduck, 'T. Walduck's Letters from Barbados', 148.

p. 248   'well planted with provisions': *Cal Col* 1702, no. 912.

p. 249   'rebellious negroes . . . have been so bold to come down armed and attack our out settlements to Windward': ibid.

p. 249   Beckford had sent out four parties, one of which, consisting of only 20 men: Craton, *Testing the Chains*, 79.

p. 249   'the negroes faced our men so long as they had any ammunition left' *Cal Col* 1702, no. 978.

p. 249   another got lost in the swamps and a quarter of the men drowned or died of fever: PRO CO 137/18; CO 137/19.

p. 249   'pretty healthy and might be kept so were it not for rumm': *Cal Col* 1731, no. 202.

p. 249   'wofull state, some companys having lost more than half their compliment chiefly owing to drunkenness': ibid., no. 415.

p. 249   a stalemate, exhausting for both sides: *Cal Col* 1732, no. 146; *Cal Col* 1733, nos. 75, 244.

p. 250   'The service here is not like that in Flanders or any part of Europe': Craton, *Testing the Chains*, 83.

p. 251   'possessed few of the external graces as far as expression and manner were concerned': Redding, *Memoirs of William Beckford*, 1:21.

p. 251   he fell in love with an unsuitable girl: ibid., 1:17.

p. 251   a 'strange and contradictory character': Hackman, 'William Beckford: The Jamaican Connection', 24.

p. 251   'a common soldier' in the island's militia: Taylor and Pringle, *Correspondence of William Pitt*, 1:185.

p. 252   seizing a large number of English vessels, including legitimate traders: Long, *History of Jamaica*, 1:293.

p. 252   almost all the 'sugar names' – Frye, Tomlinson, Warner and others: 13 October 1737, *Cal Col* 1737, no. 540.

p. 252   'Villainy is inherent to this climate': Laughton, 'Jenkins' Ear', 742.

p. 252   'At present we have nothing but Rumours of War': Wilks to Redwood, 13 October 1739, LNHA.

p. 253   'Universal dejection prevailed': Smollett, *An account of the expedition against Carthagene*, 342.

p. 253   during the fighting in Europe at the same time, the British army lost just 8 per cent of its strength to fighting and disease: *TLS*, 30 July 2010, p. 12, 'Black and yellow' by Gabriel Paquette.

p. 253   in the West Indies, 'whatever is attempted in that climate must be done *uno impetu*': 11 September 1758, Taylor and Pringle, *Correspondence of William Pitt*, 1:353.

p. 254   'damage and disgrace': Smollett, *An account of the expedition against Carthagene*, 342.

p. 254   'We flow in Money': *Gentleman's Magazine* 1744, p. 393.

p. 254   'the People of this Island were intent on nothing so much as encouraging Privateers': Leslie, *A New and Exact Account of Jamaica*, 305.

p. 254   'But I was surprised to find that no matters of philosophy were brought upon the carpet': Chapin, *Rhode Island Privateers in Kings George's War*, 12.

p. 255   Colonel Peter Beckford . . . had complained about ships from 'our Northern Plantations' supplying the Spanish: *Cal Col* 1702, no. 733.

p. 255   This money was then taken to St Eustatius or the French islands, where it was used to purchase cheaper sugar or molasses: *Journal* 1749–50, 130.

p. 256   he had seen 16 or 17 vessels from the North American colonies brazenly loading and unloading at St Eustatius: Burns, *History of the British West Indies*, 482.

p. 256   'one or two men-of-war stationed at Rhode Island would be sufficient': *Journal* 1749–50, 131.

p. 256   'laden with provisions and Naval Stores, who bring back French Rum and Molasses': Knowles to Newcastle, 20 November 1747, BL Add. MS 32713, fol. 472.

p. 256   'he should certainly have taken Martinique': Beer, *British Colonial Policy*, 73n.

p. 256   'the prosperity of the French Islands and the ruin of our own': *Journal* 1749–50, 136.

p. 257   'building Batteries & throwing up entrenchments': Tomlinson to Redwood, 12 June 1744, LNHA.

p. 257   'We are now in the utmost distress for want of provisions & Lumber of all sorts' Tomlinson to Redwood, 24 May 1746, LNHA.

p. 257   'one of the finest gardens I ever saw in my life': *Bulletin of the Newport Historical Society* 45, no. 146 (Spring 1972); Bolhouse, 'Abraham Redwood, Reluctant Quaker'.

p. 258   hundreds of pounds' worth of books, paid for from the proceeds of his Antigua sugar: Redwood letter, 11 February 1748, LNHA.

p. 258   'almost every thing' was brought 'in the lumber vessels from America': Thompson, *Sailor's Letters*, 107.

22. Barbados, the 'Civilized Isle.'

p. 259   'very homely and great Swearers': Atkins, *A Voyage to Guinea, Brasil, and the West Indies*, 208.

p. 259   'a dry crust, burnt up and gaping': Schomburgk, *The History of Barbados*, 322.

p. 259   'The industry & integrity of its first founders is lost': Walduck, 'T. Walduck's Letters from Barbados', 28.

p. 260   'hardship, sweat, and toil of their forefathers': Anon., *Some Observations*, 22.

p. 260   'fiery, restless spirits': Burkes, *An Account of the European settlements*, 2:102.

p. 260   'Vain and shewy,' many were living way beyond their reduced means, and falling into debt: Watson, *Barbados*, 51.

p. 260   'There is no Recreation out of Business': Atkins, *A Voyage to Guinea, Brasil, and the West Indies*, 206.

p. 260   'oblig'd, for the most part, to sedentary Diversions': Watson, *Barbados*, 48.

p. 260 'Though a Creole was languishing on his death bed': Moreton, *West India Customs and Manners*, 105.

p. 260 'Dancing is too violent an Exercise in this hot Climate': Hillary, *Observations on the Changes of the Air*, xi.

p. 260 a number of the leading proprietors had followed the example of Henry Drax: Watts, *The West Indies*, 354.

p. 260 Assembly elections were frequently fixed: Walduck, 'T. Walduck's Letters from Barbados', 141.

p. 260 a judge for one of the districts of Barbados where a case against him was to be tried: *Journal*, 1714–18, 154.

p. 260 in 1728 one man held eight civil and military posts: *Cal Col* 1728–9, no. 389.

p. 261 summoned to London to answer the charges, but was cleared: Smith, *Slavery, Family and Gentry Capitalism*, 59.

p. 261 sending it to London to benefit from the higher price arising from the monopoly: *Cal Col* 1720–1 no. 713.

p. 262 'to have cut his throat and arms and across his belly': Smith, *Slavery, Family and Gentry Capitalism*, 87.

p. 262 recouped the £12,000 outlay in just one year: Sheridan, *Sugar and Slavery*, 444.

p. 262 a number of deer to grace the Gedney Clarke lawns in Barbados: Hamer, *Letters and Papers of Henry Laurens*, 2:83.

p. 262 orders came by return packet for him to be restored: Senhouse papers *JBMHS* 2, 115.

p. 263 'I am sorry I cannot say any thing pleasant about this place': Thompson, *Sailor's Letters*, 111–2.

p. 263 the ratio of blacks to whites: Deerr, *History of Sugar*, 1:166.

p. 264 most of the estates were run by newly-arrived Scotsmen: Thompson, *Sailor's Letters*, 107.

p. 264 the 1730s saw the establishment of a number of good quality schools: Watson, *Barbados*, 110.

p. 264 'the languid syllables . . .': Pinckard, *Notes*, 2:107.

p. 264 found Barbadians 'more easy, hospitable and kind': Thompson, *Sailor's Letters*, 112.

p. 264 'We do not live so flash and fast': quoted in Pares, *Yankees and Creoles*, 4.

p. 265 'carbuncled faces, slender legs and thighs': Whitson, 'The Outlook of the Continental American Colonies', 65.

p. 265 'Barbados Hotel, putting up for a sign': Watson, *Barbados*, 12.

p. 265 'fickle & Merciliss Ocean': Warren, 'The Significance of George Washington's Journey to Barbados', 5.

p. 265 'with some reluctance': Toner, *Daily Journal*, 40.

p. 266 'perfectly enraptured': ibid., 42.

p. 266 'How wonderful that such people shou'd be in debt!': ibid., 58–9.

p. 266 'extravagantly dear': ibid., 48.

p. 266 'the prospect is extensive by Land and pleasant by Sea': ibid., 48.

p. 266 'Genteely receiv'd and agreeably entertain'd': Warren, 'The Significance of George Washington's Journey to Barbados', 10.

p. 266 'After Dinner was the greatest Collection of Fruits': Toner, *Daily Journal*, 50.

p. 266 'very few who may be called middling people they are either very rich or very poor': ibid., 48.

p. 267 'Generally very agreeable, but by ill custom... affect the Negro Style': Fitzpatrick, *The Diaries of George Washington* 1: 28.

p. 267 'The planters at Barbadoes are cruel to their unhappy slaves': Handler, *A Guide to Source Materials*, 81.

p. 267 'some trivial domestic error': Thompson, *Sailor's Letters*, 113.

p. 267 'taught in their very infancy to flog with a whip the slaves that offends them': ibid.

p. 267 'knocking the poor Negroes about the cheeks': Waller, *A Voyage to the West Indies*, 26–7.

p. 267 'of a more volatile and lively Disposition': Greene, 'Changing Identity in the British Caribbean', 143.

p. 267 'Here I find every Thing alter'd': Leslie, *A New and Exact Account of Jamaica*, 1.

p. 267 'When you get to Kingston, if you had five more senses, they would be all engaged': Moreton, *West India Customs and Manners*, 16.

p. 268 'Too much blue, too much purple, too much green': Rhys, *Wide Sargasso Sea*, 1967 ed., 70.

p. 268 'hardened to the callous frankness of a Jamaica liaison': de Lisser, *White Witch of Rose Hall*, 71.

p. 268 'many a young man arrive from England with the noblest resolves and the highest ideals': ibid., 102.

p. 268 'This was Jamaica': ibid., 112.

p. 268 'I have seen these unfortunate Wretches gnaw the Flesh off their own Shoulders': Burns, *History of the British West Indies*, 766.

p. 268 'would ill suit a gentleman of your nature ... real or imaginary Crosses, which are the same in effect': Smith, *Slavery, Family and Gentry Capitalism*, 85–6.

p. 269 'The real or supposed necessity of treating the Negroes with rigour': Thomas, *Slave Trade*, 308.

p. 269 'Like wax softened by the heat': Moreton, *West India Customs and Manners*, 78–81.

p. 269 'despotick government over their poor slaves': Thompson, *Sailor's Letters*, 107.

p. 269 'terrible Whippings ...': Leslie, *A New and Exact Account of Jamaica*, 39.

23. Thomas Thistlewood in Jamaica: 'Tonight very lonely and melancholy again'

p. 270 'to enquire for Mr Beckford Esqr ... but was informed he is now in Jamaica': Hall, *In Miserable Slavery*, 9.

p. 271 in 1763 he got Benjamin Franklin's book on electricity: TD, 14 September 1763.

p. 272 'Put it upon a pole and stuck it up just at the angle of the road in the home pasture': ibid., 9 October 1751.

p. 272   'Sense of Injury which will dispose them to Revenge that may produce more fatal Consequence than desertion': ibid., 10 April 1754.

p. 272   the slaves hated him and wanted him dead: ibid.

p. 273   outnumbered by the enslaved Africans by as much as 16 to one: Walvin, *Trader, the Owner, the Slave*, 107.

p. 273   'in the Negro manner, "I will kill you, I will kill you now"': TD, 27 December 1752.

p. 273   'one saying he was sick, the others that they were in a hurry': ibid.

p. 273   'My pocket Whip is broke and Wore out': TD, 24 March 1759.

p. 274   'Had Derby well whipped': ibid., 28 January 1756.

p. 274   'made Hector shit in his mouth': ibid., 23 July 1756.

p. 274   his face chopped with a machete: ibid., 4 August 1756.

p. 274   'picketed' on 'a quart bottle neck till she begged hard': Walvin, *Trader, the Owner, the Slave*, 148.

p. 274   'the entire extirpation of the white inhabitants': Long, *History of Jamaica*, 2:447–8.

p. 275   'strange various reports with torment & confusion': TD, 26 May 1760.

p. 275   'til they force the whites to give them free like Cudjoe's Negroes': ibid., 1 August 1760.

p. 275   'was made to sit on the ground, and his body being chained to an iron stake': Craton, *Testing the Chains*, 136–7.

p. 275   'he brought to my Memory ye picture of Robinson Crusoe': TD, 1 June 1750.

p. 276   '*Sup. lect. cum Marina*': TD, 7 July 1751.

p. 276   '*Cum* Flora, a congo, *Super Terram*': ibid., 10 September 1751.

p. 276   slept with nearly 140 different women, almost all black slaves, while in Jamaica: Walvin, *Trader, the Owner, the Slave*, 118.

p. 276   'Perceived a small redness, but did not regard it': TD, 30 September 1751.

p. 276   'last night *Cum* Dido': ibid., 1 October 1751.

p. 276   'Spoke to Dr Joseph Horlock. A rank infection': ibid., 9 October 1751.

p. 276   'bathing the penis a long time': ibid., 26 November 1751.

p. 276   '*cum*' Nago Jenny: ibid., 3 December 1751.

p. 276   'ye Barb[ados] woman that was rap'd by three of them': ibid., 8 January 1751.

p. 276   'At Night Mr Paul Stevens and Thomas Adams going to tear old Sarah to pieces in her hutt': ibid., 20 March 1753.

p. 277   'haw'led Eve separately into the Water Room and were Concern'd with her': ibid., 12 March 1755.

p. 277   'Mrs Cope also examined the sheets and found them amiss': ibid., 2–5 May 1756.

p. 277   'Mr C. in his trantrums last night': ibid., 9 October 1756.

p. 277   'young and full-breasted': Thomas, *Slave Trade*, 397.

p. 277   'riot in these goatish embraces': Long, *History of Jamaica*, 2:328.

p. 278   'keep a favourite black or mulatta girl on every estate': Moreton, *West India Customs and Manners*, 77–8.

p. 278   'murdered him for meddling with their women': TD, 17 December 1761.

p. 278   'Things seemed odd, but yet very pleasant': 25 February 1764, quoted in Hall, *In Miserable Slavery*, 131.

p. 278   'how strangely he looked': TD, 31 March 1765.

p. 278   'with load Huzzas': ibid., 4 April 1765.

p. 279   'Mirtilla is very ill, it is thought going to miscarry': ibid., 22 January 1755.

p. 279   'abused Mr and Mrs Mould in an extraordinary manner': ibid., 24 February 1756.

p. 280   they had sex 234 times: Burnard, *Mastery, Tyranny, & Desire*, 238.

p. 280   'I could not sleep, but vastly uneasy': TD, 19 June 1757.

p. 281   'Tonight very lonely and melancholy again': ibid., 4 July 1757.

p. 281   'She is in miserable slavery': ibid., 17 July 1757.

p. 281   the Copes had at last agreed to rent her to Thistlewood for £18 a year: Hall, *In Miserable Slavery*, 163.

p. 281   Thistlewood intervened to stop the rape of Coobah: TD, 19 February 1758.

p. 281   Phibbah was freed by a clause in Thistlewood's will: Hall, *In Miserable Slavery*, 313.

p. 281   Phibbah had already 'transcended' her state: Burnard, *Mastery, Tyranny, & Desire*, 240.

p. 282   'with a bad looseness': Hall, *In Miserable Slavery*, 94.

p. 282   entertained the white wives of two local grandees to tea: TD 16 February 1779.

p. 282   'naked for the mosquitoes to bite here tonight': ibid., 7 August 1770.

p. 282   'this offers the only hope they have of procuring a sum of money': Connell, 'Hotel Keepers and Hotels in Barbados', 162–3.

p. 282   who saw her as their friend: Craton, *Testing the Chains*, 129.

p. 283   'History of Jack the Giant Killer in 2 parts': TD, 20 August 1769.

p. 283   'become a member of Jamaica's brown elite': Burnard, *Mastery, Tyranny, & Desire*, 235.

p. 283   'very ill': TD, 1 September 1780.

p. 283   'much in liquor': ibid., 5 September 1780.

p. 283   'almost out of her senses': Brown, *Reaper's Garden*, 55.

p. 283   'putrid fever': TD, 1 September 1780.

p. 283   'in the old garden, between the pimento tree and the bee houses': ibid., 7 September 1780.

24. Jamaica: Rich and Poor

p. 285   he was worth nearly £3,000 at the time of his death: Burnard, *Mastery, Tyranny, & Desire*, 40.

p. 285   some 35 worth more than £1500. Walvin, *Trader, the Owner, the Slave*, 170.

p. 286   he only got three or four hours' sleep out of 24: Moreton, *West India Customs and Manners*, 51.

p. 286   'a dull, cheerless, drudging life': Stewart, *A View of the Past and Present State*, 189.

p. 286   'Crakka Juba': TD, 5 February 1758.

p. 286   Patrick May, was said to be 'in his house all day, drunk': ibid., 23 May 1763.

p. 286   'Yesterday afternoon John Groves like a madman amongst the Negroes': ibid., 6 January 1761.

p. 287   Ten per cent of those who held wealth owned two thirds of the island's total: Burnard, *Mastery, Tyranny, & Desire*, 40.

p. 287   from 17 shillings per hundred weight in 1733 to 43 shillings in 1747: Deerr, *History of Sugar*, 2:530.

p. 287   By 1750, nearly half of the sugar imported into the UK came from Jamaica, which also had the most productive mills: Hall, *In Miserable Slavery*, xxi.

p. 287   'not only the richest but the most considerable colony at this time under the government of Great Britain': Browne, *Civil and Natural History of Jamaica*, 9.

p. 287   worth between 20 and 30 times as much as the same man in Britain or North America: Burnard, *Mastery, Tyranny, & Desire*, 15.

p. 287   In 1774, per capita wealth in England was around £42; in Jamaica for a white man it was more than £1,000. Brown, *Reaper's Garden*, 16.

p. 287   in Jamaica the average sugar plantation in 1750 had some 200: Burnard, *Mastery, Tyranny, & Desire*, 41.

p. 287   'While we have so profitable a mine above ground': Deerr, *History of Sugar*, 1: 175n.

p. 288   owning about the same again, spread across 12 of Jamaica's parishes: Sheridan, 'Planter and Historian', 40.

p. 288   'frequently Lyes with Black women': Craton and Walvin, *A Jamaican Plantation*, 77.

p. 288   'rich a man as William Beckford, for possessions but in debt'. TD, 1 September 1757.

p. 289   'High Living': John Fuller to Rose Fuller, 10 August 1733, Crossley and Saville, *Fuller Letters*, 63.

p. 289   'Mary Johnson Rose of J'ca a free mulatto woman formerly my housekeeper': *Gentleman's Magazine*, vol. 299, (July–September 1905), 593.

p. 289   'Abundance of Business': Leslie, *A New and Exact Account of Jamaica*, 52.

p. 289   was rich enough to be lending money to Richard Beckford: Crossley and Saville, *Fuller Letters*, 253.

p. 290   'surprising to see the number of Coaches and Chariots which are perpetually plying': Leslie, *A New and Exact Account of Jamaica*, 27.

p. 290   Dresden ruffles, silver buckles and expensive belts and swords: J. Arch. Inventories, Book 36, 1756: Thomas Thompson,

p. 290   'and appear with as good a Grace': Leslie, *A New and Exact Account of Jamaica*, 34–5.

p. 290   'extraordinary good Actors': ibid., 27.

p. 290   'the noblest and best edifice of the kind': Long, *History of Jamaica*, 2:7.

p. 290   'suffered to decay': ibid., 2:3.

p. 290   some 1,200 free blacks or mulattoes: ibid., 2:103.

p. 291   'incredible number of . . . grog shops': Moreton, *West India Customs and Manners*, 35–6.

p. 291   'The People seem all sickly': Leslie, *A New and Exact Account of Jamaica*, 1.

p. 291   153 pregnancies, which produced 121 live births Burnard, *Mastery, Tyranny, & Desire*, 220–222.

p. 291 'An Account of negroes and Stock dead': William Mackinen to Redwood, 24 March 1757, LNHA.

p. 291 'One, two, tree': Renny, *An History of Jamaica*, 24.

p. 292 the proportionate, few whites died at an even greater rate: Burnard, '"The Countrie Continues Sicklie"', 71.

p. 292 20 per cent of the town's population dying every year: ibid., 53.

p. 292 'great charnel house': ibid., 50.

p. 292 'Creolians . . . seldom live to be above five and thirty years': Buisseret, *Jamaica in 1687*, 240.

p. 292 compared to two million in the Thirteen Colonies: O'Shaughnessy, *An Empire Divided*, 7.

p. 292 in the same time the population of some of the North American colonies had increased tenfold: Burnard: 'A Failed Settler Society', 64.

p. 292 'They console themselves, however, that they can enjoy more of the real existence here in one hour': Long, *History of Jamaica*, 2:285.

p. 292 'keep late hours at night: lounges a-bed in the morning': ibid., 1:375.

p. 293 as much alcohol per white as was consumed per capita in the United States in 1974: Burnard, 'A Failed Settler Society', 68.

p. 293 'the appearance of being ten years older than they really are': Waller, *A Voyage to the West Indies*, 26.

p. 293 he had lost to disease two wives and 16 children out of 21: Samuel Martin to Charles Baldwin 22 Feb. 1776 BL Add. MSS 41351, fol. 65.

p. 293 'anarchic individualism' of the West Indies: Burnard, 'A Failed Settler Society', 72.

p. 293 'The frequent occurrence' of death: quoted in Brown, *Reaper's Garden*, 58.

p. 293 of the 136 who had arrived on a ship 16 months earlier, 122 were dead: TD, 26 April 1759.

p. 293 'No Sett of Men are more unconcerned at [death's] Approach': Leslie, *A New and Exact Account of Jamaica*, 1.

p. 294 'lack of public spirit': Long, *History of Jamaica* 2:26.

p. 294 dwarfing the number of boys from North America by a factor of about seven: O'Shaughnessy, *An Empire Divided*, 21.

p. 294 preferring 'gaming' to 'the Belles Letteres': Leslie, *A New and Exact Account of Jamaica*, 38.

p. 294 'carried no Gods with them', going instead into 'the wilderness of mere materialism': J. R. Seeley, quoted in Beckles, *Inside Slavery*, 124–5.

p. 294 'have built in those islands as if we were but passing visitors': Froude, *English in the West Indies*, 256.

p. 294 'animates their industry and alleviates their misfortune': Edwards, *Thoughts on the Late Proceedings*, 29.

p. 294 'incessantly sigh for a return': quoted in O'Shaughnessy, *An Empire Divided*, 3.

p. 294 One third of Jamaican plantation owners were absentees by the 1740s, two thirds by 1800: ibid., 4–5.

p. 295 In St Kitts, half the property was owned by absentees in 1745: Pitman, *Development of the West Indies*, 39 fn 82.

25. The Sugar Lobby

p. 296 *Herald* newspaper, 23 August 1797: quoted in Keith, 'Relaxations in the British Restrictions', 16.

p. 296 'Sugar, sugar, hey? – all *that* sugar!': quoted in Pares, *Merchants and Planters*, 38.

p. 296 trebled between 1700 and 1740, and had doubled again by 1770: Sheridan, *Sugar and Slavery*, 21.

p. 296 as invented by Rebecca Price: Shephard, *Pickled, Potted and Canned*, 163.

p. 297 'Sugar is so generally in use': Long, *History of Jamaica*, 1:525.

p. 297 12 to 16 pounds of sugar be used with every pound of tea: Sheridan, *Sugar and Slavery*, 28.

p. 297 willing to accept factory discipline in order to afford their luxury stimulants: Davis, *Inhuman Bondage*, 88.

p. 297 'Among the lower orders . . . industry can only be found': Sheridan, *Sugar and Slavery*, 35.

p. 297 importing more than twice the amount as much more populous France: O'Shaughnessy, *An Empire Divided*, 72; Sheridan, *Sugar and Slavery*, 24.

p. 297 British livelihoods in the West Indies colonies depended on it: *The Country Journal or the Craftsman*, 5 June 1736, quoted in Sheridan, *Sugar and Slavery*, 345–6.

p. 297 'their rum is excellent of which they consume large quantities': Sheridan, *Sugar and Slavery*, 346.

p. 298 rum imports into England and Wales had risen to two million gallons: ibid., 347–8.

p. 298 'a constant Mine whence Britain draws prodigious Riches': Leslie, *A New and Exact Account of Jamaica*, 354.

p. 298 'necessary appendage to our present refined manner of living': Browne, *Civil and Natural History of Jamaica*, v.

p. 298 'the principal cause of the rapid motion which now agitates the universe': Williams, *Capitalism and Slavery*, 105.

p. 299 'that excited the indignation of every honest man who became acquainted with the transaction': Cundall, *Historic Jamaica*, 304.

p. 300 Francis owned lands in Hampshire and Surrey, as well as a house in Albermarle Street London: Sheridan, 'Planter and Historian', 41.

p. 300 'there were scarcely ten miles together throughout the country': Sheridan, *Sugar and Slavery*, 473.

p. 300 stocked with the best furniture, objects and paintings that money could buy: Alexander, *England's Wealthiest Son*, 34–5.

p. 300 'where expense has reached its utmost limits in furniture and ornaments': Warner, *Excursions from Bath*, 119.

p. 301 'with the appearance of immense riches, almost too tawdrily exhibited': Climenson, *Passages from the Diaries*, 166.

p. 301 'there was no such thing as a borough to be had now': Sheridan, *Sugar and Slavery*, 66.

p. 301 'West Indians', able to 'turn the balance on which side they please': quoted in Penson, *Colonial Agents*, 228.

p. 301 'West Indies vastly outweigh us of the Northern Colonies': Franklin to Collinson, 30 April 1764, quoted in Beer, *British Colonial Policy*, 136.

p. 302 his 'intelligent and perfect' 'comprehension of its essential interest': Long, *History of Jamaica*, 1:122.

p. 302 'which he could not parry': Cumberland, *Memoirs*, 97.

p. 302 'hence somewhat out of place in City epicurism': Redding, *Memoirs of William Beckford*, 1:28.

p. 303 'He is of a very agreeable disposition, but begins already to think of being master of a great fortune': Lees-Milne, *William Beckford*, 3.

p. 303 such as that of 1758 against French slave forts in Africa: Hotblack, *Chatham's Colonial Policy*, 16.

p. 303 'great guns fired out at sea': TD, 16 February 1757.

p. 303 'plundered Mr Thos. White's house': ibid., 7 December 1762.

p. 304 only 3,000 men still in action out of an original force of nearly 15,000: Rodger, *Command of the Ocean*, 286.

p. 305 several prisoners had been taken by their cruisers four times in less than two months: Stout, *Royal Navy in America*, 16.

p. 305 'sewed in the hinder part of his britches or drawers': ibid., 17.

p. 306 'a lawless set of smugglers': Beer, *British Colonial Policy*, 83.

p. 306 'illegal and most pernicious trade': Taylor and Pringle, *Correspondence of William Pitt*, 2: 320–1.

p. 306 'the large supplies they have lately received from their good friends the New England flag of truce vessels': Stout, *Royal Navy in America*, 17.

p. 306 he was taken to Williamsburg: JCBL, Obadiah Brown Records, Series IV, Maritime records, Sub-Series F: Brigantine *Prudent Hannah*.

p. 306 In fact the *Prudent Hannah* carried 47 barrels of flour: Rhode Island Historical Society, Providence, RI, Obadiah Brown papers I, Series 2, Subseries 4, Box 2x, Folder 5:1758 Vice-Admiralty Court Case against brig *Prudent Hannah*, Virginia.

p. 306 'they Looked on me as an Enemy and Trator to my Country': letter of 26 August 1758, JCBL, Obadiah Brown Records, Series IV, Maritime records, Sub-Series F: Brigantine *Prudent Hannah*.

26. Luxury and Debt

p. 311 'Sugar, sugar, is the incessant cry': Ramsay, *Essay on the Treatment and Conversion of African Slaves*, 80.

p. 311 'epidemical disorder': Sheridan, *Sugar and Slavery*, 443.

p. 311 'Threats, Arguments & the force of money': Smith, *Slavery, Family and Gentry Capitalism*, 116.

p. 311 'Thus I am placed in his shoes': ibid., 130.

p. 312 'the greatest failure that ever happened here': ibid., 190.

p. 313 had by the 1770s accumulated more than 26,000 acres across 11 parishes: Craton and Walvin, *A Jamaican Plantation*, 79.

p. 313   'a very fine piece of water, which in winter is commonly stocked with wild-duck and teal': Long, *History of Jamaica*, 2:76.

p. 313   'that respectable but unfortunate family': Cundall, *Historic Jamaica*, 262.

p. 314   'fraudulent Trading of the Sugar Planters': Massie, *Brief Observations concerning the Management of the War*, 8–9.

p. 314   'the interest of the home-consumer has been sacrificed': Smith, *Wealth of Nations*, 274 (T. Nelson ed., 1868).

p. 315   the only impulse is to eat as much as possible and do as little work as possible. ibid., 159.

p. 315   two-thirds of all American slaves worked for the sugar barons: Thomas, *Slave Trade*, 447.

p. 316   'Some happier island . . .': Pope, 'Essay on Man', 1:107.

p. 316   'a place of great wealth and dreadful wickedness, a den of tyrants, and a dungeon of slaves': Boswell, *Life of Johnson*, 2:559, 561.

p. 316   'negro whipping Beckford': quoted in O'Shaughnessy, *An Empire Divided*, 14.

p. 316   'For B . . . f . . . d he was chosen May'r . . .': quoted in Drescher, *Capitalism and Antislavery*, 178–9.

p. 316   'made in less enlightened times than our own': Beilby Porteus, quoted in Ryden, *West Indian Slavery and Abolition*, 185.

p. 317   'The status of slavery is so odious that nothing can be suffered to support it but positive law': Deerr, *History of Sugar*, 2:299.

p. 317   'I absolutely deny all Slave-holding to be consistent with any degree of even natural Justice': Wesley, *Thoughts on Slavery*, 31.

p. 318   'the inconsistency of holding slaves': Clarkson, *The History of the rise . . .*, 1:152.

p. 318   'without seeing the inconsistency of such conduct': Benezet, *A Caution*, 11.

p. 318   'Wherefore we', the Newport Quakers resolved, 'on that account do Disown him': Bolhouse, 'Abraham Redwood', 31.

p. 319   '1 boye slave Dyed': Brig *Sally* Account Book, 86, JCBL.

p. 319   'and forced overboard eighty of them which obliged the rest to submit': Donnan, *Documents Illustrative of the History of the Slave Trade*, 3:213.

p. 320   'than the taking of Fort William Henry did in 1757': Stout, *Royal Navy in America*, 40.

p. 320   'What are the people of England now going to do with us?': Tench Francis to Nicholas Brown, 16 September 1763, JCBL Box 7, Folder 4, Letter 7.

p. 320   'What method will be best for us to Take': Letter to Nicolas Brown & Co., 28 October 1763, quoted in Wiener, 'Rhode Island Merchants and the Sugar Act', 471.

p. 320   'open a correspondence with the principal merchants in all our sister colonies': *Boston Evening Post*, 19 December 1763.

p. 320   'in order to . . . Join with Those of the other Colonys': Nicholas Brown to David Van Horne, 24 January 1764, quoted in Hedges, *Browns of Providence Plantations*, 200.

p. 320   the first to lodge an official protest against the Sugar Act: Donnan, *Documents Illustrative of the History of the Slave Trade*, 3:203.

p. 321 'rich, proud, and overbearing Planters of the West Indies': *Providence Gazette*, 14 January 1764.

p. 321 'excessive contraband Trade carried on at Rhode Island': Stout, *Royal Navy in America*, 65.

p. 321 'without the concurrent Assistance of *Swaggering Soldiers*: *Providence Gazette*, 3 December 1763.

p. 322 'they ceased firing before we had convinced them of their error': Smith to Colvill, 12 July 1764, Bartlett, *Records of the Colony of Rhode Island*, 6:430.

p. 322 'There was not a man on the continent of America who does not consider the Sugar Act': Sheridan, *Sugar and Slavery*, 355.

p. 322 'every one is convinced of the Necessity of a Unanimity amongst the Colonies': 31 July 1764, JCBL, Box 7. Folder 2, Letter 20.

p. 322 'Rummagings and Searchings, Unladings & Detainings': Crane, *Benjamin Franklin's Letters*, 66–7.

p. 322 'can walk the streets without being affronted': Stout, *Royal Navy in America*, 76.

p. 322 criticism of the term 'mother country': *Providence Gazette*, 18 August 1764.

p. 323 producing nearly 80 per cent of Stamp Act revenue before the measure's repeal in February 1766: O'Shaughnessy, *An Empire Divided*, 81.

p. 323 'I was at the House of Commons yesterday' letter of 17 February 1767, LNHA

p. 324 'George Grenville and his Stamp Act raised the foul fiend': Taylor and Pringle, *Correspondence of William Pitt*, 3:203.

p. 324 'natural appendages of North America': O'Shaughnessy, *An Empire Divided*, xi.

27. The War Against America

p. 325 'nothing will save Barbados and the Leewards': Handler, *A Guide to Source Materials*, 1:43.

p. 325 'You will starve the islands': quoted in O'Shaughnessy, *An Empire Divided*, 142.

p. 325 as early as 1652 Barbados had requested representation in Parliament: *Cal Col* 1574–1660, p. 373.

p. 326 'the horrors of a Civil War': quoted in O'Shaughnessy, *An Empire Divided*, 141.

p. 326 'too many friends of America in this island': ibid., 142.

p. 326 'the North Americans might beat the English': Burnard, *Mastery, Tyranny, & Desire*, 94.

p. 327 'the total reduction of the colonies by the Administration': Silas Deane to Robert Morris, 26 April 1776, quoted in Clark and Morgan, *Naval Documents of the American Revolution*, 4:1275.

p. 327 'falsely imagining that he might declare his mind here': *London Chronicle*, 25–7 July 1776.

p. 327 'to inspire [them] with courage to beat the Yankee Rebels': quoted in O'Shaughnessy, *An Empire Divided*, 149.

p. 328 'entirely covered with Blood': *Public Advertiser*, 21 October 1779.

p. 328 'to sweeten his tea for breakfast by Christmas': quoted in O'Shaughnessy, *An Empire Divided*, 170.

p. 329 'My God! It is all over': Rodger, *Command of the Ocean*, 352.

p. 329 'The attack on Jamaica makes more noise than all North America': Nankivell, 'Rodney's Victory over DeGrasse', 119.

p. 330 'miserably shattered': Bridges, *Annals of Jamaica*, 2:472.

p. 330 'the decks were covered with the blood . . .': Blane, *An Account of the Battle*, 10.

p. 330 'to prepare an elegant Marble Statue of your Lordship': J. Arch., Stephen Fuller letter book, Volume Two, 1B/5/14/2.

p. 330 'No Man has their Interest more at Heart than myself': ibid., 1B/5/14/1.

p. 331 'the invincible law of absolute necessity': Ragatz, *Fall*, 295.

p. 331 'They can neither do without us, not we without them': quoted in Deerr, *History of Sugar*, 2:421.

p. 331 'Our Governors and Custom-house officers pretended': Johnstone, 'Nelson in the West Indies', 521.

28. The West Indian 'Nabobs': Absenteeism, Decadence and Decline

p. 333 'Despair . . . has cut off more people in the West-Indies': Beckford, *Descriptive Account*, 2:332.

p. 333 when locally owned than when it passed into the hands of the absentee William Beckford: Armstrong, *Old Village and the Great House*, 43.

p. 334 leaving an estate worth about £120,000: Sheridan, 'Planter and Historian', 45.

p. 334 an 'uncommon beauty': Anon., 'Biographical Sketch of William Beckford, Esq.', 261.

p. 334 'to view the romantic wonders of his estates': ibid., 261.

p. 334 'covered with a sapphire haze': Beckford, *Descriptive Account*, 1:21.

p. 334 'less romantic than, the most wild and beautiful situations of Frescati, Tivoli, and Albano': ibid., 1: 8–9.

p. 335 'the vegetation here, and the stamina of the land are of such a nature': Brumbaugh, 'An Unpublished Letter', 6.

p. 335 'vacant and inactive': Beckford, *Descriptive Account*, 2:366.

p. 335 'The situation of Hertford is one of the pleasantest in the country': Dallas, *A Short Journey in the West Indies*, 140.

p. 335 costing nearly £10,000: Anon., 'Biographical Sketch of William Beckford, Esq.', 261.

p. 335 'My native country' and 'paternal soil': Brumbaugh, 'An Unpublished Letter', 4.

p. 335 'I shall carry Mrs Beckford back': ibid., 5.

p. 335 'Looked over many Folio Volumes of excellent plates': TD, 11 June 1778.

p. 336 'preserves the strength of the whole': Beckford, *Descriptive Account*, 2:347–8.

p. 336 'idle, drunken, worthless and immoral': ibid., 2:380.

p. 336 be lent some of his impressive collection of books: TD, 22 August 1786.

p. 336 'The heat becomes intolerable': Dallas, *A Short Journey in the West Indies*, 31.

p. 336 'to almost its whole value': ibid., 66.

p. 336 'really the locusts of the West Indies': ibid., 6.

p. 337 'With some exceptions': ibid., 4.

p. 337 'accomplished mild and pleasing': ibid., 113.

p. 337   'superfluous coppers, stills and stores': Beckford, *Descriptive Account*, 2:24.

p. 337   'a design full of accident': BL Sloane Mss 3984, fol. 217.

p. 337   'so treacherous a plant': Beckford, *Descriptive Account*, 2:39.

p. 337   no money had been repaid four years later: Sheridan, 'Planter and Historian', 56.

p. 337   'My blood rebelled against the blow': Dallas, *A Short Journey in the West Indies*, 11–12.

p. 337   'tyranny, cruelty, murder': ibid., 109.

p. 337   'There is a kind of intoxication': ibid., 66.

p. 338   'daily sicken'd at the ills around me': Ashcroft, 'Robert Charles Dallas', 97.

p. 338   'I feel such repugnance . . . [for] negro slavery': Watson, 'Pollard Letters', 100.

p. 338   'about flogging the Negroes. Mr K. can't bear to see them flogged': TD, 22 February 1782.

p. 338   'I had imbibed in the course of my education in England': Ashcroft, 'Robert Charles Dallas', 98.

p. 338   'stream of misery . . . repugnant to our religion': Beckford, *Remarks upon the Situation of Negroes*, 3.

p. 338   'harrowing': ibid., 7.

p. 338   'excruciating bodily sufferings': ibid., 30–1.

p. 338   so 'desperate' that they committed suicide: ibid., 22fn.

p. 339   'if it can be done without infringing': ibid., 40,

p. 339   'in which they may take delight': ibid., 37.

p. 339   'labouring poor': ibid., 38.

p. 339   'to taste the comforts of protection': ibid., 98.

p. 339   'humanity' of the Africans: ibid., 17.

p. 339   'The negroes are slaves by nature': Beckford, *Descriptive Account*, 2:382.

p. 339   'the largest property real and personal of any subject in Europe': MSS Beckford C. 84, fol. 54.

p. 340   '& the whole was blown up': Lees-Milne, *William Beckford*, 28.

p. 341   'We are waiting in this most detestable town': MSS Beckford C. 15, fol. 3.

p. 341   'I cannot help confessing that no one ever embarked': ibid., fol. 25.

p. 341   three chefs and one confectioner employed in the kitchen: Lees-Milne, *William Beckford*, 41.

p. 341   'Infernal rascal this Wildman!': 14 April 1789, Beckford MSS C. 15, fols. 13–14.

p. 341   'Between this harpy and two brothers': Thorne, *House of Commons*, 578.

p. 341   'My Works at Fonthill Building planting': 5 August 1790, Beckford MSS C. 15, fol. 123.

p. 342   'Some people drink to forget their unhappiness': Lees-Milne, *William Beckford*, 50.

p. 342   the skies looked 'very wild': TD, 2 October 1780.

p. 343   Heavy cannon were carried 100 feet from the forts: Schomburgk, *History of Barbados*, 46–7.

p. 343   'the most Beautiful Island in the World': Burns, *History of the British West Indies*, 508.

p. 343   15,000 dying on Jamaica alone: ibid., 538.

p. 343 'not greatly injured, or entirely destroyed': Beckford, *Descriptive Account*, 1:106.

p. 343 Several puncheons had to be 'immediately staved': ibid., 116.

p. 343 'occasioned a kind of pestilence': ibid., 115.

p. 343 'rapacious and unfeeling' mortgage holders: Sheridan, 'Planter and Historian', 56.

p. 344 utterly unqualified to run tropical agriculture enterprises and who had never even seen the West Indies: Edwards, *History, Civil and Commercial*, 2:35.

p. 344 'Come not to Jamaica': 29 September 1784, MSS Beckford C. 26, fols. 67–70.

p. 344 'of no heart, no feeling'. Alexander, *England's Wealthiest Son*, 186.

p. 344 'the plaguey climate': Brumbaugh, 'An Unpublished Letter', 3.

p. 344 'Somerly determined to come to England': Dallas, *A Short Journey in the West Indies*, 143n.

p. 344 'to recover a constitution broken down by sickness and affliction': Beckford, *Descriptive Account*, 2:404.

p. 344 'What a place – surrounded with fresh horrors!': Cundall, 'Jamaica Worthies', 358.

29. Peace and Freedom

p. 345 180 sugar factories and 200 plantations destroyed: Deerr, *History of Sugar*, 2:319.

p. 345 was killed by being passed though his own sugar mill: ibid., 2:323.

p. 346 'I am sorry to inform you St Domingo is totally evacuated': 23 November 1798, MSS Beckford C. 37.

p. 346 'Tho' we lament the principal cause of such high prices': Ragatz, *Fall of the Planter Class*, 206.

p. 347 'the principal source of national opulence': Edwards, *History, Civil and Commercial*, 1: Dedication.

p. 347 'being, as I am informed, selected with great expense': ibid., 2:124.

p. 347 'Such eating and drinking I never saw!': Cundall, *Lady Nugent's Journal*, 78.

p. 347 'saying dis and dat and toder': ibid., 102.

p. 347 'suffer much, submit to much and lead a life of misery': Beckford, *Descriptive Account*, 2:377.

p. 348 'a canoe, containing three or four black females': Renny, *An History of Jamaica*, 241.

p. 348 'they were thrown alive into the sea, it would be the loss of the underwriters': Donnan, *Documents Illustrative of the History of the Slave Trade*, 2:555.

p. 349 'The whole Body of a roasted Negro': Deerr, *History of Sugar*, 2:296.

p. 349 'no nation has plunged so deeply into this guilt': Thomas, *Slave Trade*, 235.

p. 350 'I have the great pleasure to inform you that on Thursday last': letter book of Stephen Fuller 1784–92, J. Arch. 1B/5/14/1.

p. 350 'in a great measure, built up by the blood of the poor Africans': Samuel Hopkins to Moses Brown, 29 April 1784, quoted in Donnan, *Documents Illustrative of the History of the Slave Trade*, 3:335.

p. 350 'created not to ruin only one good citizen but to ruin many hundreds': quoted in *Providence Journal*, 16 March 2006.

p. 350 John 'Drew his Brothers with him into a Voyage in that Unrighteous Traffic': Hedges, *Browns of Providence Plantations*, 341.

p. 351 'exert himself to support the West India Int. in the next Parliament': Thomas Wildman to James Wildman, 6 November 1793, MSS Beckford C. 499.

p. 351 'I was exposed not only to the sight, but also to the practice of severities': Knutsford, *Life and Letters of Zachary Macaulay*, 7–8.

p. 352 By 1805 it had fallen from over £100,000 to somewhere in the region of £30,000: Lees-Milne, *William Beckford*, 77.

p. 353 'one of the very few possessors of great wealth who have honestly tried to spend it poetically': *Times*, 6 July 1822.

p. 353 'a desert of magnificence, a glittering waste of laborious idleness': quoted in Knight, *Gentlemen of Fortune*, 125.

p. 354 'having an antique appearance': Pierre F. M'callum, quoted in Handler, 'Addenda to a Guide', 282–3.

p. 354 'natural tendency to extravagance': Faulks, *Eighteen Months in Jamaica*, 23.

p. 355 'The very building shook at the strange yet sacred joy': Hinton, *Memoir of William Knibb*, 261.

p. 356 'an inferior social and economic organisation': Williams, *Capitalism and Slavery*, 23.

p. 356 'perhaps as disgraceful a portion of history as the whole course of time can afford': Southey to John May, 7 March 1824, Southey, *Life and Correspondence of Robert Southey*, 5:170.

Epilogue

p. 359 'Jamaican history is characteristic': quoted in Thomson, *The Dead Yard*, 2.

p. 360 'miserabell Negros borne to perpetuall slavery they and Thayer seed': Whistler, *Journal of the West India Expedition*, 146.

p. 361 'spel very prettily and repeat the Creed and Lords prayer': Klingberg, *Codrington Chronicle*, 99.

p. 362 Sir Simon Codrington reported: *Times* 2 November 1982.

p. 363 falling to a nadir of 5,000 tons: Deerr, *History of Sugar*, 1:198–9.

p. 363 shrank from over 500 to just 77: Thomson, *The Dead Yard*, 49.

p. 363 'The island has always been and still is run for the whites': Albert Edwards, *Panama, the Canal, the Country, the People*, 21.

SELECT BIBLIOGRAPHY

Abbreviations

CUP	Cambridge University Press
HUP	Harvard University Press
JBMHS	*Journal of the Barbados Museum and Historical Society*
JCH	*The Journal of Caribbean History*
OUP	Oxford University Press
UNCP	University of North Carolina Press
UWIP	University of the West Indies Press
WMQ	*William and Mary Quarterly*
YUP	Yale University Press

'A. B.' *A Brief relation of the beginning and ending of the troubles of the Barbados*. London, 1653

Acts of Assembly, Passed in the Charibbee Leeward Islands. London, 1734

Acts of Assembly passed in the Island of Barbados, 1648–1718. London, 1732

Adams, John. *Novangulus, and Massachusettensis, or Political Essays Published in the Years 1774 and 1775*. Boston: Hews & Goss, 1819

Alexander, Boyd. *England's Wealthiest Son: A Study of William Beckford*. London: Centaur Press Ltd., 1962

Amussen, Susan Dwyer. *Caribbean Exchanges: Slavery and the Transformation of English Society, 1640–1700*. Chapel Hill, NC: UNCP, 2007

Andrews, Evangeline W., and Charles M., eds. *Journal of a Lady of Quality*. New Haven, Conn., 1923

Anon. *A full Account of the Late Dreadful Earthquake at Port Royal in Jamaica, Written in two Letters from the Minister of that Place*. London, 1692

Anon. *A State of the Present Condition of the Island of Barbadoes*. London, c. 1698

Anon. *A State of the Trade carried on with the French on the Island of Hispaniola*. London, 1760

Anon. *A True and Perfect Relation of that ... terrible Earthquake in Port-Royal Jamaica.* London, 1692

Anon. 'Biographical Sketch of William Beckford, Esq.' *Monthly Mirror* (May 1799): 259–64

Anon. *Bloudy Newes from the Barbadoes.* London, 1652

Anon. 'From aboard the Rainbow in Carlisle Bay'. *Mercurius Politicus* no. 90, (1652)

Anon. *Great Newes from the Barbadoes.* London, 1676

Anon. *Interesting Tracts, Relating to the Island of Jamaica.* St Jago de la Vega, Jamaica: Lewis, Lunan and Jones, 1800

Anon. *Letters Concerning the English Expedition into the Spanish West Indies in 1655.* Rawlison Mss. D. 1208. fol. 62, Bodleian Library; reprinted in Firth, *Narrative of General Venables*, 127–43

Anon. *Some Memoirs of the first Settlement of the Island of Barbados.* Bridgetown, 1741

Anon. *Some Observation, Which May Contribute to Afford a Just Idea of Our West-India Colonies.* London, 1764

Anon. *The truest and largest account of the late Earthquake in Jamaica, June the 7th, 1692. Written by a Reverend Divine there to his Friend in London.* London, 1693

Appleby, John C. 'English Settlement in the Lesser Antilles during War and Peace, 1603–1660'. In Paquette and Engerman. *Lesser Antilles in the Age of European Expansion.* 86–104

Archer, James Henry Lawrence. *Monumental Inscriptions.* London: Chatto & Windus, 1875

Armitage, D. *The Ideological Roots of the British Empire.* Cambridge: CUP, 2000

Armitage, David and Braddick, Michael J., eds. *The British Atlantic World, 1500–1800.* Basingstoke, England: Palgrave Macmillan, 2002

Armstrong, Douglas. *The Old Village and the Great House.* Urbana, Ill.: University of Illinois Press, 1990

Ashcroft, Michael. 'Robert Charles Dallas'. *Jamaica Journal* 44 (1980): 94–101

Aspinall, Algernon. *West Indian Tales of Old.* London: Duckworth & Co., 1912

Atkins, John. *A Voyage to Guinea, Brasil, and the West Indies.* London, 1735

Bailyn, Bernard. *The New England Merchants in the Seventeenth Century.* Cambridge, Mass.: HUP, 1955

Bailyn, Bernard, and Morgan, Philip D. *Strangers within the Realm: Cultural Margins of the First British Empire.* Chapel Hill, NC: UNCP, 1991

Bartlett, John Russell. *History of the Wanton family of Newport.* Providence: S.S. Rider, 1878

────── ed. *Records of the Colony of Rhode Island and Providence Plantations in New England.* 10 vols. Providence, 1856–65

Baxter, Richard. *A Christian Directory.* London, 1673

Beckford, William. *Descriptive Account of Jamaica.* 2 vols. London: T. & J. Egerton, 1790

────── *Remarks upon the Situation of Negroes in Jamaica.* London: T. & J. Egerton, 1788

Beckles, Hilary M. *Black Rebellion in Barbados.* Bridgetown, Barbados: Antilles Publications, 1984

────── 'The Economic Origins of Black Slavery in the British West Indies, 1640–1680: A Tentative Analysis of the Barbados Model'. *JCH* 16 (1982): 36–56

────── 'English Parliamentary Debate on "White Slavery" in Barbados, 1659'. *JBMHS* 36:4 (1982): 344–52

────── *The History of Barbados: From Amerindian Settlement to Nation State*. Cambridge: CUP, 1990

────── 'The "Hub of Empire": the Caribbean and Britain in the Seventeenth Century'. In Canny, ed. *Origins of Empire*, 218–40

────── *Inside Slavery: Process and Legacy in the Caribbean Experience*. Kingston: Canoe Press, UWI, 1996

────── 'Land Distribution and Class Formation in Barbados, 1630–1700: The Rise of a Wage Proletariat'. *JBMHS* 36:2 (1980): 136–43

────── 'Sugar and White Servitude: An Analysis of Indentured Labour during the Sugar Revolution of Barbados, 1643– 1655'. *JBMHS* 36:3 (1981): 236–47

────── *White Servitude and Black Slavery in Barbados, 1627–1715*. Knoxville, Tenn.: University of Tennessee Press, 1989

Beer, George Louis. *British Colonial Policy, 1764–65*. London: Macmillan, 1907

Behn, Aphra. *Oroonoko: or the Royal Slave, A true History*. London: Will. Canning, 1698

Belgrove, William. *A Treatise on Husbandry or Planting*. Boston: D. Fowle, 1755

Bell, Sir H. Hesketh. 'The Caribs of Dominica'. *JBMHS* 5 (Nov. 1937): 18–31

Benezet, Anthony. *A Caution to Great Britain and her Colonies . . .* Philadelphia: Henry Miller, 1766

Bennett, Hazel and Sherlock, Philip M. *The Story of the Jamaican People*. Kingston: Ian Randle, 1998

Bennett, J. H. *Bondsmen and Bishops, Slavery and Apprenticeship on the Codrington Plantations of Barbados 1710–1838*. Berkeley and Los Angeles: University of California Press, 1958

────── 'Cary Helyar, Merchant and Planter of Seventeenth-Century Jamaica', *WMQ* 3rd series, 21:1 (Jan. 1964): 53–76

────── 'The Problem of Slave Labor Supply at the Codrington Plantations.' *Journal of Negro History*, 36:4 (Oct. 1951): 406–441

Black, Clinton V. *The History of Jamaica*. London: Collins, 1958

Blane, Gilbert. *An Account of the Battle Between the British and the French Fleets in the West Indies, on the Twelfth of April, 1782*. London, 1782

Bliss, Robert M. *Revolution and Empire: English Politics and American Colonies in the Seventeenth Century*. Manchester: Manchester University Press, 1990

Blome, Richard. *Description of the Island of Jamaica*. London: T. Milbourn, 1672

Bolhouse, Gladys. 'Abraham Redwood: Reluctant Quaker, Philanthropist, Botanist'. *Newport History* 45, Part 2, Issue 146, 17–35

Bourne, Ruth. *Queen Anne's Navy in the West Indies*. New Haven, Conn., 1939

Bowen, H.V. *Elites, Enterprise and the Making of the British Overseas Empire, 1688–1775*. London: Macmillan, 1996

Braithwaite, Edward. *The Development of Creole Society in Jamaica 1770–1820*. Oxford: Clarendon Press, 1971

Brandow, James. *Genealogies of Barbados Families*. Baltimore: Genealogical Publishing Company, Inc., 1983

Brenner, Robert. *Merchants and Revolution: Commercial Change, Political Conflict, and London's Overseas Traders, 1550–1653.* Princeton: Princeton University Press, 1993

Breverton, Terry. *Black Bart Roberts: the greatest pirate of them all.* Glyndwr Publishing, 2004

Bridenbaugh, Carl. *Fat Mutton and Liberty of Conscience: Society in Rhode Island, 1636–1690.* Providence: Brown University Press, 1974

—— and Roberta Bridenbaugh *No Peace Beyond the Line: The English in the Caribbean, 1624–1690.* New York: OUP, 1972

Bridges, George Wilson. *The Annals of Jamaica.* 2 vols. London: John Murray, 1828

Brown, Vincent. *The Reaper's Garden: Death and Power in the World of Atlantic Slavery.* Cambridge, Mass.: HUP, 2008

Browne, Patrick. *The Civil and Natural History of Jamaica.* London, 1756

Bruce, John, ed. *Letters and Papers of the Verney Family.* London: Camden Society, 1853

Brumbaugh, Thomas B. ed. "An Unpublished Letter of William Beckford of Hertford'. *Jamaica Monograph No. 17,* Rhodes House, Oxford, 1954

Buisseret, David. *Historic Jamaica from the Air.* Kingston: Ian Randle Publishers, 1969

—— ed. *Jamaica in 1687.* Kingston: UWIP, 2008

Burke, William and Edmund. *An Account of the European settlements in America.* 2 vols. London: R. & J. Dodsley, 1757

Burnard, Trevor. "'The Countrie Continues Sicklie": White Mortality in Jamaica, 1655–1780'. *Social History of Medicine* 12:1 (Apr. 1999): 45–72

—— 'A Failed Settler Society: Marriage and Demographic Failure in Early Jamaica'. *Journal of Social History* 28 (Fall 1994): 63–82

—— *Mastery, Tyranny, & Desire: Thomas Thistlewood and his Slaves in the Anglo-Jamaican World.* Chapel Hill, N.C.: UNCP, 2004

—— 'Not a Place for Whites? Demographic Failure and Settlement in Comparative Context: Jamaica, 1655–1780'. In Monteith and Richards, eds. *Jamaica in Slavery and Freedom,* 73–88

Burns, Sir Alan. *The History of the British West Indies.* London: Allen & Unwin, 1954

Bush, Barbara. *Slave Women in Caribbean Society 1650–1838.* London: James Currey Ltd., 1990

—— 'White "Ladies", Coloured "Favourites" and Black "Wenches": Some Considerations on Sex, Race and Class Factors in Social Relations in White Creole Society in the British Caribbean'. *Slavery & Abolition* 2:3 (Dec. 1981): 245–62

Butler, Mary. 'Mortality and Labour on the Codrington Estates, Barbados'. *JCH* 19:1 (May 1984): 48–67

Byam, William. *An Exact Relation of the Most Execrable Attempts of John Allin, Committed on the Person of His Excellency Francis Lord Willoughby.* London, 1665

Campbell, P.F. 'Aspects of Barbados Land Tenure, 1627–1663' *JBMHS* 37:2 (1984): 112–58

—— 'More About Richard Ligon'. *JBMHS* 37:4 (1985): 415–16

—— 'Richard Ligon'. *JBMHS* 37:3 (1985): 215–38

—— *Some Early Barbadian History.* Barbados: Caribbean Graphics, 1993

Canny, Nicholas P. *Colonial identity in the Atlantic world, 1500–1800.* Princeton, NJ: Princeton University Press, 1987

—— ed. *The Origins of Empire.* Oxford: OUP, 1998

Carrington, Selwyn H.H. *The British West Indies during the American Revolution*. Providence: Foris Publications, 1988

Carswell, John. *The South Sea Bubble*. London: Cresset Press, 1960

Cary, John. *An Essay on the State of England, in Relation to its Trade*. Bristol, 1695

Chandler, Alfred D. 'The Expansion of Barbados'. *JBMHS* 13 (1946): 104–14

Chandler M. J. *A Guide to Records in Barbados*. Oxford: Basil Blackwell, 1965

Chapin, Howard M. *Rhode Island Privateers in Kings George's War, 1739–1748*. Providence: Rhode Island Historical Society, 1926

Clark, William Bell, and Morgan, William James, eds. *Naval Documents of the American Revolution*. 10 vols. Washington DC: US Navy Dept., 1964–9

Clarke, C.P. 'Imperial Forces in Barbados'. *JBMHS* 32:4 (Nov. 1968): 174–80

Clarkson, Thomas. *The History of the rise, progress and accomplishment of the abolition of the African Slave Trade by the British parliament*. 2 vols. London: Longman, Hurst, Rees and Orme, 1808

Climenson, Emily J., ed. *Passages from the Diaries of Mrs Philip Lybbe Powys, of Hardwick House, Oxon., A.D. 1756 to 1808*. London: Longmans & Co., 1899

Codrington, R.H. *Memoir of the family of Codrington of Codrington Didmarton*. Letchworth: Arden Press, 1910

Colley, Linda. *Britons: Forging the Nation, 1707–1837*. New Haven, Conn.: YUP, 1992

——— *The Ordeal of Elizabeth Marsh*. London: Harper Press, 2007

Colt, Sir Henry. 'The Voyage of Sir Henry Colt'. In Harlow, ed. *Colonising Expeditions to the West Indies and Guiana*, 54–102

Connell, Neville, ed. and trans. 'Father Labat's Visit to Barbados in 1700'. *JBMHS* 24 (Aug. 1957): 160–74

——— 'Furniture and Furnishings in Barbados During the 17th Century'. *JBMHS* 24 (1957): 102–21

——— 'Hotel Keepers and Hotels in Barbados'. *JBMHS* 33 (Nov. 1970): 162–85

Coughtry, Jay. *The Notorious Triangle*. Philadelphia: Temple University Press, 1981

Crain, Edward E. *Historic Architecture in the Caribbean Islands*. Gainsville, Fl.: University Press of Florida, 1994

Crane, Elaine F. '"The First Wheel of Commerce": Newport, Rhode Island and the Slave Trade, 1760–1776'. *Slavery and Abolition* 1:2 (Sept. 1980): 178–98

Crane, V. W. ed. *Benjamin Franklin's Letters to the Press, 1758–1775*. Chapel Hill, NC: UNCP, 1950

Craton, Michael. *Sinews of Empire: A Short History of British Slavery*. London: Temple Smith, 1974

——— *Testing the Chains: Resistance to Slavery in the British West Indies*. Ithaca, NY: Cornell University Press, 1982

Craton, Michael and Walvin, James. *A Jamaican Plantation: The History of Worthy Park, 1670–1970*. London: W. H. Allen, 1970

Crossley, David, and Saville, Richard. *The Fuller Letters 1728–1755: Guns, Slaves and Finance*. Lewes: Sussex Record Society, vol. 76, 1991

Crouse, Nellis M. *The French Struggle for the West Indies, 1665–1713*. New York: Columbia University Press, 1943

Crow, Hugh. *Memoirs of the late Hugh Crow of Liverpool.* London and Liverpool: Longman, Rees, Orme, Brown and Green; and G. and J. Robinson, 1830

Cumberland, Richard. *Memoirs of Richard Cumberland.* Philadelphia: Samuel F. Bradford, 1806

Cundall, Frank. *Historic Jamaica.* Kingston: Institute of Jamaica, 1915

────── 'Jamaica Worthies, VII. William Beckford Historian'. *Journal of the Institute of Jamaica* 1:8 (December 1893): 349–60

────── ed. *Lady Nugent's Journal.* London: West India Committee, 1939

Dallas, Robert (published as 'Anon'). *A Short Journey in the West Indies.* London: J. Murray, 1790

Davies, John, trs. *History of the Caribby-Islands.* London: J.M. for Thomas Dring and John Starkey, 1666

Davis, David Brion. *Inhuman Bondage: The Rise and Fall of Slavery in the New World.* Oxford: OUP, 2006

Davis, N. Darnell. *The Cavaliers and Roundheads of Barbados, 1650–1652.* Georgetown, Guyana: Argosy Press, 1877

────── ed. 'Papers Relating to the Early History of Barbados'. *Timehri* 5 (1891): 51–60

────── ed. 'Papers Relating to the Early History of Barbados and St Kitts'. *Timehri* 6 (1892): 327–49

Deerr, Noel. *The History of Sugar.* 2 vols. London: Chapman and Hall, 1949–50

Dexter, Franklin Bowditch, ed. *Literary Diary of Ezra Stiles.* New York: Scribners, 1901

Donnan, Elizabeth, ed. *Documents Illustrative of the History of the Slave Trade to America.* 4 vols. Washington DC: Carnegie Institute of Washington, 1930–5

Drax, Henry. 'Instructions which I would have observed by Mr Richard Harwood in the Managment of My plantation according to the Articles of Agreement betwene us which are heare unto Annexed'. Rawlinson Mss A348. Bodleian Library, Oxford. Reprinted in Thompson, 'Henry Drax's Instructions', 565–604

Drescher, Seymour. *Capitalism and Antislavery.* Oxford: OUP, 1986

Dresser, Madge. *Slavery Obscured: The Social History of the Slave Trade in an English Provincial Port.* London: Continuum, 2001

Duke, William. *Memoirs of the First Settlement of the Island of Barbados . . . to the Year 1742.* In Campbell, *Some Early Barbadian History,* 197–245

Dunn, Richard. 'The Barbados Census of 1689 – Profile of the Richest Colony in English America'. *JBMHS* 33 (Nov. 1969): 57–75

────── 'The Glorious Revolution and America'. In Canny, ed. *Origins of Empire,* 445–66

────── *Sugar and Slaves: the Rise of the Planter Class in the English West Indies, 1624–1713.* Chapel Hill, NC: UNCP, 1972

Eaden, John, ed. *The memoirs of Père Labat, 1693–1705.* London: Constable, 1931

Edmundson, William. *A Journal of the Life, Travels, Sufferings and Labour . . . of William Edmundson.* London, 1774

Edwards, Bryan. *The History, Civil and Commercial, of the British Colonies in the West Indies.* 2 vols. London, 1793

────── *Thoughts on the Late Proceedings of Government Respecting the Trade of the West India Islands with the United States of North America.* 2nd ed., London, 1784

Eltis David. 'The British Transatlantic Slave Trade Before 1714: Annual Estimates of Volume and Direction'. In Paquette and Engerman. *Lesser Antilles in the Age of European Expansion*, 182–205

——— *The Rise of African Slavery in the Americas*. Cambridge: CUP, 2000

Equiano, Olaudah. *The Interesting Narrative of the Life of Olaudah Equiano, or Gustavas Vassa, the African*. London, 1791

Esquemeling, John. *The Bucaniers of America*. London, 1684

Faraday, M. A., ed. *Herefordshire Militia Assessments of 1663*. Camden Fourth Series, Vol. 10. London: Royal Historical Society, 1972

Faulks, Theodore. *Eighteen Months in Jamaica; with Recollections of the Late Rebellion*. London, 1833

Firth, C. H., ed. *The Narrative of General Venables*. London: Longmans, Green, and Co., 1900

Fisher, P. *The Catalogue of Most of the memorable Tomes, Grave-stones*. London, 1668

Fitzpatrick, John C., ed. *The Diaries of George Washington, 1748–1799*. 4 vols. Boston and New York: Houghton Mifflin, 1925

Flannigan, Mrs. *Antigua and the Antiguans: A Full Account of the Colony and its Inhabitants from the Time of the Caribs to the Present Day*. London: Saunders & Otley, 1844

Forbes, Allyn B. et al., eds. *Winthrop Papers, 1498–1649*. 5 vols. Boston: The Massachusetts Historical Society, 1929–47

Ford, Worthington C. *The Commerce of Rhode Island 1726–1800*. Boston: Massachusetts Historical Society Collections, 7th Series, Vols. IX–X, 1914–15

Fortescue, J. W. et al., ed. *Calendar of State Papers, Colonial Series, America and the West Indies* (multivolume). London: HMSO, 1860–1969

Foster, Joseph. *London Marriage Licences, 1521–1869*. London: Bernard Quaritch, 1887

——— ed. *The Visitation of Middlesex began in the Year 1663*. London, 1887

Foster, Nicholas. *A Briefe relation of the late Horrid Rebellion Acted in the Island of Barbados*. London, 1650

Fox, George. *A journal or historical account of the life, travels of . . . George Fox*. 2 vols. London, 1694–8

——— *To the Ministers, Teachers and Priests (So Called, and so Stiling your Selves) in Barbadoes*. London, 1672

Fraser, Henry, and Hughes, Ronnie. *Historic Houses of Barbados*. Bridgetown: Barbados National Trust, 1982

French, G. *Answer to a Scurrilous Libel*. London, 1719

Froude, James Anthony. *The English in the West Indies or the Bow of Ulysses*. London: Longmans, Green, 1888

Fuertado, W.A. *Official and Other Personages of Jamaica from 1655–1790*. Kingston, 1896

Gage, Thomas. *The English-American*. London, 1648

Galenson, David. *Traders, Planters, and Slaves; Market Behaviour in Early English America*. Cambridge: CUP, 1986

——— *White Servitude in Colonial America: An Economic Analysis*. Cambridge: CUP, 1981

Games, Alison F. 'Opportunity and Mobility in Early Barbados'. In Paquette and Engerman. *Lesser Antilles in the Age of European Expansion*, 165–81

Gardyner, George. *A Description of the New World.* London, 1651

Gaspar, David Barry. *Bondmen and Rebels: A Study of Master-Slave Relations in Antigua with Implications for Colonial British America.* Baltimore: Johns Hopkins University Press, 1985

Godwyn, Morgan. *The Negro's and Indians Advocate.* London, 1680

Gordon, William. *A Sermon Preach'd at the funeral of the Honourable Colonel Christopher Codrington.* London: G. Strahan, 1710

Goveia, Elsa V. *Slave Society in the British Leeward Islands at the End of the Eighteenth Century.* London: YUP, 1965

Gragg, Larry. *Englishmen Transplanted: The English Colonization of Barbados, 1627–1660.* Oxford: OUP, 2003

—— 'Puritans in Paradise: The New England Migration to Barbados, 1640–1660', *JCH* 21:2 (1988): 154–167

Greene, Jack P. 'Changing Identity in the British Caribbean: Barbados as a Case Study'. *JBMHS* 47 (Nov. 2001): 106–65

Gregory, W. *The Beckford Family.* Bath: Queen Square Library, 1887

Gunkel, Alexander, and Handler, Jerome S., ed. and trans. 'A German Indentured Servant in Barbados in 1652: The Account of Heinrich Von Uchteritz'. *JBMHS* 33 (May 1970): 91–100

—— 'A Swiss Medical Doctor's description of Barbados in 1661'. *JBMHS* 33 (May 1969): 3–13

Hackman, Wm. Kent. 'William Beckford: The Jamaican Connection'. *JCH* 32 (1998): 23–45

Hall, Clayton Colman, ed. *Narratives of Early Maryland, 1633–1684.* New York: Scribner's, 1910

Hall, Douglas. *In Miserable Slavery: Thomas Thistlewood in Jamaica.* London: Macmillan, 1989

Hall, Richard, ed. *Acts, passed in the Island of Barbados From 1643 to 1762 inclusive.* London, 1764

Hamer, Philip, ed. *Letters and papers of Henry Laurens.* 3 vols. Columbia, SC: University of South Carolina Press, 1968

Hamshere, Cyril. *The British in the Caribbean.* London: Weidenfeld & Nicolson, 1972

Hancock, David. *Citizens of the World: London Merchants and the Integration of the British Atlantic Community, 1735–1785.* Cambridge: CUP, 1995

Handler, Jerome T. *A Guide to Source Materials for the Study of Barbados History, 1627–1834.* Carbondale, Ill.: Southern Illinois University Press, 1972

—— 'Addenda to a Guide to Source Materials for the Study of Barbados History, 1627–1834, Part II'. *JBMHS* 36:3 (1981): 279–85

—— 'The Barbados Slave Conspiracies of 1675 and 1692'. *JBMHS* 36:4 (1982): 312–33

—— 'Father Antoine Biet's Visit to Barbados in 1654'. *JBMHS* 32 (May 1967): 56–76

—— 'Sources for the Study of Preemancipation Sugar Plantations in Barbados'. *Caribbean Archives* 5 (1976): 11–21

—— *Supplement to A Guide to Source Materials for the Study of Barbados History, 1627–1834.* Providence, RI: John Carter Brown Library, 1991

—— *The Unappropriated People.* Baltimore: Johns Hopkins University Press, 1974

Harding, Richard. *Amphibious Warfare in the Eighteenth Century: The British expedition to the West Indies, 1740–1742*. Suffolk: The Boydell Press, 1991

Haring, C.H. *The Buccaneers in the West Indies in the XVII Century*. London: Methuen & Co., 1910

Harlow, Vincent T. *Christopher Codrington, 1688–1710*. Oxford: Clarendon Press, 1928

—— ed. *Colonising Expeditions to the West Indies and Guiana, 1623–1667*. London: Hakluyt Society, 1925

—— *A History of Barbados, 1625–1685*. Oxford: Clarendon Press, 1926

—— ed., *The Voyage of Captain William Jackson, 1624–1645*. London: Royal Historical Society, 1923

Hedges, James B. *The Browns of Providence Plantations: The Colonial Years*. Cambridge, Massachusetts: HUP, 1952

Hickeringill, Edmund. *Jamaica Viewed*. London: J. Williams, 1661 (2nd ed.)

Higham, C.S.S. *The Development of the Leeward Islands Under the Restoration, 1660–1688*. Cambridge: CUP, 1921

—— 'The Negro Policy of Christopher Codrington'. *Negro History* 10:2 (Jan. 1925): 150–3

Higman, Barry W. *Jamaica Surveyed: Plantation Maps and Plans of the Eighteenth and Nineteenth Centuries*. Kingston: Institute of Jamaica, 1988

Hill, Christopher. *God's Englishman: Oliver Cromwell and the English Revolution*. London: Weidenfeld & Nicolson, 1970

Hillary, William. *Observations on the Changes of the Air, and the Concomitant Epidemical Disease of Barbodoes*. London, 1759

Hinton, John Howard. *Memoir of William Knibb, Missionary in Jamaica*. London: Houlston & Stoneman, 1847

Hosmer, James Kendall, ed. *Winthrop's Journal, 1630–1649*. 2 vols. New York, 1908

Hotblack, Kate. *Chatham's Colonial Policy: A Study in the Fiscal and Economic Implications of the Colonial Policy of the Elder Pitt*. London: Routledge, 1917

Hotten, John Camden, ed. *The Original Lists of Persons of Quality ... and Others Who Went from Great Britain to the American Plantations, 1600–1700*. London, 1874

Howard, Robert Mowbray, ed. *Records and Letters of the Family of the Longs of Longville, Jamaica and Hampton Lodge, Surrey*. 2 vols. London: Simpkin, Marshall, Hamilton, Kent & Co. Ltd, 1925

Hughes, Griffith. *The Natural History of Barbados*. London, 1750

Hughes, Ronald. 'Samuel Osborne, 1674–1736: Barbadian Sugar Planter Extraordinary'. *JBMHS* 34:4 (Mar. 1974): 158–65

Hulme, Peter. *Colonial Encounters: Europe and the Native Caribbean*. London: Methuen, 1986

Hutchinson, Thomas. *The History of the Colony of Massachusetts Bay*. London: M. Richardson, 1760 (2nd ed.)

Hutson, J. Edward, ed. *The English Civil War in Barbados, 1650–1652*. Barbados: Barbados National Trust, 2001

Ingram, K. E. *Sources of Jamaican History, 1655–1838*. 2 vols. Zug, Switzerland: Inter Documentation Co., 1976

Innes, F. C. 'The Pre-sugar Era of European Settlement in Barbados'. *JCH*1, (1970): 1–22

'Instructions unto Generall Robert Venables giuen by his Highnes by aduice of his Councel upon his expedition to the West Indies'. BL Add. Mss. 11410, fol. 41. Reprinted in Firth, ed., *Narrative of General Venables.* 111–15

'I.S'. *A brief and perfect Journal of the late Proceedings and Success of the English Army in the West Indies.* London, 1655. Reprinted in Park, ed., *Harleian Miscellany*, 3:510–23

Israel, Jonathan I. 'Empire: The Continental Perspective', In Canny, ed. *Origins of Empire.* 423–44

James, Sydney V. *Colonial Rhode Island: A History.* New York: Scribner's, 1975

Jeaffreson, John Cordy, ed. *A Young Squire of the Seventeenth Century.* 2 vols. London, 1878

Jesse, Rev. C. 'Barbadians Buy St Lucia from the Caribs: the Sale of St Lucia by Indian Warner and Other Caribs to the Barbadians in A.D. 1663'. *JBMHS* 32:4 (Nov. 1968): 180–6

Johnstone, Robert. 'Nelson in the West Indies'. *Journal of the Institute of Jamaica* 2 (Mar. 1899): 521–71

Jones, Alison. 'The Rhode Island Slave Trade: A Trading Advantage in Africa'. *Slavery & Abolition* 2:3 (Dec. 1981): 227–44

Jones, Augustine. *Moses Brown: His Life and Services. A Sketch.* Providence: Rhode Island Printing Co., 1892

Journal of the Commissioners for Trade and Plantations. 14 vols. covering 1704–82. London: HMSO, 1920–38

Keith, Alice B. 'Relaxations in the British Restrictions on the American Trade with the British West Indies, 1783–1802'. *Journal of Modern History* 20 (Mar. 1948): 1–18

Kimball, Gertrude Selwyn. *Providence in Colonial Times.* Boston & New York: Houghton Mifflin, 1912

King, Bruce, ed., *West Indian Literature.* London: Macmillan, 1979

Klingberg, Frank Joseph. *The Anti-Slavery Movement in England: A Study in English Humanitarianism.* New Haven, Conn.: Yale Historical Publications, 1926

——— *The Codrington Chronicle: An experiment in Anglican Altruism on a Barbados Plantation, 1710–1834.* Berkeley and Los Angeles: University of California Press, 1949

Knight, Derrick. *Gentlemen of Fortune: The Men Who Made their Fortunes in Britain's Slave Colonies.* London: Muller, 1978

Knutsford, Vicountess. *Life and Letters of Zachary Macaulay.* London: Edward Arnold, 1900

Krise, Thomas W., ed. *Caribbeana: An Anthology of English Literature of the West Indies, 1657–1777.* Chicago: University of Chicago Press, 1999

Kriz, Kay Dian. *Slavery, Sugar and the Culture of Refinement.* New Haven, Conn.: YUP, 2008

Labat, Jean B. *Nouveau Voyage aux isles de l'Amerique.* Paris: La Haye, 1724

Laughton, J.K. 'Jenkins' Ear'. *English Historical Review* 4 (1889): 741–9

Lees-Milne, James. *William Beckford.* London: Century, 1976

Leslie, Charles. *A New and Exact Account of Jamaica.* Edinburgh: R. Fleming, 1740

Lewis, Matthew. *Journal of a West India Proprietor*. London: J. Murray, 1834

Ligon, Richard. *A True and Exact History of the Island of Barbados*. London, 1657

Littleton, Edward. *The Groans of the Plantations*. London: M. Clark, 1689

Livingstone, Noel. B. *Sketch Pedigree of Some of the Early Settlers in Jamaica*. Kingston: Education Supply Co., 1909

Locke, John. *Two Treatises on Government*. London, 1689

Lockwood, Alice. *Gardens of Colony and State: Gardens and Gardeners of the American Colonies and of the Republic before 1840*. 2 vols. New York: Charles Scribner's Sons, 1934

Long, Edward. *The History of Jamaica*. 3 vols. London: T. Lowndes, 1744

Lords Journals. London: HMSO, multivolume.

Lovejoy, David S. *Rhode Island Politics and the American Revolution, 1760–1776*. Providence: Brown University Press, 1958

Lowe, Robson. *The Codrington Correspondence, 1743–1851*. London: Robson Lowe, 1951

MacMurray, William, ed. *The Records of Two City Parishes*. London: Hunter & Longhurst, 1925

Makinson, David H. *Barbados, a Study of North American–West Indian Relations, 1739–1789*. New York: Mouton & Co., 1964

Marks, Jeanette. *The Family of the Barrett*. New York: Macmillan, 1938

Marsden, R. G. 'Early Prize Jurisdiction and Prize Law in England'. *English Historical Review* 24 (1909): 675–97

Martin, Bernard, and Spurrel, Mark, eds. *Journal of a Slave Trader*. London: Epworth Press, 1962

Martin, Samuel (writing as Antegonianus, Agricola). *An Essay upon Plantership*. Antigua: T. Smith, 1750

Massie, Joseph. *Brief Observations concerning the Management of the War, and the Means to prevent the Ruin of Great Britain*. London, 1761

McCusker, John J., and Menard, Russell R. *The Economy of British America, 1607–1789*. Chapel Hill, NC: UNCP, 1985

—— 'The Sugar Industry in the Seventeenth Century: A New Perspective on the Barbadian Sugar Revolution'. In Schwartz, ed., *Tropical Babylons*, 289–330

McDonald, Roderick A. ed. *West Indies Accounts: Essays on the History of the British Caribbean and the Atlantic Economy in honour of Richard Sheridan*. Bridgetown, Barbados: UWIP, 1996

Menard, Russell R. 'Plantation Empire: How Sugar and Tobacco Planters Built their Industries and Raised an Empire'. *Agricultural History* 81:3 (Summer 2007): 309–32

—— *Sweet Negotiations: Sugar, Slavery, and Plantation Agriculture in Early Barbados*. Charlottesville and London: University of Virginia Press, 2006

Metcalfe, George. *Royal Government and Political Conflict in Jamaica 1729–1783*. London: Longmans, 1965

Mintz, Sidney W. *Sweetness and Power: The Place of Sugar in Modern History*. New York: Penguin, 1985

Monteith, Kathleen E. A., and Richards, Glen, eds. *Jamaica in Slavery and Freedom: History, Heritage and Culture*. Barbados: UWIP, 2002

Moreton, J. B. *West India Customs and Manners*. London, 1790

Moulton, Phillips P., ed. *The Journal and Major Essays of John Woolman*. New York: OUP, 1971

Nankivell, Commander, RN. 'Rodney's Victory over DeGrasse'. *Journal of the Institute of Jamaica* 2:2 (Apr. 1893): 114–20

Nickalls, John L., ed. *The Journal of George Fox*. London: Religious Society of Friends, 1975

Ogilby, John. *America*. London, 1671

Oldmixon, John. *The British Empire in America*. 2 vols. London, 1708

Oliver, Vere Langford. *Caribbeana*. 6 vols. London: Mitchell, Hughes and Clarke, 1909–19

——— *The History of the Island of Antigua*. 3 vols. London: Mitchell & Hughes, 1894–9

O'Shaughnessy, Andrew Jackson. *An Empire Divided: The American Revolution and the British Caribbean*. Philadelphia: University of Pennsylvania Press, 2000

Paquette, Robert L., and Engerman, Stanley L., eds. *The Lesser Antilles in the Age of European Expansion*. Gainsville, Fl.: University Press of Florida, 1996

Pares, Richard. *Merchants and Planters*. Cambridge: CUP, 1960

——— *War and Trade in the West Indies, 1739–1763*. Oxford: Clarendon Press, 1936

——— *A West-India Fortune*. London: Longmans, Green & Co., 1950

——— *Yankees and Creoles: The Trade Between North America and the West Indies Before the American Revolution*. London: Longman, Green & Co., 1956

Park, Thomas, ed. *Harleian Miscellany* Vol. 3. London, 1809

Patterson, Orlando. *The Sociology of Slavery: An Analysis of the Origins, Development and Structure of Negro Slave Society in Jamaica*. London: MacGibbon & Kee, 1967

Peck, Louis F. *Life of Matthew G. Lewis*. Cambridge, Mass.: HUP, 1961

Penson, Lilian M. *The Colonial Agents of the British West Indies*. London: University Press, 1924

Pepys, Samuel. *The Diary of Samuel Pepys*. 1890 ed., 5 vols.

Pestana, Carla Gardina. *The English Atlantic in an Age of Revolution, 1640–1661*. Cambridge, Mass.: HUP, 2004

Peterson, Rev. Edward. *History of Rhode Island*. New York, 1853

Pinckard, George. *Notes on the West Indies*. 3 vols. London: Longman, Hurst, Rees, and Orme, 1806

Pinder, Richard. *A Loving Invitation to Repentence and Amendment of Life, unto all the Inhabitants of the Island Barbados . . .* London: R. Wilson, 1660

Pitman, Frank Wesley. *The Development of the West Indies, 1700–1763*. New Haven, Conn.: Yale Historical Publications IV, 1917

——— 'Slavery on British West Indian Plantations in the Eighteenth Century'. *Journal of Negro History* 11:4, (Oct. 1926): 584–668

Poyer, John. *History of Barbados*. London, 1808

Poyntz, John. *The Present Prospect of the Famous and Fertile Island of Tobago*. London: George Larkin, 1683

Puckrein, Gary. *Little England: Plantation Society and Anglo-Barbadian Politics, 1627–1700*. New York: New York University Press, 1984

Ragatz, Lowell Joseph. *The Fall of the Planter Class in the British Caribbean, 1763–1833*. New York and London: Century, 1928

────── *A Guide for the Study of British Caribbean History*, 1763–1834. Washington DC: American Historical Association, 1932

Ramsay, Reverend James. *Essay on the Treatment and Conversion of African Slaves in the British Sugar Colonies.* London: James Phillips, 1784

Rappleye, Charles. *Sons of Providence: The Brown Brothers, the Slave Trade, and the American Revolution.* New York: Simon & Schuster, 2007

Rawson, Geoffrey, ed. *Nelson's Letters from the Leeward Islands.* London: Golden Cockerel Press, 1953

Redding, Cyrus. *Memoirs of William Beckford.* 2 vols. London: C.J. Skeet, 1859

Renny, Robert. *An History of Jamaica.* London: J. Cawthorn, 1807

Richardson, Bonham C. *The Caribbean in the Wider World, 1492–1992: A Regional Geography.* Cambridge: CUP, 1992

Robertson, James. 'Re-writing the English Conquest of Jamaica in the Late Seventeenth Century'. *English Historical Review* 117:473 (Sept. 2003): 813–39

Robertson, Rev. Robert. *A Detection of the State and Situation of the present Sugar Planters of Barbados and the Leeward Islands.* London: J. Wilford, 1732

Rodger, N. A. M. *The Command of the Ocean: A Naval History of Britain, Volume Two 1649–1815.* London: Allen Lane, 2004

Rous, John. 'A warning to the Inhabitants of Barbadoes'. London, 1656

Ryden, David. *West Indian Slavery and Abolition 1783–1807.* Cambridge: CUP, 2009

Salt, Mary C.L. 'The Fullers of Brightling Park'. *Sussex Archaeological Collections,* Vols. 104 (1966): 63–87 and 106 (1968): 73–88

Sanders, Joanne McRee, ed. *Barbados Records: Baptisms, 1637–1800.* Baltimore: Genealogical Publishing Co., 1984

────── ed. *Barbados Records: Marriages, 1643–1800.* Houston: Sanders Historical Publications, 1982

────── ed. *Barbados Records: Wills and Administrations, 1639–80.* Marceline, Mo: Sanders Historical Publications, 1979

Sandiford, Keith. *The Cultural Politics of Sugar: Caribbean Slavery and Narratives of Colonialism.* Cambridge: CUP, 2000

Sanford, Peleg. *The Letter Book of Peleg Sanford of Newport Merchant (Later Governor of Rhode Island), 1666–1668.* Providence: Rhode Island Historical Society, 1928

Schama, Simon. *A History of Britain 2, 1603–1776.* London: BBC, 2001

Schlesinger, A. M. *The Colonial Merchants and the American Revolution, 1763–1776.* New York: Columbia University Studies, 1917

Schomburgk, Sir Robert H. *The History of Barbados.* London: Longman, Brown, Green and Longmans, 1848

Schwartz, Stuart B., ed. *Tropical Babylons: Sugar and the Making of the Atlantic World, 1450–1680.* Chapel Hill, NC: UNCP, 2004

Scott, John. 'The Description of Barbados'. In Campbell, *Some Early Barbadian History.* 246–59

Senior, Bernard. *Jamaica.* London: T. Hurst, 1835

Shamas, Carole. *The Pre-Industrial Consumer in England and America.* Oxford: Clarendon Press, 1990

Shephard, Sue. *Pickled, Potted and Canned: The Story of Food Preserving*. London: Headline, 2000

Sheppard, Jill. *The Redlegs of Barbados: Their Origins and History*. Millwood, NY: KTO Press, 1977

Sheridan, R. B. 'The British Credit Crisis of 1772 and the American Colonies'. *Journal of Economic History* 20:2 (1960): 161–86

—— *Doctors and Slaves: A Medical and Demographic History of Slavery in the British West Indies, 1680–1834*. Cambridge: CUP, 1985

—— 'Planter and Historian: The Career of William Beckford of Jamaica and England, 1744–1799'. *Jamaican Historical Review* 4 (1964): 36–58

—— 'The Rise of a Colonial Gentry: A Case Study of Antigua, 1730–1775.' *Economic History Review*, 2nd series Vol. 8 No. 3 (Apr. 1961): 342–57

—— 'Simon Taylor Sugar Tycoon of Jamaica.' *Agricultural History* 45:4 (Oct. 1971): 285–296

—— *Sugar and Slavery: An Economic History of the British West Indies 1623–1775*. Barbados: Caribbean Universities Press, 1974

—— 'William Beckford (1744–1799), Patron of Painters in Jamaica'. *Register of the Museum of Art, University of Kansas* 3:8–9 (Winter 1967): 46–61

Shilstone, E. M., 'The Washingtons and their Doctors in Barbados'. *JBMHS* 20:2 (Feb. 1953): 71–80

Simmons, George C. 'Towards a biography of Christopher Codrington the Younger'. *Caribbean Studies* 12 (Apr. 1972): 32–50

Sloane, Sir Hans. *A Voyage to the Islands of Madeira, Barbados, Nieves, St Christophers and Jamaica*. 2 vols. London, 1707

Smith, Abbot Emerson. *Colonists in Bondage: White Servitude and Convict Labor in America, 1607–1776*. Chapel Hill, NC: UNCP, 1967

Smith, Adam. *An Inquiry into the Nature and Causes of the Wealth of Nations*. London, 1776

Smith, Captain John. *The True Travels, adventures, and observations of Captain John Smith*. London, 1630

Smith, S.D. *Slavery, Family and Gentry Capitalism in the British Atlantic*. Cambridge: CUP, 2006

Smollett, T. *An account of the expedition against Carthagene*. London, 1756

Souden, David. '"Rogues, Whores and Vagbonds"? Indentured Servant Emigrants to North America, and the Case of Mid-Seventeenth-Century Bristol'. *Social History* 3 (1978): 23–41

Southey, C. C., ed. *The Life and Correspondence of Robert Southey*. 6 vols. London, 1849–50

Southey, Thomas. *Chronological History of the West Indies*. 3 vols. London, 1827

Spencer, Thomas. *A true and faithful relation of the proceedings of the forces . . . against the French . . .* London, 1691

Stewart, John. *A View of the Past and Present State of the Island of Jamaica*. Edinburgh: Oliver & Boyd, 1823

Stout, Neil R. *The Royal Navy in America, 1760–1775: A Study of Enforcement in the Era of the American Revolution*. Annapolis, Md.: Maryland Naval Institute Press, 1973

Strachan, Ian. *Paradise and the Plantation*. Charlottesville, Va.: University of Virginia Press, 2002

Strong, Frank. 'The Causes of Cromwell's West Indian Expedition'. *The American Historical Review* 2 (Jan. 1899): 228–45

Symmons, C., ed. *The Prose Works of John Milton*. London: J. Johnson etc., 1806

Taylor, S. A. G. *The Western Design: An Account of Cromwell's Expedition to the Caribbean.* Kingston: Institute of Jamaica, 1965

Taylor, W.S., and Pringle, J.H., eds. *Correspondence of William Pitt*. 4 vols. London: J. Murray, 1838–40

Thomas, Dalby. *An Historical Account of the Rise and Growth of the West-India Collonies.* London, 1690

Thomas, Hugh. *The Slave Trade: The History of the Atlantic Slave Trade: 1440–1870*. London: Picador, 1997

Thompson, Edward. *Sailor's Letters, Written to his select friends in England, during his voyages and travels in Europe, Asia, Africa, and America. From the year 1754 to 1759.* 2 Vols. Dublin: J. Hoey & J. Potts, 1766–7

Thompson, Mack. *Moses Brown, Reluctant Reformer.* Chapel Hill, NC: UNCP, 1962

Thompson, Peter. 'Henry Drax's Instructions on the Management of a Seventeenth-Century Barbadian Sugar Plantation'. *WMQ*, 3rd Series, 66:3 (July 2009): 565–604

Thomson, Ian. *The Dead Yard: Tales of Modern Jamaica*. London: Faber and Faber, 2009

Thorne, R. G. *The House of Commons, 1790–1820*. 5 vols. London: Secker and Warburg, 1986

Toner, J. M., ed. *The Daily Journal of Major George Washington*. Albany, New York: Joel Munsell's Sons, 1892

Troyer, Howard William. *Ned Ward of Grub Street: A Study of Sub-Literary London in the Eighteenth Century*. London: Frank Cass & Co. Ltd, 1946

Turner, M. *Slaves and Missionaries: the disintegration of Jamaican slave society, 1787–1834.* Urbana, Ill.: The University of Illinois Press, 1982

Tyron, Thomas (published as Physiologus, Philotheos). *Friendly Advice to the Gentlemen-Planters of the East and West Indies*. London, 1684

Verney, Frances Parthenope, ed. *Memoirs of the Verney Family During the Civil War*. 2 vols. London: Longmans, 1892–9

Walduck, T. 'T. Walduck's Letters from Barbados, 1710'. *JBMHS* 15:1 (Nov. 1947): 27–51; *JBMHS* 15:2 (Feb. 1948): 84–88; *JBMHS* 15:3 (May 1948): 137–49

Waller, J. A. *A Voyage to the West Indies*. London, 1820

Walvin, James. *Black and White: The Negro and English Society, 1555–1945*. London: Allen Lane, 1973

———*The Trader, the Owner, the Slave: Parallel Lives in the Age of Slavery*. London: Jonathan Cape, 2007

Ward, Edward. *A Trip to Jamaica: With a True Character of the People and Island*. London, 1698

Warner, Aucher. *Sir Thomas Warner, Pioneer of the West Indies, A Chronicle of his Family.* London, 1933

Warner, Revd Richard. *Excursions from Bath*. Bath: R. Cruttwell, 1801

Warren, Jack D. 'The Significance of George Washington's Journey to Barbados'. *JBMHS* 47 (2001): 1–34

Watson, Karl. *Barbados, The Civilised Island, A Social History 1750 to 1816*. Barbados: Caribbean Graphic Production Ltd., 1979

———— 'The Pollard Letters: A Case Study in Alienation'. *JBMHS* 36:2 (1980): 94–107

Watts, David. *The West Indies: Patterns of Development, Culture and Environmental Change Since 1492*. Cambridge: CUP, 1987

———— 'Dung Farming: A Seventeenth-century Experiment in Barbadian Agricultural Improvisation.' *JBMHS* 34:2 (May 1972): 58–63

———— *Man's Influence on the Vegetation of Barbados, 1627 to 1800*. Occasional Papers in Geography 4, University of Hull, 1966

Wesley, John. *Thoughts on Slavery*. London: R. Hawes, 1774

White, Father Andrew. 'A Briefe Relation of the Voyage Unto Maryland, By Father Andrew White, 1634'. In Hall, *Narratives of Early Maryland*, 25–45

Whistler, Henry. *Journal of the West India Expedition*. BL Sloane Mss 3926. Extracts printed in Firth, *Narrative of General Venables*, 114–69

Whitson, Agnes. 'The Outlook of the Continental American Colonies on the British West Indies, 1760–1775'. *Political Science Quarterly* 45:1 (Mar. 1930): 56–86

Wiener, Frederick Bernays. 'The Rhode Island Merchants and the Sugar Act'. *The New England Quarterly* 3:3 (Jul. 1930): 464–500

Williams, Eric. *Capitalism and Slavery*. Chapel Hill, NC: UNCP, 1944

———— *From Columbus to Castro: The History of the Caribbean 1492–1969*. London: André Deutsch, 1970

Wright, Richardson. *Revels in Jamaica 1682–1838*. New York: Dodd, Mead & Co., 1937

Yorke, Philip C., ed., *The Diary of John Baker 1751–1778*. London, 1931

Zahedieh, Nuala. 'Overseas expansion and Trade in the Seventeenth Century'. In Canny, ed., *Origins of Empire*, 398–422

PICTURE SOURCES

Section One:

Tobacco Farmers: engraving by Aldert Meijer, from Carel Allard, *Orbis habitabilis oppida et vestitus . . .*, Amsterdam, 1680.

Drax Busts: author photographs, used with permission of the Church of St. Anne and St. Agnes, Gresham Street, London.

Drax Will: National Archives, UK. Prob/11/307, image 355. Used with permission.

St Nicholas Abbey: author photograph

Drax Hall: author photograph

Ruins of Drax factory: author photograph

Barbados Map: from Richard Ligon, *A True and Exact History of Barbados*, London, 1657.

Duchess of Portsmouth: © National Portrait Gallery, London. NPG 497, used with permission.

Charles II and pineapple: attributed to Hendrick Danckerts. From the collection of the Dowager Marchioness of Cholmondley. Photo: The Arts Council of Great Britain, used with permission.

Battle of Pointe de Sable: From Nellis Crouse, *The French Struggle for the West Indies*, New York, 1943.

Prospect of Bridgetown: by Samuel Copen, 1695, engraved in London by Johannes Kip. Library of Congress, Washington.

Cane-holing and Sugar Factory: from Noel Deerr, *The History of Sugar*, London 1949-50.

Colonel Peter Beckford: © National Portrait Gallery, London. NPG D31549, used with permission.

Peter Beckford the Younger: portrait by Benjamin West.

Sir Henry Morgan: from Edmund Ollier, *Cassell's History of the United States*, Vol. 1, London, 1874.

Port Royal before and after: from Patrick Browne, *A New Map of Jamaica*, London 1755.

Earthquake Illustration: From *A True and Perfect Relation of that most Sad and Terrible Earthquake at Port Royal in Jamaica*, London, 1692.

Section Two:

Christopher Codrington the Younger: © National Portrait Gallery, London. NPG D13732, used with permission.

Old Drawing of Codrington College: from William Mayo, *A New & Exact Map of the Island of Barbadoes in America according to An Actual & Accurate Survey*, London, 1722.

Codrington College: author photograph

Surinam Planter: engraving by William Blake from John Stedman, *Narrative of a Five Year Expedition against the Revolted Negroes of Surinam*, London, 1806

Bartholomew Roberts: from Charles Johnson, *Historia der Engelsche Zee-Roovers . . . In het Engelsch beschreeven door . . .* Amsterdam, 1725.

The Torrid Zone: drawing attributed to Abraham James, 1806. Used with permission of the Wellcome Library, London.

Drax Hall, Jamaica: from Barry Higman, *Jamaica Surveyed*, Kingston, 1988.

Roaring River: an engraving by Thomas Vivares from a painting by George Robertson. Published by John Boydell, London, 1778.

Beckford miniature by John Smart.

Alderman Beckford: from Boyd Alexander, *England's Wealthiest Son*, London, 1962.

Fonthill Splendens: from William Angus, *The Seats of the Nobility & Gentry in Great Britain and Wales*, London 1787.

William Beckford of Fonthill: portrait by Romney, from James Lees-Milne, *William Beckford*, Tisbury, 1976.

Ruins of Fonthill: from Boyd Alexander, *England's Wealthiest Son*, London, 1962.

Battle of the Saints: painting by Thomas Luny, © National Maritime Museum, Greenwich, London, used with permission.

Model of Slave Ship: © Wilberforce House Museum: Hull Museums. Used with permission.

Slaves packed together: from, R. Walsh, *Notices of Brazil*, London, 1830.

African insurrection: from Carl Bernard Wadström, *An Essay on Colonization*, London, 1794.

Hanged Slave: engraving by William Blake from John Stedman, *Narrative of a Five Year Expedition against the Revolted Negroes of Surinam*, London, 1806.

Revenge taken by the black army: Library of Congress, Washington.

Haitian Revolution: From Michael Craton, *Testing the Chains*, New York, 1982.

Gillray Cartoon: © National Portrait Gallery, London. NPG D12417, used with permission.

Anti-Slavery Convention: © National Portrait Gallery, London. NPG 599, used with permission.

While every effort has been made to trace copyright holders, the publisher is happy to correct any omissions in future editions.

ACKNOWLEDGEMENTS

I am grateful to the K. Blundell Trust, administered by the Society of Authors, for a grant towards the costs of researching this book.

My greatest debt is to the scholars who have produced a rich academic literature on West Indian history, including transcriptions of key documents. Their help with identifying and interpreting the primary sources has been very valuable.

Writing about West Indian history has, unsurprisingly, been dominated by a concern with slavery and, influenced in part by the nature of a lot of the source material, with the economics of the plantation system. For this reason, I have tried to focus on other aspects of the time, although, of course, neither can be ignored, and specialists on these topics have also helped shape this book. In particular, I would like to acknowledge my great debt to (and recommend as further reading): Susan Amussen, Bernard Bailyn, Hilary Beckles, the Bridenbaughs, Vincent Brown, Trevor Burnard (especially), Linda Colley, Michael Craton, Noel Deerr, Richard Dunn, David Eltis, David Galenson, Larry Gragg, Douglas Hall, Vincent Harlow, Russell Menard, Sidney Mintz, Vere Oliver, Andrew O'Shaughnessy, Gabriel Paquette, Richard Pares, Lowell Ragatz, Richard Sheridan, Simon Smith, Peter Thompson, Karl Watson and Eric Williams.

I am grateful to all the academics who shared their research and gave this project encouragement, as well as others who sent me letters or pictures, or provided leads and contacts: Tim Anderson; David Beasley, Librarian, The Goldsmiths Company; Chris Codrington of Florida; Professor Madge Dresser; Michael Hamilton; Charles Freedland; Maya

Jasanoff, Steve Jervis; Louisa Parker; Victoria Perry; Derek Seaton; Paul Vlitos; Brian Wessely.

I am much indebted to the staff of a number of local and national archives in the UK including: the British Library, especially the staff of the Rare Books and Manuscripts reading rooms; the Bodleian Library in Oxford, in particular Lucy McCann; the Public Records Office and the county archives of Sussex and Lincolnshire. I am indebted for help with picture research to the brilliant staff of the National Portrait Gallery in London. In the United States, I was given valuable assistance by Kim Nusco in the John Carter Brown Library, Bert Lippincott at the Newport Historical Society, and by the staffs of the Rhode Island Historical Society and the Redwood Library. From Jamaica I would like to thank John Aarons, Audene Brooks at the Jamaica National Heritage Trust, George Faria, Tony Hart, Geoffrey and Patricia Pinto, as well as all at the National Library, the National Archives in Spanish Town and the Jamaica Institute. Special thanks to the late, much-missed Ed Kritzler, who showed me another world in Roaring River, Westmoreland. In Barbados, I was lucky enough to enjoy the enthusiastic support and local historical expertise of Mary Gleadall, and the assistance of Joan Braithwaite at the Barbados Museum archives, and of the staff of the National Archives at Black Rock.

A thousand thanks to Professor Barbara Bush for her careful checking of the manuscript and for her enthusiasm and advice. All errors, remain, of course, my own.

I was immensely lucky that the excellent Martin Brown was able to spend the time to draw the maps for the book, and in my copy-editor Jane Selley, proof-reader Mask Handsley and indexer Andy Armitage.

Indeed, books like this are a team effort. I have been fortunate to have two editors of huge experience and expertise in Tony Whittome at Hutchinson and George Gibson at Walker Books in the US, both of whom took the time to roll up their sleeves and get involved in the nitty-gritty of the manuscript, as well as providing encouragement and advice. I am grateful to Caroline Gascoigne and all at Random House and Walker Books who have helped with publishing this book, and for their patience when the research took much longer than planned. Thanks also to my agents Julian Alexander in London and George Lucas in New York, and to all my friends and family who have read and commented on drafts, in particular my father David Parker, and my father-in-law Paul Swain.

Lastly, much love and thanks to Hannah, Milly, Tom and Ollie, my most special ones.

INDEX

(key to initials: CC1 = Christopher Codrington I;
CC2 = Christopher Codrington II; CC3 = Christopher
Codrington III; PB1 = Colonel Peter Beckford Sr;
PB2 = Peter Beckford Jr)